MASSACHUSETTS

A GUIDE TO ITS PLACES AND PEOPLE

AMERICAN GUIDE SERIES

MASSACHUSETTS

A GUIDE TO ITS PLACES AND PEOPLE

Written and compiled by the Federal Writers' Project of the Works Progress Administration for Massachusetts

---

FREDERIC W. COOK, SECRETARY OF THE COMMONWEALTH, COOPERATING SPONSOR

Illustrated

HOUGHTON MIFFLIN COMPANY - BOSTON

The Riverside Press Cambridge

Republished 1973
SOMERSET PUBLISHERS – a Division of Scholarly Press, Inc.
22929 Industrial Drive East, St. Clair Shores, Michigan 48080

COPYRIGHT, 1937, BY GEORGE M. NUTTING, DIRECTOR OF PUBLICITY
COMMONWEALTH OF MASSACHUSETTS

Library of Congress Cataloging in Publication Data

Federal Writers' Project. Massachusetts.
  Massachusetts.

  Reprint of the 1937 ed., issued in series: American
guide series.
  Bibliography: p.
  1. Massachusetts--Description and travel--Guide-books.
I. Series: American guide series.
F70.F295 1972   917.44'04'4   72-84481
ISBN 0-403-02150-2

ONE MOMENT, PLEASE!

WHEN the Federal Writers' Project was set up in Massachusetts, and the staff received its first instructions from the central office in Washington, the editors blithely embarked on a task of whose magnitude they had little conception: the job of adequately describing the 316 towns and 39 cities of the Commonwealth, and of presenting, as concisely, accurately, and simply as possible, the facts about the State, from its Architecture to its Zoology, from the year ?00,000,000 B.C., when its geological history began, to A.D., 1937 when its social history has by no means ended.

All over the Commonwealth, field workers began to interview local historians, consult town records, talk with oldest inhabitants, tramp miles of country roads. In district offices, research workers checked and re-checked data against all available sources. Officials of State and local governmental agencies were pressed into service; volunteer consultants — geologists, architects, historians, anthropologists, travel experts, critics — read, criticized, and corrected copy. Photographers clicked cameras, cartographers wrought maps, tour checkers clocked mileage.

In the State office, bulky parcels began to arrive. The mailman staggered upstairs with piled envelopes of field copy, heavier each day. Readers struggled desperately to keep up with incoming copy; typists and copyreaders trod water in pools of manuscript. Batteries of steel files became crammed; a hundred wooden file boxes hungered and were fed. Meanwhile, a small administrative staff labored at the vital job of keeping accounts straight and records accurate, and of seeing that each worker received — many of them for the first time in months — his or her weekly pay check.

Out of several millions of words there slowly grew a book — nay, a *BOOK*, some 650,000 words long. The editors, abandoning a momentarily considered idea of publishing a volume of 2000 pages mounted on wheels with a trailer attachment, sharpened a gross of blue pencils and attacked the typescript to condense it to a portable size. Chapters became pages, pages became paragraphs, paragraphs became sentences. Tempers wore thin as cherished passages were cruelly blue-penciled, and editorial conferences developed into pitched battles. But out of it all, writers of varied ability and training and of widely differing temperament, thrown together on the common basis of need, shared a new experience — an adventure in co-operation.

Although comprehensive, this book is not an encyclopedia. Its purpose is not to catalogue all the facts, but to present and preserve significant facts. Designed to serve the needs of the tourist, this guide will be, it is hoped, more than a manual for the casual traveler. Tours there are in plenty, and thousands of points of interest are located and described. But the adventurous-minded will discover herein other excursions, less precisely marked, along highways of letters, history, art, and architecture.

In the midst of editing this book, the Federal Writers' Project of Massachusetts compiled and edited other guides, brochures, bibliographies, etc., some of which have already been published, others of which are still in preparation.

The editors are deeply obligated to many governmental agencies, Federal, State, and local, to commercial associations and travel agencies, to historical societies, and to hundreds of individuals, for information and assistance. They must content themselves, however, with brief and totally inadequate acknowledgment to the State Planning Board, the State Departments of Conservation and of Labor and Industries, to many local planning boards, the New England Council, the New England Hotel Association, the Boston and Albany, Boston and Maine–Central Vermont, and New York, New Haven, and Hartford Railroads, the Boston Elevated Company, other transportation companies. Professor E. A. Hooten, of the Department of Anthropology of Harvard University, criticized the article 'First Americans'; Professor A. M. Schlesinger, of the Department of History, Harvard, read 'Enough of Its History to Explain Its People'; Professor Lawrence LaForge, of the Department of Geology, Harvard, assisted in the preparation of 'Natural Setting,' of which Professor David Potter, of the Department of Biology, Clark University, reviewed the sections of flora and fauna. Professor Walter Piston, of the Department of Music, Harvard, made suggestions for the first section of the essay 'Music and the Theater'; and Mr. Leverett Saltonstall contributed the major portion of the article 'Government.' Miss Dorothy Adlow contributed the essay 'Art.' In addition, all the above, as well as many others not named, were frequently consulted for information and advice on matter lying within their several fields. The American Antiquarian Society, the Massachusetts Historical Society, the

State Library, the Bostonian Society, the Boston Athenæum, and numerous local historical societies and libraries generously made their collections available to research workers. Selectmen, town clerks, librarians, and others freely lent their aid.

The four-line stanza by Emily Dickinson in the article 'Literature' is quoted by special permission from 'Poems of Emily Dickinson,' 1937, edited by Martha Dickinson Bianchi and Alfred Leete Hampson: Little, Brown and Company, Boston.

This volume was prepared under the editorial direction of Joseph Gaer, Editor-in-Chief of the New England Guides and Chief Field Supervisor of the Federal Writers' Project.

RAY ALLEN BILLINGTON, *State Director*

BERT JAMES LOEWENBERG ⎫
MERLE COLBY ⎭ *Assistant State Directors*

CONTENTS

MASSACHUSETTS: THE GENERAL BACKGROUND

II. MAIN STREET AND VILLAGE GREEN

(City and Town Descriptions and City Tours)

III. HIGH ROADS AND LOW ROADS

(Mile-by-Mile Description of the State's Highways)

LIST OF MAPS

ILLUSTRATIONS

Illustrations marked * are by W. Lincoln Highton of the Works Progress
Administration; those marked † by courtesy of Goodspeed's Book Shop,
Boston; all uncredited photographs are by the staff photographer of the
Federal Writers' Project of Massachusetts.

GENERAL INFORMATION

Railroads: Boston & Maine (B. & M.), Boston & Albany (B. & A.), New York, New Haven & Hartford (N.Y., N.H. & H.), Central Vermont (C.V.).

Highways: 101 State highways. 6 Federal highways, as follows: 1, Fort Kent, Maine, to Miami, Fla.; 3, Canada via Colebrook, N.H.; 5, Quebec via Newport, Vt.; 6, Greely, Colo.; 7, Quebec via St. Albans, Vt.; 20, Yellowstone Park. (For routes throughout State see folding map.) Highway patrol to safeguard traffic and enforce traffic regulations.

Bus Lines: Intrastate: 155 lines connecting principal towns and cities. Interstate: Boston & Maine Transportation Co. (Boston to Portland, Me., Boston to White River Junction, Vt., Boston to Keene and Concord, N.H.); New England Transportation Co. (Boston to Hartford, Conn., Boston to Poughkeepsie, N.Y.); Berkshire Motor Coach Lines (Boston to Poughkeepsie, N.Y., via Worcester, New Haven, and New York City); Blue Line (Worcester to New York, via Springfield); Blue Way Lines (Portland, Me., and Boston to New York, via Springfield and Worcester); Eastern Greyhound Lines, Inc., of New England (Boston and Portland, Boston and New York); Frontier Coach Lines (Boston and Montreal); Greyhound Lines (national coverage); Interstate Busses Corporation (Providence, R.I., to Schenectady, N.Y., via Springfield and Pittsfield); I.R.T. Co., Inc. (Boston to Providence, R.I.); P.H.N. Lines, Inc. (Boston and Norwich, Conn., via Worcester); Old Colony Coach Lines, Inc. (Boston to Concord, N.H., Boston to Bar Harbor, Boston to Montreal and Quebec); Short Line System (Springfield to Portland, New York, Waterbury, Worcester, and Boston).

Airlines: Intrastate: Boston to Cape Cod and Nantucket (summer service). Interstate: American Airlines (Boston, Providence, Hartford, New Haven and New York; Boston–Buffalo and all points west). Boston–Maine–Central Vermont Airways (Portland, Augusta, Waterville, Bangor, Bar Harbor during summer, Manchester, Concord, White River Junction, Barre–Montpelier, Burlington).

Waterways: Regular service by steamship to New York and ports south via Cape Cod Canal from Boston or Fall River. Many trans-Atlantic liners call at Boston. Regular trips to Canada and the West Indies.

New Bedford, Martha's Vineyard, and Nantucket Steamship Co. (operated by New England Navigation Co.) to Woods Hole, Martha's Vineyard, and Nantucket (year-round service). Cape Cod Steamship Co., Boston to Provincetown (summers only).

Traffic Regulations: Non-residents may operate motor-cars within the State for 30 days without permit. Penalty for violation thereafter.

Speed: For State highways, regulations prescribe speed that is 'reasonable and proper': not to exceed 30 m. p. h. outside of a thickly settled or business district. Within a thickly settled district or at any place where operator's view of the road is obstructed, not in excess of 20 m. p. h. Curves not to be negotiated in excess of 15 m. p. h.

Lights: 'Every automobile operated during the period from one half an hour after sunset to one half an hour before sunrise shall display at least two white lights, or lights of yellow or amber tint, or if parked within the limits of a way one white light nearer the center of the way. And every motor vehicle shall display at least one red light in the reverse direction. No spotlights to be used unless approved by the registrar of motor vehicles.'

Brakes: Brakes must be adequate to control the movement of such vehicles, must conform to rules and regulations, and must be in good working order.

Accommodations: State is well provided with hotel accommodations. Accommodations in private houses are also available in nearly all towns. Tourist camps are located in all parts of the State. Municipal ordinances require rigid enforcement of rules on sanitation and hygiene. Most of these establishments are privately owned, but there is every evidence of their being orderly and well regulated. As most of the camps are within easy reach of trading centers, food supplies as well as emergency clothing are quickly obtainable.

Climate and Equipment: State has variable climate with temperatures ranging from the nineties in summer to sub-zero in winter. Visitors should carry clothing such as sweater and topcoat for sudden changes in summer, and in winter special heavy clothing for coasting, skiing, skating, and other outdoor sports. In winter snow trains leave Boston regularly for New Hampshire, Vermont, and Maine, destinations depending somewhat on the conditions of ice and snow.

Fires: 'No person shall set, maintain or increase a fire in the open air at any time unless the ground is substantially covered with snow, except by written permission ... granted by the forest warden or chief of the fire department in cities and towns ... or the fire commissioner. Persons above the age of eighteen may set or maintain a fire for a reasonable purpose upon sandy land, or upon salt marshes or sandy or rocky beaches bordering on tide-water, if the fire is enclosed within rocks, metal or other non-inflammable material.' Consult local fire warden.

Poisonous Plants and Reptiles: Poison ivy grows somewhat profusely in certain sections, generally along stone walls and fences in pasture and woodland, and occasionally along the seashore. Antidotes obtainable at any drugstore. Rattlesnakes at times are seen in certain sections of the Blue Hills in the eastern part of the State and in the Berkshires in the West.

Information Bureaus: The New England Council, Statler Building, 20 Providence Street, Boston; the various chambers of commerce, hotels, and railroads are equipped to give information on travel, resorts, recreational opportunities, and road conditions.

RECREATION

Golf: Massachusetts had the first golf course in America, the Country Club of Brookline, founded in 1882, and courses are well distributed throughout the State. On Cape Cod, on the adjacent islands of Nantucket and Martha's Vineyard, and in many other ocean-front cities and towns, courses overlook the sea. The eastern and central portions of the State provide numerous 'sporty' courses on rolling and varied terrain. The courses of western Massachusetts in the Berkshire Hills are set in the midst of rugged hills and valleys. Distributed throughout the State are approximately 215 courses, varying in size from six to thirty-six holes, the majority of which are open to the general public. Tournaments and special matches, both amateur and professional, are held during the season on representative courses.

Tennis: Tennis courts are provided as part of the recreational development of the Myles Standish State Forest in Plymouth, and on certain Metropolitan District Commission reservations. Many courts, available for public use for a fee, at specified times, are under the administration of colleges, private schools, private organizations, and municipalities.

Yachting: The State's hundreds of miles of coastline offer splendid opportunities for yachting. Large fleets of yachts and boats annually dot Massachusetts waters, engaging in races, regattas, and general cruising. There are approximately 130 yacht and boat clubs, including motor-boat and dory clubs distributed among the nine eastern and southern counties of the State. In the central and western portion there are four such clubs, the primary interest of which is motor or speed boating. Most yacht and boat clubs are, of course, in Essex County on the North Shore, in Suffolk County on the Central Shore, and in Barnstable County on the South Shore. Essex and Barnstable County clubs serve primarily the non-resident yachtsman; Suffolk County clubs serve the resident.

Beaches: The Commonwealth has more than one thousand miles of ocean front. Many towns which have acquired and developed ocean beaches have restricted the use to their own residents. There are now eight State-owned ocean beaches, one administered by the Department of Conservation, one in charge of the Department of Public Works, and six controlled by the Metropolitan District Commission.

Picnicking: The State forests, which have been expanded both in size and in facilities, offer convenient provisions for picnicking. Of the sixty-nine State forests, approximately thirty-nine have one or more developed picnic areas equipped with tables, benches, fireplaces, and sanitary facilities, and often have additional facilities for camping, such as tent sites, trailer sites, and cabins, as well as swimming facilities. In the remaining thirty State forests, picnicking is allowed, but there are few facilities, and fires are prohibited.

There are numerous other opportunities for picnicking in the two State parks, eleven State reservations, eight semi-public reservations, and fourteen reservations controlled by the Metropolitan District Commission, all of which permit picnicking in some form and provide some of the necessary facilities, such as tables and benches. Opportunity for picnicking is not limited to the State-provided facilities. Many cities and towns have large parks or lakeside reservations where non-residents may picnic. There are also many commercial picnic grounds, camp-grounds, and beaches.

Fairs: In 1935, approximately twenty outstanding fairs were held throughout the State, attracting some 750,000 people. More than fifty per cent of the attendance was at the two major fairs — the Brockton Fair and the Eastern States Exposition.

Horse and Dog Races: Horse and dog racing, under the pari-mutuel system of betting, has become increasingly popular. In 1935, the first year of operation of horse and dog racing under the pari-mutuel system, four flat running-horse tracks, four harness-horse tracks, and three dog tracks were licensed.

Auto Races: Auto racing is engaged in primarily as amateur competition and as a feature event at certain of the major fairs. For amateur competition for midget cars, two dirt tracks have been built, one at Wayland and one at Marstons Mills on Cape Cod. On these tracks several races are scheduled during the summer and early fall. All types of cars are used, and the usual length is fifty miles. Professional and semi-professional auto racing is limited to the major fairs.

Winter Sports: The State Department of Conservation, in co-operation with the National Park Service and the Civilian Conservation Corps, has extended the winter-sports facilities in the State forests and reservations, and is still developing them. Climatic conditions and natural topography make certain sections of the State ideal for extensive winter-sports developments. The Berkshire Hills area is the best-developed section, but new trails have been constructed in the Wachusett region, more favorably located in relation to principal centers of population than the Berkshires. There are approximately seventy-five areas devoted to skiing, with many miles of trails and acres of open slopes. Jumps are few in number, only thirteen being available. Probably more than 75 per cent of the skiing facilities are concentrated in the four western counties, the major portion of these being in Berkshire County. On the Mount Wachusett State Reservation, two new downhill trails have been developed or improved. In the eastern part of the State are a few facilities: Mount Hood Memorial Park, Melrose, the two trails on the Metropolitan District Commission's

Blue Hills Reservation, and a few small municipal or private open slopes and jumps. Many golf clubs allow the use of open slopes on the courses for skiing. 'Snow trains' leave Boston regularly in winter.

There are seventeen ski and outing clubs, most of which are in central and western Massachusetts. The Western Massachusetts Winter Sports Council is the largest combined organization actively promoting winter sports in the State. The Berkshire Hills Conference also encourages winter sports.

Practically every city and town in Massachusetts has sufficient water area for skating. Several ponds or lakes on State reservations and forests are kept cleared during the season.

Tobogganing has a few facilities, widely scattered over the State. On most State reservation lands, no constructed chutes are necessary because natural conditions, dependent on suitable snow cover, are sufficient. The same is true for most municipal parks.

Snowshoeing is dependent on the quality and condition of snow. Since it requires no special areas or trails, there are adequate opportunities for it in every section of the State when there is snow. Existing foot trails or minor back roads may be used.

Hiking: Perhaps the best-known hiking route is the Appalachian Trail (*see Tour* 9), extending from the Connecticut boundary to the Vermont line and forming a link in the route from Georgia to Maine. There is also the Wachusett–Watatic Trail (*see Tour* 11A), covering a distance of more than twenty miles from the Mount Wachusett Reservation to a point near the New Hampshire line, where it connects with the Wapack Trail. The State forests and reservations provide a total of 225 miles of local trails, constructed by the Department of Conservation in co-operation with the National Park Service and the Civilian Conservation Corps during the past four years. The Metropolitan District Commission has developed a number of trails on its reservations, particularly the Blue Hills (*see Tour* 25) and Middlesex Fells (*see Tour* 5).

Several organizations are actively engaged in the promotion and construction of foot trails, preparation of guide books, and the establishment of trail shelters. Prominent among these are the Berkshire Chapter of the Appalachian Mountain Club, the Connecticut Valley Trails Conference, the Massachusetts Forest and Park Association, the outing clubs of colleges and preparatory schools, the American Youth Hostel, Inc., the New England Trails Conference, and the Massachusetts Department of Conservation.

Riding: Bridle trails in Massachusetts consist of several local municipal units, some few miles developed on the State forests and reservations, a few miles developed by the Metropolitan District Commission on their reservations and parkways, and the Capes-to-the-Berkshires Trail (*see Tour* 12), a through trail 450 miles in length. Throughout the State there are many miles of old wood roads and minor back roads which serve as bridle paths. Excluding these roads, there are more than 500 miles of existing bridle trails in Massachusetts. Eighty-six riding academies and many local outing clubs are distributed throughout the State. Many of these are on or near the Capes-to-the-Berkshires Trail, and offer shelter to horse and rider.

Bicycling: There are no bicycle trails as such in Massachusetts. The American Youth Hostel, Inc., has laid out a bicycle loop trip through New England, utilizing back roads and portions of the Capes-to-the-Berkshires Trail.

Hunting: Hunting is permitted in 64 State forests, comprising more than 150,000 acres. In thirty of these forests, hunting is strictly regulated by permit; and portions of ten forests, comprising approximately 3200 acres, are set aside for game preserves, on which no hunting is allowed. Public lands available for public hunting (State forest lands) are widely distributed throughout the State, with the largest percentage, both in number and acreage, in the central and western portions. The Division of Fisheries and Game carries on extensive stocking of covers, particularly with quail, pheasants, hares, and rabbits. Game preserves, under a variety of classifications and organizations, are numerous. The State contains 33 or more preserves, varying in size from 12 to 8600 acres, and representing a total of approximately 21,300 acres. Included in the total are the various State reservations, under the control of County and Special Commissioners, which unless otherwise specified are closed to hunting. There are four game farms, varying in size from 23 to 132 acres, and comprising a total of 364 acres. All are under the direct control of the Division of Fisheries and Game of the Department of Conservation, 20 Somerset St., Boston. For hunting license consult the Division, or the local game warden.

Fishing: While a large part of the brook fishing is still in private unposted land, more and more streams seem destined to be closed to the public by individuals and private clubs. However, opportunity for public fishing is fairly extensive. Under the General Laws of Massachusetts, the Director of the Division of Fisheries and Game is permitted to acquire, by gift or lease, fishing rights and privileges in any brook or stream in the Commonwealth, with rights of ingress and egress, unless it is a source of or tributary to a public water supply. There are eleven such areas in the State, comprising some eighty miles of stream. In addition to these streams, the ponds of the State, with the exception of those used for water supply, are public for the purpose of fishing, hunting, and boating. There are 1302 such ponds, of which approximately two hundred are used for water-supply purposes. Certain others are controlled either by the Division of Fisheries and Game for breeding purposes, or by cities and towns. For fishing license, consult the Division, 20 Somerset St., Boston, or the local game warden, who will supply lists of stocked streams and ponds.

For salt-water fishing no license is required. At most harbors, boats and equipment are available to parties for deep-sea fishing. During the summer deep-sea fishing excursion boats leave T Wharf, Boston (foot of State Street) daily. Surf-casting is increasing in popularity, and equipment and instruction are available at many resorts.

TRANSPORTATION

JOSIAH QUINCY in his Journal thus describes a trip from Boston to New York in 1773: 'I set out from Boston in the line of stages of an enterprising Yankee, Pease by name, considered a method of transportation of wonderful expedition. The journey to New York took up a week.... We reached our resting place for the night, if no accident intervened, at 10 o'clock, and after a frugal supper, went to bed with a notice that we should be called at three, which generally proved to be half past two, and then, whether it snowed or rained, the traveler must rise and make ready... and proceed on his way over bad roads, sometimes getting out to help the coachman lift the coach out of a quagmire or rut, and arriving in New York after a week's hard traveling, wondering at the ease, as well as the expedition with which our journey was effected.'

At the time that Josiah made his memorable journey, little progress in transportation methods had been made since the founding of the Plymouth Colony. Though primitive forms of wheeled vehicles were used as early as 1650, the colonists usually traveled on horseback, and few attempts were made by them to improve the condition of the roads. Action taken at early town meetings to compel able-bodied men to work on the roads or pay tax money to hire substitutes did not suffice to keep the roads in good condition. Road-building in the early days was simply not considered an important undertaking. The first settlements were made on the coast, and the colonists maintained communication largely by water because it was more convenient for them.

In the seventeenth and eighteenth centuries more traveling by land was done in the winter than during any other season of the year. Sleighs drawn by oxen or horses were used on small streams and frozen rivers.

By the year 1683 a few private coaches began to appear in the larger towns, like Boston and New York. The earliest were of three types: one was patterned after the heavy two-horse family carriage used in England; the others were better adapted to conditions in America, and drawn by one horse. Road conditions did not permit their use outside the limits of the towns.

Some of the wealthier inhabitants in the larger towns began to use sedan chairs, but public opinion in the Colony decidedly frowned on the use of such vehicles. Governor Winthrop had received a sedan chair as a gift, but he did not dare to use it.

During the second half of the eighteenth century, stagecoach service was established between a few of the larger communities along the New England coasts, such as Boston and Providence.

The first stagecoaches were crude in form. They usually had four wooden benches without any backs, seating a maximum of nine passengers. Baggage was placed either on the passengers' knees or under their legs. The coach had a top usually made of some heavy woven material, with leather curtains at the sides and rear. It had no springs, and the traveler who had not to hobble when he arrived at his destination was very fortunate and very rare.

The end of the Revolutionary War marked the opening of a new era. People began at last to recognize the need of adequate transportation facilities. New industries established in different sections of the State, and expanding municipalities demanded better facilities for moving people and freight overland.

The question was, however, who was to build the roads? The War had impoverished the local communities and the State. Neither was financially able to undertake the construction of roads which demanded an outlay of millions of dollars. Out of these difficulties grew a new method of private financing and control, whereby the roads were built by private companies incorporated under acts passed by the State Legislature. These roads, called turnpikes, were constructed by private capital, privately owned, and operated for the revenue derived from the collection of tolls.

Both the rates of toll and the number of gates that could be erected were fixed in the charters granted to the various corporations. The gates were erected at intervals of about ten miles, and rates had to be displayed on large signs. Certain persons were exempt from paying toll: Any person going to or from his usual place of public worship; any person passing with his horses, team, or cattle to or from his farm, in connection with work to be performed there; any person passing on military duty. If the toll-gatherer were not present to receive the toll, the gate had to be left open and everybody was permitted to pass without paying.

The opening of the turnpikes was followed by the establishment of regular stagecoach lines between all sections of Massachusetts. In 1801, one hundred and sixteen coaches arrived and departed from Boston each week. There were twenty-six lines to as many different places. The running time to New York was then about forty hours, and some lines reduced the time between cities by traveling all night instead of stopping at a tavern.

The improved type of stagecoach used between 1800 and 1840 was built of wood and sole leather, and was shaped somewhat like a football. It had no springs, but was swung on several thick strips of leather riveted together and called thoroughbraces; the average coach seated nine passengers and was usually drawn by four horses. In these new coaches strips of leather were nailed lengthwise to provide backs for the benches. Meanwhile the top of the coach had assumed a flat shape, and, with the installation of railings, baggage could be carried on the roof. The 'Concord Coach,' first built in Concord, New Hampshire, about 1828, was considered the acme of luxury. So highly were these coaches regarded by the traveling public that the railroads used them mounted on railway trucks, as their first passenger coaches.

In the winter time, the stagecoach lines often placed their vehicles on sled bodies instead of on wheels, and thus maintained their service with but a small decrease in speed. On occasions when the coach was too heavy to be drawn through the snow, its use was temporarily abandoned in favor of small, open, boxlike conveyances, with the travelers exposed to every inclemency of the weather.

Distances were commonly reckoned in miles intervening between taverns, and not, as one would expect, between towns. Taverns were the important landmarks of any journey. There the weary passengers alighted to seek refreshment and stretch their cramped limbs while assembled townsfolk pressed about them and questioned them eagerly about the news from the outside world.

About 1800 a new and radically different method of transportation was devised. This was the canal. The stagecoach was not adapted to freight traffic. A number of surveys were made, but nothing was done. Despite popular enthusiasm, only one large canal, the Middlesex, completed in 1808 and extending from the Merrimack River near Lowell to the Charles River in Boston, was built in Massachusetts, and its period of usefulness was very short. The rapid railroad development all over the State from 1835 to 1850 solved the problem.

In spite of advantages which were obvious to the foresighted, Massachusetts was slower than some other sections of the country in accepting the new method of transportation. Just as the first coaches to appear on the streets were severely censured, so were the first railroads. Puritanism was always suspicious of anything that made for physical comfort. Many people were sincerely convinced that the use of these iron highways would lower the prevailing standards of morality.

During the building of the Western Railroad from Worcester to Springfield in 1837, so much adverse criticism was directed against this project that the owners of the road sent a letter to all the churches of the State asking that *sermons be preached on the beneficial moral effect of railroads*.

The first three important New England railroads were all completed in 1835 in this State. They were the Boston and Lowell, the Boston and Providence, and the Boston and Worcester.

The reaction of the people to the new method of transportation is found in the newspapers of the day. In the issue of the *Maine Farmer* of July 18, 1835, a newspaper published in Worcester, there is the following comment concerning the trip between Boston and Worcester: 'The usual passage is performed in two and a half or three hours, including stops — A few years ago, 14 miles an hour would have been considered rapid traveling. . . . So great are the advantages gained, that already one of the principal dealers here has offered to lay a side track from the road to his own storehouse . . . A person in business here informed me that he left Worcester one day at 12 o'clock, arrived in Boston, had one and a quarter hours to transact his business, returned by the four o'clock car, and arrived here at seven o'clock in the evening — thus traveling 88 miles in eight and three quarter hours. . . . Some of the passenger cars on this road are very elegant, and will hold from twenty to thirty persons. The motion of the cars upon the road is so easy that I saw a little child walking from seat to seat, as if in a parlor.'

Parallel to the development of steam railroads was that of a similar type of intercity transportation. The first street railway in Massachusetts was built in Boston in 1836. Horse-car systems were replaced about 1890 by the use of electricity as a motive power. Then came the automobile, and an entirely new and revolutionary method of transportation slowly began to undermine both the street railways and the railroads, culminating in the employment of busses both for local and long-distance passenger and freight service.

An integral part of the success of the new method was the development of an improved highway system throughout the State. After the failure in 1850 of most of the turnpikes, the roads had reverted to the control of the cities and towns in which they were located. In 1893 the Legislature established the Massachusetts Highway Commission as the result of an investigation which disclosed that the roads of the State were in a deplorable condition. The Commission was authorized to take over, lay out, and maintain roads, and to unite the more important cities by trunk lines of large traffic capacity. The first State appropriation, amounting to $300,000, was made in 1894. By 1916 a total of $11,767,000 had been spent. Obviously some portion of this gathering cost had to be turned back in some way to those who benefited. The old turnpike toll in a different form is paid by motorists of today. In 1925 the State Legislature established the Highway Fund, whereby the proceeds of motor-vehicle fees and fines and of the tax on gasoline are pledged to the construction and maintenance of both State and local highways. During the past twenty-five years the cost of new road construction in Massachusetts has been approximately $105,000,000.

Today five types of transportation, all highly developed, are open to the traveler in Massachusetts. The most expeditious is by air. Josiah Quincy, who thought a week was a remarkably short time for the journey from Boston to New York, would hardly have believed that a century and a half later the traveler would board a plane at Boston and make a happy landing at Newark Airport on the edge of New York City in eighty-four minutes.

Besides Boston, thirty-six cities of Massachusetts have airplane landing facilities, and seaplane landings can be made at Boston, Gloucester, Squantum, and New Bedford. In 1937 recognized commercial air service was provided by two large airlines, one of which connects Boston, via New York and via Albany, with all the other important air routes of the country, and the other of which reaches the cities of upper New England. During the summer seaplanes fly between Boston, Provincetown, Hyannis, Nantucket, and Martha's Vineyard.

Next in speed, but with certain superior elements of practicability, come the railroads. At present three major lines serve Massachusetts and link it with the south and southwest, the west, and the north; and five others operate within the State.

Next in speed to the railroad but with more flexibility and usually at less cost, passenger and freight service are given by bus and truck lines, which cover the State with a fine network. Three main operators, controlled by three railroads, and several lesser lines handle the long-distance traffic, while about one hundred and sixty bus lines are engaged in intrastate traffic.

The development of motor transportation has seriously curtailed the operation of street railways, especially interurban and suburban lines. The street railway mileage has been steadily decreasing since 1920. Although the Boston Elevated Railway, the largest line in the State, which serves the thickly settled Greater Boston district, has been able to retain much of its suburban traffic through its tunnel lines, it also operates an increasingly large number of motor coaches.

The private automobile began to be a factor in transportation following the World War. In 1920, 223,112 automobiles were registered in Massachusetts; the number has steadily increased, and the average during the past few years has been near the 900,000 mark. For the automobile traveler, as well as for bus and trucking companies, the interior roadway system offers easy access to all important points. Four United States highways (20, 3, 1 to the north, and 1 to the south) radiate from Boston, besides a large number of other main roads. Routes 1, 3, 202, 5, and 7 are the major north and south arteries of the State; number 20 is the main western line. The total highway mileage in 1935 was 18,802, including 2400 miles of State highways. Inland water transportation is negligible except that through the Cape Cod Canal, which considerably reduces the time and increases the safety of the passage between Boston and New York. Forty-one steamship lines give foreign service out of the port of Boston, and twenty lines give domestic or coastwise service. A steamship line, connecting two old whaling ports and a summer resort, plies between New Bedford, Martha's Vineyard, and Nantucket via Woods Hole, and summer steamers run from New Bedford to New York and from Boston to Provincetown. Passenger service by steamship between Boston and Portland was discontinued about 1935. The Commonwealth has several smaller ports besides Boston, the most important in volume of traffic being Fall River, followed by New Bedford, Beverly, Salem, and Lynn, in this order. Boston has the largest drydock on the continent, constructed by the Commonwealth and later sold to the United States Government.

CALENDAR OF EVENTS

Events are arranged first by frequency of occurrence (Annual, Seasonal, Bi-Annual), and next by date within cities, which are grouped together.

ANNUAL

(nfd = no fixed date)

Jan.	last Sat.	Boston	Knights of Columbus Track Meet, Boston Garden, North Station.
Jan.	20 to Feb. 19 (1 day)	Boston	Chinese New Year.
Jan.	nfd	Springfield	Springfield Art League, exhibit at Museum of Fine Arts.
Jan.	1	Stoughton	Old Stoughton Musical Society Concert, Town Hall.
Jan.	nfd	Worcester	Union Agricultural Meetings.
Feb.	1st wk	Boston	N.E. Sportsmen's and Boat Show, Mechanics Bldg., Huntington Ave.
Feb.	1st Sat.	Boston	Boston Athletic Association Games, Boston Garden, North Station.
Feb.	nfd	Boston	Boston Society of Independent Artists, no-jury exhibit, Boston Art Club, 150 Newbury St.
Feb.	last 2 wks	Boston	Boston Society of Water Color Painters, exhibit, Vose Galleries, 559 Boylston St.
Feb.	21–22	Boston	Eastern Dog Club Show, Mechanics Bldg., Huntington Ave.
Feb.	22	Boston	International Music Festival, Symphony Hall, Huntington Ave.
Feb.	22	Boston	'Handshake ceremony,' State House.
Feb.	1st & last week-ends	Melrose	Winter Carnivals on Mt. Hood Reservation sponsored by National Ski Assn.
March	last wk	Boston	Spring Flower Show, Massachusetts Horticultural Society, Mechanics Building, Huntington Ave.
March	17	South Boston	Evacuation Day. Ceremonies and Parade.
March	1st 2 wks	Worcester	Spring Flower Show, Worcester Horticultural Society, Horticultural Hall, 30 Elm St.
April	19	Boston	Patriots' Day. Celebration and Marathon.
April	last wk	Boston	Pension Fund Concert of Boston Symphony Orchestra, Symphony Hall, Huntington Ave.

April	19	Lexington	Revolutionary Pageant on Common.
April	nfd	Provincetown	Portuguese festival in honor of Santo Christo.
May	5	Boston	Opening of Boston Symphony 'Pops' concerts continuing to July 3, at Symphony Hall, Huntington Ave.
May	1st wk	Boston	National Music Week celebrated by Boston Public Schools.
May	1st Sun.	Boston	Annual Concert of Boston Music School Settlement, Jordan Hall, Huntington Ave.
May	1st wk	Boston	Ford Hall Forum Banquet, Ford Hall, Ashburton Place.
May	May Day	Boston	Labor groups and others celebrate with music and speeches on Common.
May	last 3 wks	Boston	'Paradise of Blossoms,' Arnold Arboretum.
May	nfd	Boston	American Unitarian Associations' Convention, 'May Meetings.'
May	1st wk	Boston	Tournament sponsored by National Guild of Piano Teachers, Steinert Hall, Boylston St.
May	1st Sat.	Cambridge	Massachusetts Institute of Technology, Open House.
May	3 Sundays	Gloucester	Portuguese Festival of Penticost at Church of Our Lady of Good Voyage.
May	nfd	Ipswich	Rights for 'Alewife run' sold to highest bidder.
May	3d wk	Lawrence	Three Day Carnival sponsored by International Institute. Fourteen or more national groups appear in folk costumes to re-enact native pageantry.
May	6th Sun. after Easter	New Bedford	Portuguese religious celebration.
May	mid-May	Wellesley	Wellesley College celebrates 'Float Night' on Lake Waban.
May	nfd (2 days)	Nashoba Valley Towns	Nashoba Apple Blossom Festival.
June	1st Mon.	Boston	Installation of Officers and Drum Parade of Ancient and Honorable Artillery Company, on Common.
June	mid-June	Boston	Peony and Rose Show, Horticultural Hall, Massachusetts Ave.
June	nfd 1 wk	Boston	Boston National Home Show, Mechanics Building, Huntington Ave.
June	19	Brookline	Opening of State Singles Tennis Championship Tournament, Longwood Cricket Club.
June	16–26	Cambridge	Harvard Commencement exercises, Harvard Yard, Cambridge; Class Day at Harvard Stadium, Brighton.
June	2d Tues.	Cambridge	Alumni Reunion at the Massachusetts Institute of Technology.

June	16	Charlestown	Bunker Hill Banquet, Armory, Bunker Hill St.
June	17	Charlestown	Bunker Hill Day Celebration and Parade.
June	28 to July 23	Concord	Choral Programs by students of Concord Summer School of Music, usually in Unitarian Church.
June	near 15	Northampton	Gaily decorated floats on Paradise Pond, stage for Smith College Glee Club Concert, Class Day.
July	1st Sat. and Sun.	Bridgewater	Portuguese celebrate Holy Ghost Festival.
July	near 1st	Dennis	Opening of two-month season of summer stock company at Cape Playhouse.
July	Near 1st to end of month	Boston	Esplanade concerts by members of Boston Symphony Orchestra.
July	4–18	Wellesley	Wellesley College Summer Institute for Social Progress, Wellesley College.
July	nfd	Gloucester	Italian religious festival, Old Fort section.
July	nfd— to middle of Sept.	Gloucester	North Shore Art Association, exhibits, East Gloucester Sq.
July	nfd — to middle of Sept.	Gloucester	Gloucester Society of Artists, exhibit of members' work, near Hawthorne Inn.
July	4 wks	Northfield	Conference of Ministers and Missionaries, Northfield Seminary.
July	nfd	Provincetown	Beachcombers' Ball, costume affair, by artists, writers and others.
July	4 to Labor Day	Provincetown	Art exhibits at galleries of Provincetown Art Association.
July	nfd	Rockport	North Shore Art Association opens three months' exhibitions concurrent with two months' showings of Rockport Art Association.
July	last wk	Amherst	Farm and Home Week.
Aug.		Falmouth	Sessions at Marine Biological Laboratory, Woods Hole.
Aug.		Falmouth	Sessions at Oceanographic Institute, Woods Hole.
Aug.		Falmouth	Sessions at United States Bureau of Fisheries, Woods Hole.
Aug.	nfd	Beverly	Sam-Sam Carnival, midway, flower show and fireworks.
Aug.	nfd	Boston	Mid-summer exhibition of Massachusetts Horticultural Society, Horticultural Hall, Massachusetts Ave.
Aug.	nfd	Boston	Products of Children's Gardens Exhibition, Horticultural Hall, Massachusetts Ave.
Aug.	23	Brookline	Beginning National Championship Doubles and Mixed Doubles Tennis Tournament, Longwood Cricket Club.

Aug.	nfd	Gloucester	Gloucester Fishermen's Memorial Day Services at the site of the Gloucester Fisherman's Memorial.
Aug.	2d wk	Marblehead	Annual Cruise, Eastern Yacht Club.
Aug.	near 15	Marblehead	Marblehead Race Week, yachting.
Aug.	nfd	Marshfield	Marshfield Fair.
Aug.	10–28	Mattapoisett	Special events in connection with cruise of New York and Eastern Yacht Clubs in harbor.
Aug.	nfd	Provincetown	Art Association Ball, costume affair, Town Hall.
Aug.	near 15 (2 evgs)	Rockport	Cape Ann–North Shore Music Festival, Fort Park.
Aug.	3d wk	Rockport	Artists' Ball, Rockport Art Association.
Aug.	near 15	Stockbridge	Berkshire Symphonic Festival, three concerts by Boston Symphony Orchestra.
Sept.	2d wk	Boston	Late summer exhibition of Massachusetts Horticultural Society, Horticultural Hall, Massachusetts Ave.
Sept.	3d wk	Brockton	Brockton Fair, held annually since 1784.
Sept.	Fri. & Sat. before Labor Day	Middlefield	Middlefield Fair.
Sept.	3d wk	Springfield	Eastern States Exposition.
Sept.	Labor Day week-end	Topsfield	Topsfield Fair, Treadwell Farm.
Oct.	1st wk	Worcester	Worcester Music Festival, four concerts including one oratorio.
Nov.	1st wk	Worcester	Worcester Horticultural Society, Chrysanthemum Show, Horticultural Hall, 30 Elm St.
Nov.	nfd	Amherst	Horticultural Show of the Mass. State College.
Dec.	24	Boston	Christmas Eve Carol Singing on Beacon Hill (principally in Louisburg Sq.). 'Open House' in many homes.
Dec.	near 24	Boston	Handel's 'Messiah' by Handel and Haydn Society, Symphony Hall, Huntington Ave.
Dec.	or Jan.	Boston	National Winter Sports Exposition, indoor skiing, skating, reproductions of famous winter resorts, Boston Garden, North Station.
Dec.	21	Plymouth	Forefathers' Day, observance of landing of Pilgrim Fathers.
Dec.	last wk	Provincetown	Portuguese celebrate with open house, oldtime parties and dances.
Dec.	Christmas Sun.	Worcester	Handel's 'Messiah' by Worcester Oratorio Society, Memorial Auditorium.

SEASONAL

April — Sept.	Boston	American and National League professional baseball games at Fenway and National League Parks.
May — June	Boston	College Crew Races, Saturday afternoons, Charles River.
June — Sept.	Brookline	Federal Music Project concerts, Tuesday and Thursday evenings, Brookline Shell, Dean Rd.
July 6 — Aug. 10	Cambridge	Free concerts, Tuesdays at 8.15 P.M., Longy School, 44 Church St.
Sept. 1 — June	Boston	Fenway Court Concerts, Sundays, 1–4 P.M., Isabella Stewart-Gardner Museum, Fenway.
Oct. — Nov.	Boston	Professional football games.
Oct. — Nov.	Throughout State	College football games.
Oct. — May	Cambridge	Free concerts, Tuesdays at 8.15 P.M., Longy School, 44 Church St.
Oct. — April	Boston	Boston Public Library Lectures and Concerts, Sundays at 3 P.M. and 8 P.M., and Thursdays at 8 P.M., Lecture Hall, Boston Public Library.
		Community Church of Boston, Sundays at 10.30 A.M., Symphony Hall, Huntington Ave.
		Ford Hall Forum, Sundays at 8 P.M., Ashburton Pl.
		Ford Hall Youth Forum, Mondays at 8 P.M., Ashburton Pl.
		Old South Forum, Sundays at 3 P.M., Old South Meeting House, Washington St.
		Symphony Concerts, Saturday and Monday evenings and Tuesday and Friday afternoons, Symphony Hall, Huntington Ave.

BI-ANNUAL

Jan. 1st Thurs. after 1st. Wed. (odd years)	Boston	Inauguration of Governor, State House.
June	nfd (even years)	Democratic Convention.
	nfd (even years)	Republican Convention.

I. MASSACHUSETTS: THE GENERAL BACKGROUND

CLUES TO ITS CHARACTER

TO THE seeker of a clue to the character of Massachusetts people, the rubric of the east wind may be useful. Time and again a salty breeze has blown through this most conservative of commonwealths. It wafted the first rebels to Cape Cod, dying down soon after. It burst forth again to blow steadily through most of the eighteenth century, when victories were won not only for political freedom but for education and religious toleration. During the period of Federalism it abated, but by the 1840's the faint whisper which had fanned the cheeks of mill girls in Lowell, mechanics in Boston, and scholars in Cambridge and Concord was roaring in a gale that shook the rafters of the nation. It blew fitfully throughout the later nineteenth century, dying to a flat calm at the beginning of the twentieth. From about 1909 to 1927 it let loose a window-rattling blast or two before subsiding again.

Many symbols have been devised to explain the Bay Stater. He has been pictured as a kind of dormant volcano, the red hot lava from one eruption hardening into a crater which impedes the next; as a river, with two main currents of transcendental metaphysics and catchpenny opportunism running side by side; as an asocial discord consisting mainly of overtones and undertones; as a petrified backbone, 'that unblossoming stalk.' To these may be added the cartoonist's Bluenose, the debunker's Puritan, the Gentleman with a Green Bag, Aunt Harriet with her *Boston Transcript*, and the late unlamented Little Waldo of the spectacles and painfully corrugated brow.

That so many symbols have been created for the State hints at the complexity of its people. Any almanac or book of facts can inform the clue-seeker that the population is roughly three-fifths native, one-eighth from other states, and a quarter foreign-born or of mixed foreign-born and native parentage; that half the land area consists of farms, yet only a tiny proportion of the four and one-third million inhabitants are farmers; that about half the residents are church members, of whom three-fifths are Catholics; that an Indian boldly figures on the State seal, but only 874 residents today report themselves as descended from Massachusetts' first families. Stumbling on the fact that the State has more public libraries than any other save New York, and more volumes per capita than any other, the seeker cries *Aha!* — only to learn a few moments later that Ohio, with one-third fewer library books, has at least as many library readers. Told that no non-native resident ever feels at home for his first twenty-five years, the seeker is surprised to discover that more than a third of the State's residents were born outside its borders. At long last he is likely to emerge from the almanac with the information that citizens of the State live a little longer than the dromedary, rather less than the ostrich, and for a much shorter span than the fresh-water mussel; or that from the State came three Presidents, seven Secretaries of the Navy, a host of cabinet officers, and the man who first went over Horseshoe Falls in a rubber ball.

Clearly a symbol is necessary. Let it be, then, the east wind, and let the east wind blow to these shores in the early 1600's, not companies of large-minded and open-handed gentlemen-adventurers, but small, close-knit, compactly organized groups. 'God sifted a whole nation that he might send choice grain over into this wilderness,' wrote William Stoughton in 1668, and this 'sober and judicial statement,' as Calvin Coolidge called it, indicates how the first-comers viewed the rest of the world in terms of themselves. The peculiar combination of individualism and conformity which still marks the State was given divine sanction by the theology brought by the first inhabitants. Calvinism, which had deposed heaven's hierarchy of saints, increased the prestige of the individual; but the doctrine of Providence, which taught that God's gifts must not be used for selfish ends, permitted the individual to act only as the group decreed. Individuals outside the group were feared and combated. Since conformity breeds non-conformists, rebels appeared and split off from the main group — they in turn to conform and to breed rebellion.

With the expulsion of Anne Hutchinson, Roger Williams, and their followers, the inhabitants of the Bay Colony proved, at least to themselves, their right to be winnowed grain. Succeeding Roger Williams at Salem in 1636, however, came an even more radical minister, Hugh Peter. Master Hugh, a member of the first Harvard Board of Overseers, while still in London had advocated State employment relief, slum clearance, and prison reform. In the New World he proposed the wholesale abolition of English law and the substitution therefor of a new concise legal code understandable by the common people. Perhaps it was as well for the peace of mind of the colonists that he returned to England, where unfortunately he got himself beheaded for his plain speaking. But the east wind blew; the Church of England was granted toleration, and a wider freedom of worship slowly followed. Yet worshipers still sat in their pews strictly according to rank; democracy was highly limited; and a large section of the people, including indentured servants, women, and the propertyless, remained disenfranchised for more than a century.

The gale of pamphleteering, musketeering, committee organizing, speech-making, and political scribbling which blew throughout the eighteenth century ceased abruptly late in the 1790's. A lone voice rose but was unheard, that of William Manning, Billerica farmer. 'I see,' wrote this Jeffersonian radical, painfully forming his letters, 'almost the first blood that was shed in Concord fite and scores of men dead, dying and wounded in the Cause of Libberty.... I believed then and still believ it is a good cause which we aught to defend to the very last.' The editor of the *Independent Chronicle* of Boston, to whom Manning sent his appeal, was jailed on the Federalist charge of 'seditious libel.' Meanwhile Daniel Shays and his lieutenant Luke Day had armed their cohorts of impoverished farmers near Worcester, and had been dispersed by a militia subsidized by Boston merchants. A new cloud big with wind, the rising of which farmers such as Manning and Shays could not foresee, was bulking in the sky: the young 'mechanick' class of the industrial towns.

Against the background of the demands of the skilled mechanics and factory operatives for popular education, legislative reform, and political representation which characterized the 1840's, rose transcendentalism, a kind of neo-puritanism which symbolized, on the plane of ideas, the conflict going on in the real world between the Colonial system of small self-sufficient industry and the new mode of factory production. On the social field transcendentalism had a single watchword: harmony. Not through hatred, collision, the war of class against class, transcendentalists insisted, could come social adjustment, but only through the reconciling of interests. In this belief the Unitarians founded Brook Farm and the Universalists Hopedale. Josiah Warren was holding his 'parlor conversations' and opening his 'time stores,' in which goods were paid for in scrip representing labor-time. Brisbane, aided by Horace Greeley, was moving his paper *The Phalanx* to Brook Farm and renaming it *The Harbinger*. It was a time of optimism, of revolt against tradition and convention, of faith in the infinite perfectibility of the human race — and the particular perfectibility of the Yankee. It was the glorious adolescence of the most precocious of the states.

Throughout the three hundred years of the State's history the east wind blew steadily among its women, producing such champions of women's rights as Mary Lyon, Mary Livermore, Lucy Stone, Susan

Anthony, Lydia Maria Child, and Margaret Fuller. The first attempt of women to exercise the right of free assembly was made by Anne Hutchinson, who after being tried on a joint charge of sedition and heresy was banished from Boston in 1638. Mary Dyer, twice banished, returned to Boston in 1660 to test the legality of the law which sentenced to death Quakers who visited the colony after being expelled, and was publicly hanged. An early rebel against the discrimination suffered by women in industry was Louisa Morton Green, who refused to do man's work at a spindle in a Dedham woolen mill unless she was paid man's wages. Working fourteen hours a day for two dollars a week and board, she found time to study to be a school teacher, and later became active in the anti-slavery cause, industrial reform, and woman suffrage. An early organizer of the Red Cross, and its first president, was Clara Barton. In medicine, religion, astronomy, physics, education, and the arts, scores of Massachusetts women battled for their sex. Phillis Wheatley was one of a long line of Negro women of Massachusetts who contributed to the State's literature, art, and social movements.

Nowhere has the east wind blown so vigorously in the State as through the schools. The spirit of the famous Act of 1647, which required each township of fifty families to have a primary school and each township of one hundred families to establish a grammar school, remained in force for two hundred years. An early governor of the State, James Sullivan, urged its citizens to throw off 'the trammels they had forged for us' — *they*, of course, being the English — and called for an American system of general public education, remarking, 'Where the mass of people are ignorant, poor and miserable, there is no public opinion excepting what is the offspring of fear.' As late as 1834 the Association of Farmers, Mechanics, and Other Workingmen demanded at its convention a better quality of instruction in the public schools. Not until Horace Mann fought his bitter battle as Secretary of the Board of Education did the State acquire a decent system of graded schools, with properly qualified, trained, and compensated teachers.

For more than two centuries the State has been predominantly industrial and commercial. As early as 1699 Edward Ward complained: 'The Inhabitants seem very Religious, showing many outward and visible signs of an inward and Spiritual Grace: But tho' they wear in their Faces the Innocence of Doves, you will find them in their Dealings as Subtile as Serpents. Interest is their Faith, Money their God, and Large Possessions the only Heaven they covet.' Although the nineteenth century, with its wind of liberalism, proved these strictures one-sided, it is worth recalling that the Massachusetts Bay Company was a joint stock company organized solely for profit, that the State early became a centre for the accumulation of capital employed in the South and West, and that the first corporation as the term is understood today arose in the State.

The essentially urban character of the people is emphasized by the fact that every citizen literally lives 'in town,' as the 316 towns and 39 cities comprise the total area of the State. At the town meetings, still held in ninety-three per cent of corporate communities in New England, qualified voters elect their selectmen, the chairman or moderator, and administrative officers. Under pressure from large and mixed populations, certain towns still unwilling to adopt representative city government have devised the 'limited town meeting,' attended by elected delegates chosen by vote according to precinct. Although the town meeting is supposed to favor the perpetuation of what has been called 'a sort of untitled squirarchy,' its champions maintain that this method of government at least keeps public officials under constant public scrutiny.

In spite of the 'town' character of its political life, there are farmers in the State — 163,219 of them. Regardless of their low birth rate and in the face of no growth of the farming population in the United States as a whole, they are increasing. The value of their holdings is slowly going up, and most of them own their farms. Here the Massachusetts tendency to smallness is manifest, as the farms are of few acres and well distributed, just as the State Forests are more numerous — and smaller — than in any other state.

When Boston was Tory, rural Massachusetts was Whig. When Boston was Federalist, rural Massachusetts was Republican and radical. Even today a rural resident of the State when not a Republican is a different breed of Democrat. The hinterland's distrust of the political power of the metropolis is apparent in the fact that the Boston police force is under the control not of the mayor but of a commissioner appointed by the Governor — who, although he no longer need be certified as 'a Christian worth £1000,' receives a lower salary than the Mayor of Boston. But the farmer, with all his political difference, partakes of the racial admixture and the turn of mind of other residents of the State. He, too, is very likely to be a trader, though he may do most of his trading with 'summer people' visiting the Berkshires or the Cape.

Making a campaign speech for Lincoln at Philadelphia in 1860, Charles Francis Adams of Massachusetts, facing what he termed 'the most con-

servative city in America,' half apologized for coming from 'a more
excitable community.' The State has always been full of stimulating
cross-winds. Life within its borders has never been conditioned by the
slow swing of the seasons, the easy tilling of an abundant earth. Ma-
rooned on a rocky soil, Massachusetts men had to be ingenious to survive,
and they early became skilled at devising shrewd 'notions,' commercial
and intellectual. Used to dealing with people, they learned to think in
small and individual terms rather than in broad geographical concepts.
The ideal supposed in Europe to be the tenet of all Americans, that because a thing is bigger it is somehow better, was never adopted by
Massachusetts.

Skillful of hand, sharp at a bargain, stubborn of mind, the Bay Stater
possesses a character which with its mixture of shrewdness and idealism
is often labeled hypocrisy. He exhibits a strong tendency to conform —
provided he thinks conformity is his own idea. But let conformity be
thrust upon him, and the east wind again begins to thrum! The blowing
of that wind brought to the State much early social legislation: the child
labor law in 1836, a law legalizing trade unions in 1842, the first State
board of health, the first minimum wage law for women and children,
and the first State tuberculosis sanatorium. Against general opposition,
first use was made of inoculation and of ether as an anesthetic within the
State.

Massachusetts is parochial, yet it is never long out of the main currents of American life. It is a State of tradition, but part of its tradition
is its history of revolt. Its people are fiercely individualistic, yet they
have fierce group loyalties. It is noted for conservatism, yet it exports
not only shoes and textiles but rebels to all corners of the earth. Its
sons and daughters live in small houses, worship in small churches,
work in small factories, produce small things, and vote in small political
units, yet time and again their largeness of spirit has burst beyond State
borders.

NATURAL SETTING

THE land of Massachusetts is a product of millions of years of wearing down and building up; erosion by water, wind, and ice; lifting of plains and seashore; filling in of valleys and troughs; eruption of volcanoes; intrusions of lava; and the invasion of continental glaciers. Rocks that must have had their origin thousands of feet below the surface may be found cropping out all over the State. Formations that once were simple and deposited on level planes are now complex and metamorphic rocks, warped, truncated, and steeply dipped — the results of physical and chemical changes that could have taken place only under extreme heat and at times of terrestrial cataclysms. Everywhere is the evidence that once-lofty mountains have been worn down to plain-level, and that one-time deep valleys have been filled in and raised to great heights.

At the beginning of known geologic time, three mountain masses of granitic rock, alternating with sea channels, extended northeast across the State. Strata were deposited on the shore of the Champlain Channel west of the Hoosac Mountain, in the narrow gulf which ran from Gaspé Point to Worcester, and in the trough from Rhode Island to the Bay of Fundy. Then came the period of the making of the Appalachian Mountains, of which the Hoosac Mountain and its continuation in the Green Mountains represented the axis. As a result of this cataclysm, the older Paleozoic clastics were metamorphized — limestone into marble, muds and gravels into slate and schist, and some of the sandstone into quartzite.

This raising of surface was followed by a renewed activity of the streams in wearing down the land masses. By the carboniferous era, the whole State had been reduced to a peneplain, and coal measures had been deposited in the Rhode Island-Nova Scotia basin, and in the Gaspé-Worcester trough.

In the next geologic era, the rock formations of the Connecticut Valley region had slipped down, and the sea had inundated the latter up to the northern boundary of the State. This twenty-mile-wide estuary gradually filled from the higher levels with materials that later were to become the sandstones, shales, and conglomerates of the valley. But during the formation of these rocks there occurred great outflows of lava, which covered in some places the older weak formation and, forming the traprock, resisted erosion so that they stand today as the prominent elevations of the valley.

All New England in a later period was reduced by erosion to a base-level, with the southeastern margin of Massachusetts submerged under a shallow sea. But by the end of this geologic era, the whole of the Appalachian region was uplifted, and Massachusetts was raised to a plateau of moderate elevation. The rivers again appeared to repeat the process of erosion, and the dissected topography of the uplands of the State is a present indication of that activity.

In recent geologic time, the continental ice-sheet, originating in the Laurentian region, crept down over New England, advancing as far south as Martha's Vineyard, Nantucket, and Long Island. During its advance, it picked up rocks which became embedded in the ice, and with these it scraped the soil and ground the mountains. It dammed rivers and changed courses, formed lakes, and deeply altered the character of the land. Upon its retreat, it left behind a terminal moraine which made and shaped Cape Cod, Martha's Vineyard, and Nantucket. Over the whole land it spread glacial débris of soil, rocks, and boulders.

The complex geologic history of Massachusetts has resulted in a widely varied landscape patchwork. Within a small area, the State offers a great variety of terrain — rugged coasts, barren sand beaches, wild mountains, green valleys, and upland plateaus.

The State as a whole, however, may be divided into four physiographic types: coastal lowlands, interior lowlands, dissected uplands, and residuals of ancient mountains.

The coastal lowlands spread out at Narragansett Bay, cutting through the middle of Rhode Island and across Massachusetts to the New Hampshire line near the Merrimack River. Thus they take in the eastern part of the State, including the Cape Cod peninsula and the islands off the mainland. The whole coastline of Massachusetts, with its rugged mountainous shore and deep indentations, is evidence of an early submergence and a later uplift of the area. The submerged river mouths, the many good harbors and bays of Boston, Buzzard, and Narragansett, are prominent features of the topography of Massachusetts. Farther inland, the effect of the lowering of the coastal plain is found in the falls and rapids of the rivers.

In the northeastern section of this division the bed-rock is near the surface, and rock-outcrops are found in many places. It is this out-cropping along the coast that gives the North Shore of Massachusetts its rugged and picturesque character. This division is also characterized by the many shallow troughs and basins that are eroded on the softer rocks and enclosed by the higher lands of resistant formations. The two largest and most important of these depressions are the Boston and Narragansett Basins.

The most outstanding feature of the division is, without doubt, the peninsula of Cape Cod, which extends for sixty-five miles in the form of an arm bent upward at the elbow. This owes its origin to the glacier, and was refashioned by the sea and wind. Near here are also many islands of the same origin — Martha's Vineyard, Nantucket, and the sixteen Elizabeth islands. The glacial outwash plains of Martha's Vineyard and Nantucket are now broad grassy heaths. The southern side of the delta-like plain of Cape Cod has been cut along high cliffs by the surf and waves. Here the plain is covered with a growth of pitch pine and scrub oak. Much of the 'forearm' of the Cape is a bleak grassy country, while the outer end is a wild and desolate region with long yellow beaches. Lacking land fit for farming, the Cape and Islands have reared a distinctive type of hardy men who 'farm' the sea.

In the interior of Massachusetts, there are two lowlands or valleys: the Connecticut River Valley and the Berkshire Valley. Each of these is enclosed by uplands. The Connecticut River Valley is a lens-shaped trench extending from the northern boundary of the State to Long Island Sound, and is drained throughout its length by the Connecticut River. Its weak red sandstones give its soil a distinctive ruddy tint. The landscape throughout the valley is dominated by curved wooded ridges that run longitudinally and owe their origin to intrusive trap-lava which resisted erosion after the weaker layers were worn away. Some of these traprock elevations rise, in the southern part, high above the valley, ranging from 954 feet to 1628 feet in Mounts Holyoke, Tom, Toby, and Grace.

The Connecticut Valley, with its rich soil and mild climate, has become a productive agricultural country, as well as the seat of many prosperous and populous cities and towns. Its broad open meadows, reddish soil, and tobacco and onion fields present an aspect somewhat unusual in New England.

The Berkshire Valley, shut off by the Berkshire plateau in the east and the Taconic Mountains in the west, is an isolated world of its own. The northern part of the valley is watered by streams that cut through the Taconics to the Hudson, and the southern part by the headwaters of the Housatonic. From Pittsfield northward it is only six miles wide;

but southward it opens up into the meadowlands of Great Barrington, Lenox, and Sheffield. The valley with its green meadows is largely devoted to dairy farming, and lives a peaceful, isolated life.

The uplands of Massachusetts are two divisions separated by the Connecticut River, but joining north of the valley to form the great central upland of northern New England.

The western uplands, or, as they are commonly known, the Berkshire Hills, are a continuation of the Vermont Green Mountains, deeply dissected and composed of a number of ranges and small valleys. The Taconic Range, on the extreme border of the State, attains its highest elevation in Mount Greylock at 3535 feet, and decreases to the south, where Mount Washington in the southeastern corner of Massachusetts rises 2624 feet. The Hoosac Range, farther east, varies in altitude from 1200 to 1600 feet, with Spruce Hill at 2588 feet as its highest point.

In the Vermont Green Mountains, only the valleys are cultivated and inhabited; but here in Massachusetts, farms and hamlets are found on the tops of the elevations, often at high altitudes. This is the country of the famous 'hill towns' of the Berkshires, which attract many visitors during the summer to enjoy the health-giving atmosphere and surrounding scenic beauty. The best known of these hill towns are Florida and Peru. East of these ranges, the uplands slope southeasterly toward the Connecticut River Valley, and are deeply cut by such streams as the Deerfield, Westfield, and Farmington Rivers. The most picturesque of these rivers is the Deerfield, which has an impressive canyon-like valley through the plateau.

The eastern uplands of Worcester County rise gradually from the Connecticut River Valley eastward to an elevation of 1100 feet in the middle of the State, then slope down toward the coast. This plateau is an extension of the White Mountains of New Hampshire, which cross Massachusetts into Connecticut. The outstanding features of the plateau are the monadnocks of Mount Wachusett and Mount Watatic, solitary remnants of once lofty mountains.

In general, the topography of Massachusetts is a varied patchwork of physiographic features, the eroded remnants of once high mountains, leveled to a plateau which has been deeply dissected by streams, and scraped and reformed by glaciers. It affords, from its indented and rocky coast in the east to its lofty hills in the extreme west, a cross-section of the Appalachian Mountain system in its old age, when it was covered by the continental ice-sheet. Moreover, this varied topography has had a great influence upon the lives and occupations of its people — the fishermen of the coast, the urban dwellers of eastern cities, the industrial workers along the waterways of the mill towns, the suburban farmers, the large-scale planters of the Connecticut Valley, and the Berkshire natives, still somewhat isolated and provincial.

FLORA

Massachusetts lies in an area characterized by a forest cover composed mainly of trees which shed their leaves yearly about the time of approaching winter. Nevertheless, within the State are to be found well-defined areas with quite different floristic makeup. These subdivisions might be called: the Cape Cod region; the area of the sea margin extending from Cape Cod to the New Hampshire line; the upland region of Central Massachusetts; and the rugged area of the Berkshires in the western part of the State. To the above might also be added the tops of the two highest points of land within the State, Mount Greylock and Mount Wachusett.

In the morainal and outwash area characterizing Cape Cod is found a floristic composition similar in certain respects to that of southern New Jersey, since the Cape is really the only close approach to coastal plain within the State.

Northward along the seacoast are many plants which do not stray far from the influence of the sea. Examples range from the low-growing beach plants to the marsh grasses, sedges, and rushes.

By far the largest area of the State is included in the upland region, which is covered by a typical northern deciduous forest of maples, birches, beeches, oaks, with a scattering of pine and an occasional stand of hemlock and larch. The forest floor is covered with a host of low-growing herbs varying according to their particular habitat. In the low marshy spots will be found many early spring plants such as skunk cabbage, American white hellebore, marsh marigold, white and blue violets; while on the drier slopes grow the false spikenard, Solomon's-seal, trailing arbutus, wild oats, and various trilliums. From early spring to late fall there is a constant parade of gorgeous color with such striking plants as rhodora, azalea, mountain laurel, shad, dogwood, viburnum, augmented by innumerable herbaceous types. The ferns add materially to the charm of the landscape, from the low, delicate maidenhair spleenwort to the large, graceful osmundas.

The Berkshires offer still another scenic and floristic type, much more rugged than the last, and to some much more beautiful. The forest is still of the deciduous type, but with a ground cover differing in certain respects, for here will be found plants more often associated with cooler regions of the North.

Space does not permit mention of the great variety of plants growing within the State, but there are available at least three collections of mounted plants. The herbarium of the New England Botanical Club, located at the Gray Herbarium at Harvard University, has an excellent representative collection. The herbarium of the Hadwen Botanical Club, located at Clark University in Worcester, specializes in the flora of Worcester County, which is of the general upland region; while that at Amherst College in Amherst contains plants of the western region. All three of these herbaria are available to the genuinely interested person. Harvard University also maintains the famous Arnold Arboretum where trees and shrubs are appropriately planted and labeled.

FAUNA

The effigy of a codfish hanging since 1784 in the assembly room of the State House on Beacon Hill, and the fact that early settlers used beaver skins as currency, testify to the firmness with which the existence of early Massachusetts men was rooted in the abundance of wild life. Fishing has maintained its economic importance through three centuries, but when in 1636 William Pynchon removed to the wilderness of Springfield to trade in beaver, he signified the beginning of a process of extinction of Massachusetts fauna halted only in recent years.

The forests preserve today a much narrower range of wild life. The gray wolf and the black bear have been extirpated. The lynx, once common, only accidentally finds its way into the mountainous portions of the State at long intervals. The beaver is gone. The northern Virginia deer, almost driven out during the nineteenth century, has appeared in larger numbers in late years, but is scarce. Of the larger forms of wild life, only the fox holds its own. In spite of hunters, the red fox, cross fox, and black fox are still commonly seen.

Of the family Leporidae, the eastern varying hare or white rabbit is occasionally seen. The northern cottontail or gray rabbit is more uncommon. The family Muridae is represented by many varieties of mice

and rats and by the muskrat. The skunk is very common in open woodlands and fields. There are two varieties of weasels: the little brown
weasel, often seen in stony places, and the New York weasel, which is
not very common and usually lives in the woods. The large brown mink is
sometimes found along the coast. Shrews and moles exist in numbers,
and several varieties of bat are common. Especially large is the family
of Rodentia, whose members are the northern gray squirrel and the
southern red squirrel, the chipmunk or ground squirrel, the woodchuck
or groundhog, the rare Canadian flying squirrel, and the more common
southern flying squirrel. A most remarkable creature, the one member
in the State of the family Zapodidae, is the Hudson Bay jumping mouse.

Whales, though no longer numerous, are sometimes sighted off the
coast or washed up on the beach. Many varieties of snakes are found, as
are lizards, tortoises, and toads, frogs, and salamanders.

The seacoast and secluded streams and ponds inland are the home of
a large variety of water, marsh, and shore birds, including the diving
birds, the grebe, the puffin, guillemot, murre, razor-billed auk, little auk,
and loon. The great northern loon and the red-throated loon visit the
State during part of the year.

The gulls and terns are the best-known members of the long-winged
swimmers. In this same class are the skuas and jaegers, virtually sea-
hawks, with powerful wings, beaks, and claws.

The tube-nosed swimmers, having tubular nostrils and exceptional
powers of flight, are represented by fulmars, shearwaters, and petrels.
The four-toed, fully-webbed, Totipalmate order of water birds includes
gannets, cormorants, and man-o'-war birds.

Among the better-known river ducks are the black, red-legged black,
baldpate, and wood ducks. Rarer varieties include the mallard, European
widgeon, golden teal, blue-winged teal, and American pintail. The sea
ducks are the canvasback, scaup, lesser scaup, golden-eye, bufflehead,
old-squaw, eider, and scoter ducks, as well as the rare ring-necked and
harlequin varieties. The Canada and brant goose visit the State during
part of the year, though not in great numbers, and the whistling swan is
a rare migrant.

Of Herodiones are the great blue heron, little blue heron, green heron,
black-crowned night heron, bittern, and the rare least bittern. A few
examples of the order Paludicolae still remain, chiefly the sora, Virginia
rail, and coot; gallinules are rare, and the crane is merely an accidental
visitor.

The shore birds are waders differing from herons and marsh birds in that their breasts are plump and rounded, with a less prominent sternum. Generally they are small in size, and have short tails and long legs.

The ground-dwelling, scratching game birds are found in diminishing numbers. Probably the ring-necked pheasant is the most common. Bobwhites, which flourished locally when introduced and protected, are now uncommon. The ruffed and Witlow grouse and the heath hen remain in only a few places. The domestic dove or pigeon is found in the larger cities, less commonly in rural districts; and the mourning dove is frequently seen.

Among the birds of prey are such accidental visitors as the turkey vulture and the eagle. The hawk family has many members in the State, as has the owl family.

The cuckoos and the belted kingfisher comprise an order by themselves. Another order includes the woodpeckers. The Macrochire family, with peculiar wing development and frail feet, has for members the whip-poor-will, nighthawk, chimney swift, ruby-throated hummingbird, and the very rare goatsucker.

The Passeres, or perching birds, are the largest of all orders. Of the so-called songless perching birds the kingbird is familiar. The songbirds of the Passeres are very numerous, including the larks and starlings, the blue jay, bobolink, cowbird, blackbird, meadowlark, oriole, rusty blackbird, and grackle. The Fringillidae or finches, the largest family of perching songbirds, are represented in Massachusetts by about thirty species.

Fish caught in the lakes and rivers and along the coast of Massachusetts include alewives, bass, rockbass, bluefish, bonito, butterfish, carp, catfish, cod, cunners, cusk, eels, flounders, haddock, hake, halibut, herring, kingfish, mackerel, Spanish mackerel, perch, pickerel, pollock, salmon, scup, shad, skate, smelt, sturgeon, swordfish, tautog, tom-cod, trout, turbot, and weakfish. The State is well known for its shellfish: clams, lobsters, oysters, scallops, and shrimp.

By a not unusual human phenomenon, as wild life has declined, interest in natural history has increased. In the mid-nineteenth century Agassiz laid the basis for a pre-eminence in the field of biology retained by Massachusetts institutions to this day. Agassiz's pioneer work in classification was carried on by his son, and his students became foremost scientists — Jeffries Wyman, Nathaniel Southgate Shaler, Burt G. Wilder, among others. The biological museum at Harvard bears Agassiz's name, and he founded the Marine Biological Institute at Woods Hole. The splendid theoretical and practical work being done by the Massachusetts Bureau of Fisheries, the biological departments of Massachusetts universities, the New England Society of Natural History, the State Department of Conservation may be properly said to owe much to the pioneer labors of the Swiss-American scientist.

Massachusetts philosophers and naturalists from Thoreau to Dallas Lore Sharp have drawn much of their inspiration from native wild life. Artists, too, have turned to birds and animals for their subjects, notably Frank W. Benson, the well-known painter and etcher of waterfowl, whose work may be seen in many private galleries and in the Boston Museum of Fine Arts, as well as Charles Heil, whose studies of birds in water-colors are exceptional.

Of the organizations which foster the study of nature in a broader sense, the New England Society of Natural History, founded in 1830, itself the outgrowth of the Linnaean Society dating back to 1814, is evidence of the early interest in the subject. The Audubon Society, the Field and Forest Club, the Appalachian Mountain Club, the Green Mountain Club, and numerous bird clubs throughout the State serve to center the interest of nature-lovers today.

FIRST AMERICANS

THE remote ancestors of the Indian tribes in Massachusetts were a hunting and fishing people without agriculture. They had learned to fashion several varieties of stone implements, but did not use either tobacco, pottery, or axes. These early people were probably related to the Beothuk red Indians of Newfoundland, and burial places belonging to their culture have been unearthed at Marblehead and near Fresh Pond in Cambridge. Excavations at Grassy Island in Berkley on the Taunton River indicate the presence of an ancient village, established by the depth of the salt peat overlay as being at least one thousand years old.

The Indians encountered by the first Europeans in Massachusetts belonged to the Algonquin linguistic stock, and occupied the large area ranging from the Maritime Provinces of Canada to the Gulf of Florida and as far west as the Mississippi. The old Algonquins of Massachusetts came from the west, gradually pushing the pre-Algonquin inhabitants to the coast, where they were finally assimilated or wiped out. Favorite camping places were the areas near the falls of the larger rivers, which were later picked by the white men as sites for dams and factories.

Roger Williams has preserved the legend that a crow brought a grain of corn in one ear and a bean in the other from the field of the great god Kauntantouwit in the southwest. This fable assumes historical importance in view of the fact that it was precisely the old Algonquins, coming from the west and south, who introduced agriculture. They also brought with them the art of pottery-making, although its forms were restricted to tobacco pipes and cooking vessels. Many of the vessels had pointed bases, made to be supported by hearthstones and not suspended over the fire. Ornamentation consisted largely of lines and dots arranged in zones or other patterns, one of the most persistent of which was a zigzag design commonly found in pottery from the mound groups of the Ohio region.

Like their white successors, the earliest Massachusetts Indians got much of their food from the sea. Some of the tribes made desultory visits to the salt water; others lived permanently near the shore. Clams, quahogs, scallops, and oysters formed an important addition to their food supply, and the shells heaped up in the course of many years have aided in preserving fragments of their pottery and the more perishable implements used in their rude arts. An invasion of the Iroquois separated the old Algonquin and later Algonquin cultures. Shell beads belong almost invariably to the later Algonquin period. Pottery vessels shaped in globular form for suspension over the fire and terra cotta pipes of the later Algonquins show Iroquois influence. The purple quahog shell wampum and the white wampum were borrowed from the Dutch of Long Island.

The occasional presence in early Indian graves of porcelain and glass beads and of copper and brass ornaments emphasizes the fact that early contact of Europeans with Massachusetts Indians did not begin at Plymouth. In the year 1578, for example, no fewer than four hundred European vessels were engaged in whaling and fishing along the New England coast, and most of these traded with the Indians. The 'Skeleton in Armor' found at Fall River in 1831 wore a brass breastplate about fourteen inches long, and around his lower torso was a belt of brass tubes closed together lengthwise. The fact that similar tubes arranged in like manner had been found in Denmark made Longfellow believe that the grave was that of a Norseman, and in this belief he wrote his poem. Later examination showed that the skeleton was that of an Indian not antedating 1650, and as no Indian could have manufactured brass, the 'armor' was probably hammered from a brass kettle received in trade.

On Dighton Rock, a sandstone boulder, eleven feet high, on Assonet Neck in Berkley, appear pecked incisions of questionable origin, some apparently alphabetical and some pictorial. Certain authorities have read among them a Latin record of a visit of the Portuguese Miguel Cortereal some years after he and his ship disappeared from history on the rocky coast of Newfoundland in 1502, supporting their case by recalling a local Indian legend that strange men in a wooden house came up the river and fought with the natives.

However vague pre-Colonial history of the Indians must remain, we know that during the early Colonial period seven tribes inhabited Massachusetts: the Massachusetts, the Wampanoags, the Nausets, the Pennacooks, the Nipmucks, the Pocumtucs, and the Mohicans.

The Massachusetts dominated the territory enclosed in a circle drawn through Boston and Charlestown harbors, Malden, Nantucket, Hingham, Weymouth, Braintree, and Dorchester. Before the arrival of the first settlers the Massachusetts had reached the height of their importance. The plague of 1616–17 wrecked their power, and by 1631 they numbered only about five hundred. Ultimately they were gathered into the villages of the Christianized or Praying Indians — almost the last act of a tragic drama.

The Wampanoags held sovereignty over the whole tract from Cape Cod to Massachusetts Bay, with some control over the petty tribes of the interior.

The Nausets, a friendly tribe who accepted the white man as a brother, occupied Cape Cod and the adjacent islands under the dominion of the Wampanoags. Most of them became Christianized before King Philip's War. Nauset Light at Eastham commemorates these gentle red men.

The Pennacooks, allied with the quarrelsome Abenaki of Maine who continually raided the lands of the Massachusetts, originally inhabited northern Massachusetts. At the close of King Philip's War in 1676 the remnant of the Pennacooks migrated to Canada.

The Nipmucks roamed the eastern interior of Massachusetts from Boston on the east to Bennington, Vermont, on the west. Concord, New Hampshire, on the north, and Connecticut and Rhode Island on the south bounded their territory, which centered in Worcester County.

The Pocumtucs, whose chief village was near the present town of Deerfield, dominated all the Indians of the Connecticut Valley in Massachusetts.

Like the Massachusetts, the Mohicans, popularly memorialized in Cooper's novel, were decimated by the plague of 1616–17. This tribe had originally ranged from New York into the upper portions of the Housatonic Valley. In 1664 their Council moved its fire from Albany to Stockbridge, Massachusetts. From Stockbridge some of the Mohicans migrated to the Susquehanna River, but the remnants of this picturesque people were gathered into a mission at Stockbridge — a forlorn hope for perpetuation.

All these Indians were typical long-headed Algonquins, with smooth skins, swarthy complexions, black hair and eyes, and high foreheads. They had broad shoulders and brawny arms, but lean bellies, flat knees, and small hands and feet. Their skins were redder and less coppery than those of their western relations.

The men wore in winter a costume later adopted by white hunters — leggings, dressed buckskin shirts, breech clouts and moccasins, and sometimes fur caps. In summer the breech clouts and moccasins formed a complete costume. Women wore leggings and long gowns. Garments were decorated with fringes and sometimes painted with simple designs.

Both sexes painted their faces. Tattooing was confined to the cheeks, upon which totemic figures were permanently placed by the insertion of black pigment beneath the surface of the skin. The men plucked their beards, and hair was dressed in various styles according to the sex, age, and station of the individual.

The primary weapon was the wooden bow strung with moose sinew, and wooden arrows tipped with stone or bone and carried in quivers of otter skin. In warfare the usual offensive weapon was the tomahawk, with bark shields serving to some extent for defense.

Communities were built on hunting and agriculture. The members of the tribes or communities were the recognized proprietors of certain hunting, fishing, and agricultural lands, held as a rule in common. The winter villages were usually situated in warm, thickly wooded valleys near a lake or river. The early spring was spent on the fishing grounds, and when the planting season arrived the tribe moved to its summer fields. Each family had its garden of corn, beans, pumpkins, squash, artichokes, and tobacco, cultivated with hoes of stone, wood, or clam shells and fertilized by herring and shad. Wild berries, roots, and nuts furnished other sources of food, supplemented by fish and by the meat of the larger mammals preserved by cutting in strips and smoke-drying.

The Indians divided themselves very strictly into three social classes: those of royal blood, including the sachems, shamans, elders of the council, and subordinate chiefs; commoners or freemen with rights to the tribal lands; and 'outsiders' of alien blood, usually captives, with no tribal rights. Descent was commonly reckoned through the female line, and the office of head chief or sachem was hereditary. If tribes were large and important they might be governed by several under-chiefs, and each tribe had a council of elders of noble blood. The shamans or pow-wows possessed great influence. They were partly seers, partly wizards, and partly physicians. When, as occasionally happened, the offices of sachem and shaman were combined, the person vested with this dual authority held tremendous power.

Polygamy was fairly common, and divorce was approved and frequent, the right being exercised as freely by women as by men. Justice was a simple matter. If any tribesman was wronged, all related to him were bound to see that proper restitution was made. Murder was avenged or suitably punished by the kinsmen of the victim.

The Algonquins believed that Manitou, a supernatural power, was inherent in all things. An evil power personified as Mattand was feared and placated. Elaborate communal ceremonies celebrated the harvest, and rituals concerned with sun, rainfall, and a plenitude of game were performed religiously. In all these ceremonies, as in secular matters, smoking had definite significance.

On a day in March, 1621, a flurry was created among the citizens of Plymouth when a strange Indian suddenly appeared, quite alone, in the middle of Leyden Street. He caused even greater excitement when, with an air of grave friendliness, he spoke two words in English: 'Welcome, Englishmen!' The stranger was Samoset, a member of one of Massachusetts' first families come to offer aid to these white aliens. He had learned a few words of English from casual fishermen at Monhegan, and he spoke them with unconscious drama, unaware that they spelled the doom of his race.

When the Pilgrims first arrived in the new country, they settled on lands belonging to Massasoit, chief of the Wampanoags, whose favorite residence was at Pokanoket (Mount Hope, Bristol, Rhode Island), a spot which was to witness the death not only of his son Philip but of the hopes of his race. On April 1, 1621, on Strawberry Hill, Plymouth, Massasoit in solemn council ratified the first treaty between Indian and white man. The treaty, effected by the good offices of Samoset, was faithfully supported by Massasoit, and lasted the fifty-four years of his lifetime. Massasoit was never converted to Christianity, but without his generous help the settlement of Massachusetts would have been infinitely more difficult and perhaps impossible.

Another Indian who gave the Pilgrims much practical aid in their adjustment to the conditions of life in a wild country among savage peoples was Squanto, who served as an interpreter. He was one of five Indians carried to London in 1605 by Captain George Weymouth. In 1614 he was brought back to Cape Cod by John Smith, but in the same year he again visited England — this time with Captain Thomas Dernier. Returning to America in 1619, he fell in with the Pilgrims at Plymouth. He is supposed to have been the only Indian to escape the Patuxet (Plymouth) plague.

Not all tribes, of course, were friendly to the first settlers. Before the arrival of the Pilgrims the savage Pequot (destroyer) Indians had fought their way through from the west and settled in what is now eastern Connecticut. In 1636 Boston joined the towns of Hartford, Wethersfield, and Windsor in a concerted attack against the Pequots with the aid of the Mohicans. The remnants of the tribe were sold to the Bermudans, who purchased no bargain, as the Indians proved to be 'sullen and treacherous.' They were poor laborers in the fields, but as whalers and sailors they developed considerable skill and daring.

One of the most determined foes of the white settlers was King Philip, who believed that the continued encroachment of the white men must end in the extermination of the red men, and that the colonists were consciously working toward this end. The gradual extension of the colonists for two generations brought about a condition in which Indian and white land claims conflicted. Roger Williams had once in a letter to Governor Bradford hotly protested the validity of the land titles of the colonists. 'Why lay such stress,' he demanded, 'upon your patent from King James? 'Tis but idle parchment. James has no more right to give away or sell Massasoit's lands and cut and carve his country than Massasoit has to sell King James' kingdom or to send Indians to colonize Warwickshire.' In addition, the colonists had gained presumption with power, and insisted on administering justice to everybody. To the Indians this not only seemed an unwarrantable interference with their rights, but also made it difficult, if not impossible, for them to obtain fair hearings in the English courts.

Along with his belief that the Indian must drive out the intruder or be exterminated, Philip had perhaps a personal reason for his hatred of the whites — a belief that his brother Wamsutta had been murdered. At all events, he prepared for war secretly and with intelligence. Shortly before the outbreak of hostilities in 1675 the Governor of Massachusetts sent an ambassador to Philip asking him to pledge peace. Philip returned a proud but not undiplomatic reply: 'Your governor is but a subject of King Charles of England. I shall not treat with a subject. I shall treat of peace only with the King, my brother. When he comes, I am ready.'

Philip undoubtedly intended a simultaneous movement of all the tribes on the North Atlantic seaboard against the white men. An unexpected event, however, precipitated war a year sooner than he had intended and destroyed his plans: the treachery of Sassamon.

The latter, one of Philip's tribe, had been converted to Christianity, had lived at Harvard College for a short time, and was a school teacher in the Praying Town of Natick. He became Philip's secretary, and it was he who imparted news of Philip's plans to the Governor at Plymouth. Philip learned of the treachery, and Sassamon's body was found in Assawompsett Pond in Middleborough. The implication was obvious, and the English authorities promptly apprehended three of Philip's tribesmen and brought them to trial.

In order to give a semblance of fairness to the trial, six Indians were included on the jury. The concurrence of the six in a verdict of guilty could reasonably be counted on. But the court took no chances. Before the six Indians were empaneled, a legal jury of twelve good (white) men and true had been drawn. In case of a 'bolt' by the Indians, a legal conviction was still assured. The Indians were executed in June, 1675, creating the overt act which forced Philip's hand. Before this event no hostilities had been undertaken by Philip or his warriors against the whites: now he immediately attacked Swansea.

Town after town fell before him. While the English forces were marching in one direction, the Indians were burning and laying waste in another. The Narragansetts had not yet heartily engaged in the campaign, though there is no doubt that they stood pledged to it. In order to secure their strong support, Philip went to their country. This tactical necessity, forced upon him by the precipitation of war, turned out to be fatal. In December an army of fifteen hundred English concentrated upon this region where Philip was known to be. The whole Narragansett Nation was trapped in an immense swamp at South Kingstown, Rhode Island, and Philip was overwhelmingly defeated.

This was the turning-point of the war. When success in Massachusetts no longer attended Philip's cause, his southern allies began to desert him. He was driven from place to place, losing more and more of his warriors. His wife and son were captured and sold into slavery; his heart and courage were broken. He took shelter at last in his ancient seat at Pokanoket, but even here there was no longer any refuge. He was driven out and slain by one of his own men, in vengeance, according to the English report, for the life of a brother who had been shot by Philip.

A few miles south of Kingstown, a stone shaft by the railroad track marks the grave of the Narragansett Nation. The barrel of the gun with which Philip was killed is now in Pilgrim Hall, Plymouth, and its lock is in the keeping of the Massachusetts Historical Society of Boston.

With the death of King Philip the power of the tribes of southern New England was completely destroyed. The war dragged on for two years more, until 1678. After Philip's rout, however, there was never any doubt as to its outcome. During its course the Wampanoags and their lesser allies, as well as the Narragansetts, were all but wiped out. The few survivors fled northward or westward beyond the Hudson.

The extermination of the red men was not accomplished without dreadful casualties among the English. One in every ten of the five thousand Englishmen of military age in the Massachusetts and Plymouth colonies is estimated to have been killed or captured. It was forty years before the devastated frontiers were reoccupied.

Not only among the Indians were there idealists who, like Samoset and Massasoit, believed that there could be brotherhood between red men and white. Such idealists existed also among the colonists. One of the most active of these was John Eliot, the 'Apostle to the Indians.' Eliot was a sincere evangelist and a man of tremendous industry. He mastered the Algonquin language and translated the Bible into this tongue so that his converts might read it for themselves. He believed that before the Indians could be converted they must first be civilized, and in that belief the famous Praying Towns were conceived.

In founding these centers of Christian education, Eliot associated with himself Gookin, Mayhew, and other men of intelligence and altruism. They established some thirty Praying Towns with schools and a teacher in each. The first was at Natick in 1651. A set of by-laws was formulated and an Indian named Waban was appointed justice of the peace. In the following year another Praying Town was established at Concord, and soon there were others sprinkled over the territory from Cape Cod to Narragansett Bay. Eliot traveled from one to another, preaching, teaching, and supervising. At first he was violently opposed by the local chiefs and priests, who feared the undermining of their power, but behind Eliot's gospel teachings loomed the heavy shadow of the English authorities, and gradually opposition was emptied of force. By 1674 there were eleven hundred converts in Massachusetts — five hundred in Plymouth and the rest in Nantucket and Martha's Vineyard. Many of these conversions were no doubt genuine, but whether they were due more to religious conviction than to friendship for the white teachers is problematical.

Eliot's plan embraced the possibility of higher education for his protégés. The first brick building at Harvard College was erected for Indian students, but they did not make use of it in numbers sufficient to justify the building, and it was transformed into a printing shop. One Indian, Caleb Cheeshahteamuck, was graduated from Harvard in the class of 1665; at least three others studied at the college but did not graduate.

The Indians on Cape Cod and the adjacent islands had been in large part Christianized before the outbreak of King Philip's War. It is probable that some of them left the Praying Towns to join Philip, as did many from the Praying Towns around Boston.

It was the undeserved fate of the Christian Indians to be treated by Philip as allies of the English and to be suspected by the English of treacherous commerce with Philip. One of the blacker pages in the history of the relations of the colonists and the Indians is the chronicle of English treatment of the Christianized Naticks. Without overt act on the part of the latter to justify any suspicion of their loyalty, they were ordered to emigrate in the dead of winter. The Praying Town at Wamesit (Tewksbury) was broken up, and its inhabitants driven out to Long Island and Deer Island. The Indians suffered terribly in their confinement at such a season to an area where they had neither shelter nor stores. After several weeks the General Court, yielding to adverse public opinion, gave permission for their removal from the islands — providing, however, that this must be done without expense to the colony. Those who had survived were taken to Cambridge, where a humane citizen, Thomas Oliver, gave them refuge on his lands along the Charles River until spring, when most of them returned to the ruins of their homes. Ill, weakened by exposure and hunger, they were too feeble to maintain many towns, and the remoter ones were abandoned.

This setback dealt a death blow to any further attempts to Christianize the Indians. The 'Apostle to the Indians' strove in vain. Six years after the conclusion of King Philip's War, only four Praying Towns remained out of some thirty thriving centers which John Eliot had established. His life work had been undone.

The Indians at Natick, who at one time held all the town offices, were gradually replaced by white men, and their land titles extinguished. At various times and places Indian reservations were established. In 1861 there were reservations at Chappequiddick, Christiantown, Gay Head, Herring Pond, Natick, and Ponkapog. But this restricted life was not favorable to the red man. Mentally and physically, the Indians degenerated with the taking on of the white men's vices.

Today there are only two places in Massachusetts where the Indians have been able to preserve a semblance of their ethnic identity: Mashpee and Gay Head. The former town, incorporated in 1871, comprises Mashpee, South Mashpee, and a part of Wakeby. It has a public library, a town hall, and two churches; one of the latter, the Indian Mission Church, founded in 1684, is of interest to visitors. But the real sight in Mashpee is the cranberry bogs, the principal support of the town, which belong mostly to the white non-residents who employ the Indians as pickers. In the season, bending their backs over the bog, can be seen the half-breed descendants of the proud and friendly savages who once roamed the windswept dunes of Cape Cod.

On the farthest tip of Martha's Vineyard, across Menemsha Pond, rises a peninsula that ends in cliffs composed of strata of incredibly variegated clays — red, blue, orange, tan, and black — alternating with a

HISTORICAL LANDMARKS

A GOOD many landmarks in the history of Massachusetts are still standing. The pictures of some of these landmarks are reproduced here: the house of John Alden, who was one of the heroes of Longfellow's poem, 'Miles Standish'; the Paul Revere House; the Old South Meeting-House; the Old State House, which saw the Boston Massacre take place beneath the stately carvings of the Lion and the Unicorn which adorn its roof.

Also included among the pictures are two ships, for the sea has always been important in the making of Massachusetts. First is the 'Arbella' — a reconstruction — which floats on the waters of the Salem Harbor not far from the spot where the original vessel dropped anchor in 1630. And there is the frigate 'Constitution,' famous for its victories in the War of 1812, and the subject of Holmes's poem, 'Old Ironsides.'

THE ARBELLA, SALEM

JOHN ALDEN HOUSE, DUXBURY

L REVERE HOUSE, BOSTON

COMMODORE'S QUARTERS, U.S. FRIGATE CONSTITUTION

By the rude bridge that
    arched the flood,
Their flag to April's
    breeze unfurled,
Here once the embattled
    farmers stood,
And fired the shot heard
    round the world.

THE MINUTEMAN STATUE, CONCORD

OLD SOUTH MEETING HOUSE, BOSTON

LEYDEN ST., PLYMOUTH, FIRST STREET IN MASSACHUSETTS

OLD STATE HOUSE, BOSTON

JOHN QUINCY ADAMS HOUSE, QUINCY

dazzling white sandy substance. This is Gay Head. From these bright clays the Indians, who have kept their racial stock more nearly pure here than elsewhere, fashion small vases and jars which preserve the designs and patterns inherited from remote ancestors. The sale of these souvenirs by silent Indian children waiting by the roadside for the hordes of summer tourists is the last reminder of a primitive culture that could not survive the rape of its free forests and wide lands.

ENOUGH OF ITS HISTORY
TO EXPLAIN ITS PEOPLE

MASSACHUSETTS (măs-să-chū'sĕts) 190 miles long, 60 to 100 miles broad, 8266 square miles in area; bounded northerly by New Hampshire and Vermont, westerly by New York, southerly by Connecticut, Rhode Island, and the Atlantic, easterly by Massachusetts Bay and the Atlantic, lies between the parallels of 41° 10' and 42° 53' north latitude and between 69° 57' and 73° 30' west latitude. Its name is a combination of three Algonquin words meaning 'near the great mountain': *adchu* (mountain or hill), *set* (location near or in the vicinity of), *massu* (great).

MASSACHUSETTS' history begins not with the landing of the Pilgrims at Plymouth but when Martin Luther dramatically nailed his ninety-five theses to the church door at Wittenberg. The Protestant Reformation from which the religious dissension of the reign of Henry VIII may be traced drove Pilgrim and Puritan to Massachusetts in quest of theological freedom for themselves if not for other religious and social dissenters.

Before religious nonconformists became the first permanent settlers, the coast of the Bay Colony had been well explored by hardy adventurers. Leif, son of Eric the Red, may have touched Massachusetts with his Norsemen in the year 1000; it is probable, too, that French and Spanish fishermen cast their nets on the Grand Banks off Newfoundland in the middle of the fifteenth century and that many of them touched Cape Cod, lured by the fish from which the sickle-shaped promontory takes its name. The first voyage definitely recorded was that of John Cabot, Venetian navigator, whose exploration in 1497 and 1498 gave England her claim to the region of North America. During the next century scattered explorers slowly added to Europe's meager knowledge of the region: John Rut, a shipmaster of the English Royal Navy, Verrazzano under the *fleur de lis*, Gomez under the flag of Spain, all sought a route to the fabled riches of Zipangu and Cathay. Unsung fishermen, too, contented with the less romantic cod of Massachusetts' shores, looked for shelter from the North Atlantic's storms in the snug harbors of the coast.

Commercial enterprise and the search for exotic Eastern treasure motivated these early voyages, and similar motives were responsible for the first attempts to settle Massachusetts. The patent for the colonization of southern New England which Sir Humphrey Gilbert obtained from Elizabeth in 1578, recognizing that permanent population must precede trade, authorized the planting of an English community beyond the seas. Sir Humphrey unfortunately died before this was accomplished; returning from his first exploratory voyage, his frail ten-ton vessel was swamped by the huge waves of an Atlantic storm, and his seamen on an accompanying ship had a last glimpse of their commander standing on the afterdeck, waving a book and shouting, 'We are as near to heaven by sea as by land.' Gilbert's patent descended to his half brother, Sir Walter Raleigh, but England, bent on harrying Spain, was too much concerned with the success of her marauding sea dogs to be interested in colony planting. A few attempts at settlement followed, but they were made in violation of the Raleigh patent. In 1602 Bartholomew Gosnold explored Massachusetts Bay, christened Cape Cod, built a fort on the island of Cuttyhunk in Buzzard's Bay, and finally returned to England with his ships loaded with sassafras.

Raleigh's waning power ended with the death of Elizabeth, and James I, the new Stuart monarch, assigned the land to a group of Plymouth merchants and adventurers known as the Plymouth Company. Commerce and profits stimulated Sir Ferdinando Gorges, Sir John Popham, and the other gentlemen who managed the destinies of this new company. Learning of the richness of the New England coast from George Weymouth, a private explorer, the Plymouth Company attempted to found the colony of Sagadahoc on the Kennebec River in what is now Maine (1607), at the time that the first permanent English colony was being established in Virginia. This venture failed completely and the company lapsed into inactivity, although lands were granted to a number of small fishing and trading colonies that sprang up along the Massachusetts coast in the early seventeenth century, inspired by John Smith's glowing accounts of the region. One visionary explorer, licensed by the company, devoted a season to gold-digging on Martha's Vineyard, but only 'spent his victuall and returned with nothing.'

The lust for trade failed to entice a population sufficient to make Massachusetts important, but where desire for gain failed the Reformation succeeded. Introduced to England by the oft-wedded Henry VIII, it had barely taken root when his successor, Mary, returned the land to Catholicism and sent Protestant leaders scurrying for their lives. Elizabeth attempted a compromise settlement that satisfied neither extreme

Catholics nor extreme Protestants, although the compromise laid the basis for the Church of England. The Elizabethan settlement was particularly distasteful to Protestants who had fled from England during the reign of 'Bloody Mary,' and had imbibed the radical teaching of Luther and Calvin while sojourning on the Continent. It was from this group that Massachusetts received its first wave of settlement.

First among these enthusiastic Protestants to reach the New World were the Separatists or Pilgrims. They believed each congregation should be entirely independent of all other congregations, and the compromise establishing the Church of England was particularly unacceptable to them. A small band of these people had been driven by the uncongenial atmosphere of their native Scrooby to seek a haven for their beliefs in Holland early in the seventeenth century, but the industrialism of Leyden displeased sons of English soil, who determined to turn instead to the New World. After securing support from London financiers they obtained a grant (1619) to settle on the James River in Virginia, and it was for that point that the 'Mayflower' set sail in 1620. Storms drove them off their course, however, and it was in Provincetown harbor that the small ship cast anchor on a bleak November day. The appearance of the countryside disturbed them: 'For sumer being done, all things stand upon them with a weatherbeaten face; and ye whole countrie, full of woods and thickets, represented a wild and savage heiw.' Disheartened at the prospects, the Pilgrims spent some time looking for more hospitable surroundings. Plymouth harbor was finally selected, and on the day after Christmas, 1620, they began to erect their first common house for themselves and their goods.

In founding their colony at Plymouth, the Pilgrims were on land to which they had no right; they were, in a sense, beyond the pale of English law which would have followed them had they reached their destination in Virginia. To protect themselves until governmental control could be made to include them, they drew up the 'Mayflower Compact' while their ship was still anchored in Provincetown harbor. By this agreement, based upon Calvinistic principles, all agreed to abide by the majority will. A pattern of democracy was cast for this first Massachusetts colony which served throughout the trying winter and allowed the colony to enter upon a period of slow but steady growth. Within a comparatively short time the London backers were paid in full and Plymouth became economically sound and independent. In this the Pilgrims made their greatest contribution: they demonstrated that a colony could be self-supporting and encouraged others to attempt the experiment.

A number of small communities were founded along the Massachusetts coast during the next decade. Nearly all were villages or posts dedicated to fishing and trade, and all secured their grants from the Council for New England, which had by this time taken over the claims of the Plymouth Company. Most famous among these early settlements was one sent out in 1622 by Thomas Weston, a London merchant who had aided the Pilgrims, at Wessagusset, now Weymouth. When abandoned by Weston, the post built by his men was taken over by Captain Robert Gorges and became a dispersing point for isolated settlements. From this point the militant churchman, Thomas Walford, commenced his trek to Mishawum, now Charlestown; Samuel Maverick, a gentleman-trader, established himself in what is now East Boston; the Reverend William Blaxton (or Blackstone), a rebel Anglican clergyman, sought solitude in what was later to be known as Beacon Hill; and David Thompson removed to the island in Boston harbor that still bears his name. The religious-minded Pilgrims had little in common with most of these adventurers, but they objected particularly to the settlement of a group of indentured servants led by Captain Thomas Wollaston and Thomas Morton at Quincy in 1625. Morton and his fellows were jolly sportsmen, and while they traded with the Indians they reserved time enough to frolic. 'They also set up a Maypole,' wrote the horrified Bradford, Governor of Plymouth, 'drinking and dancing aboute in many days togeather, inviting the Indian women for their consorts, dancing and frisking togeather like so many fairies or furies.' These 'beastley practicses of the madd Bacchinalians' did not cease until the Pilgrims sent Miles Standish to capture the post and deport Morton to England. A fishing post under the command of Roger Conant had also been established at Cape Ann in 1623 by an English trading concern called the Dorchester Company. These villages were all small and could not, unaided, have expanded into a united colony, but they gave Englishmen a foothold and an interest which, when the time was ripe, attracted migration and laid the foundations of the Commonwealth.

The later migration evolved from this insignificant Dorchester fishing enterprise on Cape Ann. Conant's failure left many of his English backers dissatisfied but still anxious to experiment in empire-building. The Reverend John White, John Endicott, and John Humphrey were the most restive spirits in this group. These men were Puritans who, unwilling to separate from the Established Church, believed that the Church might be purified from within; they hoped that a colony in America would provide an opportunity for the free exercise of their beliefs and would serve as a 'bulwark against the kingdom of Antichrist.' The Council for New England was respectfully petitioned for a grant of land, which was approved in March, 1628. The petitioners were given control of the territory between a point three miles south of the Charles River and another three miles north of the Merrimack, running from sea to sea. Armed with this grant, a shipload of settlers under Endicott set sail for Salem in 1628, where Conant and his band had moved two years before. Meanwhile royal sanction was sought and obtained, and in 1629 their 'dread sovereign' issued a charter confirming the grant from the Council of New England.

This royal act created the Massachusetts Bay Company, and it was upon the basis of this charter that the democracy and expansion of the Massachusetts Bay Colony developed. The colony was to be administered by two general courts; the first was to be made up of all the stockholders or freemen and was to hold quarterly sessions, at one of which the members of the other court were to be selected in the form of a governor, deputy governor, and eighteen assistants. The use of the term 'freemen' as a designation for members of the General Court laid the basis for the representative system as it later emerged in Massachusetts. Equally important was the failure of the charter to state that meetings of the Court must be held in England. This made it possible for the charter and the entire government of the colony to be transferred to America.

Certain prominent Puritan leaders in England, notably John Winthrop, recognized this vital fact. They perceived that if the charter was removed to America the colony would virtually be free of English control and could, therefore, become a Puritan commonwealth governed by Biblical principles. Winthrop's arguments prevailed, and the company resolved to move entirely to Massachusetts and to change from a trading company with Puritan sympathies to a Puritan colony. In return, Winthrop agreed to emigrate with his considerable group of followers. In March, 1630, they set out confidently, and with them went the charter. A new type of English colony was automatically established, and Massachusetts became a self-contained corporate colony markedly different from earlier proprietary colonies like Virginia.

Salem, which had pleased Roger Conant, did not please Winthrop, who had become the colony's first governor, and he moved first to Charlestown and then to Boston, leaving the other communities as towns to join those that grew up around Boston harbor. A period of almost unprecedented growth followed, and by 1640 sixteen thousand people had joined in the Great Migration to Massachusetts, for which English religious and economic conditions were largely responsible. The Puritans had joined forces with the Parliamentary Party, which opposed James I and had lost. Charles I dissolved his third Parliament in 1629, and entered upon an eleven-year period of personal rule designed partly to stamp out dissent and entrench the Anglican Church. Puritan dissatisfaction was aggravated by economic distress, particularly in the eastern and southeastern counties, the principal sources of emigration to America. Puritan discontent was reflected in the number of settlements — Medford, Roxbury, Dorchester, Lynn, Cambridge — which were made on the Bay Company's land during the era of Jacobin dictatorship.

While the Massachusetts Bay charter contained intimations of democracy, growth was slow. The leaders of the colony planned a social order in which individual freedom was to be sublimated to the will of God as interpreted by His clergy. The Governor and his assistants devoted themselves to this end. They refused to summon a meeting of the General Court until one hundred and nine freemen, insisting on their charter right, demanded that this be done. So firmly did Winthrop and his clerical allies believe that they alone were the proper interpreters of the Divine will that they illegally vested nearly all governmental powers within themselves before succumbing to this popular pressure by providing that only church members could sit in the General Court. This occasioned a growing discontent which culminated in 1634, when the freemen demanded to see the charter. The Governor dared not refuse, and the indignant members of the General Court, realizing that their rights had been infringed, hastily passed legislation which would vest governmental authority for all time in their own hands.

Discontent bred of these struggles accelerated the settlement of Massachusetts and the rest of New England. As long as the magistrates could direct the course of this westward movement they approved, if only for the reason that God's word was planted in the wilderness. Land was granted freely to any group of town proprietors who were church members, and tier upon tier of frontier towns were created as population flowed westward from England through Boston. On the south shore were founded Duxbury (1632), Scituate (1633), Hingham (1636), Barnstable (1638), Yarmouth (1639), Marshfield (1640), and Eastham (1649); on the broad fields of the north shore Saugus, later named Lynn (1631), Ipswich (1634), Marblehead (1635), Newbury (1635), Rowley (1639), and Salisbury (1640), while to the west Cambridge or Newtowne (1631),

Dedham (1636), Braintree (1640), Concord or Musketequid (1635), and Sudbury (1639) steadily advanced the course of settlement.

While the peopling of Massachusetts continued, Boston was sending out its inhabitants to settle other New England colonies. In 1635 the Reverend Thomas Hooker's congregation at Cambridge, dissatisfied with the ruling hand of John Cotton and other Boston clergy, and moved by 'a strong bent of their spirits for change,' gave Connecticut its first English inhabitants by founding Hartford. In the same year Wethersfield and Windsor, Connecticut, were established by mass migrations from Watertown and Dorchester, and in 1636 a group from Roxbury laid out the first fields of Springfield. From Massachusetts Bay, too, went Roger Williams and Anne Hutchinson, expelled for their principles, to found Providence and Portsmouth in Rhode Island; John Wheelwright, likewise banished, made the weary journey to Exeter, New Hampshire, to establish a more democratic church. The same spirit of revolt against the established order that had sent Puritans to America thus led to a dispersion of their numbers and ideas in the wilderness.

The social, economic, and spiritual influences which have distinguished Massachusetts from the other States were implanted in these towns. Nature ordained small-scale agriculture as the basis of Colonial economic life in Massachusetts. Rough, rocky soil made the clearing and cultivation of large plots of land impossible, and only interested labor could make it reasonably productive. Slavery was tried during Colonial days, but when found to be unprofitable was soon abandoned. The cold winters of Massachusetts made a compact form of settlement imperative; homes were clustered about a central green or common and the fields scattered nearby. Even though this encouraged sociability, the Puritan farmer preferred to utilize the long winter months in making furniture, harnesses, and the many other things needed by his family that his meagre income from the soil would not permit him to buy. Thus developed the fabled New England jack-of-all-trades whose descendants were equipped to take over mechanical tasks when mills began to invade Massachusetts early in the nineteenth century.

Situated on the village common in the center of the towns was the church. A closely knit settlement mitigated the influence of the frontier, which might have arrested the formal observance of religion. Long winter evenings afforded ample opportunity for introspection and made the Puritans more righteous and godly than their English brethren. In such society the minister became an outstanding figure; he was each town's acknowledged leader and frequently, in addition, its lawyer, doctor, and schoolmaster. His rule was not absolute, however, for each community was governed by a town meeting, in which every church member had an equal voice. This essentially democratic institution was one of the most enduring contributions of Massachusetts, through which its people received the training necessary to provide political leadership in the Revolution.

These town meetings not only managed ordinary governmental functions, but the life of each inhabitant was carefully regulated. Individual liberty was sacrificed to detailed legislation regulating habits and social conduct. Even dress was regarded as a legitimate field for official scrutiny. These 'blue laws,' as they have since been called, represented a desire for simplicity natural to a group that had rebelled against the ceremony of the Established Church; they reflected, too, the realization that hard work was necessary to conquer a wilderness. The shiftless were 'warned out' of Massachusetts towns, holidays such as Christmas were forbidden, Maypoles and similar frivolities were discouraged. There was work to be done, and the town fathers were determined to see that no one shirked. The Sabbath alone was exempted, not solely because of Biblical injunction but because a day of rest was required by hard-working colonizers.

The Church gave Massachusetts more than blue laws. It initiated, among other things, the educational development of America. Puritanism presupposed an intelligent clergy capable of interpreting Scripture, and literate worshipers who could understand the Bible and the long sermons to which they were subjected. Schools, therefore, were essential for the training of clergymen as well as their congregations. In 1636 the General Court appropriated a sum of money to start the College of Newtowne or Cambridge, a college endowed by John Harvard with his books, his money, and his name. Popular education, however, dates from 1647, when a law requiring elementary schools in towns of fifty families and secondary schools in those double that size or larger was enacted. Although not free, these schools were open to all, and laid the foundation of the American educational system.

Massachusetts was permitted to develop its peculiar social and religious institutions because of the preoccupation of the mother country. From the time of its founding until 1660 the colony was virtually independent of England, then engrossed in civil war and the Cromwellian Protectorate. The Puritan colonies were able in 1643 to form the New England Confederation as a bulwark of defense against the Indians and the Dutch of New York. With the restoration of Charles II in 1660, however, Massachusetts entered upon a new era which saw the Bible Commonwealth gradually evolve into an orderly crown colony, similar to Virginia or the other English outposts along the coast.

This change was possible partly because Puritan excesses had led to a declining interest in religion in Massachusetts. In the 1650's, for example, all of the forces of Puritanism were focused on a few troublesome Quakers who had made their way into the colony. They were beaten and banished, only to return in quest of martyrdom, with which the magistrates unwittingly provided them. Such willful persecution turned the people against the clergy and magistrates who had for so long dominated Massachusetts. The younger people who had not suffered for their religion as had their parents and the rising secular commercial class demanded a government less completely dominated by the Church. They won their first victory in 1657 with the adoption of the Half Way Covenant, which allowed baptized as well as converted church members to exercise the franchise, but it was not until the overthrow of the Massachusetts charter in 1684 that the Bible Commonwealth completely vanished.

The withdrawal of the charter on which the Bay Colony had rested its early governmental system was a natural result of the Stuart Restoration. The tendency throughout the Empire after 1660 was toward tightening imperial control and drawing the colonies closer together that they might be useful to the mother country. This the Massachusetts leaders, undisciplined by twenty years of imperial inefficiency, resisted vigorously, refusing to grant liberty of conscience or citizenship to members of the Church of England, openly snubbing royal commissions or agents sent to investigate conditions, and flagrantly violating the laws with which Parliament was attempting to regulate the Empire's trade. Justly indignant, the English Government began court proceedings against Massachusetts that culminated in 1684 in a decree cancelling the Massachusetts charter.

A new government known as the Dominion of New England was provided for Massachusetts. This was an attempt to centralize all the northern colonies so that royal control could be effected. Massachusetts, Rhode Island, Connecticut, New Hampshire, and Maine and later New York and New Jersey were united into a single governmental unit under the control of Sir Edmund Andros. Although an able administrator, he immediately provoked colonial wrath by what were considered tyrannical acts. For a time Massachusetts resisted his orders in every conceivable way and the Reverend Increase Mather, President of Harvard College, was sent to England to protest directly to James II. When the news of the Glorious Revolution in England (1688) which toppled the last of the Stuart monarchs from the throne and elevated William and Mary in their stead reached the colony, the Puritans seized the opportunity to stage their own revolt against Andros. The Dominion of New England was overthrown, and a provisional government was set up until the will of the new rulers could be learned.

Massachusetts hoped for a restoration of its old charter, but this was not in conformity with the new Colonial policy. The new instrument of government issued by William and Mary in 1691 created a royal colony similar to Virginia or Maryland, established boundaries, and solidified institutions in a form that was to endure until the Revolution. During its period of independence Massachusetts had launched an imperialistic policy of its own and had annexed Maine and New Hampshire; now New Hampshire was taken away, but Massachusetts was given jurisdiction over Plymouth and the islands south of Cape Cod. The Governor of the Bay Colony was henceforth to be appointed by the Crown, and the old assistants became the Governor's Council, elected by the Assembly. Two legislative houses (which had actually existed in Massachusetts since 1644, when a dispute between the assistants and freemen over the ownership of a stray sow drew them to separate chambers) were recognized by the new charter. One of the most important provisions of the new charter abolished church membership as a prerequisite for voting; Massachusetts was to be a civil rather than a Bible Commonwealth.

The changed governmental structure embodied in the charter of 1691 initiated the forces which almost a century later were to lead Massachusetts and the other colonies to the brink of revolt. Massachusetts farmers, accustomed to virtual freedom since 1630, resented the interference of a governor appointed by the Crown. The charter gave the Governor the right to veto laws passed by the Assembly, but this advantage was balanced by the Assembly's right to vote the Governor's salary. Conflict between these two branches of government, one representing the Crown, the other representing the settlers, who were jealous of what they had come to regard as their rights, was continual after 1717. England's efforts to control the trade of her increasingly rebellious colony was the crux of the controversy.

The people of Massachusetts were peculiarly sensitive to commercial regulation, for by the beginning of the eighteenth century they were finding in the sea the riches which nature had denied them elsewhere. Starting with scattered fishing ventures, their trade had become in-

creasingly profitable as Yankee shippers used the abundant harbors and
the plentiful supply of lumber for the construction of ships which scoured
the seven seas in search of profits. Massachusetts gradually emerged as
the carrier for America; her ships hauled the sugar of the West Indies and
the tobacco of Virginia to the mother country, and returned laden with
manufactured goods and luxuries for Colonial planter and merchant.

Engaged largely in trade, Massachusetts felt the effect of commercial
regulation more than any other colony. Under the restrictions of the
Restoration and the eighteenth century the market for many of the
essential products of Colonial enterprise was confined to England, and
the colonists were forbidden to secure their manufactured goods except
through the mother country. These laws did little harm to the staple-
producing colonies. Virginia could exchange her tobacco for the luxuries
available in England, and Barbadoes could do the same with her sugar.
But Massachusetts produced nothing that the mother country desired,
her fish competed with those of Britain's fleets, and her agricultural goods
found little market in a country still predominately rural. Yet the Bay
Colony's growing population needed the products of English mills and
factories, and Massachusetts in order to circumvent these commercial
restrictions developed the famous Triangular Trade. Sugar and molasses were brought from the West Indies in return for foodstuffs, lumber,
livestock, and codfish. Molasses was transformed into rum, which was
traded in Africa for slaves, who were then sold in the sugar-growing West
Indian islands to obtain the gold required for English luxuries. While
England had numerous possessions in the Caribbean region, the British
islands were not large enough to absorb so great a volume of trade. The
continued economic existence of the colony depended on an uninterrupted trade with French, Spanish, and Dutch sugar islands, a trade
made illegal by English commercial legislation.

Massachusetts did not feel the full weight of these burdensome laws for
some time. England made few attempts to enforce them, and smuggling
went on with the open connivance of royal governors and their agents,
many of the colony's great fortunes being founded in this illegal but
respectable trade. It was not until the close of the long series of wars
with France which filled much of the eighteenth century that the mother
country realized the full extent of commercial laxity. This conflict between the two great colonial powers, which lasted for more than half
a century, reached its culmination in the Seven Years' War (1756–63),
which was touched off in America and offered a true test of the colony's
loyalty to Crown and Empire. As in the previous contests, the Massa-

chusetts back country was subjected to a series of raids by French and Indians who swept down the Champlain Valley from Canada. Eastern shippers, impervious to barbarities on the frontier, blithely continued their illicit traffic with the French sugar islands and with Canada. The French armies were supplied by this means with the foodstuffs necessary to ravage the Massachusetts hinterland. Enticed by the greater profits of wartime, thrifty Yankee captains carried on this trade with the enemy so extensively that England's superior navy was completely unable to starve the French West Indian possessions into submission; in fact, foodstuffs sold there more cheaply than in British islands. British officers found it cheaper to import grain from England than to compete in America's markets with traders who were anxious to sell to the enemy. Massachusetts, along with the other colonies, refused to provide adequately for its own defense or to bear what the home government considered a just share of the war's expenses.

This scandalous conduct convinced England that her whole Colonial administration needed reform, but it was this reform which finally led to America's successful struggle for independence. In that clash of mother country and colony Massachusetts played a leading part, not only because a democratic tradition had been bred in her citizens for generations, but also because she, more than any other colony, was adversely affected by the new imperial policy. The first of these measures, the Sugar Act of 1764, made effective earlier prohibitions on trade with French or Spanish possessions; the second, the Stamp Act enacted a year later, provided for revenue stamps which were to be affixed to publications and to legal and commercial papers. Through these two measures the Crown hoped to raise a part of the revenue to maintain a body of troops in America necessary for the protection of the colonists against Indian attack, made imminent in 1763 by the serious outbreak of border warfare known as Pontiac's Rebellion.

These two measures actually did much harm to Massachusetts. The Sugar Act practically ended the foreign trade on which the colony depended for its currency supply, while the Stamp Act drained the little money remaining away from Boston. Furthermore, Massachusetts was undergoing the usual post-war depression, which magnified the effects of the new acts. It is little wonder that Boston merchants, hurriedly retrenching, agreed to wear no more lace and ruffles or that Boston tradesmen were willing to appear only in American-made leather clothes. It is easy to understand, too, why Sam Adams and the little group of political leaders who gathered with him at the picturesque Boston tavern, the

Green Dragon, could stir up mobs which forced the resignation of the Massachusetts stamp collector and despoiled the house of Lieutenant Governor Thomas Hutchinson. Amidst this popular discontent a general boycott of English goods, in which Boston merchants joined with those of Philadelphia and New York, was easily accomplished, and it was this boycott, seriously injuring British manufacturers, who were already suffering from a depression similar to that being felt in America, that caused the repeal of the Stamp Act and the revision of the Sugar Act in 1766.

Peace, however, was not for long. In 1767 a series of revenue measures, the Townshend Acts, which levied duties on paint, glass, tea, and other products imported into the colonies, again stirred Massachusetts to a fever of resentment. Boston shippers were particularly alarmed by re-forms in the customs service that accompanied the Townshend Acts. A Board of Customs Commissioners was placed in the Bay Colony, and that threatened to bring to a complete end the little smuggling which was carried on after the passage of the Sugar Act. Again merchants, those of Boston this time taking the lead, protested by refusing to import English goods; again mobs roamed the Boston streets, harrying before them luck-less agents of the Crown. Mob rule reached its height when an angry crowd tried to prevent a customs agent from collecting duty on a cargo of wine that was about to be landed by John Hancock. The agent was, as he expressed it, 'hoved down' into the hold while the patriots gleefully carried the wine ashore. Protests such as these, together with a shifting point of view in England, finally led to the repeal of the Townshend Acts in 1770, but they also led to the establishment of a garrison in Boston that peace might be preserved in that turbulent city. The inevitable clash between these soldiers and the overwrought citizenry of Boston came on the night of March 5, 1770, when a mob that was taunting a sentry at the customs house was fired upon, giving first blood to the revolution not yet formally begun, and to history the 'Boston Massacre.'

For three years after the repeal of the Townshend Acts the controversy subsided. Prosperity returned and people everywhere forgot the few years of turbulence. They forgot that England still taxed their tea and molasses, and Sam Adams worked in vain to stir up sentiment against the mother country. Even John Adams, staunch patriot though he was, drank tea at John Hancock's home, and hoped it had been smuggled from Holland but did not take the pains to inquire.

This calm was broken in 1773 with the passage of the Tea Act, which gave the East India Company a monopoly for the sale of that beverage in the colonies and lowered the duty until it could no longer be smuggled profitably. Shippers who had illegally imported tea in the past were swept from business, as well as the merchants who handled its shipping and sale. The Tea Act alarmed Colonial business classes, who, fearing Parliament might create similar monopolies on other products in the future, were driven once more into the hands of the radicals. Sam Adams was in his glory. In a series of carefully planned meetings he worked Boston sentiment to a new height, then, at the climax of a great gathering in the Old South Meeting House, sent a group of disguised laborers and tradesmen to dump the tea on three East India Company ships into Boston Harbor.

The reaction both in England and America to this wanton destruction of property was one of instant revulsion, particularly among the merchant group that had aided the patriots in the past; nevertheless a wise handling of the situation would probably have quieted revolutionary agitation for some time to come. Instead, the British Ministry blundered badly. A series of Coercive Acts were hurriedly passed by Parliament closing the Port of Boston to trade, altering the charter, revising the legal system, and inflicting penalties on Massachusetts which were to be removed only when restitution for the destroyed tea should be made. Most of the Colonial merchants, even in Boston, were willing to take this step, but the Coercive Acts had put the radicals in control again. Unable to secure merchant co-operation in a boycott of England, they determined to attempt united political action, and from Massachusetts and other colonies a call for a Continental Congress was issued. The Boston Tea Party gave the patriot forces of the Revolution the unity required for success.

The Massachusetts Assembly chose its delegates to this first Congress with the door of the legislative chamber locked, and with Governor Thomas Gage vainly shouting through the keyhole that the legislature was dissolved and could transact no further business. Under these conditions, duplicated in other colonies, the delegates selected were naturally of the radical wing, and the Continental Congress quickly showed their domination. They endorsed the Suffolk Resolves and enforced a general boycott of English goods. As yet the members had no thought of independence; it remained for further developments in Massachusetts to lead them to the point where relations with the mother country could be severed.

Tension had been high in the Bay Colony ever since the arrival of General Thomas Gage, who had been sent with a large force of troops to enforce the Coercive Acts. Clashes between the soldiers and patriots were narrowly averted on several occasions during the fall and winter of 1774–75, and only served to hurry the process by which the colonists were arming themselves, drilling their militia, and forming groups of Minutemen who were ready to swing into action against the British at a moment's notice. On April 19, 1775, the opportunity came. General Gage had resolved to send a detachment of troops to Concord to overawe the countryside by a show of British strength and to secure the supplies accumulated there by the colonists. The march began on the night of April 18, but the patriots were prepared for such a step and immediately dispatched two riders to warn their countrymen. One rider, Paul Revere, was captured before he could reach Concord; the other, William Dawes, succeeded in spreading the alarm. Minutemen began gathering immediately. A small group assembled on the village Green at Lexington, where they were met by the larger British force. In the scuffle that followed a shot was fired — the shot heard round the world. The troops then marched on to Concord, destroyed the stores, and returned to Boston, with a rising countryside following their steps and keeping up a steady fire that lasted until the last British soldier was safe in Boston.

The siege of Boston followed naturally, for the English had retreated to the safety of that city and it was inevitable that the colonists should decide to keep them there. The city then lay at the tip of a narrow peninsula, so that this could be accomplished easily if all avenues to the mainland were properly guarded. One such avenue lay across Boston Neck; this was carefully watched by the army of twenty thousand men authorized by the Assembly, and commanded first by General Artemus Ward and after July 2 by George Washington. Another possible route was across Charlestown Neck, and to protect this the Americans had to fortify Bunker Hill. This was done on the night of June 16. Actually it was Breed's Hill that was fortified rather than Bunker Hill, and it was there that the famous battle was fought the following day. The poorly prepared American forces were driven slowly backward, but acquitted themselves well, and demonstrated for the first time that the colonists could cope successfully with the supposedly invincible British arms.

After Bunker Hill, the siege of Boston became one of quiet waiting until the spring of 1776. Not until cannon which Ethan Allen had captured at Ticonderoga were sledded to Boston was it possible for Washington to attack. These new arms, mounted on Nooks Hill, Dorchester Heights, commanded the entire city, and immediately began to throw shot upon the helpless British. Finally General Howe, now in command, recognized the inevitable. On March 17 the evacuation of Boston took place and the entire British army, together with many Tory citizens, sailed away to Nova Scotia. Massachusetts had not only launched the military phase of the Revolution, but had given the patriot cause its first major victory. For the remainder of the war, the State was free of hostile troops.

Independence was inevitable after this first clash of rival arms, and with the separation of colonies from mother country Massachusetts was faced with the problem of erecting a new governmental structure that would perpetuate ideals of liberty and freedom. The last General Court held under the old provincial charter convened in 1774, and from that time on Massachusetts was governed by a Provincial Congress that had no legal basis for existence and was not representative. Objections naturally arose, particularly in Berkshire County, where the independent farmers refused to allow courts to sit until they had been given a government in which they had a voice. A constitution to meet this demand was drafted by the Provincial Congress in 1777–79 and submitted to the people for ratification — the first state constitution to be tested by popular vote — but that constitution contained few provisions for separation of powers and no Bill of Rights, and was promptly rejected. Finally in September, 1778, a popularly elected Constitutional Convention met in Cambridge, and after due consideration accepted a frame of government drawn up largely by John Adams. This was submitted to the people on March 2, 1780, and ratified on June 7. Massachusetts was the last of the States to adopt a written constitution, yet so wisely had its framers labored that today the same instrument still governs the Commonwealth, a record of which no other state can boast. Moreover, that constitution of 1780, drawn up by a popularly elected convention and submitted to the people for ratification, set a pattern that was to be followed in the framing of the Federal Constitution.

In Massachusetts, as in the other States, the Revolutionary period was one of social and economic as well as political upheaval. Many of the great commercial and governmental leaders of the past became Tories and followed the retreating British armies to Canada or England. In their place a new aristocracy arose which drew its wealth, as in Colonial days, from the sea. More and more, as their operations increased, were the financial resources of the Commonwealth concentrated along the coast, leaving the dissatisfied farmers of the interior struggling vainly against the stubborn soil. This dissatisfaction was fanned to open rebellion by the economic depression which swept over the newly created United States after the war. In the hilly country around Worcester and in the Berkshires the farmers began to demand legislative relief in the form of paper money and stay laws which would prevent mortgage foreclosures. These discontented elements united under the leadership of Daniel Shays, a Revolutionary war veteran. In 1786 he and his disheveled followers closed the courts of Worcester and threatened to capture Boston until an army, hastily formed by Governor Bowdoin and financed by Boston merchants, quelled the uprising.

This show of popular discontent alarmed the propertied classes of Massachusetts. They were now more disposed to support the growing movement for a new constitution to displace the Articles of Confederation, which had proved so useless in fostering trade, stabilizing finance, and protecting the interests of property. Actually, Massachusetts became the sixth State to ratify the Federal Constitution, but this was accomplished only after much adroit manipulation. A majority of the ratifying convention which assembled in Boston was opposed to the new form of government, with the farmers of the interior hilly region, the Berkshires and Maine, then still a part of Massachusetts, most outspoken in their opposition. Conservative leaders finally won over John Hancock, who, as was usual when he had an important decision to make, had retired to his home with an attack of gout until he determined the direction of popular sentiment. This was accomplished only by offering him the governorship of the State and, if Virginia did not ratify and make Washington eligible, their support for the presidency; but it was effective, for Hancock was the idol of the lower classes, and his support made ratification possible. In taking this step, however, Massachusetts submitted a series of proposed amendments to the Constitution; this practice was followed by the remaining States, and from them grew the first ten amendments to our national Constitution, the so-called Bill of Rights.

With the inauguration of the new government under Washington, Massachusetts entered on a period of prosperity and peace. While her old trade routes within the British Empire were now closed to her, new ones were soon discovered, particularly that immensely profitable trade with China which thrived unchecked until iron steamships supplanted American sailing vessels. In every other corner of the world, too, ships of daring Yankee masters began to appear, seeking cargoes and fortunes for themselves and their State. After 1793, with England and France locked in the first of the series of wars that followed the French Revolution, Massachusetts took over a large share of the carrying trade formerly monopolized by those powers. From every quarter new wealth was flowing into the Commonwealth; the depression that had given birth to Shays' Rebellion was now only a fast dimming memory.

This prosperity naturally shaped the political bent of the people, and when the shuffle of political fortunes which had gone on through Washington's two administrations finally ended, Massachusetts was firmly wedded to the principles of the Federalist Party. This conviction was strengthened while John Adams, one of the Commonwealth's own sons, was Chief Executive. Many in the State even supported the Alien and Sedition Acts through which the Federalists sought to solidify national power during the French Naval War of 1798. Jefferson's election in 1800 was looked upon as a major calamity; pious Massachusetts ladies concealed their Bibles lest that Francophile atheist burn them, and conservative merchants and shipowners prepared for a disaster which they thought certain. Instead, the State's prosperity continued to increase, and by 1804 Massachusetts was ready to desert the Federalist column for the first time and support Jefferson's re-election.

Those who had taken this step soon were ready to admit their mistake, for the tangled foreign policy of Jefferson's second administration bore harder on Massachusetts than on any other State. The Embargo with which the President attempted to combat French and English interference with American shipping led the Commonwealth once more into the slough of depression. The wealth of Massachusetts still came from the sea, and its people still protested against interference with their trade, as they had when burdened by English Navigation Acts. Those protests, voiced first by newspaper editors who spelled Embargo backward as 'O Grab Me,' swelled to a final chorus of rebellion when Jefferson's successor, Madison, responded to demands of the expansionist West and carried the United States into the War of 1812 against England. For the three years of that war the trade of the Commonwealth was at a standstill, driven from the seas by the superior British navy; and for those three years the people gave vent to their resentment in every conceivable manner. Massachusetts refused to allow her militia to be used outside the state borders, she gave only lukewarm financial support to the national cause, she held celebrations to cheer English victories over Napoleon, and she was instrumental in calling the Hartford Convention of 1814, where delegates from the several New England States talked vaguely of secession from the Union and nullification of the Constitution.

With the close of the war in 1815, Massachusetts entered a new phase of her history. It was during this period that the basis for her later industrial development was laid, and the commercial aristocracy which had shaped her destinies for so long was successfully challenged for the first time. American manufacturing began with Jefferson's Embargo, which stopped the importation of manufactured goods from England; it grew steadily during the war that followed, when the United States, cut off from European sources, was forced to become self-supporting; and it was given a permanent basis by the protective tariff of 1816, designed to insure the infant industries which had developed between 1807 and 1815. At first this manufacturing was scattered through the Eastern States, but as time passed it concentrated more and more in New England and particularly in Massachusetts. There the Yankee farmers, long accustomed to the production of household goods, had a training in handicraft that equipped them to organize and manage the mills that dotted the countryside. The many streams that coursed the State's valleys furnished a plentiful supply of water-power. Labor could be secured as in no other section of the Union, for thousands of Massachusetts farmers were ready to abandon their unequal struggle with a stubborn soil and drift into industrial employment. Hence the Commonwealth was able to take full advantage of Francis Cabot Lowell's perfection of the first power loom which, originally installed at a mill in Waltham in 1814, revolutionized the textile industry and turned Lowell, Lawrence, Fall River, and other towns into manufacturing centers. By the time of the Civil War, Irish immigrants were flocking in to perform the labor in these factories and Massachusetts was fast assuming the appearance of a modern industrial state.

The rise of manufacturing coincided with a decline in agriculture. This was partly due to the greater opportunity for profit available in the infant industries; more responsible, however, was the growth of Western agriculture, with which the farmers of Massachusetts could not compete. Western farm products penetrated Eastern markets as soon as the Ohio Valley frontier was established, but it was only after 1825, when the opening of the Erie Canal allowed the cheap and rapid movement of Western products to the East, that the full impact of this new competition was felt. Grain from the Ohio Valley could now undersell grain from the Berkshires in the Boston markets, and Massachusetts' farmers were faced with the alternative of going to the cities to become workers in the growing factories or of migrating westward themselves. Many of them chose the latter course, moving in a constant stream across New York to settle the northern tier of the Old Northwest States. Rural decay in Massachusetts began. Cultivated fields were allowed to return to a state of nature, and abandoned farms alone remained as dreary reminders of former prosperity.

The flow of Massachusetts population to the West was not without its effect on the Commonwealth. Leaders of the State, alarmed at the exodus of their sons, engaged in a bit of Puritan self-scrutiny to discover the cause. They agreed that one expelling force was the antiquated governmental and religious system still in use, and that only a reform in that system could stem the exodus. Politically, this reforming spirit found expression in the release of Maine and in a Constitutional Convention of 1820. This convention yielded to the demand of the people for a greater voice in their own government by drafting ten amendments to the Constitution providing for the incorporation of cities, the abolition of property qualifications for voting, the removal of religious tests for office-holders, and other much needed reforms. The religious expression of this social change reached its culmination in 1833, when another constitutional amendment was adopted completely separating the Church and State and placing Congregationalism, hitherto favored by governmental support, on the same plane as other sects. The last vestiges of aristocratic Puritanism were swept from the statute books, and the ideals of democracy were brought nearer reality.

The reforming spirit in Massachusetts was not stilled by these concrete gains. Unitarianism, begun in America at King's Chapel (Boston) just after Independence, was sweeping through the Commonwealth under the fostering guidance of William Ellery Channing. Its refreshingly liberal doctrines threatened to bury the Congregational Church under an avalanche of popular disapproval, and only the valiant efforts of the Reverend Horace Bushnell, who sought to reconcile the old Calvinistic theology with the gentle humanitarianism of the new era, saved Congregational power and influence. In Concord, Emerson, Thoreau, and a whole school of disciples began to feel the first vague resentment against the machine, and preached the cult of individualism and the doctrine of the nobility of man in immortal verse and prose. Dorothea L. Dix shocked the state of Massachusetts into providing the first decent care for the insane before beginning her country-wide crusade in behalf of these little understood unfortunates. Horace Mann agitated valiantly and successfully in behalf of the revolutionary doctrine of universal education, and through his efforts elevated Massachusetts to a position of leadership in this important sphere. Total abstinence societies, formed first in Boston in 1826, were spreading like wildfire through the State and nation, beginning that organized movement that was to end in the Eighteenth (and Twenty-First) Amendments. At Brook Farm, near Boston, at Fruitlands, near Harvard, and elsewhere bewildered idealists like Hawthorne, Alcott, and Margaret Fuller sought refuge from a changing world in the simple life and communism — an experiment gently but effectively satirized by Hawthorne in 'The Blithedale Romance.'

From this mad, shifting world emanated the crusade against slavery, centered in Boston and New York State, where the revivalism of the Reverend Charles G. Finney whipped his disciples into action against 'the peculiar institution' of the South. It was in Boston that William Lloyd Garrison established his newspaper *The Liberator* in 1831, committed to the immediate emancipation of all humans held in bondage and vitriolic in the abuse which it heaped on slaveholders. It was in Boston that the New England Anti-Slavery Society was formed in 1832, which within a year became the American Anti-Slavery Society and spread over the North, stirring sentiment everywhere in favor of uncompensated emancipation. The movement that was to plunge the nation into a civil war within two decades was launched in Massachusetts.

Garrison and his fellow reformers did not have an easy path to follow. They were opposed by many milder men, led by William Ellery Channing, who favored legal and peaceful methods of freeing the slaves, and by most of the respectable elements of society, who soon became alarmed lest the agitation check the flow of cotton from the South, on which the Massachusetts textile industry depended. Although Garrison's followers were initially of little importance, the movement soon attracted such men as John Quincy Adams, Wendell Phillips, and John Greenleaf Whittier, and later included a large group of outstanding Massachusetts men and women. These abolitionists strongly opposed the Fugitive Slave Act, established 'Underground Railroad' stations to hurry escaping slaves to freedom in Canada, and organized the New England Emigrant Aid Company, through which Eli Thayer of Worcester vainly tried to win Kansas for the North by peopling it with freedom-loving individuals who would bar slavery from that territory.

The turbulence of those trying days was soon translated into Massachusetts politics, where the reforming spirit was as clearly discernible as in the idealism of Brook Farm or the fanaticism of Garrison. The Federalist Party had passed from existence by 1824, engulfed in a tide of disapproval which followed its opposition to the War of 1812, and from that time Massachusetts steadfastly supported either the Whig Party or an independent candidate of its own. The reforming zeal of its people was expressed first not against the slaveholders but against the foreigners, for the 1840's and 1850's saw a steady stream of Irish immigrants pouring into the Commonwealth until many of the larger cities were predominantly Celtic in composition. Alarmed by this alien invasion, Massachusetts gave its vote in the state elections of 1854 and 1855 almost solidly to the American or Know Nothing Party, which was pledged to check immigration and combat the growing power of the Catholic Church. By 1856, however, the Republican Party with its anti-slavery principles invaded the Commonwealth, and the votes of Massachusetts went for its candidate, John C. Frémont, and helped elect Abraham Lincoln to the presidency in 1860.

Thus did Massachusetts, the birthplace of abolitionism, remain true to its genius. Nor did this loyalty lessen when a panic of fear swept the Southern States toward secession and plunged the nation into civil war. When President Lincoln called the North to arms on April 15, 1861, the first state to respond was Massachusetts, which within four days sent fifteen hundred men to Fort Monroe. Massachusetts blood was also the first to be shed in the Civil War when on April 19, 1861, just eighty-six years to the day after the battles of Lexington and Concord, a mob attacked the Sixth Regiment in Baltimore. The State was aroused, a wave of patriotism in which factional differences were forgotten swept Massachusetts, and support of the Union became the major issue. For the four trying years of this sectional struggle the Bay State contributed freely in men, money, and effort that the Union might be preserved.

Appomattox closed a chapter in American life, and the next scene in the drama of American history was sketched against the background of industrialism. With the acceleration of industry and the revolutions which took place simultaneously in agriculture and mining, the medieval period of America drew to a close.

The sea, upon which the fortunes of Massachusetts had been built, was a factor of decreasing significance. Exports declined with monotonous regularity, but imports continued to be a consideration of consequence; for although Massachusetts did not serve as a distributor beyond the confines of New England, her own industries required a growing volume of raw materials. The great white sails which once cleared out of Salem and New Bedford were never succeeded by the funnels of the steamship, and only Boston remained a vital point in Massachusetts commerce. Fishing alone continued to thrive, and although riches were still sought in the traffic lanes of the Atlantic, a new economy had begun. Improved methods of steel production and the development of the petroleum industry assured the success of the new industrialism, but it marked the end, among other things, of the whalers. Civil War and Arctic disasters hastened the decline. The glamour of whaling boats like clipper ships faded into history and legend, but a supply of fluid capital had been created which poured into Western railroads as well as Massachusetts industry.

The industrial evolution of Massachusetts is the economic history of the United States in miniature. Manufacturing, like population, continued to be drawn by the magnetic attraction of the West, but in many fields Massachusetts held undisputed pre-eminence until the end of the century. More than one-third of all the woolens of the nation were produced in this State, and in the eighties Fall River led the field in cotton manufacture, Lawrence, Lowell, and New Bedford closely following. Partly because of its climate New Bedford became famous for its fine grade of cotton goods, while the northern New England mills developed the heavier fabrics. By 1890 Lawrence had become the third most important city in America in the manufacture of woolens, and Lowell was a close fourth.

The boot and shoe industry had already made considerable progress, but as a result of technological advances in power manufacture the importance of the industry increased tremendously. In 1866, for example, Lynn possessed 220 factories whose annual output was $12,000,000, while the State output was $53,000,000, increasing to $88,000,000 by 1870. In 1890 Lynn's industry alone was evaluated at $26,000,000, and the extent to which the manufacture of boots and shoes was concentrated in Massachusetts is evidenced by the fact that Brockton, Haverhill, Marlborough, and Worcester were all leading shoe centers. Despite the rivalry of New York and the Middle West, Massachusetts resisted serious competition until 1900, by which date the State was producing almost fifty per cent of the nation's output in this field.

Considerable success had been achieved in the manufacture of machinery, partly as a by-product of industrial eminence. Power looms to feed its textile mills were locally produced. Shoe machinery was made at an immense plant in Beverly and smaller ones at Boston and Waltham. Paper mill machinery was constructed at Lowell, Pittsfield, Lawrence, and Worcester. As competition developed at points nearer the source of raw material, however, the metal industry underwent a radical change. Lighter grades of machines, tools, and mechanical equipment were found to be more profitable, and native Yankee ingenuity developed a fine skill in their production.

Industry and the rise of cities attracted scores of workers who sought peace and security in the New Canaan. The immigrant invasion which resulted changed the social complexion of the State: sixty-six per cent of all the white stock in Massachusetts contains a foreign strain. Before the Civil War immigration was drawn largely from western Europe, but beginning with the decade of the eighties the majority came from the southern and eastern sections of the Continent, with the result that almost every racial group is represented in the population. The most rigid type of immigration control was in effect up to 1849, and Massachusetts contained a relatively small racial admixture; today it has more foreigners than any other State except New York. French-Canadians, Greeks, Poles, Czechoslovakians, Russians, Finns, Letts, Lithuanians, and Turks live side by side with the descendants of Bay Colony settlers. Many new strands have been added to Anglo-Saxon culture. Slavic, Semitic, and Celtic influences have permeated Massachusetts thought, enriching folkways, enlivening speech, and giving a new perspective to graphic art, music, and literature. The effect of immigration may also be traced in the new direction of the labor movement, as well as in an increase of the Catholic and Jewish religious groups.

The establishment of factories and the concentration of population was paralleled by a growth in workers' organizations. Trade unions after the Civil War grew from seventeen to forty two in number, and in many cases the State was the focal point of their growth. Organization of the boot and shoe industry proceeded quickly, largely because labor and not machinery was the important element. Organization of the textile industry was not so simple; here the lower skills demanded of the workers retarded unionization. The National Cotton Mule Spinners were organized in 1889, but it was not until the United Textile Workers came upon the scene in 1901 that any semblance of success was achieved. American society was unprepared for such an economic revolution, social relations were severely strained, and the latter nineteenth century was marked by industrial strife. Illinois had its Haymarket, Pennsylvania its Homestead, and Massachusetts its Lawrence (1912). To contemporaries it seemed as though the long-cherished ideals of American life and institutions were disintegrating, but calmer reflection indicated that this was merely another stage in the evolution of industrial society.

As a result of organized effort many gains accrued to labor and society as a whole. A department of labor and industry was established (1912), and legislation was adopted for the protection of health, the investigation of industrial diseases, and the recognition of occupational hazards. Under the new law (1933) a person might no longer be coerced into an agreement not to join a union as a condition of employment. Massachusetts law today requires that employers who advertise for labor during a strike must state specifically that a state of strike exists. No woman or child may be employed for more than forty-eight hours a week, and children under fourteen are forbidden to work at all. Minors in the age group of fourteen to sixteen years must complete the sixth grade of elementary school, and may not work more than six days a week or eight hours a day.

By the beginning of the nineteenth century the influx of immigration and the growing development of industry brought about corresponding changes in government. The New England town meeting, generally economical, simple, and efficient, did not lend itself to this hurried expansion and was found inadequate to meet the problems of urban life. A constitutional amendment of 1820 had given the General Court the right to charter cities, and by 1885 there were twenty-three cities containing sixty per cent of the population. The commission form of government, which places all phases of city government in the hands of five persons, though tried, was never successful: Gloucester, Haverhill, Lynn, Lawrence, and Salem all attempted it at one time or another.

Education experienced a revival after the Civil War. The rise of the cities, now the dominant factor in American life, presented new problems which it was hoped education would solve. The movement initiated by Horace Mann in the earlier decades of the nineteenth century was completed, and the scope of the public school system expanded, largely by the increase in the number of free public high schools. But it was in the upper levels of education that the results of economic maturity were most apparent. Wealth created by industrialism supplied the endowments necessary for the establishment of new institutions. In an era notable for the founding of colleges and universities throughout the country — many as a result of State aid — fifteen were founded in Massachusetts (1863–1927). In an era in which American education achieved international recognition because of its great educators and administrators, Andrew Dickson White of Cornell, James McCosh of Princeton, John Bascomb of Wisconsin, Noah Porter of Yale, Massachusetts produced four: Charles William Eliot of Harvard, Granville Stanley Hall of Clark, Francis A. Walker of the Massachusetts Institute of Technology, and Alice Freeman (Palmer) of Wellesley. The emancipation of women, quickened by modern conditions, was furthered by opportunities for advanced study, and the contribution of Massachusetts was distinguished. Wellesley was founded in 1870, Smith College (Northampton) in 1871, Radcliffe (Cambridge) in 1879, and Simmons (Boston) in 1899. Facilities for preparation in engineering and related subjects were provided by the creation of the Massachusetts Institute of Technology (Boston) and the

Worcester Polytechnic Institute (Worcester), both established in 1865. Responding to the demands of urban conditions, seventy-five cities and towns established industrial schools. Latterly educational facilities have been developed to reach people outside the public school system and the universities. Many of the larger trade unions offer a variety of courses for workers and their families, and the University Extension Division of the Department of Education has supplied an increasing number with vocational, technical, and cultural training.

An important adjunct of the educational system in Massachusetts is the library. Not only is there a free public library in every city and town (since 1926), but the State has many important special libraries and collections. There are few places with more varied materials for the study of American history; bibliophiles and historians, as well as others less fervent, make use of its varied treasures. The American Antiquarian Society (Worcester), rich in newspapers, periodicals, and manuscripts, is amply supplemented by the Massachusetts Historical Society (Boston), the Bostonian Society, the Boston Athenaeum, the Essex Institute (Salem), and the Boston Public Library, the last possessing a significant assortment of Americana, including the private libraries of Thomas Prince, John Adams, Theodore Parker, and Thomas Wentworth Higginson. In addition, the college and university libraries with their specialized interests, seldom duplicated, make Massachusetts a State with unusual opportunities for research and study.

Simultaneously with industrialism came a renewal of intellectual speculation; science was stimulated by fresh winds of doctrine from Europe and endowments of industrialists. Education and science were electrified by the concept of development which coursed through America in the period after the Civil War. Darwin, Spencer, Tyndall, and Huxley became symbols of scientific achievement as well as abroad. Massachusetts furnished one of the leading defenders of the disturbing views of Darwin in the person of Asa Gray, Fisher Professor of Botany at Harvard, and also its most eminent opponent, Louis Agassiz. Agassiz, who taught geology and zoology at Harvard, stamped his personality on every scientific movement, and like another Massachusetts man — Benjamin Franklin — was the greatest popularizer of his time. The doctrine of evolution initiated a scientific renaissance in which Massachusetts shared. Modern research revived the colonial tradition of scholarship currently typified by two distinguished scientists, James Bryant Conant of Harvard and Karl Taylor Compton of the Massachusetts Institute of Technology.

The industrial trend was not without its effect upon organized religion. European scholarship and the rapid rise of urban communities confronted the churches with a changing world, and in this critical period of religious history Massachusetts played a significant rôle. Christian Science, founded by Mary Baker Eddy (Lynn, 1867), provided a refuge for many who were dissatisfied with conventional theological forms. Another vital aspect was the development of social Christianity, which was partly a reaction to an increasing absorption in practical affairs. A declining interest in doctrinal matters was the inevitable consequence of secularism, but social Christianity arose because industrialism presented America with new complexities. The churches tempered this transition stage by a revival of the social gospel emphasizing the intimate relation between religion and life. All denominations awakened to the realization that there was a real connection between slums and morals, and a growing concern with systematic relief was manifested by the clergy. Reform became the current text which was preached with eloquence by many Massachusetts men — Francis G. Peabody, Professor of Christian Morals at Harvard Divinity School, Phillips Brooks of Trinity Church, Minot Judson Savage of the Church of the Unity, Octavius Brooks Frothingham and William Joseph Potter, leading Unitarian radicals — who successfully emulated such national leaders as Washington Gladden, Lyman Abbott, Josiah Strong, and Cardinal Gibbons. Emphasis on sociology rather than cosmology was a reflection of the scientific temper, which soon became universal, enlisting the efforts of those outside Christianity, notably two Jewish leaders, Charles Fleischer and Solomon Schindler, both rabbis at Temple Israel in Boston. In 1889 the Society of Christian Socialists was founded in Boston for the purpose of awakening 'members of the Christian churches to the fact that the teachings of Jesus Christ lead directly to some specific form or forms of Socialism.'

The development of Massachusetts may be divided into three major periods: from its founding until the election of Thomas Jefferson to the presidency; from 1800 to the Civil War; and from 1865 to the present. The destinies of the seventeenth and eighteenth centuries were moulded by mighty forces, momentarily visible in Massachusetts, which during the first period symbolized the development of the nation. Carver and Bradford, Winthrop and Cotton, the Mathers, Samuel Sewall, and Franklin belong to America; John and Samuel Adams, James Otis, Paul Revere, and John Hancock were the patriots of the Revolution. During the second period this situation slowly changed. Colonial radicals found they had exchanged the interest of British imperialists for the interests of

Federalist shipowners who, while flying a new flag, shared a like philosophy. While the rest of America moved westward to cotton belt and farmland, Massachusetts continued to devote herself to trade and developed a point of view peculiar to New England. A brief interlude of nationalism followed the War of 1812, after which Massachusetts reverted to a spirit of sectionalism typified by the Hartford Convention (1814), characteristic not only of New England but of the nation. Although Federalism disappeared and industry took the place of commerce, the National Republicans and later the Whigs gradually borrowed Federalist doctrine to the end that Massachusetts and New England might endure. The third period ushered in the economic revolution which transformed the American scene. Currents of New England individualism still flow from Massachusetts, typified in recent years by such men as Henry Cabot Lodge and Calvin Coolidge, but such currents are simply tributaries to the main stream. Provincialisms have been dissipated in the steam of locomotives and the blast of airplane propellers, while iron and steel labor to bring forth a new nation.

GOVERNMENT

FOR three centuries Massachusetts has been carrying on an experiment as old as human history: the effort of men to govern themselves. One governmental form has succeeded another as each generation, with population increasingly pressing and conditions of living continuously changing, developed new solutions to its governmental problems.

The earliest form of government in Massachusetts was that of Plymouth Colony. Having no charter, the Pilgrims based their authority upon a patent granted in 1621 to the Plymouth Company, and in 1636 definitely outlined the powers of their officials: the Governor was to be elected annually by the people, and his assistants were to govern and to act as a judiciary. Legislation, however, originated with the people, as all freemen were admitted to the General Court, a condition which existed until 1639, when, because of increased population and migration, deputies were chosen.

The first Massachusetts Colonial charter was given by Charles I in 1628. Later he tried unsuccessfully to have it abrogated. The form of government was different from that of Plymouth in that the first Governor and assistants were appointed by the Crown. Matthew Craddock, the first Governor, never came to America. Subsequent Governors, however, were elected annually until James II appointed Joseph Dudley in 1685. Sir Edmund Andros, Dudley's appointed successor, essayed to be a vice-regal dictator and was promptly deposed. In the intercharter period which followed, Simon Bradstreet headed the Colony.

The second, or Province Charter, a grant of King William and Queen Mary, arrived in 1692. It brought Plymouth Colony, Maine, and a portion of Nova Scotia under one jurisdiction. It was a far less liberal charter than the first. The Governor, Lieutenant-Governor, and State Secretary were appointed by the Crown. In 1726, King George sent over an explanatory modifying charter which limited the Governor's authority to adjourn the General Court, but made the election of the Speaker subject to the veto of the Governor. Control of money, bills, and the right of electing the councillors curbed somewhat the Governor's immense power. The last General Court held under the Provincial Charter was in 1774.

INDUSTRY EARLY AND LATE

THE geography of Massachusetts is largely responsible for its industry, for it combines water-power with good harborage. Mills and the maritime trades consequently predominate. Once established, the mills grew long after the need for local water-power had disappeared. So, in the pictures that follow, there is an old stone mill and a giant, modern weaving-room. There is boat-building as it was done two hundred years ago and still is done in Essex today. And also there is a picture of the shipyards at Fore River with much modern equipment.

There are also pictures of fishermen and their varied crops, cranberry bogs which need the level, sandy soil of the Cape, clam beds, glass-making which was undertaken at Sandwich where glass was made by a process now lost, and printing which is not an inheritance from the geography of the State, but a result of the solemn studiousness of Boston's earliest settlers which left its mark in generously scattered colleges and printing shops throughout the State.

RE RIVER SHIPYARD, QUINCY

SHIPYARD, ESSEX

HOISTING SAIL

CHAINS
WOODS HOLE BUOY YARD

OLD MILL, SUDBURY

'CHARLES W. MORGAN,' NEW BEDFORD

SEEDING CLAMS

CRANBERRY BOG

SANDWICH GLASS

NETS DRYING, GLOUCESTER

HERRING RUN, WAREHAM

WEAVING

PRINTING

In the following period, before the State Constitution was accepted, patriots and a Provincial Congress ran the affairs of State. James Bowdoin and a Council were in charge. The government was the people's own after June, 1774, but there was agitation, particularly from Berkshire County, to confirm this in a constitution. The General Court of 1777–78 drew up such an instrument making Massachusetts the first State to submit a new constitution to the people, but it was rejected. The citizens properly felt that such a momentous covenant should be drawn by a body elected solely for that purpose and, moreover, the first draft contained no bill of rights or separation of powers.

The people next voted in favor of a constitutional convention. It convened at Cambridge in September, 1779. James Bowdoin was chosen presiding officer. A sub-committee of prominent citizens eventually turned over the task of drawing up the new instrument to John Adams, indisputably the best-qualified man of his day. Adams, paying tribute to the pioneer liberals, later said it was 'Locke, Sidney, and Rousseau and De Mabley reduced to practice.' The new Constitution was submitted March 2, 1780, and was ratified June 7. John Hancock was elected Governor. Although Massachusetts had been the first of the States to establish a government of its own, it was the last of the thirteen Colonies to adopt a written constitution.

Massachusetts is today the only State in the Union still governed under its original constitution. This has endured chiefly because of its broad provisions and flexible character. It was the first such document boldly to establish the principle of the separation of powers of the various branches of government. It contains assurance of the protection of inalienable rights. Among its more important provisions were the right of the Governor and Council or the Legislature to require opinions from justices of the Supreme Judicial Court, the removal of judges by address, and the inapplicability of martial laws to citizens except with the consent of the Legislature.

There have been three constitutional conventions since 1779: in 1820, 1853, and 1917. More than seventy amendments have been made to the Constitution, but the general plan of government it erected is still essentially in operation. While power has been increasingly centralized in the Chief Executive and the State Government, the Constitution is still the bulwark of individual freedom and rights. As in the case of other State constitutions, it is a more powerful instrument than the Federal Constitution, because it has all powers not explicitly delegated to the Federal Government, while the Federal Government enjoys only powers specifically granted.

The town was the earliest unit of government. It was not for some century and a half that there was a formal statute declaring the town 'a body politic and corporate,' capable of suing and being sued; yet it was early in the history of the Colony that in practice the town became a self-governing unit — a miniature republic. The difficulties of travel, the dangers of leaving frontier farms open to Indian pillage, and inveterate distrust of arbitrary power acted jointly in favor of local independence. The General Court at Boston among its first actions granted the scattered infant towns incorporation and the right to make regulations, although at first these were made to apply only to stray swine. Gradually thereafter the townsmen assumed local authority.

In 1632 the Cambridge elders ruled that, under penalty of a fine, every person must appear at the monthly town meeting within half an hour of the sounding of the bell. Definite local officials began to appear. Dorchester was at first ruled by the clergy and magistrates. In what is asserted to be the oldest self-rule document extant in the United States, the Dorchester town meeting record of 1633, the citizens were summoned by the rumble of a drum and twelve men acting as a 'steering committee.' The next year, 1634, Charlestown organized the first Board of Selectmen. This system, which provided a civil agency of government, was promptly adopted by other towns. This spontaneous organization of government within the towns, rather than any intention of the first charter, in 1635 led the General Court, in recognition of an accomplished fact, to make the first grant of local self-government in America. Given at Newe Towne, March 3, it granted the towns the right to dispose of common property, order civil affairs, and choose their own officers. By 1640, twenty town governments were in existence.

Expansion of the duties of the town officers and an increase in the number of town officials followed. In 1642 the General Court directed the 'chosen men' of each town to see to education, a humble act which gave birth to the public school system in America. Ten years after, the town of Cambridge vested the taxing power in their 'townsmen,' a privilege exercised by the Selectmen of Dorchester since 1645. In addition to expanded duties for the Selectmen — who were even directed to remove oyster shells from the public highways — so many duties were heaped upon the town Constable — among them taking charge of smallpox funerals, levying fines, and catching Quakers that anyone declining the job was assessed the sizable fine of £10. Until 1684 the officeholders and town duties continued to grow. Gaugers, viewers of pipestaves, cullers of brick, and measurers of salt appeared on the public rolls. Town legislation multiplied.

So vigorous was the growth of the towns that between the formal end of the Colony and beginning of the Province, 1684–92, the town organization and privileges were recognized. The efforts of Governor Andros to tax the towns, command public assemblies, and interfere with the town meeting were no small factors in arousing the towns to depose him. Convinced of the inalienability of their right of self-rule, the towns maintained it until the provincial charter from William and Mary arrived in 1691. When the new charter was found to be without a provision guaranteeing local self-government, the first act passed by the General Court hastened to make that guaranty.

In the eighteenth century, growth of the towns was spasmodic because of the unsettled times and perils of the frontier. Tax lists show 111 towns in 1715; 156 in 1742; 161 in 1752; 199 in 1768; and 239 in 1780. At times the frontier hazard was so acute that the General Court passed a law by which persons abandoning a frontier town would forfeit their estates.

The same passion for self-rule, displayed at the time of Sir Edmund Andros, prompted the towns to embrace the principles of the Revolution. They voted to support the Declaration of Independence, provided supplies and ammunition, and voted bounties to volunteers. The towns, impelled by the ideals of the first settlers, were the backbone of the revolt.

The Constitution of 1780, after one hundred and fifty years of doubt, confirmed local autonomy. A General Act on towns, passed in 1786, treated application of the principle at length. It named the officers to be elected, the right to assess taxes, make by-laws, and punish offenders. The people were guaranteed the right to place an article in a town warrant or even compel a Justice of the Peace to convoke a town meeting. There were then about three hundred communities with about 400,000 population.

In 1820 a constitutional amendment gave the General Court the right to charter cities. Two years later Boston, which had made five attempts since 1784 to discard the town system, was incorporated. The genesis of city government was in the chartered borough of Colonial times. New York in 1686 had the first borough charter. It was modeled on the English Community corporation, with the Mayor and the Council or Aldermen acting as opposing checks.

At first committees of the Council handled matters like public works and water supply, but separate departments were finally created for such purposes. Wherever a Mayor secured the veto power, the Council declined in importance. Inefficiency in departments, laxity in enforcing

State laws, squandering of public funds, and poor policing led to increasing State interference in the years preceding the Civil War. After the Civil War, towns continued to shift to city government. In 1865 there were 14 cities and in 1875 19, with more than fifty per cent of the population. In 1885 there were 23 cities with sixty per cent of the population.

As the tide of immigration rose, general optimism prevailed; and with the population interested in business pursuits, public debts, inefficiency, and the spoils system flourished. By the turn of the present century the reform of city government was a major issue and, as a consequence, many towns of increasing population were seeking to discover a modified town system and avoid city organization with its maze of problems.

By a law passed in 1915, called the Optional Charter Law, the Massachusetts Legislature, which has authority to grant or annul a city charter, made four choices possible: Mayor and Council elected at-large; Mayor and Council elected partially by wards and at-large; the Commission form or City Manager form. In this State, the system of providing a charter by special acts is followed, thus theoretically basing each charter on the particular needs of the community.

However, the city form has not appealed to many large towns. In 1915 Brookline tried the limited or representative town meeting to regulate its size. Any citizen may speak, but only duly elected citizens may vote. Watertown followed this example in 1919, Arlington in 1921, and about twelve others up to the present date.

Although there is a belief that the traditional town meeting is to be found only in small communities on the Cape or in the Berkshires, there are still large communities which retain not only their town designation, like Braintree, Plymouth, and Natick — all over 12,000 in population — but also towns which, although larger than some cities, retain what has been sometimes called the 'last refuge of pure democracy,' the unlimited town meeting; among them is Framingham, a community of about 23,000.

The county system which developed in Massachusetts was at first patterned after the English model familiar to the first settlers. Its organization here was chiefly for judicial purposes. In the West, as in the English counties in Saxon days, the county has developed legislative powers; but in the Bay State the towns and cities, some of whose officers are today county commissioners, were too strong to permit it. The first counties were organized in 1643 as Suffolk, Middlesex, Essex, and Norfolk. By the time of the Revolution, 12 of the present 14 counties were in existence. Franklin was organized in 1811 and Hampden, the last, in 1812. The early officers were appointed. After the Revolution, most of them became elective.

Originally all malefactors were brought before the General Court at Boston. This resulted in such congestions and delay that in 1635 the General Court established courts at Ipswich, Salem, Newtowne, and Boston to handle all but capital cases. The General Court became a court of appeal. As courts for various purposes developed, the General Court, for convenience, located them in the four 'shires' organized in 1643. Growth of the judicial and penal system from then on was rapid. In 1647 local magistrates were appointed for smaller cases. In 1655 each county was ordered to establish a House of Correction. In 1685 came the authority to probate wills and establish Chancery Courts for equity cases. In 1699 the 'beadle' became the Sheriff, and as such was made keeper of the House of Correction.

There were few changes in the Provincial period. Judges, sheriffs, and justices were still appointed by the Governor and Council. In 1699 the Inferior Courts for common pleas were established in each county (there then being ten counties), and a Superior Court of Judicature was established by the Province. The same year legislation making the Sheriff general keeper of the jails was passed.

When the Commonwealth period began in 1780, the Superior Court of Judicature became the Supreme Judicial Court. Two years later the Inferior Courts became the Courts of Common Pleas, and in 1811 they were succeeded by the Circuit Court of Common Pleas with a Chief Justice and assistants, to be succeeded in 1859 by the Superior Courts. The present Municipal Courts are successors of the old police courts or courts of Justice of the Peace.

Although the courts, as organized in the counties, are creatures of the General Court, they constitute one of the great trinity of independent branches of our government. The independence of the courts is based upon the Constitution, for it is within their power to void even legislation when it is not consonant with constitutional provisions. Common law, just as in Colonial times, is the basis of Massachusetts jurisprudence, modified and developed, however, during the past three hundred years in accordance with legislative enactments and judicial decisions.

The courts, when in session, are open to all citizens. There are two chief divisions, for criminal and for civil business. Minor cases may be disposed in the District Courts. Major matters are customarily considered in the Superior Courts, although litigants of even minor matters have the right to carry their cases to the Superior bench. The Supreme Judicial Court is the highest court of appeal in the Commonwealth.

In Massachusetts the Legislature is known as the General Court, although it has long since created courts for the judicial affairs of the State. Today the General Court is exclusively a lawmaking body. Bicameral, it consists of a lower popular body, the House of Representatives, over which the Speaker presides, and a smaller upper body, the State Senate, over which the President presides.

The first General Court under the Constitution met in Boston October 25, 1780. The number of its members varied considerably. At times it had more than 400. The establishment of Maine as a separate State helped to reduce the number, but it was not until 1857 that a constitutional amendment fixed it at the present membership of 240 for·the House and 40 for the Senate. The Acts of 1926, which established representative and senatorial districts, determined there should be one Senator for every 103,000 persons and one Representative for every 17,000.

While most States have biennial sessions, Massachusetts retains annual sessions. Under the right of free petition, any citizen of the Commonwealth, by requesting either a Representative or Senator, may introduce a petition to alter or abolish an old law, or establish a new one. Although such petitions are pigeonholed in many States, in Massachusetts a report has to be made on each one.

Similarly, if introduced in the Senate, such a petition is given a reading in the Senate and is referred to the proper committee. Next it is printed and a public hearing is given in order that both proponents and opponents may be heard. The committee then reports on the petition. If the report is favorable, the petition, now in the form of a bill, faces three readings either in the Senate or House, depending on the officer who introduced it. If it survives the third reading, there is then a vote to be engrossed. If engrossed, it then goes to the other legislative body, and through the same readings and engrossment. Differences between the branches may be ironed out in a conference committee.

Theoretically the laws are supposed to be administered by the Governor with the aid of his Council. In reality the Governor, having a dual rôle because of his position as head of a political party, originates much legislation. With this practice of inspiring legislation and with an enormous amount of patronage under his control, the Governor's position is no longer one merely of dignity and honor, but of constantly increasing power.

Under the Colonial charter, all Governors save the first were elected by the people for a one-year term. James II, before he was deposed, broke this procedure. Thereafter, under the charter of William and Mary, the Governor was subject to appointment by the Crown. He became vice-regal, a military figure with power to prorogue or dissolve the General Court. Since 1780 the Governor has been elected at-large. John Hancock, the first Constitutional Governor, was elected six terms. A majority vote was required, resulting in 1855 in a change to a plurality vote after the election had several times been forced into the General Court for selection of the winner. Since 1917 the Governor's term has been for two years instead of one.

The Governor is Commander-in-Chief of the State's Militia and Naval forces. With advice of the Council he may prorogue the House and Senate and appoint all judicial officers, may appoint and remove State department heads, and exercises the power of pardon for every verdict but impeachment.

Only Maine, New Hampshire, and Massachusetts still have a Governor's Council. The seven assistants of the Governor of Plymouth Colony constitute the historical origin of the Council. The charter of Charles I provided for the election of eighteen assistants. The charter of William and Mary provided for the election of twenty-eight councillors. The first draft of the State Constitution omitted them, but the instrument of 1780 retained them, as did the Constitutional Convention of 1820, although their number was reduced to nine. These were elected from the group of forty, who were elected jointly Senator-Councillor, leaving a Senate of thirty-one members. It is an interesting fact that many declined the councillorship, regarding the Senate seat as more important.

In 1840 the thirteenth constitutional amendment was passed, providing for the selection of the Councillors by the House and Senate from the people-at-large. A committee of the Constitutional Convention of 1853 voted abolition of this measure, but the vote was rejected. Two years later another amendment was passed providing for eight councillor districts and direct election.

The Council has been attacked on the grounds that it is a dispensable Colonial relic, that it makes impossible a concentration of responsibility, that its pardon proceedings are secret, that its revision of sentences is prejudicial to the courts, that its work could be performed by the Senate, and on the grounds of economy. It has been defended as a check on the power of the Governor, and for the reason that numerous duties now performed by it would otherwise have to be delegated elsewhere.

In order to carry out the policies formulated by the Legislature, there has developed and been placed under the supervision of the Governor a number of State departments. These departments, with an ever-widening scope in community activities, are distinct from such primary governmental units as the departments of the Secretary of State, the State Treasurer, and the Attorney-General.

With early industrialization came an increase in the number of public welfare cases. Many of the towns and cities sought to evade their obligation toward these victims of the changing economy, with the result that a State Board of Charity, forerunner of our present Department of Public Welfare, was established by the Legislature.

Public health was another vital need which called for State intervention. Boston in 1799 established its own Board of Health. In 1828 Salem, Marblehead, Plymouth, Charlestown, Lynn, and Cambridge had similar boards. But in 1849, when there was a devastating epidemic of cholera, these Boards of Health were not able to cope with the peril, with the result that the State Board of Health was established.

In 1852 a law prohibiting the sale of alcoholic liquors was passed. Its enforcement was extremely difficult. A special committee which investigated the situation in 1863 publicized the weaknesses of local enforcement. Two years later, despite the opposition of some localities, the office of Constable of the Commonwealth was established. With his deputies he was to regulate, not only the liquor shops, but also to suppress gambling and vice. In 1875, when State prohibition of the sale of liquor was repealed, the enforcement unit was reorganized into what is today the State Police.

The development of the State Board of Education had similar small beginnings. In 1826 each town was required to choose a school committee, usually of five members, and give an annual report to the Secretary of State. In 1834 a State School Fund was established from the sale of land in Maine and from claims against the Federal Government. Three years later the State Board of Education came into being.

Practically every phase of human activity came under supervision of the State. New departments, some later consolidated, were organized: in 1838, the State Banking Commission; in 1853, the Board of Agriculture; in 1855, the Insurance Commission; in 1865, the Tax Commission; in 1869, the Bureau of Labor Statistics; in 1870, the Corporation Commission; in 1887, the first registration board.

INDUSTRY AND LABOR

MASSACHUSETTS has been devoted to industry almost from the time of its first settlement. The Puritan fathers who founded the Massachusetts Bay Colony soon learned that the rocky soil would give them existence alone and that they must seek their prosperity in the sea. Within a decade of the earliest settlement vessels from a dozen ports were regularly visiting the near-by Newfoundland Banks, and the cod had won an honored place on the Puritan's bill of fare. So important was this industry considered that in 1639 those engaging in it were exempt from military duty and fishing paraphernalia was declared free from taxes for seven years.

Codfish was dried and exported, either to the Catholic countries of southern Europe or to the sugar islands of the West Indies. There the fish was traded for tropical articles that New England could not produce, particularly sugar and molasses. Distilleries began to spring up in the Colony to convert the molasses into rum which could be sold in Europe, or traded for slaves along the coast of Africa. These slaves were sold in the West Indies for more molasses and sugar and some cash. Thus was created the famous triangular trade between New England, the West Indies, and Africa. Boston thrived as the 'mart town of the West Indies.'

Ships were needed for this commerce, and shipbuilding became one of the major industries of Colonial Massachusetts. The first shipyard was built at Salem Neck in 1637; others were soon established at Gloucester, Essex, Newbury, Ipswich, Salem, and Boston, and the Bay Colony's vessels became famed throughout the world for their speed and rugged beauty. Shipbuilding fostered a number of other industries, among which was the first ropewalk for the production of ropes and lines, opened at Boston in 1642; ironworks began operation at Lynn in 1643, and at Braintree, Taunton, and in the western part of the Colony. Surface bog iron was converted into ships' hardware.

Massachusetts also had the usual home-manufacturing, centered particularly in the interior agricultural regions where the farmers and their wives had to produce their own crude goods and implements. The spinning wheel was as symbolic of Colonial Massachusetts as the codfish;

woodworking and leather-working were regular home occupations. Wherever water-power was available, sawmills were erected to replace the laborious saw-pits. The textile industry, on which so much of the Commonwealth's later prosperity was built, had its beginning at this time. The first woolen and fulling mill in the Colonies was built at Rowley in 1643, and in 1737 a spinning school, supported by public funds, was opened in Boston. While most spinning and weaving were done in the homes, the movement toward a factory system was under way by the end of the eighteenth century with the grouping of several weaving machines under one roof.

These infant industries were far less important, however, than the commerce that laid the grounds for American independence. Massachusetts traders, unable to obtain a sufficient volume of commerce through contact with the British West Indian possessions, insisted on carrying cod and slaves to French and Spanish islands. Such a trade was opposed to England's own best interests and a series of Navigation Acts passed after 1660 made it definitely illegal. These acts the Massachusetts shippers openly flaunted; the poorly enforced measures of a distant parliament seemed less important than the wealth yielded by commerce. For a time England allowed the violation of her laws to go on, but the close of the wars with France in 1763 offered an excuse to reshape the whole imperial system. Heavy duties were levied against articles secured from French or Spanish island possessions, a Board of Customs Commissioners was set up in Boston to collect the duties, and the smuggling upon which Massachusetts had depended was brought to a sudden end. Boston merchants, ably reinforced by those of Salem, Gloucester, and other ports, fought back, and in doing so unwittingly carried their Colony into a war with the mother country.

The period of the Revolution was a disastrous one for New England shippers. A powerful British navy made even coastwise voyages unsafe, and while some vessels reaped fortunes for their owners as privateers, more were tied rotting at their docks or were captured while trying to run the blockade. Capital that had been drawn from the sea now turned to the land; agriculture experienced a revival and small industries sprang into being to supply the needs of Washington's ragged armies. Iron furnaces in eastern New England were busy casting shot and shell, gunpowder was made in many towns, leather and shoes were manufactured by the skilled Lynn workmen, and Springfield began to produce firearms and other metal goods.

But Massachusetts had been too long wedded to the sea to break off suddenly this profitable union. By 1778 her enterprising merchants were beginning to seek means of trade revival, and the close of the war in 1783 ushered in a new era of commercial prosperity. A coastwise trade with the Southern States replaced the West Indian voyages. Spain, Portugal, and France gradually opened their ports and those of their colonies to the ships of Yankee captains. In 1785 a Boston sloop completed its return voyage from China, and from that time on vessels regularly made their slow way around South America, loaded with furs on the Pacific coast, and pushed on to the Orient.

Fishing, checked as had been commerce by the Revolution, likewise experienced a revival when new trade routes opened new markets. Whaling, which had been carried on in a haphazard way since the middle of the seventeenth century, entered upon a period of fabulous growth as first Nantucket and then New Bedford became the whaling centers of America.

During the years between 1783 and 1807, Massachusetts attained the climax of her early commercial prosperity; her ships handled thirty-seven per cent of the nation's foreign trade, while her fishing fleet amounted to eighty-eight per cent of the American total.

This golden period of commercial activity came to a sudden end in 1807 when Jefferson resorted to an embargo as a means of punishing France and England, then locked in war, for their violation of American neutral shipping rights. American ships were forbidden to leave their ports, while their Massachusetts owners, horrified by the loss of profits, waxed indignant against the government. The War of 1812 climaxed their ruin. Newburyport, Salem, and Plymouth never recovered, and while Boston forged ahead to a position of greater commercial importance, her new fleets could never match the glory of her earlier proud vessels.

But while Massachusetts' marine industry was eclipsed during the War of 1812, manufacturing rose to challenge the supremacy long held by maritime commerce in the State's economic life. The Commonwealth now assumed a position of leadership in manufacturing unchallenged by other States for decades. Capital was available, released from the sea by the ruinous effect of the embargo and the war. Power was available, for the Bay State had an abundance of swift-flowing small streams ready to turn the wheels of mills. Labor was available, for Massachusetts farmers were willing to allow their wives and daughters to work and increase the meager family income. By 1815 Massachusetts was well launched on the road toward an industrial revolution.

This upheaval, while its coming was inevitable, was hastened by the genius of some of the State's own sons. Chief among these was Francis Cabot Lowell, whose close study of English manufacturing methods enabled him to perfect the power loom. This he installed in a factory at Waltham, making possible for the first time the complete manufacture of cloth under one roof, and revolutionizing the textile industry. Factories employing water-power for the production of cotton and woolen cloth began to spring up throughout the Commonwealth.

The period that followed was one of continuous industrial expansion. On the sea the perfection of the clipper ship brought Massachusetts a brief revival of world maritime supremacy. On the land the railroad appeared, the first in America being built in 1826 as a three-mile tramway from the granite quarries of Quincy to the Neponset River. In 1830 the State began chartering railroad lines and by 1836 they were reaching out from Boston to Lowell, Worcester, and Providence, opening new markets as they went. At the same time the completion of the Erie Canal in 1825 threw Massachusetts farmers into competition with the new agricultural areas of the West. The rough, hilly soil of Massachusetts made impossible the use of newly invented agricultural machinery which might have been the farmers' salvation; instead they were forced either to go West themselves or drift into the mills. The labor supply was augmented too by the arrival of large numbers of Irish immigrants, driven from their native land by the Potato Famine of 1845. Massachusetts and the other New England States were thus provided with an adequate number of workers, usually difficult to obtain in a new country.

The development and expansion of factories and mills under these conditions brought a gradual modification of the dog-eat-dog competition that characterized the State's early industrial development. Corporate ownership, first established in cotton manufacturing and other branches of the textile industry, soon became common in the larger industrial centers. Two important manufacturing towns, Lowell and Fall River, were ruled by single companies that discouraged, if they did not prevent, ingress by any potential competitor. In other milling centers a community of interest among owners began to be discernible; they adjusted production to minimize competition with each other, exchanged patent rights, and sold their output through the same channels. In this movement toward consolidation before the Civil War, Massachusetts led all other States.

This solidarity of capital was matched by the beginnings of solidarity in labor. Organization was a new and untried weapon for working men in the 1820's, when a few leaders began to preach the need of unity as the only means of obtaining concessions to labor's needs. Factory hands labored long hours at low wages — in Lowell, for instance, the working day in the mills varied from eleven and a half to thirteen and a half hours, and the wages from one dollar to five dollars a week. Three thousand poor were annually imprisoned for debt in Massachusetts. Fluctuating currency and compulsory military service penalized workingmen. Young children were widely employed at wages much lower even than their parents'.

To combat these conditions, workers began to drift into societies or unions of particular skilled crafts. A Typographical Society existed among the Boston printers as early as 1809, and others, such as the 'Columbian Charitable Society of Shipwrights and Calkers,' formed in 1823, followed. A shipbuilders' strike in Medford in 1817 brought no results, and an attempt of six hundred journeymen carpenters of Boston to secure the ten-hour day in 1825 collapsed when they met determined opposition from the 'gentlemen engaged in building' and received no support from members of other trades.

During the 1830's, however, the organization of workingmen in Massachusetts went on rapidly, inspired partly by the Jacksonian Democracy of that day and partly by the rapid price rise that preceded the Panic of 1837. Wages failed to keep pace with advancing price levels, and laborers began to feel for the first time that their problems could be solved only by united action. Trade unions multiplied throughout the Commonwealth, one of the most famous being the 'Female Society of Lynn and Vicinity for the Protection and Promotion of Female Industry,' which numbered more than one thousand members by the close of 1834. More significant was the formation of city trade unions, composed of representatives of all craft unions in a particular region. Boston organized such a trade union in 1834.

This solidarity gave labor new confidence and resulted in a series of strikes in the middle of the 1830's, both for higher wages and for the ten-hour day. Eight hundred girls employed in the Lowell mills walked out when their demands for a fifteen per cent wage increase were refused, and they returned only when public sentiment, horrified at this example of feminism, turned against them. A strike of the Boston carpenters, masons, and stonecutters for the ten-hour day, although lost, precipitated similar ones in other cities, many of which were successful and led directly to the general adoption of ameliorative legislation.

The Panic of 1837 abruptly changed the character of the Massachusetts labor movement. For the workers the period between the Panic and the Civil War was one of continuous depression. Commodity prices began to increase again in 1843 and advanced steadily for the next two decades, particularly after 1849, when the inflationary effect of the California gold discoveries was felt in Massachusetts. A conservative estimate in 1851 indicated that a family of five required $10.37 a week for the barest necessities of existence, yet salaries in most trades were woefully below this figure and constantly declining. Lynn shoemakers did not average more than four or five dollars a week, while women shoe-binders, by working fourteen to seventeen hours a day, 'if uninterrupted by domestic cares,' earned $1.60 to $2.40 weekly. Moreover, these wages were seldom paid in cash, but in orders on the Lynn Mechanics' Union or other company stores where goods were exorbitantly priced. By the end of the 1840's wages of power-loom operators in Lowell averaged $1.93 a week plus board, although a wage of $1.75 weekly without board was not uncommon. Nor could the board be relied upon. One Holyoke manager found his hands 'languorous' in the early morning because they had breakfasted. He worked them without breakfast and was gratified to find that they produced three thousand more yards of cloth each week.

While workers were thus degraded, the factory owners were enjoying increasing prosperity. Textile mills paid regular dividends varying between five and forty-three per cent each year. The Lawrence Company stock averaged earnings of 10.26 per cent, while the mills at Lowell, over this period, paid their investors from five to fourteen per cent each year. There was a growing discrepancy between the reward of labor and of capital. Wages were falling or remaining stationary, production costs were declining, and prices and profits were advancing.

For twenty-five years trade unions did not dare risk strikes. Since immediate relief was impossible, organized labor accepted the leadership of philosophical liberals who sought to secure ultimate relief by radical social reform. Other men, more practical of mind, tried to develop the co-operative movement, and in this movement Massachusetts played a leading part. As early as 1831 the possibilities of co-operation were discussed at Boston by an 'Association of Farmers, Mechanics and Other Working Men,' and a year later the journeymen cordwainers of Lynn tried an actual experiment in co-operation. In 1845 the 'Working Men's Protective Union' was formed and began a process of expansion that lasted to 1852, when it was distributing to its members goods valued at nearly two million dollars. A schism in 1853 started a decline in the Massachusetts co-operative movement and the Civil War brought it to an end.

The war grew in part from the evolution of industrial Massachusetts

The Bay State symbolized the North with its system of wage labor, absolutely antagonistic to the slave labor of the South. The clash of the two systems not only divided the nation into warring camps, but ushered Massachusetts into its greatest period of industrial prosperity. Under the press of wartime orders manufacturing boomed as never before. New factories were built, old ones were remodeled and enlarged, new machinery and new processes were introduced. By 1865 the State's industrial products were valued at more than half a billion dollars and were absorbing the labor of some 270,000 workers.

This period of hothouse growth put new emphasis upon the consolidation of Massachusetts industries. Manufacturers were made aware by the wartime profits of the advantages of large-scale production and hastened to unite into combinations that would lessen competition and transform the small-scale economic system of 1860 into the Titanic and closely interrelated financial-industrial structure of 1900.

Increased mechanization led to greater output, and in the manufacture of woolens, where new machinery was being constantly introduced, the Commonwealth produced in 1870 more than one-third of all the woolen goods consumed in the United States. During the 1880's Fall River was unmatched in the production of cotton goods, followed by Lowell, Lawrence, and New Bedford. By this time the small factory had virtually disappeared and combinations controlled the entire textile industry. Typical were the New England Cotton Yarn Company, operating cotton mills throughout the southeastern part of the State, and the American Woolen Company, which maintained twenty-six mills and a large portion of the nation's machinery devoted to the production of men's wear.

The boot and shoe industry, which had reached the factory stage by the end of the Civil War, entered at that time on a period of rapid technical development as a result of improvements in power machinery. Lynn led the nation's cities in this industry in 1890, with 323 factories producing goods worth $26,000,000. Brockton followed, turning out shoes to the value of $16,000,000 in her 73 factories. Not until the 1890's did the Bay State's shoe industry encounter serious competition, and even then it was able to resist the encroachments of New York and the Middle West for another twenty years.

The paper mills of Massachusetts, fed by the water-power of the Connecticut River and the streams of the Berkshires, also prospered after the Civil War, supplying one-fourth of the paper produced in the United States. Holyoke led the world in the manufacture of fine paper in 1890, its

22 mills producing 180 tons every day. In the manufacture of metal products, light machinery, furniture, and clocks, Massachusetts kept pace with the leading producers of the country.

Periods of industrial prosperity normally lead to a burst of labor activity. At first workers were not sure what method should be used to cope with labor problems incidental to rapidly expanding factories, and attempts were made to revive many panaceas that had been advocated before the Civil War. Thus Ira Steward, a Boston machinist, developed the theory that a general eight-hour day would solve all problems of capital and labor. His 'Grand Eight-Hour League of Massachusetts' became the model for similar organizations in other States and greatly influenced legislation toward shorter hours. Others believed labor should imitate capital and organize along national lines. Of the national trade unions that became prominent in this period, one of the most important, as far as Massachusetts was concerned, was the Knights of St. Crispin, a secret union of shoe workers formed at Milwaukee in 1867. A third solution for the dilemma of the worker was offered by the Greenbackers, who became prominent in Massachusetts during the 1870's under the leadership of Wendell Phillips and Governor Benjamin Butler. By their ambitious plans, the State would finance with fiat money co-operative associations of workmen who would eventually drive private capitalism out of existence by the competitive route.

When these schemes brought few results, labor drifted back toward a policy of unionism and tried two great experiments along national lines. The first was an attempt to organize all workers regardless of craft or skill into one body known as the Knights of Labor. After 1886, the Knights were beginning to crumble and a new organization, the American Federation of Labor, was rising. Unions affiliated with this national organization formed a Massachusetts Federation of Labor in 1887.

The first attempt at a general organization of the State's textile workers was made in 1889 when the National Cotton Spinners' Union was formed. Within a short time ring spinning had swept the trade of mule spinning from existence, and in 1901 a new union, the United Textile Workers, was organized along industrial lines. Although designed to include all textile workers, regardless of craft, its development was slow, partly because of the large numbers of women and children employed in the textile industry. More success was enjoyed by the Boot and Shoe Workers' Union, which began organizing the shoe trades in 1900.

The rise of these strong unions and employers' efforts to combat them led to many labor disputes. Between 1881 and 1900 there were 1802 recorded strikes and lockouts, Massachusetts ranking fourth among the States in strikes and third in number of lockouts.

After 1900 Massachusetts slowly relinquished the dominant industrial and commercial position she had gained in the last part of the nineteenth century. Only Boston remained an export port of any consequence and even this leading New England city, while enjoying temporary commercial growth as the smaller ports declined, after 1901 suffered a steady shrinkage of its shipping. This declining trade in the first quarter of the twentieth century paralleled and reflected a growing depression in manufacturing. In an age of general business consolidation Massachusetts found herself with a number of diversified industries that did not lend themselves to mass production. The absence of coal and oil in the State and the resulting increased costs of production handicapped many industries. Distance from raw materials, particularly from those utilized in textile and steel mills, was a factor of decisive importance in the industrial impoverishment of the State. Her nearness to foreign markets was offset by the greater advantage enjoyed by New York as the traditional shipping center of the East; and her supply of highly skilled labor, once jealously guarded, became an additional burden to industries striving to match the low wages paid untrained workers in the mass-production factories of other States.

The textile industry was particularly hard hit by these forces. Destructive competition from States nearer to the source of supply, where living standards were lower and cheap, labor easier to obtain, led to the long idleness or abandonment of cotton mills in Lowell, Fall River, Lawrence, and New Bedford. In Lowell alone, between 1919 and 1929, manufacturing employment fell off nearly forty-three per cent. In scores of Massachusetts towns silent mills were gaunt reminders of a bygone prosperity.

In the boot and shoe industry competition at home and abroad, and labor difficulties following the failure of shoe concerns to meet their skilled workers' demands, influenced Lynn, Brockton, and Haverhill plants to migrate to other States. Of the metal industries only the production of electrical machinery increased between 1919 and 1929.

Of the major industries of Massachusetts, only fishing continued to thrive. With the richest fishing area in the world lying off her coast, where cod, haddock, mackerel, and lobsters abound, the Bay State has remained an outstanding fishing center for the entire country; Boston, Gloucester, Provincetown, and other fishing ports have steadily increased their landings of fish since the beginning of the century. Modern methods of catching and packing, the development of the steam trawler and the use of mechanical refrigeration, have increased fishing profits in recent years.

Declining trade and industry ushered Massachusetts into a period of serious labor difficulties. The skilled workers whose abilities had erected the State's industrial empire naturally resented attempts of employers to lower wages to match declining production. The factory owners, on the other hand, felt that they could face new competition only by slashing labor costs and establishing wage levels comparable to those given unskilled workers in other States. This clash of interests led to a rapid organization of the industrial workers of Massachusetts and to friction along the entire labor front. Three events in this struggle gained nationwide attention: the Lawrence strike in 1912, the Boston police strike in 1919, and the Sacco-Vanzetti case which was before the public eye between 1920 and 1927.

The Lawrence strike was called to protest a wage reduction in that mill city. According to the report of the United States Commissioner of Labor, 'the average amount actually received [in Lawrence] by the 21,922 employees, during a week late in 1911, in which the mills were running full time, was $8.76.' The strike was managed by the Industrial Workers of the World, an industrial union organized a few years before in an attempt to unite unskilled workers under one banner. Even though the I.W.W. had only a few hundred actual members among the workers — another union, the United Textile Workers, had far more — the vigorous leadership of Joseph Ettor, William ('Big Bill') Haywood, and other I.W.W. leaders soon closed the mills and brought most of their operatives out on strike. The number of men involved and the presence of outside organizers frightened city officials. When mass picketing was begun on January 15, the Mayor requisitioned four regiments of troops. The next day the mills were reopened under the protection of bayonets, but this only increased the tension. On January 19 the skilled operatives joined the strike; on January 29, a woman was killed in a huge demonstration and the city council voted to turn the town over to the command of the militia, then reinforced by ten more companies of infantry and two of cavalry. Meanwhile conditions in the strikers' homes were becoming intolerable, for no adequate funds were available to care for the workers. Partly to call attention to their plight and partly because they needed actual care, several hundred of the strikers' children were sent to New York — the famous 'Refugee Children' who attracted widespread attention in the nation's press. Finally, after the organization of a picket line containing some twenty thousand persons, the strike was settled with the workers winning a slight wage increase and the guarantee of no discrimination against union members.

Even more attention was attracted by the Boston police strike seven years later. In August, 1919, the Boston Social Club, an organization of 1290 Boston policemen, voted to join the American Federation of Labor in a body, despite an order from the Police Commissioner forbidding members of the force to affiliate with any organizations outside the department, 'Except posts of the G.A.R., Spanish War Veterans, and the American Legion.' The policemen claimed that their wages had failed to keep pace with living costs, that the police stations were unsanitary, and that they worked overtime without compensation; organization, they said, was necessary for their own protection. This the Commissioner denied, and after a brief trial dismissed eight men of the force for violating his order by affiliating with the American Federation of Labor. The Policeman's Union promptly called a strike, to become effective on September 9. Officials refused the pleas of a citizens' committee which urged arbitration, and Boston entered on a period with no police protection.

Hoodlums poured into the city bent on reaping a harvest while the law was not functioning. The Mayor called on all 'citizens to do their part to assist the authorities in maintaining order'; Governor Calvin Coolidge called out one hundred State Police; President Lowell of Harvard appealed to students 'to prepare themselves for such services as the Governor may call upon them to render'; and Coach Fisher was reported by the press to have said, 'To hell with football if men are needed.' On the night of September 9th Boston slept virtually without protection. On the 10th volunteer police were on duty, the Metropolitan Police joined the strikers, and by noon Mayor Peters called out the tenth Regiment of Militia, which the Governor supplemented with five more regiments. Approximately five thousand militiamen took over guardianship of the city, an assignment which, for some of them, continued into November. The volunteers were dismissed on the 11th; by that day seven persons had been killed and sixty wounded.

This disorder turned opinion rapidly against the striking policemen. President Wilson denounced the strike and Samuel Gompers, president of the A.F. of L., ordered the strikers back to work. With the support of the Federation lost, the policemen were beaten and their union voted on September 12 to return to work. Gompers appealed to Governor Coolidge to reinstate the strikers, at the same time completely disavowing the strike. Coolidge disclaimed the power of reinstatement, and added that he was opposed to the 'public safety again being placed in the hands of these same policemen.' A new force was on duty November 10, and the defeated strikers sought jobs elsewhere. The reputation gained by Calvin Coolidge in the Boston police strike has always been considered a decisive factor in his career.

The Sacco-Vanzetti case hinged about two members of an anarchist group, Bartolomeo Vanzetti, a fish peddler, and Niccola Sacco, a shoe worker, who were arrested in 1920 on the charge of murder and robbery in connection with the theft of a $15,000 payroll. Many were convinced that the evidence used against the defendants was circumstantial and inadequate, that their alibis were truthful, and that they were being condemned to the chair more because of their radical views than because of their guilt. During the seven years that elapsed between the murder and execution of the sentence, protest demonstrations were held throughout the world. The case was twice passed upon by the Supreme Court of Massachusetts, and applications for a new trial denied. President Lowell of Harvard, President Stratton of the Massachusetts Institute of Technology, and Judge Robert Grant were invited by Governor Fuller to weigh the evidence and advise him. They upheld the finding of the court and Sacco and Vanzetti were executed on August 23, 1927. It was contended by liberals and radicals that, although legal forms were observed, the determining factor in the case was the affiliation of the two men with an unpopular minority political group.

Recent developments in the Massachusetts labor situation have indicated some of the difficulties that both industry and the workers face in the Bay State. Textile employees, entrenched in the United Textile Workers since the beginning of the century, staged a series of spectacular strikes in 1934, but secured no great concessions from an industry sadly crippled by the depression. The union was weakened by this loss of prestige, and in 1936–37 deserted the American Federation of Labor to cast its lot with the Committe for Industrial Organization.

Recent attempts to organize the shoe industry have led to serious internal disputes within labor organizations and to the migration of many shoe factories to other States. One bitter struggle occurred in 1929 when the shoe workers of Lynn, Boston, Chelsea, and Salem struck, with the major demand for recognition of their union, the United Shoe Workers of America, as opposed to the Boot and Shoe Workers' Union, an A.F. of L. affiliate. The strike lasted six months and strike-breakers were imported from neighboring States, but it was finally broken by a court injunction based upon findings that the strike was illegal. During this strike many runaway shops left Massachusetts and moved to non-union centers in other States. The frequency with which these shops have moved has earned them the title of 'factories on wheels.' Again in 1933 an attempt to unite all shoe workers into a national union, the United Shoe and Leather Workers' Union, resulted in internal dissensions and wholesale factory removals. In 1933-34 there were twenty-one shoe factories in Boston employing some seven thousand workers; by 1935-36 there remained only four factories, employing about two thousand. In 1937 a movement again developed toward industrial unionization, this time as an affiliate of the Committee for Industrial Organization. At present there is a growing conflict between two types of organization, the one, craft unionism, most strongly entrenched in the building and metal trades, the other, industrial unionism, centered in the mass-production phases of textiles and shoes.

Out of the struggle between employer and employee in the State have come results of which Massachusetts is justifiably proud. The Commonwealth long led in the enactment of progressive legislation for the benefit of workers. Child labor first received legislative attention as early as 1842 when a ten-hour day was established for children under twelve. In 1867 employment of children under ten was forbidden and subsequent statutes made it illegal for children between ten and fourteen to work while schools were in session. The Uniform Child Labor Law (1913), setting an eight-hour day for children between fourteen and sixteen, was the first workable law of that nature passed by an important textile State. Despite this willingness to act against child labor, Massachusetts has consistently refused to ratify the national Child Labor Amendment. National opposition centered in this State because the Amendment — giving Congress power 'to limit, regulate, and prohibit the labor of persons under eighteen years of age' — was submitted to a referendum here in November, 1924, the first year in which it was before the States. A majority of the voters then recorded themselves as against the Amendment, and the General Court has consistently refused to ratify, despite active efforts by proponents of the measure, each year from 1933 through 1937. The decisive defeat by referendum, although in a campaign notable for the participation of partisans from outside Massachusetts, was used in other States as an argument against ratification by their respective legislatures. The fight for the Amendment has been led by the State Federation of Labor and the Massachusetts League of Women Voters; the fight against it by the Massachusetts Associated Industries, affiliated with the National Association of Manufacturers. Many prominent citizens, including Cardinal O'Connell and A. Lawrence Lowell, opposed the Amendment.

A progressive spirit has been shown by the General Court in dealing with hours of labor and workers' safety. A ten-hour day and sixty-hour week for women and children under eighteen, set by statute in 1874, proved the entering wedge. In 1911 a fifty-four-hour law was passed and in 1919 a forty-eight-hour law. A whole series of measures regulates the labor of women and minors in dangerous or unhealthy occupations and at night. The first American law designed to protect workers in dangerous occupations has been on the State's statutes since 1877. A Workingmen's Compensation Act was passed in 1887, making employers liable for injuries or death of their employees under certain conditions where negligence could be shown. An Act of 1911 was voluntary, but it authorized insurance companies to do business with employers and excluded from the right of compensation only those workers injured because of their own serious and wilful misconduct.

Massachusetts was also the pioneer among her sister States in minimum-wage-law legislation. An Act of 1912 authorized a commission to investigate salaries paid women in any branch of industry and recommended wages considered adequate to provide a proper living standard. The commission was authorized to publish the names of firms that refused to accept its recommendations. The commission, while not mandatory and depending on publicity for its results, called national attention to this type of legislation. In 1934, minimum-wage standards for women and minors, supported by effective enforcement regulations and penalties, displaced the earlier measure.

Massachusetts has consistently sought to ease difficulties arising between employers and employees. Its bureau for investigation of labor conditions was established in 1869, the first of its kind in any State. This, by scientific investigations and impartial reports, made easier the solution of difficulties arising between workers and factory owners. A more important step was the creation, in 1886, of a State Board of Conciliation and Arbitration, one of the first of its kind in the United States. This board, composed of a representative of the employer, one of the employee, and an impartial third person, has prevented many labor difficulties and benefited both the worker and the owner. Its work has been supplemented by a Commission of Labor and Industry, now (1938) functioning as an arbitration board in industrial disputes.

ARCHITECTURE

FOR generations historians have been telling us that when the 'Mayflower' dropped anchor off what is now Plymouth, our ancestors went ashore and proceeded immediately to build log cabins. This would mean that, upon the spur of the moment, these workmen invented a new type of building — a construction such as they had never seen in England, of a kind unknown even to the Indians. A widely publicized painting illustrating this fanciful theory pictures a double row of such log houses reaching up the hillside of Leyden Street at Plymouth. Far from supporting this tradition, all accounts of day-by-day happenings following the settlement of the coastal villages give ample proof that, so far as material and labor permitted, the first settlers in New England reproduced the homes they had left in Old England. The wooden versions of the English yeoman's cottage were not the first to be built by the settlers. The exigency of immediate shelter forced a direct retrogression to a type much earlier and more primitive than those left behind. But as there were skilled artisans and carpenters among the early settlers who were qualified by long apprenticeships in England to construct permanent houses, there is no need for giving more than a passing mention to the first temporary makeshift structures. The common folk were first housed in conical huts constructed of slanting poles covered with brush, reeds, and turf, sometimes with a low wall of branches and wattle plastered with clay. These were the 'English wigwams' referred to in chronicles, and were simply a transplantation of a type then in use by charcoal-burners in England. Some of these temporary shelters were cellars built into the sides of banks, walled and roofed with brush and sod. In Salem a 'pioneer village' was built in 1930, and reproductions of some of the early shelters and houses may be seen there.

Soon after landing, the colonists dug saw pits in the English manner and began to produce boards in quantity suitable not only for the construction of their own houses but for exportation as well. In the summer of 1626, when the ship 'Fortune' sailed from Plymouth, bound for England, 'clapboards and wainscott' were listed as part of her lading. In the summer of 1623 Bradford mentions the building 'of great houses in pleasant situations,' and later writes that 'they builte a forte with good timber.' Isaac de Rasières described the structure in 1627 as 'a large square house made of thick sawn planks, stayed with oak beams.' When the fort was taken down at the close of King Philip's War in 1676, the timber was given to William Harlow, who built the Harlow House, which is still standing in Plymouth.

The usual type of permanent dwelling-house was a two-story structure, the second story overhanging, with two rooms upstairs and down, a small entry, and a mammoth chimney between. Lean-tos were often added later. The Fairbanks House in Dedham (1636), solidly framed of oak, rejoices in an unadorned simplicity lost in later and more academic structures. The Boardman House in Saugus (1651) combines two characteristic features of the medieval Colonial: the overhang and the original innovation of the lean-to. The long, unbroken slope of its roof is well suited to stream-line the cold north wind. Ornament occurs in the Parson Capen House at Topsfield (1683), where heavy carved pendrils or drops depending from the bottom of the jetty or overhang lend an Elizabethan flavor. As the overhang, however, had been evolved in England for the purpose of gaining additional floor area above the street line, in a new and spacious country it dwindled and soon disappeared.

The earliest ecclesiastical architecture was similarly influenced by English medievalism. The only church building of the seventeenth century still standing in the State, the Old Ship Church in Hingham, was erected by ship carpenters in 1681. Its roof, built in the form of a truncated pyramid, is surmounted by a belfry and lookout station. This early church, constructed to fulfill the simple needs of its congregation, is devoid of frivolity or pretense. Here, as frequently elsewhere in early Massachusetts architecture, deliberate indifference to any esthetic concept resulted in an effect of restraint and dignity.

The first indications of a more studied architecture came at the opening of the eighteenth century with the adoption of less steep roofs, the use of sash windows instead of casements, and a growing tendency to employ a uniform cornice with a hip roof. William Price, a Boston print-seller, designed Christ Church (the Old North Church) in 1723, adorning its simple front with a lofty wooden steeple reminiscent of Wren. A more imposing structure, the Old South Church, erected seven years later from plans by Robert Twelve, is in this same style, which strongly influenced ecclesiastical architecture in the colonies during the entire century. The architectural ambitions of the builders were satisfied by the steeple, little effort at further adornment being made beyond an occasional elaboration of the eaves into a classical cornice.

Independent of architectural pomposities of the mainland, the fishermen along the bended elbow of the State were erecting their huddled little 'Cape Codders.' Built on flat surfaces of the dunes, these one-and-a-half-story cottages with lean-tos hugged the earth for warmth over shallow unfinished cellars. Entrance to the cellar was provided by a trapdoor inside the house or by an outside bulkhead, its ungainliness hidden by a lilac or other flowering shrub. Since the first story was usually not over seven feet high, the half story used as a storeroom and as sleeping quarters for the children provided little headroom. The typical Cape Codder had a shingle roof, a large central chimney, a clapboarded front, sometimes painted, and unpainted shingled sides which the salt air weathered to a dull silver. The windmill, with its shingled walls and skeleton-like vanes silhouetted against the dunes, is peculiar to the Cape and Nantucket.

The floors were of pine, wide-cut, painted or 'spattered.' The doors ordinarily had six panels and opened with a thumb latch. The first-floor windows had four 'lights' each, those in the upper floor but three. Smaller windows, set irregularly in the walls, provided light for closets. The parlor, more carefully finished than the kitchen, contained a 'chair rail,' a narrow moulding running around the wall about two and a half feet from the floor. So simple a cottage made up for its bareness by the bright polish of its window-panes and the gleam of its scrubbed floor.

The 'half-a-cape,' a plain dwelling with a chimney at one end, derived its name from the fact that its owner always hoped the day would come when he could add the other half and convert his cottage into a proper house with a central chimney. The 'salt-box' — the origin of the name no longer so apparent now that salt comes in cardboard containers — has a northerly lean-to roof. The 'rainbow roof' rises in a convex curve to the ridgepole, with the appearance of an inverted boat's hull. The familiar roomy gambrel roof is occasionally but not often seen on the Cape.

As the seaboard towns grew in wealth, and tools and materials were more easily secured, builders began to indulge in the free classic details of the Queen Anne and the Georgian styles. The result was Georgian colonial, which had a profound influence upon American domestic architecture along the eastern seaboard. In New England, Georgian colonial buildings were almost invariably harmonious; details in most instances were delicate and refined; errors were apt to be on the side not of coarseness, but of smallness and reserve. The first phase of New England Georgian occupied the period between 1720-25 and 1740-45, of which the Royall House (1723) in Medford and the Dummer Mansion in Byfield are fine examples. The second phase, from 1745 to 1775-80, is exemplified in the Lee Mansion in Marblehead. The transition from Georgian to classicism, showing a strong Adam influence, was dominant in the last phase, and included some of the best work of Bulfinch and McIntire.

In the absence of professional architects in Massachusetts during the eighteenth century, cultivated amateurs turned to the drafting board. Sir Francis Bernard, for nine years Colonial Governor of Massachusetts, designed Harvard Hall (1765) in Harvard Yard. Near-by Massachusetts Hall had been erected in 1720 from designs prepared by John Leverett, president of the college, and Benjamin Wadsworth, later president. John Smibert, portrait-painter, drew the plans for Faneuil Hall (1742) in Boston, later enlarged and modified by Bulfinch. Peter Harrison, a contemporary of Smibert, although he had no professional training, became the most distinguished architect of the Colonial era. In 1749 he designed King's Chapel in Boston, in which the influence of Wren and his successor Gibbs can be seen. The exterior is dour, but the interior, with its rich sobriety, repose, and studied suavity of proportion, remains one of the finest in existence. Harrison also designed Christ Church (1761) in Cambridge.

The first professional architect of the Republic began his career as a cultivated amateur. Charles Bulfinch (1763–1844), born of a well-to-do family, made an architectural 'grand tour' of Europe. As a gentleman of means and taste he designed houses for his friends. He planned the State House on Beacon Hill in Boston, the original red brick core of which, known as the Bulfinch Front, stands sandwiched between two white annexes.

Bulfinch went bankrupt in 1796, and fortunately for architecture made extended use of his talent to earn his living. In his handling of detail and ornament the influence of Adam and Chambers is obvious, but in the sterner matters of plan and composition Bulfinch struck out in new directions, and his designs, characterized by slender proportions, a delicacy well suited to execution in wood, tall pilasters of slight projection, light cornices and balustrades, slender columns, shallow surface arches, and fan-lights and side-lights with tenuous tracery, were a departure in line and detail. Bulfinch had studied to good effect Chambers's fine new Somerset House in London, as is apparent from a comparison of his first sketches for the State House, submitted in 1787, with the façade of the English structure containing the Navy Office. A volume which Bulfinch purchased abroad, 'Le Vignole Moderne' (Paris, 1785), contains some of the motives used on the portico of the State House, as well as a good dome. His work in directing the completion of the Federal Capitol Building in Washington after 1817, when at President Monroe's invitation he replaced Latrobe as architect of the Capitol, indicates that his fresh and bold approach had become somewhat restrained.

The Elias Hasket Derby Mansion in Salem profited by the combined efforts of Bulfinch and McIntire. Derby was so situated economically that he could demand the best talent available, so Bulfinch, who was considered the best, was asked to submit designs, which he did. Dissatisfied, Derby called in McIntire, the local master, and he carried the job to completion. He designed the house almost independently, but incorporated in it some of the features by Bulfinch.

As chairman of the board of selectmen of Boston, Bulfinch had much to do with turning the Common from a meadow into a park, and during this period he drew the plans for the warehouses on Boston's India Wharf. Other buildings of significance by Bulfinch remaining today in Massachusetts are Faneuil Hall (addition and revision, 1805), the Harrison Gray Otis House (1796), the Sears House (second Harrison Gray Otis House, 1800), Wadsworth House (third Harrison Gray Otis House, 1807), Bulfinch Building, Massachusetts General Hospital (1818) — all in Boston; University Hall, Harvard (1813-15); enlargement of Faneuil Hall (1805); Lancaster Church (1810); Meeting House, Taunton; Pearson Hall (1818) and Bulfinch Hall (1818) at Phillips Academy in Andover.

As the depression of the 1780's was succeeded by better times, Yankee vessels began to pour wealth into Boston, Salem, and other seaboard towns. Port towns soon were clustered with the square white houses of shipowners and sea captains, their roofs crowned with roof decks known as 'captain's walks' or 'widow's walks,' originally lookout places for scanning the harbor. Many of the builders of these houses had been ship carpenters, taught by the exacting demands of their craft economy of line and material. As a result their houses possessed a fluidity of line seen at its best in the work of McIntire.

The work of Samuel McIntire (1757-1811), carver-architect and contemporary of Bulfinch, shows the influence of European masters, notably Robert Adam. But McIntire possessed too much native genius to be content with servile adaptation. 'He borrowed, but he repaid with interest.'

McIntire houses, many of which, happily, are preserved in Salem, had little exterior grace. They were big, four-square, three stories high. Like their mistresses, the captains' ladies, these Salem houses guarded themselves from the world by a prim, even prudish exterior. Within, however, was amiability, charm, and finely studied and eloquently executed detail, apparent in the broad staircases with their carved balusters and twisted newels, the wooden mantels enriched with figured ornament, the raised paneled dadoes, and delicate cornices with dentils and modillions. The exteriors were usually flanked with great pilasters or quoins, surmounted with cornices of well-proportioned members, and the houses were not infrequently enclosed with elaborate wooden fences.

McIntire's last houses, built from 1805 to 1811, were of brick. The use of this less pliable material and a growing classical influence gave his later work a more austere character. Outstanding examples of his architecture are the Pierce-Johonnot-Nichols House (1782), Samuel Cook House (1804), John Gardner House (1805), David P. Waters House (1805), Dudley L. Pickman House (1810), all in Salem; the Elias H. Derby House (1799), and 'Oak Hill' (1800) in Peabody. Three complete McIntire rooms from 'Oak Hill' have been installed in the American Wing of the Museum of Fine Arts in Boston.

Asher Benjamin, a contemporary of McIntire, designed the Old West Church (1806) and the Charles Street Church (1807) in Boston. Possessing the native genius of neither Bulfinch nor McIntire, Benjamin made an important contribution to American architecture through his frequent publications, from 'The Country Builder's Assistant' (1797) to 'The Practical House Carpenter' (1830).

The Greek revival, started in the beginning of the nineteenth century by Benjamin Henry Latrobe with his design for the Bank of Pennsylvania, did not spread to New England until the second decade. Alexander Parris and Solomon Willard, the planners of Bunker Hill Monument in Charlestown (1825-42), were its chief exponents in Massachusetts, and as such they designed Saint Paul's Cathedral (1820) in Boston. Later, with Quincy Market (1825) in Boston and the Stone Temple in Quincy (1828), Parris essayed other monuments to this revived style.

Long after the ebbing of the tide of Greek influence, one of the most studied efforts in this style was built in Boston: the United States Custom House (1847). Designed by Ammi B. Young and Isaiah Rogers, this building was originally crowned with a dome. Later a tall shaft was added, transforming it into Boston's first skyscraper and an apt tombstone to the movement. The dome was not removed from the interior, but the lower floors were allowed to hide it and form a shell about it. Later examples of the Greek revival travestied the classic style rather than copied it. It became common practice for the designers of commercial buildings to make imitations of Greek porticoes and entries and to attach them without discrimination to the façades of banks and markets. Allied to little in the Massachusetts tradition, the Greek revival inevitably disintegrated.

After the Greek revival came experimentation in many directions. Dwelling-houses took the form of Italian villas, or of mansard-roofed boxes — the shadows of English shadows. The result was a tedious parade of mediocrity, punctuated here and there by an outstanding atrocity. French influence fared somewhat better than English, and the Athenæum (1849), the Arlington Street Church, and the old Technology building (now Rogers Hall), all in Boston, were intelligent adaptations of Renaissance motifs.

Up to the end of the Civil War no academic training of architects was given in the State. In 1865, however, the Massachusetts Institute of Technology established the first American school for architects, in which something like the organized teaching of the École des Beaux Arts was attempted, with William R. Ware as its first director.

The period immediately following the Civil War was infected by Ruskin's fervent advocacy of medievalism and his sweeping condemnation of Renaissance architecture as 'immoral.' Ruskinian or Victorian Gothic, derived by an adoption of Italian Gothic detail and characterized by a confusion of aims frequently accompanied by mediocrity of achievement, has its monument in Memorial Hall (1878) at Harvard, William R. Ware, architect. Probably the most severely condemned of its contemporaries, 'Mem Hall' shows the laboring of an architect of taste and scholarship fatally hampered by a pernicious style. Boston's Copley Square, originally a swamp dear to none but duck-hunters, was filled in, and architects cast about for suitable designs for its new buildings. The Old South Church (1876) was designed by Cummings and Sears, who had obviously saturated themselves with Ruskin. A no less apparent study of the work of Sir Gilbert Scott, however, makes this building one of the more bearable examples of the Ruskinian episode in the United States. The old Museum of Fine Arts, devotedly Ruskinian (1876, no longer standing), built from designs by John Sturgis, was the first structure in which domestic terra cotta was used.

Just across the square Henry Hobson Richardson was burying the corpse of Victorian Gothic and raising a splendid structure, Trinity Church (1872–78). The bold individuality of Trinity, the most important example of 'Richardson Romanesque,' can be fully appreciated, even by trained eyes, only after detailed study. Taking as its point of departure the Romanesque of southern France, Trinity is characterized by its strong, vigorous and picturesque masses of rock-faced stonework and its rich and individual ornament. John LaFarge's windows and interior decorations are in keeping with the richness of the exterior.

Richardson was the second American to study at the École des Beaux Arts and in Paris he worked for Labrouste, the architect of that extraordinary building, the Bibliothèque Sainte Geneviève in Paris. Trinity Church, considered Richardson's most important work, is antedated by the First Baptist Church of Boston (formerly New Brattle Square Church, 1874), a failure acoustically, but notable for its tower. When Richardson designed the tower he sent for Bartholdi, a fellow student at the Beaux Arts, to execute the heavy frieze. Bartholdi became so engrossed in his new surroundings that he was moved to design his 'Light of Liberty,' eventually reproduced in New York Harbor. Other noteworthy examples of Richardson's work in the State are Sever Hall at Harvard, the public libraries at Quincy, Woburn, and North Easton, and the railroad stations at Auburndale and Chestnut Hill.

The Richardsonian Romanesque was widely imitated, but seldom worthily adapted. An excellent adaptation of this style to a commercial purpose, however, is the Ames Building (1891), one of Boston's first tall office buildings and the last to employ all masonry instead of steel construction, designed by Shepley, Rutan, and Coolidge, who carried on Richardson's work.

The epochal achievement of the nineteenth century which began a direct revival of classical forms was Charles Follen McKim's Albertian Boston Public Library (1888–95). Using the simple, unbroken lines of Labrouste's Bibliothèque Sainte Geneviève in Paris, he fused with this influence the more robust character of Alberti's San Francesco at Rimini. The building is monumental, yet chaste in ornamentation. It has dignity and restraint, severity without coldness.

Contemporaneous with, but independent of, the classic revival, Ralph Adams Cram began a revival of medieval Gothic forms. In Henry Adams, Massachusetts produced a scholar who sought in medieval architecture a key to the present; in Ralph Adams Cram the State possesses an architect who turns from the present to the medieval past, notably in his All Saints' Church in Ashmont; Saint Stephen's, Cohasset; First Unitarian, West Newton; All Saints' and the Church of Our Saviour in Brookline. For many years the work of the serene medievalist profited by the more restless genius of Bertram Grosvenor Goodhue. The firm of Cram, Goodhue and Ferguson led the neo-Gothic movement.

Up to the time of the Chicago Exposition in 1893, when the steel skeleton and the elevator had definitely severed architectural practice

ARCHITECTURAL MILESTONES

WHEN the settlers first came to America, they built something very like an English charcoal burner's hut. Reproductions of these early huts can be seen at the Pioneer Village in Salem. Thereafter, as soon as the people were established, they built houses as much like the familiar houses of Elizabethan England as their materials permitted. Many of these houses were afterward enlarged by the building of a 'lean-to' on the northern side which protected the house from the prevailing northerly winds. The interiors were spacious and agreeable.

Later, in the time of McIntire and Bulfinch, the architecture in Massachusetts reached a second peak. Chestnut Street in Salem shows the houses of this period at their best. On the same page with the picture of Chestnut Street is a picture of the Hill of Churches in Truro. It is included for contrast, for architecture in Massachusetts, like the people, reaches extremes of barrenness as well as beauty.

Besides Chestnut Street, two other Salem houses are shown, and several interiors and a doorway; also an early example of church architecture; Bulfinch's masterpiece, the State House; and finally two later examples of Massachusetts architecture.

WHIPPLE HOUSE, IPSWICH

KITCHEN OF JOHN WARD HOUSE, HAVERHILL

HARTSHORNE HOUSE, WAKEFIEL

ILL OF CHURCHES, TRURO

CHESTNUT ST., SALEM

ASSEMBLY HOUSE, SALEM

PIERCE-NICHOLS HOUSE, SALEM

LEE MANSION

OLD STATE HOUSE

HOUSE OF SEVEN GABLES, SALEM

STATE HOUSE, BOSTON

HOLDEN CHAPEL, HARVARD

'CONNECTICUT VALLEY' DOORWAY, MISSION HOUSE, STOCKBRIDGE

PUBLIC LIBRARY, BOSTON

TRINITY CHURCH, BOSTON

from tradition, Massachusetts held its place in the forefront of American architecture. But since the birth of the modern movement, architecture here seems to be dormant, almost oblivious of the changes taking place elsewhere. The development of a more modern style here has been prejudiced by conditions, and these for the most part have been largely sociological. In the desperate effort to keep alive her inherited British culture, Massachusetts has kept her architecture steeped in the confines of tradition and precedent. Yet in spite of this seeming retrogression, Massachusetts' influence upon modern architecture has been great. This was not in the manner of recently constructed buildings, but in the sporadic strokes of genius that formed the roots of the radical school.

Paradoxical though it may seem, the contemporary movement in architecture began in Boston; in Richardson's audacious use of elementary masonry forms, gestation of modern architecture began. Not since Wren has an architect left such a profound impress of his own personality, both through his work and that of his successors. With few exceptions, Richardson's successors were a parade of puppet kings wielding the monarch's scepter. Their work was bold, unabashed, and ugly, and its manifestations were not joyous; nonetheless it had promise. Of this work Montgomery Schuyler wrote, 'It is more feasible to tame exuberances than to create a soul under the ribs of death. The emancipation of American architecture is thus ultimately more hopeful than if it were put under academic bonds to keep peace.'

A highly significant architecture such as this was being designed in the office of Furness and Hewitt at Philadelphia when a young Bostonian — fresh from Massachusetts Institute of Technology, and bound for the École des Beaux Arts in Paris — began work there. Louis Henry Sullivan is the internationally recognized father of the radical school of architecture. On Richardson's foundation he laid the cornerstone of modern architecture. He was the link between two great masters, Richardson and Frank Lloyd Wright. It is not unreasonable to believe that Sullivan saw before him in Boston too much tradition to overcome and that this influenced him to go West to start the radical school. In Sullivan's work we see the transition from Richardson's masonry to the lighter and more supple forms of steel construction. Yet Sullivan is probably more significant as Frank Lloyd Wright's *Liebermeister* than for his own designs. Sullivan's best ideas found expression in Wright more convincingly than in his own work. It was in Wright's architecture that the transition from old to new was completed. From it the world movement evolved.

Contemporary work in Massachusetts shows few buildings strictly modern in conception. More significant is the work of keeping alive the traditional New England Georgian architecture. Prominent in this important phase of American architecture has been the work of Coolidge, Shepley, Bulfinch, and Abbott, with such superior designs as Lowell and Dunster Houses at Harvard. The recently completed restoration at Williamsburg, Virginia — the largest project of this nature ever undertaken in the country — was done by Perry, Shaw and Hepburn, a Boston firm. Longfellow Hall at Radcliffe College in Cambridge is another important work by the Boston architects. Despite its fine detail a strain of Southern influence is apparent, doubtless absorbed by the designers while working in this tradition at Williamsburg.

Strictly modern architecture in Massachusetts is negligible. The Motor Mart Garage, in Boston, and Rindge Technical High School, in Cambridge, by Ralph Harrington Doane are more truly functional than others of the modern type. Boston has its share of mechanically good structures, a few of which are even clothed in pseudo-modern shells. Heading this group is the new Federal Building by Cram and Ferguson. Credit, or blame — according to one's taste — is not wholly due to the Boston firm, for its design was subjected to regimentation at the hands of the Federal Architect's Office in Washington, as are designs for all Federal Buildings. One is inclined to wonder, if the ardent medievalist had been given a free hand to indulge his fancy, whether the resultant structure would not have been more compatible with the functions within.

Evidence that Boston architects have been able to lift themselves out of their traditional environment and do modern work elsewhere is seen in the superior designs of the New York Hospital and Cornell Medical School Building in New York, completed in 1932 by Coolidge, Shepley, Bulfinch and Abbott. In this mammoth project, the Boston architects demanded a frank and independent solution, with an inflexible insistence upon adjustment of means to end. The result set a precedent in modern hospital-design.

Thus the reactionary trend in Massachusetts architecture is attributable not so much to poverty of thought on the part of its architects as to a lack of fortunate opportunities and an intrenched conservatism on the part of patrons.

LITERATURE

IT MUST have been with some astonishment, to put it mildly, that the first settlers of Boston — who of course actually, to begin with, had planted themselves in Charlestown — found Boston itself to be already an English city, with a population of exactly one soul. This city, to be precise, consisted of William Blackstone or Blaxton, B.A., a graduate of Cambridge University, and one of the most curious and suggestive figures in the whole early history of the colonization of America. A member of the ill-starred Gorges expedition of 1625, Blackstone had spent two years in Wessagussett, now Weymouth. It appears that he had cast in his lot with Gorges not much more for reasons of Puritan conscience than because he simply wanted to be alone. At any rate, in what is now Boston, in the year 1630, 'William Blackstone, a solitary, bookish recluse, in his thirty-fifth year, had a dwelling somewhere on the west slope of Beacon Hill, not far from what are now Beacon and Spruce Streets, from which he commanded the mouth of the Charles. Here he had lived ever since his removal from Wessagussett, in 1625 or 1626, trading with the savages, cultivating his garden, and watching the growth of some apple trees.' Further, it is known that in 1634, reserving only six acres of land for himself — a parcel bounded roughly by Beacon, Charles, Mount Vernon, and Spruce Streets — he sold to the colonists the whole of Boston peninsula, which he himself had previously bought from the Indians; and 'being tired of the "lord brethren," as he had before his emigration been wearied of the "lord bishops,"' he then removed himself to an estate in Rhode Island, of which he was thus the first white inhabitant. This estate — to which he had presumably brought his books, as well as seeds and cuttings from his garden — he called Study Hill, and here he was destined to spend the rest of his life. Just once did he reappear in Boston, a good many years later, and then only for long enough to acquire a wife. He took this lady off to the wilderness with him, and Bostonians saw him no more.

It is an arresting and delightful figure, this young Cambridge graduate with his books and his apple trees, his conscience, and his passionate desire for privacy; and one cannot think of his perpetual centrifugal retreat from civilization, whenever it managed to catch up with him, without visualizing him as a symbol, or a charming figurehead, of the individualism which was to be so striking a characteristic of New England in the centuries to come. It was not that he was a misanthrope — not in the least. For it was at his own express invitation and because of his real concern for their plight that the wretched half-starved settlers of Charlestown were first brought across the river to the healthier slopes and the better springs on his own land. No, he was simply the first exemplar, the prototype of that profound individualism which has so deeply marked the American character ever since, and of which Massachusetts — especially in the field of letters — has been the most prodigal and brilliant source.

Of that fact, surely, there can be little question. In any summary, no matter how brief, of America's contribution to the world's literature, Massachusetts would be seen to have contributed most, not only in sheer quantity and quality, but — and this is much more important — in that particular searching of the conscience and the soul, and of the soul's relationship to the infinite, which has almost invariably been the dominant feature of American literature at its best. Jonathan Edwards, Benjamin Franklin, Emerson, Thoreau, Hawthorne, Longfellow, Lowell, Melville, Holmes, Whittier, Emily Dickinson, Henry Adams, and the brothers Henry and William James — not to mention the historians Parkman, Prescott, and Motley — the mere recital of the names is quite enough to prove that without the Massachusetts authors American literature would amount to very little. It is a wonderful galaxy; and it is no exaggeration to say that the only absentees from it who are of comparable stature are Poe, Whitman, Mark Twain, and possibly Howells — and of these, Poe was himself at least a native of the State, for he was born in Boston.

This amazing outburst fell almost wholly within the confines of the nineteenth century; and in fact, within about a half of that, the years from 1830 to 1880. But if the quality of it is even more astonishing than the quantity and the range, what is more interesting, whether to the historian of morals and customs or to the psychological student of the origins and function of literature, is precisely the William Blackstone motif, which, as was mentioned above, has so persistently given it its character. New England individualism — and that is tantamount, of course, to saying Massachusetts individualism — has often enough been referred to, but one wonders whether it has ever been given quite its due as the real mainspring of New England letters. One reason for this has been the very widespread notion that it should simply be seen as the natural obverse of the excessive Puritanism and Calvinism from which it was in part a reaction; the individualists, in short, were nothing but small boys who had managed to escape from a very strict school. But this is a very superficial view of the individualist, and an equally superficial view of the Puritan. It might be fruitful to consider whether in point of fact the New England individualist was not just our old friend the Puritan writ large; and conversely, whether also the Puritan was not a good deal of an individualist.

The truth is, of course, that the two terms need not at all be mutually exclusive, and that we are facing here one of those charming but misleading over-simplifications with which the history books so constantly regale us. It is so much easier, and so much more flattering to the nineteenth century and all its works, to ascribe everything, *en bloc*, to the final overthrow of a sort of crippling Frankenstein monster, and to make out Puritanism as one of the most diabolical repressive hypocrisies with which a misguided mankind ever afflicted itself. Much can be said in support of this point of view, and much has been said; and it would be idle to deny that at its worst New England Puritanism became a dreadful thing; if the witch-hanging hysteria of the seventeenth century was the most violent culmination of it, it brought also in its train other forms of spiritual disaster which, if less conspicuous, were scarcely less terrible. The free Protestantism which the Pilgrims had brought with them from England had gradually hardened, under the influence of John Cotton and his descendants the Mathers, into a theocracy. 'None should be electors nor elected, ... except such as were visible subjects of our Lord Jesus Christ, personally confederated in our churches. In those and many other ways, he propounded unto them an endeavor after a *theocracy*, as near as might be, to that which was the glory of Israel.' So remarks Cotton Mather of his grandfather, whose advice had been asked as to a revision of the 'civil constitution' of the State.

But the fact is, that though the theocrats had their way a good deal, they did not have it entirely: and this for the very simple reason that the Protestantism of New England, as it had been based to begin with on the passionate belief of the individual in his right to believe and worship in his own way, still carried in itself these stubborn seeds of freedom. Roger Williams, 'first rebel against the divine church-order in the wilderness' (again to quote Cotton Mather), submitted to a charge of heresy, and abandoned Salem, rather than surrender the tolerance which had outraged the church fathers. Another William Blackstone, he escaped to Rhode Island, and there wrote the first liberal document in American history, 'The Bloody Tenent of Persecution for Cause of Conscience, discussed in a Conference between Truth and Peace.' 'A spiritual Crusoe, the most extreme and outcast soul in all America,' he was, like Blackstone, though for very different reasons, a direct forebear of the great individualists of the nineteenth century. It is indeed essential that we should bear in mind this passionate belief in the freedom of conscience which underlay from the very beginning the foundations of New England culture. Its defeats and obscurities at the hands of the theocrats and zealots were at most only temporary; and there was never a time, even in the darkest passages of Massachusetts history, when it was not somewhere in evidence. It is as evident in Jonathan Edwards's fierce conviction that the sacrament should be administered only to those who had had a radical experience of conversion — and who could properly judge of this save the individual himself? — as in the Northampton congregation which dismissed him, after twenty-three years, because it did not agree with him. And it is as evident again in the calm fortitude with which Edwards accepted his exile, devoting the last six years of his life to a mission among the Indians of Stockbridge — the years, incidentally, during which he somehow managed to write his great philosophical treatise on the freedom of the will.

It was a period — the years from 1620 until the end of the Revolution — during which we must remember, in fact, that the congregation never surrendered its power both to choose and to dismiss its minister: it scrutinized his thought, and indeed his conduct, quite as closely as he scrutinized theirs. He might be tyrannical in his pursuit of his particular idea or ideal, but so, just as well, might they. Since God's grace was so arbitrarily bestowed, might it not fall upon Smith and Jones? Smith and Jones certainly thought so; and the result was a fierce co-operative and communal search for absolute truth, with a powerful clergy sometimes leading, but almost as often led by a powerful Church. The clergy might and did ally themselves and form a caste; but despite all their efforts, the Church remained essentially democratic, and essentially dictated — even when most misguided — by the original Puritan belief in freedom of conscience.

Meanwhile, during this period of nearly two hundred years it is scarcely an exaggeration to say that the liberal arts or anything even remotely like a literature simply did not exist in Massachusetts; and indeed it is difficult to conceive of their finding a place in a community so passionately surrendered to religious and moral preoccupations. But intellectual and spiritual and esthetic sinews were there, none the less;

the elements were ready; and it needed only the right catalyst, and the right moment, to release them in forms which probably nobody could have foreseen. The catalyst, or at any rate the most important of the catalysts, was the gradual rise of Unitarianism during the latter half of the eighteenth century, and then the phenomenal swiftness with which, early in the nineteenth, it effected an almost complete social conquest of Massachusetts. Here once more, but more clearly voiced than ever, was the Puritan insistence on freedom of conscience; but along with it also the revivifying force, almost impossible to gauge, of the Unitarian discovery that man's nature was not inevitably evil and inevitably doomed, but actually perhaps contained in itself the seeds of virtue. 'How mournfully the human mind may misrepresent the Deity,' wrote William Ellery Channing in 1809, in the course of a frontal assault on Calvinism, and, 'We must start in religion from our own souls. In these is the fountain of all divine truth.' What must have been the effect of this all-liberating doctrine on the subtle-minded New Englander, after his long winter of Calvinism? It was a blaze of sunlight, of course, and such a warming and thawing and freeing of locked energies as from this distance we perhaps cannot possibly conceive. And it was into this sudden summer, this sudden blossoming of New England into something almost like gaiety, with its wonderful discovery that virtue might go hand in hand with happiness, that the group of children were born who were destined to become the flower — and the end — of Massachusetts individualism. Prescott in 1796, Alcott in 1799, Emerson in 1803, Hawthorne in 1804, Longfellow and Whittier in 1807, Holmes in 1809, Motley in 1814, Dana in 1815, Thoreau in 1817, Melville in 1819, Emily Dickinson in 1830 — these great-grandchildren of the New England genius were born by an inevitable conspiracy of time into just such an air as they needed for their purpose. What had shaped them — the ghost of William Blackstone, the proud and frontier-seeking independence of the Puritan conscience — they would themselves turn and shape to its final and beautiful mortal perfection.

The first quarter of the nineteenth century was for Massachusetts its period of greatest prosperity—nothing like it had been seen before, nothing like it has been seen since. The shipping trade was at its height, Boston and Salem had become great international ports, and in these and in New Bedford, where the whale trade had become a thriving industry, family fortunes were being founded almost overnight. Along miles of Cape Cod roadside, almost every cottage or house contained a blue-water sea captain, who knew St. Petersburg and Canton as well as he knew India Wharf in Boston. Everybody began to travel, Massachusetts had suddenly become cosmopolitan, and what for two centuries had been a queerly isolated and in many respects an extraordinarily innocent community on the way to nowhere, now began for the first time to feel itself in very close contact with the rest of the world. A new and infinitely richer sense of background became the common property of the people; the whole world was at Boston's door; new ideas were as common and as exciting as the exotic spices brought from Java and China.

An immense advantage, this, for the young Emerson and the young Hawthorne, who, if they were caught willy-nilly in the new liberalism which was sweeping New England, were also caught in strange currents of rumor and echo from abroad. From England, from France, from Germany, came news of extraordinary developments in the literary world: the great secondary wave of romanticism, which followed by a generation the French Revolution, had begun to break in its thousand forms. What Channing's bold religious teaching had begun, the riotous brilliance and variety of the English romantic poets and the heady philosophy of Germany, at its most metaphysical, were to complete. The New England individualist who had first been a Puritan, and then a Unitarian, was now to reach his logical end in the lovely transparent butterfly hues of Transcendentalism.

When Emerson, who had been trained for the church and who preached for three years at the Second Church in Boston, resigned his pastorate in 1832 because he no longer believed in the communion and could not bring himself to administer it even in the abbreviated form then in use among the Unitarians — remarking characteristically that he simply 'was not interested in it' — he was dedicating himself to the new wilderness and the new freedom, exactly as Roger Williams had done before him. Once more a frontier had been reached, but this one the most perilous of all — that frontier within man's consciousness where the soul turns and looks fearlessly into itself, where the individual, like a diver, plunges into his own depths to sound them, and in so doing believes himself effectually to have sounded the world. Man, according to Emerson, was to be self-sufficient, self-reliant, for his divinity was within himself. He must trust his instincts and his intuitions absolutely, for these were his direct communion with the Over-Soul, or God, with which he was in a sense identifiable. This direct knowledge of the divinity was not through the senses — not at all. It was a mode of apprehension that transcended one's sensory knowledge of the phenomenal world and all the experience of the senses, and it was this notion of a 'transcendental' knowledge which gave its name to the little group which, after the publication of his first book 'Nature' in 1836, formed itself about Emerson in Concord and Boston. 'If the single man plant himself indomitably on his instincts, and there abide, the huge world will come round to him.' 'For solace, the perspective of your own infinite life' — this was almost or could easily be, the *reductio ad absurdum* of individualism, for it implied a negation of all authority, whether religious or social, and the complete autonomy of the individual soul.

Patently, this doctrine with its ancillary notions bore within itself the seeds of an intellectual and utopian anarchy; and it is interesting to notice, in this connection, how very flimsy and impractical, how absurdly and charmingly innocent, were such ideas of social awareness as this group entertained. It is hardly an exaggeration, in fact, to say that they were none of them concerned with society as such at all. The passionate search for a moral and religious center, a significance, a meaning, had led them steadily inward, never outward; and if they thought of the social problem at all, it was only to wave it away with the sublime assurance that, as man was essentially good, the social problem would quite nicely take care of itself. If the relationship of the Ego to God was satisfactory, then everything else would follow of course. The experiment at Brook Farm and Bronson Alcott's lesser adventure in a Utopia at Fruitlands were the natural, if humiliating, outcome of such beliefs, quite as much as Thoreau's attempt at a formal secession from society. Even the sole apparent exception to this indifference toward social problems, the anti-slavery agitation, in which practically without exception the transcendentalist joined, turns out on inspection to be not quite all that it purports to be. For here again the problem was looked at from the point of view, not of society, but of the individual; even the Negro should bow to no authority save God's, which was the authority within himself.

Emerson's influence, nevertheless, in spite of a good deal of misunderstanding, not to mention occasional downright derision, was immense and profoundly fructifying, both on his own generation and on that which followed. He was the real center of his time, and his mark is everywhere. Thoreau's 'Walden,' both the experiment and the book, were but the carrying into practice of Emersonian self-sufficiency; and if they add a literary and speculative genius which is Thoreau's, the spirit of Emerson is indelibly in them. Not least, either, in the very conspicuous indifference, not to say contempt, for form. The method could hardly be more wayward; it is as wayward as Emerson's, who admittedly when he wanted an essay or a lecture just ransacked his copious notebooks, extracted a random selection of observations and gnomic sayings, and strung them together on a theme as best he could. And it is as well to observe in this connection that a comparative indifference to form was a perhaps inevitable attribute of yatic individualism — everything must be spontaneous, a direct and uncontrolled uprush from the divine well of the soul; one was merely a medium for the divine voice, and in consequence there could not logically be any such thing as a compromise with so external and strictly phenomenal an affair as form or style. Communication — yes, but only such as came naturally. Nor need one bother overmuch with consistency.

This individualist attitude to form is noticeable everywhere in the literature of the Massachusetts renaissance, as much in the work of the conservative Boston and Cambridge group — Longfellow, Holmes, and Lowell — as in that of the Concord radicals. To consider a poem or an essay or a novel as a work of art, was this not to yield oneself to a kind of outside authority, and to compromise or adulterate the pure necessity and virtue of revelation? Revelation was the thing; and everything depended on the swiftness with which one brought it up from the depths of one's awareness, so that not a spark of the light should be lost. The result was a kind of romantic mysticism which was at its most lucid in Emerson, at its sunniest and serenest in Thoreau, at its profoundest in Herman Melville, and at its most vapid and ridiculous in the orphic sayings of Bronson Alcott. And the result also was a pervading looseness and raggedness, a kind of rustic and innocent willfulness, whether in prose or verse, in practically all the work of the Massachusetts galaxy. It is evident in Emerson's crabbed and gnomic free verse and his homespun couplets quite as much as in his prose, where image follows image and idea idea with little or no regard for nexus or pattern, to say nothing of rhythm. It is evident again in that cryptic unintelligibility, the sibylline phrase, which, if it has a meaning, sometimes guards it all too well from the bewildered reader. The poor reader, indeed, was given no quarter, he must simply shift for himself; and presumably it was Emerson's idea, as it was Alcott's and Thoreau's, that it was a sufficient privilege for the reader that he thus overheard, as it were, the words of the oracle at all. The words were the words of the divinity, and must not be altered: all that was needed was that they should be received with an understanding equally instinctive and divine.

The truth is, the glorification of the individual and of individualism had reached such a pitch of egoism and self-absorption, accompanied by such an entire indifference to the external world, that had they not been geniuses, literary geniuses, none of these men would have escaped disaster. Only a genius can be artless with impunity, and of all this wonderful group only one was a genuine artist, Nathaniel Hawthorne. Hawthorne listened carefully to everything the others had to say, he was himself something of a transcendentalist, he even stayed for a while at Brook Farm; but he remained always a little detached, he was essentially both in his life and in his work a moral and social observer; and it was this carefully kept moral and esthetic distance which enabled him alone of his group to understand the necessity for form and to achieve an individual mastery of it. Alone, too, was Hawthorne in having a quite definite social awareness, and in seeing precisely to what sort of bankruptcy the doctrine of uncontrolled individualism might lead. Emerson may not have realized it, but 'The Scarlet Letter' was, among other things, a very grim comment on the doctrine of self-reliance; and 'The Blithedale Romance' as well.

If in this sense Hawthorne was the only commentator on transcendental individualism, and the one analyst and chronicler of the final phases of the evolution of the Puritan passion for freedom of conscience, he was also the only link between the Concord group and the writer who carried farthest and deepest that perilous frontier of mystic consciousness which had always been the Puritan's fiercest concern: Herman Melville. 'Moby Dick' was dedicated to Hawthorne, and it was written while Hawthorne and Melville were neighbors in Pittsfield. Without any question the greatest book which has come out of New England, and one of the very greatest works of prose fiction ever written in any language, it is also the final and perfect finial to the Puritan's desperate three-century-long struggle with the problem of evil. Hunted from consciousness into the unconscious, and in effect beyond space and time, magnificently sublimated so that it becomes not one issue but all issues, a superb and almost unanalyzable matrix of universal symbolism, the white whale is the Puritan's central dream of delight and terror, the all-hating and all-loving, all-creating and all-destroying implacable god, whose magnetism none can escape, and who must be faced and fought with on the frontier of awareness with the last shred of one's moral courage and one's moral despair. Man against God? Is the principle of things, at last, to be seen as essentially evil? And redeemable only by war à outrance? Impossible, at any rate, to surrender; one's freedom to feel toward it what one will, whether hatred or love, must be preciously preserved. One must grapple with it, and alone, and in darkness, no matter whether it lead to a death throe or to an all-consuming love.

Melville, writing to Hawthorne about this extraordinary book, which was destined for half a century to be considered just a good romance for boys, likened himself to one who strips off the layers of consciousness as one might strip off the layers of an onion, and added that he had come at last to the central core. And indeed to all intents he had; when a year later, at the age of thirty-three, he published 'Pierre,' he had really finished his voyage. And he had carried William Blackstone with him to such strange borderlands as that bold explorer of Rhode Island never dreamed of. Perhaps it is worth noting that Melville himself denied that 'Moby Dick' had any allegorical intention — if only to point out that the denial can really have no meaning. 'Mardi' was quite obviously allegorical; allegory and parable came almost instinctively to the hands of a group so vitally concerned with moral and religious matters, and as a 'form' it very likely seemed no more artificial or unusual to Hawthorne or Melville than that, say, of a poem: it was something which played with meaning and which gave out meanings on many different levels, and that was the end of it.

And indeed 'Moby Dick' may be said to have been the great poem, the epic of the Puritan civilization, and to have marked a turning-point in its evolution, if not quite its end. There could not again be any such violent imaginative projection of the problem; the problem itself was beginning to dissipate and break up, to disappear in the dishevelment of analysis: individualism was to turn outward again. It could receive in the hands of Henry James a fine symphonic abstraction, or in the hands of William James a bold social and scientific externalization and analysis, but the creative poisons were all but drained from it. The worlds around were changing, new winds of doctrine brought new seeds and spores, and in 'The Education of Henry Adams' one has almost the spectacle of a dead civilization performing an autopsy on itself. The note of retrospect, the backward-looking eye — this could have only one meaning, that the Puritan struggle was at last, in all important senses, over. One genius remained yet to be heard from, and this the most exquisitely characteristic of all — Emily Dickinson. In her life of hushed and mystic and self-absorbed sequestration, no less than in her work, where we watch the lonely soul alembicating itself that it may test its own essence, we have the very mayflower of the Puritan passion for privacy and freedom. How strict was that soul with itself, when there was none to watch! Was it not her own epitaph that she wrote — or can we say that it was an epitaph for a whole phase of the human soul — in the lines:

Lay this laurel on the one
Too intrinsic for renown.
Laurel! veil your deathless tree —
Him you chasten, that is he!

This wonderful pride and immense strength in solitude which could give up as worth nothing any notion of fame or acclaim if only its soul's house be in order and its accounts straight with heaven — perfectly content, and serenely self-sufficient, so long as the windows which looked on the Eternal were kept clear — this was the final rededication of the spirit of William Blackstone, who had come to Boston when it was still a wilderness, was found there by the first settlers 'watching the growth of some apple trees,' and moved on to another wilderness and another privacy when the 'lord brethren,' his neighbors, came too close.

Emily Dickinson was the last of her line, the last of the great Massachusetts frontiersmen; and with her it may be said that the literature of Puritanism, as a purely local phenomenon, came to an end. Henceforth its heirs were to be sought farther afield, dispersed inconspicuously, but perhaps none the less indestructibly, in the consciousness of the country at large. Amy Lowell had little of this temper in her; and if in the contemporary scene it has any ambassadors, they are Robert Frost and T. S. Eliot. But the movement itself is complete and at an end.

LITERARY GROUPS AND MOVEMENTS

THE tendency among writers to form groups around political, social, or literary ideas began very early in Massachusetts. The voluminous religious tracts of the seventeenth century concealed, under a garb of godly language, the warring concepts of two opposed groups — the advocates of theocracy and the champions of democracy. The theocrats were victorious, and for nearly one hundred years the clergy dominated the press. Not until the founding of the Hell Fire Club and the publication of the first number of *The New England Courant* by James Franklin in 1721 did secular ideas have currency. In the exciting decade of 1760–70 a battle of the books took place between two political factions, a battle which enlisted Tories like Thomas Hutchinson on one side and revolutionaries such as James Otis on the other.

Even those ardent individualists, the writers of the literary renaissance of the 1840's, betrayed a decided affinity for the society of their peers, and together they organized literary clubs, publishing ventures, and Utopias. The informal group generally known as the Transcendental Club included at one time or another Emerson, James Freeman Clarke, Amos Bronson Alcott, George Ripley, Theodore Parker, Margaret Fuller, Orestes Brownson, Thoreau, Hawthorne, Charles T. Follen, William H. Channing, and that complete mystic and arch-individualist, Jones Very. An early literary magazine, *The Monthly Anthology* (1803–11), was carried on as the organ of 'a society of gentlemen,' the Anthology Club of Boston. *The North American Review* was established by a group which had for its purpose the emancipation of American literature from subservience to England. *The Dial* (1840–44), although proclaiming itself 'A Magazine for Literature, Philosophy, and Religion,' was notable for expressing, under the editorship of Margaret Fuller, the ideas of the Transcendentalists, as *The Harbinger* (1845–49) expressed those of the co-operativists. Such group expression was strongly characteristic of early magazines: they were oriented, not as most magazines are today, toward their readers or their advertisers, but toward their writers. Even as late as the 1850's, *Atlantic Monthly* dinners ranked in importance with

Atlantic pages, and younger writers outside New England bitterly accused the magazine of being a kind of closed club. Hawthorne had founded the 'Potato Club,' a literary society, at Bowdoin while still an undergraduate. Thoreau, so anti-social as to get himself jailed for non-payment of taxes, may be said to have betrayed a certain longing for society when he reproached Emerson for not sharing his cell; and Whittier said flatly, 'I set a higher value on my name as appended to the Anti-Slavery Declaration of 1833 than on the title-page of any book.'

After the Civil War, literature in Massachusetts for the first time since the eighteenth century was motivated and reinforced by scientific method and invigorated by new political currents. Realism and the Anti-Poverty Society made a simultaneous appearance, and reading Boston was divided into those who admired William Dean Howells's novels and those who despised them. Again, during the brief renaissance of 1912–16, cut short by the war, Massachusetts poets revolved around a brilliant if not fixed star, Amy Lowell.

Certain distinguished authors remained aloof from their fellow writers — notably Herman Melville and Emily Dickinson. But with few exceptions it can be said that the history of literature in Massachusetts is the history of its diverse and divergent literary groups and movements.

When the Puritans, who desired a theocratic hierarchy, arrived in Massachusetts, they found the Plymouth congregation, a group of democratic dissenters, before them; and to their alarm the Salem church shortly fell under this radical influence. In the resulting battle of words the conservatives were represented by John Cotton; Nathaniel Ward, author of 'The Simple Cobler of Aggawam' (1647); the ingenuous apostle to the Indians, John Eliot; Samuel Sewall, the diarist; Cotton Mather, harsh and dogmatic in religion, progressive in natural science and medicine; and subtle-minded Increase Mather. The democrats counted fewer but on the whole more trenchant writers: Hugh Peter, Nathaniel Morton, Edward Johnson (author of 'Wonder-Working Providence,' 1654), Roger Williams, John Wheelwright.

The first press to be set up in the new country was that of Stephen Daye in Cambridge, under the control of clerical Harvard College. The Daye press issued the 'Bay Psalm Book,' that monument to early printing and bad rhyme, in 1640. Daye was succeeded by Samuel Green, who printed John Eliot's Indian New Testament in 1661 and the entire Bible in 1663. In 1669 Green issued Morton's 'New England's Memorial,' noteworthy for having not only a printer but a publisher, 'H. Usher of

Boston,' the latter probably a bookseller, in the days when booksellers combined the functions of importer and publisher. John Dunton, Scots bookseller, remarked in 1686 that there were eight bookshops in 'Boston village.' Not until 1675 was Boston's first press established, by John Foster.

Not only theological tracts and sermons by Massachusetts writers were published during the seventeenth century. Mary Rowlandson's account of her captivity among the Indians, written in a vivid style without literary pretense, appeared in a second edition in 1682 (no copy of the first edition has survived). The anonymous 'Relation,' descriptive of Plymouth and its settlement, appeared in 1622; and two years later was published Edward Winslow's 'Good News from New England,' simply written, like a letter home describing the wonders of the new country. William Bradford, governor from 1621 to 1657 save for five years, wrote a 'History of Plymouth Plantation' in 1630–46, the manuscript of which was lost for two hundred years, finally turning up to be published by the Massachusetts Historical Society in 1856. But Captain Nathaniel Morton had access to the manuscript, for he used much of it in his 'New England's Memorial' (1669). Verse flourished no less than prose: Peter Folger's satire, 'A Looking-Glass for the Times,' appeared in 1677; Benjamin Tompson's 650-line epic on King Philip's War, 'New England's Crisis,' in 1676; Anne Bradstreet's 'The Tenth Muse, Lately Sprung up in America,' in London in 1650 and in Boston in 1678; and Michael Wigglesworth's 'Day of Doom' (1662), an epic of the last judgment, was widely read for a hundred years.

Many of the products of these first presses, as well as some priceless manuscripts, were in the library of the Reverend Thomas Prince of Boston, which, stored in the tower of the Old South Church, was dispersed and partly destroyed when British troops were quartered in the church during the American Revolution. Among these manuscripts was William Bradford's 'History of Plymouth Plantation.' Prince published in 1736 the first volume of his 'Chronological History of New England in the Form of Annals,' which he unsuccessfully endeavored to continue in six-penny serial parts. His careful use of sources makes him the first trustworthy American historian: 'I cite my vouchers to every passage,' he said — and did.

For almost one hundred years, before a Massachusetts printer dared publish a book he had to secure what practically amounted to an *imprimatur*; and if an author wrote a book with an heretical taint, he published it, if at all, in England. This condition existed until the first quarter of the eighteenth century, when Benjamin Franklin's brother James founded the lively *New England Courant* (1721) with the aid of the Hell Fire Club, hardly a clerical organization. Benjamin Franklin, while employed in his brother's printshop, contributed the satiric 'Silence Dogwood' papers to the *Courant*, slipping the first of them anonymously under the door. The *Courant* was a sort of American *Spectator*, differing in its liveliness and its literary tone from the *Boston Gazette*, already established in 1719. Two years after the *Courant* first appeared, Benjamin went to Philadelphia, and his direct connection with Massachusetts ended.

The editors of the *Courant* continually jeered at the dullness of its contemporaries, their staleness, their lack of American news and political comment. In self-defense, perhaps, *The New England Weekly Journal* was founded by a more sober group. The *Journal* had something of the liveliness of the *Courant*, but it was conservative in tone, and endeavored to offset the damage to faith, morals, and politics being worked by the Franklins' paper.

During the brave times of 1770–76 Isaiah Thomas published *The Massachusetts Spy*, which pleaded the cause of revolution. This enterprising publisher, founder of the American Antiquarian Society, later became the publisher of *The Royal American Magazine* (1774–75), chiefly remembered for containing engravings by Paul Revere; *The Worcester Magazine* (1786–88); and *The Massachusetts Magazine* (1789–96). Other early Massachusetts magazines were *The American Magazine and Historical Chronicle* (1743–46) and *The New England Magazine* (1758–60).

During this period of political pamphleteering, every agitator was an author and every author an agitator. James Otis the younger, advocate-general, was the most brilliant of these; 'The Rights of the British Colonies Asserted and Proved' (1764) and the 'Letter to a Noble Lord' (1765) are perhaps the best known of his writings. Oxenbridge Thacher, John Adams, and Josiah Quincy all produced political pamphlets, as did Noah Webster, author of the dictionary and the blue-backed speller, who proved to be as radical in politics as he was later to be in spelling. Samuel Adams, with his Committees of Correspondence, his 'Massachusetts Circular Letter' (1768), is the prototype of them all.

A new note among Colonial historians appeared with the publication of the first volume of the 'History of the Colony of Massachusetts-Bay' in 1764. Its author, Thomas Hutchinson, was a descendant of Anne, and as unpopular as the latter, though for different reasons. He was a merchant, with conservative leanings, and the rising revolutionary temper of the people made Bostonians actively mistrust him as a Tory. His history was the first account of the Colony to be written without theological bias, and notwithstanding its conservative tone, it displays a considerable political sense. The Reverend William Gordon of Roxbury wrote a history of the Revolution in 1788; and Mercy Otis Warren, sister of James Otis, produced a popular history of the same period in 1805. George Richard Minot's 'History of the Insurrection in Massachusetts' (1788) dealt with Shays's Rebellion of 1786, and Minot also continued Hutchinson's history.

The North American Review was founded in 1815. The short-lived *Pioneer*, whose three issues included contributions by Poe and Hawthorne, was published in 1843 by James Russell Lowell, who became the first editor of *The Atlantic Monthly* in 1857. With the establishing of *The North American Review* and of two great publishing houses, Ticknor and Company (1833), later Ticknor and Fields, the direct predecessors of Houghton Mifflin Company — and of Little and Brown (1837), literature in Massachusetts had a firm underpinning. In 1837, the year in which Charles C. Little and James Brown put up their sign, William Lloyd Garrison was publishing *The Liberator* (1831–65). 'Poems' by William Cullen Bryant had appeared sixteen years before; Ralph Waldo Emerson had recently moved to Concord and had just published 'The American Scholar'; Whittier was an agent of the Anti-Slavery Society; R. H. Dana, Jr., and Henry David Thoreau had just graduated from Harvard, where Henry Wadsworth Longfellow had begun to teach and James Russell Lowell was an unruly undergraduate; Hawthorne was struggling at Concord; Oliver Wendell Holmes had just begun to practice medicine; Prescott was about to publish his 'Ferdinand and Isabella'; the Saturday Club was eleven months old; Ticknor's Old Corner Bookstore was a literary gathering place; and Annie Fields's literary salon had not yet begun.

Until the first third of the nineteenth century, authorship was the avocation of amateurs and gentlemen of means. As late as 1842 Channing remarked that Hawthorne was the only American who supported himself by writing. Channing was mistaken, although not very much so. Jedidiah Morse (1761–1826) of Charlestown, America's first geographer, had been one of the few writers in America to make writing pay, although his school geographies and gazetteers scarcely rank as literature. In 1790, Congress passed a law designed to protect literary property. But in the absence of substantial publishing houses or magazines that paid for contributions, and in view of the continual pirating of books by English and American authors on both sides of the Atlantic, authorship was a poor enough business. Even after the great Boston magazines and publishing houses were established, Bryant had to edit anthologies and a newspaper; Whittier struggled desperately until the publication of 'Snow-Bound'; Mrs. Stowe made less than a living from her books until the phenomenal success of 'Uncle Tom's Cabin'; and Prescott was the first historian to achieve financial success from his writings. None of these authors received any income from the European editions of their works. It was not until writers organized in the American Copyright League (1883) and publishers in the American Publishers' Copyright League (1887) that international piracy was halted by the copyright agreement of 1891.

Mrs. Fields tells the story of Dr. Holmes's indignant exclamation, one morning when hearing the doorbell ring, that he was afraid it was 'the man Emerson.' Holmes, driving the twin horses of medicine and essay-writing, had learned to guard himself from intrusion. But it is significant that most of the writers responsible for the New England renaissance of the 1840's and 1850's not only called upon one another, but formed inter-locking circles of friendship, and embarked together in publishing schemes, in literary cenacles, and in such ventures as Fruitlands and the Brook Farm Institute of Agriculture and Education. Amos Bronson Alcott, ostracized by proper folk for teaching young children in his school the plain facts about birth and for refusing to dismiss a Negro pupil, was stoutly defended by his fellow transcendentalists, who, tolerating his orphic doings and sayings, yet recognized his progressive attempt to bring modern educational methods to New England. One of the sources of strength of the New England movement, in fact, was its awareness of contemporary European culture. Emerson, for example, brought Car-lyle, and through him German currents of thought, to American atten-tion; Prescott and Motley made Spain and the Netherlands homegrounds to Yankees; and Longfellow devotedly presented to his contemporaries the best of European literature, from the Finnish saga through Dante to Lamartine and Victor Hugo. In addition, established writers encouraged younger writers. Two of many examples are familiar: Whittier's encour-agement of a Lowell mill operative, Lucy Larcom, whose poetry is prop-erly forgotten, but whose 'A New England Girlhood' survives as a valua-ble social document; and Thomas Wentworth Higginson's careful foster-ing, however inept, of Emily Dickinson's brittle genius.

With Richard Hildreth (1807–65) and his 'History of the United States, 1492–1821,' nineteenth-century historical writing began. Hildreth was followed by John Gorham Palfrey (1798–1881), one of the editors of the *North American Review*, who defended the old régime in his 'History of New England.' George Bancroft (1800–91), an historian of enormous patience and learning despite his bias, made careful use of sources now available in the Massachusetts Historical Society, founded by Jeremy Belknap, an historian of New Hampshire, in 1791. Jared Sparks (1789–1866), also an editor of the *North American Review*, edited Franklin's and Washington's writings, and inaugurated the 'American Biography Series.' In preparing Washington's letters for the press, Sparks altered them, as he thought for the better, and the resulting hot discussion among scholars as to the necessity for accurate textual presentation of documents probably had a wholesome effect on contemporary historical editing.

William Hickling Prescott (1796–1859), published his 'Ferdinand and Isabella' in 1838, his 'Conquest of Mexico' in 1843, and his 'Conquest of Peru' in 1847; John Lothrop Motley (1814–77) made the United Netherlands his life study; and Francis Parkman (1823–93) concentrated on the history of Colonial United States. With these three authors, American historical writing came of age. Justin Winsor (1831–97), in his 'Narrative and Critical History of America,' published 1886–89, was the first to offer full bibliographical and source material to the reader of American history. Francis Parkman and John Fiske (1842–1901) belonged to a youngeï generation, as did Charles Francis Adams's three sons, all historians — Charles Francis, Jr., Brooks, and the brilliant Henry.

Four bright philosophical planets had orbits which centered in Harvard University. Two of these were Massachusetts men, William James (1842–1910), psychologist and stylist, and Charles S. Pierce (1840–1914), a remarkable scientific realist. Two others were not Yankees, but have come to be identified with Massachusetts: Josiah Royce (1855–1916) and George Santayana (b. 1863). Louis Agassiz (1807–73), nourished on idealistic philosophy, remained during twenty-five professorial years at Harvard the storm center of opposition to the shockingly novel ideas of Darwin, and was accused by his skeptical European contemporaries of trading his scientific birthright for a mess of Puritan pottage. His students became evolutionists to a man.

After the Civil War and the economic depression which followed, a different tone came into Massachusetts letters. The precursors of this new spirit were perhaps Harriet Beecher Stowe's 'Uncle Tom's Cabin,' the poems of Whittier and of Lucy Larcom, and the novels and tales of Herman Melville — that powerful realist who warned himself of the fate of those who 'fell into Plato's honey head and sweetly perished there.'

Barrett Wendell, lecturing on literature at Harvard, and popularly supposed to base his critical estimates on the family trees of authors rather than on their writings, solemnly warned a generation of Harvard students against 'democracy overpowering excellence.' Yet, despite Wendell, currents of the Populist movement, of industrial unrest, of new social doctrines, were flowing into Massachusetts.

In 1885 a shabby traveler emerged from the old Hoosac Station in Boston and, clutching an imitation-leather valise, turned his face, brown from the Dakota sun, toward the Common. This was Hamlin Garland, come (like Ravignac to another city) to capture Boston, the cradle of liberty, the home of literature. Alas, Emerson, Thoreau, and Hawthorne were dead, and the Reverend Doctor Cyrus Augustus Bartol, of the old West Meeting House, remained the sole survivor of the Concord school. Undaunted, young Garland sought out the literary giants of the day. Holmes, Whittier, and Lowell were still living, but none of these did he contrive to meet. Living on forty cents a day, battling the cockroaches in his six-dollar-a-month room, he consoled himself with reading 'Progress and Poverty,' 'at times experiencing a feeling that was almost despair.'

Garland's ingenuous narrative, 'A Son of the Middle Border,' contains many valuable indications of intellectual currents of the 1880's in Massachusetts. He soaked himself in the writings of the evolutionists — Darwin, Spencer, Fiske, Haeckel. In the reading-room of the Boston Public Library the universe resolved itself into harmony and secular order, as it had done a generation before for the European realists, as it was doing for the new generation of American writers. Literature in Massachusetts during the 1880's, for the first time since the eighteenth century, was motivated by science and invigorated by political revolt. This new temper was expressed directly and artlessly by Edward Bellamy in 'Looking Backward,' which, published in 1888, had sold more than 370,000 copies by 1891; realistically by William Dean Howells; triply-distilled in Henry James's cerebral novels.

Howells was a transplanted Bostonian, born in Ohio in 1837. 'The most vital literary man in all America at this time,' Garland thought him, adding that Boston was divided as to the worth of this American disciple of Balzac, Zola, and Tolstoi. Howells turned the minds of his contemporaries from Europe back upon America, satirizing the worship of European places and ideas so common among the middle class, indicating in his novels that America was a land of new hopes — a country with a greater future than Europe. He cut through the sentimental treacle in which the 'golden age' was now immersed, turning Massachusetts into the stream of the new realism which answered the readers' sudden cry, 'Give us people and places as they are!' Half of Boston stood aghast at this coarse new literature, but the other half applauded. The West was coming East, and the old traditions were finally shattered when in 1871 Howells became editor-in-chief of the organ of New England Brahmanism, *The Atlantic Monthly*. Yet with all his democratic ideas, Howells stood for careful art, and his own style was finished and pure.

Realism brought forth regionalism — which again Mrs. Stowe had foreshadowed, in 'Poganuc People' and 'Oldtown Folks.' Her approach was sentimental, however, while the regionalist's was scientific. Bred in a generation which exalted scientific method, the regionalists applied science in a special way. The novel was conceived of, though not always consciously, as a scientific experiment, and an experiment to be scientific must be controlled in all its particulars. Hence the deliberate narrowness of range, the careful naturalism of style, the absence of vagueness, fancy, or mysticism, the conscientious documentation. A regionalist chooses a narrow geographical sector, as Henry James chose a narrow stratum of society; he revives his memories of that sector, checks his memories with facts, employs real characters rather than invented ones, and never once allows his tale to stray from under the bell-glass. Mary E. Wilkins (1852–1930), Sarah Orne Jewett (1849–1909), and Alice Brown (b. 1857), are representatives of this school in the novel, as James Herne (1839–1901), the author of 'Shore Acres,' is its representative in the drama. All of them were careful recorders of New England's decline.

The rather large body of persons who have always believed, in the face of much evidence to the contrary, that virtue is inevitably rewarded and that poverty can always be conquered, found an exponent in one of Massachusetts' most widely read authors. Horatio Alger, Jr., born in 1834, the son of a clergyman of Revere, was known throughout his boyhood as 'holy Horatio.' After attending Harvard Divinity School he spent a season in Paris, where he performed some naughty deed, never divulged, for which he was sorry all his life. He never married. In all, he produced some one hundred and nineteen boys' books, among them 'Ragged Dick,' 'Luck and Pluck,' 'Tattered Tom,' 'From Canal Boy to President,' 'From Farm Boy to Senator.' Like the heroes of his books, he acquired riches; unlike them, he died in poverty.

The revolt against the genteel tradition, 1912–16, had its seeds in the 'muck-raking era.' Massachusetts furnished one muck-raker — Thomas

W. Lawson, who made and lost a fortune on the stock market, then pilloried the market in 'Frenzied Finance' (1902). To the poetry renaissance which began in Chicago about 1912 Massachusetts contributed several poets — T. S. Eliot, S. Foster Damon, Conrad Aiken, Robert Hillyer, among others — who were at first encouraged by Amy Lowell (1874-1925) and then satirized in 'A Critical Fable,' patterned after her great-uncle James Russell Lowell's satire. Miss Lowell introduced to young American poets the French symbolists and impressionists of the 1890's along with the Imagists, and her free verse and polyphonic prose forms had direct influence on many of them. The entire movement of 1912-16, so promising in its inception, was fatally cut off by the World War.

In 1937, literary prognosticators in Massachusetts were wetting their fingers and testing the wind. Some faint signs of a literary revival were evident in the air. Massachusetts writers again began to preoccupy themselves with contemporary Massachusetts material — an encouraging sign. Impressive gains of organization among industrial workers offered a hint of a new audience of hundreds of thousands. The New England renaissance of the 1840's had coincided with an upsurge of organization among workers, and in the social, economic, and political ferment of that decade many writers of the 'golden age' were directly concerned. The direction of the Massachusetts labor movement in 1937 was perhaps symptomatic of what might occur in literature — not as cause and effect, but as twin manifestations of the same forces. Critics dared predict a new literary renaissance in New England — unless war again intervened to blast it at the roots.

MUSIC AND THE THEATER

WHEN one considers the early evolution of the fine arts in New England — and especially music and the drama — it is essential to remember that whereas in England Puritanism was never wholly without opposition, in the New England Colonies it very early established a pseudo-theocracy which in its fundamentals was to remain unshaken for nearly two hundred years. With the Restoration, the opposition came back to power in England, and with it the enormous release of energies which was to produce the second great period of English drama. In Massachusetts, on the other hand, no such development was even remotely possible. When Henry Vane failed of re-election as Governor in 1637 and returned to England, defeated in his struggle with Winthrop and the town fathers for a more liberal policy, it was really the end of any chances there might still have been for a gentler and more humanistic New England culture. The decision of the General Court in the same year 'that none should be received to inhabit within this Jurisdiction but such as should be allowed by some of the magistrates' — which was tantamount to saying that they could exclude or banish anyone whose customs or opinions they disliked — became exactly what it was intended to be: a drastically effective social filter. The little Puritan community was henceforth to be on one pattern, heresy was to be a crime, and liberalism was to go underground for a hundred and fifty years.

Small wonder, therefore, that the Restoration could export little of its brilliance and gaiety to a shore so inhospitable. Music, the theater — these reached the ears of the Bostonians only as rumors of dreadful unbridled license. In 1686, Increase Mather, stern upholder of the proprieties and decorums, published a 'Testimony Against Profane and Superstitious Customs,' in the course of which he bemoaned the fact that there 'is much discourse now of beginning Stage Plays in New England.' He need not have worried; the 'much discourse' came to nothing; and the drama, like music and dancing — 'gynecandrial' dancing was their wonderfully contemptuous word for dancing between the sexes — remained an alien and unknown quantity. The truth is, of course, that our admirable forefathers knew nothing whatever about the arts, cared little for them, and brought into the world children who 'had but an imperfect

idea of their bearing, and in their ignorance deemed the theater the abode
of a species of devil, who, if once allowed to exist, would speedily make
converts.' In such a situation, any liberalizing influences from without
had perforce to wait on the Puritans' gradual self-liberalization from
within; and the few early attempts to import stage plays into Massachusetts — even after the theater had begun to make headway in New
York, Philadelphia, and Providence — served only to enforce the restrictions against them. Plays were occasionally given in the first half
of the eighteenth century, but only privately, and seldom; and perhaps
with a fear that they might, if indulged in too often, lead to the building
of a playhouse — an outcome too terrible to think of.

It was probably some such consideration which led, in 1750, to the
passage of 'An Act to Prevent Stage Plays and Other Theatrical Enter-
tainments,' as likely to 'occasion great and unnecessary expense, and
discourage industry and frugality,' and as also tending to 'increase im-
morality, impiety, and a contempt for religion.' The occasion for this
was a performance of Otway's 'Orphan, or Unhappy Marriage' at a
coffee house in State Street, Boston, by two enterprising young English
actors, 'assisted by some volunteer comrades from the town.' The
General Court, fearing this might be the entering wedge, made the
provisions of the act extremely stringent. Twenty pounds was the fine
to be paid by anyone who let or permitted the use of his premises for
such a purpose. And any actor or spectator present 'where a greater
number of persons than twenty shall be assembled together' was subject
to a fine of five pounds. The law was effective, and effectively enforced;
and on the whole it was supported by public sentiment. The more so,
perhaps, as it did not make strictly 'private' performances, or very un-
remunerative ones, absolutely impossible.

But the tide of public opinion was steadily if imperceptibly rising.
The more liberal elements in the community, and those whose business
took them occasionally to New York, where the theater was already well
established, pressed for the repeal of the act many times in the latter half
of the eighteenth century. Such an attempt failed in 1767; and more
daunting still was the resolve of the Continental Congress, in 1778, that
any officeholder under the United States who should be so neglectful of
his duties as to attend a play should at once lose his position. Despite
this, however, and despite the fact that in 1784 the anti-theater act of
1750 was re-enacted in Massachusetts, the moment was at hand when
the law was simply to be allowed to become a dead letter. As a test case,
the New Exhibition Room — a theater in everything but name — was

opened in what is now Hawley Street, Boston, in 1792, with a performance
in the nature of a variety show. 'Monsieur Placide will dance a hornpipe
on a Tight-Rope, play the Violin in various attitudes, and jump over a
cane backwards and forwards.' This was followed by Garrick's 'Lethe,'
and that by Otway's 'Venice Preserved,' which was announced, with the
customary bland hypocrisy of the times, as 'A Moral Lecture in Five
Parts.' And subsequent performances were given — likewise billed as
'moral lectures' — of 'Romeo and Juliet,' 'Hamlet,' and 'Othello.'
Rhymed couplets, in the handbills, drove home the moral lessons, lest
they be missed: from the bill of 'Othello', for example:

> Of jealousy, the being's bane,
> Mark the small cause and the most dreaded pain.

With these performances, and with the consequent arrest and discharge
— on a technicality — of the manager, Joseph Harper, the real history
of the theater as such in Massachusetts may be said to have begun.
The worthy citizens of Boston were now well persuaded that the drama
was actually of great social benefit; and accordingly many of the most influential people took an active part in the financing, planning, and building — with Bulfinch as architect — of the Boston Theatre, which was
completed at the corner of Federal and Franklin Streets in 1794. They
must, presumably, have closed their eyes to such unedifying sights as
were billed at Mr. Bryant's Hall, a temporary theater during this period,
where one might see, for example, Mr. Manly 'balance his whole body on
the edge of a candlestick, pick up two pins with his eyes, and a dollar at
the same time with his mouth' — all the while, moreover, rolling like a
whale in the sea. Culture was to be the thing; and they pursued it with
characteristic zeal. Despite the bankruptcy of the Boston Theatre at
the end of its first season, a second theater, the Haymarket, was built a
year later; and until 1803, when the Haymarket was torn down, a lethal
competition made prosperity impossible for either.

And in fact it is hardly an exaggeration to say that the theater was
never destined, in Boston, to very great prosperity, and that in a sense
Boston has never been really a 'theater' city. The Boston Theatre did
moderately well for a quarter of a century — with a very fine stock
company to play around such visiting stars as Kean, Macready, Forrest,
and Junius Booth — and later in the century, from 1860 to 1880, the
Boston Museum, in Tremont Street, maintained one of the finest stock
companies in the country. But the 'star' system, lamented as early as
1880 by William Clapp, one of the leading dramatic critics of the period,

was gradually to make Boston what it is today, a theatrical dependency of New York. And attempts in the present century to run stock companies in Boston, despite the temporary successes of John Craig and Mary Young at the Castle Square, and of Leon Gordon, Edmund Clive, and Henry Jewett, have invariably ended in failure. More interesting to record, in an otherwise somewhat drab history, is the vigor of the Little Theater movement in Massachusetts, with the famous Provincetown Players and the People's Theater of Northampton conspicuous for their contribution; and the very great influence of Professor George Pierce Baker's '47 Workshop' on the American theater at large. Of Massachusetts playwrights, it is perhaps sufficient, if melancholy, to quote William Clapp, who fifty years ago remarked that 'no Boston author has as yet written a play which is likely to keep the stage.'

II

If music has fared better in Massachusetts — and especially in the past fifty years, when Boston has deservedly taken its place as one of the foremost musical centers of the world — its early history in the State was quite as humble as that of the drama, and if anything even more inconspicuous. Music had, and could have, no place in a strictly Puritan community — even its controversial value was less considerable than that of the drama, for it was clearly less of a 'temptation.' Copies of Henry Ainsworth's psalter, published in 1612, were aboard the 'Mayflower,' and the first book to be printed in America — the 'Bay Psalm Book' (Cambridge, 1640) — was to go through eight editions before 1698; but neither of these actually contained any music. The psalms were sung by rote, to one of the five or six tunes then in use, the precentor chanting the psalm line by line, the congregation echoing him — a dreary business at best. And this — literally — was all the music the Puritan fathers knew.

So dreadful, however, did this rote-singing finally become that a movement arose in the Church itself — not without furious opposition — to introduce singing by note; and in 1698 the ninth edition of the 'Bay Psalm Book' contained thirteen tunes in two-part harmony — the 'oldest existing music of American imprint.' A year later, 1699, the Brattle Street Church voted unanimously 'that ye psalms in our public Worship be sung without reading line by line.' In 1714 or 1715 appeared what may be described as the first musical textbook to come out of

America — 'A very plain and easy Introduction to the Art of Singing Psalm Tunes: With the Cantus, or Trebles, of Twenty-eight Psalm Tunes contrived in such a manner as that the Learner may attain the Skill of Singing with the greatest Ease and Speed imaginable,' by the Reverend John Tufts. This book was published in Boston, and ran through ten editions by 1744. It was the forerunner of other such instruction books, and coincided with the formation of the first singing schools — one such is said to have existed as early as 1717.

Thus far, the psalm-singing was unaccompanied. But in 1714, when the first pipe-organ in America was installed in King's Chapel, the organist, Edward Enstone, just arrived from England, brought with him a 'choice Collection, of Musickal Instruments, consisting of Flageolets, Flutes, Hautboys, Bass-Viols, Violins, Bows, Strings, Reads for Hautboys, Books of Instruction for all these Instruments, Books of ruled paper.' Clearly, there was already a definite interest in instrumental music, and it was not long before the first concerts began to be given — usually for the benefit of the poor. The first advertisement of a concert in America seems to have been that in the *Boston News-Letter*, December 16–23, 1731: 'There will be a Concert of Music on sundry instruments at Mr. Pelham's great Room, being the House of the late Doctor Noyes near the Sun Tavern.' In 1732 the *New England Weekly Journal* advertised 'Conserts of Musick performed on sundry instruments at the Concert Room in Wing's Lane near the Town Dock' — a room in the George Tavern, in what is now Elm Street. In 1744 a vocal and instrumental concert was given in the newly built Faneuil Hall; and from this time on concerts became frequent, and instrumental music began to take a natural place in the home.

Perhaps the opening of the theaters, in the last decade of the eighteenth century, did much to stimulate the public interest in music, and to improve its taste — at all events, it is not without significance that there was on the program for the opening night of the Boston Theatre, February 3, 1794, 'to precede the drawing up of the curtain,' a 'grand symphony by Signor Haydn,' amongst other pieces. Here, too, the custom was introduced of 'allowing the audience to call upon the orchestra for such pieces of music as suited the popular taste,' a custom which prevailed for many years. Obviously, the Puritan terror of music had at last broken down, music was beginning to come out of the church, and all that now was needed was organization — a creative discipline and direction.

For this, some of the spade-work had already been done by the gradual formation and training of the church choirs, the founding of singing schools, partly to the same end, and the development of musical societies. Among the latter may be mentioned one of the earliest, still in existence, the Stoughton Musical Society, 1786, founded by America's first native composer, William Billings. Billings's 'New England Psalm Singer' (1770), and subsequent collections, may be said to be the beginning of American composition; and his spirited 'fuguing' style did much to free church music from the everlasting Puritan drone.

But these were modest beginnings at best, and it was really with the nineteenth century that things began to happen. In 1808 a group of students at Harvard founded the Pierian Sodality, and with it 'an unbroken chain of cause and effect' which was to lead, via the Harvard Musical Association — founded by graduates of the Pierian in 1837 — to the Boston Symphony Orchestra. This little society, for the encouragement of instrumental music, may be said to have been of the profoundest significance in the development of music, not only at Harvard, but throughout the country. Two years later came a similar venture, though not so lasting, when Gottlieb Graupner, music publisher and engraver, ex-oboist in Haydn's Orchestra in London, formed a group of professional musicians, together with a few amateurs, for weekly concerts of an informal character. This, the Philharmonic Society, lasted till 1824, thus overlapping the Handel and Haydn Society, 1815, in the founding of which Graupner again had a hand.

With the Philharmonic Society playing the symphonies of Haydn and Mozart, and the Handel and Haydn giving a performance of the whole of Handel's 'Messiah' as early as 1818, progress was clearly being made; but the discipline and training for precision-playing was to come a good deal later. A further step in this direction came with the establishment of the Boston Academy of Music, in 1833, by Lowell Mason. This admirable institution — long since defunct — gave free vocal instruction to upwards of a thousand children, and five hundred adults, a year; and in 1837 it succeeded in introducing music into the Boston public schools. Its services to the teaching of music were inestimable, but perhaps even more fraught with consequence was its decision, in 1840, under the leadership of Samuel A. Eliot, its president, then Mayor of Boston, to give up teaching and 'to engage the best orchestra it can afford and give classical instrumental concerts.' The immediate result was the first hearing of Beethoven in Boston, the First and Fifth Symphonies being performed by the Academy of Music Orchestra in its first season of eight concerts. The orchestra was small — twenty-five to forty — and by no means perfect; but its seven-year existence made the coming of the Boston Symphony Orchestra inevitable.

Other stages were to intervene — the visits of the Germania Orchestra, from 1848 to 1854; the foundation of the Harvard Musical Association in 1837, and its seventeen years of symphony concerts, from 1865 onward, under Carl Zerrahn; the popularization of chamber music by the Mendelssohn Quintette Club — but everything now tended obviously to the obvious thing, the foundation of a Boston Symphony Orchestra. This, finally made possible by the generosity and unflagging devotion of Henry Lee Higginson, began in 1881 the career which was to make it for many years the finest orchestra in the United States, and to make Boston famous for its music. Its history, under such leaders as Nikisch, Gericke, Muck, Rabaud, Monteux, and Serge Koussevitzky, is a story in itself, beyond the scope of these pages; it must be sufficient to note that out of it have come such notable institutions as the Kneisel Quartet, the Longy Club and Longy School of Music, and the Flute-Players' Club, and that as a great orchestra it continues to give Boston precisely the creative focus for music that it needs.

It remains simply to note that in the New England Conservatory of Music — founded in 1867 by Doctor Eben Tourjee — Massachusetts possesses one of the most famous schools of music in the country, and that in the field of musical composition the State stands almost alone. Among those born in the State or resident there have been such composers as George Chadwick, C. M. Loeffler, F. S. Converse, Arthur Foote, Edward Burlingame Hill, Walter Piston, Carl Ruggles, Bainbridge Crist, and Roger Sessions, to mention but a few. As a creative musical center, Boston is today in many respects unrivaled.

ART

MASSACHUSETTS is rich in the substance of the arts. It has a good tradition in handicraft; it was once the stronghold of eminent Colonial portrait-painters; it counts among its residents renowned scholars in art and discerning collectors. Within its boundaries are treasures of enviable importance. The number of art museums is exceptional, and the State is honeycombed with historic houses fitted with Colonial furnishings. The early history of Massachusetts was virtually the history of art in the United States, for many of the outstanding painters and sculptors were either born in the State or had a foothold here. The people of Massachusetts in their enthusiasm or indifference, their Puritanism or limited taste, are as responsible for the peculiarities of native art as the craftsmen themselves.

In the ways in which scholarly research can enrich understanding of the arts, Massachusetts is at an advantage. Museums are outwitting each other in acquisition of rarities and in publication of researches. While museums show increasing range of interest, each in its way has a splendid collection or a department in which it excels. The Boston Museum of Fine Arts is particularly notable for superb Far Eastern treasure, while the Worcester Art Museum draws attention by its magnificent mosaics of the Middle Ages. The Smith College Art Museum has concentrated on modern French pictures, and at the Fogg Art Museum, Harvard, there is an exceptional display of Italian primitives. The Addison Gallery of American Art at Andover is one of the most important specialized collections of American art in the land. The latter and the Germanic Museum at Harvard show a marked interest in living art through exhibition and purchase. Other museums specialize in the historic, remaining comparatively indifferent to the problems of the living artist.

Since its earliest days, Massachusetts has not been a particularly hospitable environment for the living artist. Restraints of economic necessity and puritanic bias prevented a free expression in the arts from the very beginning. Colonial handicraft was directed toward articles of household use, furniture, utensils, pewter, silver, textiles, and in some solemn likenesses of early worthies. Based upon English prototypes, the articles were made to conform to local needs and, viewed today in the historic houses or museums, they show good taste and adaptation of materials. Puritanism was opposed in principle to art, and there was not the impulse of native taste or the urgency of demand to propel the imagination of artists. Years later, it was personal pride, luxurious indulgence, a forgivable conceit which prompted Americans to have their portraits painted, revealing unmistakably their forceful characteristics and newly acquired finery. It was a painting of form and feature, flounce and frill, with rarely a sidelong glance at nature, or critical observation of society. The early limners held forth with reserve, as artisans who had branched from the more useful calling of coach or sign painting, and some, in the well-known matter-of-fact manner, peddled their wares from house to house. They carried portraits painted completely except for the face, to be bargained for by the impending client.

The early portraits are flat and descriptive, lacking the lifelike character and subtle handling of European portraiture of the time; possessing, on the other hand, the decorative beauty which to present-day taste is so appealing in provincial art. Some most interesting early portraits are to be seen in the Worcester Art Museum. On loan for many years has been 'Mrs. Freake and Baby Jane,' one of the handsomest and most touching of seventeenth-century portraits. 'John Freake' is there too, an imposing likeness in which particular attention has been paid to ornate costume. Not far from the Worcester Art Museum, in the American Antiquarian Society, are portrayals of Samuel and Increase and Cotton Mather (the latter painted by Peter Pelham about 1695–1751). Portraiture developed in the eighteenth century into a specialty. John Smibert (1688–1751) came from Scotland to Boston to paint, and incidentally designed Faneuil Hall in Boston. Joseph Blackburn (flourished 1753–1763), Robert Feke (about 1705–1750), Ralph Earle (flourished 1751–1761) were among the early exponents, and their portrayals are on exhibition at Harvard University and in the museums in Boston, Worcester, and Andover. The art of portraiture attained a notable height in the canvases of John Singleton Copley (1738–1815). In the opinion of many, Copley executed his finest pictures here at home, before he departed — in what was to become a too common practice among Massachusetts artists — to England to live. There was something in the native environment, in the types of personages he portrayed, in the limited tradition out of which his style developed that proved salutary to Copley. In England he lost individuality, acquired suaver traits. Colonial personalities, humble, smug, forceful, are clearly characterized in the Copleys shown throughout Massachusetts.

Gilbert Stuart (1755–1828) settled in Boston, where he painted outstanding Americans of the early republican days. The Athenæum portraits of George and Martha Washington hang in the Boston Museum among other portraits by Stuart, which differ from the Copleys in the swift summary handling and the emphasis upon facial features and expression, with comparative indifference to costume. Portraits in smaller dimension are scattered throughout the State. Besides its three hundred painted portraits, Essex Institute in Salem possesses a fine collection of silhouettes. Miniatures by Edward Greene Malbone (1777–1807) are in the Worcester and Boston Museums. Wax miniatures are displayed here and there in historic collections.

During the same period the household arts surpassed by far the pictorial arts. Cotton Mather had written that within a dozen years after the granting of the charter to the Massachusetts Bay Colony 'artificers to the number of some thousands came to New England.' Among early silversmiths of Boston were such notables as Robert Sanderson (1608–1693), who instructed many in the art, Jeremiah Dummer (1645–1718), John Coney (1655–1722), and, in the eighteenth century, the versatile Paul Revere (1735–1818), who, in addition to tankards, punchbowls, and candlesticks, made silver dental plates which he advertised as 'of real Use in Speaking and Eating.' The first articles of furniture of artistic significance to be made in the State were carved oak chests, which slowly evolved into highboys and writing-desks. John Goddard (1723–1785), who produced stately pieces in Santo Domingo mahogany, was born in Massachusetts but practiced his craft in Rhode Island. As early as 1638 crude glass lamps and bottles were being manufactured in Peabody, but Deming Jarves (1790–1868), head of the Boston and Sandwich glass works, revolutionized the glass industry with his new methods of furnace construction, his rediscovery of the method of manufacturing red lead, and his inventions in color-mixing. The Decorative Arts Wing of the Boston Museum has many interesting period rooms. The historic houses throughout the State give evidence of excellent handiwork, indicating the changes in taste from the early days of rigorous thrift to later luxury and finesse. Objects of folk-interest — samplers, coverlets, mourning pictures, painted Bible pictures — reveal imaginative qualities which painters in a more formidable craft lacked.

The art of carving found a particularly touching expression in gravestones, which apparently deserved special attention in the solemn judgment of Colonials. Such memorials are extant in burying grounds of Deerfield, Salem, Concord, Boston, and towns on Cape Cod. They bear indications of an authentic talent for carving in decorative borders, sacred symbols, and ruminative epitaphs. It was an original and appropriate manner of commemoration, with far more vitality in design and feeling for the craft than was revealed in native plastic art of later date. The demand for portraiture continued in the early days of the Republic. Painters went abroad for study and stimulus. Massachusetts, which had such a favorable atmosphere for the ripening of Copley's style, could not hold its painters. They would wander afar, to London and Paris, and they were not shrewd enough to ally themselves with the best teachers, but contented themselves with the guidance of lesser lights. Benjamin West (1728–1820) took young Americans under his wing. Samuel F. B. Morse (1791–1872), seeking instruction abroad, boasted of having studied with Washington Allston (1779–1843), whose unfinished masterpiece, 'Belshazzar's Feast,' is in the Boston Museum. Massachusetts artists were eager, but they lacked taste and tenacity. Abroad they responded to the official and obvious, and when they painted compositions they seemed to favor the literary and rhetorical. Morse gave up painting, as there was no market, no recognition, and turned to inventing, where his successes never consoled him for his failure as an artist. His 'Self Portrait' hangs in the Addison Gallery in Andover. Chester Harding (1792–1866) carried the portraiture tradition well into the nineteenth century, when changes were taking place with the rapid growth of the Republic and there were reverberations of political and industrial upheaval abroad.

James Abbott McNeill Whistler (1834–1903) and Winslow Homer (1836–1910) were both born in Massachusetts. There was little at home to foster the talents of a painter. One escaped to the solace and enhancement of European life; the other withdrew to solitude at Prout's Neck on the coast of Maine. Whistler possessed skill and wit. He had far better taste than most Americans, and his pictures are an odd mixture of influences from Turner to Degas, from the Pre-Raphaelites to the Japanese. Whistler did not follow his fellow countrymen to the academy; not for him the sleek and photographic and artificial. He had a fine decorative sense, and a taste for the diffuse and atmospheric. His etchings give him rank with masters in that medium. Nevertheless he remained a wanderer, lacked a mooring, and fell short of greatness as a painter. Winslow Homer went abroad, but he did not stay for long. He found water color a more responsive medium for his direct, decisive reaction to the outdoors. He painted what he saw with the impact of the first fresh impression. It was straightforward, realistic portrayal, and it marks him one of the first Massachusetts painters with a dynamic style. Homer furnishes the moral to escaping artists. He helped to deliver the artists of New England from a sense of inferiority, from the uncontroverted domination of foreign ideas which were not too well selected, not too thoroughly assimilated. Homer has risen in esteem, especially in recent years, for his peculiarly native qualities, and for the fact that he found his vigorous style through self-discovery.

Albert Pinkham Ryder (1847–1917), born in New Bedford, also painted the sea, but his portrayal was veiled in poetry, shaded with mysticism, softened with sentiment. Ryder also avoided the American scene, not as Homer or Whistler had chosen to do, but by withdrawing into himself, painting from personal resource, inner feeling. In Deerfield dwelt another native artist who painted in a gentle sentiment, George Fuller (1822–1884). Boston-born Abbott H. Thayer (1849–1921) lavished tenderness upon his canvases of womanhood.

William Morris Hunt (1824–1879) exercised considerable influence upon Bostonians through his great interest in the Barbizon school in France, especially F. D. Millet. The atmosphere at home seemed unsympathetic to him, too, and he longed for what was lacking: an impetus to paint. An entire gallery of his paintings is in the Boston Museum. His pupil and friend, John La Farge (1835–1910), was commissioned by Henry Richardson, architect, to paint murals in Trinity Church on Copley Square. On the same square stands the Boston Public Library, where murals cover the walls on the second and third floors. There is one series by the French néo-classicist, Puvis de Chavannes (1824–1898), the illustrative 'Quest of the Holy Grail' series by Edwin Abbey (1852–1911), and the elaborately wrought theological sequence by John Singer Sargent (1856–1925), to some his greatest performance. The Boston Public Library murals are very interesting and very provocative. All three differ in treatment, color, effect; they also differ greatly from the mural painting which has come rather suddenly into prominence in recent years with emphasis on scenes in history, social forces, and daily life.

Sculptors of Massachusetts have worked under a handicap that is more universal, for their special craft struggles to survive in a world which seems to find no urgent need of it. That native Americans enjoyed whittling and carving is apparent in their early houses, furniture, ship figureheads, gravestones, weather-vanes, wild fowl decoys, scrimshaw (there is an interesting collection in the Whaling Museum in New Bedford); but when they applied their gift to the formal art of portraiture, they showed little taste and insufficient vitality. Samuel McIntire (1757–1811) had a peculiar gift for carving portals and architectural decorations with the wholesome application of craft to function. That peculiar attribute of functionalism in style which is so often discussed today is rooted in the craft of Massachusetts. The most classical example is that of the Shaker workshops, which provided a variety of articles for daily use, admonishing the maker to do the job as efficiently as possible, with an eye to simplicity and usefulness.

Horatio Greenough (1805–1852) was one of the native sculptors who went to Italy to assimilate neo-classical ideas. But such ideas could not somehow be redirected with conviction by a native of Massachusetts. The sculptors, like so many painters, possessed enthusiasm and eagerness, but no commensurate creative imagination. Artistically they lacked roots. There were sculptors like Henry Kirke Brown (1814–1886), Harriet Hosmer (1830–1908), Thomas Ball (1819–1911), who did an equestrian statue of George Washington that stands in the Public Garden in Boston. Many pieces are on view throughout the State, generally Italianate or official in character. Most native are the diminutive groups executed by John Rogers (1829–1904) of Salem, ingenuous portrayals of everyday life of Americans and realistic scenes of the Civil War, a descriptive sculpture, illustrating life in America, and true to life and aspirations in Massachusetts. At Essex Institute there is a very large collection of Rogers groups.

Counted among outstanding sculptures in Massachusetts are the 'Shaw Memorial,' a high relief in bronze by Augustus Saint-Gaudens opposite the State House in Boston, and 'Dean Chapin' by the same sculptor in Springfield. The 'Minuteman' in Concord and 'John Harvard' in Cambridge were executed by Daniel Chester French, who had studied sculpture under a Boston teacher. Cyrus Dallin, sympathetic portrayer of the American Indian, is the sculptor of 'Appeal to the Great Spirit,' which stands in front of the Boston Museum of Fine Arts.

In Massachusetts until recent years a conservatism has prevailed, which resists stubbornly the experimental methods practiced in the world of art. The arbiters of taste have clung to Victorianism, or have released their energies in the study of art of remote times and remote places. The State has avoided the rapids of the main stream of contemporary art, and has thus been safeguarded against the attendant risk and deprived of the inevitable exhilaration. Exhibition places, such as the Boston Art Club, the Copley Society, the Guild of Boston Artists, have been rather inflexible, showing works of acceptable stamp, often capably wrought, depictions in a conventional or photographic manner, softened renderings of Hals or Manet, with reminiscences of Munich, Pre-Raphaelitism, and the French Academy. Pictures there are in abundance of the pursuit of wild fowl, clippers at full sail, swelling surf, flowers and fruits and bric-à-brac in a rose-gold ambience, the New England countryside, woodland retreats, pools and freshets and marshlands, and pleasant people. Boston has had its special style, its exponents. Sargent set the pace in portraiture, brisk painting of texture, fleet, skillful rendering of features. Among members of the Boston group may be counted today Frank Benson, Edward Tarbell, Marian Sloane, Herman D. Murphy, Laura Coombs Hills, John Lavalle, Margaret Fitzhugh Browne.

Ideas are blowing across the boundaries. Resourceful and probing performers have infused a new spirit into the atmosphere. Art schools are altering their point of view; museums are enlivened by new and enterprising directors. During the summer American painters have gravitated toward Provincetown and Gloucester, where the weather-beaten shacks and fisheries and townsfolk and dunes and surf and old-fashioned gardens provide choice subject matter. At Provincetown some talented artists live throughout the winter, among whom are Karl Knaths, Oliver Chaffee, Agnes Weinrich.

Among painters of the State, water color has been a popular medium. Winslow Homer, John Singer Sargent, and Dodge Macknight are admired and emulated — Homer for realism, Sargent for skilled grasp of surface texture, Macknight for bold, translucent color. Macknight provoked Bostonians to well-known vituperation when he sent his brightly colored aquarelles from France in the 1890's. The reaction paralleled that of the French middle class at the Impressionist Exhibition of 1874 in Paris. There is a Bostonian water-color style based upon these forebears, rarely, however, as powerful or as concentrated as the originals. John Whorf is the most successful and most popular exponent of this local inherited style. Other aquarellistes of more independent spirit should be noted for peculiarly expressive handling of pigment, and for some engaging theories which they have invented. Among them are Carl Gordon Cutler, Harley Perkins, Katherine Sturgis, and Charles Hopkinson. The latter is interesting as a sort of dual personality, for he does able official portraits in a manner which is highly acceptable, then turns to water color apparently as a release for his fancy, to indulge an insatiable devotion to color, and to work out some tricky compositions.

The Boston Athenæum, founded in 1807, initiated in the community the policy of having annual exhibitions of pictures painted by local artists, or borrowed from local collectors. An Athenæum catalogue of 1831 lists with exceeding pride the 'Head of a Madonna' by Carlo Dolci. Taste in Boston today runs to early rather than late Renaissance pictures.

In 1855 the Boston Art Club was organized with the purpose of promoting social intercourse among artists and for the general advancement of art. Today, there are many art centers and schools. There are clubs of hobby artists; there is the Society of Independent Artists. There is furthermore the energetic group of artists in the Federal Art Project. But the range of interest in art is no longer a local matter. Some of our best craftsmen are young and not yet known; some are newcomers to the State with fresh points of view. The pace today is set by leadership elsewhere, in sources which have been more harmonious with present-day tendencies. Massachusetts is losing its peculiar qualifications, for better, for worse, in the broadening scope of taste and of activity in cosmopolitan art centers.

But handicrafts in Massachusetts are sustained by tradition and by an inherited taste for well-made objects. Despite the influence of the machine, craftsmen are still working industriously upon textiles, ceramics, woodwork, basketry, silverware, jewelry, and leatherwork. Just forty years ago the Society of Arts and Crafts of Boston was organized with high and very strict standards of workmanship. It became the model for the arts and crafts movement throughout the country.

A field of craftsmanship in which Boston excels is the making of stained glass. Many eminent artists today work in Boston, where large and busy workshops may be visited. While glassmaking of the past century is illustrated in many examples of opaque glass to be found in the State, modern glass workers find their inspiration in the fine medieval windows and are adapting a 'lost' art to present-day needs. Much of the best stained glass installed in recent years throughout the United States was made in Boston. Outstanding pioneers in the making of glass were Harry Eldredge Goodhue and his son, Wright Goodhue. Active workshops today are those of Wilbur Herbert Burnham; Reynolds, Francis and Rohnstock; and Charles J. Connick.

II. MAIN STREET AND VILLAGE GREEN

Some cities and towns could not be conveniently described among the tours in Section III because of the amount of historical matter and the number of points of interest. For that reason, though appearing on the tours, they are described here, as well as all municipalities of 35,000 population or over, all seats of colleges, a number of historic shrines, and a few centers of varied interest.

The altitude is usually that of the municipal center, sometimes, if the former was not available, that of the railway station. Population is according to the 1935 State census. If you find a date of settlement twenty years earlier or later than one given here, yours is probably right, too. The same dates — and data — often differ in half-a-dozen reference books, and the Oldest Inhabitant's memory can rarely be trusted. When sources differed too widely to be reconciled, the editors made a reasonable choice, or took refuge in such a phrase as 'the mid-nineteenth century.'

Brief general information is listed at the beginning of each town: railroads, inter-State bus service, piers and boat service, airports, accommodations, and information centers. Local information centers, each happily situated, like Anatole France's dog, in the exact center of the universe, are equipped to answer more specific questions.

A tour has been arranged for each city or town, starting at the municipal center except where, as in Boston and Cambridge, some other starting point was considered to be more convenient. Points of interest which are concentrated or easy to find are merely numbered and listed with street addresses; otherwise driving directions are given. If the inordinate length of some of the tours within towns or cities appals you (Pittsfield's motor tour is over 30 miles long), console yourself, as you halt on a country road to shoo a flock of geese, that you are still 'in town,' as townships were abolished in Massachusetts by an Act of the General Court on August 23, 1775.

A M H E R S T . *An Adventure in Quietude*

Town: Alt. 302, pop. 6473, sett. 1703, incorp. 1775.

Railroad Station: Main St., opposite Gray St., for Central Vermont R.R.

Accommodations: Four hotels and several tourist houses.

Information: The Lord Jeffrey, Boltwood Ave., cor. Spring St.

AMHERST, on its pleasant valley plateau within a circle of hills, is a dignified college town, the seat of two institutions of higher learning. Its quiet dwellings, elm-shaded streets, and general air of academic calm make it attractive and individual. It was named for Lord Jeffrey Amherst, a British general in the French and Indian War. The town was originally a part of Hadley. Farming was the exclusive occupation of the community for three quarters of a century.

Later its two streams furnished water-power for a diversity of small and in general ephemeral industries. Shortly after the Revolution, a paper factory made its appearance, followed by three others in the next seventy years. About 1809, an abortive effort was made to spin yarn by machinery. Twenty-eight years later, improved processes made it possible to operate two woolen mills successfully. The fabrication of palmleaf hats and the temporarily popular 'Shaker' hoods for women marked the high spot of Amherst's mass-production. Miscellaneous items such as sleds, baby-carriages, and rifles complete the catalogue of the town's manufactured goods.

The agrarian skill of the inhabitants and the lusty health of their cattle as shown in annual fairs attracted State-wide interest which culminated, in 1863, in the founding of Massachusetts Agricultural College, which later, with a broadened curriculum, became Massachusetts State College. The college was established as a result of the Morrill Land Grant Act of 1862, which allotted to Massachusetts the sum of $208,464 realized from the sale of 360,000 acres of land granted by the Federal Government. From a perpetual fund set up for the promotion of education in agriculture and the 'mechanic arts,' one third was to be given to the Massachusetts Institute of Technology and two thirds to the Agricultural College.

Today the Agricultural College possesses a well-equipped dairy farm that is a model for the whole country. It also owns an outstanding entomological collection. Since 1882 the State Agricultural Experiment Station has been located on forty-eight acres of land leased from the college. An agricultural extension service was begun in 1912.

More than forty years before the founding of the Agricultural College, a purely academic institution had chosen Amherst as its site. Founded in 1821, with the simple ideal of educating 'promising but needy youths who wished to enter the Ministry,' Amherst College had an initial enrollment of forty-seven pupils, with a teaching staff of two professors and the president. For many years emphasis was placed on missionary work and Amherst sent many graduates to the home and foreign fields.

Shortly after 1830, the slavery question nearly split its academic ranks. Financial stringency threatened to complete the ruin, but by heroic effort the college weathered this crisis and succeeded in establishing itself on a firm basis. Liberal education instead of mere vocational training has been the steadfast aim. Amherst was the first institution in the land to adopt student-government.

It is one of the most noted of the smaller colleges for men in the United States, and its standards of plain living and high thinking are well illustrated by the characters of two of its best-known graduates, Henry Ward Beecher and Calvin Coolidge. Noah Webster, Helen Hunt Jackson, Emily Dickinson, Eugene Field, and Ray Stannard Baker ('David Grayson') all lived at one time or another in Amherst. Their presence fostered a literary atmosphere very congenial to the college, enhanced in later years by the addition of Robert Frost, the poet, to its faculty.

TOUR — 3 m.

S. from Amherst Common on Pleasant St. (State 116).

1. The *Amherst College Campus* crowns an elm-shaded knoll at the center of the town. The college buildings are of brick, stone, or wood, in a variety of architectural modes reflecting its growth. Their grouping is spacious and dignified, and considerable beauty is achieved by wide lawns shaded by ancient trees and outlined by barberry hedges.

College Hall (open), at the west end of the Common, resembles a New England Colonial church, with yellow-painted brick walls, a white-pillared portico, and a low octagonal belfry.

North and South College (private), are the oldest dormitories, resembling army barracks, but much beloved by reason of tradition and long, honorable service. Between these two dormitories stands the brick *Johnson Chapel (open)*, another time-honored landmark, with three-story white-pillared portico and square white belfry.

Morgan Library (open), next door to College Hall, is a gray-stone building now an Art and Historical Museum. Exhibits include an exquisite Della Robbia Madonna from the study of Clyde Fitch, noted playwright, Class of 1886; Henry Ward Beecher's Chair; Lord Jeffrey Amherst's Chair; and the immortal 'Sabrina,' a semi-nude statue donated to the college in 1857 to adorn a fountain, and for many years the prize of the Freshman and Sophomore battle. The trustees, at length wearying of these Homeric contests, fastened Sabrina into the structural walls of Morgan Library with such heavy masonry that only dynamite could now dislodge her.

The *Babbott Room (open)*, occupies the tower of The Octagon, a stucco building on the campus. In this room Robert Frost talks informally to the students.

The *Natural Science Museum* designed by McKim, Mead and White, houses the biological and geological laboratories in a large building on the southern end of the campus overlooking Hitchcock Field. In the *Biological Museum* is a large collection of shells and a celebrated Audubon Collection of birds. The *Geological Museum* contains minerals collected throughout Europe and America and a collection of fossils and vertebrates. Adjoining is a large room containing the famous Hitchcock ichthyological collection of fossil footprints.

2. The *Helen Hunt Jackson House* (*private*), 83 Pleasant St., a two-and-a-half-story yellow frame dwelling with white pilasters and a gabled roof, was the home of 'H. H.,' the pseudonym under which Mrs. Jackson wrote 'Ramona' and other popular novels.

Retrace Pleasant St.; R. from Pleasant St. on Spring St. at the Common.

3. The *Lord Jeffrey Inn* (*open*), is a charming replica of a Colonial brick tavern, white-painted, with 40-paned windows on the lower story. It houses the Plimpton Collection of French and Indian War prints, maps, and autographed letters and papers of Jeffrey Amherst, George Washington, William Pitt, General Wolfe, George II and Louis XV.

L. from Spring St. on College Ave.; R. from College Ave. on Main St.

4. The *Home of Emily Dickinson* (*not open for public inspection; those interested in Emily Dickinson memorabilia may consult the collection next door*) stands above Main Street, behind a high evergreen hedge. It was the first brick dwelling-house in Amherst, and was built about 1813 by her grandfather, Samuel Fowler Dickinson, one of the chief founders of Amherst College. Here was born in 1830, lived her life apart, and died in 1886, the poet and mystic who, after her death, was acclaimed as one of the very few great American poets and one of the leading women poets of all time. Her gradual withdrawal from the world, following a youthful renunciation of love, became almost complete during her later years as she devoted herself to a life of thought — and the writing of the hundreds of poems she was to leave to the world. With the exception of two or three, none of these was published during her lifetime, it remaining for her sister Lavinia, and then for her niece and heir, Martha Dickinson Bianchi, to make her work available to the public. More than nine hundred of her poems are now collected in one volume. Nothing relating to the Dickinsons now remains in the old family mansion, but the Emily Dickinson memorabilia are preserved at *The Evergreens*, the home of the poet's only brother, the late William Austin Dickinson, just across the lawn, which is now the home of her niece and biographer, where during the summer months they may be seen by those especially interested in Emily Dickinson's work.

Retrace on Main St.; straight ahead on Amity St.

5. *Jones Library* (*open: summer, weekdays 9–6; winter, Tues., Thurs., Sat. afternoons and evenings. Sun. afternoons*) is a gambrel-roofed field-stone building recognized as one of the most luxurious small public libraries in the United States. The interior is divided into twelve large rooms and sixteen smaller ones in the manner of a private mansion. All are paneled in Philippine white mahogany or walnut. Many have Oriental

rugs and comfortable chairs and divans; many are hung with valuable paintings. In the *Room of Amherst Authors* are representative and extensive editions of the works of Emily Dickinson, Robert Frost, Eugene Field, Helen Hunt Jackson, Noah Webster, and others.

6. The *Strong House* (*open Tues. and Sat.* 2–5; adm. free), corner of Amity and North Prospect Sts., is a three-and-a-half-story gambrelroofed brownish frame dwelling of 1744, now the home of the Amherst Historical Society. It is the oldest house in town, and was built by local craftsmen of entirely hand-hewn timber and hand-wrought hardware.

Retrace Amity St.; L. from Amity on N. Pleasant St.

7. *Massachusetts State College*, fondly known as 'Aggie,' a contraction of its former title of Massachusetts Agricultural College, occupies a large open campus, on the edge of farming country. Its brick buildings, utilitarian rather than decorative, are grouped in a long semicircle, at the center of which stands *Goodell Library* (*open*), with high white Ionic portico, giving access to 100,000 reference works.

> The *State College Science Museum* in Fernald Hall, headquarters of the geology and entomology departments, contains unusual specimens of insect life, and one of the most interesting existing collections of insects injurious to cultivated plants and trees. It was started early in the history of the college by Professor Fernald, one of the first presidents and head of this department.
>
> The *Veterinary Science Museum* is in the Veterinary Science Building on the western side of the campus. It contains interesting specimens of abnormal animal growth.

ARLINGTON . *History and Homes*

Town: Alt. 30, pop. 38,539, sett. about 1630, incorp. 1867.
Railroad Station: B. & M. R.R., Mystic and Mass. Ave.
Bus Station: Arlington Center for B. & M. Transportation Co., Champlain Coach Lines, and Frontier Coach Lines.
Accommodations: Boarding and rooming houses.
Information: Robbins Memorial (Town) Hall, Mass. Ave.

VICTIM of a series of industrial and agricultural frustrations, never quite fulfilling its destiny as a producing center, Arlington is a residential suburb.

The story of Arlington begins just after the Revolution. Industrial development started with the establishment of William Whittemore and Company (1799), card manufacturers, founded on the invention of Amos Whittemore of a machine for the manufacture of cotton and wool cards.

Prosperity was blighted in 1812 by the general wartime depression, culminating in the sale of the Whittemore plant to a New York firm, and Arlington lost its main industry. In 1827, after the expiration of the original patents, card manufacturing was revived, but never regained its vigor, and when the factory burned down in 1862, it was never rebuilt.

In 1832, James Schouler, a calico printer, moved from Lynn to Arlington. Other lesser enterprises combined to give the town a sense of industrial importance which temporarily seemed justified. By 1850 the Wood Ice Tool Company and Gage, Hittinger and Company, ice-cutters who shipped Spy Pond Ice to various parts of the world, were established. Arlington's industrial importance was at its crest.

Agriculture developed parallel to industry, but was accompanied by far less acclaim. Natural conditions and proximity to Boston markets made truck gardening the chief gainful occupation, and by 1850 Arlington produce became famous along the North Atlantic seaboard.

Just as industrial development reached a climax and then declined, so did agriculture. Farms were broken up into house lots as the increasing residential value of the land, coupled with proportionate increases in tax assessments, made it unprofitable for market-gardening.

The early city fathers had been faced with such knotty problems as the purchase of a town hearse, or the installation of a public bathtub 'for the use of the inhabitants, but to be in the custody of the treasurer.' Their successors had to gird themselves for a different sort of task — a struggle against outside turnpike companies seeking franchises through Arlington along routes considered inimical to the town. Hardly was the battle won, and hardly were the roads established along routes agreeable to all, when the victory crumbled to dust. Business men of Arlington and Lexington built a railroad to Cambridge in 1846 and turnpikes lost their significance. Horsecar lines (1859) and electric lines (1897) followed, and Arlington developed into a residential suburb.

TOUR — 6 m.

S. from Massachusetts Ave. into Pleasant St.

1. The *Ancient Burying Ground* is at the rear of the Unitarian Church. Toward the farther side of the cemetery, close to the main path, is a *Monument* over the graves of 12 Americans killed on the retreat from Concord and Lexington, and buried 'without coffins, in the clothes they had worn when they fell.'

2. *Spy Pond* was so christened, says tradition, when a company of white men, seeking Fresh Pond to procure water, 'spied' this instead. It acquired some reflected glory later on from the fact that old Mother Batherick was digging dandelions on its bank on April 19, 1775, when six British grenadiers came along, fleeing from the 'old men of Menotomy,'

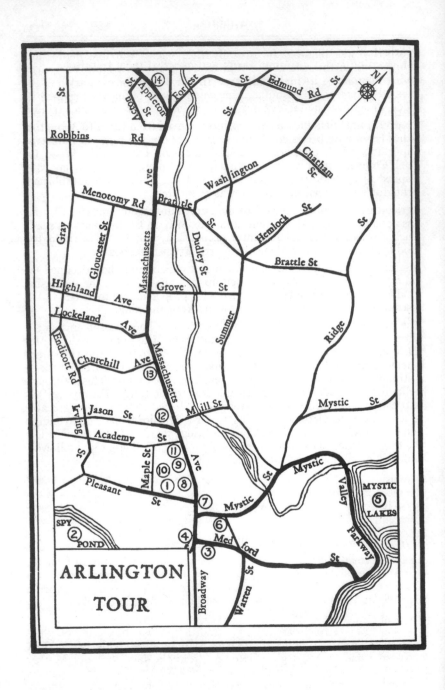

as Arlington was originally (1637–1732) called. The brave old woman took them off guard, captured them, and marched them to prison.

Retrace Pleasant St.; R. from Pleasant St. into Massachusetts Ave.

3. The *Site of Cooper Tavern*, corner of Medford St., Arlington Center, is identified by a tablet. In the Tavern, two aged men, Jabez Wyman and Jason Winship, sitting over their toddy, were killed on April 19, when the Redcoats, rushing through the town, fired blindly through the windows.

4. The *Site of the Black Horse Tavern* is opposite Linwood St. Here the Committee of Safety and Supplies of the Provincial Congress convened on April 18, 1775. The following day a British searching party surprised Vice-President Gerry and Colonels Lee and Orne, who escaped by making a hasty exit and concealing themselves in a near-by field.

Retrace on Massachusetts Ave.; R. from Massachusetts Ave. on Medford St.; L. from Medford St. into Mystic Valley Parkway.

5. The *Mystic Lakes* are popular as a resort for swimming and boating in summer and skating and ice-boating in winter.

L. from the Parkway on Mystic St.

6. *Russell Park* is one of the recreational areas of Arlington. A tablet at the rear of the school records the exploits and longevity of Samuel Whittemore, the hero who survived a bullet and a bayonet wound and very nearly lived to see his hundredth birthday.

R. from Mystic St. into Massachusetts Ave.

7. A marker on the Green identifies the *Site of the John Adams House* (1652), which served as a hospital for the Provincial soldiers during the siege of Boston.

8. In front of the *Unitarian Church* (L) is a tablet which recalls the Arlington Minutemen. It reads as follows: 'At this spot, April 19, 1775, the old men of Menotomy captured a convoy of 18 men with supplies on the way to join the British at Lexington.' When word came that a British supply train was coming through with only a small guard, the 'old men' made ready for its capture. Crouching behind a wall, they arose as the British approached, covered them with leveled muskets, and forced a surrender; the contents of the supply wagon were distributed to the farmers.

9. The *Arlington Public Library* (*open weekdays* 10–9), known as the Robbins Memorial Library, designed in 1892 by Cabot, Everett and Mead of Boston, is constructed of Ohio limestone in Italian Renaissance style. Engaged Corinthian columns support the arches over the windows. The entrance is similar in style to the main door of the Cancellaria Palace in Rome.

The *Indian Hunter*, by Cyrus E. Dallin (*see below*), stands in the park between the library and the Town Hall.

10. The *Whittemore-Robbins Mansion*, behind the library, is a Federal three-story building with a hip roof, a cupola or watch-tower, and four chimneys.

11. The *Town Hall* designed by R. Clipston Sturgis and built about 1914, is a contemporary adaptation of Colonial design. Two stories in height, the 'great hall' is surrounded on three sides by administrative offices.

L. from Massachusetts Ave. on Jason St.

12. The *Jason Russell House* (*open weekdays except Mon. 2–5, Apr.–Oct.*), 7 Jason St., a wooden two-story dwelling with pitched roof and central chimney, was built in 1680. A number of Minutemen, almost surrounded by the British on that memorable April 19, dashed into it for cover. A few who fled to the cellar were unharmed, but Jason Russell and 11 others who hid upstairs were killed. The house was occupied by descendants of the Russell family until 1890. It is now the headquarters of the Arlington Historical Society.

Retrace Jason St.; L. from Jason St. on Massachusetts Ave.

13. A tablet at 840 Massachusetts Ave. identifies the *Site of the Deacon Joseph Adams House*, from which British soldiers stole the communion service of the First Parish during their retreat from Lexington and Concord.

L. from Massachusetts Ave. on Appleton St.

14. The *Benjamin Locke House* (*private*), 21 Appleton St., was built (1726) by a captain of the militia. When the British passed by, about two o'clock on the morning of April 19, Captain Locke was awakened and rushed out to arouse his neighbors. In a short time he was able to muster 26 men. By the afternoon the band grew to 52, which, with companies from surrounding towns, joined in harassing the rear of Percy's retreating column.

15. *St. Anne's Chapel* (*open*), between Hillside and Claremont Aves., was designed by Cram and Ferguson and completed in 1916. It is built in Romanesque style, the interior and exterior being of local field-stone. It is furnished with ancient ecclesiastical furniture, most of which came from Spain and Italy.

L. from Appleton St. into Claremont Ave.; L. from Claremont Ave. into Florence Ave.; R. from Florence Ave. into Cliff St.; R. from Cliff St. into Oakland Ave.

16. The *Home of Cyrus E. Dallin* (*private*), 69 Oakland Ave., also serves as the eminent sculptor's studio. Mr. Dallin (1861–   ), a native of Utah, is well known for his understanding portrayals of the American Indian. Among his most noted works are 'Appeal to the Great Spirit,' which stands before the Museum of Fine Arts in Boston, and 'Medicine Man,' in Fairmount Park, Philadelphia.

L. from Oakland Ave. into Park Ave.

17. The *Water Standpipe* (*open to visitors each second Sun.*) rises 50 feet above the loftiest point on Arlington Heights, emphasizing the great difference between the lowest and highest altitude of this town. From a balcony near the top, Boston and the harbor are visible to the east; to the west Mt. Monadnock and Mt. Wachusett are dim blue shapes on the horizon.

B O S T O N . *The Hub of the Universe*

City: Alt. 8, pop. 781,188, sett. 1625, incorp. town 1630, city 1822.

Railroad Stations: North Station, 120 Causeway St., for B. & M. R.R., Rutland, Central Vermont, and Canadian Pacific R.R.s.; South Station, Atlantic Ave. corner of Summer St., for N.Y., N.H. & H. and B. & A. R.R.s.; Back Bay Station, 145 Dartmouth St., for N.Y., N.H. & H. R.R.; Trinity Place Station, Trinity Place and Dartmouth St., for B. & A. R.R.

Bus Stations: 8 Broadway for Berkshire Motor Coach Lines, Inc., and Victoria Coach Line, Inc.; 2 Park Square for Blue Way Trail Ways, Inc., Granite Stages, and Quaker Stages Co.; Hotel Brunswick, 520 Boylston St., for Gray Line Inc. and Royal Blue Line, Inc.; 51 Scollay Square for Black Hawk Lines, Inc.; 36 Park Square for B. & M. Transportation Co. and New England Transportation Co.; 222 Boylston St. for Greyhound Lines; 30 Boylston St. for I.R.R. Co., Inc.; 620 Atlantic Ave. for Rawding Lines, Inc.; 10 Park Square for Capitol Stages.

Piers: Commonwealth Pier No. 5, South Boston; B. & A. Docks, East Boston; Pier 3 for Cunard-White Star Line; Pier 4 for Anchor and U.S. Lines; N.Y., N.H. & H. Piers, South Boston; Pier 2 for M.M.T. Co.; Hoosac Docks, Charlestown; Pier 42 for Ocean S.S. Line and Pier 44 for Dollar Line; Mystic Docks, Charlestown; Pier 46 for Furness-Withy Line; India Wharf and Central Wharf, Atlantic Ave., Boston, for Eastern S.S. Co.; Long Wharf, Atlantic Ave., Boston, for United Fruit Co. and Cape Cod S.S. Co.

Airports: Boston Airport, East Boston, 2 *m.* from city; American Air Lines, B. & M. Airways, Mayflower Line (Boston & Cape Cod, summers); taxi fare 85¢, plus 15¢ toll fare for East Boston Tunnel.

Accommodations: Thirteen large hotels and many small ones.

Information Service: Chamber of Commerce, 80 Federal St.; New England Council, Statler Bldg., 20 Providence St.

BOSTON during its three hundred-odd years of existence has become so
encrusted with legends that the true Boston of today is almost completely
obscured by them. According to time-honored tradition, this city is the
Hub of the Universe, its intellectual center, its cultural center, populated
by superior persons all of whom have at least one ancestor who came over
in the 'Mayflower' or the 'Arbella,' a closed society of 'Brahmins.'

Visitors arriving in Boston with such preconceived notions are likely to
have them confirmed for all time by the sight of a gentleman crossing the
Common carrying a green bag, or a lady emerging from the New England
Historical and Genealogical Society with her *Transcript* under her arm.

Nothing could be farther from the truth. Boston has its share of intellectuals, its share of culture, its share of 'old families'; it still plays its part
in world affairs and fills an important rôle in national politics. By no
means do all its citizens, however, live serenely on the waterside of
Beacon Street or the sunny side of Commonwealth Avenue, nor do they
all read the *Atlantic Monthly*, or spend their summers with relatives on the
North Shore and eternity with their ancestors in Mount Auburn Cemetery.

As for the legend of ethnic homogeneity, that is so much pernicious
twaddle. Boston has greatly changed from the city of which President
Timothy Dwight of Yale wrote in 1796: 'The Bostonians, almost without
an exception, are derived from one country and a single stock. They are
all descendants of Englishmen and, of course, are united by all the great
bonds of society — language, religion, government, manners and interest.'

Today five minutes' walk from the State House will take the visitor to
any one of several sections of the city where English is a foreign language.
A social statistician has said that every third person whom you meet on
the street in Boston today is foreign-born and three out of every four are
of other than English descent. The old New England stock still largely
controls leading banks, numerous business enterprises, museums, hospitals, and universities, but numerically it is insignificant. The contemporary scene is decidedly more cosmopolitan than Calvinistic. The
'New Canaan' of the English founders is now a political new Canaan for
the Irish. Celt outnumbers Saxon.

The modern fable, however, that Boston is an 'Irish city' is no better
founded than the Puritan myth. The largest number of Boston's 229,356
foreign-born come from Canada (45,558). Three groups closely follow the
Canadians: the Irish Free State (43,932), Italy (36,274), and Russia,
chiefly Jews (31,359). Great Britain and Ireland have contributed
22,653, and Poland, Norway and Denmark, Germany and Lithuania have
sent sizable quotas in the order named, with many Jews in the Polish and
German groups. There are also in Boston 20,574 Negroes.

Equally without foundation is the frequent impression that Boston is
still the old peninsula plus the Back Bay; bounded on the north by the
North Station, on the south by the South Station, on the east by the

Atlantic Avenue wharves, and on the west by Copley Square with an extension along the Esplanade. This area, which the visitor usually thinks of as 'Boston' contains, it is true, Boston Common, the Public Garden, Beacon Hill and both State Houses, the old graveyards, the waterfront, the market, the business district, the main shopping area, and most of Boston's historic houses and shrines, but it shelters actually less than one-sixth of Boston's residents. Outside its confines Beacon Street and Commonwealth Avenue stretch along parallel to the Charles River to the vast Brighton–Allston area (annexed in 1874) in whose modern hive of apartment houses and small homes live Boston's professional and clerical workers to the number of 67,000 — a fair-sized city in itself. East Boston, an island across Boston Harbor to the northeast, has been a part of the city since 1636 and houses about 62,000 persons. South Boston has a population of more than 55,000. Charlestown, north across the inlet where the Charles River and Boston Harbor meet (annexed in 1874), contains the United States Navy Yard, Mystic Wharves, Bunker Hill, and the residences of about 30,000 Bostonians. Roxbury (annexed in 1868), West Roxbury, Jamaica Plain (annexed in 1874), and Dorchester to the south (annexed in 1874) have a combined population of approximately 450,000, a large majority of them Boston's less well-paid workers. Hyde Park has over 25,000 and 'The Islands' have 2663 inhabitants.

Bearing these facts in mind, it is a mistake for the visitor to think of Boston in any single term. Boston is a composite. It is a composite of Silas Lapham's Boston — southerly Beacon Hill, the Charles River Embankment, Beacon Street and Commonwealth Avenue, all of which William Dean Howells knew so well — and the Boston symbolized by what was once Ward 8, the kingdom of Boss Martin Lomasney, densely populated, scornfully ignorant of the proprieties of the prunes-and-prisms school, but vigorously alive. It is the paradoxical city which has inspired twenty novels of the Boston scene in the past twenty-five years. It is the Boston of wide streets overarched by spreading elms, of crooked narrow streets called 'quaint,' of magnificent parks, fine public buildings, handsome residences, and a general air of well-scrubbed propriety and gracious leisure. It is the Boston where acres of ugly wooden tenement houses line the drab streets; where ten dollars a month rents a three-room flat in a wooden fire trap without heat, lighting, or any sanitary facilities; where, despite a magnificent park system, thousands of children still must play on sidewalks. It is the Boston of the music-lovers, centered about Symphony Hall, the Opera House, the New England Conservatory of Music; the Boston of the art-lovers, centered about the Museum of Fine Arts, the Gardner Museum, the Public Library; the Boston of the well-to-do churches and the prosperous universities. It is the Boston that produces eighteen per cent of the total goods manufactured in Massachusetts by the toil of fourteen per cent of the workers in the State; the Boston of 2104 manufacturing establishments (1934), representing a capital investment of $227,315,188 and a total value of manufactured products to the amount of $332,176,950; the Boston engrossed in printing and publishing, clothing manufacture, sugar refining, boots and shoes, bread and pastries, confectionery, cutlery, foundry and machine-shop products, malt liquors and wholesale meat-packing.

Note: Because of space limitations, duplication of statement has had to be minimized. For a complete picture, the historical account of Boston which follows should be read in conjunction with the essays in Section I, *Massachusetts: The General Background.*

Boston's first settler was William Blackstone, a recluse of scholarly and probably misanthropic mental cast, formerly a clergyman of the Church of England. He had built himself a hut on the western slope of what is now Beacon Hill, planting his orchard on what later became Boston Common. At that time the wilderness occupied the peninsula, which was about one-third the size of the present Boston peninsula. Almost an island, it jutted out into the bay, joined to the mainland by a long narrow neck like the handle of a ladle. It was a mile wide at its widest, three miles long, and the neck was so narrow and so low that at times it was submerged by the ocean. Blackstone's realm was bounded on the west by a mud flat (the Back Bay); on the north by a deep cove (later dammed off to make a mill pond); on the east by a small river which cut off the North End and made an island of it, and by a deep cove (later known as the 'Town Cove'); and on the south by another deep cove. Here the disillusioned clergyman read his books, farmed a little, traded a bit with the Indians, and breathed air uncontaminated by any other white man.

His idyllic solitude was rudely shattered after four or five years, however, by the arrival of John Winthrop with a company of some eight hundred souls who settled in what is now Charlestown, just across from his paradise. Their miseries were many. The water at Charlestown was brackish; and their settlement could not easily be defended against Indian raids. Blackstone visited them and was melted by the spectacle of their plight. He invited them to come across to his peninsula and the company eagerly accepted his hospitality.

Thus in 1630 Boston actually began. Winthrop's settlers called it 'Trimountain,' possibly because of three hills later known as Beacon Hill, Copp's Hill, and Fort Hill (now razed), or possibly because of the three mounded peaks of Beacon Hill (later shaved down).

The first year acquainted the Englishmen and their families with the rigors of the New England climate, and as it was too late to plant crops, more than two hundred died of starvation and exposure. The following spring a ship laden with provisions, long overdue, dropped anchor in the bay, and famine was averted. The freshly tilled soil later yielded a good crop and the Colony survived and grew.

Fisheries were established. Fir and lumber created an export market. The foundation of trade and agriculture were early laid. Within four years more than four thousand Englishmen had emigrated to Boston and its vicinity. Twenty villages ramified out of the peninsula town to form a definite Puritan Commonwealth.

The early Bostonians spent their days in labor from which the Sabbath alone released them. Women, with spinning, weaving, and all the family clothes to make, with large numbers of children to rear, had little time to cultivate the amenities of social intercourse. Pioneer life was hard, drab, and offered few comforts. Wood, for example, was the only source of fuel, and as late as 1720 Cotton Mather complained, ' 'Tis dredful cold, my ink glass in my stand is froze.'

Divines were preoccupied with dismal theological abstractions, but the statute books reveal the fact that there were secular souls who displayed a wholesome proclivity for life. 'Tobacco drinking' (smoking) tippling, card-playing, dancing, and bowling identified the colonists with their Elizabethan forbears, but caused the town fathers much alarm. Sunday strolls or street kissing — even when legitimate — were subject to heavy fine, and an attempt was made to legislate 'sweets' out of existence. Christmas, reminiscent of 'popery,' was immediately placed under the ban and the elders often boasted that none of the holidays of old England survived the Atlantic passage.

A breach of these regulations resulted in punishment which was based upon the theory that ridicule was more effective than the isolation of imprisonment. Market squares were embellished by the erection of punitive apparatus — bilboes, stocks, pillories, and ducking stools. Public floggings were common and offenders were often forced to display on their persons the initial letter of the crime committed.

Offenses against Puritan theology were severely punished. Boston, dedicated to Calvin, neither understood nor admired toleration. Quakers and other non-conformists were ruthlessly persecuted and martyrdom became a commonplace in the Puritan town. Roger Williams was banished for having 'broached and divulged diverse new and dangerous opinions against the authority of the magistrates.' Mistress Anne Hutchinson, a 'heretic,' followed Roger Williams into banishment. Mary Dyer, a Quaker, was hanged on old Boston Common in 1660; Mary Jones, Mary Parsons, and Ann Hibbins were hanged as witches. The town fathers were content to sacrifice freedom in their attempt to achieve unity. The Reverend Nathaniel Ward, speaking for all good Puritans, remarked, 'All Familists, Anabaptists, and other Enthusiasts shall have free liberty to keepe away from us.'

In spite of a narrow religious and moral outlook, her commerce insured Boston's future greatness. Scarcely a year after the Puritans had invaded the splendid isolation of Mr. Blackstone, Governor Winthrop launched the 'Blessing of the Bay.' The Puritan 'Rebecca' sailed to Narragansett and purchased corn from the Indians. Vessels called at the Bermudas and returned to Boston with cargoes of oranges, limes, and the equally exotic potato. They traveled up the Delaware in search of pelts. Frequently they put in at New Amsterdam to traffic with Dutch burghers, and twelve years after the founding (1642) ships laden with pipe staves and other products tied up safely at English docks. Thus began the

maritime history of Massachusetts with Boston as its center. Shipbuilding, fishing, whaling, industry and exchange made the Colony a bustling
outpost of imperial Britain.

From 1630 to about 1680, Great Britain was 'so absorbed in troubles at
home that, notwithstanding the Navigation Act of 1651, she gave little
attention to regulating the enterprise of her infant Colonies. In 1691
a royal governor was sent; in 1733 the Molasses Act was passed; but the
Colonial merchants had virtually free trade until 1764 when Grenville
began the vigorous enforcement of the mercantilistic measures. From
then on friction increased rapidly and the Colonies developed a burning
sense of grievance.

The American Revolution resulted from a series of bewildering subtleties,
but many dramatic episodes, seemingly reflecting the broad issues of the
controversy but actually telescoping them, took place in Boston's crooked
streets. The Boston Massacre (1770) on King Street (now State) occurred
in the shadow of the Old State House. News of the British advance on
Lexington and Concord was semaphored to Paul Revere by the glimmer
of a lamp which swung from the belfry of the Old North Church. The
rafters of Faneuil Hall rang with the impassioned oratory of the champions
of liberty. The Old South Meeting House was the point from which fifty
men disguised as Indians rushed to Griffin's Wharf where British merchantmen rocked idly in the harbor, their holds crammed with East
Indian tea (1773). It was the Boston Tea Party which confronted the
British Cabinet with the choice of capitulation or force, replied to by the
Port Act, which marked the beginning of a policy of coercion and led
swiftly to open warfare. The battle of Bunker Hill in near-by Charlestown was one of the early engagements of the war. Boston was regarded
by the British as a most important objective, and the failure of the siege
and the evacuation of the city by the Redcoats was the first serious blow
to Tory confidence.

Commerce suffered a temporary eclipse in the depression of the post-war
years, but the discovery of new trading possibilities in the Orient offered
an opportunity which enterprising Yankee merchants were quick to
perceive. The development of the China trade and the exploitation of
the Oregon coast rich in sea otters restored Boston to its former eminence.
Wealth poured into the coffers of merchants, traders, and shipmasters.
In 1780, 455 ships from every quarter of the globe docked in Boston
Harbor, while 1200 vessels engaged in coastwise traffic out of Boston.
During a single year (1791), seventy Yankee merchantmen cleared Boston
for Europe, the Indies, and Canton.

Boston's maritime prosperity was stimulated by the wars between England and France which followed the accession of Napoleon. In 1807 the
shipping of Boston totaled 310,309 tons or more than one-third of the
mercantile marine of the United States. The Jefferson Embargo and the
War of 1812 seriously crippled the city's maritime development. Although she recovered, and although the era of the clipper made Massa-

chusetts famous throughout the world, and although the 'Sovereign of the Seas,' built by Donald McKay in East Boston (1852), was the envy of the British Admiralty, the War of 1812 really marked the beginning of the end of Boston's maritime supremacy. Thereafter manufacturing and industry gradually supplanted commercial interests.

In 1822, Boston became a city; railroads were being built from 1830 on and played an important part in urban development; the first horsecar line, connecting Cambridge and Boston, was built in 1853. Between 1824 and 1858, the Boston peninsula was enlarged from 783 acres to 1801 acres by cutting down the hills and filling in the Back Bay and the great coves with the excavated gravel as a basis for reclamation. The Neck, which William Blackstone could not always cross on foot because of the tidewater, was raised and broadened, so that what was once the narrowest part of Boston proper is now the widest.

During the era between the War of Independence and the Civil War, Boston ideas underwent a parallel transformation from the provincial to the urban. Stimulated by European currents of thought and the philosophy of the frontier, Boston began to revolt against the theology of Calvin, a revolt typical of the democratic spirit of the nineteenth century. Unitarianism under the leadership of William Ellery Channing threatened to dissolve the entire system of Puritan Congregationalism (1825). The new doctrines were embraced by Harvard and the fashion of Boston, but hardly had the rebellion subsided when new dissension broke out within Unitarian ranks. Ralph Waldo Emerson shocked his parishioners of the Second Church (1832) by tendering his resignation and retiring to Concord to ponder the mysteries of Transcendentalism. Theodore Parker, another Unitarian minister, immersed in German philosophy, Biblical criticism, and evolutionary geology, began to preach a new variety of natural religion which rejected conventional theological forms and banished the supernatural.

Coinciding with the democratic movement and partly as a result of it, a flurry of philanthropy and reform arose. John Lowell, Jr., bequeathed a fortune to establish Lowell Institute (1839) in order to provide the people of Boston with free lectures by 'foremost scholars and thinkers of the English-speaking world.' This democratization of education was supplemented by the creation of the Boston Public Library (1852). Horace Mann devoted his reforming spirit to the development of formal education. Dr. Samuel Gridley Howe dedicated his efforts to the emancipation of the deaf and blind. With the financial assistance of Thomas H. Perkins, the Perkins Institution and Massachusetts School for the Blind (first located in South Boston, later removed to Watertown) was founded, a unique institution for its day (1832). The first public surgical operation which made use of ether as an anesthetic was performed (1846) at the Massachusetts General Hospital. A controversy between the two claimants of discovery, William Thomas Green Morton and Charles T. Jackson (the claim of a country doctor in Georgia had not yet been advanced), was temporarily settled by a tactful verdict of the French

Academy which awarded each claimant a similar amount, one for the discovery of ether and the other for its application.

Nowhere was the reforming spirit more active than in the anti-slavery movement. William Lloyd Garrison had no respect for the interests of cotton, whether expounded by planters or manufacturers. He invaded Boston and founded the *Liberator* (1831) and was rewarded in 1835 with physical violence at the hands of a mob partly composed of Boston gentility. The development of cotton manufacture in Lawrence and Lowell was not without its effect on State Street and Beacon Hill. Respectable elements of society thought best to refrain from emotional language or harsh criticism after Southern statesmen began to ask pertinent questions concerning workers in Lowell and Lawrence mills. Garrison attacked the Constitution because it recognized slavery as legal, and Boston patriots could hardly suffer so sacred a document to be disparaged; but Garrison's fervor attracted Wendell Phillips, a brilliant orator whose lineage was almost as old as Boston, and he became an equally zealous advocate of the cause. Other converts were enlisted — Channing, Parker, Lowell, Longfellow, Dana — and under the championship of such ultra-respectable persons, the anti-slavery crusade gained ground rapidly.

Boston played a less important rôle in the Civil War than in events preceding it. Unable to meet the prescribed quota of soldiers by voluntary enlistment, the city fathers first employed the draft in 1863, precipitating the Boston Draft Riots. The poorer classes, irritated when their rich neighbors purchased immunity from compulsory service for the sum of three hundred dollars, objected so strenuously that the militia was called out to quell the disorders. Among the regiments which did march South to uphold the honor of Boston, one of the most famous was commanded by Colonel Robert Gould Shaw, an abolitionist 'of gentle birth and breeding.' Composed of Negroes, this regiment led the attack on Fort Wagner where Colonel Shaw and nearly half of his followers fell.

Although some Bostonians had indicated a reluctance to support the Northern cause during the war, the celebration of peace left little to be desired. The moving spirit of the great Peace Jubilee held in June, 1869, was Patrick S. Gilmore, an exuberant Irish bandmaster, whose grandiose plans for this occasion made P. T. Barnum seem a novice by comparison. A coliseum seating 30,000 people was erected near the site of the present Copley Plaza Hotel housing an Angel of Peace, thirteen feet high, together with an extinguished torch of war, frescoes, doves and angels, medallions, emblems and flags, as well as the largest bass drum in the world, constructed for the occasion, and four organs that required relays of twelve men to pump. Ten thousand choral singers combined with an orchestra of 84 trombones, 83 tubas, 83 cornets, 75 drums, 330 strings, and 119 woodwinds, produced an awe-inspiring 'Niagara of harmony.' At one stage of the celebration, a hundred members of the Fire Department, clad in red shirts, blue pants, and white caps, suddenly appeared and beat upon a hundred anvils in what was doubtless the loudest performance of the Anvil Chorus from 'Il Trovatore' ever given. President Ulysses S.

Grant, who attended, appeared unimpressed, and John S. Dwight, foremost music critic of the day, fled to Nahant in order to escape the din.

This amazing exhibition reflected the American adoration of size as well
as the immaturity of the new wealth which the rise of industry was
bringing to Boston. The proud and graceful clippers that had sailed from
Boston Harbor had been displaced by smoke-belching steamships which
were largely of British ownership. Says Samuel Eliot Morison, in his
'Maritime History of Massachusetts':

> The maritime history of Massachusetts... ends with the passing of the
> clipper. 'Twas a glorious ending! Never, in these United States, has the
> brain of man conceived, or the hand of man fashioned, so perfect a thing
> as the clipper ship. In her, the long-suppressed artistic impulse of a practi-
> cal, hard-worked race burst into flower. The 'Flying Cloud' was our
> Rheims, the 'Sovereign of the Seas' our Parthenon, the 'Lightning' our
> Amiens; but they were monuments carved from snow. For a few brief
> moments of time they flashed their splendor around the world, then dis-
> appeared with the sudden completeness of the wild pigeon. One by one
> they sailed out of Boston, to return no more. A tragic or mysterious end
> was the final privilege of many, favored by the gods. Others, with lofty
> rig cut down to cautious dimensions, with glistening decks and topsides
> scarred and neglected, limped about the seas under foreign flags, like faded
> beauties forced upon the street.

Money formerly invested in shipping now flowed into the mills and
factories that sprang up in large numbers in Boston and its suburbs. The
shoe and textile industries, which had boomed with the artificial demand
of wartime conditions, continued their advance under the stimulus of
capital released from maritime pursuits. Other manufacturing establishments followed the trail to Boston, and by the turn of the twentieth
century, the intellectual 'Hub of the Universe' had become the industrial
hub of New England.

A new commerce grew from this new industry. It was neither so romantic nor so important as that of pre-Civil War days, but it sufficed
to establish Boston as one of the leading ports on the Atlantic seaboard.
Shipping became an adjunct of manufacturing plants; raw materials,
such as cotton and wool for textiles and leather for shoes, were brought
to the factories and the finished products carried to the remotest markets
of the world. In 1901 ships sailing out of Boston Harbor carried goods
valued at $143,708,000, while imports in that year amounted to $80,000,000.

By the end of the nineteenth century, Bostonians could (and did) boast
of other things in addition to a thriving industry and commerce. Boston
had at least two much-touted claims to fame: John L. Sullivan, the greatest fighter of his time, and the first passenger-car subway in America,
a two-mile stretch from Arlington and Boylston Streets to the North
Station. The last horsecar was discarded in 1910, and while bicycles,
drays, and carriages were still dashing along at the reckless speed of eight
or ten miles an hour, electric surface lines were being built in every
section of the city. An elevated railroad (begun in 1909) pushed into

the suburb of Forest Hills; downtown Boston was transformed by steel, cut stone, and marble; the National Shawmut Bank, the buildings of William Filene's Sons Co., and Jordan Marsh Company, all erected shortly after 1907, set a pattern of utilitarian beauty which changed the external character of the city.

The growth of industry was paralleled by the growing consciousness of labor. One of the most spectacular strikes in the history of the labor movement was the Boston police strike of 1919, based on the formal complaint of an organization of 1290 Boston patrolmen, that their wages had failed to keep pace with living costs, that the police stations were unsanitary, and that they worked overtime without compensation.

A number of factors defeated the policemen and they voted to return to work. Governor Coolidge, however, disclaimed the power to reinstate the strikers, stating that he was opposed to 'the public safety again being placed in the hands of these same policemen.' Mayor Peters worked all during September 15 on a revised wage scale — for the new policemen.

Hardly had the excitement of the police strike subsided when Boston became the storm center of another crisis, concerning the arrest, trial, conviction, and execution of two obscure Italian laborers, the anarchists Sacco and Vanzetti. (*See Industry and Labor*, p. 76.)

Such spectacular events as these are exceptional in the city's history. Boston, however, as the seat of State government and in itself a cross-section of all major State industries, has been conscious of consistent effort along the labor front. This was the theater of the pitched battle in 1924 over ratification of the Child Labor Amendment. The friction resulting since 1929 from the decreased prosperity of industry and the resistance of labor to wage reductions has burst out sporadically, notably in the textile and shoe trades. Debate over craft or industrial organization has been heated, but not to the critical point reached in some cities.

For twenty years Boston, stimulated by an exposition ambitiously announcing as its goal, 'Boston 1915 the Finest City in the World,' had been consciously building its physical self into a fine, clean, and beautiful city. Shortly before the nation-wide depression overtook it, it became obsessed also by a desire to put its spiritual house in order. Celestial roundsmen under the aegis of the 'New England Watch and Ward Society' inaugurated a virulent campaign against 'lewd and indecent' books and plays. What is salacity? It was like the time-honored stickler: How old is Ann? Other cities indulged in loud guffaws over the antics of the Boston censors as the latter grew hotter and hotter and more and more bothered over the perplexing problem. 'Banned in Boston' came to be the novelist's and dramatist's dream of successful publicity — 'a natural' in advertising. The greatest furore was occasioned by the refusal of the authorities to permit the Boston production of Eugene O'Neill's 'Strange Interlude.' The producers promptly moved their company to Quincy, where the play had a tremendous run, playing to audiences packed with Boston residents.

The tragic vagaries of the stock market, the headlines of 1927, censorship with all its trail of Rabelaisian mirth, the police strike, though it made Calvin Coolidge Vice-President and subsequently President — all were temporarily forgotten in the great Tercentenary Celebration which ushered in the third decade of the century. Even the cloud of the approaching depression, considerably larger already on the horizon than a man's hand, cast no shadow on gala preparations.

The Boston Tercentenary Committee, in conjunction with State-wide subcommittees, mapped out a gigantic program. The ceremonies, conducted with considerable pomp, were formally opened by a 'Great Meeting held on Boston Common, where the chief address was delivered by the Right Honorable H. A. L. Fisher, Warden of New College, Oxford. 'Little did the founders reckon,' said Professor Fisher in his oration, 'that a time would come when ... in the fullness of years, their New England would be followed by a New Ireland, a New Italy, a New Germany, a New Poland, and a New Greece, all destined to be merged into a great and harmonious Commonwealth.'

The story of the economic collapse, which followed hard upon the very celebration itself, is better not written except where it may be dissected and analyzed. Boston, for all its rigidity of pattern and form, continues to be a paradox. In spite of the depression, which affected it with the utmost seriousness, it is today still the metropolis of New England, the commercial, financial, and industrial center of a densely populated area, second to none in the diversity of its manufactures and the skill of its labor. And in spite of censorship it is still a cultural center, maintained so by the perennial optimism and courage of its artists, and the warm support of a great body of art-loving citizens. And in spite of its undeniable intolerance, it is still the home of militant liberalism. Here Unitarianism and Universalism make their home; here liberal education waged a spectacular fight against the Teachers' Oath Bill; and Boston liberals picketed the very State House one dramatic afternoon in championship of the Child Labor Law. Boston is still the Boston of the Lowells, the Lodges, the Cabots, but it is from newer stocks that it derives much of its color, its hope, and its unquenchable vitality.

FOOT TOUR 1 (*Back Bay and Beacon Hill*) — 3 *m.*

W. from Clarendon St. on Boylston St.

Copley Square is more photographed than any other plaza in Boston, owing to the stately architectural beauty of two sides of its triangular green, which is now marred by the contrasting stretch of shops, banks, and offices on its third side.

1. *Trinity Church* (Episcopal) (*open daily*) faces west on Copley Square. At the time it was built, in 1877, American architecture had for twenty

years languished in an unprecedented state of decadence. To the perversions of the then prevalent Victorian Gothic the genius of Henry Hobson Richardson vigorously superimposed, and with his Trinity Church began the emancipation of American architecture.

The shape of the lot, triangular in form, bounded by three streets, made impossible the usual long nave and dominant entrance front, and invited the defiance of tradition. Richardson found in the Romanesque of southern France a medium well suited to the problem. He turned also to the 11th-century work of the cities of Auvergne in central France where the central tower was developed to such proportion as to become the main portion of the structure. The resultant plan was compact and cruciform with all its limbs nearly equal — apse, nave, transepts, and chapel forming the base of the tower obelisk. The massive tower is the dominant feature of the design and the composition as a whole is a romantic and picturesque mass studied for its effectiveness from all angles. For the tower design, Richardson was inspired by the cathedral of Salamanca, in Spain.

The architect early decided that Trinity should be a 'color church.' The walls are of yellowish Dedham granite laid up in rock-faced ashler with trim of reddish-brown Longmeadow freestone. Cut stone, in alternating patterns of light and dark, decorates some of the walls. Throughout, the building is animated by rich and powerful carvings, the best of which are seen in the West Porch, a posthumous work completed in 1897, from Richardson's designs, by Evans and Tombs of Boston.

Richardson entrusted the decoration of the interior to John La Farge under whose direction the great barrel vaults came to glow with some of the fire of San Marco. The dominant color of the interior walls is red, the great piers a dark bronze green with gilded capitals and bases. The best of the windows were by Sir Edward Burne-Jones, executed by William Morris, John La Farge, and by Clayton and Bill of London. Trinity stands as the masterpiece of the 'Richardsonian Romanesque' which gave rise to a new though short-lived school, which nevertheless formed the first milestone in the radical school of architecture of today.

Adjoining the church outside, on the Huntington Avenue side, is the Saint-Gaudens statue of *Phillips Brooks and Christ*, still adversely criticized in Boston. By optical illusion the placing of the pastor in front of a slender figure of Christ, and on a lower level, suggests a short, stocky man, whereas Phillips Brooks was six feet four inches tall, a fact which undoubtedly added to his singularly magnetic personality. The union of symbolism and realism is also regarded as unhappy by many critics. Ninety-five thousand dollars had poured in in voluntary public contributions for this statue, and the disappointment of the donors was keen.

2. *The Boston Public Library* (*open weekdays* 9–10; *Sun.* 2–9; *June* 15– *Sept.* 15, 9–9; *closed holidays*) faces east on Copley Square. The strong tide of classicism that emanated from the Chicago Exposition of 1893 found its first important expression in this Albertian building finished in

1895 from plans by McKim, Mead and White. For inspiration, Charles Follen McKim turned to the bold lines of Labrouste's Italian Renaissance masterpiece, the Bibliothèque Sainte Geneviève in Paris. Not content, he fused with this influence, the more robust character of Alberti's *San Francesco* at Rimini. The interior court, one of the finest features, is an almost servile adaptation of the *Palazzo della Cancelleria* in Rome.

Situated at the west end of Copley Square the 'great palace of books' stands upon a granite platform elevated by six broad steps above the level of the Square. The façade consists of thirteen deep raked arches, separated by massive piers. The entrance or central motif is composed of three lofty and deeply revealed arches, above which are exquisitely sculptured panels by Saint-Gaudens illustrating the seals of the Library, the City, and the Commonwealth.

The structure's salient function being to house one of the largest collections of books in the world, its plan shows a directness and general simplicity of arrangement. The walls of the vestibule are of unpolished Tennessee marble. The three doorways leading into the Entrance Hall are copies from the Erechtheum at Athens. The double bronze doors, which contain graceful, allegorical figures in low relief, were designed by Daniel Chester French. The Entrance Hall itself, with its low mosaic-covered vaults and arches supported by walls and massive square columns of Iowa sandstone, is Roman in design. The walls of the Stair Hall are of rich-veined yellow Siena marble and the steps of French Échaillon marble lead to the Main Corridor. The upper walls of the stair hall are divided into eight arched panels and within these spaces and on one wall of the Main Corridor are symbolic murals by Puvis de Chavannes. Bates Hall, the main reading-room, has a rich barrel vault with half domes at the ends, and stretches the full breadth of the façade, 218 feet. Abbey's large frieze, 'The Quest of the Holy Grail,' occupies the upper portion of the walls of the Delivery Room. On the upper or special libraries floor is a corridor known as Sargent Hall and on its walls are Sargent's murals depicting 'The Triumph of Religion.'

Besides its vast collection of volumes for circulation or reference, the Boston Public Library houses special collections of particular significance. Outstanding among these is the Sabatier collection, an unusual assortment of books dealing with Saint Francis of Assisi. Likewise important is its remarkable newspaper collection, covering every city of importance in the world. Of note also are the libraries of John Adams, Nathaniel Bowditch, George Ticknor, and the Reverend Thomas Prince (which includes the first book printed in the English Colonies of America — the 'Bay Psalm Book'); a comprehensive assortment of manuscript letters relating to the anti-slavery movement in the United States; Webster's 'Reply to Hayne,' in manuscript; Bentley's collection of accounting books before 1900; the Lewissohn collection of Washingtoniana; and a collection of Benjamin Franklin's books and engravings. The unique Trent Defoe collection and the collection of incunabula are especially noteworthy.

3. The *Old South Church (Third)*, 645 Boylston St., corner of Dartmouth St., built in 1875 from the plans of Cummings and Sears, is probably the least distressing example of the Ruskinian or Victorian Gothic trend that corrupted taste in the late nineteenth century. The campanile, which soars to a height of 248 feet, was for many years the 'leaning tower of Copley Square.' Built on filled ground and entirely of massive masonry work, the tower sank out of plumb. When, in 1932, it was in danger of toppling, it was removed, each stone catalogued and stored away. In 1937, steel skeleton anchored to deep-sunk piles chased the superficial form and the original masonry followed its course. So now, the 'leaning tower' — its spine once more erect — serves as an effective companion piece to the Library Building.

4. *Boston University*, 688 Boylston St., founded in 1869 by Lee Claflin, Isaac Rich, and Jacob Sleeper, with its first department the Boston Theological Seminary, has grown to be one of the largest universities in the United States. Despite its name, it is not a city college, but is supported, like any other private institution, by endowments and tuition fees. Its present student body numbers about fifteen thousand, representing every State and thirty-two foreign countries. The three founders were religious men, but the noteworthy thing is that, although all were Methodists, they showed themselves broader, more tolerant, and more liberal than the founders of almost any other privately endowed institution in the State; for from the very beginning they prescribed that the University should never discriminate on denominational or sectarian lines. To these liberal tendencies which still endure may be attributed the rapid growth of the University.

Boston University is co-educational, with the exception of the *College of Practical Arts and Letters* and the *Sargent College of Physical Education*, which last was transferred to Boston University in 1929. Both are exclusively for women.

The proposed site for a new building to house the entire University except the Law and Medical Schools is on the banks of the Charles River where Alexander Graham Bell, a professor at Boston University, will be signally honored by a memorial tower 375 feet high.

In 1937 the University had no definite campus. The different schools were housed in various parts of the city as follows:

College of Liberal Arts, 688 Boylston Street.
College of Business Administration, 525 Boylston Street.
College of Practical Arts and Letters, 27 Garrison Street.
College of Music, 25 Blagden Street.
Sargent College of Physical Education, 6 Everett Street, Cambridge, Mass.
School of Theology, 72 Mt. Vernon Street.
School of Law, 11 Ashburton Place.
School of Medicine, 80 East Concord Street.
School of Education, 84 Exeter Street.
School of Religious and Social Work, 84 Exeter Street.
Graduate School, 688 Boylston Street.

Retrace Boylston St.; L. from Boylston St. on Dartmouth St.

A FLASHBACK IN
EARLY PRINTS

FOR a flashback on the Massachusetts scene prior to photography we are indebted to early artists, engravers, and lithographers. The prints that follow afford a fair prospect of old Boston that has all but disappeared, and make pictorial historical events that we still celebrate. The Remick drawing recalls the provision of 1643 by which Governor Winthrop set the Common aside for a 'trayning field and pasture for cattell.' The house beyond the fence on the top of the hill is the Hancock Mansion; the wooden tower back of it is the old beacon which for a century and a half surmounted the hill. In the picture of forty years later, the Bulfinch State House stands on the land where Hancock's cows grazed, while the old beacon has been replaced by a monument.

As shown in the Bird's-Eye View of the city, a water-line still existed in 1850 along Charles Street below the Common. Here in 1775, before the extension of Beacon Street blocked the way, the British soldiers boarded their boats and rowed across to Cambridge on the eve of their battle in Concord.

Less than a century after the settlement of the Bay Colony, an Englishman, describing the activity in Boston Harbor, said the masts of the ships here 'made a kind of wood of trees.' The city grew with its commerce, gradually encroaching on the harbor as well as on the back bay. Water Street in Post Office Square was the original shore-line. One of the prints shows a dock just below Quincy Market and Faneuil Hall; the market was built on made land in 1825.

The set of four prints of the Old State House reveals the changes this building underwent and the variety of its architectural expressions. Today the lion and the unicorn uphold their corners of the roof as they did in the Paul Revere picture of 1770.

Engraving from one of America's earliest historical paintings, by Earle in 1775

TH BRIDGE, CONCORD

ON COMMON IN 1768, SHOWING THE HANCOCK HOUSE AND THE OLD BEACON

From a Renick water color

THE OLD STATE HOUSE AND THE 'BLOODY MASSACRE,' 1770

THE OLD STATE HOUSE IN 1801, THE LION AND UNICORN REMO

STATE HOUSE FIRE, 1832. Note new balconies and chimneys

OLD STATE HOUSE IN 1876 WITH MANSARD ROOF AND ADVERTISEMENTS

SOUTHEAST VIEW OF BOSTON IN 1743, FROM THE HARBOR

THE CITY IN 1848, VIEWED FROM EAST BOS

Lithograph after the Price engraving

OLD BEACON ON BEACON HILL IS THE NINTH SPIRE FROM THE LEFT

THE NEW STATE HOUSE IS JUST RIGHT OF THE CENTER OF THE PICTURE
Lithograph by Whitefield

BIRD'S-EYE VIEW OF BOSTON AROUND

Lithograph by Pend

FANEUIL HALL AND THE OLD SHORE LINE

NEW STATE HOUSE AND THE BULFINCH BEACON, ABOUT 18

Lithograph by Pendlet

5. The *Boston Art Club Gallery* (*open to the public during exhibitions*), corner of Dartmouth and Newbury Sts., features exhibitions of contemporary painting and sculpture of New England artists.

L. from Dartmouth St. on Commonwealth Ave. (*central gravel mall*).

Commonwealth Ave., Marlborough St., and Beacon St., parallel thoroughfares, are 'The Three Streets' of Boston — impeccable residential addresses in their lower numbers.

6. The *Statue of William Lloyd Garrison* in the center of the walk, memorialized (1886) the celebrated Abolitionist. The declaration inscribed beneath his statue is dynamic: *I am in earnest. I will not equivocate. I will not excuse. I will not retreat a single inch, and I will be heard.* Yet the seated figure by Olin L. Warner shows him as a kindly deacon. It was James Russell Lowell who said:

> There's Garrison, his features very
> Benign for an incendiary.

Retrace on Commonwealth Ave.

7. The *First Baptist Church* (formerly New Brattle Square Church), corner of Clarendon St., designed by H. H. Richardson and built in 1870–72, marks the beginning of the architect's professional maturity. The exigencies of the corner site resulted in an asymmetrical composition, with the entrance located on a side street and the tower placed on the corner. The first Richardsonian work definitely Romanesque rather than Victorian Gothic, its style is still far from true Romanesque and not typically 'Richardsonian Romanesque.' Once vacated because of its failure acoustically, the church is notable mainly for its tower, with the heavy frieze by Bartholdi, a fellow student of Richardson at the École des Beaux Arts. This frieze of trumpeting angels is responsible for the irreverent but affectionate name: 'The Church of the Holy Beanblowers.' Bostonians like their Beanblower tower so well that a group of them have purchased it privately, so that it can never be torn down without their consent.

L. from Commonwealth Ave. on Berkeley St.

8. The *First Church in Boston* (Unitarian) (*open daily 9–5, through Marlborough St. entrance, or on Sunday by main entrance on Berkeley St.*), corner of Marlborough St., originally Congregational, was formed by Governor Winthrop in 1630 as the first parish. A bronze *Statue of Winthrop*, by R. S. Greenough, stands on the lawn at the side.

Retrace Berkeley St.; L. from Berkeley St. on the Commonwealth Ave. mall.

9. The *Statue of Alexander Hamilton*, is a nine-foot, full-length granite carving by William Rimmer, a self-taught Boston sculptor and teacher of Daniel Chester French. Rimmer had a theory, ahead of his time, of working impressionistically without models. Though contemporary criticism was violently adverse, the statue was admired by Hamilton's own family for its graceful and somewhat aloof pose, characteristic of its subject. Its ultra-modern qualities receive present-day recognition.

Straight ahead into the Public Garden; L. from entrance on first path within the Garden.

10. The *Public Garden*, with its academically labeled trees of rare varieties, its formal flower beds and its celebrated swan boats, has been a treasured feature of Boston ever since it was laid out in the middle of the nineteenth century on the 'made land' along the Charles. All the newer fashionable residential district west of this point was once a broad marshy tidal basin: this region is still called 'the Back Bay.'

11. The *Ether Monument* (1867), is not an artistic masterpiece, but none commemorates a greater humanitarian achievement than 'the discovery that the inhaling of ether causes insensibility to pain, first proved to the world at the Massachusetts General Hospital in Boston, October, 1846.'

12. The *George R. White Memorial Fountain,* by Daniel Chester French, is a tribute to a citizen who bequeathed a large fund to the city for use in health education.

L. from the Public Garden path on Beacon St.; R. from Beacon St. on Embankment Rd.

13. The *Esplanade* is a grassy promenade along the Charles River where in an open shell summer evening concerts are given by members of the Boston Symphony Orchestra.

R. on Chestnut St.

Beacon Hill is a conservative residential section where new buildings are considered extremely regrettable, though occasionally necessary. The correct building material is plain red brick.

This level end of Chestnut St. was once popularly known as Horse-Chestnut St. because the stables of the wealthy householders of the Hill were here. Some of these stables may still be seen, converted into studios. Crossing Chestnut St. is Charles St., once the home of Boston's literati, but now widened and lined with small markets and antique shops.

L. from Chestnut St. on Charles St.

14. *Charles Street Church*, at the corner of Charles and Mt. Vernon Sts., was built in 1807. The red-brick Federal structure with well-designed façade and low cupola was designed by Asher Benjamin, who, as author of 'The Country Builder's Assistant' and other preceptorial works on architecture, propagated the mode set by Bulfinch and McIntire.

Retrace on Charles St.; L. from Charles St. on Chestnut St.

15. *Francis Parkman's House (private),* 50 Chestnut St., with its arched recessed doorway, slate hip roof, and high flues, was built in 1824 and was for many years the home of the noted historian.

16. The *Home of Edwin Booth (private),* 29A Chestnut St., has a few of the original purple window-panes once favored in this district, which sun and time have transformed to a lilac hue, the despair of imitators. To have a house with original purple panes is practically to have a patent of Bostonian aristocracy. This house has the small, wrought-iron second-

story balconies introduced by Bulfinch and Benjamin. It is the only house on the street with a main entrance at the side, facing a small lawn. The arched Georgian doorway with Corinthian portico is beautiful, and the entire house has a princely, brooding air suggestive of 'Hamlet,' Booth's most famous rôle.

17. The *Home of Julia Ward Howe* and later of *John Singer Sargent* (*private*), 13 Chestnut St., is attributed to Bulfinch. It is a four-story brick structure, with a delicate-columned Georgian doorway, ivory-color, and second-story long windows with wrought-iron balconies. Such windows indicate a second-story drawing room, a hallmark of fashion in Boston. For many years this house was the meeting-place of the Radical Club that succeeded the noted Transcendental Club.

L. from Chestnut St. on Walnut St.

18. The *Ellery Sedgwick House* (*private*), 14 Walnut St., the home of the recently retired editor of the *Atlantic Monthly*, built in 1805, is the most individualistic house on the Hill. It has three stories and gray-painted brick ends, with black blinds, the south side wall being of wood painted gray. On that side is a large tree-shaded garden, which, owing to the slope of the Hill, is elevated high above the street and buttressed by a base-wall of hand-hewn granite blocks.

R. from Walnut St. on Mt. Vernon St.

19. *Thomas Bailey Aldrich's House* (*private*), 59 Mt. Vernon St., is distinguished by its white marble portico and a white marble band between the second and third stories.

20. The *Home of Charles Francis Adams, Sr.* (*private*), 57 Mt. Vernon St., is of a conservative elegance to be expected of the Civil War Ambassador to England, son of John Quincy Adams, and father of the author of 'The Education of Henry Adams.' Its four substantial stories face a trim lawn. The white doorway has an unusual richly carved lintel. There are tall second-story windows, the one over the door distinguished by a covered balcony.

Retrace Mt. Vernon St.

21. The *Sears House* (*Second Harrison Gray Otis House*, 1800) (*private*), 85 Mt. Vernon St., is a good example of Bulfinch's domestic design, somewhat resembling his notable group on Franklin Crescent. The square house with roof balustrade is excellently proportioned and has the typical Bulfinch arched recesses surrounding the lower windows. The upper stories are enlivened by four Corinthian pilasters. Although somewhat altered, the architecture of this dignified Federal mansion remains impressive.

R. from Mt. Vernon St. into Louisburg Square.

22. *Louisburg Square*, looking much like some square in London's Mayfair, is the epitome of Beacon Hill style. Noted residents have included William Dean Howells, Louisa May Alcott and her father, Amos Bronson Alcott, Jenny Lind, and Minnie Maddern Fiske. The houses, inhabited by

elderly and ultra-conservative families, are large three- or four-story brick dwellings, mostly with bow-fronts and plain doorways, the whole in synchronous monotone. The central green, enclosed by an iron fence with no gate, belongs to the proprietors of the Square. The small statue of Aristides the Just, at the south end, and that of Columbus at the north, have been adopted affectionately by the residents through many years of custom, but when their donor, Joseph Iasigi, a wealthy Greek living at No. 3, included also a fountain, it was hastily removed.

At Christmas each year the Square echoes with Christmas carols, sung by trained voices usually selected from musical groups with sufficient social prestige to be asked to contribute carolers. Bellringing and the keeping of open house are additional features of the program.

R. from Louisburg Square on Pinckney St.

Pinckney St. was named for South Carolina's Charles Cotesworth Pinckney, famous for his reply to Talleyrand: 'Millions for defense, but not one cent for tribute.' The street is the border-line between wealth and poverty and beyond it a less proud district slopes down the back of the Hill.

L. from Pinckney St. on Joy St.; R. from Joy St. on Cambridge St.

23. The *Harrison Gray Otis House* (*open*, 10–5, *fee* 25¢), 141 Cambridge St., built in 1795, has been since 1916 the headquarters of the Society for the Preservation of New England Antiquities. The interior has not been greatly altered, and the Society has restored the exterior to its former beauty by replacing on the façade the semi-circular porch, Palladian window, and third-story fan window that are the main decorative features. This square hip-roofed mansion has an interior finished with unusual refinement and delicacy. It is attributed to Bulfinch.

24. The *Old West Church* (West End Church) was built in 1806 from designs by Asher Benjamin, architect-writer. Characteristic of his work, it is of well-studied proportions, but more solid and masculine than the work of his contemporaries, Bulfinch and McIntire. Its façade, with stepped gable and lofty tower, is capped by a square gilt-domed cupola. The church has for some time been converted to the uses of a branch library.

Retrace Cambridge St.; L. from Cambridge St. on Joy St.; R. from Joy St. on Beacon St.

25. The *Women's City Club* (*open by permission*), 40 Beacon St., although built in 1818, is believed to be a Bulfinch work. Today, beautifully preserved, it exemplifies the gracious tradition of Post-Colonial architecture. Its beautiful spiral stairway is as fine as any in New England.

26. The *Wadsworth House* (*Third Harrison Gray Otis House*) (*private*), 45 Beacon St., built in 1807, reveals the influence of Bulfinch's sojourn in France by his use of an oval drawing-room on the garden side and perhaps also by his placing the entrance at ground level and the important

rooms on the story above. The façade shows a uniform range of five windows, with a novel departure from Colonial precedent in the type of enframement. The entrance, too, is unusually handled, a rectangular portico with four columns — coupled columns and coupled pilasters behind — being used as the door enframement. The house is a fine example of an aristocratic city mansion of the Federal period.

Retrace Beacon St.

27. The *Robert Gould Shaw Memorial*, facing the State House from the edge of the Common, is a notable group statue in high relief, by Augustus Saint-Gaudens. Colonel Shaw, his horse, and the Negro troopers are all sculptured with remarkable sensitivity to the medium and the subject. Charles F. McKim designed the frame, a wide pink granite exedra with crouching eagles, Greek urns, and low benches, shadowed by two enormous English elms.

28. The *State House* (*open weekdays 9–5*), with its golden dome, crowns the Hill. Built in 1795, the 'Bulfinch Front' of the State House stands as a monument to the architectural genius of Charles Bulfinch and as an expression of classicism in American design. Unhappily, this original portion of the present State House is now sandwiched between huge, inept wings. The 'Bulfinch Front' cannot be seen merely as a unit of the structure; its quality sets it apart as a thing to be known and revered independent of its setting. Bulfinch was the first professional architect of the Republic. The State House was his greatest work. He spread across its front a colossal portico; he completed it with a high and dominating dome. The Corinthian colonnade that surmounts the projecting arcade of the first story, the arched windows with classical enframement, the pediment that breaks the line of the dome, the sweep and lift of the dome itself, contribute to the classicism vibrant in Bulfinch's work, strongly influenced at this period by that of Sir William Chambers, an older London contemporary.

Doric Hall contains portraits of some of the Massachusetts Governors. Just beyond is a more imposing white marble hall with historical murals. The *Hall of Flags* opening from this displays State regimental flags of the Civil, Spanish-American, and World Wars. The dome bears the seals of the Thirteen Original States. In the *House of Representatives* (third floor rear, left) hangs the Sacred Cod, the State emblem symbolizing a historic basic industry.

At the front of the lower floor, a left turn down a passage leads to a unique memorial very characteristic of Boston, always appreciative of its 'dumb animal' friends, the *Dog and Horse Tablet* (in the through corridor from the Hooker Statue to Mt. Vernon St.), a tribute to the dogs and horses that served in the World War.

Traverse the corridor from Beacon St. to Mt. Vernon St., passing into the greensward square behind the State House. Straight ahead on Ashburton Place.

29. *Ford Hall*, which houses the Ford Hall Forum, 15 Ashburton Place, in a tall office building, is a modern stronghold of Boston liberalism, entrenched in the very shadow of the State House.

FOOT TOUR 2 (*The Old City*) — 2 *m.*

E. from Park St. on Beacon St.

30. The *Boston Athenæum* (*open to scholars by guest card obtained at the desk*), is at 10½ Beacon St. The building (1847–49) was designed by Edward C. Cabot — a minor Renaissance gesture in the Palladian style that seemed significant then. The Athenæum, which contains one of the most famous private libraries in the country, is a descendant of the 'Anthology Club' formed in 1807 by the father of Ralph Waldo Emerson. Among its 200,000 volumes are rare collections of news on international law, of State papers and historical documents, of books published in the South during the Civil War, and most of George Washington's private library.

Retrace Beacon St.; L. from Beacon St. on Park St.

31. The *Park Street Church* (Congregational), corner Tremont St., was built in 1809 and was the only building designed by Peter Banner. It bears little evidence of the Classic Revival felt in contemporaneous work; it maintains closely the character of earlier work. An unusual feature is the use of the semi-circular porches between the tower base and the body of the main building. The tower proper is probably as fine as any extant. The church originally housed a Trinitarian congregation formed in protest to the spreading Unitarian movement. It stands on the site of the Granary where the sails of the 'Constitution' were made. This site is known as 'Brimstone Corner,' because in the War of 1812 gunpowder was stored in the basement. When Henry Ward Beecher, a believer in a literal Hell, preached vigorous guest sermons there, the Unitarians slyly said that the corner was well named.

L. from Park St. on Tremont St.

32. The *Old Granary Burial Ground* (*open*), hemmed in by business blocks and Tremont St., contains the graves of three signers of the Declaration of Independence (John Hancock, Samuel Adams, and Robert Treat Paine), Paul Revere, Peter Faneuil, the parents of Benjamin Franklin, the victims of the Boston Massacre, nine early Governors of the State, and Mother Goose (a real person actually named Mary Goose).

33. *Tremont Temple* (Baptist), 82 Tremont St., stands on the site of an earlier temple in which Jenny Lind sang (1850–52). Founded in 1839 because the Charles Street Church, then Baptist, decreed that any member bringing a Negro into his pew would be expelled, it is one of the most popular evangelical congregations in Greater Boston.

34. *King's Chapel* (Unitarian) (*open daily* 9–5), corner of School St., built in 1749, was designed by Peter Harrison, who had been a student of Sir John Vanbrugh, a younger contemporary of Sir Christopher Wren. It was from this intimacy with the mode set by Wren and his successor, Gibbs, that the architecture of King's Chapel is derived. But the Newport gentleman-architect possessed too much native genius for his design to be a servile copy of the British masters. The bold and somewhat cold masonry exterior is headed by a low, squat base intended to support a tower which was never built. The interior, replete with aberrations characteristic of its designer, is perhaps the finest Colonial church interior extant. Its rich sobriety, its repose and studied suavity of proportion proclaim it a work of genius. It ranks in historic fame with the Old South Meeting House and the Old North Church, for King's Chapel is both the first Episcopal church in New England and the first Unitarian church in America; and its establishment in both faiths was accompanied by storm. The present building was built in 1754 around a wooden building which was then dismantled.

35. *King's Chapel Burial Ground* (1630), adjoining the church, is the oldest burial ground in Boston. Here lie Governor Winthrop, John Cotton, and Mary Chilton Winslow.

Retrace Tremont St.; L. from Tremont St. on School St.

36. The *Boston Public Latin School Tablet* on the wall of the *Parker House* marks the site of the first Public Latin School (1635) in America.

37. The *Old Corner Bookstore Building* (1712), at the corner of School and Washington Sts., is an ancient three-and-a-half-story brick building with gambrel roof. From 1828 to 1903, it housed the most famous bookstore in Boston, and at one time the offices of Ticknor and Fields, who published the early works of all major New England poets. Through its doors strolled Hawthorne, Emerson, Longfellow, Lowell, and Holmes, as well as Whittier, the latter rarely, for he was shy and confused by the roar of nineteenth-century traffic.

R. from School St. on Washington St.

38. The *Old South Meeting House* (1729) (*open daily, summer* 9–5, *winter* 9–4; *adm.* 25¢), corner of Milk St., shared with Faneuil Hall the most fervid and momentous oratory of Revolutionary days, and an Old South meeting was always a danger signal to Burke and Pitt. It is still used for public meetings of civic or social protest. The church building, designed by Robert Twelve, has a simple mass with severely plain exterior of brick laid in Flemish bond. The wooden steeple rising 180 feet is of conventional design, more impressive than that of its predecessor, the 'Old North Church.' Its double row of .arched windows is especially effective in the interior, where interest centers in the great arched recess above the altar. The Old South greatly influenced later ecclesiastical design in the Colonies.

The interior with its gate-pews was restored after the British had used it for a riding-school during the Siege; in 1876 the pews were again removed when the building ceased to be used as a church. The only remaining parts of the original building are the walls and their framework, including the windows and doors, and the double tier of white galleries, in the topmost of which sat Negro slaves. The high broad white pulpit is a replica of the one which resounded to the voices of Otis, Samuel Adams, Quincy, Warren, and Hancock. Here began the line of march of the Boston Tea Party, and here General Warren, prevented by the British from entering the pulpit by the stairs, climbed into it through the window at the rear. The beautiful gilded *Gallery Clock*, surmounted by a spread eagle bearing in his beak a double string of gilded balls, is a reproduction of a famous pattern designed by Simon Willard, a Boston clockmaker (1753-1848). The women of Massachusetts purchased and thus saved this noted landmark from destruction in 1876, when it was proposed to sell it, because of the great increase in value of the land. The parish, formed in 1669 (Congregational), worships at the 'Old South Third' in Copley Square.

L. from Washington St. on Milk St.; L. from Milk St. on Congress St.

39. The *United States Post Office* and *Federal Office Building* is a massive new granite building in modern style designed by Cram and Ferguson. It occupies the entire block between Devonshire, Congress, Water, and Milk Sts. A tablet on the Milk St. frontage of the former Post-Office block commemorates the fact that the great Boston fire of 1872, that raged November 9-10, sweeping 60 acres and destroying $60,000,000 worth of property, was halted here.

L. from Congress St. on State St.

40. The *Site of the Boston Massacre*, 30 State St., is marked by a brass arrow pointing into the street where a cobblestone circle indicates the exact spot where the first patriots fell when fired upon by British soldiers.

41. The *Old State House* (*open daily except Sun. and Holidays*, 9-4.30; *Sat.* 9-1), Washington and State Sts., built in 1713 on the site of its predecessor, has been restored to its original robust appearance after successive alterations. Its steeply pitched roof with stepped gables at either end, its tower with gracefully telescoped members finished by a fine cupola rising from the middle of the building, are enhanced by the aloof position of the building. Upon the stepped gables, strangely enough Dutch in derivation, ramp the British lion and unicorn. Classic details in doors, windows, and cupola are a new note in this period. The famous building, the identity of whose architect is a mystery, is markedly important as an influence upon the architecture of its time.

This was the State House of the British in the eighteenth century, until the Revolution, and thereafter of the Commonwealth until the new State House was ready in 1798. In 1881, it was proposed to demolish the Old State House, because the land was valued at $1,500,000. At this juncture, Chicago offered to transfer the building to Lincoln Park on Lake Michigan and take care of it, paying all the expense of removal and reassembly. The offer stung Boston so sharply that the City Fathers agreed to stand the loss on the land in perpetuity, and never again to threaten the building with removal or destruction.

Within, the spiral stairway is the best architectural feature, but is not coeval with the original structure. The building is the headquarters of the Bostonian Society and houses intimate historical relics and a fine marine museum.

Straight ahead from State St. on Court St.

42. The *Ames Building*, corner of Washington St., Boston's first sky-scraper, 13 stories high, was erected in 1891 from plans made by Shepley, Rutan and Coolidge, successors of Richardson. It is among the rare instances of skillful adaptation of the Richardson Romanesque to commercial purposes.

43. The *Site of the Franklin Printing Press* is marked by a tablet on the Franklin Ave. frontage of the building at No. 17 Court St. Here Benjamin Franklin learned the printer's trade from his brother and composed ballads that he later disparaged.

Retrace Court St.; L. from Court St. on Washington St.

44. The *Site of Paul Revere's Goldsmith Shop*, 175 Washington St., is marked by a bas-relief tablet. The patriot who rode to Lexington to give his memorable alarm was a great artist in gold and silverware. Any of his work now commands fabulous prices. Examples are at the Museum of Fine Arts (*see below*).

R. from Washington St. into Dock Square.

45. *Dock Square*, so named because the docks of the present Atlantic Ave. waterfront once extended here, is now the market district of Boston. From earliest dawn till dusk it is in constant turmoil, with huge vans unloading whole carcasses of meats, and crates of fruits and vegetables piled over the sidewalks. The predominant human type is the market-man, in soiled apron and inevitable straw hat, but many a humble shopper is also here, bargain-hunting.

46. *Faneuil* (Fan'l) *Hall* (*open daily 9–5, Sat. 9–12, closed Sun.*) was called the 'Cradle of Liberty' because many important meetings of protest were held here before the Revolution. It was the first Colonial attempt at academic design, completed in 1742 from the plans of John Smibert, the Colonial portrait-painter, and given by Peter Faneuil, a Boston merchant. It contained a town hall above and a public market below. The original structure, two stories and a half of brick, with open arches below and a bell-tower above, was considered impressive and ornate. When fire destroyed the building in 1762, it was promptly rebuilt on the original plan. In 1805, Charles Bulfinch added a third story and doubled the original 40-foot width, but retained the original style of the building. Its weathervane, a grasshopper, is the most noted steeple adornment in Boston, modeled by Shem Drowne of Hawthorne's story, 'Drowne's Wooden Image.' The leading Faneuil historian says that

Drowne chose a grasshopper because while chasing one as a small boy he met the man who started him on the road to success. An American consul once tested those claiming Boston citizenship by asking them what is on top of Faneuil Hall. Its chief present treasure is G. P. A. Healy's gigantic painting of 'Webster's Reply to Hayne.'

Faneuil Hall is protected by a charter against sale or leasing. It is never rented, but is open to any group upon request of a required number of citizens agreeing to abide by certain prescribed regulations. The lower floor is occupied by market stalls handling all sorts of produce, a busy and fascinating spectacle.

Two flights upstairs from the hall are the rooms (*open weekdays* 10–4, *Sat.* 10–12) of the *Ancient and Honourable Artillery Company*, oldest military organization in America (1638), which still parades in Boston on important occasions, dressed in elaborate historical uniforms.

47. *Quincy Market* (*open*), adjacent to Faneuil Hall and sometimes called New Faneuil Hall, is architecturally a product of the Greek Revival, designed in 1826 by Alexander Parris.

L. from Dock Square on Union St.

48. The *Union Oyster House*, 41 Union St., Boston's renowned sea-food restaurant, has been situated for the past 110 years in this low, angular three-story brick tavern with the small-paned windows, all of 200 years old. The lower floor contains very old semi-private eating-booths, and a small bar at which Daniel Webster used to drop in for a toddy on cold days. Several other excellent restaurants in the vicinity are located in less historic buildings.

R. from Union St. on Marshall St.

49. The *Boston Stone* is embedded in the back wall of the last building on the right, just around the corner of the side alley. It is a granite block (1737), surmounted by a spherical granite paint-grinder about the size and shape of a cannon ball. The block and the ball constituted a hand paint mill for Thomas Child from 1693 to 1706. The stone was later used as the starting-point for the measurement of mileages from Boston.

R. from Marshall St. on Hanover St.

Hanover St., now the main thoroughfare of the Italian North End, was once favored by wealthy sea captains and leading patriots of the Revolution. The finest houses are gone, but here and there are old wooden dwellings, flush with the street between cheap modern brick tenements, Italian food stores, and clothing shops. The North End is one of the most congested sections in any major American city.

R. from Hanover St. on Prince St.; R. from Prince St. into North Square.

50. *Paul Revere's House* (*open daily* 10–4, *adm.* 25¢), 19 North Square, which was a century old when it became the home of the famous patriot

and silversmith, is the only 17th-century structure now standing in downtown Boston. Claimed by some to have been built in 1660, there is more proof that it stands on the plot once occupied by the Increase Mather Parsonage that burned in the great fire of 1676, so it is likely that it was built within the next year. During its long life it has undergone many changes, but in 1908 it was rescued from the encroachments of progress by the Paul Revere Memorial Association and restored to its original condition. Characteristic of the medieval influence which dominated all seventeenth-century architecture in Massachusetts, it has the overhanging second story with ornamental drops or pendrils, the small casements with diamond-shaped panes, and a simple floor plan with massive end chimney.

The house has only four rooms and an attic, and contains some beautiful old furniture and china (not much of it Revere's); two enormous fireplaces with brick ovens and ancient utensils; portions of wallpaper of 1750, depicting in block pattern the Church of Saint Mary le Bow in London; and some of Revere's etchings and manuscript letters.

Retrace North Square; L. from North Square on Prince St.; R. from Prince St. on Salem St.

Salem Street, narrow at best, is so crowded with pushcarts laden with fruits and vegetables that locomotion is difficult. Here is the heart of the Italian quarter, noisy, garrulous, good-natured, and vital.

51. The *Old North Church* (Christ Church, Episcopal) (*open daily 9–5; voluntary contributions; Sun. services* 10.45), 193 Salem St., had a belfry known to every American child by Longfellow's lines: 'One if by land and two if by sea, and I on the opposite shore will be.' The eight melodious bells in the tower are inscribed: 'We are the first ring of bells cast for the British Empire in North America.'

The church was built in 1723. The design of this historic building was made by William Price, a Boston print-seller and draftsman who, while in London, made a study of Christopher Wren churches. During a violent gale in 1804 the steeple was blown down, and in 1808 a new one, built after a model by Charles Bulfinch, replaced the old. Although following closely the design of the original, the new tower was lowered in height by 16 feet. The interior, although obviously the product of an untrained man, is modeled after the designs by Wren. The galleries are supported by square columns carried through to the roof. The pews carry small brass plates inscribed with the names of eighteenth-century merchant-prince owners. Some are still held by descendants; others have become prized possessions of old Boston families.

FOOT TOUR 3 (*Waterfront*) — 1.5 *m.*

S. from Salem St. on Charter St.; L. from Charter St. on Hanover St.; R. from Hanover St. on Commercial St.

This tour covers the old waterfront, once the port for all ships, now devoted to coastwise shipping and fishing boats. Vessels from European ports now dock in East or South Boston.

52. *Constitution Wharf*, 409 Commercial St., at the foot of Hanover St., is occupied chiefly by a high brick warehouse which cuts off the harbor view. A bas-relief tablet on the Commercial St. wall commemorates the launching (1797) of the famous U.S. Frigate 'Constitution' ('Old Ironsides') the Queen of the Navy, which made history in the War with Tripoli and the War of 1812.

Straight ahead on Atlantic Ave., Commercial St. having slipped unobtrusively off to the right, after the manner of Boston streets.

Just beyond Lewis's Wharf, 32 Atlantic Ave., is the first delightful glimpse of the actual waterfront, with freighters using the same slips as the humble power-boats of small fishermen. Along the quays are marine hardware shops and numerous lunchrooms for sailors. On the hottest summer day, the air has a cool salty tang, becoming definitely fishy as one passes the brief row of fish-markets.

53. *T Wharf*, 178 Atlantic Ave., is one of the most famous and picturesque fishing piers in the country. The entrance, obscure and poorly marked, is just beyond the huge brick warehouse of the Quincy Cold Storage Plant. Suddenly the gaudy small trawlers of Italian and Portuguese fishermen appear, outlined against the long, low yellow shed of the pier — a shed with many small-paned windows, which give upon fish-brokerages and small restaurants specializing in New England fish dinners.

This is the center of the 'Little man's fishing industry,' for the larger boats go to the modern great Fish Pier at South Boston. Knots of Latin fishermen are always gathered here mending nets, repairing buoys, or baiting lines, and animatedly discussing the weather, the catch, and current prices.

54. *Long Wharf* (1710), 202 Atlantic Ave., was once a great deal longer, beginning in fact up by the present Custom House which now soars in the background. From here a century and a half ago the British embarked for home (March 17, 1776), and from here today hundreds of summer tourists embark daily for Provincetown. In the late eighteenth century, the wharf, then privately owned, was a center for fashionable smugglers, said to have included Governor Hancock.

R. from Atlantic Ave. on State St.

55. The *United States Custom House* (*open* 9–5 *daily*), (1847) designed

by Ammi B. Young and Isaiah Rogers, was among the last monuments of the Greek Revival. A dome with which it was originally crowned is concealed within the tall shaft of floors which in 1915 transformed the building into a 500-foot skyscraper and a fitting mausoleum to the era of Greek affectation. The tower shows a similarity to that of the Metropolitan Building in New York, although on a much smaller scale. Peabody and Stearns were the architects of the super-structure. A balcony near the top offers a splendid panorama of Boston.

Retrace State St.; R. from State St. on Atlantic Ave.

56. *India Wharf,* which begins at 288 Atlantic Ave. and continues for four piers, now serves the Eastern Steamship Lines. The ancient lofts of the two middle piers were once occupied by riggers and sail makers.

57. *Rowe's Wharf,* 344 Atlantic Ave., a small but busy railroad terminal, was the scene of the seizure and deposition of Governor Andros (1689). The Nantasket steamer, which sails from here and offers a good view of the harbor islands, is a Boston institution.

58. The *Boston Tea Party* (Dec. 16, 1773) took place at the northeast corner of Atlantic Ave. and Pearl St., then *Griffin's Wharf,* when a group of patriots disguised as Indians boarded British tea-ships and threw the cargo overboard. A tablet on the Atlantic Ave. wall of the commercial building now occupying the site gives the Boston version of the party.

FOOT TOUR 4 *(Downtown)* — 2.5 *m.*

N.E. from Atlantic Ave., at South Station, on Federal St.

59. The *Shoe Museum* of the United Shoe Machinery Corporation *(open weekdays 9–5),* 140 Federal St., exhibits 1500 pairs of shoes of all periods, styles, and countries; Egyptian sandals dating back to 2000 B.C.; boots worn by Henry IV of France; postilion boots weighing 12 pounds each; Spanish shoes made especially to protect against snakebite. Pictures and models illustrate the many stages and varied machinery involved today in making a single pair of shoes.

Retrace on Federal St.; R. from Federal St. on High St.; R. from High St. on Summer St.; straight ahead from Summer St. into Winter St.; L. from Winter St. on Tremont St.

60. *Saint Paul's Cathedral* (1819–20), opposite the Common, the seat of the Episcopal Bishops of Massachusetts, is Boston's earliest example of the Greek Revival. The architects were Alexander Parris, who later built the Quincy Market, and Solomon Willard. The Ionic capitals were carved by Willard. The white interior is severely plain, with high stall-like pews and no stained glass. Daniel Webster, a pewholder, was on the building committee. The dome of the present chancel is a reproduction of that in Saint Paul's, London.

61. *Boston Common*, part of a tract set aside by Governor Winthrop as a cow pasture and training field, retains as paved walks the casual paths worn by grazing cattle. Here stocks and pillory once stood, as well as a pen where those who desecrated the Sabbath were imprisoned. Several Quakers are thought to have been hanged and buried on the Common. Both British and Massachusetts regiments were mustered on it, and it is still used on occasion as a drill ground.

Free speech has always been a privilege on the Common. Group arguments on social and economic problems are in daily progress around the Grecian *Parkman Bandstand* and orators address the public along the *Charles Street Mall*. The *Frog Pond* in the center is now a shallow artificial pool patronized during hot weather by little boys in various stages of undress.

62. The *Crispus Attucks Monument* (set back on lawn) commemorates the 'Boston Massacre' (1770), which John Adams and Daniel Webster united in calling the origin of the Revolution. Crispus Attucks, a Negro, was one of several persons killed when soldiers, taunted by a group of excited citizens, fired on the crowd.

L. from Tremont St. into Boylston St.

63. The *Liberty Tree Site*, facing Boylston St. on Washington St., is covered by a business block, bearing on its wall a carved tree commemorating this Revolutionary landmark, scene of Stamp Act meetings and frequent hangings in effigy of well-known Tories.

L. from Boylston St., diagonally across Washington St. into Essex St.; R. from Essex St. on Harrison Ave.; L. from Harrison Ave. on Beach St.

64. *Chinatown* begins at Harrison Ave. and Beach St. with a group of small native shops, principally markets, the latter displaying in their windows strings of strange-looking sausages and small wire hanging baskets of ancient eggs. At the corner of Oxford St. (L) is the *Chinese Bulletin*, a news sheet in native characters, posted daily.

R. from Beach St. on Hudson St.

Near-by is a district crowded with Chinese restaurants and Oriental curio shops.

R. from Hudson St. on Kneeland St.

Kneeland Street is the center of the ready-made dress business of New England. Wholesale houses and workshops crowd the district, and on warm days the hum of hundreds of sewing machines can be heard through the open windows.

Straight ahead on Stuart St.; L. from Stuart St. on Tremont St.

65. The *Wilbur Theatre*, built in 1913 from plans by Blackall, Clapp and Whittemore, is an adaptation of late Georgian Colonial architecture. It is one of the first auditoriums to be designed with scientific knowledge of acoustics, Professor Sabine of Harvard, pioneer in the field, being the consultant.

Retrace Tremont St.; L. from Tremont St. on Stuart St.; straight ahead into Eliot St.; R. from Eliot St. through Park Sq.; L. from Park Sq. on Boylston St.

66. *Statues along Boylston Street Mall* are: (1) *Wendell Phillips*, 'Champion of the Slave' (1811–84), done in bronze by Daniel Chester French; (2) Theo Alice Ruggles Kitson's handsome young *Thaddeus Kosciuszko* (1746–1817), the popular Polish patriot who served under Washington; (3) *Charles Sumner*, one of the leading abolitionist senators, by Thomas Ball.

67. *Boylston Street Subway* (1897), its streetcar entrance opposite the Sumner statue, was the first transportation subway in the United States.

68. The *William Ellery Channing Statue*, by Herbert Adams, corner of Boylston and Arlington Sts., is a tribute to a leader (1780–1842) of the Unitarian movement in America.

69. The *Natural History Museum* (*open weekdays* 9–4.30; *Sun.* 1–4.30), corner of Berkeley St., a Palladian structure of brick and brownstone, houses collections of minerals and fauna of New England.

FOOT TOUR 5 (*Fenway District*) — 2.5 m.

E. from Massachusetts Ave. on Huntington Ave.

70. The *Christian Science Church* (*open Wed. and Fri.* 10–5; *services Sun. morning and evening and Wed. evening*) is The Mother Church. Christian Science was discovered in 1866 by Mary Baker Eddy, who developed the theme into a Christian Science textbook, 'Science and Health with Key to the Scriptures,' and published it in 1875. In 1879, she organized the Church of Christ, Scientist, and reorganized it in 1892. The present organization, including all its branches and activities, is the direct outgrowth of her work. The Publishing House across the street issues *The Christian Science Monitor*, widely read throughout the English-speaking world. A large terraced grass plot on Huntington Avenue, adorned with shrubs and small trees, allows the buildings to be seen in perspective.

Two church structures in actual contact with each other are connected by an interior passage. The smaller one of gray rough-faced granite with a square granite tower, erected in 1894, is the first Christian Science church building in Boston, though its congregation dates from 1879. The main church (1904), in Italian Renaissance with a great central dome, is of limestone, trimmed with granite below and with glazed white tiles above. Its vast open nave, seating 5000 people, rises 108 feet from floor to dome, with no support of pillars. The doors and pews are of San Domingo mahogany, richly carved; the walls of limestone, with windows of clear glass. The wide pulpit contains two lecterns, one for the First Reader, a man, and one for the Second Reader, a woman.

The *Publishing House* (*open daily*, 9–11.30 *and* 1–4, *guide service*) occupies a three-story limestone building, covering a city block and surmounted by six additional stories in a recessed tower, capped by yellow tiles.

Beyond the white marble entrance hall is the *Mapparium*, unique in the world, a spherical room, thirty feet in diameter, with walls of colored glass depicting a world map. Passage through the room is by a glass bridge.

Throughout the building marble corridors lead from room to room opulently paneled in rare woods, beautifully tiled or carpeted, hung with Venetian blinds and tapestries. Even in the halls of the presses is spotlessness, quiet, and order.

Retrace on Huntington Ave. across Massachusetts Ave.

71. *Symphony Hall*, northwest corner of Massachusetts Ave., a low, oblong, red-brick building trimmed with granite, is a subdued adaptation of Renaissance forms designed by McKim, Mead and White (1900) and admirably suited to its specific function. The concert hall, with two balconies, seats 2500 persons. In a side room is the *Casadesus Collection of Ancient Musical Instruments* (*open during concert hours*). The Boston Symphony Orchestra, founded in 1881, by Major Henry Lee Higginson, is recognized as one of the finest in the country. In early summer a reduced orchestra gives a ten-week season of popular concerts, affectionately known to all Boston as 'the Pops.' For this series Symphony Hall assumes a gala appearance with gay lattices adorning the stately walls and the floor occupied by small square tables at which refreshments are served.

72. The *New England Conservatory of Music*, at the corner of Gainsborough St., occupies a three-story, square, flat-roofed building of gray brick, trimmed with granite and marble. It is one of the oldest institutions (1867) of its kind in America, as well as one of the best, offering co-educational instruction in instrumental and vocal music, in composition and teaching. It has a distinguished faculty, and many of its 140,000 graduates have attained eminence.

Within the building, reached from the Gainsborough St. entrance, is *Jordan Hall*, the leading recital hall in Boston, with perfect acoustics and a seating capacity of 1000.

73. *Northeastern University* (incorporated 1916), 316 Huntington Ave., is a co-operative educational institution with a total enrollment (1937) of 5293. The student is enabled to combine classroom instruction with supervised employment, effectively uniting theory and practice. Among its professional branches the divisions of law and engineering are well known.

74. The *Boston Opera House* (1906), corner of Opera Place, is a massive brick building of somber Neo-Classic design. The front wall is plastered with billboards advertising downtown theatrical attractions, except during brief visiting engagements of operatic companies. On November 8,

1909, this building was the scene of the brilliant début of the new Boston Opera Company, founded and maintained at a heavy loss for three years by Eben D. Jordan, a Boston merchant.

75. The *Museum of Fine Arts* (*open daily except Mon.*, 9–5, *winter* 9–4, *Sun.*, 1–5; *closed Thanksgiving, Christmas,* 4*th of July*) occupies several buildings. These, grouped by halls and loggias, are of granite, admirably situated in a broad quadrangle on the open, sunny lawns of the Fenway. The not-too-well-designed Neo-Classic buildings derive their impress from the massiveness of the group. Directly in front of the entrance is the 'Appeal to the Great Spirit,' Cyrus Dallin's renowned American Indian on ponyback, his face lifted skyward, both arms outstretched in supplication.

The largest showings of individual painters are of Millet, Copley, and Stuart. The American Colonial silver is very fine, and includes many examples of the work of Paul Revere. Equally memorable are the Colonial interiors, consisting of entire rooms transferred from New England houses, together with their original period furniture. Notable among these in the American Wing are three complete rooms designed and executed by Samuel McIntire from his 'Oak Hill' in Peabody.

The Dancing Bacchante, a copy of a statue by Frederick MacMonnies, in the central courtyard, has a piquant past. A nude figure of a young dancer, holding aloft in one arm an infant whom she tantalizes with a bunch of grapes held high in the other hand, the original statue was placed in the courtyard of the Public Library in 1895, where it roused a storm of protest still clearly remembered by middle-aged citizens. Morals, especially the morals of youth, were regarded as imperiled and a suggestion was made in all seriousness that the sculptor be asked to clothe the figure. The original young lady is now in the Metropolitan Museum of Art, New York.

76. *Wentworth Institute* (*open Sept.–May,* 9–4, *except Sat. and Sun.; in summer to shops and laboratories not in use*), corner of Ruggles St., trains young men in the mechanical arts. It occupies a wide, four-story yellow-brick building trimmed with granite, set well back on a spacious lawn.

R. from Huntington Ave. on Longwood Ave.

77. The *Massachusetts College of Pharmacy*, corner of Worthington St., was instituted in 1823, as an association of Boston pharmacists who fostered the training of apprentices in apothecary shops.

78. The *Angell Memorial* (*animal*) *Hospital* (*open* 9–9 *daily; Sunday and holidays for emergency only*), named for George T. Angell, founder and first president of the Massachusetts Society for the Prevention of Cruelty to Animals and editor of *Our Dumb Animals*, occupies a handsome three-story brick and granite building at 180 Longwood Ave., opposite the Massachusetts College of Pharmacy.

79. The *Harvard Medical School* (1903–06), built entirely of white Ver-

mont marble, from designs by Shepley, Rutan and Coolidge, is of simple classic design adapted from the Greek and made impressive by its formal setting upon a terrace.

The *Four Laboratory Buildings*, set upon a lower level than the Administration Building, are symmetrical in design. The *Administration Building*, approached by broad steps leading up from the terrace to a gigantic Ionic portico is monumental in character. On its ground floor is a great hall of design conforming to the classic exterior, and a marble staircase rises on the axis of the building.

R. from Longwood Ave. on Avenue Louis Pasteur.

80. The *Boston Public Latin School* (1635) now occupies a three-story brick building, three blocks deep, with granite Corinthian columns. It is the oldest public Latin school still in existence.

L. from Avenue Louis Pasteur on Fenway.

81. *Emmanuel College*, 400 Fenway, a massive four-story brick and granite edifice in English Collegiate Gothic, with a broad, square, open bell-tower and wide lawns adorned with shrubbery, is a non-resident Catholic institution for women, directed by the Sisters of Notre Dame de Namur.

Retrace on Fenway.

82. *Simmons College* (for women), 300 Fenway, occupies a wide three-story yellow-brick building dating from 1902. It was the first college for women in the United States to recognize the desirability of giving students such instruction as would fit them to earn an independent livelihood. It offers courses in science, household economics, literary and secretarial work, and is affiliated with schools of physical education and store service. It has more than 1600 students.

83. The *Isabella Stewart Gardner Museum* ('Mrs. Jack Gardner's Venetian Palace') (*open Tues., Thurs., Sat.* 10–4, *adm.* 25¢; *Sun.* 1–4, *free, closed in August*), at junction of Fenway and Worthington St., built in 1902, is a composite of fragments and materials from Venice and other parts of Italy. Although Edward H. Sears, an architect, drew the plans, the edifice is obviously the work of a collector indulging an unbridled fancy. The Museum houses works of Raphael, Titian, Rembrandt, Cellini, and many other old masters. Chamber-music concerts are given in the romantic setting of the *Tapestry Room* (*Tues., Thurs., Sat. at* 2.45, *Sun. at* 2, *no extra fee*).

Mrs. John Lowell Gardner, known to Boston during her lifetime as 'Mrs. Jack Gardner,' was the most picturesque figure in the social, art, and music world of Boston in the Mauve Decade. The daughter of a wealthy New York merchant with an artistic and musical flair, she was witty and independent, flaunting social tradition, and gathering about herself a salon of artists and musicians. Her shrewd acceptance of drawbacks in her personal appearance, and her capitalization of her good points, is somewhat cryptically embodied in the small portrait of her by Zorn, representing her as flinging open her palace doors, her face a mysterious vague blur without features, but her shapely arms and hands very prominent, even reflected in the doors.

Straight ahead from the front of Gardner Museum.

84. The Back Bay Fens, commonly called *The Fenway*, are reclaimed mud flats. This stretch of charming parkway, following the beautified meanderings of a sluggish brook far from lovely in itself, gives a rustic touch to the surrounding residential district and the art and educational institutions. The Fens, with their bridle paths and motor roads, begin a long strip of parkway winding through Brookline and Roxbury.

On the right is the *Museum of Fine Arts* (north front), and just beyond, the marble walls of the *Forsyth Dental Infirmary for Children*.

85. The *Boston Medical Library* (*open Mon. and Wed.* 9.30–10; *Tues., Thurs., Fri.* 9.30–6; *Sat.* 9.30–5), 8 Fenway, is a modern three-story yellow-brick building trimmed with granite, built in 1901.

R. from Fenway on Boylston St.

86. The *Massachusetts Historical Society* (*open weekdays* 9–5; *Sat.* 9–1; *museum open Wed.* 2–4), 1154 Boylston St., corner of Fenway, occupies an incongruously modern bow-front granite and yellow-brick building. Founded in 1791, the oldest historical society in the United States, it is primarily a library, rich in early books, historical documents, newspapers, manuscripts, and engravings. Of special interest are a suit of clothes worn by Benjamin Franklin in Paris, of lilac poplin, with cuffs of pleated lawn, Governor Winthrop's Bible, Shem Drowne's Indian weathervane from Province House, Peter Faneuil's mahogany wine chest, and a British drum from Bunker Hill. Casually tucked away among these is the pen with which Lincoln signed the *Emancipation Proclamation*.

MOTOR TOUR 1 (*South Boston, Roxbury, and Dorchester*) — 23 m.

E. from South Station, Boston, on Summer St.

87. The *Commonwealth Pier*, built by the State just before the World War, is a fine passenger and freight pier. Twelve hundred feet long and 400 feet wide, it provides berths for five 600-foot vessels at a time, and is used by a number of transatlantic lines.

88. The *Army Base* (*open by approval of Officer of the Day*), corner of Harbor St., comprises a 2000-foot pier and an 8-story concrete warehouse 1600 feet long. Built during the World War, it is the Army Quartermaster depot for New England, and the second largest Army base in the United States. The adjacent drydock is the largest in this country.

Straight ahead from Summer St. on L St.; L. from L St. on East Broadway.

The *City Point Section* of South Boston is traversed by East Broadway, bordered by old bow-front brick residences reminiscent of the fashionable·

forties. It has the finest situation, with respect to the harbor, of any district of Boston, and one of the best beaches near the Metropolitan Center.

89. The *Boston Aquarium* (*open* 10–5 *daily*), corner of Farragut Rd., is a low stucco building with octagonal, red-tiled tower and a fish weathervane.

L. from East Broadway on Gardner Way.

90. *Castle Island*, so named by Governor Winthrop, who thought its natural contours resembled a castle, is a peninsular headland park, its 20 rolling acres capped in the center by the solid stone walls of *Fort Independence* (*yard only open*), erected in 1801 and abandoned about 1880. When exposed fortifications were of service in warfare, this fort was of great strategic value in the defense of Boston, for the harbor channel passes within a stone's throw of its northern face.

In 1827, Edgar Allan Poe, at eighteen, enlisting under the name of Perry, did five months of army service here. In 1905, an amazing parallel to Poe's story, 'The Cask of Amontillado,' was disclosed by the finding, in a sealed casemate within the fort, of a skeleton clothed in army uniform.

> Motor cars may proceed only to the 'island's' edge. The short footpath around the fort offers an interesting panorama. To the northwest, surmounted by another abandoned stone fort, is *Governor's Island*, one of Governor Winthrop's three Boston homes. To the north is *Winthrop* (*see Tour 1A*), huddled at the foot of a silvergray water-tower. Northeast is *Deer Island*, identified by the long red-brick buildings of a city penitentiary.
>
> Due east on the far horizon rises the white tower of *Boston Light*, the oldest lighthouse in America, not to be confused with the nearer white tower of *Long Island Light*, a trifle southeast of it, marking the entrance to *Nantasket Roads*, where the British gathered their departing fleet in 1776.
>
> Directly opposite the *Clipper Ship Monument* to Donald McKay (*see NEWBURYPORT*) is the *Ship Channel* of the inner harbor, busy at all hours with passing vessels, large and small.

Retrace Gardner Way; straight ahead on Columbia Rd.

91. The *L Street Baths*, at the junction with L St., are built on the European plan of enclosed bathing areas, one for men, one for women and girls, and one for boys. The enclosure is roofed over to hold the bathhouses; the walls extend out, surrounding open-air sections of beach and water. A group of intrepid bathers popularly known as the 'L Street Brownies' go into the ocean here every day of the year.

R. from Columbia Rd. on L St.; L. from L St. on East Broadway.

92. The *Site of the Old Mount Washington Hotel*, later the first building of Perkins Institution for the Blind (*see WATERTOWN*), is covered by the South Boston Municipal Building, 535 East Broadway.

L. from East Broadway on G St.; R. from G St. on Thomas Parkway.

93. The *Dorchester Heights Monument* (*not open*), summit of Thomas Park, is a square white marble tower 80 feet high, commemorating the

gunfire from this hill that was a contributive factor in the British evacuation of Boston on March 17, 1776.

R. from Thomas Parkway on Telegraph St.; R. from Telegraph St. on Mercer St.

94. *Old Saint Augustine's Chapel* (*open upon application at Saint Augustine's Church, one block left on Dorchester St.*) (1819) stands in the walled cemetery at the junction of Mercer and Dorchester Sts. The tiny brick chapel, with its irregular slate-tiled roof and its arches, small-paned clear-glass windows, nestling in a century-old graveyard under giant English elms, inevitably suggests Gray's 'Elegy.'

L. from Mercer St. on Dorchester St.; L. from Dorchester St. on Old Colony Blvd.

95. *Old Harbor Village* (R), framing the expansive area of Columbia Circle, is one of the largest ventures of the Federal Housing Projects in New England. Occupying 20 acres, this group comprises 1016 apartments in a block of three-story buildings with penthouses, play yards, and social halls. The buildings are centrally heated. The apartments have 3 to 5 rooms and rent at a moderate figure. The smaller structures, called 'low houses,' have from 3 to 6 rooms, each section with its own private entrance.

R. from Old Colony Blvd. on Columbia Rd. to the junction with Pond St.

96. The *Blake House* (1648) (*owned by the Dorchester Historical Society, open upon application*), corner of Pond St., is a two-and-a-half-story shingled cottage with steep pitched roof and diamond-paned windows. The interior, consisting only of four rooms and an attic, has hand-hewn cross-beams, slightly arched, and 'S' hinges. By the front doorsill is the *Dorchester Milestone.*

97. The *Site of Edward Everett's Birthplace*, corner of Boston St., Edward Everett Square, Dorchester, is marked by a tablet, just across the square from his *Statue*, by W. W. Story. Congressman, Governor, Minister to England, Secretary of State, President of Harvard, and U.S. Senator, Edward Everett (1794–1865) was in addition a graceful orator, without whom no commemorative exercises in the New England of his day were considered complete.

R. from Columbia Rd. on Boston St.; L. from Boston St. on Willow Court.

98. The *Clap House* (*open by arrangement*), 23 Willow Court, early 17th-century, still retains its gambrel roof.

Retrace Willow Court; R. from Willow Court on Boston St. to Edward Everett Sq.; R. from Edward Everett Sq. on East Cottage St.; L. from East Cottage St. on Humphreys St.

99. The *Bird-Sawyer House* (*private*), 41 Humphreys St., is a two-and-a-half-story gray clapboarded dwelling built in 1637 with broad windows, a green door with a brass eagle knocker of Federal date, and a square central chimney. Additions were made in 1804.

R. from Humphreys St. on Dudley St.; R. from Dudley St. on Shirley St.

100. The *Shirley-Eustis House* (*not open*, 1937, *but present ownership plans to restore as a museum*), 31 Shirley St., was once a gubernatorial mansion in the grand manner. It is a four-story square frame structure with dormer windows and cupola built in 1748. Two wide stone flights of steps lead to the second or main floor. The west flight gives access to the entrance hall, while the east flight opens into a two-story banquet hall with a musicians' gallery. The east doorway is treated with pilasters, a fan-light, and side panels of glass. The house itself is also pilastered, and has an elaborate carved cornice. The windows of the main floor reach from floor to ceiling. Originally there were piazzas north and south. Occupied by Governor William Shirley until his death in 1771, it passed through a succession of merchant princes and then to William Eustis, Governor from 1823 to 1825. Its guests have included Washington, Franklin, Lafayette, Webster, Clay, Calhoun, and Aaron Burr.

Retrace Shirley St.; L. from Shirley St. on Dudley St.; R. from Dudley St. on Columbia Rd.; L. from Columbia Rd. on Hancock St.; R. from Hancock St. on Winter St.

101. The *First Parish Church* (Unitarian) in Dorchester (*open 9–5 daily by the vestry entrance*), Meeting House Hill, houses a *Roman Mosaic* from Dorchester, England, dating from the Conquest of Britain by Caesar. In the vestry is an Anglo-Chinese clock of 1770, the works English, the case Chinese, beautifully lacquered. This case, larger than needed for the clock, was used just before the Revolution for smuggling tea, an undertaking then considered so patriotic as not to disturb the conscience of the church when the gift of the clock was made.

L. from Winter St. on Adams St.; R. from Adams St. on Dorchester Ave.; L. from Dorchester Ave. on Ashmont St.

102. *All Saints' Church*, constructed in 1894, was the initial success of the contemporary medievalist, Ralph Adams Cram. In his autobiography he wrote: 'Into it I put all I knew or suspected of Gothic — which to tell the truth was not much.... It struck a new note in the cacophony of disintegrating Romanesque and an arid Victorianism.'

Retrace Ashmont St.; R. from Ashmont St. on Talbot Ave.

103. *Franklin Field* has facilities for baseball, football, tennis, and bowling.

R. from Talbot Ave. on Blue Hill Ave.

104. *Franklin Park*, 527 acres of open, rolling terrain, beautifully wooded and watered, contains a public golf course and motor and bridle paths. The park forms a unit in a parkway chain which circles Boston southwest and south from Commonwealth Ave. to the Blue Hills.

> *Franklin Park Zoo* (*open daily* 10–5), corner of Seaver St., is one of the ranking zoos of America. Boston follows its news with absorbed interest, and new arrivals, whether by ship or by stork, are an occasion for headline stories and pictures in the press.

Retrace Blue Hill Ave.; R. from Blue Hill Ave. on American Legion High-way; R. from American Legion Highway on Morton St. (second unmarked road within park).

105. *Forest Hills Cemetery* (*plan and information furnished at office*), famous for its rhododendron hedges, is the largest cemetery in New England and is known as one of the most beautiful in the United States. Here are buried Joseph Warren, William Lloyd Garrison, Fanny Davenport, and Edward Everett Hale. 'Death Staying the Hand of the Sculptor,' a memorial by Daniel Chester French, marks the grave of Martin Milmore.

Straight ahead from Morton St. on Arborway; L. from Arborway on Washington St.

106. *Stony Brook Reservation*, West Roxbury, 464 acres, is the one forest park in Metropolitan Boston. It is densely wooded with pine, oak, and birch, but traversed by trunk motor highways and many paths, some of the latter leading to knolls which offer delightful views of the Charles River Valley.

R. from Washington St. on La Grange St.; L. from La Grange St. on Centre St.

107. The *Roxbury Latin School*, corner of St. Theresa Ave., the third oldest school still existing in the United States, is remarkable because it was for 250 years the oldest, if not the only, free school not aided by public funds. It was established by the Apostle John Eliot and 60 families of Roxbury — practically the entire town in 1645 — by generous contributions of land, money, and labor.

R. from Centre St. on Spring St.; R. from Spring St. on Baker St.

108. *Brook Farm* (*open as the Martin Luther Orphans' Home*), 670 Baker St., was the scene of an early experiment (1841–47) in communal living by the Transcendentalists. Among actual members or associate participants were Hawthorne, Emerson, Bronson Alcott, Theodore Parker, George W. Curtis, and Margaret Fuller. Everyone had some share of work, and all members shared in educational and social enjoyments. Under the influence of Albert Brisbane, father of the late Arthur Brisbane, the associates adopted the phalanx according to the plan of Fourier, and established primary departments of agriculture, domestic industry, and mechanic arts. In March, 1846, one of the main buildings, the Phalanstery, was burned. At this heavy financial blow, the group, already somewhat discouraged, lost heart completely and disbanded in October, 1847.

Retrace Baker St.; L. from Baker St. on US1; R. from US1 on Arborway.

109. The *Arnold Arboretum* (*for pedestrians only*), just beyond US1, is the largest living-tree and shrub museum in the country as regards foreign introductions. In May and early June its 223 acres are a paradise of blooming lilac hedges and cherry trees, forsythias, plum trees, magnolias, rhododendrons, and azaleas. Endowed (1872) by the late James

Arnold, a New Bedford merchant, the Arboretum is owned by Harvard University (*see CAMBRIDGE*) and contains the buildings of Harvard's *Bussey Institute of Horticulture and Agriculture.*

Retrace Arborway; R. from Arborway on Centre St.

110. The *Loring-Greenough House* (1758) (*open by special arrangement*), 12 South St., in Whitcomb Square, is set in sizable grounds which once extended half a mile to Jamaica Pond. It is a square two-story frame mansion, with dormer windows, painted white, black blinds, a dentiled cornice, a slate mansard roof, white roof-rail, and white chimneys. There are three formal doorways, one of which opens from a porch (added later). Another has an iron lock eighteen inches wide and a keyhole the size of the human eye. The wide hall is especially fine, having a hand-carved stair-rail imported from early Georgian England, and landscape wallpaper of the same period. The large square rooms are wainscoted in white and furnished with valuable and beautiful antiques. A feature of the house is a large vault, built between two chimney flues. The house was first the home of Commodore Joseph Loring, a Tory naval officer who distinguished himself in the conquest of Canada. In 1775, it was the headquarters of General Greene, and later a hospital for American Revolutionary soldiers.

Sharp L. from Whitcomb Square on Eliot St.; R. from Eliot St. on Pond St.

111. The *Children's Museum* of Boston (*open daily except Monday 9–5; Sun. 2–5; free*), 60 Burroughs St., is a modern stucco building with white wood trim. Founded in 1913 and maintained by private subscription, its purpose is to stimulate the interest of children in the wonders and beauties of nature. Natural history specimens, including animal skeletons, stuffed animals and birds, are displayed; and a collection of variegated minerals illustrates the simpler stages of geologic history. There is a small but instructive industrial exhibit, as well as a collection of dolls, ancient and modern, dressed in typical costumes of various countries.

112. *Jamaica Pond* (*refreshments and rowboats available; also fishing, by permit from Fish and Game Commission*), junction of Pond St. and Arborway, a beautiful 65-acre expanse of fresh water, is encircled by 55 acres of parkway in the Boston Park Department.

Straight ahead from Pond St. on Jamaicaway; R. from Jamaicaway on Perkins St.; straight ahead from Perkins St. on Centre St.

113. The *First Church in Roxbury* (Unitarian) (*open Tues. and Thurs. 1–3; Sun. service* 11), Eliot Square, erected in 1804, was built after the design of the First Unitarian Church in Portsmouth, New Hampshire, and was known as the Church of John Eliot, Apostle to the Indians. It is a typical New England meeting house, simple and dignified, with a clock-tower and open belfry.

The interior, in ivory color and brown, has broad lateral galleries supported by columns. There is a balcony pulpit, raised halfway between the floor and the galleries. Treasures of the church are John Eliot's

Chair and a Simon Willard Gallery Clock, surmounted by a spread eagle, holding in its beak two strings of gilded balls. This famous design has often been copied, but this clock is one of the two or three authentic examples.

114. The *Dillaway House* (*open daily* 9–5), 183 Roxbury St., originally the parsonage, built 1714, is a fine type of the two-and-a-half-story gambrel-roof dwelling with dormer windows. Some of the rooms show the supporting corner posts; some have rounded corners. The wide, uneven floor boards and the hand-hewn timbers of the roof, are original, as well as the door-knobs, hinges, and massive locks.

Straight ahead on Roxbury St.; R. from Roxbury St. on Guild Row; L. from Guild Row on Dudley St.; R. from Dudley St. on Warren St.

115. *General Joseph Warren's Statue* by Paul Bartlett, Warren Square, shows the physician and Revolutionary hero as a handsome, imperious young man in his early thirties. Quite indifferent to personal danger, Warren had been a marked man to the British ever since he had outwitted their guard at the Old South Meeting House and climbed through a second-story window over the heads of British soldiers, to address the patriots within. His death at the battle of Bunker Hill was mourned throughout Boston.

Retrace Warren St.; straight ahead from Warren St. on Harrison Ave.; L. from Harrison Ave. on Massachusetts Ave.; R. from Massachusetts Ave. on Tremont St.; L. from Tremont St. on Dartmouth St.; R. from Dartmouth St. on Montgomery St.

116. The *Boston English High School* founded in 1821, one year before Boston became a city, is the oldest high school in the United States.

Straight ahead from Montgomery St. on Tremont St.; R. from Tremont St. on Castle St.; L. from Castle St. on Shawmut Ave.

117. *Morgan Memorial* at the junction of Shawmut Ave. and Corning St., occupies a group of buildings. Here are the central offices of the far-famed Morgan Memorial activities, founded in 1868 by Henry Morgan. The various branches of this social service have been so extended that they provide useful employment for many people unable to find work in other fields. The best-known of these projects is the Goodwill Industries, which collects discarded clothing, furniture and household equipment of all sorts for resale.

MOTOR TOUR 2 (*Charlestown*) — 5 m.

N. from North Station, Boston, across Charlestown Bridge on Main St.; R. from Main St. on Chelsea St.; R. from Chelsea St. on Wapping St.

118. *United States Navy Yard* (*open daily* 9.30–4.30; *adm. to cars and pedestrians*), popularly known as the Charlestown Navy Yard, and con-

tinuously operated since 1800, occupies 123 acres in a narrow, high-walled strip extending 1½ miles along the waterfront. The great attractions of the yard are the U.S. Frigate 'Constitution' ('Old Ironsides') (*open during yard visiting hours*), and the *Rope Walk*, a long stone building where the great hempen cables of the fleet are carded, twisted, and wound. Ships in port may usually be visited.

Retrace on Wapping St.; straight ahead on Henley St.; R. from Henley St. on Warren St.; R. from Warren St. on Winthrop St.

119. *Bunker Hill Monument* on Breed's Hill (*open 9–5, May to Sept.; 9–4, Oct. to April; adm.* 10¢) is a granite obelisk about 220 feet high, designed by Solomon Willard, a noted architect, and erected between 1825 and 1842. Its design shows the influence of the Greek Revival which lamentably dominated American architecture at the time. At the base of the monument is a *Statue of Colonel William Prescott* ('Don't fire until you see the whites of their eyes'), in a spirited pose, sculptured by William Wetmore Story. A small museum contains portraits, statues, and engravings of battle participants, both British and American.

L. from Winthrop St. on High St.; L. from High St. on Cordis St.

120. The *Webb–Adams House* (*private*), 32 Cordis St., with yellow clapboards, low hip roof, small-paned windows, and semi-circular white Doric portico, is the best remaining example of the pleasant homes of nineteenth-century Charlestown (1801). It has the frequent Charlestown feature of a front door at the garden side of the house, away from the street, frequent in Southern cities, but unusual in New England.

Retrace on Cordis St.; L. from Cordis St. on High St.; L. from High St. on Green St.

121. The *Boys' Club of Boston* (*open daily, 9–9; visitors welcome*), founded in 1898, by Frank S. Mason, represents in its broad two-story brick building, surrounding a flagged terrace, one of the finest civic undertakings in Boston. The combined membership, consisting of boys from 7 to 21, is 7500.

R. from Green St. on Main St.

122. The *Site of the Birthplace of Samuel F. B. Morse*, inventor of the telegraph, 195 Main St., is marked by a white marble tablet.

L. from Main St. on Phipps St.

123. The *Phipps Street Burial Ground*, at the end of the street, dates from 1638. Here lies John Harvard, founder of Harvard College, beneath a granite shaft, erected in 1828, 190 years after his death, through popular subscription directed by Edward Everett, who limited contributions to one dollar a person, in order to give a large number of people a chance to participate.

MOTOR TOUR 3 (*East Boston*) — 5 *m.*

N.E. from Haymarket Sq., Boston, through Sumner Tunnel.

124. The *Sumner Tunnel (fare for passenger car*, 15¢), constructed (1931–34) by the city at a cost of $19,000,000, was named for General William H. Sumner, founder of East Boston. At the Boston terminal is a brick and granite administration building. The tunnel is more than a mile long and serves the seaboard north of the city, passing under the harbor and emerging in East Boston. Blow-plants at either end supply air-conditioning.

L. from Sumner Tunnel on Porter St.; L. from Porter St. on Meridian St. into Central Square.

125. The *East Boston Social Centers Council (open)* occupies an old redbrick building, formerly a church, in Central Square. Endowed by Jewish philanthropists, it offers to all creeds and races recreation, instruction in arts and crafts, music, drama, and health education.

R. from Meridian St. on Paris St.; L. from Paris St. on Henry St.

126. The *Lutheran Seamen's Home*, 11 Henry St., occupying a pair of old bow-front brick dwellings, is a Scandinavian bethel, where comfortable shelter, regardless of the recipient's ability to pay, is provided and leavened by a measure of home life and wise counsel.

R. from Henry St. into Maverick Square; L. from Maverick Square on Sumner St.; R. from Sumner St. on Orleans St.; L. from Orleans St. at its end on unmarked Marginal St.

127. *Saint Mary's House for Sailors (open* 8–10), 120 Marginal St., a recreational center founded in 1890 by Phillips Brooks, furnishes reading and game rooms, shower baths, and foreign money exchange service free. In a wing is *Saint Mary's Church for Sailors* (Episcopal).

128. The *United States Immigration Station*, 285 Marginal St., is not very busy in these days of restricted immigration.

L. from Marginal St. on Jeffries St.

129. The *Boston Airport (daily airplanes to New York, Albany, Burlington, and Bangor connecting at those cities for all other points)* occupies a two-story yellow brick terminal, surrounded by five hangars.

Retrace Maverick St.; R. from Maverick St. on Chelsea St.; R. from Chelsea St. on Route C1.

130. Suffolk Downs, a mile-long racing track, has two 30-day horse-racing sessions. Pari-mutuel betting is legalized.

B R O C K T O N . *City of Shoes*

City: Alt. 120, pop. 62,407, sett. 1700, incorp. town 1821, city 1881.

Railroad Stations: 104 Center St., 41 Station Ave., 31 Riverside Ave., and 847 North Montello St. for N.Y., N.H. & H. R.R.

Bus Stations: 104 Center St. and 233 Main St., for New England Transportation Co.; Legion Parkway and Main St. for Great Eastern Line and Grey Line; 117 Main St. for Interstate Transportation Co.

Accommodations: Four first-class hotels.

Information: Chamber of Commerce, Legion Parkway.

BROCKTON is one of the two great shoe-manufacturing centers of New England. The middle of the city is occupied by block after block of factories making shoes and shoe findings. From this core stretch the areas crowded with the homes of the workers, tenements, and small houses. Beyond these, chiefly toward the south, lie residential areas.

In 1649 the lands now occupied by this city were deeded by the Indians to Miles Standish and John Alden for approximately thirty dollars. The district including Brockton was part of the town of Bridgewater until 1821, when it was set off as North Bridgewater.

The Revolutionary War did not vitally affect the everyday lives of the townsfolk of North Bridgewater, the scene of actual hostilities being comparatively remote. But the post-Revolutionary depression found them vigorously opposing the ruthless laws affecting small debtors. Militant townsmen snatched their hunting guns from the walls and came out into the street in sympathy with Shays's Rebellion.

Continuing their democratic traditions, the inhabitants of North Bridgewater played an important rôle in pre-Civil War days. The skilled shoe workers, most of whom had fled their respective countries to escape the tyranny of the old order and had come to America to help build a new and free world, felt a ready sympathy with the Negroes of the South. They became devoted followers of William Lloyd Garrison, and developed an intricate system of 'Underground Stations' to facilitate the escape of runaway slaves.

In the second quarter of the nineteenth century, just prior to the Civil War, the invention of the McKay sewing machine, which made it possible to sew together the uppers and soles of shoes instead of pegging them, changed North Bridgewater from a small unimportant farming center to one of the foremost industrial cities in Massachusetts.

Civil War days brought unparalleled prosperity to the owners of the shoe factories. Government orders for army shoes during the Civil

War made it the largest shoe producing city in America. Half the Union Army was shod by North Bridgewater.

Workers streamed into town, and by 1880 the population of Brockton — the name adopted in 1874 — had more than tripled. William Cullen Bryant in describing the city said: 'The whole place resounds, rather rattles, with the machinery of shoe shops, which turn out millions of shoes, not one of which, I am told, is sold in the place.'

Before the Civil War the social life of Brockton consisted almost wholly of church functions characterized by a minimum of gaiety — a residuum from Puritan days. With the influx of foreign-born workers communal gatherings assumed a livelier cast. Public dances became the vogue. The Swedish workers were the first church group to sanction dancing, holding their parties in the church vestry. Volunteer firemen grouped themselves into engine companies and soon became leaders in the social life of the community. The Firemen's Ball became the most brilliant and colorful social event of the year. Local dramatic groups produced such plays as 'Uncle Tom's Cabin' and 'Ten Nights in a Bar-Room.' The young bloods formed secret societies and musical clubs. The workers organized into trade unions, and various foreign-language groups erected halls which were later to become community centers.

Civic improvement kept pace with the rapid industrial and social growth of the town. It is claimed that the first central power station in the United States from which power was distributed through three-wire underground conductors was located here, becoming the present Edison Electric Company. An early experimental street railway especially built for the use of electric power was developed here, and Thomas Alva Edison came to Brockton to see the first car run over the line. In 1893, Brockton worked out a solution of the sewage disposal problem for inland cities, and investigating committees came from foreign countries as well as from many cities of the United States to learn the Brockton system and arrange for its adoption.

In 1929, in the neighborhood of Brockton there were thirty thousand skilled shoe workers employed in sixty factories. Three of the largest shoe manufacturing corporations in America are today located in Brockton, as are also several of the largest plants producing tools and supplies for the shoe industry.

During the last few years the emigration of shoe industries from New England, due to attractive offers of cheap unorganized labor and tax rebatements in other States, has noticeably affected Brockton. This movement, along with antiquated production methods and lack of foresight on the part of the manufacturers, has been a primary factor in the decline of the shoe industry. Between 1919 and 1929 local production fell off forty-nine per cent.

On the whole, Brockton has been remarkably fortunate in relationships between employer and employee. Aside from two large strikes, the city did not participate in the series of violent industrial revolts that swept the country at the beginning of the twentieth century. A majority of the shoe workers are affiliated with the Brotherhood of Shoe and Allied Craftsmen and the balance with the Boot and Shoe Workers' Union of the A.F. of L.

POINTS OF INTEREST

1. The *Brockton Fair Grounds*, on Belmont St., are the property of the Agricultural Society. The Brockton Fair, held here in September, has been famous since 1874. It includes agricultural, industrial, and educational exhibits, vaudeville acts, an automobile show, horse and automobile races, and other popular attractions.

2. The *Bryant House* (*open; present occupant, a relative of the poet, permits visitors*), 815 Belmont St., corner of Lorraine Ave., is a simple unpainted frame dwelling. Here William Cullen Bryant lived for a time while studying law, and here the famous New England poet is said to have composed 'Yellow Violet' and a part of 'To a Waterfowl.'

3. *Stone House Hill*, opposite 330 Belmont St., has a boulder-studded, pine-covered crest from which, or from a rock near-by, according to tradition, the Indians relayed smoke signals from Plymouth to the Blue Hills.

4. The *Public Library* (*open weekdays* 9–9, *Sun.* 3–9), White Ave. and Main St., will eventually house the Walter Bryant Copeland Collection of American Masters of Art, which was bequeathed to the city with a fund to maintain it.

5. The *Walk-Over Shoe Factory and Club* (*open; permission at office*), 82 Perkins Ave., occupies the old Keith plant, which includes a hospital with health clinics, clubhouses, and a park.

6. The *W. L. Douglas Shoe Factory* (*open; permission at office*), occupies 133–173 Spark St. Begun in 1876 by W. L. Douglas with a capital of $875 and a small group of carefully chosen workmen, it has grown into a $10,000,000 business.

7. *D. W. Field Park*, Oak St., beautified by woods, gardens, ponds, and artificial waterfalls, is one of the show places of the State. From a tower in the grounds it is possible to see Plymouth and Massachusetts Bay. Municipal golf links adjoin the park, which was named after a citizen who helped to create it — Daniel Waldo Field (1856), leading shoe manufacturer, agriculturist, dairyman, philanthropist, and author.

B R O O K L I N E . *Opulent Comfort*

Town: Alt. 18, pop. 50,319, sett. about 1638, incorp. 1705.

Railroad Station: Brookline Station, Station St., for B. & A. R.R.

Bus Station: Blueway Line, Boston to Springfield, stops at Brookline Village, 115 Washington St.

Accommodations: Three hotels and several private houses.

Swimming: Municipal Pool, Tappan St. (*fee* 10¢). Separate hours for men and women.

Annual Events: National championship tennis matches at Longwood Cricket Club; horse show and races at Brookline Country Club.

Information: Chamber of Commerce, 306 Harvard St.

BROOKLINE is almost exclusively a residential town. Over its three hills, Fisher Hill, Corey Hill, Aspinwall Hill, and along Beacon Street and Commonwealth Avenue, around the Reservoir and over into Chestnut Hill, spread the homes of people who find their source of income in the business districts of Boston. In the first decade of the twentieth century, Brookline was popularly known as the 'Town of Millionaires.' By 1910, however, it had begun to open its doors to residents of far more modest means. Restricted areas are still occupied by hedged and landscaped estates, handsome showplaces of the metropolitan area. In other sections the beautiful old estates have begun to be split into house lots; apartments have appeared, especially along the boulevards; large private dwellings have been turned into rooming houses. Half of Brookline still remains the closed citadel of wealth and leisure; the other half has become a modern residential hive for the better paid of the busy workers of Boston.

In 1630, the Company of Massachusetts Bay, bringing the Charter and its Governor, John Winthrop, arrived from London. Shortly afterward the worthy citizens of old Boston found their Common overcrowded with cows, and the town fathers found it needful to seek a new place to the west for grazing.

Governor Winthrop first mentions 'Muddy River Hamlet' in his writings in connection with early allotments made for 'planting.' John Cotton, urbane, affable, and of easy fortune, as his well-fed embonpoint testified — the foremost divine of Boston — was granted the first tract of land. Following him, other distinguished citizens of Boston hastened to secure for themselves generous grants, until by 1639 the available acreage began to run decidedly short. After the first famous allotment of January 8, 1638, the grants were smaller, more numerous, and made to less well-known applicants.

In the earliest days, agriculture was naturally the most important industry. Truck farms raising produce for sale in Boston, and fields, were under cultivation as early as 1662, and a clerk of market was appointed to represent the Muddy River farmers at Old Faneuil Hall Market, Boston. Growth of the little village went forward, and in 1705 it was granted recognition as the separate town of Muddy River Hamlet (now euphemistically called Brookline), having been named for the estate of Judge Samuel Sewall, of witchcraft fame, who owned a large tract in Muddy River.

During the Revolution much property in Brookline owned by Boston Tories was confiscated. A Mr. Jackson, living near the present Public Library, sold his home and moved away when he was forced to provide quarters for Continental soldiers. The house of Henry Moulton, mandamus counsellor for the British Government, was mobbed by a crowd of boys who broke the windows with stones.

By the middle of the nineteenth century a larger town hall was built; the first railroad ran through the town; telegraph posts and wires were beginning to appear; the Coolidges had a store near the spot later to be known as Coolidge Corner.

As time passed, many leading citizens of Boston were attracted to this flourishing suburb, so far removed in appearance as well as in name from the Old Muddy River Hamlet. Taxes were low. Brookline was near Boston and could be reached by train and trolley in a short time at a moderate fare. It was an ideal commuter's town.

In 1870, Boston attempted to annex Brookline. Aroused, the citizens gathered in town meeting and blocked this proposal. Five times more did Boston attempt to pull out this coveted plum from the political pie, but each time met with failure, though at times the margin of votes was narrow. Brookline is today an 'island' almost entirely surrounded by Boston. A modified form of town government is still maintained to avoid expense and political complications, although the population of Brookline makes it by far the largest town in New England. In the last forty years the racial character of the general population has materially changed; it is now about equally divided among native inhabitants, foreign-born residents, and those of mixed parentage. Among the latter, the Irish strain predominates, with the Jewish influence second.

Among the famous citizens of Brookline was Hannah Adams, said to be the first woman in America to follow the profession of literature. In recent times the roll of honor has included such diverse personalities as Serge Koussevitzky, conductor of the Boston Symphony Orchestra; Jack Sharkey, the former heavyweight champion prize-fighter of the world; Roland Hayes, renowned Negro tenor, whose work furthered acceptance of the Negro Spiritual as an art form; and the brilliant Amy Lowell, who during her later years was one of the striking figures in contemporary American poetry. She lectured widely. Among her contributions to poetry, which include 'A Dome of Many-Coloured Glass' and 'What's O'Clock,' must be reckoned the perfecting, in her best work.

of the technique of free verse; her almost unrivaled command of the vocabulary of sensuous impressions; the wide range of the themes to which she has given poetical expression; and the clarity and restrained beauty of many of her shorter poems. Her most important critical work was the biography of John Keats.

TOUR — 14 m.

W. from State 9 (Boylston St.) on Washington St.

1. The *Brookline Public Library* (*open weekdays*, 8.30–9; *Sat.* 2–9), at 361 Washington St., was designed by R. Clipston Sturgis and erected in 1910. It is set well back from the street in landscaped grounds. The library houses the Desmond Fitzgerald Collection of Paintings, in which among other artists are represented Maufra, Bloos, Banderweiden, and Dodge MacKnight.

R. from Washington on School St.; L. from School on Harvard St.

2. The *Harvard Congregational Church*, Harvard and Marion Sts., is a low rambling brownstone building in Gothic style with a high tower which contains an unusually fine set of chimes. It was designed by E. Tuckerman Potter and erected in 1873.

L. from Harvard St. into Marion St.; L. from Marion into Beacon St.

3. *All Saints' Church*, 1773 Beacon St., consecrated in 1926, and like the cathedrals of Europe built slowly over a period of years, was one of the first large churches undertaken by Cram, Goodhue, and Ferguson. It shows the influence of the 'perpendicular' churches of England — late Gothic design. The high walls, low-pitched roof, and restrained use of carving are characteristic. The rose window, by Charles J. Connick of Boston — the American authority on stained glass — is a notable feature.

Retrace Beacon St.; L. from Beacon into Summit Ave., a steep grade.

4. The *Corey Hill Outlook* (alt. 265) is the best vantage-point of Brookline. Beneath it, to the west, lie the towns of Brighton and Watertown, with the tower of Perkins Institution for the Blind, and the Watertown Arsenal, a group of gray-brick buildings, standing out among the huddle of roofs. To the north the horseshoe of the Harvard Stadium is easily distinguished, with the towers of the college buildings on its right. To the east the Charles River widens to its greatest breadth and merges with Boston Harbor in the distance.

Retrace Summit Ave.; L. from Summit Ave. on Beacon St.

5. The *Brookline Trust Company*, at 1341 Beacon St., has the Ernest B. Dane Collection of Tapestries, which includes four Gobelin tapestries valued at $2,000,000.

L. from Beacon St. on Harvard St.

6. The *Edward Devotion House* (*open Sat.* 2–4; *adm.* 10¢), at 347 Harvard St., was built in 1680 by Edward Devotion, town perambulator, town constable, fence viewer, and tythingman. The neat cream and yellow two-and-a-half-story frame house with small-paned windows, gambrel roof, and central chimney stands on the premises of the Devotion School. Two old maples shade and partly hide the little house, which is now the headquarters of the Brookline Historical Society.

Retrace Harvard St.; L. from Harvard St. on Beacon St.; L. from Beacon St. on Amory St.

7. *Hawes Pond* (*skating*), lies in the Amory St. Playground. Tradition has it that a white horse and wagon once sank in its reputedly bottomless depths, and for many years thereafter it was known as White Horse Pond.

Retrace Amory St.; R. from Amory St. on Beacon St.; L. from Beacon St. into Kent St.; L. from Kent St. on Aspinwall Ave.; L. from Aspinwall Ave. into Netherlands Rd.

8. The *Netherlands House* (*private*), is a close copy of the Stadthuise at Franeker in Fresland (16th century). From the World's Columbian Exposition held at Chicago in 1893, where it served as the Dutch Cocoa House, it was moved piece by piece and set up in its present location. The door frame, embellished with stone animals, is a replica of the doorway of the Enkhaisen Orphanage.

Retrace Netherlands Rd.; L. on Aspinwall Ave.; R. from Aspinwall Ave. on Brookline Ave.; R. from Brookline Ave. on Boylston St.; R. from Boylston St. on Buckminster Rd.; L. from Buckminster Rd. on Seaver St.

9. The *Zion Research Library* (*open daily* 1.30–4.30), 120 Seaver St., is a non-sectarian institution for the study of the Bible and church history. The building, a brownstone mansion of 60 rooms, once John Munro Longyear's private residence in Bay City, Michigan, was carried stone by stone to its present location on the crest of Fisher Hill.

Retrace Seaver St.; R. from Seaver St. into Buckminster Rd.; R. from Buckminster Rd. into Summer St.; across Boylston St., entering Warren St.

10. The *Davis-Cabot-Goddard Home* or Green Hill (*private*), 215 Warren St., on one of the tall inner chimneys bears the inscription, 'Greenhill 1730.' The first-floor windows and their sturdy green blinds are ten feet high. The wallpaper in the living-room is of the design known as *Les Rives du Bosphore*, and was printed in colors from wooden blocks by Joseph Defour in Paris; the dates ascribed to this design vary from 1816 to 1829. The rear wing, with its floors three feet lower than those in the original house, is a long, low, rambling addition.

L. from Warren St. into Cottage St.; R. from Cottage into Goddard Ave.

11. *Green Hill* (The Goddard House; *private*), 235 Goddard Ave., was built as a farmhouse for Nehemiah Davis in 1732. The great drawing-room with chambers above was added in 1797, and subsequent alterations have been made. This house is one of the oldest in Brookline. Just beyond the house is a cone-shaped pudding-stone boulder set in an alcove of young

evergreens, with a bronze tablet to Hannah Seaver Goddard and her husband John Goddard, loyal patriot and wagonmaster-general during the Revolution. In the barn, long since demolished, were secreted military stores which Goddard carted to Concord in 1775.

Straight ahead into Newton St.; R. from Newton St. on Clyde St.

12. The *Country Club* (*adm. by invitation*), claimed to be the oldest course in the United States, was established in 1882. Along Clyde St. the grounds, over 100 acres, are enclosed by a high wooden beanpole fence. Here are perpetuated the ancient sport of curling and various turf sports, as well as the more modern horse-racing, steeple-chase, and golf. In the dining-room are several interesting murals depicting hunting scenes, painted by Karl Yens.

Retrace Clyde St.; R. from Clyde St. on Newton St.; straight ahead into West Roxbury Parkway.

13. The *Municipal Golf Course* is one of the finest public courses in the vicinity of Boston (*available to transients; small fee*).

R. from West Roxbury Parkway on Hammond St.

14. The *Longwood Cricket Club* is at the junction of Hammond and Boylston Sts. This organization sponsors national annual tennis tournaments.

Retrace Hammond St.; L. from Hammond St. on Boylston St.

15. A Tercentenary Marker opposite Reservoir Park indicates the *Site of the Zabdiel Boylston House*. Here, in 1736, lived Dr. Zabdiel Boylston, the first American physician to inoculate for smallpox. In 1721, despite popular prejudice, he inoculated his son and two slaves. As a consequence of the success of this experiment, smallpox inoculations gradually became general, public hostility was reduced, and smallpox finally ceased to be a scourge.

CAMBRIDGE . *University City*

City: Alt. 9, pop. 118,075, sett. 1630, incorp. town 1636, city 1846.

Railroad Station: Cambridge Station near Porter Square, for B. & M. R.R.

Bus Stations: Bence Pharmacy, 1607 Mass. Ave., for B. & M. Transportation Company; Leavitt and Pierce, Harvard Square, for Frontier Coach.

Accommodations: Five hotels, including 3 apartment hotels, and a large number of certified tourist homes.

Swimming: Magazine Beach, Memorial Drive.

Annual Events: Ride of William Dawes, April 19.

Information Service: Booth at Harvard Square (summers only).

ON THE northwest bank of the beautiful Charles River, occupying a level plain broken only by Mt. Auburn, lies the city of Cambridge, bisected by the busy arteries of Massachusetts Avenue and Mt. Auburn Street and bordered by the leisurely sweep of Memorial Drive. In reality four cities occupy its confines. Here in elm-shaded streets, in fenced dooryards and landmarks that preserve treasured memories, still live Old Cambridge and that second Cambridge which succeeded it, the Home of the Literati. And here, visible in contemporaneous lusty existence, are two other cities: the University City and one other — the Unknown City.

The University City shelters ten thousand people within the walls of the Harvard dormitories, and Harvard Yard is a hive of learning vaster than any Tibetan monastery. The University City houses a thousand Radcliffe students in beautiful Georgian Colonial brick buildings. The University City may claim the Massachusetts Institute of Technology (1861), the leading technical institute in the United States, and one of the foremost in the world, with 2600 men and women students.

This Cambridge is famous. The story of its historic shrines, its illustrious authors and poets, its learned scholars and scientists, has been told and retold. But the story of Cambridge, the Unknown City, has seldom been told.

Yet this is a very real Cambridge. A hundred and fifty thousand people throng its streets, stores, and crowded subway stations. Five hundred distributing and manufacturing plants pour out a score of nationally known products. The streets of its mercantile sections are lined with banks, motion-picture theaters, department stores, and more than one thousand small retail stores. It presses in between Harvard Yard and the vast Technology Unit; it surges toward the elegant Embankment; it encroaches on the placid dignity of Brattle Street and Lincoln Lane; the city of which one seldom hears but which no one should ignore: Cambridge the Industrial City.

This Unknown City is the second of Massachusetts in the value of goods manufactured; it is third in all New England, outranked only by Boston and Providence. Huge factories pour forth goods, including candy, bread, and soap, into the great stream of American commerce and industry. Within its confines over a hundred thousand workers dwell.

So they stand, interlocked, interpenetrated, Cambridge the University City and Cambridge the great Industrial City; and behind them and within them in surviving landmarks lie the shadows of two other cities: Old Cambridge and the Home of the Literati.

OLD CAMBRIDGE dates back over three centuries. In 1630, the Company of Massachusetts Bay arrived from London with its charter and its Governor, John Winthrop. A fortified place was needed for a capital, protected against the enemy most to be feared — not the Indians, but the warships of King Charles. 'Wherefore they rather made choice to enter further among the Indians, than hazzard the fury of malignant adversaries that might pursue them . . . and erected a town called New Towne, now named Cambridge.'

Great pains were taken in laying out and building the 'New Towne.' One of its earliest visitors describes it as 'having many fair structures with many handsomely contrived streets — one of the neatest towns in New England. The inhabitants, most of them, are very rich.'

An early episode had much to do with determining New Towne's destiny. In October, 1636, the General Court of the Massachusetts Bay Colony agreed to give £400 towards a school or college — a sum equal to the whole colony tax. It remained to select the place.

The preceding year a solemn synod of the teaching elders had been called at the little meeting house on Dunster Street, Cambridge, to put down the dangerous and disturbing doctrines of Mistress Anne Hutchinson of Boston, a strong-minded and brilliant New England woman who took the liberty of expressing lively doubts as to the Boston clergy's being the recipients of divine inspiration. This first New England synod was dominated by the Rev. Mr. Shepard of New Towne; and Mistress Hutchinson was condemned by the General Court together with about eighty others — for opinions 'some blasphemous, others erroneous, all unsound.'

As the country was 'miserably distracted' by a storm of Baptists and other 'unorthodox sects,' and as 'the vigilancy of Mr. Shepard preserved the congregation from the rot of these opinions,' Cotton Mather, the eminent Puritan divine, says that Cambridge was selected as the site of the new college because it was 'under the soul-ravishing ministry of Mr. Thomas Shepard.'

At the time there was living in Charlestown a young dissenting minister, John Harvard, and as the friends of higher education 'were thinking and consulting, how to effect this great work . . . it pleased God that he died, and it was then found he had bequeathed his library to the proposed college, and one-half his estate — in all, some £1,700.' It was therefore decreed that the new college should bear John Harvard's name. The Court also ordered that 'New towne shall henceforth be called Cambridge,' the name of the Old English University town.

Less than a decade later, once more in solemn synod, the solid men of the town assembled to set forth a document of all known opposites to the Church of England. This was the famous 'Cambridge Platform,' wherein the powers of the clergy were minutely defined, and the duty of the common people stated to be 'obeying their elders and submitting themselves unto the Lord.' By this action Church and State were united by law, and the rule of the clergy was made absolute.

In spite of all this, there shortly appeared in Boston 'an accursed and pernicious sect of heretics lately risen up in the world, who are commonly called Quakers.' The plague spread, and the horrified people of Cambridge beheld Elizabeth Horton passing through the streets crying, 'Repentance! Repentance! A day of howling and sad lamentation is coming upon you from the Lord!' Elizabeth was soon laid hold of by a mob and cast into jail; then tied to a whipping-post and lashed ten stripes with a three-stringed whip having three knots at the end. Then they carried her, miserably torn and beaten, many miles into the wilderness, and toward night 'left her among the wolves, bears, and wild beasts.'

The Devil, however, continued to afflict Old Cambridge; and the Mathers, father and son, as God's appointed judges, jousted vigorously with him.

At Harvard, Bible study was most important. The student was expected to live under a monastic code. The main aim of his life was 'to know God and Jesus Christ.' All his acts were performed under the vigilant eye of the Town Watch. He was to read the Scriptures twice a day, and not to 'intrude or inter-meddle on other men's affairs.' He could not 'buy, sell, or exchange anything above the value of a sixpence,' nor could he use tobacco without permission of the president or prescription of a physician, and then only 'in a sober and private manner.'

In spite of all this praiseworthy regulation, however, the infant college, which should have been a stronghold of piety, was not free from the taint of 'willfulle heresie.' There was the painful conduct of President Dunster, who obstinately would neither renounce nor conceal his opposition to infant baptism, and who was therefore haled before a Grand Jury and removed from office for 'poisoning the minds of his students and thus unfitting them to become preachers of the truth.' By the early quarter of the eighteenth century the College had fallen into a sad state of decay. Its buildings were dilapidated, the number of students reduced, and all available funds did not amount to £1000.

Cambridge in those days was still primitive. The forest was still near at hand and the town had not yet 250 taxable inhabitants. 'A great many bears are killed at Cambridge and the neighboring towns about this time,' wrote student Belknap of Harvard.

But the town had its elegant sophistication. The wealthy and aristocratic families who gave social strength to the Church 'made a superior figure to most in the country.' The Phipses, Inmans, Vassalls, Sewalls, Lees, Ruggles, Olivers, and Lechmeres were all in easy circumstances. The whole easterly part of the town was divided into a few great farms, and the luxurious estates stretching along Brattle Street on the highway to Watertown won for it the name of Tory Row.

Tories were, however, soon to become decidedly unpopular in Cambridge. In 1768, delegates from ninety-five towns met in patriotic protest at Faneuil Hall — among them two Cambridge delegates. On March 8, 1770, the solemn tolling of the bell in the meeting house in Cambridge mingled with the tones of the bells at Charlestown and Roxbury while the victims of the Boston Massacre were carried through the streets of Boston to their burial. In May of that year, the House of Representatives sat in the halls of Harvard College. In 1772, events were moving rapidly toward the crisis. Cambridge elected a revolutionary committee of ten despite the efforts of William Brattle, its Tory Moderator, to prevent it. The night following the famous Boston Tea Party thousands of people assembled round the courthouse steps, forcing the Crown's officials to resign, including High Sheriff, Judges, and Councillors.

One evening a party of British soldiers dined in Cambridge, arousing great suspicion. That night, hoofbeats echoed in the frosty air — Paul Revere set out on his midnight ride; William Dawes, his comrade, galloped over the Great Bridge into Cambridge to arouse the town. The women and children, awakened by the 'horrors of that midnight cry were bidden to take refuge near Fresh Pond away from the Redcoats' line of march.' From all quarters, small companies of militia and Minutemen were hastening to Cambridge.

By the end of the week a rude army of fifteen to twenty thousand men had assembled. For the next year, after the nineteenth of April, 1775, Cambridge became the headquarters of the first American army.

Shortly after the Battle of Bunker Hill, a cavalcade of citizens and a troop of light horse gathered by the Watertown road. There they were met by General George Washington, newly commissioned Commander. The weathered bronze tablet on the Common gate tells the rest of the story:

Near this Spot
on July 3, 1775
George Washington
took command of the American Army.

Through a glass, from a 'crow's-nest' erected in the branches of a tree, Washington surveyed the surrounding country. A citizen wrote: 'Thousands are at work, every day from four until eleven o'clock in the morning. ... There is a great overturning in Camp. Generals Washington and Lee are upon the line every day. Everyone is made to know his place, and keep in it or be tied up and receive forty lashes.'

On the first day of the new year, over the camp a new flag of thirteen stripes was unfurled, symbolizing the union of the thirteen Colonies. On the second day of March, the booming of cannon and mortar announced that the bombardment of Boston had begun. A sortie and counter attack by the British was expected; but on the seventeenth day of March the British troops were seen moving out of the city. Boston was evacuated and Washington left for New York soon after. The military days of Cambridge were ended.

After the Revolution, the life of the little town flowed along. The church gave an impulse to the college, the college to the town, and a scholastic and literary atmosphere took form, regarded as the epitome of American culture even by critical European intellectuals. Cambridge, borne on a sluggish but smooth and comfortable current, was entering upon the second chapter of its existence, as the *Home of the Literati.*

Oliver Wendell Holmes, the kindly 'Autocrat of the Breakfast Table,' brilliant talker and disarming wit, too sympathetic to practice medicine despite his brilliant contribution in the discovery of puerperal fever, at fifty had embarked on a new career — literature. Associated with him was a young Harvard professor of modern languages, Henry Wadsworth Longfellow. No poems of the era entered more deeply into the life of the people than Longfellow's. 'The Psalm of Life' was translated before the century was out into fifteen languages. The children of Cambridge subscribed to give him an armchair from the wood of the 'spreading chestnut tree.' James Russell Lowell, also a Harvard professor, and also a poet, author of the famous 'Biglow Papers,' was twice appointed United States ambassador, once to Spain and once to the Court of St. James's. In London his popularity was tremendous in literary circles.

Now appeared the *North American Review*, devoted to the 'true revival of polite learning,' its editors and its foremost contributors mainly from Cambridge. Similarly came into being *The Dial*, the journal of the famous Transcendental Club, edited by the brilliant Margaret Fuller. Two famous presses, the University Press and The Riverside Press, were a practical factor in this literary domination.

The history of Cambridge is peppered with the names of scholars, historians, and scientists. Among the historians are Henry Adams, Ticknor, John Fiske, and Palfrey. To these may be added distinguished European scholars, among them the great scientist Louis Agassiz from Switzerland; Francis Sales, that living Gil Blas in hairpowder and pigtail, from France.

By the last quarter of the eighteenth century, Cambridge the *University City* was far beyond the embryo stage. 'This business of teaching, lodging, boarding and clothing and generally providing for the [Harvard] students [who numbered five hundred] was the occupation of the majority of the households of the Old Village.' College and town, mutually dependent, grew steadily during the next century.

One evening in 1878, Dr. Gilman, a noted teacher, historian, and author, invited Prof. Greenough and his wife to come to his house to talk over a very important matter, namely, the foundation of a college for women.

Radcliffe was created, unofficially, in 1879, as a mere association of Harvard instructors, who agreed that in response to popular demand they would give women 'some opportunity for systematic study in courses parallel to those of the University.' There was no official connection with Harvard until 1894. In that year the new college was formally named Radcliffe, in honor of Ann Radcliffe of England, donor of the first Harvard scholarship fund. The new institution of learning was long known among the irreverent as Harvard Annex, and serious qualms were felt by the respectable citizenry of Cambridge at the idea of 'hosts of young women walking unescorted through the town.'

Today, though Radcliffe has its own President and other administrative officers, the counter-signature of the President of Harvard on all diplomas officially establishes standards of scholarship equal to those of Harvard.

In 1916 another and most distinguished institution of learning added itself to Cambridge, the Massachusetts Institute of Technology. Late one August afternoon, a procession, its members clad as Venetian sailors and led by a marshal in the crimson and velvet of a Doge, moved slowly to the river edge in Boston. Followed by a group of men in gowns and crimson hoods, and bearing a great gilded and ornamental chest containing charter and archives, the solemn procession moved forward. They were met by a Venetian barge, which, under the eyes of ten thousand spectators, bore them away to the other shore.

The processional solemnity, the colorful spectacle, the silent throngs massed on both banks of the river, the hovering sailboats and motor craft, constituted a peculiarly appropriate celebration of a civic event of tremendous import: the University City had come of age.

So, too, but without heralds or fanfare, the date unnoticed and unrecorded, had the *Industrial City*.

While Washington was still President, the building of the Unknown City began. One of its founders was a lad who walked ninety miles from a New Hampshire farm to make his fortune. From good Deacon Livermore he learned to make brown soap. Today from his efforts stands the Lever Brothers Soap Works, one of the largest in the country.

One of its founders was a cook on a Nova Scotia fishing schooner, a boy of sixteen who came to Cambridge to seek his fortune, paying his toll over the bridge with a lead pencil. He learned to make coffins, and today his business is part of the National Casket Company.

Two of its founders, named Little and Brown, were clerks in a bookstore. They, with Henry O. Houghton, founder of The Riverside Press, established two great publishing houses in Boston.

The stories of these men and a hundred more read like those of Oliver Optic, and are stranger than fiction. Among them were the farsighted men who built the town buildings on the edge of a marsh in the far corner of the town and reclaimed the useless mud flats along the river, where great factories stand today. They made the laws, freed the bridges from tolls, founded the banks, and kept the town records. Old residents still recall the hundred and twenty-four foot chimney of the New England Glass Company, and the great banquet held on its top the day that it was completed.

Before mid-century the Unknown City was a going concern with eight times as many workers in its factories as there were students in the college.

Today the country's first ladder factory and the great carriage works are but memories. So, too, are the immense ice cuttings on Fresh Pond, from which the ice trade of the country was controlled. But here, laying the foundations of today's industrial city, was made the first galvanized iron pipe, relieving thousands of tinsmiths from making their pipe by hand. Here were the machines that produced the first piano keys, and,

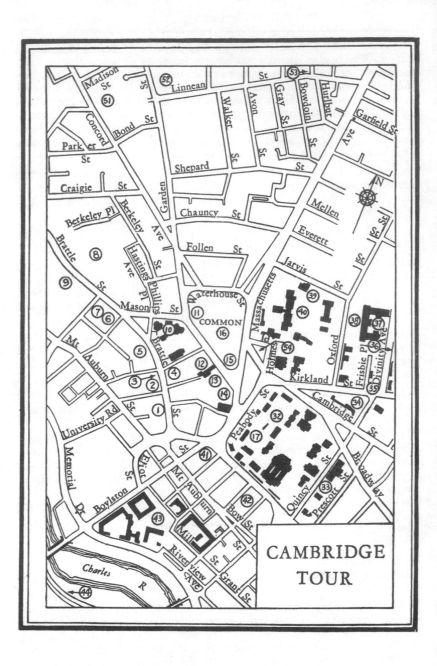

CAMBRIDGE
TOUR

in humbler fields, perfected flowerpots, the famous reversible collars, waterproof hats, and the first mechanical egg-beater. Call the roll of the industries today and 'Kendall Square will answer: Ink, machineries, and foundries; glass, rubber, food and cracker factories. Call the roll and North Cambridge and Cambridgeport will answer: Binderies, printeries, and paper boxes; wire cable, valves, and boilers.

Here it lies, crowded in between and around two great universities: a city of workers, most of whose thousands never even dreamed of going to college, many of whom never even completed high school; yet a city no less real than its intellectual other self, with no less lusty a heritage and no less potent and problematic a future.

FOOT TOUR 1 — 1.5 m.

SW. from Harvard Square on Brattle St.; R. from Brattle St.

1. The *Brattle Mansion* (*open*), 42 Brattle St., is a three-story, clapboarded, gambrel-roofed house with dormer windows, shorn of much of its former glory, but otherwise well preserved as the home of the Cam-

bridge Social Union. Built in 1727, it was one of the 18th century show houses of Cambridge.

Later it was the home of Margaret Fuller (1810–50), the most brilliant American woman of her day, a friend of Emerson and other transcendentalists, first editor of the *Dial*, author of 'Woman in the Nineteenth Century,' literary critic and teacher. Holmes, who went to grammar school with her, described Margaret Fuller as a queer child; and the urbane and customarily gallant Lowell went as far as to call her 'that dreadful old maid.' In her thirties, however, she married the Marquis D'Ossoli in Italy and bore him a son. On their return voyage to America she perished with him and the child in a shipwreck off New Jersey.

2. The *Site of the Village Smithy* immortalized by Longfellow is marked by a stone at the corner of Story St.

3. The *Cock Horse Tearoom* (*open*), 56 Brattle St., was built in 1811 as the home of Dexter Pratt, the village blacksmith ('The smith a mighty man was he'). The main house, to which have been added quaint and harmonious ells, is of two stories with brown clapboards and green blinds.

4. The *Read House* (*private*), 55 Brattle St., was built in 1725. It is a two-and-a-half-story yellow frame dwelling distinguished by a white doorway framed by wedge-shaped wood quoins. Though encroached upon by the business district, it maintains a front garden stretching back 60 feet from the sidewalk to the house.

5. *Mary Longfellow Greenleaf's Home* (*private*), 76 Brattle St., is a two-and-a-half-story brown frame dwelling with a flat-roofed ell. Its one-time owner was a sister of the famous poet. Another brother, Samuel, wrote several fine hymns still in general use.

6. The *House that John Fiske Built* (*private*), corner of Ash St., is a Victorian dwelling with a tower, which the eminent historian (1842–1901) was building at the time of his sudden death. An early champion of the then heretical theory of evolution, Fiske was not invited to teach at Harvard. After the University embraced the theory it still thought Fiske a little too 'popular' to adorn its faculty, but awarded him an honorary degree.

7. The *Belcher House* (*private*), 94 Brattle St., is an impressive mansion of yellow frame, with a mansard roof and white roof-rail. Having main entrances both east and west, it could easily be mistaken for a double house, and as a matter of fact the west end was constructed first — some experts say as early as 1635, because of its use of shell plaster in the chimney. The east end, a harmonious block, dates from 1700. Although the house has undergone alterations, it is still a dignified example of the more massive type of Colonial home.

8. The *Craigie-Longfellow House* (*study and grounds open Sat. 2–4*), 105 Brattle St., the home of Henry Wadsworth Longfellow and now occupied by his grandson, Henry Wadsworth Longfellow Dana, has a mellow prosperous dignity very characteristic of the poet himself. Built in 1759 by Major John Vassall, a Tory, the house is a three-story square yellow

clapboarded mansion with white Ionic pilasters, a white roof-rail, and yellow brick chimneys capped with ornamental hoods. Side piazzas, east and west, overlook wide lawns, and in front of the house a small formal park runs down almost to the Charles River.

This was one of the seven famous houses that made up Tory Row. When Major Vassall fled to Boston in 1774, General Washington made the house his headquarters. Martha Washington joined him in December, and on the sixth of January they celebrated their wedding anniversary here. Later the house was occupied by Dr. Andrew Craigie, who added the banquet hall behind the study and entertained lavishly. He died bankrupt, and his wife rented rooms.

Young Longfellow came here to lodge in 1837, in his second year of teaching at Harvard College, and was installed in the second-floor rooms at the right of the entrance. His study at that time had once been Washington's private chamber. In this historic atmosphere, the poet wrote 'Hyperion,' 'The Psalm of Life,' 'The Wreck of the Hesperus,' and other early poems. Here he brought his second bride, Frances Appleton of Boston, whose father gave them the house as a wedding present. In 1845 the poet's former study became the nursery, and the study was transferred to the right-hand front room on the lower floor of the mansion.

Here in his later years were held the meetings of the Dante Club. At the Wednesday evening gatherings, to which Lowell, Norton, and other scholars and friends were invited, Longfellow read his translation of 'The Divine Comedy,' and welcomed suggestions for revision. The evenings always ended with a good supper, good wine and good conversation.

9. *Longfellow Park*, opposite the Craigie-Longfellow House, was named after the poet and later given to the city by his family and friends. At the lower end of the park stands a *Memorial Monument* by Daniel Chester French, embellished in bas-relief with figures of some of the poet's best known characters, including 'The Village Blacksmith,' 'Miles Standish,' 'Evangeline,' and 'Hiawatha.'

Retrace Brattle St.; L. from Brattle St. on Mason St.

10. The *Campus of Radcliffe College* for women occupies a block bounded by Garden, Mason, James, and Brattle Sts. and Appian Way.

The architecture of the college buildings, like those of Harvard, derives from the Georgian; but the more modern of them are tempered with a strain of refinement — especially in interior work — which distinguishes and feminizes them. Unlike Harvard, where the architecture runs the full gamut from early Georgian through Victorian Gothic and Richardsonian Romanesque to revived Colonial forms, Radcliffe has maintained a certain consistency of style.

> *Fay House*, the Administration Building, is the oldest structure. It was built in 1807 by Nathaniel Ireland as a private home from, according to tradition, designs by Charles Bulfinch. *Agassiz House* and *Bertram Hall* were designed by the architect, Alexander W. Longfellow. The *Library* was designed by Winslow and Bige-

low, and *Hemenway Hall*, the gymnasium, was built in 1899 from designs by McKim, Mead, and White.

Alice Mary Longfellow Hall, completed in 1931, brought to its architects, Perry, Shaw, and Hepburn, award of the Parker medal. The design of this building, which is devoted to lecture halls, is based upon that of University Hall, a Harvard building designed by Bulfinch. Besides the base course of cut granite, a special brick of a pink salmon color was used in the structure to match that of Fay House.

R. from Mason St. on Garden St.

11. The *Site of the Washington Elm*, under which Washington took command of the Continental Army in 1775, is marked by a circular plaque with bronze letters.

12. *Christ Church*, designed by Peter Harrison and built in 1761, is the oldest church building in Cambridge, and was used in the Revolution as a barracks for the Colonial troops. The gray flush-board exterior and the small squat wooden tower, visibly leaning forward, and only relieved by small lunette windows at front and sides, are not particularly prepossessing, though their humility has a certain charm; and they give little idea of the great beauty of the interior. It is, in fact, among the four or five best church interiors in or near Boston, and is a jewel of Georgian Colonial. The simplicity of the seven tall windows at each side, and the six white wooden columns in each of the side aisles, give it, though small, a great deal of dignity; and the mahogany-colored pew-backs add the necessary touch of warmth. An unusual feature is the presence of heavy two-piece slatted shutters *inside* the church, folded back so as partly to obscure the white wooden pilasters between the windows. These do much to enrich the whole effect of the interior, and to give it depth. The windows, of plain glass, are heavily muntined in the early Georgian manner. The fine crystal chandeliers were given in memory of Mrs. Francis Sayre, daughter of Woodrow Wilson. The tower holds the Harvard Chime, a set of thirteen bells given in 1860 by Harvard graduates. The original organ loft remains, but the metal pipes of the original organ were melted into bullets during the Revolution.

13. The *Old Town Burying Ground* (*open to visitors*) lies adjacent between Christ Church and the First Parish Church and dates from 1636, the year Harvard College was founded. Here lie buried most of the early settlers and the earlier presidents of Harvard College.

R. from Garden St. on Massachusetts Ave.

14. The *First Parish Church* (Unitarian) houses the oldest church organization in Cambridge, dating from 1633. Among its early pastors was Thomas Hooker, who, disagreeing with some of the policies of the Massachusetts Bay clergy, quietly and peaceably led his flock to Hartford, Connecticut. The present building, a gray wooden edifice with a latticed belfry, was erected in 1833. Harvard College commencements were held here from 1833 to 1873, and a number of Harvard Presidents, including Dr. Eliot, were inaugurated here. Its most popular minister was the late Samuel McChord Crothers, genial wit and essayist, who after listening to the speeches at a certain Harvard Commencement re-

marked that he gathered that the world had been in great danger, but that all would now be well.

Retrace Massachusetts Ave.

15. The *George Washington Memorial Gateway* to the Common at the corner of Garden St. was dedicated on the sesquicentennial of Washington's taking command of the Continental Army.

16. The *Common* was originally the common pasture and was called the 'cow common.' On it criminals were punished, and it was the scene of several executions.

FOOT TOUR 2

(Harvard University)

E. from Harvard Square on Massachusetts Ave.

17. The *Wadsworth House (semi-private housing the Alumni Association)*, which stands at the edge of Harvard Yard opposite Holyoke St. was built in 1726. It is a typical yellow clapboarded Colonial house of two-and-a-half-stories, and is of considerable dignity. The ell is of brick; the roof gambrel, with dormers; green blinds set off the 24-paned windows on the lower floor. Harvard presidents, from Wadsworth to Leverett, lived here, and Washington stayed here briefly in 1775.

L. from Massachusetts Ave. into the Yard by the McKean Gate, the first gate E. of Wadsworth House.

18. The *Harvard Yard*, which is the university campus, is the original center of the College, and still keeps much of its Old World charm. Not unlike Lincoln's Inn Fields and Gray's Inn, in London, and roughly contemporary with them, it shares much of their characteristic blending of Georgian stateliness and mellowed red brick. On the whole, the modern additions to the Yard have been tactfully adapted to their surroundings, with but a few exceptions, to be noted later. It may well be described as one of the most beautiful college campuses in America.

19. The *Chinese Student Memorial* is a granite shaft 10 feet high, carved with dragons at the top, its base resting on a dragon-headed mythical monster. An inscribed tablet explains in Chinese that it was presented at the Harvard Tercentenary in 1936 by 1,000 Chinese alumni of the University.

20. The *Widener Library (open Mon.–Fri.* 8.45–10; *Sat.* 8.45–5.30), on the south side of the Yard, is a huge red-brick edifice which unfortunately somewhat dwarfs its surroundings, and has therefore been adversely criticized. A wide cascade of shallow stone steps leads up into the deep Corinthian portico, with its 12 lofty columns, the main floor being considerably above ground level. Designed by Horace Trumbauer and built in 1913–14, the Library is a memorial to Harry Elkins Widener, class of 1907, who was drowned with the sinking of the 'Titanic.' The much-marbled interior, at its worst in the pillared entrance hall, has been considered too lavish to be quite in keeping with the general character of the college buildings. On the stairway above are John Singer Sargent's *World War Murals*.

The *Treasure Room*, reached from the southwest corner of the entrance hall, is allotted to such rare books and manuscripts as need special supervision. Here are a collection of the various editions of the 'Imitatio Christi,' a similar series of the issues of the 'Compleat Angler,' the 'George Herbert Collection,' given by George Herbert Palmer, and a remarkable theater collection. Among examples of fine printing is the collection of books designed and printed by Bruce Rogers. Also of interest is a case containing an approximate reproduction of the library of books bequeathed by John Harvard.

The *Widener Memorial Room*, on the first landing of the main stairway, entered between the two Sargent murals, contains a portrait of Widener and his own collection of rare books, among them an almost unrivaled collection of Stevensoniana. This room, finished in carved English oak, is approached through an octagonal reception room executed in white Alabama marble.

The *Poetry Room*, on the third floor, west of the staircase, dedicated to George Edward Woodberry, contains the valuable Amy Lowell collection, especially interesting for its Keats manuscripts.

21. The *New Yard*, on which the Library faces, bounded on the west by University Hall, on the north by Memorial Church, and on the east by Sever Hall, was the scene of the tercentenary exercises in 1936.

22. *University Hall*, at the left, designed by Charles Bulfinch and built in 1813–15, is one of the most beautiful buildings in the Yard. Its gray Chelmsford granite body, white wooden pilasters and white chimneys, provides an excellent foil for the Georgian red brick which everywhere surrounds it. Particularly effective, in the unusual impression of lightness which they give, are the six tall round-topped windows of the second story which light the *Faculty Room*. Within is a flight of granite stairs, each step a single granite block, so designed that they appear to climb to the second floor unsupported. With its white wainscoting and pilasters, green-tinted walls, and the twelve tall windows with deep-paneled reveals, the Faculty Room is easily the handsomest room in the university. One regrets the presence of a good many indifferent portraits of Harvard worthies. To be noted, however, is the very fine portrait of Nicholas Boylston by John Singleton Copley, one of the painter's most brilliant works.

23. The *Statue of John Harvard*, which stands in front of University Hall, was done by Daniel Chester French in 1880, and is an imaginary likeness; no portrait of Harvard is known to exist.

24. *Massachusetts Hall* was erected in 1720 with funds granted by the Province of Massachusetts, and designed by John Leverett, then president of the college, is the oldest of all the Harvard buildings, and in recent years has been used as the archetype from which the style of the new buildings has been evolved. Standing opposite University Hall, but endlong to it, it plays a lesser part in the general impression of the Yard than the houses which face directly on the Yard. Simple in line, with gambrel roof, end-chimneys, and white roof-rail, the belt-courses of brick between the stories and the somewhat heavy woodwork of the windows (as in the thick muntins) give it an air of great solidity. It is this effect which has been sought, for the most part in the recent additions to Harvard — an earlier and heavier type of Georgian Colonial, with the emphasis on weight and simplicity.

25. *Harvard Hall*, to the North of Massachusetts Hall and parallel with it, built in 1766 from the design of Sir Francis Barnard, has been largely spoiled by later additions, in 1842 and 1870, but traces of the 18th century character may still be seen in the upstairs lecture rooms.

26. *Hollis* and *Stoughton Halls*, to the North, are almost identical twins, the former built in 1763 from the design of Colonel Thomas Dawes, the latter being frankly modeled after it. They are not quite identical, however, for Hollis has belt-courses between stories, and looks heavier than the more graceful Stoughton.

27. *Holworthy Hall* (1812), which closes the north end of the Yard, does most, along with University, Hollis, and Stoughton Halls, to give the Yard its character.

It was named for Sir Matthew Holworthy, a generous English benefactor of the college, and its architect, Loammi Baldwin, was a graduate of the college, class of 1800. The building is a very nearly perfect example of the essential unobtrusiveness with which, in such groupings as this, the Georgian Colonial style makes its effect. Seen from any part of the Yard, with its simplicity, in which no detail, not even the admirable doorways with their stone trim and splayed steps, is conspicuous, it affords the perfect counterfoil to University Hall, and the perfect end-piece for the finest part of the Yard. The brick work is very good without being quite as good as that of Hollis and Stoughton — both of the latter having a color of brick probably not to be matched in beauty today.

28. *Holden Chapel* (between Hollis and Stoughton) is a tiny building of which the most conspicuous feature is the huge coat of arms with elaborate mantling (much imitated in the new college Houses) which adorns the bright blue flush-board gable of the eastern end. But it is also the most complete small example of pure Georgian Colonial architecture to be seen in the Yard, and one of the finest in America. Built in 1744, its plans were probably drawn in London. Its anonymous architect set an example of purity which is now probably more intelligently appreciated than in his own day.

Recross the Yard and pass University Hall to the N.

29. *Appleton Chapel* or *Memorial Church* (*open daily by the west door,* 9–5), built in 1932 as a War Memorial for Harvard men, was designed by the firm of Coolidge, Shepley, Bulfinch, and Abbott, who were also architects of the new Houses. It tries at one and the same time to oppose the mass of Widener to the south and the dead weight of Thayer Hall to the west, with a portico of heavy Doric columns directed toward each. A doubtful success, though admired by some, the building seems on the whole to be at odds with its surroundings, and not too well synthesized in itself: the needle-fine white spire appears much too elongated for so squat and massive a structure. Part of this effect is due to the excessive fatness of the wooden Doric columns, and to the fact also that the pediment above the south portico breaks the otherwise admirable long roof-line. The interior, very much in the Wren tradition, is carried out almost wholly in white, with white Colonial pews, Corinthian columns, and pilasters between heavy-muntined rounded windows. The pulpit is of the Colonial wineglass design, and advanced into the body of the church.

At the right of the nave is the *Memorial Room*, which commemorates the 373 Harvard men who died in the World War. The pseudo-classic treatment, carried out in Italian travertine, is too opulent, and out of key with the rest of the church. The low-relief figures on the north wall, by Joseph Coletti, and the sculptured group by Malvina Hoffman do little to redeem it.

30. *Robinson Hall*, to the east, built in 1901 by McKim, Mead, and White, houses the Schools of Architecture and Landscape Architecture. The entrance is properly from the south, the side which faces Emerson, which, together with Sever and the Fogg Museum (across Quincy St.), forms what is known as *Sever Quadrangle*, one of the pleasantest quadrangles in the Yard, and the scene of the Harvard Commencements. The small brick columns which intersperse the windows of the second story, together with the wide shallow steps, set with urns before the doorway, and the sculptured plaques inlaid in the walls right and left of the door, combine to give an air of spaciousness to a small quadrangle which might easily have looked a little cramped.

31. *Sever Hall* (1880), a red-brick building which forms the west side of the Sever Quadrangle, was designed by Henry Hobson Richardson, famous for his adaptations of the Romanesque style. Not too fortunate a specimen, it was the first, and remains the most glaring note of incongruity in an otherwise harmonious grouping of Georgian Colonial buildings. Of interest is the brick carving, comparatively rare, over the doors at front and back.

32. *Emerson Hall* (1905), designed by Coolidge, Shepley, Bulfinch, and Abbott for the Philosophy Department, is a somewhat heavy building whose massive brick columns and pilasters, of Doric design, dominate Sever Quadrangle from the

south. Beyond this, in the southeast corner of the Yard, are the *President's House* (1912) (*private*), a brick Colonial house designed by Coolidge, Shepley, Bulfinch, and Abbott, and the *Dana-Palmer House* (1820) (*private*), built by Thomas Foster. To the west of this, behind Widener, and somewhat cramped for room, is *Wigglesworth Hall* (1931), which together with *Straus Hall* in the southwest corner of the Yard, and *Lionel and Mower Halls* in the northwest (1926-31), are the most recent additions to the Yard, showing on the whole a very skillful adaptation of the style of Massachusetts Hall.

Exit from the Yard by the SE. gate; L. from gate on Quincy St.

33. The *Fogg Art Museum* (*open weekdays* 9-5; *free*) is an admirably designed Georgian Colonial building of red brick in which function and appearance have been skillfully combined. It was built in 1927 from the designs of Charles A. Coolidge, with the co-operation of Henry R. Shepley and Meyric Rogers. In addition to its use for lectures and class-work, it houses an extremely good art collection. Noteworthy are two very fine Spanish sculptures in wood of the 13th century, a superb group of Copley portraits, some excellent Italian primitives, fine Tintorettos and El Grecos, and a very large collection of prints.

34. *Memorial Hall* (*open Mon.-Fri.*, 9-5; *Sat.* 9-1), the one fantastic building in all the Harvard group, is an immense pile of red brick in Victorian Gothic style, with a gargoyled tower which is a landmark for miles. Dedicated as a memorial to Harvard men who died in defense of the Union in the Civil War, and built between 1870 and 1878 from the designs of Ware and Van Brunt, this remarkable building is fascinating if only as a monument in a style now wholly discredited. The *Great Hall*, at the west end, was formerly used as a dining-hall, and *Sanders Theatre*, the *Auditorium* at the east end, is now used for part of the Commencement exercises and for symphony concerts.

R. from Quincy St. into Kirkland St.

35. The *Germanic Museum* or Adolph Busch Hall (1917) (*open weekdays except holidays from* 9-5; *Sun.* 1-5), corner of Divinity Ave., is a curious and very interesting stucco and limestone building with red-tile roof. It was done from designs by Prof. Germain Bestelmeyer of Munich, in the pre-war Munich 'kunstlerisch' style, the designs then being adapted to local conditions by Dean H. Langford Warren of the Harvard School of Architecture. The low clock-tower is not unimpressive, the outdoor courtyard, with a cast of the Brunswick Lion, charming, and the interior affords an admirable progressive survey of the characteristic features of Romanesque, Gothic, and Renaissance styles. It contains also a collection, outstanding in America, of reproductions of great medieval sculpture.

L. from Kirkland St. into Divinity Ave.

36. The *Semitic Museum* (*open weekdays* 9-5; *Sun.* 1-4.30) houses collections which relate to the history and arts of the Arabs, Aramaeans, Assyrians, Babylonians, Hebrews, and Phoenicians. Among Assyrian reproductions are bas-reliefs from the palace of Ashurnazirpal, King of Assyria (884-860 B.C.) and the Black Obelisk of Shalmaneser III (860-825 B.C.). In the Babylonian collection is the oldest known map (dating

from 2500 B.C.) and discovered by a Harvard expedition. Of importance in the Palestinian collection is a model of the hill of Zion with its modern buildings and a tentative reconstruction of Herod's Temple, made, in 1903, by Dr. Konrad Schick of Berlin. Other conjectural reconstructions include the Tabernacle and the Temple of Solomon.

37. The *Biological Laboratories*, housed in what is certainly one of the most distinguished of the university buildings, form a three-sided court five stories in height, and offer a superb example of modern 'functional' architecture. Largely the design of Henry Shepley (Coolidge, Shepley, Bulfinch, and Abbott), and built in 1931 with the help of the Rockefeller Foundation, this lovely brick building, with its harmoniously spaced tall windows and exquisite use of plane surfaces, is a gentle reminder of what might have been done with Widener Library. The frieze of animals carved in the brick of the upper facing by Miss Katherine Lane, and so skillfully done that the shadows resulting from the slant-cut carving enhance the effect of the line, affords just the requisite offset of richness to the beautiful simplicity of the building as a whole; and Miss Lane's colossal bronze rhinos and carved doors complete a distinguished architectural unit.

L. from Divinity Ave. by footpath to Oxford St.

38. The *University Museum* (*open weekdays* 9–4.30; *Sun.* 1–4.30), opposite Jarvis St. is a six-story rambling brick structure. Its most celebrated and popular exhibit is that of the *Glass Flowers*. Glass models of the humbler flowers of field and wood are realistically produced with an astonishing delicacy of detail and complete botanic accuracy. The secret of this art was discovered in the 19th century by a German family named Blaschka, and it remains with them.

Stuffed specimens of *North American Birds* form one of the most complete collections and the *Harvard Forest Models* depict the history of land-clearing and reforestation.

L. from Oxford St. into Jarvis St.

39. The *Children's Museum of Cambridge* (*open weekdays except Sat.* 8.30–4.30; *Sun.* 1–4.30; *closed on Sat.*), 5 Jarvis St., is a small red wooden building, a department of the Cambridge Public Schools and indirectly connected with Harvard University through the study privileges accorded at University Museum. The Children's Museum is less an exhibition hall than a classroom and club center for visual education in geography and nature study. Some of the instruction is given at the museum, some at the public schools, and much of it in the fields. There are, however, Indian and Eskimo models, small collections of mineral and stuffed birds, and exhibits of such popular hobbies as postage stamps and airplane modeling.

L. from Jarvis St. into footpath at W. end of Children's Museum.

40. The *Harvard Law School* mainly occupies Langdell Hall, a long two-story limestone building with an Ionic colonnade. This is the oldest law

school now in existence in the United States. Its library of over 460,000 volumes is claimed to be the most complete law library in the world, and contains the statutes, judicial decisions, and legal treatises of every country on the globe. Portraits of eminent lawyers and judges within its walls include canvases by Lawrence, Raeburn, Romney, Lely, and Stuart.

R. from footpath into Cambridge St.; L. from Cambridge St. into Peabody St.; straight ahead on Massachusetts Ave. through Harvard Square.

41. A Tercentenary Marker, corner of Dunster St., marks the *Site Of The First Meeting House*, where Thomas Shepard, that 'holy heavenly sweet affecting and soul-ravishing' preacher, held forth.

This same corner is the *Site Of The House Of Stephen Daye*, the first printer in British America, who arrived here in 1638 and set up his press under the auspices of Harvard.

R. from Massachusetts Ave. into Linden St.

42. The *'Bishop's Palace'* (Apthorp House) (*private*) is half hidden in a courtyard, reached by a footpath. It is a fine three-story mansion with white clapboards, dentiled cornice, and large inner chimneys, built in 1760 by the first minister of Christ Church (Episcopal) and named irreverently by Provincial dissenters. It now serves as the residence of the Master of Adams House, the nearest to the Yard of the 'New Houses.'

R. from Linden St. into Mt. Auburn St.; L. from Mt. Auburn St. into Holyoke St.; L. from Holyoke St. into Holyoke Place.

43. These *'New Houses,'* seven in number, lie between Winthrop St. and the Charles River, from north to south, and between Boylston Street and McCarthy Road, from west to east. Something more than dormitories for the three upper classes, they serve as units for special types of study concentration, with resident masters and tutors, and their own libraries and dining-halls. Some of them were built originally as Freshman dormitories, but their amalgamation into the Houses has done a good deal to shift the center of the University toward the river, and has created a little university town of great charm. Of the completely new Houses — Lowell (1930), Dunster (1930), and Eliot (1931), all designed by Coolidge, Shepley, Bulfinch, and Abbott — perhaps Lowell, which is the largest, is also the handsomest. In all of them may be seen the following-out of the Georgian Colonial motif, with now and then a heavy leaning on Holden Chapel (as in the frequent use of arms and mantling on the gables) and University Hall (as in the dining-hall of Lowell, which bears a close resemblance to the Faculty Room). The rapidity with which they were built has made them possibly a shade too uniform, despite the deliberate attempt of the architects to vary them.

Retrace Holyoke Place; L. from Holyoke Place into Holyoke St.; L. from Holyoke St. into Mill St.; R. from Mill St. into Plympton St.

44. Across the Charles River from Memorial Drive is the *Harvard Business School* (graduate), visible on the opposite shore like another

fine group of the 'colleges within the college,' extending on either side of the white-columned *Baker Library* (*open*) with its white steeple. The establishment of the school in 1902 was accompanied by a sharp protest from scholars in the liberal arts against its association with cultural Harvard, but such comment has now largely disappeared. Baker Library contains 135,000 volumes and pamphlets relating to commerce and trade.

45. The *Harvard Stadium*, rising 60 feet in air and approximately two city blocks in length, is impressively visible across the river, just west of the Business School. It is not the largest in the country but was the first, and is still considered, with its ivy-clad arches and classic colonnade, one of the most beautiful. It seats 22,000 on the concrete, and with additional steel stands and temporary seats can accommodate a total of 57,750. It was constructed under the direction of Prof. Lewis Jerome Johnson, Class of 1887, and Joseph Ruggles Worcester, Class of 1882. The general architectural design was worked out by George Bruns de Gersdorff, Class of 1888, under the direction of Charles Follen McKim, Master of Arts, Harvard 1890. The stadium, 570 feet long by 420 feet wide, encloses a field 478 by 430 feet on which are held, in addition to the usual athletic events, part of the Class Day festivities and outdoor theatrical performances of note.

Tourists especially interested in Harvard University are referred to the following additional points of interest:

> Radcliffe College (10), First Parish Church (4), in list above; Mt. Auburn Cemetery (47), Cambridge Observatory (51), and the Botanic Garden and Gray Herbarium (52), below; also the Harvard Medical School and Arnold Arboretum (*see Boston*), the Thayer Bird Museum (*see Tour* 7, *LANCASTER*) and the Harvard Astronomical Observatory (*see Tour* 7, *HARVARD*) and the Black Brook Plantation (*see Tour* 1A, *HAMILTON*.

CAMBRIDGE MOTOR TOUR — 6 m.

SW. from Harvard Square through Brattle Street; R. from Brattle Street into Mt. Auburn St.

46. *Elmwood* (*private*), corner of Elmwood Ave., was the home of James Russell Lowell. It is a fine three-story yellow clapboarded mansion with white roof-rail and square yellow chimneys.

The house was built in 1767, and was first the home of Lieutenant Governor Oliver, the last of the royal deputies in Massachusetts, who in 1774 was forced by 4000 Cantabrigians to write his resignation and seek safety in Boston. In 1810 Elbridge Gerry lived here while he was Governor, just before becoming Vice-President in 1812. Lowell was born here and made it his lifelong home, except for his absences as United States minister to Spain and England (1877–85). Here he wrote his 'Vision of Sir Launfal' and the first of the 'Biglow Papers.'

47. *Mt. Auburn Cemetery (free map at gate)* has famous graves of nearly every one of note who has died in or near Boston for the past hundred years.

> Individual graves may be found by circling left from the gate, as follows: Mary Baker Eddy, Halcyon Ave.; Oliver Wendell Holmes, Lime Ave., in the Jackson plot of his wife's relatives; James Russell Lowell, Fountain Ave., next to the stone of the child immortalized in 'The First Snowfall'; Henry Wadsworth Longfellow, Indian Ridge Path, next to Grave Alice of 'The Children's Hour' (Laughing Allegra and Edith with Golden Hair became Mrs. Thorp and Mrs. Dana, respectively); Charlotte Cushman, Palm Ave. *(the trustees of the cemetery would be glad to hear of any of her heirs)*; Charles Sumner, Arethusa Path; Louis Agassiz, Bellwort Path, under a boulder taken from a glacier near his birthplace in Switzerland; Margaret Fuller, Pyrola Path; Edwin Booth, Anemone Path; Phillips Brooks, Mimosa Path; William Ellery Channing, Greenbrier Path.

> In Mt. Auburn are buried also Julia Ward Howe, Samuel G. Howe, Edward Everett, Hosea Ballou, Joseph Story, Rufus Choate, and the historians Prescott and Parkman.

The reason for the choice of Mt. Auburn by the families of so many celebrities, before it became so historically noted, was that it was for many years the only garden cemetery in the environs of Boston. It is still one of the two most beautiful. Its grounds are thickly wooded with rare trees and shrubs, landscaped with occasional ponds, and they rise to a commanding hill, from which is a dreamy view of the winding Charles River, Cambridge, Boston, and distant hills.

Retrace Mt. Auburn St.; L. from Mt. Auburn St. into Brattle St.

48. The *Nichols-Lee House (private)*, 159 Brattle St., is a heavy-set oblong three-story dwelling, clapboarded, except for a stone west end, in cinnamon color, with ivory-colored wood quoins, and surmounted by a roof-rail and a central chimney 12 feet wide, with six hoods. The 20-paned windows have brown blinds. A broad doorway, ivory colored, with pilasters in the Doric, fronts upon a lawn enclosed by a picket fence. The house dates from 1660, and was occupied at the time of the Revolution by Joseph Lee, a mild and kindly Tory who thought best to flee, but who was such a general favorite as a citizen that he was allowed to return after the war without confiscation of his property. When he died at over 90 years of age the entire city mourned.

49. *American Thomas Lee's House (private)*, 153 Brattle St., is one of several sumptuous and beautiful old mansions to be seen hereabout. It is a three-story, clapboarded house (1685), with mansard roof, dormer windows, white roof-rail, and massive chimneys painted white with black hoods. It is set behind an ornamental white picket fence, on a lawn shaded by horse chestnut trees, and broken by a terrace with a low white rail.

50. *Baroness Riedesel's House (private)*, 149 Brattle St., is of interest as having been the home of the Baron and Baroness Riedesel, prisoners of war in the days of the Continental Army's second major success. The Baron was Burgoyne's chief staff officer at Saratoga, and the Baroness's gay and vivid letters about her social life in Cambridge are evidence that the city treated her well, in spite of its Revolutionary sympathies. After

the Baroness left, Washington gave the house to 'English Thomas Lee,' a former Tory who changed over to the American Cause. English Thomas was so named to distinguish him from his neighbor 'American Thomas Lee.'

L. from Brattle St. into Craigie St.; R. from Craigie St. into Concord Ave.; L. from Concord Ave. into Garden St.

51. The *Cambridge Observatory of Harvard University* (*open weekdays* 9–5; *closed Sun. and holidays*), 60 Garden St., is in the unmarked hilly landscaped grounds just across the street from the Botanic Garden (*see No. 52, below*).

There is a public exhibit of *Astronomical Pictures* on glass plates lighted from behind. These are magnified examples of some of the famous collection of 400,000 glass plates which the University has made in studying motions, magnitudes, and variations of celestial objects. This collection is studied by astronomers from all over the world, and some of the plates come from another observatory of the University in South Africa. The beehive-like houses in the Cambridge grounds are shelters for powerful photographic telescopes and sky-patrol cameras, which on every clear night swing the circuit of the universe, noting everything that happens for some billions of miles.

52. The *Botanic Garden of Harvard University* (*open weekdays* 9–5; *closed Sun. and holidays*), corner of Garden and Linnaean Sts., was established in 1807 for the cultivation of all herbaceous plants hardy in this climate. From 1842 to 1872 Asa Gray, the celebrated botanist, was director. There are a rock garden, a rose garden, a water garden, and a greenhouse. In the grounds is the building of the *Gray Herbarium* (*open only to botanists*), containing 750,000 sheets of mounted specimens.

Retrace Garden St.; L. from Garden St. into Linnaean St.

53. The *Cooper-Frost-Austin House* (*open Thurs.* 1–5; *adm.* 25¢), 21 Linnaean St., built in 1657, is the oldest house in the city, except possibly for one block of the Belcher House at 94 Brattle St. It is a two-and-a-half-story clapboard dwelling with lean-to and central chimney, furnished in early Colonial style and owned by the Society for the Preservation of New England Antiquities.

R. from Linnaean St. into Massachusetts Ave.

54. The *Site of Oliver Wendell Holmes's Birthplace* is marked by a granite tablet beyond the triangular green opposite the Common. Here as a young physician he first displayed his shingle, on which he considered inscribing: 'The smallest fevers thankfully received.'

L. from Massachusetts Ave. into Peabody St.; R. from Peabody St. into Kirkland St.; L. from Kirkland St. into Irving St.

55. *Shady Hill* (*private*), 136 Irving St., is a broad two-story mansion of 1790 with a long front piazza, crowning a landscaped knoll. Its chief interest lies in its occupancy by Charles Eliot Norton (1827–1908), Harvard Professor of Art, and personal friend of Browning, Ruskin,

Carlyle, and the pre-Raphaelites. Norton was one of the most admired American scholars of the 19th century, and exerted a profound influence on all Harvard graduates of his day. Like Ruskin, however, he was deeply concerned with the moral implications of art, and it was once slyly said that his art courses were 'Lectures in Morals as Illustrated by Art.'

Retrace Irving St.; R. from Irving St. into Cambridge St.; L. from Cambridge St. into Felton St.; L. from Felton St. into Broadway.

56. The *Cambridge Public Library* (*open* 9–9), corner of Trowbridge St. (1889), is in the Romanesque style, of granite trimmed with sandstone. Murals in the reading room depict 'The Evolution of the Printing Press.' A collection of copies of paintings by old masters includes subjects by Correggio, Domenichino, Van der Werff, Murillo, and Raphael, and an original painting 400 years old (*artist unknown*), 'St. Jerome Interpreting the Scriptures.'

R. from Broadway into Inman St.

57. The *Site of General Putnam's Headquarters* during the Siege of Boston is marked by a tablet near the rear of City Hall. Putnam's troops had erected a small earthworks, known as Fort Washington, on the present Waverly Street, and had on the present Otis Street a battery which fired by mistake on the Brattle Square Church in Boston.

L. from Inman St. into Massachusetts Ave.; L. from Massachusetts Ave. into Main St.

58. *New Towne Court*, corner of Windsor St., a Federal Housing project, is an attempt to provide attractive low-cost homes for people of small incomes. It consists of six large and two small brick apartment buildings, entrance to all of which is gained from the court, which runs from one end of the unit to the other. It contains 294 modern apartments of three, four, and five rooms, with a central heating plant. Rentals are moderate and include the utilities: heat, water, electricity, gas, and refrigeration. On the corner stood the house in which Elias Howe, inventor of the sewing machine, lived and perfected his model.

Retrace Main St.; L. from Main St. into Massachusetts Ave.

59. The *Massachusetts Institute Of Technology*, corner of Memorial Drive, occupies an 80-acre campus in a beautiful location facing the broad terminal basin of the Charles River and, across this, the Boston skyline. Its 46 so-called separate buildings, of limestone and yellow brick, in restrained neo-Classic style, are in reality almost a single massive unit, connected by interior corridors, forming a U-shaped hollow square. A terraced lawn spreads before them, landscaped by rhododendrons, poplars, and small elms, and ornamented by formal rows of decorative lamp-posts. The central or administration building, with a low central dome and Ionic portico, is known simply as 'Number 10.' All the buildings are illuminated by flood-lights at night, and with their reflection in the beautiful waters of the Charles they constitute an outstanding attraction of Boston and Cambridge.

To scientists, every department of the Institute contains equipment and exhibits of absorbing interest. The general public, however, finds special features of more comprehensive appeal. In the lower right hand corridors of *Building* 10 are representative exhibits, changed frequently, from the Institute's noted *ceramics collection*, which comprises beautiful pottery and glass from all ages and lands, including specimens from the Chinese dynasties from 206 B.C. to A.D. 1850. In the dome of Building 10 is the *Library*, one of the best in the United States in scientific and engineering subjects.

In Building 5 is a *Ship Model Museum*, a part of the Institute's distinguished School of Naval Architecture and Marine Engineering, which fosters one of Tech's most popular sports, sailboat-racing in the Charles River Basin. In Building 4 is *The Colossus of Volts*, a giant electrostatic generator which created the highest steady direct voltage ever achieved by man. In the basement of Building 6 is *The Round Table of Light Camera*, a great circular table, hollow at its core, with a grating of optical glass, which has no rival as an apparatus for spectroscopy.

The *Guggenheim Aeronautical Laboratory* (Separate Building No. 35) has interesting wind-testing machines. Adjoining this laboratory, in Separate Building 20, is a large *Model of the Cape Cod Canal*, through which water is operated at the various levels and forces of the tides in the actual canal.

The *Walker Memorial*, a separate unnumbered building, is the student social and athletic center, distinguished by a lofty and handsome restaurant hall adorned with a vast mural by Edwin H. Blashfield, representing 'Technology Saluted by the Hosts of Science.' The building contains also reading rooms and a gymnasium.

Four main schools, the School of Science, the School of Engineering, the School of Architecture, and the Graduate School, together offer over 900 subjects of instruction. In the words of President Compton, the Institute 'pioneered in extending the laboratory method of instruction as an indispensable educational technique. It virtually created the modern profession of chemical engineering. Its courses in electrical and aeronautical engineerings and in applied physics were probably the first in the world.'

C H E L S E A . *City of Transformations*

City: Alt. 29, pop. 42,673, sett. 1624, incorp. town 1739, city 1857.

Railroad Station: Washington Ave. and Heard St. for B. & M. R.R.

Bus Station: Markell's Drugstore, Chelsea Square, for Greyhound Lines.

Accommodations: Hotels and rooming houses.

Information: Chamber of Commerce, 445 Broadway.

CHELSEA is a city of transformations. Humbly beginning as a trading post, it has been successively a manorial estate, an agricultural community, a ferry landing, a summer resort, a residential suburb and finally an industrial city. Its principal manufactures today are rubber, elastic webbing, boots and shoes, and paper stock.

In 1624, Samuel Maverick, a youth of twenty-two, saw possibilities in a permanent trade with the Indians of Winnisimmet, now Chelsea, and with some followers he set up his homestead, the first permanent one on Boston Harbor.

Ten years later he sold out his large holdings to Governor Richard Bellingham, one of the most extensive landowners about Boston. A leader in the political affairs of the Bay Colony, he must have been somewhat scandalously erratic from the Puritan point of view. Quite soon after his first wife's death, he married a woman betrothed to another man, performing the ceremony himself. When prosecuted for this breach of law and decorum, he, being a judge, refused to leave the bench, thereby trying and freeing himself.

With equal independence, he adopted a procedure with regard to his land which was not customary in New England. Dividing it up into four farms in manorial fashion, he leased out each quarter to a tenant farmer.

When in his eightieth year the old Governor was gathered to his fathers, he left behind him as his final self-assertion a last will and testament that was to torment legal minds for a century to come. The contest over this memorable will had no parallel in the country, and by tying up the property it effectively retarded the development of early Chelsea.

Though the original Bellingham purchase transformed Chelsea from a fur-trading post into an agricultural community, geographic location singled it out for another and more impressive function. Boston, practically insular until after the Revolution, was reached by land from towns to the north by a route which entailed a whole day's journey. For north-country folk, the nearest point of mainland to Boston was Winnisimmet (Chelsea) but a mile distant by water. Consequently, the General Court enacted a subsidy to encourage a ferry route between Boston, Charlestown and Winnisimmet. This was the first ferry in New England and probably in North America.

The Court also kept an eye on the ferry business, regulating fares and schedules and imposing suitable penalties for neglect of duty. The convenience and safety of the passage was a matter of vital concern to these early legislators. The difficulties they themselves experienced in crossing are vividly described in Cotton Mather's diary: 'A fearful hurricane and thunderstorm overtook us, just as we got out of Winnisimmet Ferryboat (a ferry three miles wide), which, had it overtaken us four or five minutes earlier, we had unquestionably perished in ye waters.'

The hazards of wind and tide often delayed travel; so, before long, taverns sprang up near the ferry, where, besides a night's lodging, 'strong waters' might be had to console or embolden the traveler.

Throughout much of the nineteenth century Chelsea was a well-known summer resort, offering not only country landscape, but also three miles of beautiful sandy beach (now Revere).

Paradoxically, the steam ferry made and then ruined Chelsea as a summer resort. The efficient operation of the Winnisimmet Company made commuting to Boston possible. In a phenomenally short period, Chelsea's population passed the ten thousand mark. After a while, manufacturing and shipping usurped the waterfront; the residential section was pushed back from the sea, and congestion of population followed. Its rustic appeal gone, many of the older inhabitants packed up and went elsewhere. Many remaining commuters departed after the great Chelsea fire burned their homes to the ground.

A century's upbuilding vanished in smoke on Palm Sunday morning, April 12, 1908. Because of a heavy gale, the flames spread with remarkable rapidity and within ten hours all buildings burned were in ruins. By nightfall the city was a devastated waste of smoldering embers: seventeen thousand four hundred and fifty people were homeless. It is said that in the entire burned area there was not enough combustible material left to start a kitchen fire.

In the reconstruction of the city, the business section was considerably enlarged and the population took on a decidedly cosmopolitan cast. Today Irish Catholics, Jews, Italians, Poles, and Armenians represent over eighty per cent of the total population.

POINTS OF INTEREST

1. *City Hall*, Broadway, in Bellingham Square, is in the Georgian Colonial style, its design having been based on that of Independence Hall at Philadelphia.

2. The *Thomas Pratt House* (about 1662) (*occasional visitors welcome*), 481 Washington Ave., occupied by a descendant of the original owner, sets back from the road, its steep sloping roof and huge chimneys distinguishing it from the modern dwellings which surround it on every side. The shingled exterior is in need of repair, but the interior has been well preserved and retains the spirit of the original design. The hand-hewn ceiling beams in the living-room and the warped floor boards are of special interest.

3. The *Bellingham-Cary House* (*open Thurs.* 2-5, *at other times through courtesy of the resident caretaker; adm. free*), 34 Parker St., is a square hip-roofed frame house with interior chimneys. The original portion was built in 1629 and was at one time the home of Governor Bellingham. It was remodeled by Samuel Cary in 1791-92, and was purchased by the Cary House Association in 1912. In it Washington quartered the last outpost of the left wing of the Continental Army besieging Boston.

4. *Powder Horn Hill*, Hillside Ave., is so named because it was believed sold by the Indians to the early settlers for a horn of gunpowder. On its

summit, 200 feet above sea level, is *Soldiers' Home*, a haven for 2500 veterans.

5. The *Forbes Lithograph Co.* (*permission at office*), Forbes St., off Crescent Ave., has a national reputation for unique color processes.

6. The *U.S. Lighthouse Service* (*permission from officer in charge*) has a depot at 37 Marginal St. where gaudy-colored buoys line the quays and bright-hued lightships arrive from and depart to their lonely vigils along the Atlantic coast.

7. The *Samuel Cabot Co.* (*open*), 229 Marginal St., a pioneer in the field of chemical experimentation, manufactures the commercial product known as Sylpho-Nathol. This firm is also nationally famous for its research in the field of shingle stains.

8. The *Pulaski Monument*, Chelsea Square, a medallion head on a granite shaft, was erected by the Poles of Chelsea, and dedicated in 1931 in honor of the great Polish patriot of the Revolutionary War.

9. The *Chelsea Clock Co.* (*permission at office*), 284 Everett Ave., is internationally known for its marine clocks.

C H I C O P E E . *The Future-Minded*

City: Alt. 92, pop. 41,952, sett. 1652, incorp. town 1848, city 1890.
Railroad Stations: Chicopee Station, Exchange St., and Willimansett Station, near Prospect St., for B. & M. R.R.
Bus Station: 276 Exchange St. for Blue Way Line.
Accommodations: Hotels and tourist houses.
Swimming: Municipal pools in Nash Field (Willimansett), and on Front St.

CHICOPEE, a manufacturing city just above Springfield on the Connecticut River and across the river from Holyoke, consists of three separate units, Chicopee, Chicopee Falls, and Willimansett. These are all manufacturing centers, but the outlying districts have a rural character. Of its 41,952 inhabitants, over half are of foreign-born parentage, with French-Canadian predominating. It has sixteen large industrial plants, those outstanding being A. G. Spalding Company, specialists in sporting goods, and the Fisk Rubber Company, the second largest rubber factory in the world.

The residential parts of the manufacturing sections are crowded with the homes of the workers, individual frame or brick dwellings with little tree-shaded yards, or solid blocks of tenements. Springfield Street, in the better residential quarter, has a look of considerable prosperity and Victorian charm.

The Chicopee River, bisecting the city from east to west, is so banked with factories as to be hidden from sight, but where it joins the Connecticut River there are broad, elm-shaded meadows. These meadows and the river attracted the first settlers.

On April 20, 1641, the Indian Nippumsuit deeded land now included in Chicopee to William Pynchon in return for 'fifteen fathom of wampum by tale accounted and one yard and three quarters of double shagg bags, one bow, seaven knifes, seaven payer of sessars and seaven owles with certaine fish hooks and other small things given at their request.' The region remained a part of Springfield until its incorporation as a town in 1848.

Down to the last days of the eighteenth century Chicopee continued a quiet farming community. Then certain industrial-minded men of the town perceived possibilities in the water-power of the Chicopee River, which cut through the main section of the town into the Connecticut River. Others set about mining bog iron (iron ore) and erecting blast furnaces. In 1805, Benjamin Belcher bought out from his two partners an iron foundry on the Chicopee River and prospered.

In 1822, Edmund Dwight, of the Boston and Springfield Manufacturing Company, decided upon Chicopee for the site of a textile factory. He located at a natural waterfall, now called Chicopee Falls, and the corporation he founded is today the Chicopee Manufacturing Company.

Later, in 1829, Nathan Ames and his father and brother were settled in Chicopee, busily manufacturing edged tools and cutlery, electro-plated silverware, and swords. Heretofore, Army and Navy swords had been imported from abroad, but the Ames brothers began filling government contracts, their products rivaling the illustrious blades of Toledo and Damascus. By 1853 the Ames Manufacturing Company had expanded to include a department of bronze statuary, the first of its kind in America.

The first friction matches in the country are claimed to have been made in Chicopee in 1835; some of them are still in the possession of old Chicopee families.

By 1845 the town of Chicopee, with a population of 8000, had set up its own government. The citizens, feeling that they had interests foreign to those of Springfield, broke away from that city. Chicopee was then known as Cabotville, not taking its present name until a later period.

Prior to the Civil War, Chicopee was one of the stations in the Underground Railroad to Canada. A. G. Parker, a shoe manufacturer, harbored numerous fugitive slaves in his home on Chicopee Street. Not infrequently funds were raised to buy freedom for runaway Negroes.

One illustrious son of Chicopee, Edward Bellamy, became internationally famous. Within ten years of publication, almost a million copies had been sold of his 'Looking Backward,' best known of American Utopias.

Translations into German, French, Italian, Russian, Arabic, Bulgarian, and several other languages and dialects brought this Chicopee man's name into many parts of the world.

POINTS OF INTEREST

1. *City Hall*, Front and Springfield Sts., is an Italian Gothic building in red brick designed by Charles Edward Parker and erected in 1871. It is arresting because of its very high, slender, square tower, capped by a pointed roof, and its second-story stained-glass windows and beautiful rose window.

2. The white Victorian *Stebbins Mansion* (*private*), Springfield St., now a part of the College of Our Lady of the Elms, is a typical American Victorian dwelling of the best type, complete with a little tower, narrow projecting ells, offering bay windows, and a little porch with fretwork pillars. It is reminiscent of the Swiss chalet.

3. The *Ames Mansion* (*at present still occupied by an Ames descendant, but open free as a museum at suitable daylight hours*), Front St., corner of Grape St., is a square two-story brick residence of 1844, with an almost flat hip roof, and is set in a gardened lawn behind a picket fence. It contains some delightfully personal mementoes of sorts: a bronze wall candelabrum taken from the White House when gas was installed, an invitation to dinner with President Lincoln, a punchbowl brought from Japan by Commodore Perry in 1851, a landscape by Albert Bierstadt painted surreptitiously by him as a present to his host, a presentation autographed photograph of Mary Garden.

4. *Edward Bellamy's Birthplace* (*private*), 93 Church St., Chicopee Falls, is a small two-and-a-half-story plain white clapboarded house with a small ell and two porches. Here the son of a Baptist minister mused on the theme of social equality later to be treated by him in 'Looking Backward' and 'Equality.'

C O N C O R D . *Golden-Age Haven*

Town: Alt. 135, pop. 7723, sett. about 1635, incorp. 1635.

Railroad Station: B. & M. R.R. (Fitchburg Division), Thoreau St.

Bus Stations: B. & M. Transportation Co., Colonial Inn, Monument Square, and R.R. Station; Grey Line sightseeing tour from Hotel Brunswick, Boston.

LITERARY LANDMARKS

ONE might suppose that the authors of Massachusetts had been influenced by the dignity and spare simplicity of the houses which sheltered them. Elmwood, the Cambridge home of James Russell Lowell, and the Craigie-Longfellow House are graceful Georgian mansions. The two views of the rooms in the Antiquarian House in Concord reflect Emerson's love of ingenuous, homely order. The rambling country house where Longfellow set the scene of the 'Tales' is still the Wayside Inn, Sudbury; Fruitlands, in Harvard, is where Alcott and his 'English Mystics' struggled with farming for their ideal of a consociate family. And the Orchard House, on the main Concord road, is today very much as it was when Bronson and Louisa May Alcott lived in it, with sister May's sketches still preserved on the walls and doors of the girls' rooms.

It was in the Salem Custom House that Hawthorne spent unhappy years as a clerk. After he had left Salem, he wrote 'The House of the Seven Gables,' a story which is vividly recalled by the tinkle of the bell above the door through which visitors enter. The tale of Moby Dick, the white whale, was written at Arrowhead, in Pittsfield, where Melville worked, and on the same page is pictured the house (austere as his writings) where Thoreau lived.

The stately, shadowed house in Amherst is the Emily Dickinson home. On the right, in the second story, is the 'window facing west.' The Dickinson memorabilia may be seen in The Evergreens, the house across the lawn, built by Emily's brother in 1856.

WOOD (JAMES RUSSELL LOWELL HOUSE), CAMBRIDGE

CRAIGIE-LONGFELLOW HOUSE, CAMBRIDGE

CUSTOM HOUSE, SALEM

EMERSON ROOM, ANTIQUARIAN HOUSE, CONCORD

WAYSIDE INN, SUDBURY

FRUITLANDS, HARVARD

ORCHARD HOUSE, CONCORD

HOUSE OF SEVEN GABLES, SALEM

ARROWHEAD (BUSH-MELVILLE HOUSE), PITTSFIELD

THOREAU'S HOUSE, CONCORD

EMILY DICKINSON HOUSE, AMHERST

Accommodations: Several inns and rooms in private houses.
Information: Independent Information Bureau, 26 School St.

CONCORD, situated where the Sudbury and Assabet join to form the Concord River, is rich in historical and literary associations. It shares with Lexington the honor of being the birthplace of the American Revolution; later, in the 'Golden Age' of American literature, it was a haven for poets, authors, naturalists, and philosophers.

The Concord River has not attracted great industries, so that the village is predominantly residential, retaining much of its quiet Colonial atmosphere. Around the Green are grouped the trim red-brick and clapboarded shops of the business district. Along the river, so slow-moving that Hawthorne said he lived beside it for weeks before discovering which way it flowed, stand fine white houses on broad lawns that slope down to the water's edge. Tall elms shade other homes distinguished by the beautifully proportioned doorways and panelled interiors that are a heritage of eighteenth-century craftsmanship. Outlying fields are given over to farms.

In 1635, scarcely five years after Boston had been settled, Simon Willard, a fur trader, and the Reverend Peter Bulkeley led about a dozen families to this spot, then the Indian village of Musketaquid. It was the furthermost inland point in the wilderness. With garments, hatchets, knives, and cloth the settlers purchased from the Massachusetts tribe a plantation described as 'six myles of land square,' then clinched the bargain by smoking the pipe of peace with the Indian chieftains. The name 'Concord' commemorates this friendship, a friendship that was never broken.

It went hard with the settlers during the first winters, but the settlement slowly grew, in the latter half of the century becoming a county seat. The first county convention to protest against the Acts of Parliament met here in August of 1774; the First Provincial Congress in October of the same year. From March 22 until four days before the Battle at the Bridge, the Second Provincial Congress held sessions in the town. Throughout this period Concord was a depot for military stores and consequently a focal point for British attack. On April 19, 1775, after Dr. Samuel Prescott and William Dawes had carried Paul Revere's message to Concord, the British redcoats appeared and, as the Concord Minutemen advanced across the Old North Bridge, fired the 'shot heard round the world.'

During the siege of Boston that followed, so many patriots took refuge in Concord that a Boston town meeting was called here. Again, while Harvard served as a barracks for American forces, the university classes were conducted in Concord. The town was the seat of the Middlesex field of Shays's Rebellion.

Following a post-war period of readjustment, Concord entered upon its second phase — this time as an important center of American culture.

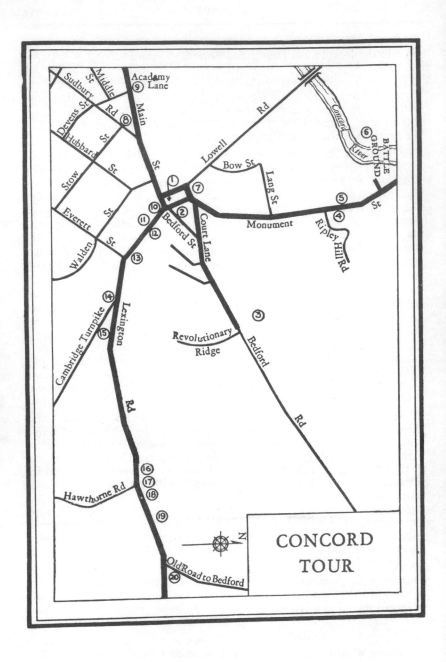

CONCORD
TOUR

Here Ralph Waldo Emerson wrote his greatest essays, poems, and journals, and revived the philosophy of Transcendentalism. Closely associated with the Transcendentalist movement were Nathaniel Hawthorne, novelist; Franklin B. Sanborn, journalist, philanthropist, and biographer; and William Ellery Channing the poet. While not residents in Concord, Margaret Fuller, editor of the School of Philosophy's organ the *Dial*, and Elizabeth Peabody, Boston educator who established the first American kindergarten, were of this literary group.

By the shores of Walden Pond, Emerson's intimate friend, Henry David Thoreau, the naturalist, fled from society, built his hut and studied the trees and birds he was to write about in 'Walden, or Life in the Woods.'

In the building known as Hillside Chapel, Amos Bronson Alcott opened his School of Philosophy, while his more practical wife and daughters wrestled with the humdrum problem of making ends meet. As a result of their struggles, Mr. Alcott's daughter Louisa May wrote her series of books, the most autobiographical of which, 'Little Women,' has taken its place among children's classics. Margaret Sidney (Mrs. Harriet Mulford Stone Lothrop) was another Concord author, and Jane Austin wrote here the 'Nameless Nobleman.' Daniel Chester French (1850–1931) of Concord has won fame for his sculptures. These are represented in his home town by the *Minuteman*, the *Melvin Memorial*, and a statue of *Emerson*.

Concord men have made contributions outside the field of the arts. Harrison Gray Dyer erected the first telegraph line in this country and William Monroe made the first lead pencils in America. In 1853 Ephraim Bull bred the Concord grape, a development which began the commercial production of table grapes in America.

Though Concord, with its many memories, seems so much a part of an older New England, it is nevertheless a flourishing modern village. Today ten small factories and a busy tourist trade supplement the revenue that comes to Concord from its position as trading center for farm and garden products. Many Boston families have in recent years established their homes here, since Concord is within commuting distance.

CONCORD MAP INDEX

TOUR — 7.0 *m.*

NW. from Lexington Rd. through Monument Square.

1. *Monument Square* has three war memorials on its Green. In the center is the huge granite shaft of the *Civil War Memorial;* the *Boulder* at the north end of the Green commemorates the heroes of the Spanish War; the *World War Memorial*, a boulder now almost covered with ivy, bears Emerson's words:

> 'So nigh is grandeur to our dust,
> So near is God to Man,
> When duty whispers low, "Thou must,"
> The youth replies, "I can."'

2. In front of the Town Hall, NE. of the square is the *Emerson Elm*. Under this tree for the past three generations Concord men on their way to battle have been addressed by a member of the Emerson family.

R. from Monument Square into Monument St.; R. from Monument St. into Court Lane; straight ahead into Bedford Rd.

3. *Sleepy Hollow Cemetery*, lying in an oval basin surrounded by high ridges and tall trees, holds the graves of many of Concord's notable dead — Emerson, Hawthorne, Thoreau, the Alcotts, Elizabeth Peabody, William Ellery Channing, Frank Sanborn. Here lie Colonel Prescott and members of the Hoar family, prominent in national politics during the last century. The tombstone of Ephraim Bull, who lacked the shrewdness to profit by his development of the Concord grape, bears the significant epitaph: 'He sowed, others reaped.'

Retrace Bedford Rd. into Court Lane; R. from Court Lane into Monument St.

4. *Bullet-Hole House* (*private*), 36 Monument St., the original portion of which was built in 1644, is probably the oldest house in Concord. It is a two-and-a-half-story white, yellow-trimmed structure with a plain board front, a clapboarded ell, and a mansard roof. During the battles of Concord and Lexington, Elisha Jones, a Minuteman, guarded Colonial military supplies stored in this house. When the British began their retreat, Elisha rashly appeared at the door and was fired upon. The bullet-hole is still to be seen, enclosed in a glass case at the left of the door in the ell.

5. *Old Manse*, adjacent to the Battleground (*open weekdays* 10–6; *Sun.* 12–6), a dark gray, clapboarded, three-story structure with a gambrel roof, was built in 1765 by the Rev. William Emerson, the militant minister, grandfather of the writer Ralph Waldo Emerson. Hawthorne lived here for a time and made it the setting for 'Mosses from an Old Manse.'

L. from Monument St. into footpath.

6. *Battleground*, made famous in 1775. The *Minuteman*, the first statue by Daniel Chester French, guards this site. Too poor to afford a model, the sculptor is said to have used as model a statue of Apollo Belvedere arrayed in the dress of the Minutemen. Near-by is a concrete reproduction of the original wooden Concord Bridge over which the Americans crossed in pursuit of the British attacking force. A tablet marks the graves of two British soldiers.

Retrace to Monument St.; R. from Monument St. into Monument Square.

7. *Colonial Inn*, 11 Monument Square (*open the year round*), faces the Concord Green at its northern end. The inn, a long rambling yellow structure formed by joining together three adjacent houses, is in an excellent state of preservation. The original unit was built in 1770. The taproom holds its original fittings besides Revolutionary relics.

R. from Monument Square on Main St.

8. *Public Library*, corner of Sudbury Rd., a red-brick structure lately modernized, has French's statue of Emerson, cabinets of Indian relics, volumes by Concord authors, paintings, and other objects of historic and artistic interest.

9. *Thoreau–Alcott House* (*private*), 75 Main St., a buff-colored dwelling, is the house in which Thoreau died.

Retrace Main St.; R. from Main St. into Lexington Rd.

10. *Wright Tavern* (*open as a hotel*), 2 Lexington Rd., built in 1747, is the oldest existing tavern in Concord. The exterior, hip-roofed, with two large chimneys, retains much architectural charm. Here Major Pitcairn had his headquarters on April 19, 1775, and here he made his boast that before night he would 'stir the blood of the damned Yankee rebels.'

11. *First Parish Church* (Unitarian) is on the site of the building in which sat the First and Second Provincial Congresses, with John Hancock presiding and William Emerson as chaplain.

12. *Concord Art Association* (*open April–Oct.* 15), 15 Lexington Rd., housed in a white clapboarded building with a central chimney, has permanent exhibits of unusual historical interest. During the summer months resident artists hold exhibitions.

12a. *The Concord Summer School of Music*, 21 Lexington Rd., founded in 1914, and directed by Thomas Whitney Surette, gives a series of three public chamber music concerts each summer. Public classes (*free*) in folk dancing are also conducted.

13. *Reuben Brown House* (*open as tearoom*), 27 Lexington Rd., a red clapboarded structure with white trim and with a central chimney, was the home of Reuben Brown, a saddler by trade, who brought back from Lexington the news of the outbreak of hostilities. The British fired his house, but it was saved.

14. *Emerson House (open weekdays* 9.30–11.30, 1.30–3.30 *and by appointment!),* Lexington Rd. and Cambridge Turnpike, is a square white dwelling in a setting of pines. In 1820 Emerson himself built the house, and here he lived from 1835 until his death in 1882, except for the period of his European tour, when Thoreau occupied the house. The Victorian interior shows furnishings, portraits, hangings of Emerson's day as well as the philosopher's fine library of classics and first editions.

15. *Antiquarian House (open weekdays April* 19–*Nov.* 11, 10–5.30, *Sun.* 2–5; *after Nov.* 11, 10–5; *adm.* 25¢), Lexington Rd. at Cambridge Turnpike, is one of the most important museums in Concord. The two-and-one-half-story brick structure with green blinds, has a pitched roof and two wings. The museum contains several authentic New England period rooms, in which are admirably displayed furniture, glass, and china dating from the 17th to the 19th centuries. The *Emerson Room* reproduces the philosopher's study with its furnishings kept just as they were when he died. Thoreau's books, flute, and surveyor's chain, as well as articles from the Walden hut, are exhibited in the room bearing his name.

16. *School of Philosophy,* Lexington Rd., once known as the Hillside Chapel, is a small, unpainted building with Gothic doors and windows. Here for nearly a decade Bronson Alcott gathered together leaders of American thought.

17. *Orchard House (open weekdays April* 19–*Oct.* 31, 10–6, *Sun.* 2–6; *adm.* 25¢), a tan two-and-a-half-story house with central chimney and small paned windows, was the second home of the Alcotts. The old house, considered unlivable, was shaded by great elms in front. In the rear was an apple orchard. The members of the Bronson family repaired, painted, and papered the house. The interior and the Alcott furnishings, books, and pictures are all preserved. Drawings by 'Amy' are still on the doors and walls of her room. It was here at 'Apple Slump,' as she called it, that Louisa May Alcott wrote the first part of 'Little Women.'

18. *Wayside (open daily May* 3–*Nov.* 11, 9–6; *adm.* 25¢), near Hawthorne Rd., was known as Hillside during the residence of Bronson Alcott in 1845–48. Here Louisa and her sisters spent part of their girlhood, and here in the barn they staged their early plays. Hawthorne, upon purchasing the property in 1852, named it Wayside, and lived here until his death in 1864. In the tower that he built as a refuge from visitors, Hawthorne wrote 'Tanglewood Tales' and the 'Marble Faun.' Margaret Sidney, while a resident at Wayside, wrote several volumes of her children's series, 'The Five Little Peppers.' On display are photostats of pages of Hawthorne manuscript and letters, as well as furniture belonging to Hawthorne and Margaret Sidney.

19. *Grapevine Cottage (open as tearoom),* a gambrel-roofed cottage, has a tablet identifying it as the home of Ephraim Wales Bull. For many years a trellis against the cottage wall supported the original Concord grapevine. Recently this was winter-killed, but the present vine is a shoot from the same root. On the trellis is a tablet inscribed with a

quotation from Bull's journal: 'I looked to see what I could find among our wildings. The next thing to do was to find the best and earliest grape for seed, and this I found in an accidental seedling at the foot of the hill. The crop was abundant, ripe in August, and of very good quality for a wild grape. I sowed the seed in the Autumn 1843. Among them the Concord was the only one worth saving.'

20. A tablet, junction of Lexington Rd. and Old Bedford Rd., indicates the *Site of the Attack* made by the Minutemen of Concord and neighboring towns upon the British while they were retreating from North Bridge, April 19, 1775.

POINTS OF INTEREST IN THE ENVIRONS

1. *Walden Pond Reservation*, 1.5 *m*. S. of the village (*see Tour 1 C*).
2. *Concord Reformatory*, W. Concord (*see Tour 2*).
3. *Middlesex School for Boys* (1901), about 3 *m*. N. of Concord on Lowell Rd., is a college preparatory school with fine modern buildings, dormitories and equipment.

D E D H A M . *The Sober-Minded*

Town: Alt. 111, pop. 15,371, sett. 1635, incorp. 1636.
Railroad Station: Dedham Station, off High St., for N.Y., N.H. & H. R.R.
Bus Station: 380 Washington St. for New England Transportation Co.
Accommodations: Inns and boarding-houses charge reasonable rates.
Information: Board of Trade, Hartnett Square.

FEW towns in Massachusetts have changed as little in their basic characteristics between the time of settlement and the present day as has Dedham. In its earliest beginnings and through the pioneer period it was known as a sober-minded and solid community full of the well-recognized virtues of citizenship; and this reputation still endures, embodied in the substantial architecture of its center and the comfortable residential uniformity of its surrounding districts.

The permanent character of the town was determined at its very genesis by the character of the men who settled it. The Dedham settlers were not religious enthusiasts or sentimental visionaries. They cared for all the solid respectable things of life. For many of them the new land promised primarily social and economic advancement. So they chose a place on a pleasant river, well watered by subsidiary streams, and blessed with a fruitful soil. The town covenant announced their purpose of being 'a loving and comfortable society.' And in the word 'comfortable' they certainly meant to include physical comfort. It is significant that in their petition to the General Court they requested that their town should be named 'Contentment.' These were sober persons who wanted security, a congenial group, and the goods of life.

Moreover, the founders had a penchant for law and civic regulation. The Dedham town covenant antedated the first code of colony laws by several years.

Had the new town been situated on the shore, a spirit of adventure might have been stimulated. Men who go down to the sea in ships learn to take chances; the infinite variability of wind and sky and season accustoms them to change. No such salty alchemy wrought upon the men of Dedham. It was sheltered from the buffetings of circumstance. Even the Indian wars hardly touched it.

Other settlements of Massachusetts might be more conspicuous, self-assertive as leaders of Colonial development, finally revolutionary; the Dedhamites went sanely and solidly on their way, laying the foundations of a prosperous industrial and residential town.

TOUR — 6 m.

W. from Dedham Square on High St. (State 135).

1. The building of the *Dedham Historical Society (open weekdays* 2–5), 612 High St., erected in 1887, contains a collection which includes among many notable items, a mother-of-pearl tea chest, exquisitely carved, brought from China before 1775 and donated by the Quincy family; a Simon Willard clock with an unusual astronomical base made about 1780; wallpaper depicting a Roman chariot race, taken about 1819 from the dining-room of the Dickson House on High St.; and a steam jack in use about 1765 and probably the first steam machine in the country. The jack is composed of a water-compartment and an arrangement of cogs attached to a roasting-spit. The water-compartment was bedded in the fire on the hearth. As the water boiled, the spit turned and browned the roast. Among documents preserved in the vault is the original manuscript of a diary (1726–29, 1729–75) kept by Dr. Nathaniel Ames, Jr., the editor of an almanac which rivaled Benjamin Franklin's in popularity in its time.

2. The *Thayer House (private)*, 618 High St., a two-story yellow-painted clapboarded structure with two chimneys, brick ends, and a small ell, has grown shabby with the passing years, during which four generations

of Thayers have lived and died within it; but on the door gleams a brightly polished brass Masonic emblem placed there in 1831 by Dr. Elisha Thayer at the time of a national attack on the Masonic Order, when Dedham Masons were being stoned in the streets.

3. The *Norfolk County Courthouse* (1827) is an imposing edifice of gray stone with a dome and frontal columns. Within its walls have been pleaded many interesting cases. First of these was the controversy between the Natick Indians and the town over certain lands occupied by the Indians. The latter won but Dedham was allotted 8000 acres in the west (now Deerfield) in compensation.

A second noteworthy trial centered around the Fisher Tavern, later to be known as the Ames Tavern and finally as the Woodward Tavern (*see below*). Dr. Nathaniel Ames, Sr., married a Fisher. By a series of four deaths in rapid succession, the last that of an infant, the tavern came into probate court. Ames brought suit for possession and won his case, the first ruling in Massachusetts by which a father inherited a deceased child's estate.

Of prime importance was the litigation culminating in 1818 with an historic decision of the Supreme Court of Massachusetts, which gave to the Dedham Parish, rather than to the church fellowship, the right to elect ministers, and thus paved the way for the rise of Unitarianism in Massachusetts.

The most celebrated of all Dedham trials was that of Sacco and Vanzetti before Judge Webster Thayer in 1921. (*See Industry and Labor*, p. 76.) But as early as 1801 a Dedham murder case hit the public imagination when Jason Fairbanks slew his sweetheart and was sentenced to swing for it. Federalist journals pointed out in editorials on 'seditious Dedham' that the prisoner broke jail with the help of his Republican friends. Presumably Dedham was purged of the sedition taint when Jason was hanged on Dedham Common. Later the court rendered an historic decision on a legalistic issue between church and parish, then units virtually but not literally identical. Liberal members of the First Church — voting as parish members — elected a Unitarian preacher displeasing to their fellow church members of Congregationalist belief. The court sustained the exclusive right of the parish to elect public teachers, and included the minister within that definition.

4. A tablet on the Norfolk County Registry, another large gray stone building, across from the courthouse, commemorates the *Site of Woodward (Fisher) Tavern*, where was held the Suffolk Convention for the drawing-up of the Suffolk Resolves. The legend reads in part: 'They lighted the match that kindled the mighty conflagration of the American Revolution.' Another tablet marks this site as the *Birthplace of Fisher Ames* (1758–1808), a member of the Massachusetts Constitutional Convention and a distinguished Federalist, author of the Lucius Junius Brutus papers written in denunciation of Shays's Rebellion.

5. On the Church Green at the southeast corner of High and Court Sts. is the stone *Base* of the Pillar of Liberty, erected in 1766 by the Sons of

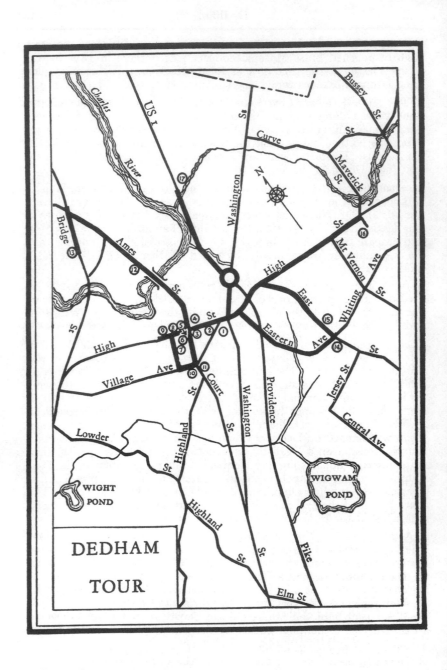

DEDHAM

TOUR

Liberty to glorify William Pitt for his vigorous opposition to the Stamp Act.

6. The *First Church in Dedham* (Unitarian) fronts on the Church Green. A dignified and simple type of American Georgian architecture, built about 1768, it is painted white and has a steeple and two round-topped doors.

7. A tablet in front of the church marks the *Site of the First Free Public School in America* (built 1649) to be supported by general taxation.

8. The *Haven House* (*open as Dedham Community House; tearoom*), 669 High St., was built by Judge Samuel Haven in 1795. Two venerable English elms standing in front of the house were set out by the judge in 1789, when he graduated from college.

9. The *Dexter House* (*private*), 699 High St., was built about 1762 by Samuel Dexter, member of the Provincial Congress, 1774–75. The interior retains its 18th-century features including the beautiful staircase with elaborate balusters, high paneled wainscoting and ample fireplaces.

Retrace High St.; R. from High St. on Bullard St.; L. from Bullard St. into Village Ave.

10. *St. Paul's Episcopal Church* is an impressive edifice of rough granite. Most of the buildings of the business section of Dover, an adjoining town, are tenants on 999-year leases of lands bequeathed to this church in 1757 by Samuel Colburn.

11. *Horace Mann's Law Office* (*private*), 74 Church St., diagonally opposite St. Paul's Church across Village Square, is now a two-and-a-half-story, broad gabled dwelling; its original character has been lost by remodeling. Horace Mann occupied it from 1828 until 1835, while he was a representative from Dedham in the General Court.

L. from Village Ave. into Court St.; straight ahead into Ames St.

12. The *Powder House*, opposite 162 Ames St., is perched on a rocky knoll. A tiny cube, hardly bigger than a large closet and surmounted by a (restored) conical roof, it was built in 1766 of bricks formed of clay from local pits and baked in a local kiln.

L. from Ames St. on Bridge St.

DEDHAM MAP INDEX

13. Granite gateposts mark the entrance to the campus of the *Noble and Greenough School* for boys, a non-sectarian institution originally established (1886) in Boston as a preparatory school for Harvard. In 1917 the Volkmann School was combined with it, and in 1922 it moved to Dedham. Well worth an extra ten minutes is the drive along the charming wooded lane with views (R) of a picturesque main building set high on a rocky eminence like a luxurious castle with red tiled roof and (L) of athletic fields, modern new buildings, and a small lake.

Retrace Bridge St.; R. from Bridge St. into Ames St.; L. from Ames St. into High St.; cross Dedham Square; R. from High St. into Eastern Ave.

14. The *Fairbanks House* (*open daily* 9–6, *Apr.* 19 *to Nov.* 1; *contribution expected*) stands at the corner of East St. Set on a mound lawn and shaded by giant elm trees this long, low, faded brown house stretches along in three sections, its lower story massed by flowering shrubs. The roof sags in two deep curves on each side from the great central chimney and slopes almost to the ground in the rear. The central block, built in 1636, with two wings of different architecture added at a later date, is generally conceded to be the oldest frame house still standing in America. Like Dedham itself in 1936, it celebrated its 300th anniversary. Furnished with family heirlooms, it is a shrine for 6000 Fairbanks families incorporated as descendants of the builder, Jonathan Fairbanks. Five doors lead from a small entrance hall to other parts of the dwelling. The step down into the kitchen is a simple log, worn concave by the feet of many generations of Fairbanks.

L. from Eastern Ave. into East St.

15. *The Avery Oak*, 80 feet in height and 16 feet in circumference, standing on the lawn of a modern frame house (R) half a block down, is under the protection of the Dedham Historical Society. This patriarch of a vanished forest was 'marked' in its prime to be used in the construction of the frigate 'Constitution,' but the Averys refused to sell it.

R. from East St. into High St.; R. from High St. into Pottery Lane.

16. The *Dedham Pottery* (*open, guide provided*) is an attractive brick building within which is made, by secret process, a famous blue-and-white porcelain reminiscent of old Chinese crackleware.

Retrace Pottery Lane; L. from Pottery Lane into High St.; R. from High St. into Washington St.; L. from Washington St. into US 1.

17. *Mother Brook*, believed to be the first canal in America, connects the Charles and Neponset Rivers. The narrow channel, long unused now, was dug, according to the tablet, 'before 1640,' to provide water for the mills of the early settlers, and was the basis of the town's industrial growth.

DEERFIELD . *A Beautiful Ghost*

Town: Alt. 204, pop. 2963, sett. 1673, incorp. 1677.

Railroad Stations: Memorial St., Deerfield and Elm Sts., South Deerfield, for B. & M. R.R.

Bus Stations: Elm St. for B. & M. Transportation Co.; Billings Drugstore for Blue Way Line.

Accommodations: One hotel open summer only, Deerfield; two hotels open all year, South Deerfield. Tourist houses.

Information: See Greenfield.

IF IT is no exaggeration to say that Deerfield is not so much a town as the ghost of a town, its dimness almost transparent, its quiet almost a cessation, it is essential to add that it is probably quite the most beautiful ghost of its kind, and with the deepest poetic and historic significance to be found in America. Salem, with its somber echoes of the witch hangings, of the brighter pages of the clipper-ship trade with the East, New Bedford with its whale-ships, Concord with its bold patriotism and its almost unexampled literary flowering — these all perhaps have a greater 'importance.' But Deerfield has something to say which none of these say, and says it perfectly. It is, and will probably always remain, the perfect and beautiful statement of the tragic and creative moment when one civilization is destroyed by another. And the wonderful ghostliness of this mile-long 'Street' of grave and ancient houses, the strange air of unreality which hangs over it, arises precisely from the fact that the little town is really saying two things at once. It is saying, 'I dared to be beautiful, even in the shadow of the wilderness'; but it is also saying, 'And the wilderness haunts me, the ghosts of a slain race are in my doorways and clapboards, like a kind of death.'

The air of unreality, moreover, is simplified and heightened by the fact that Deerfield is one of those towns which have literally and completely been forgotten by time: it has fallen asleep. To all intents, nothing has happened there for two hundred years; and the whole history of its greatness is crowded into the first three decades of its existence, the violent and dreadful years from 1672 to 1704, when it was the northwest frontier of New England, the spearhead of English civilization in an unknown and hostile country. The town of Dedham having been awarded a grant of land in 1663 (*see DEDHAM*), the site of Deerfield was 'laid out' in the Pocumtuck country just west of the Connecticut River in 1665. Not a single Dedham man settled there until 1669, when Samuel Hinsdell of Dedham, a squatter, began the cultivation of the fertile soil, where the Pocumtucks had grown their corn and pumpkins and tobacco; and by 1672 Samson Frary and others had joined him. After two expeditions to Boston, Hinsdell got the consent of the General Court to form a township.

A minister was procured and the little town throve. In 1673 it had twenty families, and two years later its population numbered 125. But seeming peace and prosperity were to prove only an illusion: with the outbreak of King Philip's War began the interminable series of Indian and French attacks on Deerfield which for thirty years kept its inhabitants in constant terror. The two most famous of these — the Bloody Brook massacre of 1675 and the great Deerfield raid of 1704 — practically emptied the town: the first, in fact, wholly, and the second of all save its garrison. In 1675 the garrison was withdrawn, the families were scattered among the towns lower in the valley, and for seven years Deerfield's houses were empty.

Not to be discouraged, the survivors in 1678 presented a petition to the General Court asking leave to return. They had their way, the town was re-established in 1682, and in 1686 was held its first town meeting. John Williams, destined to become Deerfield's most famous citizen, came to take over the church in the same year, induced by the handsome offer of 'sixteen cow-commons of meadow-land,' a 'homelott,' and a house 'forty-two foot long, twenty foot wide, with a lentoo.' Of Williams's part in the great raid of 1704, during Queen Anne's War, when half the town was burned, 49 inhabitants killed, and Williams himself with 110 others taken captive to Canada, it is sufficient here to say that Williams's own account of it in 'The Redeemed Captive' remains the best.

With its slow rehabilitation after the great raid, Deerfield had really ended its active life, and began to become the long reminiscence which it seems destined to be. Agriculturally, its importance died with the opening of the West, though it still grows its tobacco and cucumbers; a development of handicrafts late in the eighteenth century was of short duration; and a revival of them again in the early part of the present century — needlework, hand-weaving, basket-making — is only now (1937) making headway. Actually, the town's chief industry is its schools. Deerfield Academy is one of the oldest boarding-schools in the country: this and Eaglebrook, a preparatory school for boys, and Bement, co-educational, add about five hundred to the town's population.

TOUR — 1.5 m.

1. *Old Deerfield Street*, a mile long, contains none but old houses, most of them Colonial, beside a church, two schools, and a post-office. The shops of the town are elsewhere, and this one long street gives an effect of being the entire village, with glimpses of open country, fields, and far hills beyond. All the way along it, spreading elms, two hundred years old, form an arch; a setting once frequent in New England, but now rare. Some of the houses are singularly handsome and still prosperous; others

are plain but well tended; still others are on the verge of romantic decay. Two-leaf front doors, characteristic of the Connecticut Valley and rare elsewhere in New England, are to be seen here on many of the dwellings.

2. The *Frary House (private)*, in the Town Square on the southeast corner of Old Deerfield and Memorial Sts., was built — at least its north end — in 1689, and was one of the very few to escape being burned in the most disastrous Indian raid of New England. It is a long, massive, L-shaped structure of two and a half stories, of unpainted, darkly weathered clapboards, with a white portico, white sashes, and white dentiled cornice. Samson Frary, who built this old house, was murdered by the Indians. Later it became a Revolutionary tavern, where Benedict Arnold closed a contract which afforded his army much needed supplies.

N. from the Town Square on Old Deerfield St.

3. The *Willard House (private)*, built in 1768 and sometimes called the Manse, is one of the loveliest houses in Deerfield, a square Georgian Colonial mansion of yellow clapboards with white trim, set imperiously on a banking, and adorned about its doorway and windows with all the decorative detail the general conception will stand. The curious gambrel-roofed red ell in the rear was originally a separate building, the oldest in Deerfield. The Manse was the home of Dr. Samuel Willard, one of the ministers of the First Church across the way and a pioneer in the Unitarian movement in Massachusetts.

4. The *Meeting House* (Unitarian), built in 1824, was probably designed by Isaac Damon. The brick body of the church, with arched doorways, is surmounted by a pediment, roof, and closed cupola of wood, which lighten the somber dignity of the design.

5. The *Joseph Stebbins House (private;* about 1772), marked by a granite tablet in the grounds, is a massive three-and-a-half-story white Georgian Colonial house with wood quoins and gambrel roof. The front and side doorways match, except for an arched hood over the front door. Each has a top light of five panes cut in the rare pattern of a triple hood (similar to the tops of many old gravestones), the center hood rising above the two flanking ones.

6. The *'Indian House' Reproduction (open daily 9–12 and 1–5; adm.* 10¢), with its dark weathered timbers and second- and third-story overhangs, illustrates a special type of the earliest Colonial architecture. It takes its name from its survival of the Indian raid of 1704. The original house was torn down in 1848, but its door, with a hole caused by a tomahawk, may be seen at Memorial Hall. The present structure was erected in 1929 by the Deerfield Historical Society, and on a *Millstone* in the yard is inscribed the history of its predecessor. The rooms are furnished in Colonial style, and one of them contains an exhibit of handicraft and paintings by local artists.

7. *Old Bloody Brook Tavern (open daily 9–12 and 1–5; adm. free)*, in the rear yard of the Indian House, is a long one-and-a-half-story frame build-

ing with giant central chimney, now the home of the Deerfield Art School. It was built prior to 1700, and was moved here from South Deerfield.

8. The *Bardwell–Stebbins–Abercrombie House* (*private*) is a charming two-and-a-half-story gray frame dwelling with a central chimney and a gabled roof. It sits on a banking above a field-stone wall. At the rear is a low ell porch, added later, but designed with the open arches of the early New England woodshed to conform to the style of the older part of the dwelling.

9. The *Sheldon Homestead* (*open as an antique shop*) is a two-and-a-half-story unpainted clapboarded structure. It was built in 1734, and has a gable roof, and a gambrel-roof ell. Its major interest, as often in Deerfield, is its narrow two-leaf front door, framed with ornamental pilasters.

10. The *Hinsdale House* (*visitors by permission*) is a two-and-a-half-story frame house with hip roof, very well preserved, and interesting because of its unusual doorway, which has wide white paneling in the jambs and heads, framing a large fanlight and ornamental sidelights. The house was built in 1738 and remodeled in 1816.

Retrace Old Deerfield St.; R. from Old Deerfield St. on Albany Rd.

11. *Deerfield Academy* occupies several modern brick buildings in the Georgian style. It was established in 1797, and after several changes, including one period when it was a local public school, it is today one of the leading smaller preparatory schools for boys, having 275 resident students, in addition to day students.

12. The *John Williams House* (*open*) was built in 1707, a two-and-a-half-story brown frame dwelling of generous proportions and in a good state of preservation. The graceful and beautiful entrance has a broken-arch pediment over its two-leaf door. The house has a secret stairway. It belonged to the Rev. John Williams, 'The Redeemed Captive.'

13. The '*Little Brown House*' (*private*) is a broad one-and-a-half-story unpainted clapboarded house with gable roof, interesting as an adaptation to a studio by means of a large window in the north front.

Retrace Albany Rd.; straight ahead from Albany Rd. on Memorial St.

14. *Memorial Hall* (*open weekdays 9–12 and 1–5; adm. 10¢*) is a three-story brick building erected in 1798, the first building of Deerfield Academy and now a museum of the Pocumtuck Valley Memorial Association.

EVERETT . *Industrial Half-Sister*

City: alt. 31, pop. 47,228, sett. 1649, incorp. town 1870, city 1892.
Railroad Stations: West Everett, West St.; Everett, off Broadway, for B. & M. R.R.
Bus Station: Glendale Square for B. & M., Grey Line, and Greyhound busses.
Accommodations: Rooms in private houses.
Information: Board of Trade, National Bank Bldg.

EVERETT, an industrial city adjacent to Boston, today shows one hundred and forty-two manufactories with an employment roll of over five thousand, specializing mainly in coke and petroleum products, oils, chemicals, and shoes. Everett is the home of the New England Coke and Coal Company and the New England Fuel and Transportation Company, the latter one of the largest coal discharging plants in the east, with a storage capacity of two hundred thousand tons or more and with equipment to handle fifteen hundred tons hourly. Another of the city's notable enterprises is the Beacon Oil Company. A fleet of tankers plies constantly between the company's docks and Texas. Within the plant there is an underground storage room for one million barrels of crude petroleum; above ground are warehouses with storage facilities for 500,000 barrels of refined oil. The main supply of gas for Boston is manufactured on the Everett side of the Mystic River (but on Boston territory) by the Boston Consolidated Gas Company. A local plant of the General Electric Company turns out castings, while another of du Pont de Nemours and Company produces a complete line of paints and varnishes. At the Mystic Iron Works may be seen in operation the only blast furnace in New England, and one of the few on the eastern seaboard. There are many other outstanding industrial firms.

A year before John Winthrop's fleet dropped anchor in Salem Harbor, three brothers were exploring the virgin timberland along the Mystic River. Diverging a trifle from their course, they came upon a country which one of the brothers, Ralph Sprague, reported as an 'uncouth wilderness' (uncouth then meaning 'wonderful,' 'uncommon') full of 'stately timber.' This is the first record (1629) of a white man's visiting the three square miles of territory that now contain the thriving industrial city of Everett.

Since more than two centuries passed before Everett became self-governing, its history is entangled with that of Malden and early Charlestown. As early as 1649, a petition granted to some 'Mystic Side' men permitted them to separate from Charlestown and to set up a town called 'Maulden.'

In the first half of the nineteenth century, South Malden was important principally because of the commanding position which it occupied in the overland communication to Boston. A penny ferry, opened in 1640, had formerly been the most direct route to the capital. From the back country one of the oldest New England roads led to the ferry. In 1796 a country road was laid out, three rods wide, running to Malden Bridge, built ten years before to supplant the ferry. Private capital financed the construction of Malden Bridge, which the Malden Bridge Corporation owned and operated as a toll bridge for seventy-two years. During that time the round trip from Malden to Boston was costly: the tolls amounted to forty-seven cents, a heavy tax in a time when a daily wage rarely exceeded a dollar.

When the Newbury Turnpike Corporation decided upon South Malden as a terminus for the new highroad to Newburyport, the first step was taken in making the future Everett a consequential post in the transportational plan of the Commonwealth. Yet, in spite of its favorable location in the system of communication between Boston and the north country, Everett's progress before 1870 was slow. Until 1845 the town was engrossed in agriculture. In 1859 toll charges were done away with on the Malden Bridge, thus attracting more business and more residents to the town, which in 1870 was incorporated under the name of Everett, in honor of the illustrious orator, statesman, and scholar Edward Everett.

POINTS OF INTEREST

1. *Parlin Library*, Everett Square, a modern white brick building, chief public library of the city, and memorial to Albert N. Parlin, civic philanthropist, contains one of the few copies now readily available of a useful historical-descriptive booklet, 'The Straight Road,' concerning the Newburyport Turnpike, which passed through what is now Everett. On the lawn of the library grounds is a *Sundial* inscribed: 'To the children of Everett that they may measure their hours of sunshine.'

2. The *Milburn Collection of Hawthorniana* (*open only to accredited students of Hawthorne*), 88 Waverly St., is a large and exceedingly valuable treasure-house of first editions of Nathaniel Hawthorne's works and other Hawthorniana. Except for 'Fanshawe' and the two 'Carrier's Addresses' (broadsides soliciting newspaper subscriptions in Salem), the set of Hawthorne 'firsts' is complete. Among the rare items are the large paper copy of 'The Gentle Boy,' containing a frontispiece drawing by Mrs. Hawthorne and the privately printed 'Love Letters of Hawthorne.' There are also in the collection notebooks, manuscripts, and a very nearly complete compilation of all comment so far discovered in print about the great novelist, as well as association objects.

3. *Mt. Washington* (summit on Garland St., alt. 176) is one of several glacial drumlins in a chain, the others, visible from this one, being

Powder Horn Hill in Chelsea and Orient Heights in East Boston. Westward is a good view of Everett. Once there were remains of Indian forts here, testifying to the defeat of a Massachusetts tribe by the Wabanaki of Maine. Indian relics, including pottery, have been dug up at various times, indicating that the Indians also used Mt. Washington for ceremonials and encampments.

4. *Woodlawn Cemetery*, Elm St., 176 acres, planted with rhododendrons and many varieties of beautiful trees, is one of the notable burial grounds in Greater Boston, comparing favorably with Mt. Auburn and Forest Hills.

5. The *Mystic Iron Works* (*open by permission*), on the Mystic River, has a five-million-dollar blast furnace turning out 500 tons of pig iron daily, which is about 20 per cent of this type of raw material used in New England. This furnace is among the largest in the country. The great ore bridge, first object to catch the eye of the approaching visitor, has a clear span of 250 feet and is equipped with an eight-ton bucket. The plant, built in 1926, revived in Massachusetts an industry which had been lost to the State for a century and a half.

6. *Merrimac Chemical Company* (*open by appointment Mon. Fri.* 9–4.45; *guide provided*), Chemical Lane, off Broadway, is another vast and important plant, picturesquely marked for many years to travelers on the Eastern Division of the Boston and Maine Railroad by the great outdoor pile of sulphur which lies west of the buildings. This plant, formerly the Cochrane Chemical Co., was established in 1858. During the World War it did a huge business in TNT, phenol, and picric acid. It marketed the first H-acid made in the United States, and produces also fire and sagger clay, mined at Bennington, Vermont. A favorite statement is that its total output supplies the basic materials of every applied science and manufacturing process and the physical media of all the arts.

FALL RIVER. *City of Falling Water*

City: Alt. 39, pop. 117,414, sett. 1656, incorp. town, 1803, city 1854.

Railroad Station: Fall River, 860 North Main St., for N.Y., N.H. & H. R.R.

Bus Stations: North Main St., Granite Block opposite City Hall, for Eastern Mass. Ry. Co.; Union Coach Terminal for New England Transportation Co., Short Line, Inc., Union Ry. Co., and I.C.T. Bus Co.

Piers: Fall River Line Wharf, off Water St., near Anawan St.

Accommodations: Ten hotels; twenty-four lodging houses; three boarding-houses.

Information: Chamber of Commerce, N. Main and Granite Sts.

FALL RIVER, strikingly outlined against the sky on a long steep hill crest across Mount Hope Bay, looks both larger than it is and very foreign. The lofty chimneys of the great stone or brick mills and the soaring stone towers of numerous Roman Catholic churches, especially the twin pagoda-like spires of Notre Dame, give a European tone. In the foreground of the bay the white Fall River Boat to New York, one of an abandoned line long known to New Englanders, for years added a picturesque accent to the scene as it lay moored awaiting its sailing hour.

The uphill approach to City Hall and the heart of the municipality, through warehouses and mills which, architecturally unimaginative, yet stimulate the imagination sensitive to the drama in industry, is unimpressive, but the center of the business district is solid and substantial, with large stores, banks, and public buildings, mainly of granite, brownstone, or limestone. Excursions from this center bring the visitor at almost any block to sudden stretches of time-darkened mill plants, of which the Durfee Mills, all of granite, extend for eight blocks, largely closed, though some sections have been leased to small concerns. South and east of these lie large areas of shabby but self-respecting wooden tenements; toward the north the streets open into a more prosperous and pleasant residential district. The territory of the present city was settled in 1656 as part of a large land grant from Plymouth known as Freemen's Purchase. What is now Fall River was then called Pocasset, an Indian name still preserved by one of the villages in the town of Bourne on Cape Cod. In 1804 Fall River's Pocasset took the name of Troy, because of the affection of one of its citizens for Troy, New York. The present name of the city dates from 1834, and originated from the Indian name of the Quequechan River ('Falling Water'), which runs through the city and gives power to its mills.

Agricultural interests predominated until the Revolution, and thereafter no drama appears in the settlement until its sudden discovery by the industrial age. Fall River has three natural advantages as a center for cotton manufacturing: water-power, a mild, moist climate suited to the weaving of cotton fibers, and a sea harbor adequate for trade shipments. In consequence, its textile mills were among the first to be established in New England, and by 1871 they experienced a boom which from then until 1929 made the name of the city practically synonymous with cotton in the social and industrial history of the nation. Even in 1936, after seven years of depression, the city directory listed 236 industrial plants. There are upward of fifty labor unions.

Today the dominant note of the working city is French. The handsomest churches are French; French translations parallel the English inscriptions on monuments; the radios in the restaurants offer French popular songs; French newspapers are read in the trolleys.

Dark, stolid, built four-square, the Portuguese from the settlement at the far north of the city, more numerous than the French, are also principally engaged in the textile industry. Other races have spread through

the city, have intermingled by marriage, and have developed a cosmopolitan culture.

Fall River, by its very pre-eminence in cotton manufacture, has been
the hardest hit of all New England mill cities through the combination
of general business depression, the preference of modern women for
rayon or silk to cotton, and the removal of many textile factories to the
cheaper operating field of the South.

POINTS OF INTEREST

1. The *Site of the Battle of Fall River* is indicated by a Tablet on the City
Hall, North Main St. Shortly before the Revolution, Tory sentiment
was still strong, but this feeling changed, and 31 Freetown men responded
to the Lexington alarm. Colonel Joseph Durfee, who later started the
first cotton mill here, organized a home guard in 1777. On Sunday morning, May 25, 1778, boats were discovered cautiously approaching the
town. Challenged, they did not reply and were fired upon by Samuel
Reed, one of the guards. The whole neighborhood sprang to arms.
Colonel Durfee stationed his men behind a stone wall and maintained a
constant fire until the British brought cannon to bear. The Colonials
then retreated slowly to Main Street, where, near this spot, a stand was
made and the enemy was repulsed, leaving one soldier dead, one dying
and carrying a number of wounded with them.

The attacking British numbered about 150, commanded by Major Ayres.
On landing, they set fire to the home of Thomas Borden, near Anawan
and Pond Streets, and to his saw and grist mills. They fired the buildings of Richard Borden, an aged man, and took him prisoner, but released him on parole a few days later. As the boats retreated down the
bay the Colonials kept up musket fire, killing one soldier.

2. The *Sand Bank* where the skeleton in armor was found (1831) is indicated by a tablet on the gas plant at the corner of Fifth and Hartwell
Streets. This discovery inspired Longfellow to write a famous poem,
'The Skeleton in Armor.' Some of the remains are now to be found at
the Fall River Historical Society.

3. In a haunted hut on the *Banks of the Quequechan River* lived for many
years an old hag reputed to be in league with the Devil. Driven out and
stoned by her superstitious neighbors, she was left to die while they
burned her hut. Before setting the torch to it, however, they searched it,
and found — or so the oldsters say — a letter from Captain Kidd to the
crone which indicated that in her youth she had been his cherished
mistress.

4. The *Bradford Durfee Textile School*, Bank and Durfee Sts., is free to
citizens of the State who wish to make themselves more proficient in
this trade and for those who seek preliminary training. In 1933 the
school had 148 students. At the present time it is giving active attention

to courses designed to meet new trends in the textile industry, a progressive policy demanded by the recent hardships experienced in New England mills under changed conditions of trade.

5. The *Old Church House (private)*, corner of June St., is the oldest house in Fall River, a vine-covered, gambrel-roofed one-and-a-half-story frame structure, painted red, with a central chimney. Built about 1763, it is said to have been occupied by a Tory, who during the Revolutionary War lent his assistance to the British by using the house as one of the many connecting stations which sent messages to Taunton by means of flags and beacon lights.

6. *Fall River Historical Society (open to public weekdays 2–4, Sat. 10–12; adm. free)*, 451 Rock St. With its high-ceiled rooms and impressive dignity, the building lends itself well to museum purposes. On the first floor is a picture gallery with oil paintings by Bryant Chapin, Robert Dunning, and others. A false bookcase in the parlor once concealed the entrance to a wine-cellar, a station of the Underground Railroad. Mills, millmen, and streets of Fall River are represented in the room named 'Downtown of the Nineteenth Century,' where also are many interesting photographs of the steamers on the 'Old Fall River Line.'

7. The *Lafayette Monument* in Lafayette Park, Eastern Ave., County and Mason Sts., presented to the city by the Franco-Americans in 1916, depicts in bronze a youthful Lafayette on horseback. It was executed by Arnold Zocchi in Rome.

8. *Rolling Rock*, facing Lafayette Park on Eastern Ave., is a huge conglomerate resting on a granite ledge. It is said that in former times the Indians found that, by applying force, this rock could be rolled about on its base without falling off, and they used this discovery as a unique method of torture, placing captives' arms under a raised part of the rock and then rolling it onto them, crushing flesh and bone.

9. *Notre Dame Church*, Eastern Ave. at St. Joseph Street, contains 'The Last Judgment' of Cremonini painted on the ceiling of the main auditorium. This is the largest work of this famous Italian mural artist in the United States.

F I T C H B U R G . *The Farmer Goes to Town*

City: Alt. 458, pop. 41,700, sett. about 1730, incorp. town 1764, city 1872.

Railroad Station: Union Station, 264 Main St., for N.Y., N.H. & H. R.R. and B. & M. R.R.

Bus Station: 261 Main St. for Blue Way Line and New England Transportation Co. Union Station for B. & M. Transportation Co.

Accommodations: Two hotels open all year at reasonable rates.

Information: Chamber of Commerce, 560 Main St.; Y.M.C.A., 525 Main St.

NESTLED among rolling hills, in the valley along a branch of the Nashua River, Fitchburg illustrates the almost inevitable trend of many Massachusetts cities which, after more than a century's existence as small agricultural hamlets, were transformed in a few years into industrial cities. Second in size in Worcester County, Fitchburg is notable in its segregation of the industrial and residential sections. The steep slopes on the south side of the little Nashua River are covered almost entirely by dwelling houses, while the business section monopolizes the north side close to the river bank. The outlying portions, sparsely populated, are used principally for pasturing and farming.

Owing to the dominance of heavy industries, Fitchburg gives the appearance of being a man's town, although the census reports that women lead in actual numbers. A Yankee twang is at once detected in the voices, but the city is a composite of many races. There are Irish, some descended from early railroad hands, many dark French-Canadians, who came as mill workers about 1860, lean, blue-eyed Swedes, brought by Iver Johnson interests in 1890, and serious-faced Finns, introduced in the great immigration of 1880 to 1912, and Poles and Italians. The city itself has an air of substance, unleavened by imagination. It strikes a level midway between an impressive display of wealth and a marked revelation of poverty. This is due in part to the great number of small commercial enterprises owned principally by Germans, Jews, and Armenians. Racially organized co-operatives, notably the Finnish Co-operative Society, the Farmers Co-operatives, and the new German enterprise, promote an orderliness of living not usually found in 'factory towns.'

Fitchburg for fifty years after its incorporation was primarily a dairying and agricultural community, largely self-contained. In 1793 an outlet was provided by the opening of a stagecoach line between Boston and Fitchburg. At the same time the industrial potentialities of the Nashua River were recognized. As early as 1805 General Leonard Burbank established a paper mill near the 250-foot fall of the river.

The opening of the Boston and Fitchburg Railroad in 1845, and the Vermont and Massachusetts Railroad in 1848, insured still more rapid transportation facilities and attracted new industries, many of which are now in operation. The quarrying of granite from Rollstone Hill is still an important industry.

POINTS OF INTEREST

1. The *Home of the Fitchburg Plan* is the new High School, Wallace Ave., a red-brick building capped by a white cupola. The Plan, originated

in 1911, is a co-operative arrangement by which boys in engineering courses are allowed to spend three days a week at high school and three days at work in local factories, and are paid on an apprenticeship basis.

2. The *Fitchburg Historical Society* (*open Sun. and Thurs.* 2–4), 50 Grove St., occupies a modern two-story brick building with limestone trim. Rare exhibits are a Vinegar Bible published in London in 1777 ('vinegar' is erroneously used in the margin instead of 'vineyard'); also a Breeches Bible, published in 1588 ('breeches' instead of 'apron' used in Genesis III, 7). A drum used by a high priest of Haiti in the voodoo dance and an English hurdygurdy 300 years old are on display.

3. The *Fitchburg Art Center*, at the end of the Merriam Parkway (*open weekdays except Mon.* 10–12 *and* 2–5; *Sun.* 2–5), has been transformed into an attractive two-story building of brick and exposed timbers covered with woodbine. It houses a notable permanent collection of 18th-century French provincial furniture, pottery, and glass; monthly traveling exhibits are shown, with emphasis on textile weaves and designs, and on color prints.

4. *Rollstone Rock*, Main St. near Caldwell Place, is a huge glacial boulder which geologists classify as 'erratic,' since no rock of like formation or substance is found nearer than 100 miles to the north. As quarrying on Rollstone Hill progressed, it was found necessary to move the rock, but its 100-ton weight prohibited its removal in a single piece. It was consequently split into sections and reassembled.

5. The *Iver Johnson Arms and Cycle Co.* (*open to ranking technicians only*), River St. (State 2), occupies a series of long two-story brick buildings covered with woodbine. A tour of the plant and an explanation of the 4000 processes involved in the manufacture of a shotgun takes three hours. Iver Johnson was a Norwegian mechanic with a genius for firearms and organization, and a passion for fine materials and workmanship. Sporting firearms are manufactured, but not ammunition; bicycles, though originally a side-line, are now of primary importance.

6. The paper industries of the city are perhaps best represented by the large brick *Mills of the Fitchburg Paper Co.*, River St. (State 2), and the extensive series of *Mills of the Crocker–Burbank Co.*, Westminster St. (State 2) (*both open to technicians only*). The Fitchburg Paper Co. specializes in wallpaper and coated paper for lithography.

7. Mysterious *Arches*, on a terraced bank 200 feet back from Blossom St., near the summit of the hill, somewhat resemble a Roman aqueduct in miniature. They are constructed of smooth field-stones the size of a man's palm, set in cement. Early in the 20th century Andrew Whitney, a wealthy citizen with a reputation for eccentricity, started to build 'something' whose purpose he refused to divulge. He died when the structure had progressed thus far. As Mr. Whitney was interested in theatrical ventures, it is thought that he may have had in mind an outdoor theater or a home for retired actors. Saplings and brush have encroached on the arches, adding to their mystery a touch of desolation.

8. The *State Teachers' College*, at the junction of Pearl and North Sts., occupies a broad three-story red-brick building on a pleasant campus. It is one of the largest teachers' colleges in the State, and has an especially good art school. It established one of the first junior high schools in the country.

9. The *Simonds Saw and Steel Co.* (*open only to visitors with special mechanical or mercantile interests*), 5 North St., makes the largest saws in America, those used by the lumber trade.

10. The *Laurel St. Bridge*, Laurel St. (*descend on foot to see arches*), is unique in Massachusetts in that its abutments are not at right angles to the river or railroad tracks, but set at an angle of approximately 45 degrees, so that the water flows almost diagonally beneath it through a series of arches. It withstood the floods of 1936.

11. The *Cushing Flour and Grain Co.* (*seen from the bridge*) has occupied since 1868 a fascinating old stone building with a gambrel roof, small-paned windows, and white cupola.

12. *Coggshall Park* (*picnic groves, skating rink*), South St., is a beautiful natural pine grove and lake with a combined area of 200 hilly acres, noted for its profusion of laurel in June.

G L O U C E S T E R *and* R O C K P O R T

Mother Ann's Children

GLOUCESTER

City: Alt. 57, pop. 24,164, sett. 1623, incorp. town 1642, city 1873.

Railroad Station: Railroad Ave. for B. & M. R.R.

Piers: Annisquam and Eastern Point Yacht Clubs, Wonson's Cove.

Accommodations: One year-round hotel; 12 summer hotels.

Annual Events: Italian fishermen's three-day St. Peter festival early in July; the Fishermen's Memorial Service in August.

Information: Booth in summer on Western Ave., near Fisherman Statue. Chamber of Commerce, Main St.

ROCKPORT

Town: Alt. 61, pop. 3634, sett. 1690, incorp. 1840.

Railroad Station: Rockport Station on Granite St. and Railroad Ave. for the B. & M.

Piers: T Wharf off Dock Square for the Municipal Yacht Basin at the Sandy Bay Yacht Club.

Accommodations: One year-round hotel; eight summer hotels.

Annual Event: The Artists' Ball sponsored by the Rockport Art Association, third week in August.

Information: Board of Trade off Dock Square.

GLOUCESTER and ROCKPORT comprise the whole of the granite peninsula of Cape Ann. Gloucester is an up-to-date industrial city, fringed by summer resorts ranging from fashionable Eastern Point, Bass Rocks, and Magnolia to quiet Annisquam. Nevertheless the persistence of its seafaring tradition for more than three hundred years gives its wharves, its narrow streets, its skyline of weathered roofs and spires, a unique atmosphere, of which the essence is the never-to-be-forgotten smell of Gloucester, a compound of tar, salt air, and the strong fresh aroma of codfish drying in the sun. Modern Rockport is an artist's paradise, with neat wooden houses crowding close around the harbor, still looking seaward and away from the bleak and boulder-strewn moorlands of the interior Cape.

The work of innumerable artists who flock to Cape Ann every summer, Kipling's classic 'Captains Courageous,' and the salty yarns of James B. Connolly have spread the fame of the picturesque seaport of Gloucester and the tiny fishing villages of the outer Cape far beyond the confines of New England. For more than two centuries Rockport shared this tradition and a fleet of small fishing boats still rides at anchor in the minute harbor, snugly sheltered from the battering surge of the open Atlantic by natural buttresses of sea-worn granite.

Since 1623, when the Dorchester Adventurers' colony at Gloucester was established, Cape Ann men have drawn their livelihood from the sea. But with the mushroom growth of American cities during the boom days of the industrial age, Rockport found a valuable article of export in the high-grade granite that everywhere underlies the town. Riggers who had learned their trade in the lofts of Gloucester turned their talents to erecting the quarry derricks, which with their spider webs of gray wires are today still a feature of the Rockport landscape, as are the piles of faulted blocks and the deep pools of the abandoned quarries. A special type of vessel was perfected in the shipyards of Rockport and the near-by towns for carrying granite. Up to about twenty-five years ago these stone sloops were a picturesque sight as they lay loading in almost every narrow deep tongue of water along the outer Cape. The quarries attracted a colony of Finnish stoneworkers, who still remain, although the granite industry is greatly diminished in scope.

And time has brought changes to the fisheries of Gloucester. The fast schooners that once sailed out past the breakwater are giving way to smaller trawlers and gill-netters, Diesel-powered. The Anglo-Saxon population that dominated the city for more than two hundred and fifty years has recently been given vitality and color by large immigrant groups of Portuguese and Italians and a sprinkling of Scandinavians.

These men, seafarers all, have brought their own traditions to the fisheries and their allied industries, spar- and sailmaking, rigging and iron-working and to the manufactures dependent on the fisheries — glue, isinglass, and fertilizer. The fishermen seek their living upon the most dangerous waters in the world, the fog-shrouded, berg-haunted Grand Banks, with their swift currents and steep, short seas, and the treacherous shoals nearer home — Georges Bank, Stellwagen Bank, and the picturesquely named ledges along the coast. Although ten thousand men of Gloucester have been lost at sea in the three centuries of her history, the modern fishermen still pursue their calling without heroics but with skill and daring undiminished.

GLOUCESTER FOOT TOUR — 2 m.

E. from Legion Square on Middle St.

1. The *Joan of Arc Equestrian Statue*, at Legion Square, is a distinguished work of Anna Vaughn Hyatt.

2. The *Universalist Church*, corner of Church St., was erected in 1868, its octagonal steeple a copy of one on an earlier church on the same site, where was held in 1774 the first Universalist service in America.

3. The *Sargent–Murray–Gilman House* (1768) (*open in summer as a tearoom; no inspection charge to patrons; otherwise 25¢*), 49 Middle St., has a gambrel roof, denticular cornice, and quoined corners. It was, sometime after 1788, the home of the Rev. John Murray, founder of Universalism.

4. The *Sawyer Public Library* (*open weekdays 9–9, Sun. 2–9*) is a residence in the Federal style with white clapboards, quoined corners, a recessed third story and a modern red roof. The walls of the fine old stairway were adorned in 1934 with Murals of *Gloucester Scenes*, under the sponsorship of the Federal Art Project.

L. from Middle St. on Dale Ave.; R. from Dale Ave. on Warren St.; L. from Warren St. on Pleasant St.

5. The *Cape Ann Scientific, Literary, and Historical Association* (*open daily in summer, 11–4; adm. 25¢*), corner of Federal St., is a three-story Georgian Colonial house, containing ship models, period furniture, old china, pewter, costumes, minerals, and marine plants.

R. from Pleasant St. on Prospect St.

6. The Portuguese *Church of Our Lady of Good Voyage* (*open*), is known for its carillon of 32 bells. Above its door is a sensitively conceived figure of the Madonna holding a schooner in one hand, the other hand raised in blessing the waters. The *Fiesta Of Pentecost* is celebrated on three successive Sundays. Dark-skinned, brilliant-eyed children march with their elders to the church, where the pastor places crowns on the

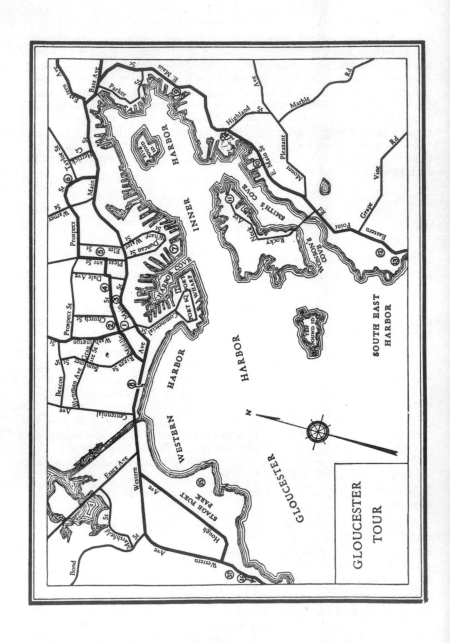

GLOUCESTER
TOUR

heads of those chosen to express the gratitude of the community for the intervention of St. Peter in their behalf during the past year.

R. from Prospect St. on Main St.

7. Below the *Waterfront* are the wharves where for more than 300 years fishing boats have discharged their cargoes. The vessels returning with their great catches from the Grand Banks and nearer waters were once all sailing ships and the crews all Yankee. Now the 40-foot power trawlers and gill-netters predominate, and most of the crews are Portuguese.

Straight ahead from Main St. on Western Ave.

8. The *Gloucester Fisherman* in bronze, executed by Leonard Craske, stands on the Esplanade, looking across the harbor to the open sea. By the statue every year on an August Sunday afternoon is held the fishermen's memorial ceremony. Flowers are placed at the feet of the Fisherman; from a point of land near Blynman's Bridge, the roll of those lost at sea during the past year is slowly read and armfuls of blossoms are strewn upon the water, to be carried out by the ebb tide to unknown graves.

The larger island in the harbor is *Ten Pound Island*, purchased from the Indians for ten pounds, and now a Coast Guard station. Farther east stretches *Eastern Point*, from the tip of which juts *Dog Bar Breakwater*. Little *Five Pound Island* was chosen as the site of the new Fish Pier, in 1937.

MOTOR TOUR 1 (*Eastern Point*), 7.3 m.

S. from Legion Square on Washington St.; L. from Washington St. on Main St.; R. from Main St. on E. Main St.

9. The *Gorton–Pew Fisheries Plant* (*open*) is a series of gray fish sheds, piers, and open-air 'flakes' for canning and drying fish.

GLOUCESTER MAP INDEX

1. Joan of Arc Equestrian Statue
2. Universalist Church
3. Sargent-Murray-Gilman House
4. Sawyer Public Library
5. Cape Ann Scientific, Literary, and Historical Association
6. Church of Our Lady of Good Voyage
7. Waterfront
8. Gloucester Fisherman
9. Gorton-Pew Fisheries Plant
10. North Shore Art Association
11. Rocky Neck
12. Gloucester Society of Artists
13. Eastern Point Yacht Club
35. Stage Fort Park
36. Hammond Museum
37. Rafe's Chasm

10. The *North Shore Art Association* (*open in summer; weekdays* 10–6, *Sun.* 2–6), on the water's edge, holds exhibitions from July to September.

R. from E. Main St. on Rocky Neck Ave.

11. *Rocky Neck* is the heart of the summer colony of artists, actors and writers, occupying bungalows, old sail lofts and remodeled sheds along the narrow peninsula. To the left lies the open bay; to the right is the inner harbor.

The *Gloucester School of the Theater* presents plays acted by its students in a red-shingled small barn (the Little Theater) at the end of the road, by the side of the marine railway.

Retrace on Rocky Neck Ave.; R. from Rocky Neck Ave. on E. Main St. and straight ahead from E. Main St. into Eastern Point Rd.

12. The *Gloucester Society of Artists* (*open in summer, weekdays* 10–6, *Sun.* 2–6, *adm.* 15¢) exhibits paintings and sculpture through the summer season, and joins in August with the North Shore Art Association in the Artists' Ball.

13. The *Eastern Point Yacht Club* (*private*) occupies a small promontory in the harbor on the edge of Niles Beach. Here begin the large summer estates.

Straight ahead from Eastern Point Rd. into Eastern Point Blvd. West.

14. *Niles Pond* is a curious and lovely natural phenomenon, a reed-bordered and lily-starred fresh-water pond divided from the sea on the east by the narrowest of causeways.

Beyond the pond the road (*barred in summer to tourists*) leads to *Eastern Point Light and Mother Ann*, a rock formation bearing a fancied resemblance to a reclining woman.

L. from Eastern Point Blvd. West, on Lake Ave.; R. from Lake Ave. on Eastern Point Blvd. East; Straight ahead from the boulevard on Atlantic Rd.; R. from Atlantic Rd. on Bass Ave.

15. *Little Good Harbor Beach* (*public; parking charge on Sun.*), is an excellent sandy bathing beach at all tides. The small rocky island just offshore is *Salt Island*; and in the near distance is *Thatcher's Island*, with the granite towers of its twin lights (erected in 1771), only one of which is now in use.

MOTOR TOUR 2 (*Cape Ann*), 19 *m.*

S. from Legion Square on Washington St.; L. from Washington St. on Main St.; L. from Main St. on Eastern Ave.; R. from Eastern Ave. on Thatcher Rd.; R. from Thatcher Rd. on Long Beach Rd.

16. *Long Beach,* one and a half miles long, is a fine sandy bathing beach on the open Atlantic.

Retrace Long Beach Rd.; R. from Long Beach Rd. on Thatcher Rd. which becomes South St., Rockport; R. from South St. on Marmion Way.

17. The *Straitsmouth Inn*, perched on the rocks overlooking Straitsmouth Island, commands a fine view. Just below the inn at the right is a *U.S. Coast Guard Station (open).*

Retrace Marmion Way; R. from Marmion Way, on South St.

The tour now plunges abruptly into the heart of ROCKPORT, rival of Gloucester in its summer art colony.

R. from South St. into short lane leading to docks.

18. *New Harbor* is the joy of artists. At the left stretches little Bearskin Neck, crowded with weathered fishermen's shacks, small gray sail lofts and piers, to which are usually moored two or three fishing smacks. At the right is the *Sandy Bay Yacht Club (private).*

'*Motif No. 1*' is the designation facetiously applied to the natural composition made by a little sail loft with a siding of vertical brown planks, which juts out into the harbor, and a small vessel usually tied alongside, because the scene has been so often painted by Rockport artists.

Retrace lane; R. from lane on South St.; R. from South St. on Bearskin Neck.

19. *Bearskin Neck* takes its name, as indicated by a marker at the turn from South St., from the capture there in early days of a bear which had been caught by the tide.

At the end of the Neck is the *Site of an Old Fort* which served the town well in the War of 1812, when Rockport was of sufficient importance to draw a naval attack from the British.

Retrace Bearskin Neck; R. from Bearskin Neck on Main St.

20. The *Ebenezer Pool Mansion (private),* 25 Main St., is a square white dwelling erected in 1805, with four great chimneys rising from a hip roof.

21. The *Rockport Art Association (open in July and Aug. daily; free),* 12 Main St., holds summer-long exhibitions, and sponsors an Artists' Ball, the great event of the Rockport season. The Association occupies *The Old Tavern,* erected in 1770, and considerably renovated.

22. The *First Congregational Church* (1803), known as the 'Old Sloop,' has a steeple rebuilt in 1814 after being demolished by a shot from the British man-of-war 'Nymph.'

R. from Main St. on Beach St.; straight ahead from Beach St. into Granite St.

23. The *Granite Quarries* represent a flourishing 19th-century industry which was crippled by the introduction of substitutes for stone in buildings and highway construction.

24. The *Old Castle (open July and Aug., and Sun. 2-5; free),* at the junction of Curtis St., is a dwelling dating to about 1700, with a lean-to roof, shingled sides, and a red door and window sashes, the whole set well back from the road in a grassy, tree-shaded yard.

L. from Granite St. on Curtis St.; L. from Curtis St. on Pigeon Hill St.

25. The *Paper House* (*open in summer daily; fee* 25¢) is a bungalow (1922) with walls and furniture constructed entirely from newspapers, rolled and glued.

Retrace Pigeon Hill St.; R. from Pigeon Hill St. on Curtis St.; L. from Curtis St. on Granite St.

26. The *Garrison Witch House* (*private*), which is nearly opposite Phillips Ave., dates in part from 1670, a gray clapboarded dwelling with unusual roof line, a later white doorway and a side second-story overhang. It is the only authentic garrison house remaining near Boston, and was probably used as a refuge during King Philip's War. Here fled Elizabeth Proctor, condemned with her husband and four other settlers as guilty of witchcraft.

R. from Granite St. on Gott Ave.

27. *Halibut Point* (*reached by footpath only, from a point* 200 *yards down Gott Ave.; parking* 25¢) is a State Reservation on a jagged rocky headland. At the beginning of the footpath is the *Gott House* (*open by arrangement*), a humble gambrel-roofed dwelling of 1702.

Retrace Gott Ave.; R. from Gott Ave. on Granite St., which becomes Washington St. in Gloucester.

28. *Lanesville* offers a view of granite cliffs and sand dunes across a stretch of ocean.

29. The *Consolidated Lobster Company* (*open to visitors*) is a large plant which makes deliveries by airplanes, keeping the crustaceans alive in pools until shipped.

30. At *Goose Cove*, Annisquam, from the bridge crossing the inlet, appears the nearest view on the Cape of sand dunes, white across the Annisquam River, and accented with sage-green beach grass. The nearer beach is *Coffin's Beach* with *Wingaersheek Beach* beyond.

31. The *Annisquam Willows*, through which the highway runs in a doubled roadbed, were planted that their interlacing roots might make a firm underpinning for the road.

L. from Washington St. on Reynard St.; L. from Reynard St. on lane marked 'To Dogtown.'

32. *Dogtown*, truly a 'blasted heath,' is a vast open, rolling moor, thickly strewn with glacial boulders and rendered yet more desolate by a sparse growth of stunted cedars. It contains the cellar holes of more than 40 dwellings, the homes in 1650 of fishermen and their families. Through war and wrecks at sea and the removal of remaining settlers closer to the harbor, the village came to be inhabited solely by poverty-stricken widows and children, protected by ferocious watchdogs from which the settlement took its name. The majority of the cellar holes have been numbered on adjoining boulders, to identify them under their owners' names in Roger Babson's 'History of Dogtown.' Here lived old Luce

George, a wild-eyed hag, and her niece, Tammy Younger, who so bewitched the oxen hauling grain past their cabin that the animals stood with lolling tongues and would not move until part of their load had been donated to the Devil, as represented by Goody George. Here, too, dwelt young Judy Rhines, heroine of Percy MacKaye's poem, casting her spells over fine strong lads; and old Peg Wesson, who, in the guise of a black crow, followed a detachment of soldiers to Louisburg in 1745 and annoyed them until the crow was shot by a silver bullet made from the buttons of a soldier's coat; at which very moment, back in Gloucester, Old Peg fell down and broke her leg and soon died — some say with a silver bullet in her.

Retrace 'Dogtown' Lane; R. from 'Dogtown' Lane on Reynard St.; L. from Reynard St. on Washington St.

33. The *Babson House* (*private*) (1740), 245 Washington St., a gambrel-roofed yellow mansion with white trimmings, contains attic pens once used for slaves.

34. The *Ellery House* (*private*), directly opposite the Babson House, dates from 1704. Its gray walls have an overhanging second story, a lean-to roof, and the typical central chimney of the period.

MOTOR TOUR 3 (*West Gloucester*), 11 *m.*

SW. from Legion Square on Middle St.; R. from Middle St. on Western Ave.; L. from Western Ave. on Hough Ave.

35. At *Stage Fort Park*, overlooking Gloucester Harbor, was the first fishing stage and the first fort on Cape Ann.

L. from Hough Ave. on Western Ave.; L. from Western Ave. on Hesperus Ave.

36. The *Hammond Museum* (*open June 1–Oct. 1 on weekday mornings only; tours under guide at 9, 10, and 11; adm. 50¢*), a stone castle in medieval style in the Magnolia section, overlooks the sea. It contains a picture gallery, rare old furniture, wood carvings and sculpture collected and arranged by John Hays Hammond, Jr.

L. from Hesperus Ave. on dirt road marked 'To Rafe's Chasm.'

37. *Rafe's Chasm* is a narrow cleft in the granite coast at sea level, in which the tide surges back and forth with a hollow boom, and from which an east wind and an incoming sea send up sheets of spray high in the air. Offshore is the small reef of *Norman's Woe*, familiar from Longfellow's 'The Wreck of the Hesperus.'

HAVERHILL

From Hardscrabble to Hats and Shoes

City: Alt. 59, pop. 49,516, sett. 1640, incorp. town 1645, city 1869.

Railroad Station: Haverhill Station, Railroad Square, off Washington St., for B. & M. R.R.

Bus Stations: Corner Bridge and Water Sts. for Eastern Mass. Ry. Co.; Lyon's Drugstore, Merrimack St., for the Blue Way Lines, Short Line, B. & M., and Checker Cab Bus; 6 Washington St. for Grey Line.

Airport: Emergency landing field only, with no refueling service; daylight landings only. Located 2 *m.* N. of the center of the city on State 108.

Accommodations: Two hotels open all the year.

Information: Chamber of Commerce, Washington Sq.

HAVERHILL, now a typical New England manufacturing city, in its three hundred years' history has developed from a hardscrabble frontier village to its present high position in the industrial world. Something of its variegated past still remains to give the city a flavor quite different from that of its neighbor Lawrence. At Haverhill's back door flows the Merrimack. New houses shoulder weathered old ones along the wide streets, and from the Haverhill bridge there unfolds upstream a panorama of factories, office buildings, and spires, while downstream lies the long, lovely perspective of rounded hills, neat farms, and broad river of an unchanged New England.

Certainly the Reverend John Ward and his twelve followers could never have previsioned more than an eventual approximation of the quiet market town of Haverhill, England, when they landed on the muddy Merrimack shore in 1640 to found a new plantation. The swift wide waters of the river were too powerful for them to harness, but they early saw modest possibilities in the rapid small streams rushing down from the hills, and they offered grants of land and other inducements to such applicants as would put them to use.

During the first century of its existence Haverhill was a frontier town cut off by the Merrimack from the more secure settlements of the coast. The settlers clearing their fields had no Indian troubles until King Philip's War in 1675, and their frontier position had many advantages. The soil of the glacial hillsides was fertile. The forests provided oak and pine timber, and the wilderness trails became the avenues for a profitable trade in skins and furs. The oaks and pines provided frames and planking for the ships which were building all along the Merrimack. The first vessel was launched from a Haverhill yard in 1697, and for nearly one hundred and fifty years the town's merchants sent their goods adventuring in their own ships. The pelts purchased from the Indians were cured in the tanneries which had flourished from 1643, and which are still a feature of the town's industrial life.

The making of hats, recorded as early as 1747, was an important industry in Haverhill throughout the last century, and continues at present on a diminished scale.

The mercantile boom that swept the cities of the Massachusetts coast to prosperity during the Federalist period gave impetus to Haverhill ship-building. Four shipyards in 1800 were turning out ships, schooners, and sloops; sometimes three were launched in a single day. Trade with the South and with the West Indies flourished. Haverhill's position as a port of entry, however, was gradually surrendered to Newburyport and other coastal cities. The larger vessels which gained favor after the Revolution were not suited to river navigation, and this was made even more difficult when a group of Newburyport merchants built the Chain Bridge across the Merrimack in 1811. Haverhill merchants turned manufacturers and invested their profits in shoe factories, hat factories, comb factories, and tanneries. In 1836 there were twenty-eight shoe factories in Haverhill.

The invention of the Goodyear turn shoe-stitching machine, patented in 1875, assured Haverhill's position as a manufacturing center of high-grade shoes. Later the local manufacturers specialized in fashionable shoes for women. As a center of shoe manufacture and allied industries, Haverhill was outdistanced only by Brockton among Massachusetts cities in 1934. Other manufactures are boxes and paper, woolens, food products, brooms, chemicals, shirts, mattresses, hats, cigars, and radio cabinets.

Haverhill, like the other Massachusetts shoe cities, Lynn and Brockton, is a center of unionism. For the student, trade-union structure and opera-tion is vividly depicted in the activities of the Shoe Workers Protective Union in Haverhill from 1900 to 1930. Thomas Norton in his 'Trade Union Policies in the Massachusetts Shoe Industry' analyzes this union and its arbitration technique. Other strong unions in the city are the Boot and Shoe Workers' Union of the American Federation of Labor, the Brotherhood of Shoe and Allied Craftsmen and the United Shoe and Leather Workers' Union, the last two independent. Recently there has been a movement to amalgamate all these groups.

The city is definitely divided into foreign quarters, whose residents are more or less segregated and intermingle with those from other quarters only during the working day at the factories. Along the Methuen high-way, Polish immigrants till their small farms. Between the end of this highway and the western side of the city, the Latin immigrants have built a little Italy. The Jewish quarter, complete with markets, clubs, and synagogues, borders both sides of Washington Street near the junction of River Street. The homes and societies of the French-Canadians dominate Lafayette Square. In the section between Washington Square, Essex, Emerson, and Winter Streets are the places of business, the coffee houses, and the homes of the Syrians and Armenians. From Winter Street to the northern outskirts of the city is the 'Acre,' as the Irish section of

Haverhill has long been called. From Monument Square toward the northeast extends that part of the city inhabited by families who took root in Haverhill soil before the industrial era.

Haverhill is one of the few cities in the east with a commission form of government. Such a system is built on the theory that the modern city is essentially a great business enterprise and should be administered by the same methods which would be regarded as efficient by any successful commercial corporation.

TOUR — 7.5 m.

N. from River St. into Main St.

1. The *Hannah Dustin Statue* (1879), occupying a small triangular Green near the junction of Summer St., depicts the heroic woman who was abducted by the Indians in March, 1697, and escaped with the scalps of ten of her captors dangling from her belt.

R. from Main St. into Summer St.

2. The *Haverhill Public Library* (*open weekdays* 9–9, *Sun.* 2–6, *Nov.–Apr.*) is rich in souvenirs of the poet Whittier, and contains a complete and valuable collection of first editions of his works.

R. from Summer St. into Mill St.; L. from Mill St. into Water St.

3. The *Rev. John Ward House* (*open Tues., Thurs., Sat.* 2–5; *adm. free*), the first frame house in Haverhill, was built about 1645 for the first minister. The Haverhill Historical Society, present owners, have restored the rooms to their original condition and furnished them in 17th-century style.

4. The *Buttonwoods* (*adm. free*), built in 1814 and now headquarters of the Haverhill Historical Society, is adjacent to the Ward House and terraced high above the Merrimack. In front of it are still standing the two sycamores of which Whittier wrote. *Tenny Hall* (*open Tues., Thurs., Sat.* 2–5; *adm. free*), is a modern annex of the old brick-end clapboarded house. It houses the Archeological and Natural History Department of the Society, containing Indian relics and other antiquities of this section.

5. The *Spiller House* or *Hazen Garrison House* (1680–1690) (*private*), on the corner of Groveland and Water Sts., is a charming dwelling carefully restored. A two-and-a-half-story brick house, its bricks laid in shell mortar, it contains unusually large fireplaces with two huge ovens shaped like beehives. The window arrangement is unusual and the hardware, which includes oak latches and hinges and strap and butterfly hinges, is for the most part original.

Retrace Water St.; R. from Water St. into Mill St.

6. The *Ayer Homestead* (*private*) overlooks the Green from the northwest

side at the intersection of Saltonstall St. This is a 17th-century dwelling with a dark weather-stained exterior, steeply pitched roof, central chimney, and interesting doorway.

R. from Mill St. into State 110 (*Kenoza St.*).

7 The *Winnikenni Reservation* (*automobiles must park at entrance*) contains tennis courts, bridle paths, and hiking trails. In the background loom the massive gray walls of *Winnikenni Castle* (*open on application to Park Dept.*), built in 1873 and in imitation of a medieval castle in Bath, England.

8. *Kenoza Lake* (Indian, meaning 'Lake of the Pickerel') lies near-by, mirroring the wooded banks of the Reservation.

9. The *Birthplace of John Greenleaf Whittier* (*open daily* 10–*sundown; adm.* 10¢) (on State 110, 3 m. from city) is a fine example of a New England early American farmhouse. The house contains relics which include the old desk on which the poet's earliest rhymes and last poem were written. Built in 1688, it has been restored as nearly as possible to its original condition. The many landmarks identified with Whittier's poems are those of the old Haverhill, the quiet New England farming town. The gentle Quaker poet was not sensitive to the throbbing industrial city that was growing up along the Merrimack shore, and preferred to sing of country ways and the 'proud isolation' and 'self-righteous poverty' of the old stock from which he sprang.

Retrace State 110; *L. from State* 110 *into Main St.; straight ahead across Merrimack River on State* 125.

10. The *Kimball Tavern* (about 1690) (*open* 10–5; *adm. free*), stands at the corner of Salem St. The first iron stove in Haverhill was set up in this house, which is also noted for its fine woodwork and finish, its old latches and panels, its old furniture and curios.

11. The *First Church of Christ* (organized 1682; erected 1848) (*services, 11 Sun.; midweek services Thurs.* 7.30), across the Common, is an animated adaptation of the late Colonial style, adorned with Corinthian columns, an elaborate cornice, and a graceful steeple. The tower of the church was used as a model for that of the Chapel of Mary and Martha in Dearborn, Michigan, built by Henry Ford.

A *Boulder* on the church green claims the birth here in 1810 of the foreign missionary movement in the United States, through the organization of the American Board of Commissioners for Foreign Missions. In 1812, four missionaries sailed for Calcutta on the brigantine 'Caravan' 'to bring light to the moral darkness of Asia.' They were the famous Adoniram Judson (*see MALDEN*) and his wife Anne Hasseltine and Samuel Newell and Newell's wife, Harriet Atwood, the latter a resident of Haverhill.

12. *Bradford Junior College*, South Main St., occupies a well-equipped campus of 37 acres. Founded in 1803 as an Academy, it is believed to be the oldest upper school for girls in New England. None of the original buildings are now standing.

HOLYOKE . *The Power of Water*

City: Alt. 152, pop. 56,139, sett. 1745, incorp. town 1850, city 1873.

Railroad Station: Mosher St. for B. & M. R.R.

Bus Stations: 69 Suffolk St. and 443 High St. for Blue Way, B. & M., Greyhound, Interstate, and Vermont Transit Co.

Airport: Barnes Airport, on Hampton Plains, between Westfield and Holyoke.

Accommodations: Five hotels.

Information: Chamber of Commerce, 98 Suffolk St.; County Automobile Club, 129 Chestnut St.

HOLYOKE, a large manufacturing city on the Connecticut River south of Mount Tom, is built around the numerous power canals that cut across the city. Entered from the north, it is modern, well-groomed, and prosperous. To the south are a number of imposing Catholic institutions, educational and charitable. The manufacturing center, lying along the power canals, has been unusually active throughout the depression. The absence of drab slum quarters usually associated with mill towns is notable.

One factor in creating this prosperous atmosphere is the skilled type of worker employed by the numerous paper mills that manufacture high-grade writing paper, the principal support of the town. Particularly well known are the Whiting Mills. This and six other important paper mills, attracted by cheap water-power from Hadley Falls Dam, have given the town the name of 'The Paper City.'

The American Thread Company, the Farr Alpaca Company, and the Skinner Silk Company are about all that remain of what promised to be a great textile center. Cheap water-power, accessible wood for wood-pulp and rag-scrap from textile mills diverted interests to paper-making.

The waterworks and gas and electric plants are municipally owned. A daily and weekly paper in English, and one weekly each in French and German, are published. The City Hall, a striking building with a great granite tower, is an object of civic pride. Cultural pursuits are evidenced by the excellent small museum of natural history and a small art gallery, both at the Public Library, by the Holyoke League of Arts and Crafts, and by a number of musical organizations.

The first foreign-born citizens to arrive were the Irish, whose descendants constitute one third of the present population. These, with the French-Canadians, make the city an outstanding Catholic center. Poles number ten per cent of the inhabitants, and the rest are of English, Scotch, German, Italian, Greek, Scandinavian, or Jewish origin. All this foreign growth has been made in the past ninety years, but it is the very essence of Holyoke, and there is little or nothing other than the Indian arrowheads at the Public Library to remind the visitor that there was a settlement as early as 1725.

During Revolutionary years the village remained an agricultural community centered about a tavern that served as a halfway stop on the stage route between Springfield and Northampton. The potential water-power of the Connecticut River just above Hadley Falls was not long in attracting the attention of manufacturing pioneers, and as early as 1828 a dam had been constructed, and a few small textile, grain, and metal mills were in operation. Not until 1848, however, did capital appear in the form of a group of New York and Boston investors and developers who secured the rights of the old Hadley Falls Company. In 1848 a $75,000 dam was completed, and on the same day it was swept away by the terrific pressure, incorrectly calculated, of the water behind it. The story is said to have been graphically told in a series of telegrams directed to the Boston office:

10 A.M. Gates just closed: water filling behind dam.
12 A.M. Dam leaking badly.
2 P.M. Stones of bulkhead giving way to pressure.
3.20 P.M. Your old dam's gone to hell by way of Willimansett.

Within a year a second dam, twice as costly, was completed, which served until 1900. The present dam and its great waterfall are visible only from the uppermost of the three city bridges which cross the river. Known as 'The Gateway of New England Waters,' this dam proved its strength by withstanding the destructive flood of 1936.

TOUR — 5.5 m.

W. from High St. on Appleton

1. The interior of *Skinner Memorial Chapel* (Congregational) (*open daily* 9–5), Appleton and Maple Sts., is designed in Gothic style. A decorative panel in the choir stall represents the conversion of the Ethiopian eunuch by St. Philip, and is surmounted by dull stained-glass windows. The chancel floor is mosaic.

L. from Appleton St. on Maple St.

2. The *Holyoke Library and Museum* (*open weekdays* 10–5), 335 Maple St., contains exhibits of wild life, of prehistoric and Indian relics, and a gallery of paintings. Professor Burlingham Schurr, the noted naturalist, is the curator. The paintings include examples of the work of Twachtman, Whistler, Homer, Diaz, Monet, Chase, and Duveneck.

R. from Maple St. on Cabot St.

3. In the Skinner home, 'Wistariahurst,' at the corner of Pine and Cabot Sts. (*open 2.30–5; permission at office of Skinner Silk Mills, 208 Appleton St., or from curator at house opposite: 'Wistariahurst'*), is the *Belle Skinner*

Collection of musical instruments and manuscripts. The collection, numbering some ninety pieces, includes a Chinese instrument, 600 years old, and several other ancient instruments. All are kept in such perfect condition that Conductor Koussevitzky of the Boston Symphony Orchestra called it 'a collection of superlatives.'

Straight ahead from Cabot St. on Pleasant St.; L. from Pleasant St. on Dwight St., R. from Dwight St. on Northampton St. (US 5).

4. *Mt. Tom and Mountain Park (open in summer, fee)*, 3.5 *m.*, are reached by a winding drive, uphill through a marked entrance. The park has picnicking facilities and an amusement center.

Opposite the entrance, a path leads to *Dinosaur Tracks*, embedded in a ledge 150 by 30 feet.

Straight ahead on Northampton St. (US 5).

5. *Mt. Tom State Reservation (picnicking facilities)*, 5.5 *m.*, is an extensive wooded area through which winds a fine road past heavy growths of laurel. In 1932, 10 pounds of the rare mineral babingtonite were found near-by. Some geologists believe Mt. Tom was once volcanic.

L A W R E N C E . *Warp and Woof*

City: Alt. 43, pop. 86,785, sett. 1655, incorp. town 1847, city 1853.

Railroad Station: B. & M. R.R., South Canal St.

Bus Stations: Eastern Mass. Street Ry. Co., 400 Essex St.; Blue Way Line, Inc., B. & M. Transportation Co., Checker Cab bus, P.Q. Mass., Northeastern Bus Line, Mason's Bus Line, Hampshire St.

Airport: North Andover Airport, partly owned by city of Lawrence, about 7 *m.* from the city. Emergency landing field, refueling.

Accommodations: Two hotels open all year.

Information: Chamber of Commerce, Essex St.

TEXTILE mills dominate both the life and the landscape of Lawrence. From the heights above the Merrimack at Andover the city sprawls, with its forest of chimneys and acres of red-brick factory buildings regimented along the river-banks. The striking uniformity of the city is the result of a made-to-order construction program. For Lawrence is Massachusetts' only 'made city.'

In 1845 the Essex Company was formed by a group of Boston financiers to utilize the water-power of Bodwell's Falls in the Merrimack. An area of 6.75 miles was purchased, comprising parts of the townships of Andover and Methuen, which, although industrial almost since their beginning, had neither the capital nor the engineering skill to harness the river. The group of capitalists who envisioned the city on the flat plain where only some twenty families then scratched a living from the soil was headed by Abbott Lawrence as principal stockholder and first president. It included wealthy merchants long powerful in Boston maritime enterprise, who turned from foreign commerce to the mounting profits of the first textile centers.

Within a month after the incorporation of the Essex Company in March, $1,000,000 was subscribed. During the summer, work on the great dam, the heart of the whole enterprise, went forward at a tremendous rate. In the autumn of 1848, three years after the first stone was laid, the dam was completed, hills were leveled, valleys filled in, buildings erected, and a sizable imported population installed in the rows of workers' houses. The vast program of the Essex Company included also the construction of two canals running parallel into the river, the erection of a machine shop for the building of locomotives, a reservoir on Prospect Hill, gas-works, fifty brick buildings, a large boarding-house, and plants of the Atlantic Cotton, Pemberton, Upper Pacific, and Duck Mills.

The first group of immigrants were natives of England and Ireland, mechanics, artisans, printers, engravers, and weavers. The stream of immigration from other countries, mostly of unskilled workers, continued steadily, and by 1890 as many as forty-five languages were spoken. Today eighty-three per cent of the population is of foreign birth or ancestry. The Italians, who constitute the largest of the foreign-born population groups, have jealously preserved their ethnic identity. The Poles, Syrians, Armenians, and French-Canadians also form large and cohesive racial groups. The International Institute sponsors each year a three-day carnival in which fourteen or more national groups appear in the costumes of their native lands, and re-enact in exact detail the age-old pageantry of their countries.

Built and populated almost overnight, Lawrence at first was totally lacking in many of the actual necessities of community life. There was no store in the town until Amos Pillsbury in 1846 brought supplies up the river in a gondola and set up shop near the Andover bridge. In 1847, passenger train service was first introduced by the Boston and Maine Railroad. The first newspaper, the *Merrimac Courier*, was issued in 1846, and in the same year the first religious services were held in the Free Will Baptist Church. Following the granting of the city charter in 1853, Charles S. Storrow, a director of the Essex Company, was elected the first mayor.

The abnormally rapid growth of the town, coupled with the focusing of its builders' attention upon industrial production rather than on social evolution, naturally resulted in unfortunate living conditions. Sanitation, proper heating, and ventilation were lacking. Overcrowding, low wages, and long working hours prevailed. Little consideration was given in the design of factory buildings to the health or safety of the operatives.

In 1860 the roof of the Pemberton Mill crashed in. The débris took fire and 525 workers trapped within the building were killed or injured. A jury attributed the disaster to flimsy wall construction. In 1890 a tornado swept across the southern part of the city, killing and injuring many persons and destroying property. Though the misery caused by this 'act of God' had no essential connection with the wretchedness resulting from labor conditions, the psychological effect was cumulative. In 1912 the labor problem of the city reached a climax and the workers began to demonstrate in protest against allegedly intolerable conditions. The result was a strike into which the Industrial Workers of the World, led by 'Big Bill' Haywood, injected themselves with telling effect. The strikers won, although the terms of settlement were not superficially impressive — a wage increase of about one cent an hour, and the privilege of returning to work without discrimination against strikers or leaders. (*See Industry and Labor*, p. 74.)

Since 1912 Lawrence labor has led a comparatively peaceful existence, even refusing to join the widespread textile strikes of 1934. The plight of her industries, however, has posed major questions for this city to solve. When several of the great textile mills closed, thousands of employees were thrown out of work. Confronted with miles of vacant floor space and an acute unemployment problem, business men joined their efforts. In prosperous 1926, during the 'Spirit of Lawrence' week, an attempt had been made to unite business and professional men, service clubs, and labor organizations into a civic body. In 1928 the idea was revived, and before long the entire city was vitally interested, spurred by the fact that the Everett Mills — a huge cotton plant incorporated in 1860 — had recently gone out of business, throwing nearly two thousand operatives out of work.

These co-operative efforts resulted in the formation of the Lawrence Industrial Bureau, established in April, 1928, with the backing of men prominent in mercantile, banking, and real-estate fields. At that time there was no industrial department in the local Chamber of Commerce. The new Bureau had the immediate co-operation of the New England Council and the Boston and Maine Railroad. It functioned until the latter part of 1936.

From January 1, 1929, to August 6, 1936, the Bureau succeeded in reclaiming more than two and a half million square feet of vacated textile manufacturing space for production purposes. Twenty-nine new industries of varied nature were brought to Lawrence and more than three thousand workers given employment. Since that time industrial proselyting has continued, and several additional industries of various types have set up their machines in the once abandoned mills.

There are today thirty-eight local trade unions in Lawrence which send delegates to four central labor bodies, the Allied Printing Trades' Council, the Building Trades' Council, the Carpenters' District Council of Lawrence and Vicinity, and the Central Labor Union. In 1937 Lawrence was made the center of a national textile organizing campaign by the Committee for Industrial Organization. Although woolen mills still predominate, there has been a growth in diversified industries. A report of the Chamber of Commerce for 1936 gave a total of 155 industries, and an estimated payroll of $23,560,680. Besides textiles other manufactures are paper and soap. The Champion-International Paper Company is one of the largest coated paper concerns in the world, and the Wood Mill of the American Woolen Company is the largest single woolen mill.

TOUR — 5 m.

E. from Broadway (State 28) *on Haverhill St. (State* 110).

1. *St. Mary's Roman Catholic Church*, near Hampshire St., founded by the Augustinian Fathers in 1848, is in the Gothic manner.

2. The *Common*, between Haverhill and Common Sts., is surrounded by public buildings, schools, and churches. Near the pond stands a large wooden flagpole which commemorates the Flag Day celebration against the demonstrations of the I.W.W. in the strike of 1912. In the granite foundation is a tablet which reads: 'The gift of Joseph Shattuck [a Boston, Springfield, and Lawrence banker] to the people of Lawrence, as a perpetual reminder of October 12, 1912, when 32,000 men and women of the city marched under the flag for God and Country.'

L. from Haverhill St. on Jackson St.; R. from Jackson St. on Elm St.; L. from Elm St. on East Haverhill St.

3. The *Bodwell House (private)*, 33 East Haverhill St., erected about 1708 (ells added later), is the only surviving landmark of the days before the made-to-order city was built.

Retrace East Haverhill St.; L. from East Haverhill St. on Elm St.; R. from Elm St. on Union St.; L. from Union St. on Haverhill St.; R. from Haverhill St. on Prospect St.

4. From the grounds of the Lawrence General Hospital, Prospect St., there is an unparalleled *View of Industrial Lawrence*, red-brick chimneys emitting their smoke periodically; miles of red-brick factories with clock towers and small-paned windows; the canal with its dull look of cooling metal.

R. from Prospect St. on Canal St.

5. The *North Canal*, Union St., is about 5330 feet in length. This and the South Canal across the Merrimack were startling engineering feats in their

day. The North Canal was built in connection with the great Lawrence Dam in 1845, and diverts the Merrimack waters to supply the great mills which lie on the left along Canal St. The *South Canal* was built in 1866 and is about 2000 feet in length.

L. from Canal St. on Island St.

6. The *Lawrence Experimental Station* of the State Board of Health (*open*), the first institution of its kind in America, was established in 1887 for bacteriological and sewage disposal research. One of the early results of experimentation was the construction of the municipal filter, the first large sand filter in the country. The Station has been visited by sanitary and medical experts from many countries.

Retrace Island St.; L. from Island St. on Canal St.

7. The *Pacific Print Works* is the largest print works in the world. The *Lower Pacific Mill* is a worsted plant. Also in the same group is the *Pacific Cotton Mill* (*all open by permission at the office*). Extending for more than half a mile, they occupy the entire block beyond the intersection of Amesbury St. The first combing machines in the country were set up here.

Retrace Canal St.; R. from Canal St. on Union St.

8. The *Wood Mill* (*open by permission*), near Merrimack St., built in 1905 by the American Woolen Company, is the largest woolen mill in the world, more than one third of a mile long, 126 feet wide, and 6 stories high. It contains under one roof more than 30 acres of floor space.

R. from Union St. on Merrimack St.; R. from Merrimack St. on Broadway.

9. The *Great Stone Dam*, immediately above the O'Leary Bridge, was built in 1845 to furnish water-power from the falls of the river, and was a notable engineering achievement of the time. It withstood the floods of 1936, which otherwise must have devastated the city.

10. The *Arlington Mills* (*open by permission before* 1), established in 1865, were the first in the country to manufacture black alpacas and mohairs. They are devoted largely to worsted manufacture and carding and combing wool for spinners. The mills have also an exclusive process for the removal of grease from wool.

L E X I N G T O N . *A Town of Heroic Past*

Town: Alt. 201, pop. 10,813, sett. 1640, incorp. 1713.

Railroad Station: Lexington Station, Massachusetts Ave., serving B. & M. R.R.

Bus Stations: Lexington R.R. Station for B. & M. Transportation Co. Lexington Center for Granite Stages.

Local Busses: Frequent service to neighboring towns, 10¢.

Accommodations: No hotels; several inns and boarding-houses.

Swimming: Parker Field (pool).

Information: Cary Memorial Library, 1874 Massachusetts Ave.

THE town of Lexington today presents nothing of its heroic past, little of its ancient rustic calm, and still less of its brief industrial fever. It is a haven of quiet streets and comfortable homes, free of industrial ugliness and urban squalor. For 364 days of the year Lexington runs along in the placid groove of a suburb of Boston. But on each April 19 the town plunges back into the past and relives its part in ushering in the American Revolution.

There was no permanent settlement at Cambridge Farms, as Lexington was first called, until about 1642. The settlers supplied the main town of Cambridge with hay and wood, raised food for themselves, wove coarse fabrics for clothing, and erected a few rude houses. In 1691 the General Court recognized the community as a separate parish.

Lexington furnished 148 men for the wars against the French and the Indians between the years 1756 and 1763. Those who survived formed the nucleus of the militia that gathered when the threat to Boston by the British in April, 1775, roused Lexington to a quick response. The town's minister, the Reverend Jonas Clarke, sympathetic to the cause of the rebellion, led his fellow townsmen to join with Boston in resistance. He formed a Committee of Correspondence to keep in touch with developments. So lively was the resentment of Lexington's patriots that in 1773 resolutions were sent to the Legislature affirming that their people 'would be ready to sacrifice our estates and everything dear in life, yes, and life itself, in support of the common cause.'

On April 19, 1775, local farmers gathered on Lexington Green to resist the troops of General Gage. Gage had laid plans to confiscate the stores of muskets and ammunition at near-by Concord. It was believed at the time that he was also planning to capture the Revolutionary leaders, Samuel Adams and John Hancock, who had fled to Lexington after receiving a report early in April that Parliament had ordered their arrest for trial in England. It now seems probable, however, that Gage did not even know that Adams and Hancock were hiding in the region. The purpose of this expedition was undoubtedly twofold: to overawe the people by a show of British strength and thus to check a movement toward unity that was beginning to grow in the New England Colonies; and to capture the stores at Concord.

Despite the care with which Gage's plans were laid, news of them leaked out, and Dr. Joseph Warren on the eve of the battle dispatched Paul Revere and William Dawes to Concord and Lexington to warn the patriot leaders of the danger. By two o'clock in the morning the Green at Lexington was swarming with Minutemen, and the roll was called by Captain John Parker, veteran of the French wars.

At four-thirty in the morning word reached Parker that the enemy was in sight. Some fifty or sixty Minutemen lined up hastily on the Green and received the famous order from Parker: 'Stand your ground; don't fire unless fired upon, but if they mean to have a war, let it begin here.' A few minutes later the little band of farmers faced four hundred redcoats, the advance guard of British regulars, under Major Pitcairn.

'Disperse, ye rebels!' shouted Pitcairn. The men of Lexington did not stir. Twice the major repeated his command; then a musket shot rang out. The British officer ordered his regulars to open fire. The Minutemen returned it, but so inferior were their numbers that Parker ordered an immediate retreat.

When the regulars had passed on, marching toward Concord, they left behind them eight patriots dead and nine wounded. The British casualties were only two wounded. The stores at Concord were destroyed. The British retreated to Boston, harassed by the Minutemen, who followed them, firing from behind stone walls and trees. The battle had small immediate result, but the stand of the Lexington farmers was the beginning of a dogged resistance which ultimately ended in defeat for the forces of the King.

Meanwhile Adams and Hancock were hiding a few miles out of Lexington. As they ran across a field, Adams shouted, 'It is a fine day!' 'Very pleasant,' answered one of his companions, taking it to be a reference to the weather, and rather surprised at such small talk. 'I mean,' said Adams, 'this day is a glorious day for America.'

The name of Lexington spread over the land. Hunters in Kentucky baptized their camp Lexington. Twenty-four counties, cities, and towns by the name of Lexington scattered over the country testify to the pride awakened by the events of April 19, 1775.

Exhaustion and unrest were the post-Revolutionary lot of Lexington, as of most communities in Massachusetts. Debts mounted as business stagnated. Despite their passion for liberty and democracy, however, Lexington farmers did not join the insurrection of embittered debtors led by Daniel Shays; on the contrary, the town sent militia to aid in putting it down.

By the end of the eighteenth century the town had recovered a peaceful prosperity. Its population at that time was sixteen hundred, most of whom were engaged in farming. The Industrial Revolution brought a spurt of manufacturing which lasted for the first quarter of the nineteenth century. The activity had no sound basis, however, and when neighboring towns more advantageously located for power and markets surpassed it, Lexington returned to the less eventful pursuits of agriculture. In later years the town has been transformed gradually into a residential community.

TOUR — 6 m.

N. from junction of Waltham St. and Massachusetts Ave., Lexington Center, on Massachusetts Ave.

1. The *Lexington Battleground*, 'Birthplace of American Liberty,' a triangular level Green, is marked by the arresting *Minuteman Statue* of H. H. Kitson.

2. The *Marrett* and *Nathan Munroe House* (*private*), 1906 Massachusetts Ave., facing the Green, originally (1729) had a hip roof sloping to the ground in the rear from the third story. The line of the roof has been broken by the addition for the back porch, but the effect is not inharmonious.

R. from Massachusetts Ave. on Elm Ave. along N. edge of Green.

3. The *Old Burying Ground* lies just behind the white-steepled church, overlooking pleasant meadows rimmed by distant hills. Some of its slate stones with their bas-relief skulls date back to 1690. Here are graves of Revolutionary patriots and their 'agreeable consorts.' The Rev. John Hancock and the Rev. Jonas Clarke, whose successive local pastorates covered the entire 18th century, rest beneath the same stone.

4. The *Jonathan Harrington, Jr., House* (*private*), corner of Elm Ave. and Bedford Sts., is a rectangular white, two-storied frame dwelling, with green shutters. It has a Georgian Colonial doorway. The rear enclosed porch is a modern addition. During the battle on the Green, Jonathan Harrington was wounded by the British. He dragged himself to the door of his home, where he died at his wife's feet.

5. The *First State Normal School* in the United States, opposite corner of Bedford St., was founded in 1839 under the direction of the Rev. Cyrus Pierce, with three pupils. It is a two-story white building, now a Masonic Temple, at the northeast corner of the Green.

R. from Elm Ave. on Bedford St.

6. The *Buckman Tavern* (*open summer, weekdays* 10–5; *Sun.* 2–5), built in 1690 and later the rallying-place of the Minutemen, retains some interesting interior features of the 17th century, but has been greatly altered in appearance by the addition of a hip roof with dormer windows,

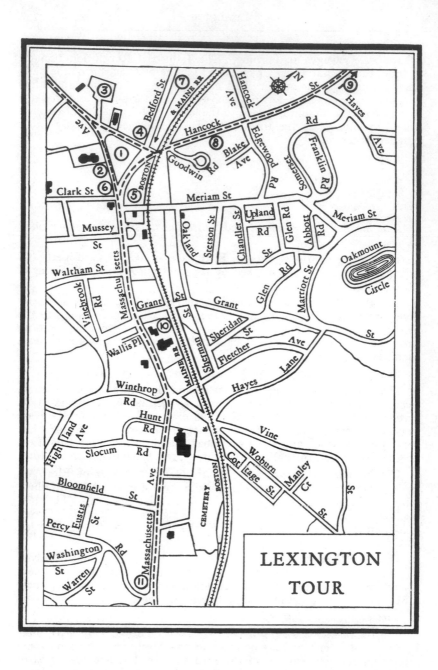

LEXINGTON
TOUR

forming a third story. Here, about the great fireplace on the morning of April 19, the Minutemen assembled to await the approach of the British troops; from the chamber windows above Paul Revere witnessed their arrival; across its threshold that afternoon were brought two wounded British soldiers, one of whom died. Since 1921 it has been maintained as a community meeting place. The inn has a small collection of old bottles, jugs, flip mugs, loggerheads, and tavern table and chairs.

L. from Bedford St. on Massachusetts Ave.; R from Massachusetts Ave. on Clark St.

7. A reproduction of the *Belfry* from which sounded the alarm to the Minutemen stands on the original site on a low hill, a stone's throw to the southwest of the Green. The bell long ago disappeared, but these weather-beaten timbers vividly commemorate the humble daily functions of its tongue, faithfully year in and year out 'summoning the people to worship, warning them at night to rake up the fires and go to bed, and tolling for them when one after another they passed away.'

Retrace Clark St.; L. from Clark St. on Massachusetts Ave.; R. from Massachusetts Ave. on Bedford St.; R. from Bedford St. on Hancock St.

8. The *Hancock-Clarke House*, 35 Hancock St. (*open weekdays 9.30–5, Sun. 2–5, Apr. 1–Nov. 1; weekdays 11–4, Sun. 2–4, Nov. Dec. March; not open during Jan. and Feb.; adm. free*), is the eleventh house across the railroad track. The one-story gambrel-roofed ell was the original dwelling, built in 1698 by the Reverend John Hancock, whose son John, father of Governor John Hancock, was born here. The frame is of hand-hewn oak and shows little sign of decay. Enlarged in 1734, at the outbreak of the Revolution it was the home of the Rev. Jonas Clarke. Here John Hancock and Samuel Adams lay hidden on the night of April 18, 1775, when Paul Revere sounded his alarm; and Dorothy Quincy, Hancock's betrothed, met them there, bringing a 'fine salmon for their dinner.' An ell contains Revolutionary costumes and the drum beaten at the battle. The large, low-ceilinged kitchen, then the real center of family life, exhibits utensils in use at the time. In all, there are 2400 pieces owned by the Lexington Historical Society which has maintained headquarters in this house since the date of its purchase by the Society in 1896.

9. The *Botanic Garden* (*open daily; free*), 91 Hancock St., was begun in

1930 to 'grow, test and display all hardy herbaceous plants.' Most of the labor is voluntarily contributed by friends and members of garden clubs. Beginning with the summer of 1937 the Garden was used as a classroom for the Summer School of the School of Landscape Architecture of Harvard University.

Retrace on Hancock St., back to Green; L. from Hancock St. on Bedford St.; L. from Bedford St. on Massachusetts Ave.

10. The *Cary Memorial Building*, 1605 Massachusetts Ave., a modern low brick structure which serves as a town hall, is worth a brief visit for the purpose of seeing the painting of the Battle of Lexington, 'The Dawn of Liberty,' by Henry Sandham, and a portrait of Lady Lexington.

11. The *Munroe Tavern (open weekdays 9.30–5, Sun. 2–5, April 19– Nov. 11; free)*, 1332 Massachusetts Ave., built in 1695 and subsequently altered, now houses beneath its hip roof a museum collection. Its old rooms, which retain many of their original features, are furnished in the manner of the period. In 1789 Washington was entertained here at a testimonial dinner and the chair, table, dishes, and hatrack which he used are preserved.

12. The *Mason House (private)*, almost opposite, 1303 Massachusetts Avenue, was built in 1680 but is still in a good state of preservation.

13. Another *Jonathan Harrington Home (private)* is at 955 Massachusetts Ave. near Joseph Rd. Its builder, a relative of the Jonathan Harrington killed in the battle, was the fifer of the Minutemen and the last survivor of the battle. Seventeen years old in 1775, he lived to be 95 and occupied a front seat at commemorative exercises of the 25th, 50th, and 75th anniversaries of the battle, shaking the hands of famous statesmen and' always referring to himself as the Minute Boy.

14. The *Ben Wellington Tablet* (R), Massachusetts Ave. and Follen Rd., commemorates 'the first armed men taken in the Revolution.'

L O W E L L . *Company Founders and City Fathers*

City: Alt. 110, pop. 100,114, sett. 1653, incorp. town 1826, city 1836.
Railroad Station: Northern Depot, Middlesex St., for B. & M. R.R. and N.Y., N.H. & H. R.R.
Bus Stations: Railroad Station and Lowell Bus Terminal, 44 Bridge St., for B. & M. Transportation Co., Vermont Transit Co., Frontier Coach Lines, Champlain Coach Lines, and Blue Way Line; 70 Central St. for Grey Line.
Accommodations: Four hotels.
Information: Lowell Chamber of Commerce, Merrimack St.

ONE hundred feet above sea level, on a plateau where the powerful Merrimack joins the sluggish Concord River, stands Lowell, one of the leading
manufacturing cities of New England. Canals and grassy plots criss-
cross the crowded metropolitan business section. On the hills beyond are
a city's homes from mansion to tenement.

The early history of this region is identified with the town of Chelmsford,
of which it was for many years a remote and insignificant part. At that
time only a settlement existed here, supporting itself by the handicrafts
of the home and the fisheries of Pawtucket Falls.

At the turn of the eighteenth century, the name of Francis Cabot Lowell,
known as the originator of American cotton manufacturing, enters the annals of this city. In England he had studied British methods of textile
operations. Returning to this country he devised and financed a practical
power loom for American use. Through Ezra Worthen, the possibilities
of the river Merrimack and the recently constructed Pawtucket Canal
were investigated. Lowell was enthusiastic, and in February, 1822 (five
years after Lowell's untimely death), the Merrimack Manufacturing Company was formed by his associates. Overnight the company founders became the first city fathers in what would today be called a huge company
town. Both men and women slept in corporation lodging houses, ate in
company dining-rooms, shopped in company stores, and were buried in
company lots. Employees worked from five in the morning to seven at
night. Women received from two dollars and twenty-five cents to four
dollars a week, men about twice that. On March 1, 1826, the district was
incorporated as the township of Lowell in recognition of its sponsor, and
the company associates promptly took over the political reins. Outside
capital poured in from the merchants of Boston and many other sources.
To the cotton manufacturing of the Merrimack Company was added the
Print Works in 1824. The Hamilton Company, with a capital of $600,000,
and the Appleton and Lowell Manufacturing Companies were among the
many that rushed in to exploit the miraculous water-power of the Merrimack. Agents of these various companies scoured Europe in search of
cheap labor, painting glowing pictures of the promised land across the sea
and luring thousands of immigrants into the maw of the hungry, growing
city.

Canals formed an integral part of this expansion. The Middlesex Canal,
built in the first years of the nineteenth century, was the first American
traction canal of a type already familiar in England and on the Continent. Much of the freight and passenger traffic of the new community
flowed between its banks.

Europe watched Lowell with something like amazement. Its rapid rise to
industrial eminence interested and astounded economists, historians, and
writers all over the world. Many of the skilled workers who first came to
the factories were the Irish and English, who now occupy prominent
places in the city life. After them came the non-English-speaking groups
who settled in their own little communities, building their churches,

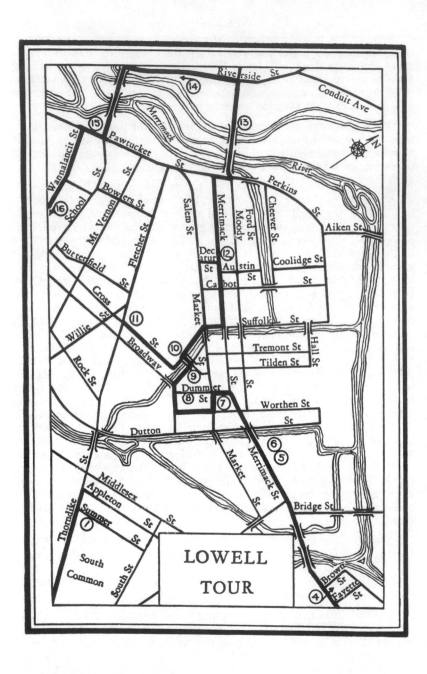

schools, and convents and preserving the culture of their homeland. The French-Canadians, the Poles, and the Greeks today have their own clubs and newspapers. The Greeks dominate so large a section of the city that Lowell has often been called a modern American Athens.

The peak of the city's industrial development was achieved in the period of artificial prosperity preceding 1924. After 1924 there was a general decrease, ending in the devastating debacle of 1929. Many of the mills moved south. Other industries were liquidated. The whole textile industry of the city was reduced by fifty per cent, and thousands of workers were left jobless and homeless. Lowell lost its position as the most important textile center in the world. It ceased to be the 'Spindle City.' Yet in place of these losses, it began slowly to make gains and to change its aspect. From a concentration on textiles it broadened its scope to include many kinds of manufactures. By 1934 it seemed to have entered the upward grind toward recovery.

TOUR — 11.7 *m.*

S. from Appleton St. on Thorndike St.

1. *South Common* is a 22-acre recreational center.

L. from Thorndike St. into Central St.; R. from Central St. into Wamesit St.; L. from Wamesit St. into Rogers St., crossing the Concord River, tributary to the Merrimack.

2. *Rogers Hall*, 196 Rogers St., facing a hilly park, is a preparatory school and junior college for girls.

R. from Rogers St. into Park Ave. and straight up the hill.

3. *Fort Hill Park*, beautifully planted in open vistas framed by birches, maples, beeches, poplars, oaks, pines, spruces, cedars, and tamaracks, has from its crest a magnificent view.

Down the hill into Park Ave.; E., as a direct return is prohibited; L. from Park Ave.; E. at cemetery into unmarked Knapp Ave.; L. from Knapp Ave. on Rogers St., bearing R. from Rogers St. into Nesmith St.; L. from Nesmith St. into E. Merrimack St.

LOWELL MAP INDEX

1. South Common
4. Immaculate Conception Church
5. St. Anne's Church
6. Lucy Larcom Park
7. Cardinal O'Connell Bust
8. Birthplace of Whistler
9. Greek Orthodox Church
10. St. Patrick's Church
11. North Common
12. Statue of Father Garin
13. Lowell Textile Institute
14. Wannalancit Park
15. Spaulding House
16. The Francis Floodgate

4. The *Immaculate Conception Church* (Catholic), corner of Fayette St., is a Gothic edifice of the gray granite which abounds in this region. The truncated tower of the church, its delicate spires, and its great rosette window on the side are reminiscent of the cathedrals of France.

5. *St. Anne's Church* (Episcopal), corner of Kirk St., is the gem of the city's smaller churches. This is a plain Norman house of worship with a square tower, constructed almost entirely of small, irregular field-stone blocks, smooth-faced and almost slate in color. The low wing of the church vestry and the rectory at its farther end break the monotony of the line.

6. *Lucy Larcom Park*, adjacent to St. Anne's, is a long, narrow strip of greensward extending along the Pawtucket Canal, which here swirls suddenly up from gatelocks after flowing for some distance beneath the city. This parkway was named in honor of Lucy Larcom, a 19th-century New England poet who wrote 'Hannah Binding Shoes' and the prose 'New England Girlhood,' which tells of her early days as a mill hand at Lowell. At the Merrimack St. end of the park is a section of the *Railroad Track* laid in 1835 for the Boston and Lowell Railroad, the first steam railroad in New England.

L. from Merrimack St. into Cardinal O'Connell Parkway.

7. The *Cardinal O'Connell Bust* surmounts a granite bird bath in the middle of the Green, commemorating the fondness of St. Francis of Assisi for the winged creatures of God. The bust is an excellent likeness of the Cardinal, a native of Lowell.

L. from the Parkway into Market St.; R. from Market St. into Worthen St.

8. The *Birthplace of Whistler* (*open weekdays* 10–5 *except Mon.; Sun.* 12–5), 243 Worthen St., is a shrine for artists who often know nothing of Lowell except that it is the birthplace of James Abbott McNeill Whistler (1834–1903), America's most renowned painter, dandy, and wit, son of an Army engineer. The house, built in 1824, stands directly on the sidewalk in what is now a shabby but quiet byway near the Greek quarter of the city.

R. from Worthen St. into Broadway; R. from Broadway into Lewis St.

9. The *Greek Orthodox Church*, corner of Jefferson St., established in 1907, was the first of its denomination in America. It is a Byzantine structure in yellow brick, with a squat central red dome surmounted by a gilded Greek cross and fronted by two still lower domed towers. This section is Little Greece, a center of humble, nondescript frame dwellings and small variety shops bearing signs in modern Greek.

L. from Lewis St. into Jefferson St., crossing the canal.

10. *St. Patrick's Church*, on Suffolk St. facing Jefferson St., is an impressive Gothic gray-stone church, distinguished by its very tall tower with tapering spire.

L. from Jefferson St. into Suffolk St.; R. from Suffolk St. into Cross St.

11. *North Common* is a recreational center, serving the Acre, a section tenanted by Irish, French, and Greeks.

Retrace Cross St.; L. from Cross St. into Suffolk St.; L. from Suffolk St. into Merrimack St.

12. The *Statue of Father Garin*, on the small side lawn of St. James's Catholic Church, was erected by the French-Canadians to their parish priest of this name. A fine bronze statue of heroic size, by Philippe Heber, it presents a tall, bareheaded, commanding figure, with strong but sensitive scholarly face.

R. from Merrimack St. into Pawtucket St.; L. from Pawtucket St. into Moody St.

13. The *Lowell Textile Institute (co-educational)*, corner of Colonial Ave., established in 1897, is probably the largest school of its kind in the world and the only one offering instruction in textile processes. Among technical schools of every nature, it ranks at the top. Of especial interest is an exhibit *(open)* of the various processes undergone by cotton from the boll to the finished cloth. In connection with this exhibit are spindles and looms in full operation.

L. from Moody St. into Riverside St.; straight ahead on Varnum Ave., the continuation of Riverside St.

14. *Wannalancit Park*, a grassy embankment shaded by trees, traversed by footpaths and dotted with benches, extends for several miles along the river.

Retrace Varnum Ave.; R. from Varnum Ave. into Mammouth Rd., crossing the bridge; R. from Mammouth Rd. into Pawtucket St.

15. The *Spalding House (private)*, 275 Pawtucket St., originally a tavern, erected in 1760, presents a carefully restored exterior of two-and-a-half stories with hip roof, its twin chimneys, later than the single central type, its yellow clapboards with white trim, and its 18-paned windows. The narrow black blinds are a variation from type. The curved iron hand rail with brass knob, at the front steps, and the green-paneled front door are restorations.

L. from Pawtucket St. into Wannalancit St.; R. from Wannalancit St. into Clare St.; R. from Clare St. into Broadway.

16. The *Francis Floodgate* consists of a guard lock of massive timber 27 feet wide, 25 feet deep, and 2 feet thick, built in 1848 and at the time known as 'Francis' Folly.' Major Francis, its builder, at that time chief engineer of the Locks and Canal Co., was the target of sharp criticism and caustic derision to the day of his death. But 88 years after its construction the gate was dropped and reinforced by sandbags, just in time to save Lowell from the havoc wrought by the river in cities to the north.

L. from Broadway into Wilder St.

17. The *Lowell State Teachers' College* (1894), 850 Broadway, is constructed of the yellow brick which Lowell favors whenever tempted from

its allegiance to gray granite. It is notable for its beautiful location in a broad-landscaped campus on a spacious hilltop.

L. from Wilder St. into Liberty St.

18. The *Lincoln Memorial*, in Lincoln Square, is a medallion head of the Emancipator by Bela Pratt, given to the city by its school-children.

L Y N N . *Machine City*

City: Alt. 34, pop. 102,320, sett. 1629, incorp. town 1631, city 1850.

Railroad Stations: Central Square for B. & M. R.R.; Market and Broad Sts. for Boston, Revere Beach, & Lynn (Narrow Gauge).
Bus Station: Costello's Book Store, 332 Union St., for Greyhound Lines.
Piers: Yacht Basin, Lynn Harbor, end of Washington St.

Accommodations: One first-class hotel, rates same winter as summer. Apartment hotels, tourist homes.

Swimming: Lynn Beach, two miles in length, end of Nahant St. Fresh water, Flax Pond, bath-houses, etc.

Information: Hotel Edison, Lynn Chamber of Commerce.

FROM the General Edwards Bridge, the industrial city of Lynn sprawls across a plain flanked by rocky hills to the north and west, and by the sea and miles of tidal flats to the east and south. The vast River Works plant of the General Electric stretches beyond the Saugus River, and ahead are the dreary Victorian buildings of the shoe factories. From the congested heart of the industrial district tenement roofs, spires, and brick walls rise in a chaotic jumble to the distant city heights, in fantastic contrast with the great woods and the several quiet lakes which lie, surprisingly, within the limits of this noisy machine city.

Lynn, first known as Saugus, was named in honor of King's Lynn in Norfolk County, England. Appropriately, *Lhyn* to the ancient Britons signified 'Place of the Spreading Waters.' Very early the town began to swing toward industrialism.

One of the first settlers was a tanner, and his establishment laid the foundation of a related industry that was to make Lynn famous throughout the industrial world. Two highly skilled shoemakers, Philip Kirtland and Edmund Bridges, settled near the tannery in 1635 and began to fashion shoes that compared favorably with those produced elsewhere. By the beginning of the eighteenth century almost every house had its 'back-yard' shop, and presently Lynn was supplying most of the foot-gear for Boston. John Adam Dagyr (1750), a Welsh shoemaker, set a high standard of workmanship which lasted for many years after his death.

The beginning of the nineteenth century brought new life, resulting in part from the activities of Ebenezer Breed, who was influential in per-suading Congress to protect the growing industry with a tariff. In 1800 the State Legislature passed an act to encourage the manufacture of shoes, boots, and 'arctics' (galoshes). An army of craftsmen toiled early and late in their small shops, and in 1810 manufactured about one million pairs of shoes.

With the introduction of the first shoe sewing machine in 1848, the fac-tory system began to take over. The domestic production units of the craftsmen were liquidated and the workers were absorbed into huge plants. With bewilderment and resentment, they saw their craftsmen's status fade into insignificance when they took their places at the alien machines. The ensuing friction brought about the shoe strike of 1867, when all shoe factories were closed down for seven weeks. Demanding better living conditions, the employees organized parades in which several thousand men and women marched with brass bands, fire companies, military organizations, and sympathizers from neighboring towns.

The new system attracted foreign workingmen by the thousand and al-tered the racial complexion of the city. The French-Canadians, the largest racial group, dispersed through the city. The Irish, second in numbers, were forced by religious intolerance to settle in a compact dis-trict. The third most numerous group, the Italians, as well as Greeks, Poles, and Armenians, formed distinctly bilingual communities but lost most of their picturesque color. The Greek district in the vicinity of Pleas-ant and Tremont Streets has several restaurants which feature native dishes, notably Turkish coffee, nutritious *yoghourt*, and *baclava*. There are five large Jewish districts where Yiddish is still widely spoken and orthodox customs are maintained.

An interesting episode of the period of immigration was the sojourn of Thomas Bata, a Czechoslovakian, who came here to learn the trade. Having observed factory methods, he returned to Czechoslovakia, and built one of the largest and most modern shoe factories in the world, capable of producing footgear at a very low cost, somewhat to the resent-ment of his industrial alma mater.

Until the last decade of the nineteenth century Lynn was the leading shoe center in the country. In November, 1889, fire ravaged thirty-one acres of the business section, with a property loss of about $5,000,000. By 1915, it had fallen to third place. The introduction of modern machinery decreased the reliance on skilled craftsmen, and manufacturers began to remove into areas of cheaper, less-skilled labor. Recently, this migration seems to have halted. There has also been a recent noticeable expansion of the leather industry.

In the period immediately following the Civil War, Lynn shoe workers joined the powerful Knights of St. Crispin, but this union declined. Never since has there been a long period when the principal crafts were unorganized, but the unions in the several crafts have not always co-operated well. At present most of the Lynn shoe workers belong to the United Shoe Workers of America, affiliated with the Committee for Industrial Organization. A company union in the Lion Shoe Company was recently dissolved by the National Labor Relations Board.

The General Electric Company set up a system of works councils in its huge plant just after the World War. In 1934, the workers organized an industrial union, and secured recognition. This union spread to other centers, and as the United Electrical and Radio Workers is affiliated with the C.I.O. The leather workers of Lynn also belong to a C.I.O. affiliate, the National Leather Workers. The workers in a number of other trades hold charters from unions affiliated with the American Federation of Labor.

Lynn's varied industries have made it possible for the city to withstand, somewhat better than single-industry communities, the tremors of economic instability. Although the shoe factories and their allied trades predominate numerically, the General Electric Company is the largest industry of the city, and in 1935 its two Lynn plants employed more workmen than any other concern in the State.

TOUR — 10 m.

E. from Central Square on Exchange St.; L. from Exchange St. into Broad St.; R. from Broad St. into Nahant St.; L. from Nahant St. into Lynn Shore Drive.

1. *Lynn Beach* (*restaurants, amusements, municipal bathhouse*), bordering on Nahant Bay, is a vast playground crowded in summer with throngs almost as brown as were the Indians who once gathered here to watch their braves in contests of strength and skill.

L. from Lynn Shore Drive into Ocean Ter.; L. (straight ahead) from Ocean Ter. into Lewis St. and then into Broad St.

2. The *Mary Baker Eddy Residence* (*free Christian Science Reading Room; open weekdays*, 10–5.30), 12 Broad St., is the house where it is thought the Founder of Christian Science (*see Tour 1A, SWAMPSCOTT*) wrote the major part of 'Science and Health.'

R. from Broad St. into Green St.

3. The *Lynn Historical Society* (*open summer Wed.* 2.30–4), 125 Green St., exhibits in its house and museum a collection of early furniture, household utensils, pewter, glassware, and historical records.

L. from Green St. into Union St.; R. from Union St. into Ireson St.; cross

Massison Sq. into Rockaway St.; L. from Rockaway St. into High Rock St.; L. from High Rock St. into Circuit Ave.

4. *High Rock* is a bold promontory, from the summit of which an observation tower 275 feet above sea level affords a magnificent view of the industrial panorama of Lynn and also of the ocean and the rocky rim of the Massachusetts Basin.

5. The *Home of Moll Pitcher* (*inaccessible*), built in 1666, stands in the shadow of this dull purple porphyry cliff. Moll's fame as a fortune-teller spread to most of the principal parts of Europe, and her memory is perpetuated in a poem of Whittier's named for her, and by a melodrama entitled 'The Fortune Teller of Lynn,' popular on the New England stage for 30 years.

Retrace on Circuit Ave.; R. from Circuit Ave. into High Rock St.; L. from High Rock St. into Rockaway St.; straight ahead into Rock Ave.; R. from Rock Ave. into Grant St.; L. from Grant St. into Rockingham St.; R. from Rockingham St. into Western Ave.

6. The *Lydia E. Pinkham Medicine Company* (*open by permission*), on Western Ave., manufactures a famous medicinal compound first made by Lydia E. Pinkham in her kitchen. Financial losses in the panic of 1873 led her to capitalize on her remedy. Once started, the fame of the cure spread rapidly through the world, and as a favorite ballad stated, 'the papers printed her face.' According to recent international advertising programs, 'although dead, she still sends her messages of hope to millions of women.'

L. from Western Ave. into Chestnut St.; straight ahead into Broadway.

7. At *Flax Pond* (*public bath-house; boating*), the pioneer women of Lynn retted flax from which to spin thread for weaving linen.

L. from Broadway into Lynnfield St.

8. The *Lynn Woods*, a 2000-acre park of wild natural beauty, begins at Lynnfield St. and Great Woods Rd. by the *Happy Valley Golf Course* (*public*).

> On Burrill Hill is an *Observation Tower*, from which there is an excellent view of the Blue Hills, Bunker Hill Monument, and the golden dome of the State House. Great Woods Rd. leads to a lovely ravine, framing the long slender mirror of Walden Pond with overhanging branches of birches and elms.
>
> *Dungeon Rock* is one of the most interesting landmarks in the Woods. According to tradition a group of buccaneers hid vast treasures here in a huge cave whose entrance was closed by the earthquake of 1658.
>
> Approaching the Penny Brook entrance the trail passes *Lantern Rock*, where pirates once hung signal lights for small boats stealing up the Saugus River under cover of night. Near Lantern Rock is *Circle Trail*, with signs designating the unusual minerals and glacial deposits, and the varieties of flora indigenous to Lynn Woods. Near-by is the *Botanical Garden* with its multitude of rare blooms.

L. from Penny Brook Entrance into Walnut St., and, following State 129, R. from Walnut St. into Kirtland St.; L. from Kirtland St. into Boston St.; R. from Boston St. into Federal St.

9. The *General Electric Company* occupies both sides of Federal St. in West Lynn (*open by permission*). Turbines, arc lights, and generators are manufactured here.

R. from Federal St. into Western Ave.

10. The *River Works Plant* of the *Lynn General Electric Co.* (*open by permission*), together with the West Lynn Plant, employs about 10,000 workers and is the city's ranking industry. Here Elihu Thomson, one of the founders of the General Electric Company and world-famous as an inventor and electrical engineer, carried on most of his experiments.

M A L D E N . *Neighbor of Boston*

City: Alt. 9, pop. 57,277, sett. 1640, incorp. town 1649, city 1881.

Railroad Stations: Malden Station on Summer St. near Pleasant St.; Oak Grove, 277 Washington St., for B. & M. R.R.

Bus Station: Eastern Mass. R.R. Busses for Lowell and Lawrence stop at Malden Square (opposite Baptist Church).

Accommodations: One hotel at reasonable rates; tourist camps.

Riding: Several miles of bridle paths, carriage roads, and trails in Middlesex Fells.

Information: Chamber of Commerce, Pleasant St.

FROM the summit of Waitt's Hill, Malden is seen to be both a residential and a manufacturing city, tree-shaded, and girt on the north and northwest by the rugged, wooded cliffs of the Middlesex Fells. Although manufacturing is actually of prominence, it is largely confined to a limited area near the Everett border, and the main impression gained by a drive through the city is of frame dwelling houses mainly of the parvenu era, schools, churches, community centers, and a number of small but pleasant parks. The proximity of Malden to the great metropolitan center of Boston is both an advantage and a drawback to its residential appeal. Inevitably with the years, its suburban identity tends to be swallowed up in the overflowing tide from the greater city. Yet there are not many apartment houses, and if there are no pretentiously wealthy districts, neither is there shabby poverty. Malden remains what it has long been, a good-sized city of comfortable middle-class homes.

The settlers of Malden, mainly Puritans, landed at Charlestown, situated in a part of the grant made in 1622 to Robert Gorges by the Northern Virginia Company. However, in 1628 the Council at Plymouth disregarded this grant and the subsequent lease and sold the land to the Massachusetts Bay Colony.

After the arrival of Governor Winthrop, in 1630, Charlestown grew rapidly and extended its boundaries. Within ten years a few settlers had crossed to the north side of the Mystic River, built homes, and founded a new town. ' Upon the petition of a committee chosen from among these persons the General Court granted, in 1649, the charter. Malden's first free school was established in accordance with the terms of the will of William Gooden, who left a portion of his estate in trust for this purpose.

Difficulty was experienced in securing men competent to teach. More than once an hiatus occurred between the release of a schoolmaster and the appointment of his successor, so that on one occasion the town was presented at Court sessions on the charge of not maintaining a school. The first schoolhouse, built in 1712, saw only eighteen years in the service of education; in 1730 it was sold to the town bellman and grave-digger. Private homes were again requisitioned for use as schoolhouses. Not until 1783, after much discussion and long delay, was the nucleus of the present school system created.

A company of soldiers known as the Malden Band was formed shortly after the incorporation of the town. Citizens also organized a company of cavalry, which saw service in King Philip's War. On September 23, 1774, the townsmen voted to instruct Captain Ebenezer Harnden, their representative in General Court, that it was their 'firm and deliberate resolution rather to rule our lives and fortunes than submit to those unrighteous acts of the British Parliament which pretends to regulate the government of this Province.' This resolution was translated into action at the outbreak of the Revolutionary War.

Until it received its city charter Malden was regulated by five selectmen chosen from churchmen in good standing. The granting of the city charter in 1881 made necessary a different form of government, and city affairs have since been administered by a mayor, a board of aldermen, and a city council.

Malden is now primarily a manufacturing center. It is within twenty-four-hour rail delivery of three quarters of the nation's markets and has easy access to the major trans-Atlantic and coastwise passenger and freight lines. Its factories, of which there are approximately one hundred and fifty, are widely representative of varied industries.

POINTS OF INTEREST

1. The *Malden Public Library*, Malden Sq., was built 1879–85, and de-signed by H. H. Richardson. Characteristic of his work, it is a personal-ized adaptation of Romanesque forms. It is an excellent example of his

later and more mature designs which came to be known as 'Richardsonian Romanesque.' Its simple and well-studied masses are entirely of brownstone, and its interior is enhanced by Romanesque-Byzantine carving.

The library contains a small but distinguished art gallery, displaying works of noted French and American artists dating from Claude Lorraine to the present day. Of historic interest is Albion H. Bicknell's large group portrait, 'The Gettysburg Address.'

2. The *Parsonage House (private)*, 145 Main St., is a two-and-a-half-story white structure built in 1724 and first occupied by the Rev. Joseph Emerson, who has been piquantly characterized by his son: 'He was a Boanerges, a son of thunder, to the workers of iniquity; a Barnabas, a son of consolation, to the mourners in Zion.' In this house in 1788 was born Adoniram Judson, the famous missionary to Burma. Judson attended Brown University and after graduation opened a private school at Plymouth, where he prepared a book entitled 'Young Ladies' Arithmetic' — presumably a gentle adaptation of the knotty subject to the young female brain. In 1808, while traveling through the United States, his mind became affected by 'infidel views' of religion and, with no decided plan for his life, he became a member of a theatrical company. In 1809, after a short but wretched period of skepticism and doubt, he joined the Third Congregational Church in Plymouth. After his ordination in 1812, he married and set out with his young bride for India, but was converted to the Baptist denomination while on board ship.

3. *Bell Rock Memorial Park* is opposite the Parsonage, near which stood the house in which the congregation of the Church of Mystic Side gathered and where preached Marmaduke Matthews, the first pastor in Malden. The bell that summoned the people to worship, sounded the alarm in times of danger, and called the freeholders to meet for action in public affairs was hung upon a rock of which only a part now remains. In the park is a replica of a small fortress, accessible from the street by a stairway, and at its summit stands a modern Civil War *Soldiers' and Sailors' Monument* by Bela Pratt.

4. The *Greene House (private)*, 51 Appleton St., is also known as the Perkins House. On what was then known as Greene Hill, James Greene built a house in 1648. The present dwelling was constructed of timbers taken from its predecessor. In 1686 a council was held in the old house to try a man named McCheever for alleged irregularities of speech and conduct. Increase Mather was the moderator, but the council, which included five ministers from Boston, could not arrive at an agreement. The upshot of the matter was that 'they left the whole matter in the hands of the Lord as an easy way out of it.'

5. *Waitt's Mount*, Leonard St., a small park which crowns the highest hill in the city, affords a fine panoramic view of the surrounding country. During the months of July and August a camp is maintained here for undernourished children.

6. *Pine Banks Tourist Camp (free)*, Main St., at the Malden-Melrose city line, is situated in a beautiful natural wooded park. It was bequeathed to the cities of Malden and Melrose by the children of Elisha Slade Converse, first mayor of Malden and former director of the Boston Rubber Shoe Company.

M A R B L E H E A D . *Where Tradition Lingers*

Town: Alt. 15, pop. 10,173, sett. 1629, incorp. 1649.

Railroad Station: 97 Pleasant for B. & M. R.R.

Piers: Marblehead Neck for Eastern Yacht Club and Corinthian Yacht Club. Front St. for Boston Yacht Club. Public landing at foot of State St. The Ferry, Ferry Lane (*harbor trips*, 10¢).

Accommodations: One large hotel, several small first class hotels and boarding houses. Winter accommodations limited.

Information: Rotary Club, Washington St.

MARBLEHEAD, in whose narrow, twisted streets traditions linger, is built upon a rock, and everywhere through the thin garment of turf protrude knobs and cliffs of granite. Along the steep, winding ways weather-beaten houses shoulder each other, with intermittent glimpses of the harbor and the sea between their grayed walls. A mass of tumbled rocks chiseled by the sea forms the grim profile of the 'Neck.'

Reckless, hardbitten fishermen from Cornwall and the Channel Islands settled Marblehead (Marble Harbor) in 1629 as a plantation of Salem. Their rude huts clung to the rocks like sea-birds' nests. Said a Marbleheader of a later day — 'Our ancestors came not here for religion. Their main end was to catch fish.' As might have been expected from such ungodliness, early Marblehead was a favorite with the powers of darkness. Many a citizen met Satan himself riding in state in a coach and four, or was chased through the streets by a corpse in a coffin. The eerie lament of the 'screeching woman of Marblehead' resounded across the harbor, and Puritan Salem hanged old 'Mammy Red' of Marblehead who knew how to turn enemies' butter to blue wool. Within a decade unruly Marblehead was without regret permitted to become a separate town, 'the greatest Towne for fishing in New England.'

The early prosperity of the fisheries was short-lived. The Reverend John Barnard, who came in 1715 to minister to the heathen, wrote, 'Nor could I find twenty families that could stand upon their own legs, and they were generally as rude, swearing, drunken and fighting a crew as they were poor.' Under his guidance markets were sought in the West Indies and Europe for the carefully cured fish, and a class of merchants began to send larger vessels to more distant ports.

As war with England approached and His Majesty's frigates lay threateningly in the harbor, the rafters of the Old Town House thundered to revolutionary speeches and all Marblehead blazed with patriotism. Her merchants patriotically extended shipping privileges to the merchants of Boston when Marblehead took Boston's place as the port of entry after the passage of the Boston Port Bill (1774). The Tory merchants fled for their lives, seafaring men turned to privateering with its promise of prize money and adventure or joined General John Glover's famous 'Amphibious Regiment' which was later with muffled oars to row Washington across the Delaware. The Marblehead schooner 'Lee,' manned by a captain and crew of this regiment, flew the Pine Tree flag and took the 'Nancy,' the first British prize.

Privateering became unprofitable as the British blockade tightened. The close of the war found Marblehead economically prostrate, the merchant fleet captured or sunk, the fishing fleet rotting at the wharves.

To relieve the distress two lotteries were organized and the fishing fleet was reconditioned with the proceeds, but just as prosperity again seemed assured, the War of 1812 tied up the fleet once more and embargo closed the ports of trade. After the war the fishing fleet gallantly put to sea, but the town with little capital could not compete with the more fortunately situated ports of Boston and Gloucester. The great gale of 1846, which took a frightful toll of men and ships, hastened the end.

Undaunted, Marblehead turned to industry. The back-yard shoe shops, a feature of every fisherman's cottage, were amalgamated into factories after 1840, and within a decade, trained hands and mass production methods were turning out a million pairs of shoes a year. Other factories produced glue, rope, twine, barrels, paint, and cigars. But the spider web of railroads that spun out across the country, tapping the resources of the West and concentrating manufacturing in the larger cities, spelled doom to Marblehead as an industrial center, a doom hastened by two disastrous fires.

Ultimately it was the sea that once more brought prosperity. The harbor, where long ago the high-sterned fishing boats rode to tree-root moorings, has become the yachting center of the eastern seaboard. Summer estates line the once bleak shore of the Neck and overlook the harbor where hundreds of sleek-hulled craft ride at anchor. In the yachting season more sails slant out past Halfway Rock, where once the fishermen tossed pennies to buy good luck and safe return, than ever did in the days of Marblehead's maritime glory.

FOOT TOUR — 2 m.

E. on Washington St. through Washington Square.

1. *Abbot Hall*, the Victorian Town Hall and Public Library, in the center of the Square, houses Willard's 'The Spirit of '76,' the familiar historical painting.

2. The *Colonel William Lee House* (*private*), 185 Washington St., is one of the network of old houses, nearly all of them pre-Revolutionary, which form the heart of Marblehead. Colonel Lee was an early merchant prince of the town, and a Revolutionary army officer. The house dates from the mid-18th century, and has the wood-block front, popular in Marblehead's fashionable dwellings. An Ionic portico and octagonal cupola add distinction.

3. The *Jeremiah Lee Mansion* (1768) (*open weekdays* 9–5; *adm.* 25¢), opposite Mason St., is one of the finest examples of the second phase of New England Georgian architecture. A three-story building, rusticated over the entire surface and accented by quoined corners, it is surmounted by an octahedral cupola. The chief embellishment is a simple portico of two fluted Ionic columns. The elaborate paneling of the 'mahogany room,' the magnificent staircase, and the rich variety of detail in wood finish give the interior exceptional interest.

R. from Washington St. on Hooper St.

4. The *King Hooper House* (*private*), 8 Hooper St., which was built in 1745, is the third of three houses built by early merchant princes. The three-story front is of wood executed to give the effect of stone coursing. Robert Hooper, the builder of the house, was nicknamed 'King' because of his great wealth and royal manner of life.

Retrace on Hooper St.; straight ahead on Washington St.

5. *St. Michael's Church* (*Episcopal*) (*open daily* 9–5), corner of Summer St., was erected in 1714, and is probably the oldest Episcopal church edifice in New England. The interior has gate pews and the typical Colonial raised pulpit, reached by a winding stair and surmounted by an overhanging sounding board.

6. The *Old Town House* (1727) needed to be sturdy of rafters to withstand the turbulent shouts of pre-Revolutionary town meetings. It is a pleasing example of the first phase of New England Georgian design — a two-story clapboarded building set high upon a granite walled basement, its corners flanked with quoins, its low gabled roof enhanced by a simple cornice.

7. The *Marblehead Art Association* (*open publicly in August for an annual exhibition, free*), 65 Washington St., has a membership of 400, with headquarters at this Colonial house.

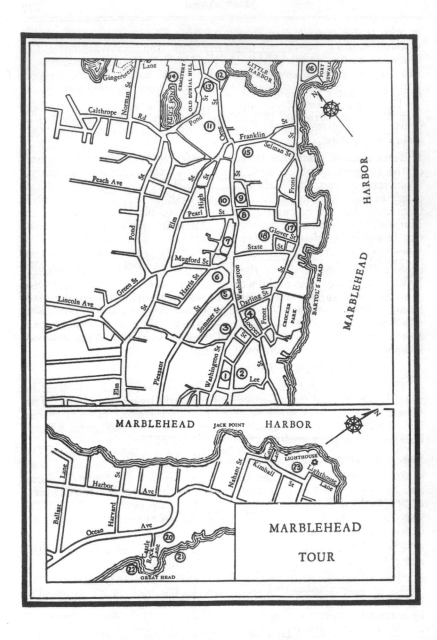

8. The *Major Pedrick House* (*now a rooming house, but also open as a Colonial dwelling,* 10–11 *and* 2–4 *daily; adm.* 15¢), 52 Washington St., is almost as fine architecturally as the Lee and Hooper mansions. It was built in 1756, a square three-story house, with wood front representing stone coursing, elaborate cornice, and huge, square chimneys.

9. The *Elbridge Gerry House* (*private*), 44 Washington St., is marked by a tablet as the birthplace of Elbridge Gerry (1744–1814), a member of the Continental Congress, Governor of Massachusetts, Vice-President of the United States during the War of 1812, and popularly known as the originator of the device of 'gerrymandering.'

10. The *Old North Church* (Congregational), opposite the Gerry House, was erected in 1824, but is the first parish in the town. The vine-covered stone church has a characteristic Colonial Georgian steeple.

L. from Washington St. into Orne St.

11. The *Azor Orne House* (*private*), 18 Orne St., was the home of Colonel Azor Orne, a member of the Revolutionary Committee of Safety which included Elbridge Gerry, John Hancock, and Samuel and John Adams.

This district is Barnegat, long ago named for the town on the New Jersey coast where 'mooncussers' lured vessels to destruction by false lights from shore, with the purpose of plundering their cargoes. (A mooncusser is one who curses the moon for its hindrance to his nefarious designs.)

12. The *Agnes Surriage Well* (*see Tour* 1C, *Ashland*) is at the end of the grassy lane leading (R) from Orne St. just beyond the Orne House.

13. The *Old Brig* (about 1720), known also as the *Moll Pitcher House*, on Orne St. opposite the lane leading to the Agnes Surriage Well, is the unnumbered low white gabled roof Colonial house with the big central chimney. It was the home of the famous psychic fortune-teller, Moll Pitcher, born here about 1743, and of her ancestor the wizard Dimond. Above this house, on the rocky summit of *Old Burial Hill*,

---

MARBLEHEAD MAP INDEX

among gravestones outlined against the sky, the awed townsfolk often saw Old Dimond's shadowy form swaying in a wild northeaster, as with brandished arms he defied the gale and shouted to invisible satanic thralls his orders for the safe guidance of the Marblehead fleet.

14. *Old Burial Hill*, just beyond the Old Brig on Orne St., dates from 1638 and contains the graves of no less than 600 Revolutionary heroes. The low white *Obelisk* on the crest of the hill honors 65 Marblehead fishermen who lost their lives in a great gale in 1846. From the hill is obtained a panoramic view of *Marblehead Harbor*, the summer yachting center of the eastern seaboard.

Retrace on Orne St.; L. from Orne St. on Franklin St.

15. The *Parson Barnard House* (*open by arrangement with its resident tenant*), 7 Franklin St., was the home of Marblehead's second and most famous pastor, during his 54-year ministry from 1716 to 1770. It was Parson John Barnard who schooled the rude fishermen in the foreign commerce which brought such great prosperity to the town before the Revolution. And it was Parson Barnard who declined the presidency of Harvard University, referring the Committee of Invitation to his rival pastor in the town, the Rev. Edward Holyoke, who accepted. When Marblehead objected strenuously to losing either clergyman, Parson Barnard appeared in his colleague's pulpit and told the Holyoke flock in no uncertain terms how great was the honor to their leader. A visitor afterward inquired for Mr. Holyoke, and was told, 'Old Barnard prayed him away.'

L. from Franklin St. on Front St.

16. *Fort Sewall*, at the end of Front St., was erected in 1742 and did good service in keeping the British at bay in the Revolution, but has long been abandoned to the pacific uses of a small seaside park.

Retrace on Front St.

17. The *Old Tavern* (*open*), 82 Front St., corner of Glover St., was built in 1680 and is now an antique shop. Its clapboards long held British shot fired at it from the harbor after a Marblehead patriot had disarmed several British officers in its bar by fencing with a mere stick against their rapiers.

R. from Front St. on Glover St.

18. *General John Glover's House* (*private*), 11 Glover St., built in 1762, bears a tablet recording the General's crossing of the Delaware and other military services. Glover was actually a sailor rather than a soldier, and his privateer vessel, the 'Hannah,' manned by Marbleheaders, was the first ship of what came to be the American Navy.

MOTOR TOUR — 4 *m.*

W. from Washington Square on Washington St.; L. from Washington St. on Atlantic Ave.; L. from Atlantic Ave. on Ocean Ave.

19. The *Causeway* and *Bathing Beach* (*bathhouses*) continue Ocean Ave. from Marblehead to *Marblehead Neck*. On the left is *Marblehead Harbor*, gay in summer with yachts. On the right is the long sandy, shelving beach, facing Massachusetts Bay.

Ocean Ave. bears (R) around the ocean side of the Neck, which until the Civil War was one great cow pasture, dotted alongshore with an occasional fisherman's shack. It is now the home of an exclusive summer colony.

20. Outstanding among the residences at Marblehead Neck is the *Gove House* on Ocean Avenue, designed by Smith and Walker of Boston after the ancient Castle of Carcassonne in Southern France and built about 1934 for the daughter of Lydia Pinkham.

21. The *Churn*, on Ocean Ave., reached by an unmarked path leading through a field (R) where the latter makes a short turn west, is a fissure in the rocks at tide level from which under an east or northeast wind great billows of spray rise to a height sometimes of 50 feet.

22. *Castle Rock*, adjoining the Churn (R), a rugged granite bluff rising sheer from the sea, offers a beautiful ocean view with a long line of shore breakers.

L. from Ocean Ave. on Follett St.

23. The *Lighthouse* (*open daily* 10–12 *and* 2–4) is a circular iron tower at the tip of the Neck. From the rocks at its base is obtained the best view of the yacht races. Just offshore, northeast, is *Children's Island*, its rocky reaches covered with the buildings of a hospital for tubercular children.

M E D F O R D . *Rum, Ships, and Homes*

City: Alt. 12, pop. 61,444, sett. 1630–35, incorp. town 1684, city 1892.

Railroad Stations: Tufts College, Boston Ave.; Medford Hillside, Boston Ave. and Winthrop St.; West Medford, High St., for Lowell Division of B. & M R.R.

Accommodations: Boarding and rooming houses; some tourist places.

Swimming: Municipal pool, Tufts Park, Main St.
Riding: Bridle trails through Middlesex Fells Reservation.
Information: Public Library, 117 High St.

MEDFORD rum and Medford-built ships, once staples of world-wide repute, today are only legend. Still Medford thrives; a paradox accounted for by its proximity to Boston, its residential attractiveness, and a fine educational system reaching its climax geographically as well as pedagogically in Tufts College. Its hustle and bustle over, today Medford has closed shop and settled back to its destiny as a community of homes.

In the early days of its settlement, rich loam near the river banks beckoned farmers, and the surging tides of the Mystic River offered thriving fisheries. Shipbuilding was soon under way. John Winthrop, a year before settling on Ten Hills Farm at Somerville, had launched the 'Blessing of the Bay' at Medford. Then followed a century of depression, until the New England rum and slave trade sprang up.

Medford rum had its start when the Hall family set up a wooden still on the site of a spring, to which the special flavor of the rum was attributed. The Hall formula, used for two hundred years, was finally destroyed by General Samuel C. Lawrence, when Medford distilling came to an end.

The navigable Mystic River was the direct cause of the other very substantial economic activity of Medford. Freighting produce to the State capital by boat became a bustling enterprise.

Medford developed into a supply shop for New Hampshire and Vermont, furnishing iron, steel, lead, salt, molasses, sugar, tea, codfish, chocolate, gunpowder, and rum at lower than Boston prices. In addition Medford merchants engaged directly in extensive trade with foreign and domestic ports. Barrel-making and slaughtering thrived.

One day in the year 1802, Thatcher Magoun, a youth on a holiday from a Charlestown shipyard, was rambling about Winter Hill. In a vision he saw a thriving shipyard on the river banks below him, himself its master. Excitedly he clattered down the hill and boarded a two-masted schooner lying alongside a distilling-house wharf. Breathlessly he plied the amazed captain with all sorts of questions. A year later he returned and laid the keel of his first ship.

Thatcher Magoun's project came at a critical moment. The English navigation laws, after the Revolution, ended American trade with the British West Indies, and New England merchants were frantically seeking new markets.

Finally Yankee ingenuity found a way out, in a new trade with China. Because their two hundred to three hundred ton capacity made possible the navigation of the shallow bays of the northwest coast, many Medford vessels were dispatched to the Pacific. 'Medford-built' found its way into the idiom of the sea.

Such Medford builders as J. O. Curtis, Hayden and Cudworth, and S. Lapham had more fast California passages to their credit, in proportion to the number of clipper ships built, than those of any other town.

Sailing vessels became definitely unprofitable with the Civil War and the introduction of steamships. In 1873 the last Medford-built ship was launched. Nor did the distilleries long survive; by 1905 they, too, had ceased.

TOUR — 10.7 m.

W. from Medford Sq. on High St.

1. Three *Hall Houses* (*private*), homes of early Medford merchants and patriots, 45, 49, and 57 High St., offer an unusual chance to compare at close range varying details of Colonial architecture. No. 57, the most ornate, has the familiar broad, square lines and cornice of the prosperous town houses of the 18th century. No. 49 has a wood front and brick ends, U-shaped double end-chimneys which serve to add height and pride, and an ornamental rail across the sloping roof. No. 45, the smallest, of frame and clapboard, is the plainest.

R. from High St. on Governors Ave.; L. from Governors Ave. into South Border Rd.

2. *Pine Hill* is approached by a wooded lane (*vehicles excluded*) which skirts a small pond. A number of footpaths wind to the summit, from which there is an excellent view of the Mystic Valley.

3. *Lawrence Observatory* (*marked footpath*), an iron tower the summit of which is 310 feet above sea level, offers a beautiful panorama of pond-studded woodland and fields, with Medford and the Mystic River waterfront in the foreground.

L. from South Border Rd. by foot on bridle path; R. from bridle path into first wagon path; L. from wagon path one-fourth mile to an open field.

4. A *Cedar Tree*, 15 ft. tall, growing out of a solid boulder, is a curious natural wonder. Its age is estimated at about 400 years.

Retrace on South Border Rd.; R. from South Border Rd. on Governors Ave.; R. from Governors Ave. on High St.

5. The *Medford Public Library* (*open weekdays* 9–9), 121 High St., formerly the residence of Thatcher Magoun 2d, was built in 1835. Within are several autographed letters of George Washington written to Medford patriots; and one of the 100 existing copies of 'The Catalogue and Investigation in Jade,' edited by George F. Kunz, Tiffany expert in precious stones, for the estate of Heber Bishop, a Medford collector of jade.

6. The *Charles Brooks House* (*private*), 309 High St., is a notable ex-

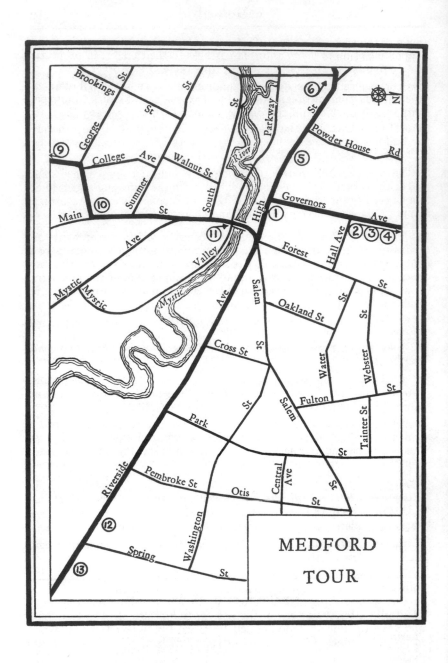

ample of the white wood front and brick-ends type, with a pair of chimneys at each side.

7. The *West Medford Railroad Station*, West Medford Square, is a bizarre structure built about 1880. In its outside walls were embedded, when it was built, various glittering minerals and semi-precious jewels, a whale's tooth, fluted seashells, and an eroded boulder which is supposed to bear a natural resemblance to the head of George Washington. Unfortunately the building has been denuded of most of its jewels, which have been picked out of their cement bed by souvenir hunters.

8. The *Route of Paul Revere* to Lexington is indicated by a board on a tree at the corner of Grove and High Sts., with the following addendum: 'On Grove St. was the home of Rev. Edward Brooks where the returning Minute Men were served with food and chocolate, BUT NO TEA.'

L. from High St. into Boston Ave.; R. from Boston Ave. into College Ave.

9. *Tufts College*, co-educational, crowns the summit of the hill. It was founded in 1852 by Hosea Ballou 2d, nephew of the famous Universalist divine of the same name, with endowment funds and land given by Charles Tufts. The Goddard Chapel (1882–83), of early Gothic style, is built of field-stone.

At one time consisting only of Ballou Hall, the college now forms an impressive group.

In the *Barnum Museum* (*open weekdays, 9–5; Sat. 9–12*) is the famous showman's extensive zoological collection, including the stuffed hide of Jumbo, an elephant beloved by the circus crowds of a past generation.

Tufts College had its origin primarily in the fact that dogmatic proselyting was an approved function of the 19th-century American college. When someone asked Charles Tufts of Somerville, a man of open mind in sympathy with liberal religion, what he intended to do with the windswept heights of Walnut Hill, in a prophetic flash, he answered, 'I will put a light on it!'

Courses are given in liberal arts, theology, engineering and law. Of particular interest is the recently founded Fletcher School of Law and Diplomacy administered in co-operation with Harvard University. Training is offered for government foreign service, international business, and research in international relations.

Tufts College is now affiliated with Jackson College for women. The total enrollment of students is 2,104, including those in attendance at Tufts Medical and Dental Schools in Boston.

Retrace on College Ave.; R. from College Ave. into George St.

10. The *Usher Royall House* (*open May–Nov. daily except Mon. and Fri.*

1–5; *adm.* 25¢) is at 15 George St. A three-story mansion, it derives from the Usher nucleus; it was built before 1697 and is one of the few existing brick houses of the 17th century. Successive alterations, mainly before 1750, have created a three-story mansion, the gabled brick ends terminating in tall chimney stacks, the wooden west front rusticated and adorned with a colossal order, the angles decorated with quoins (among the earliest examples) and the windows richly framed, with cornices — one of the most elaborate dwellings of its period extant in Massachusetts.

L. from George St. into Main St.

11. *Craddock Bridge*, a small concrete span over the Mystic River, takes the place of a timbered draw said to have been the first toll bridge in New England. To the right are replacements of the docks from which ships were launched and the famous Medford Rum was exported.

R. from Main St. into Riverside Ave.

12. *Old Sawyer House* (*private*), 306 Riverside Ave., is an unpainted story-and-a-half dwelling, with clapboarded front, shingled sides, and central chimney, typical of the more modest Colonial dwellings. It is at least 200 years old, and its present resident is a descendant of the original owner.

13. The *Peter Tufts House* or '*Old Fort*' (*open on request; adm.* 25¢), 350 Riverside Ave., sometimes called the *Craddock House*, is a landmark dating from 1677–80. It is interesting to architects as one of the earliest brick houses built from the start with a depth of two rooms in each story. Porthole windows from which to fire revivify in the mind the terrors of Indian attack. Some antiquarians believe this to be the house built in 1638 for Governor Matthew Craddock.

NEW BEDFORD . *Thar She Blows*

City: Alt. 9, pop. 110,022, sett. 1640, incorp. town 1787, city 1847.

Railroad Stations: New Bedford Station, 624 Acushnet Ave.; New Bedford Wharf Station, 41 Front St.; Weld St. Station, 81 Weld St.; all for N.Y., N.H. & H. R.R.

Bus Stations: Middle St. for Union St. Ry. Co.; Vineyard Steamboat Line Dock, Front St., for New England Transportation Co.; 'Times Lot,' 911 Purchase St., for I.C.T. Bus Co.

Steamship Piers: Merrill's Wharf, from 11 Front St. to Acushnet River, for New Bedford Cuttyhunk Line; Vineyard Steamboat Wharf, from 41 Front St. to Acushnet River, for the New Bedford, Martha's Vineyard and Nantucket Steamboat Line.

Accommodations: Three hotels, adequate modern inns and transient facilities.

Information Service: Board of Commerce, Pleasant and William Sts.; New Bedford Auto Club, 628 Pleasant St.

NEW BEDFORD, once a famous whaling port, now a textile center at the mouth of the Acushnet River, is made up of a number of interesting contradictions. Gone are the whalers, but the harbor is still busy with deep-sea fishing vessels, with small steamers plying between New Bedford and Martha's Vineyard and Nantucket, and with coastwise freighters. New Bedford, once the fourth in the United States, is still a busy secondary port.

Even the mills, employing large numbers of English and French-Canadian operatives, have not destroyed this nautical flavor, perpetuated by a whaling museum, a seamen's Bethel, and substantial old houses once the homes of captains and wealthy traders. Twelve thousand Portuguese live in the town. 'The Crowning,' a Portuguese religious festival, takes place the sixth Sunday after Easter and any Sunday thereafter throughout the summer. It takes its name from the custom established by an early queen of Portugal who, legend reports, performed miraculous cures of the sick by placing her crown on their heads. A heavy silver crown, a replica of the queen's, is kept at one of the Portuguese churches for repetitions of these crownings, performed by a priest. 'The Chamarita,' a Portuguese folk dance, is often enjoyed at carnivals and informal gatherings of these people.

Until its incorporation as New Bedford, 'Bedford Village' was a part of the town of Dartmouth. Up to 1760 there were no more than a dozen scattered farms in the village, the homes chiefly of Quakers from Rhode Island and Cape Cod. But Joseph Russell, known as the 'Father of New Bedford' because he gave the town its name in honor of the Duke of Bedford, was already engaged in whaling on a small scale, and soon afterward Joseph Rotch arrived from Nantucket, extended the industry, and presently attracted shipbuilders including George Claghorn, later to build the U.S. Frigate 'Constitution' at Boston. New Bedford's first ship, the 'Dartmouth,' was launched in 1767. In 1773 she was one of the ships whose cargoes of tea were dumped into Boston Harbor on the eve of December 16.

The Revolution temporarily halted local expansion, and New Bedford saw the first clash between the British and the Colonials on water. General Gage, isolated in Boston since April 19, 1775, had sent ships of war scouting southward for food supplies, and one of these, the 'Falcon,' seized two sloops in Vineyard Sound for use as decoys, and advanced slowly toward New Bedford. An unknown messenger made a gallant ride from Wareham with the news. Twenty-five men in a small vessel at once set out to intercept the British, and on May 14 and 15 captured both sloops, thereby discouraging the 'Falcon.' Thereafter, New Bedford Harbor was a rendezvous for American privateers, who turned the tables by preying upon British shipping. This fact prompted a British invasion of the town on September 5, 1778, with five thousand soldiers, who met with little resistance and who burned all patriot homes, vessels, and business houses, but spared those of the Tories.

Nantucket was the leading whaling port until after the War of 1812, but by 1820, with a population of 3947, New Bedford had outstripped it and thereafter led the industry, gradually absorbing almost the entire whaling of the Atlantic seaboard. The year 1845 saw New Bedford's greatest receipts from its fleet — 158,000 barrels of sperm oil, 272,000 barrels of whale oil, and 3,000,000 pounds of whalebone. Ten thousand seamen manned the ships.

While this industry brought wealth to certain sections, to the waterfront it brought rough living and exploited vice. A notorious district known as 'Hard Dig' was burned in 1826 by a mob of zealous citizens.

The discovery of petroleum in Pennsylvania in 1857 spelled the doom of the whaling industry, hastened to some extent by the growing scarcity of whales. Today almost the entire product of blackfish oil (derived from a species of small whale and by sailors called porpoise jaw oil), a lubricant for clocks and watches, is refined here.

In the years just before the Civil War, New Bedford was a station of the Underground Railway for smuggling runaway slaves into Canada. Abolition sentiments were fostered by the Quakers and by Frederick Douglass, a distinguished Negro orator, who aided in recruiting Colonel Robert Gould Shaw's Negro troops. New Bedford had a number of ships in the Stone Fleet which blockaded Southern ports by sinking vessels laden with granite at Southern harbor entrances.

The Wamsutta Mills, the first important textile plant, were chartered in 1846, but the industry grew slowly, owing to the fact that whaling was still dominant. New Bedford shared, however, in the New England textile boom of 1881–83, and from that time on the city was in the front rank as a manufacturer of fine cotton fabrics. Its mild damp climate is favorable to the handling of cotton.

About 1921 came the turn. Even before the general business depression of 1929, low-cost Southern production began to cut into New Bedford's business. A number of mills went into liquidation; others operated on greatly curtailed schedules, creating a major unemployment problem.

Matters were precipitated, April 9, 1928, by a ten per cent cut in the wages of all textile operatives except those of the Dartmouth and Beacon Mills. A six-months strike followed in which twenty-seven thousand workers were involved. About three thousand skilled workers in the Textile Council of the American Federation of Textile Operators joined with the United Textile Workers during the strike in order to gain the support of the American Federation of Labor. The more radical workers, chiefly unskilled and foreign-born, found leadership in the Textile Mill Committee, a national organization. During the course of the strike, the latter joined the vertically organized New Bedford Textile Workers'

Union, which later became the chief local of the National Textile Workers' Union, an industrial union.

A summary of national press comment showed practically unanimous country-wide sympathy with the workers. Settlement was eventually made on the basis of a five per cent reduction in wages, to be restored as soon as conditions might warrant; agreement by the manufacturers to give thirty days' notice of any future reductions; and agreement of the operatives to co-operate in a study designed to increase, if possible, the efficiency of production in the mills. Several plants, however, failed to resume operations and eventually went into liquidation.

Nevertheless, New Bedford's textile history is by no means a closed chapter. During readjustment a number of new industries have been attracted to the city, including needle industries employing thirty-five hundred in the manufacture of cotton garments.

In addition, the development of truck transportation has made New Bedford a modern fish-shipping center. Many fishing boats from Cape Cod waters which formerly unloaded their cargoes directly in Boston or New York now trans-ship their haul at New Bedford. Ten million pounds of fish were brought here in 1934.

FOOT TOUR — 1.5 m.

S. from Middle St. into Pleasant St.

1. The *Public Library* (1856) (*open* 9–9), between William and Market Sts., an impressive building fronted by massive columns, contains a collection of Quaker relics and whaling logs. Established in 1852, it is one of the oldest free public libraries in the country.

2. The *Whaleman Statue*, executed in granite by Bela Pratt, stands on the north side of the Library lawn. It was dedicated (1913) to the whaler's motto, 'A dead whale or a stove boat.'

L. from Pleasant St. into School St.; R. from School St. into Front St.

3. The *Bourne Office Building*, end of School St., is a large three-story stone survival with boarded windows, old-fashioned wooden shutters, and tightly locked doors. Jonathan Bourne, the most successful of all the whaling merchants, opened offices in this building in 1848. His counting-room furniture was transferred a decade ago to the old Dartmouth Historical Society.

The first floor contained chandlery shops and storage rooms for whaling outfits. Lofts and rigging lofts occupied the upper stories; the counting-rooms were on the second floor, with counters and iron railings fencing off the tall mahogany desks at which the bookkeepers stood up, or sat on high stools. There were few luxuries. About the walls were models of whaleships and whaling prints.

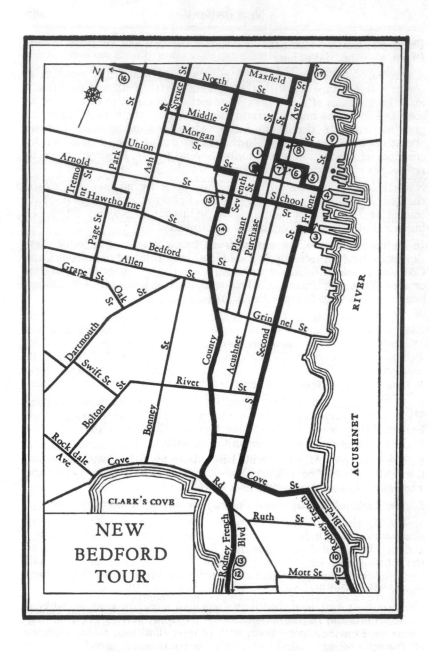

NEW
BEDFORD
TOUR

In the heyday of whaling, oil casks were loaded upon the dock in front of the building, where they were carefully covered with seaweed to prevent the sun from drying them out and spreading the seams. A pen was then built around each collection until such time as a buyer could be found.

Retrace Front St.

4. Along the east side of Front St. is the *Waterfront Area*, centered about the State Pier, and utilized today by a large fishing fleet.

L. from Front St. into Union St.; R. from Union St. into Johnny Cake Hill.

5. On the crest of the hill stand the *Museum of the Old Dartmouth Historical Society*, and the *Bourne Whaling Museum (open daily; adm. 25¢)*. The chief exhibit here is a half-size reproduction of Jonathan Bourne's favorite vessel, the whaling bark 'Lagoda.' The main floor contains smaller models and half models of hulls made by master shipbuilders to guide their workmen. Around the walls are harpoons, darting guns, lances, and other implements used in the chase. There are examples of scrimshaw work made by the whalemen in their leisure time out of whales' teeth and bone. Six hundred logbooks reward research with an almost inexhaustible yield of local color and detail.

6. The *Seamen's Bethel (open)*, facing the Museum, was dedicated on May 2, 1832, to give moral and religious inspiration to the thousands of sailors, native and foreign-born, who frequented the city. It was immortalized by Herman Melville in 'Moby Dick' and has been little changed since Melville's time. Still adorning the walls are the black-bordered, marble cenotaphs inscribed in terms of bitter and hopeless grief; once from the ship's-prow pulpit resounded the chaplain's salty sermons.

L. from Johnny Cake Hill into William St.

7. The *Customhouse*, at the corner of North Second St., on which it fronts, is a granite structure more than a century old. It has two stories, a portico in classic style, and a winding stone stairway of unusual design.

R. from Williams St. into Purchase St.

8. The *Liberty Bell Tablet*, on the eastern wall of the Merchants' Na-

tional Bank at the corner, reads in part: 'News of the passage of the Fugitive Slave Law was brought from Boston in 1851 by an express messenger who rode all night, and the bell on the old Hall was rung to give warning to fugitive slaves that U.S. Marshals were coming.'

MOTOR TOUR — 6 *m*.

E. from Pleasant St. into Middle St.

9. *Bridge Park* at the head of the State bridge, is a beautifully landscaped area.

R. from Middle St. into Front St.; R. from Front St. into Walnut St.; L. from Walnut St. into South Second St.; L. from South Second St. into Cove St.; R. from Cove St. into Rodney French Blvd.

10. *Acushnet Park (open-air dance hall, public bathing beach, clambake pavilion) (privately owned; open in summer; adm. free)*, adjacent to the Infirmary, is a public amusement park.

11. *Fort Rodman (open, visitors restricted)*, at the tip of Clark's Point, is one of the key defenses of the North Atlantic coast. Two active batteries are maintained here. The fort antedates the Civil War.

12. The *Rodney French Memorial Tablet*, at the entrance to Hazelwood Park *(public; tennis; baseball; bowling)*, was erected by the Negroes of the city in honor of an abolitionist mayor in 1853–54.

13. The *Municipal Bathing Beach (bathing suits for hire, outside showers)* was cleared and improved, walls constructed, and a children's beach created by Emergency Relief Administration and Works Progress Administration projects.

L. from Rodney French Blvd. into Cove Rd.; R. from Cove Rd. into County St.

14. The *Mark Duff Home (private)*, between Madison and Cherry Sts., was designed by Russell Warren, early 19th-century Providence architect. It is a two-and-a-half-story frame building topped by a cupola and surrounded by spacious grounds.

R. from County St. into Walnut St.; L. from Walnut St. into Seventh St.

15. The *Perry House (private)*, southeast corner of School St., a mansion of whaling days, is an excellent example of New England Georgian architecture. A winding, mahogany staircase rises through the center of the house from the street floor to the cupola or captain's walk.

L. from Seventh St. into Union St.; R. from Union St. into County St.; L. from County St. into North St.; L. from North St. into Rockdale Ave.

16. *Buttonwood Park* (west end of the city) is the largest in the city. Here is the *Barnard Monument*, a twofold tribute to the whalemen and to the promoters of the textile industry.

Retrace *Rockdale Ave.; R. from Rockdale Ave. into Mill St.* (*one-way, east*);
L. from Mill St. into Acushnet Ave.

17. *Wamsutta Mills* (*not open to the public*), between Wamsutta and
Logan Sts., the oldest of New Bedford's many textile mills, are constructed of granite.

N E W B U R Y P O R T . *City of Captains' Houses*

City: Alt. 26, pop. 14,815, sett. 1635, incorp. town 1764, city 1851.
Railroad Station: Winter St. for B. & M. R.R.
Accommodations: One hotel open all year; two open only during summer.
Information: Chamber of Commerce, 12 Pleasant St.

ONCE seagoing vessels huddled so close in the Merrimack that they
almost bridged the river from the Newburyport to the Salisbury shore.
Now the great river runs placidly by the city, and the harbor is clogged
with sand. Along the shore still stand a few factories, their red-brick
walls faded and picturesque against the background of moving water.
A dignified and charming city rises from the river level, bisected by the
gleaming Turnpike — a modern note in a setting which is otherwise
almost a monument to the glorious days of Newburyport's maritime
supremacy. Shipowners and their captains built the stately houses which
border High Street for several miles; square three-storied dwellings with
hip roofs, often crowned by cupolas, their severity of line relieved by
cornices, doorways, and window treatments, skillfully executed by men
who had learned their craft as shipwrights in the famous Newburyport
yards. Throughout the country the street is known as a distinguished
survival of the best in Federal architecture.

Newburyport's business district is that of any busy modern city, although
even in Market Square space is given to a tablet which tells the tale of
old Goody Morse, victim of the witchcraft delusion. The aroma of molasses still floats from the rum factory, and fine silver is made today in a
plant whose antecedents go back to early Colonial days. Newer manufactures have been established, and the city strives to adjust itself to the
modern tempo. Yet it is in the upper reaches of the city, where the old
jail used for British prisoners frowns over Bartlett Mall, and St. Paul's
Church rears its bishop's mitre high over the roofs of the old houses, that
Newburyport reveals its inner character.

Long before bands of sober-minded Puritans ventured northward to
found the city of Newburyport at the mouth of the Merrimack, free-

lance traders had realized its strategic position. They had tapped the rich Indian country to such an extent that the apprehensions of Governor John Winthrop were aroused. He feared lest such outsiders might secure too firm a foothold within the borders of the Massachusetts Bay Colony. In 1635, therefore, a party of colonists was dispatched to set up an outpost of virtue and commerce against these interlopers. For seven years they attempted to farm the forest at Old Newbury. In 1642 many of them gave up the thankless task and moved to the present site of Newburyport. Industry sprang up at once. Trapping and fishing were followed by whaling and international trade. The deep-channeled river and the limitless supply of lumber made shipbuilding an inevitable development. Between 1681 and 1741, 107 ships were launched from Newburyport shipyards. Subsidiary industries came to life. Along the waterfront appeared ironworks, sail lofts, and ropewalks. For a time the pre-eminence of Boston was seriously threatened, but heavy duties imposed before the Revolution by the British Crown, and the exclusion of American ships from the West Indian trade and the Newfoundland fishing banks after the Revolution, left the town economically prostrate. By 1790 Newburyport had recovered a measure of its prosperity, but it was short-lived. The ninth ship-owning community in the country, it never recovered from the disastrous effects of the Jefferson Embargo Act. The town's plight was thus mourned by a Newbury poet in 1808:

> 'Our ships all in motion once whitened the ocean,
> They sailed and returned with a cargo;
> Now doomed to decay, they have fallen a prey
> To Jefferson — worms — and embargo.'

Another blow was the fire of 1811. Fifteen acres in the heart of the city were burned to the ground. The Industrial Revolution proved Newburyport's commercial undoing. After the War of 1812, textile mills sprang up on every natural water site in Essex County; and the more farseeing mercantile families of Newburyport, such as the Lowells and the Jacksons, turned from trade to manufacture. As the country became industrialized, tariffs were enacted to protect infant industries. Such imports as India cottons, English woolens, Russian duck and canvas, and Baltic iron — backbone of Newburyport's seaborne commerce — were practically wiped out.

Shipbuilding, however, knew another day of glory in the clipper-ship era. The demand for packets to carry adventurers to the California goldfields in '49 gave the industry new impetus. Donald McKay, noted designer of clipper ships, came to Newburyport after his New York apprenticeship. Between 1841 and 1843, in partnership with John Currier, Jr., he turned out three packet vessels of such perfection that his reputation was made. Later, in the same yards, the record-breaking clipper 'Dreadnought' was built by Currier and Townsend.

A geographical position far from the mercantile centers, the ever-increasing sandbars and dangerous shoals at the harbor mouth, and the advent of steam brought to a close this last glorious era in Newburyport's history, and with its passing something of glamor and vitality seemed to leave the city. Newburyport turned to manufacturing, but without enthusiasm. Today the principal industries are shoes, iron and steel products, textiles, and cigars, besides the traditional Newburyport manufactures, rum and fine silver, that have persisted for more than two centuries.

TOUR — 6.5 m.

E. from Green St. into Pleasant St.

1. The *Church of the First Religious Society* (Unitarian), built in 1801, is virtually a duplicate of McIntire's Old South Church in Salem, and valuable — although ascribed to another architect — as an indication of the style of the Salem genius in church design.

L. from Pleasant St. into State St.; R. from State St. on Middle St.; R. from Middle St. into Federal St.

2. The *Old South Church*, corner of School St., now known as the First Presbyterian Meeting House, was built in 1756 and remodeled in 1856. Benedict Arnold and the men of the Quebec Expedition gathered here to worship on September 17, 1775. Here preached the great revivalist, George Whitefield.

R. from Federal St. into Temple St.; L. from Temple St. into State St.

3. The *Tracy House* (*open*), now the Public Library, is the red-brick building at the corner of Prince Place. This house was built in 1771 by Patrick Tracy for his son Nathaniel, who equipped and sent out the first privateer to sail from the United Colonies against England.

4. The *Wolfe Tavern* (*open as a tavern June to Oct.*), corner of Harris St., was built in 1807. The present building, three-story brick with full-length porch, replaced the original tavern built in 1762 and destroyed by the fire of 1811. William Davenport, the original proprietor of the hostelry, named it in honor of the British General Wolfe, with whom he served against the French at Quebec.

5. The *Dalton Club* (*open by special arrangement*) is directly across the street. This spacious gambrel-roofed structure was built in 1746. Particularly interesting are the fine doorway with its carved detail and the interior woodwork.

L. from State St. into High St.

6. The *Cushing House* (1808), on the corner of Fruit St., is a fine example of Federal architecture on a street noted throughout the country for its beauty. The square, three-story brick house is especially notable for its cornice. Caleb Cushing, distinguished statesman, entertained John Quincy Adams here in 1837.

7. The *Wheelwright House* (1797), now the Home for Aged Women, is

characterized by a portico supported by Doric columns and surmounted by a balustrade; a central Palladian window adds charm to the façade.

Retrace on High St.; R. from High St. into Green St.

8. The interior of the *Sumner House* (*open* 2–4; *adm. free*), corner of Harris St., is considered an excellent example of Federal architecture.

9. In Brown's Park, corner of Green and Pleasant Sts., stands the *Statue of the 'Great Liberator,'* William Lloyd Garrison, abolitionist, orator, and publisher of *The Liberator*, which championed the cause of the slaves.

Retrace on Green St.; R. from Green St. into High St.

10. Across the green stretch of Bartlett Mall is the *Old Hill Burying Ground*. Here is buried the self-styled 'Lord' Timothy Dexter (*see below*).

L. at end of Mall on Aubin St.

11. The *Old County Jail* was built in 1744 and used until 1825 as the county prison. During the Revolution many British privateersmen were confined here.

Retrace on Aubin St.; L. from Aubin St. into High St.

12. *St. Paul's Church*, corner of Market St., is said to be the oldest Episcopal parish in Massachusetts, dating from the erection of Queen Anne's Chapel in 1711. In 1797 the rector was consecrated the first Bishop of Massachusetts. Atop the vine-covered stone church is a bishop's mitre.

13. The *Historical Society of Old Newbury* (*open June–Sept. daily* 2–5; *adm.* 25¢) contains early relics of the Newbury settlements and a marine collection. This is the Pettingell-Fowler house, built in 1792.

14. The *Moseley House* (*private*), 182 High St., is a graceful building of the Federal period. Built in 1811, it has a two-story portico with Corinthian columns.

15. The *Jackson-Dexter House* (*private*), at 201 High St., was built in 1771. The ornate wood-encased chimneys, the watch-tower surmounted by a gilded eagle, the columns flanking the door, give an aspect of eccentric charm to this old dwelling, which was once the lavish residence of 'Lord' Timothy Dexter. Lord Timothy, Newburyport's self-titled eccentric, cluttered his estate with statues of the great, his own included. He beat his wife for not giving vent to sufficient grief at a mock funeral held for himself. But his 'lordship' was far from crazy. He gained a good portion of his wealth by buying up depreciated Continental currency. He made a tidy profit out of a cargo of warming-pans sent, with every appearance of lunacy, to the West Indies, and there snapped up for molasses ladles. He published in 1802 a book called 'Pickles for the Knowing Ones,' in which all the punctuation appeared at the end of the book as pages of commas and periods, bearing the unique caption 'Salt and Pepper to Taste.'

16. Atkinson Common, at the juncture with Moseley Ave., is a spacious Green in which stands a newly erected field-stone *Observation Tower*. This vantage-point affords an exceptional view of the Merrimack River, the inland country, and the sea.

R. from High St. into Moseley Ave.; straight ahead into Spofford St. (Amesbury highway).

17. The *Moseley Woods* (*parking space, tennis courts, pavilion, bathing beach, playground equipment, open fireplaces*), on the Amesbury highway at the western end of the city, is one of the larger recreational centers of Newburyport.

18. *Chain Bridge*, which crosses the Merrimack from Amesbury Rd. near the entrance to Moseley Woods, was the first bridge over the navigable waters. It was rebuilt as a suspension bridge in 1810.

Retrace on Spofford St.; L. from Spofford St. into Merrimac St.; L. from Merrimac St. into Jefferson St.

19. *Carr's Ferry Approach* is the site of the first ferry established between Newbury and Carr's Island. The original ferry was the only connecting link between Boston and the northern frontier.

Retrace on Jefferson St.; L. from Jefferson St. into Merrimac St.

20. The *Shipyard Sites* are at the foot of Ashland St. Here was launched the famous 1400-ton clipper 'Dreadnought.' Its record crossing of the Atlantic (9 days, 13 hours, from Sandy Hook to Liverpool) was the marvel of the year 1859.

21. The *Towle Company Factory* (*open by arrangement*) is a survivor of an industry for which early Newburyport was noted. This firm is today one of the largest manufacturers of sterling silverware, exclusively, in the world.

22. The *Caldwell Distilleries* (*open by arrangement*) housed in a red-brick plant on the river bank, are the only distilleries in the city still manufacturing rum, a commodity once inseparably associated with the name of Newburyport.

N E W T O N . *Commuter's Haven*

City: Alt. 142, pop. 66,144, sett. 1639, incorp. town 1691, city 1873.

Railroad Stations: Newton, Newtonville, West Newton, Auburndale, and Riverside for B. & A. R.R. (main line); Chestnut Hill, Newton Centre, Newton Highlands, Eliot, Waban, Woodland and Riverside for B. & A. R.R. (Highland branch); Newton Upper Falls for N.Y., N.H. & H. R.R. Newton Lower Falls (Wellesley) for B. & A. R.R. (Newton Lower Falls branch).

Bus Stations: Chestnut Hill, Newton Highlands, and Newton Upper Falls for Boston & Worcester Lines; Charles Pharmacy, Elm and Washington Sts., West Newton, for Victoria Coach Lines (Boston & N.Y.).

Information: Bureau of University Travel, 11 Boyd St.

NEWTON is a city built, like Rome, on seven hills; but it is suburban and residential rather than truly urban. It has its business sections and a few isolated industries, but the slopes and summits of its hills are almost entirely mantled with small or large estates or acreage not yet developed. Its roads are excellent, its parkways beautiful, and its proximity to Boston, combined with its lavish natural beauty, places it in the front rank of commuters' towns.

In few Massachusetts cities has the identity of the original villages persisted as it has in Newton. These villages number fourteen. All except Nonantum are recognized by separate railway stations; all have distinct business and civic centers; and though the confines melt into each other, each has its own individuality and is worthy of a visit on its own account.

The town had been settled for seven years when, in 1646, John Eliot first began to preach to the Indians at Nonantum, an event commemorated by the city seal. His first sermon, an hour and a quarter in length, was followed by a distribution of apples and biscuits to the children and of tobacco to the men — an apparently effective method of holding the audience. Whether the women were so interested that no reward was necessary, or whether their attendance was a matter of indifference to the preacher, the record does not state.

John Eliot was the first pastor of Newton's first church. After his death in 1690 the church was for some years without a spiritual guide, during which time various visiting ministers, objecting to the inadequate compensation offered them, sued the town for additional payment. The Court ordered the town to pay, and pay it did.

In these early days in Newton, farming was a principal occupation, and friendly Indians were helpful in introducing the pioneers to such new crops as potatoes, maize, squash, pumpkins, and beans. Some of the settlers built looms or forges or engaged in fishing. Everybody prospered. Substantial frame houses soon supplanted the original log huts.

Newton Upper Falls and Newton Lower Falls became the seat of busy industries in the early nineteenth century with two year-round hotels, many stores, and, on the Needham side of the river, a cotton mill with three thousand spindles. The rest of the Newtons developed more slowly.

During one period Newton was distinguished by the residence of outstanding leaders of culture. For a time Horace Mann lived in West Newton at the corner of Highland and Chestnut Streets. After he moved away, his brother-in-law, Nathaniel Hawthorne, occupied the same house for a year, the year in which he wrote 'The Blithedale Romance.' 'It is calm as eternity and will give you lively ideas of the same,' wrote Ralph Waldo Emerson, who in 1833 came with his mother to occupy an old farmhouse near the Upper Falls. At the Old Elms, the home of Governor Claflin in Newtonville, Mrs. Mary Claflin, author of 'Oldtime Folks' and 'Under the Elms,' entertained such distinguished guests as John Greenleaf Whittier, Henry Ward Beecher, Harriet Beecher Stowe, President Hayes, Chief Justice Chase, and others. Another literary group used to meet with Celia Thaxter and her husband, Levi Lincoln Thaxter, a Browning enthusiast, in the Thaxters' barn in Newtonville.

The 1934 census of manufactures of the Department of Labor and Industry gives the total number of manufacturing plants in operation as fifty-four. The census of 1935 indicates a shrinkage to fifteen. It is not the hum of machinery which the casual visitor hears in Newton today, but the passing of shining automobiles over well-built roads; it is not the brick walls and huddled squalor of a factory city which greets one's eye, but fine residences with spacious garages; not the soot of an industrial center which reaches one's nostrils, but the summer fragrance of carefully landscaped estates. It was not the destiny of Newton's hills to be mantled in smoke or of its glistening lakes to be filmed with a scum. When the rails of the Boston and Worcester Railroad reached out in 1834, Newton began to receive the residential overflow of the near-by metropolis, and from its earliest days it attracted a prosperous type of home-maker. Not to become an agricultural community, not to become an industrial center, but to be a city of quiet and handsome homes where the strain and uncertainty of a busy civilization seem like a distant murmur, this was Newton's destiny.

TOUR — 23 *m.*

W. from Newton Corner into Washington St. (one-way traffic); L. from Washington St. into Hall St. (short unmarked street at end of first block); R. from Hall St. into Centre St.

NEWTON CORNER is the first of the fourteen famous Newton villages. Its core, covering several blocks, is occupied by stores and office buildings, giving the effect of a busy small town. Immediately on turning into Centre St., however, the visitor enters typical residential Newton. This is one of the older sections characterized by large comfortable Victorian dwellings, some of them slightly shabby but more of them very well preserved, or by the smaller modern houses, popularly of Tudor brick and timber, which have replaced their more substantial predecessors. Here and there handsome churches and prosperous city buildings rise as appropriate civic accents in the residential scene.

1. The *Shannon House (private)*, 749 Centre St., suggests the early Victorian by its solid quiet lines and its serenely terraced lawn and shading trees. It was, however, built at a still earlier date (1798) and was one of the show houses of the town. The small conservatory was at-

tached to the house by its 19th-century owner, Miss Mary Shannon, a local philanthropist, whose hobby was gardening.

Retrace on Centre St.; R. from Centre St. into Sargent St.; straight ahead from Sargent into Kenrick St.; R. from Kenrick St. into Magnolia St.

2. The *Eliot Memorial* is a small stone terrace attractively landscaped. A tablet in the superstructure records the date of 1646, when the Apostle to the Indians preached his first sermon near the spot.

R. from Magnolia St. into Eliot Memorial Rd.; L. from Eliot Memorial Rd. into Waverley Ave.; R. from Waverley Ave. into Cotton St.; L. from Cotton St. into Centre St.; L. from Centre St. into Commonwealth Ave.

Commonwealth Avenue skirts the second and perhaps the most opulent village of all, that of *Chestnut Hill*, which Newton shares with Brookline. Here are the really large estates, to every one of which is attached some name well known in national trade, finance, or political history.

3. *Boston College* spreads its fine open campus on a hill slope overlooking the beautiful Chestnut Hill Reservoir. Four imposing gray-stone buildings in English Collegiate Gothic accommodate a large student body made up largely of day students. Its library contains illuminated manuscripts, including breviaries, books of hours, and missals, of the medieval era, and a very famous collection of the Negro folklore of Africa and the West Indies. The College is operated by the Society of Jesus.

Retrace on Commonwealth Ave.; L. from Commonwealth Ave. into Hammond St.; R. from Hammond St. into Dunster Rd.

3a. The *Chestnut Hill Railroad Station*, designed by H. H. Richardson, was built in 1881–84.

Retrace to Hammond St.; L. from Hammond St. into Beacon St.

4. The *Home of Mary Baker Eddy* (*open weekdays* 2–5; *adm. by card only, obtainable at Administration Office of Mother Church, Boston*), at 400 Beacon St., Chestnut Hill, is of modified Tudor architecture. Mrs. Eddy resided here for about three years, from 1908 to 1910.

Along here is a procession of stately homes as the visitor approaches NEWTON CENTRE, the third village, with its small focus of business, its civic buildings and churches.

R. from Beacon St. into Centre St.

5. The *Smith House* (*private*), 1181 Centre St., a broad, low frame house painted cinnamon color, was the home for many years of the Rev. Samuel Francis Smith, author of 'America.' A tablet within the grounds which refers to this as the 'site' of the house is slightly misleading, as this is not only the site but actually the house itself.

Retrace on Centre St.; L. from Centre St. into Institution Ave.

6. The *Andover Newton Theological School*, impressively crowning a salient hill, combines the former Newton Theological Institution, founded in 1825 for training young men for the Baptist ministry, and the former

Andover Theological Seminary, founded in 1808 as a training school for the Congregational ministry. The somewhat heterogeneous group of buildings is less notable than the superb view in every direction from the campus.

South is OAK HILL, the fourth village, an attractive cluster of roofs and trees half encircled by the Charles River Country Club.

Retrace on Institution Ave.; L. from Institution Ave. into Beacon St.; R. from Beacon St. into Walnut St.; L. from Walnut St. into Homer St.

7. The *Newton City Hall* and *War Memorial* (1932, Allen and Collens, architects) make a notable civic group. Apparently out in the country, actually it is very nearly in the geographical center of the city taken as a whole. A symbolic sculpture designed by Charles Collens representing History, Patriotism, and Sacrifice is executed upon the pediment of the Memorial. A popular feature in the Memorial is a group of four realistic action-groups in miniature waxwork composition containing over 200 figures and representing four important events in American military and naval history.

R. from Homer St. into Commonwealth Ave.; R. from Commonwealth Ave. into Walnut St. at front of City Hall; R. from Walnut St. into Lincoln St.

Here is the village of NEWTON HIGHLANDS, which consists of more and yet more fine residences clustered about a small business center.

R. from Lincoln St. into Woodward St.; L. from Woodward St. into Fairlee Rd.

8. The *Woodward Farmhouse (private)* (R), up a gravel lane, was built in 1681, and is occupied by a descendant of the builder. Its brown clapboards, massive central chimney, and small-paned windows blend with the tree-shaded meadows of the background.

Retrace on Fairlee Rd.; R. from Fairlee Rd. into Woodward St.; R. from Woodward St. into Boylston St.; R. on marked dip for underpass; L. into Ellis St.

Here is the village of NEWTON UPPER FALLS, a small manufacturing center. It has not the crowded look, however, of a typical mill settlement. The factories have a rather casual air and the workers' houses, many of them 100 years old or more, have an appearance of space and rural leisure.

9. Here *Echo Bridge* spans the Charles River. It was built in 1876 not for traffic but to carry the Sudbury River conduit, which brings in part of Newton's water supply. The foundations are sunk in solid rock, and the triple stone arch is one of the largest of this construction in the world. A footpath leads along the river brink to the central arch, where a shout or a laugh will be mimicked in eery echoes.

The clear dark tide flows smoothly at this point through *Hemlock Gorge*, one of the very few natural hemlock groves remaining on the eastern seaboard.

Retrace on Ellis St.; straight ahead from Ellis St. into Quinobequin Rd.

Farther to the left lie the wooded meadows not yet developed, land such as once comprised all Newton. On the right lie WABAN and ELIOT, adjacent villages with attractive and well-kept homes.

L. from Quinobequin Rd. into Washington St.

Here is NEWTON LOWER FALLS, another small manufacturing center.

10. The *Baury House* (*private*), 2349 Washington St., is a fine three-story Colonial house of the massive square type. Its recessed doorway with carved panels and ceilings, an architectural detail common in the Connecticut Valley, is rarely found in this section. The fleur-de-lis carving on the door lends a French touch incongruous but pleasing and a reminder of an early owner of French descent, who was rector of the beautiful white church (*open*) which stands in the rear. The house dates from 1750, the church from 1814. Within the latter at the ends of the old-fashioned box pews are the amusing old gate-doors.

Retrace on Washington St.; L. from Washington St. into Grove St.; L. from Grove St. into Woodland Rd.; L. from Woodland Rd. into Auburn St.; R. from Auburn St. into Commonwealth Ave.

11. *Norumbega Park* (*open, small fee*) occupies an attractive woodland stretch along the banks of the Charles River (*canoeing*).

At RIVERSIDE, the tenth village, there are also canoes for hire.

R. from Commonwealth Ave. into Ash St.; L. from Ash St. into Auburn St.

The road traverses AUBURNDALE, a residential village of pleasant, not too pretentious homes.

11 *a*. The *Auburndale Railroad Station* (1881) is H. H. Richardson's first and finest work in this field.

L. from Auburn St. into Washington St.

This leads to the village of WEST NEWTON, which has a large business center, surrounded by handsome residential areas.

12. The *First Unitarian Church* (1905–06), designed by Cram and Ferguson, forms a quadrangle around a central open courtyard. The style of the building is modified English Perpendicular Gothic; the material seam-face granite, with limestone and terra-cotta trim, and some wood and plaster in the subsidiary wings. The church proper consists of a nave seating about 800 and narrow aisles. The open timber roof is supported by heavy arched masses, resting on corbels in the form of angels.

The adjacent village, NEWTONVILLE, increases the conviction that there actually is a place in Newton where its citizens can shop without journeying to Boston; but in the outlying districts a pond or two, a wooded slope, here and there an open field, still remind the visitor of the days not so long ago, when Newton was a scattering of villages.

L. from Washington St. on Walnut St.; R. from Walnut St. on Watertown St.

The fourteenth village bears the original Indian name of the settlement, NONANTUM. This is a fair-sized manufacturing and commercial center, and its drab and huddled tenements and crowded streets come as more than a slight shock after the long tour of wide boulevards and shaded avenues bordered by charming and elegant, or at least commodious, homes and spacious opulent estates.

R. from Watertown St. on Adams St.; L. from Adams St. on Washington St.

13. The *Jackson House* (*private*), 527 Washington St., was said by the late Robert N. Cram to look 'like Mrs. John Hancock, making up her mind whether she would speak to the neighbors.' The ell of the present building is said to have belonged to the original structure (1640). The proportions of the house, a white, square two-story dwelling with clapboarded front, brick ends, and four end chimneys, are quiet and refined.

NORTHAMPTON

From Jonathan Edwards to Sophia Smith

City: Alt. 133, pop. 24,525, sett. 1654, incorp. town 1656, city 1883.

Railroad Station: Union Depot, Main St. and Strong Ave., for B. & M. R.R.
Bus Stations: New England Transportation Co., 171 Main St., 86 Green St.; Railroad Station.

Accommodations: Three hotels.

Information: Wiggins Old Tavern (Hotel Northampton), King St.; Draper Hotel, Main St.

NORTHAMPTON, a residential and industrial city on the Connecticut River, has the prosperous rural beauty of wide streets shaded by stately trees, and lined in almost every quarter by substantial homes of quiet distinction. The many parks, the Smith College Campus, 'Paradise,' Sunset Hill, and Round Hill offer agreeable strolls. A large part of its twenty-five thousand citizens are engaged in the manufacture of silk, hosiery, cutlery, brushes, indelible ink, and caskets.

About twoscore years after the Pilgrims had landed at Plymouth, a party of Connecticut men petitioned the General Court at the Colony of Massachusetts Bay for permission to settle a second 'plantation' north of Hartford.

The first crude shelters were built along a rough dirt road, now Pleasant Street. Four acres of land were presented to each householder, together with a generous portion of fair meadow. Soon the fertile soil attracted many other pioneers, and Hawley, Market, and King Streets were quickly settled.

In the beginning, Indian attacks were infrequent, for when the French and Indian Wars began, the Nonotucks had long since left the country. But other tribes began to go on the warpath and, at the beginning of King Philip's War severely harassed the settlers.

Early in the eighteenth century, Jonathan Edwards, a Puritan divine, took over the Northampton pastorate and was soon recognized as the mightiest preacher in New England. He was one of the inspired leaders of the 'Great Awakening' of 1740, America's first great revival movement. Soon in a frenzy of religious hysteria the townsfolk were falling into trances and seeing visions; even little children swooned in the streets from their 'conviction of sin.' All New England was convulsed with terror of hell-fire. Finally Edwards's Northampton career came to an abrupt end with his forced removal to Stockbridge as a missionary. It was in Stockbridge that he wrote his great philosophical treatise, 'On the Freedom of the Will.'

After the Revolution, deprived of the independence for which they had fought, the inhabitants of Northampton rose in rebellion along with many of their neighbors. Led by their preacher, Sam Ely, they stormed the courthouse, in 1782, to prevent the foreclosure of their farms. In 1786, near the tragic end of Shays's Rebellion, a crowd of angry citizens again descended on the court to keep it from holding session. On the other side of the question, in this same year, William Butler, a youth of twenty-two, founded the *Hampshire Gazette* (still published today) to combat the discontent.

Impetus was given to the development of the town by the establishment here of Smith College by Sophia Smith, a resident of Hatfield, at a period when the intellectual standards of women's colleges were very slightly superior to those of secondary schools. Her phrase, 'the intelligent gentlewoman,' expressed the ideal of the college body; the spirit of Christianity was to pervade the teachings and life of the college, but it was to be absolutely non-sectarian. Smith, which opened with 14 students in 1875, is among the largest resident women's colleges in the world (enrollment approximately two thousand). During the first two years at the college, a broad general foundation is laid. An opportunity is given for specialization during the remaining two years, and students in French, German, Italian, and Spanish may spend their junior year abroad in the respective countries. The system of departmental honors permits candidates to work at their own rate of speed.

TOUR — 9 *m.*

E. from King St. (US 5) on Main St. which becomes Bridge St.

1. *Calvin Coolidge's Law Office*, Masonic Temple, a yellow-brick building opposite Strong Ave., is still marked with his name on a second-story window. At one time Mayor of the city, in 1920 Governor of Massachusetts, Coolidge became Vice-President in 1921, and at President Harding's death in 1923 he became President of the United States.

2. The *Bliss House* (*private*), 58 Bridge St., was erected between 1655 and 1658, and is a small two-and-a-half-story white clapboarded dwelling with small ells east and west, a central chimney, and a small, modern but harmonious plain white portico, fronting a tree-shaded lawn.

3. The *Wright House* (*private*), 96 Bridge St., is a 17th-century dwelling not readily recognizable as such, owing to its additions. It is a large two-and-a-half-story gray clapboard house with white trim, hip roof, and a long rear ell, the whole set in a pleasant lawn bordered by a lilac hedge.

Retrace Bridge and Main St.; R. from Main St. on King St.; L. from King St. on Court St.

4. The *Wiggins Tavern* (*open as antique shop*) is a three-story brick hostelry built in 1786, and famous for its Currier and Ives prints, Rogers groups, glass, pewter, brass, and kitchen and table utensils. In the courtyard is a clever reproduction of a *Country Store*, such as existed as late as the turn of the present century, crammed with every conceivable product.

Retrace on Court St.; R. from Court St. on King St.; R. from King St. on Main St.; R. from Main St. on Gothic St.

5. The *People's Institute* was founded half a century ago by George W. Cable, a popular author, as a reading group. Mr. E. H. R. Lyman of Northampton gave them the old Methodist Church on Center St. and a wider program was introduced which included instruction for young women in the domestic arts, and classes in Americanization. In 1905, Andrew Carnegie made it possible to erect the present building, for all practical purposes a community center.

Retrace Gothic St.; R. from Gothic St. on Main St.

6. The *Northampton Historical Society* (*open Wed., Sat.* 10.30–12 *and* 2–4.30) is in Memorial Hall, a two-story brick building. On the grounds is a granite bas-relief of *Casimir Pulaski*, Revolutionary general, given by the Polish-American citizens of Northampton.

7. The old *Smith College* campus is bounded by Elm St., West St., and Paradise Pond. The college property, however, with its spacious lawns, driveways, and attractive quadrangles, has been expanded gradually

to take in both sides of Elm St. and an extensive area farther up Elm St.
It covers 119 acres and is prepared to house almost the entire student
body, but in order to retain the old 'cottage idea' of the founders,
dormitories have been made small and homelike. Four of these are co-
operatives for the use of students who wish to reduce expenses.

The *Grecourt Gates* (*motor cars may enter*), at the Main St. entrance to the campus,
are of wrought iron, swung from brick and stone pillars surmounted by urns.
They are a replica of the gates of the Château Robecourt, Grecourt, France, and
commemorate the work of the Smith College Relief Unit during and after the World
War, 1917–20.

College Hall (L), just inside the Grecourt Gates, is of brick, in Collegiate Gothic,
with a square clock-tower containing the melodious Dorothea Carlile Chime.
From here, right and left, is a beautiful view of landscaped, tree-shaded lawns, set
with large and handsome dormitories, lecture halls, library, gymnasium, and
Botanic Garden. The present trend in the architecture of the college favors Colonial Georgian, with buildings of red brick and white stone trim.

Paradise Pond, at the farther end of the campus, is said to have been named by
Jenny Lind. It is a limpid pool bordered by oaks and pines, a part of the college
property. On the near shore is a boathouse with canoes and rowboats, on the far
shore playing fields. Here on a June night, as part of the Class Day exercises, is
held a glee club concert, the girls singing from shadowy floats under the moon to
an audience covering the high bank of the pond.

Retrace through the campus; L. from Grecourt Gates on Elm St.

Gateway House (*private*) is a gabled brick residence with white wood trim, known
from 1875 to 1920 as 'the President's House.' The new President's House overlooks
Paradise Pond.

Tryon Art Gallery (*open weekdays* 10–6; *Sun.* 2.30–4.30; *adm. free*), opposite Bedford Terrace, is a small brick, ivy-clad building, housing one of the only two considerable collections anywhere of the magical crepuscular landscapes of Dwight
William Tryon (1849–1925), for many years visiting professor of art at Smith
College. Tryon alone of American artists was considered worthy to companion
Whistler in any extensive showing at the Freer Gallery in Washington, D.C. The
adjoining *Hillyer Art Gallery* at Smith contains less specialized examples of American art.

John Greene Hall, opposite Prospect St., is a brick assembly hall with lofty Ionic
columns on the principal façade named for John Morton Greene, Sophia Smith's
pastor and advisor, to whom is credited much of the foresight in the liberal wording
of the bequest for the college foundation.

Sessions House, 109 Elm St., was built in 1700, and is now college property. It is
the most beautiful early American house in Northampton, a large white clapboarded gambrel-roofed dwelling with a simple white portico, small-paned windows, dormer windows, and a central chimney. Although a large and irregular ell
has been added, this extension harmonizes well with the original house.

Mandell Quadrangle, between Paradise Rd. and Kensington Ave., is the seat of
two of the newest, largest, and most luxurious Smith dormitories. Colonial
Georgian in style and constructed of brick with white trim, they are beautifully
grouped with six other similar dormitories around terraced and balustraded lawns.
The loggia in *Laura Scales House* has photo-murals made from old prints of Northampton, and is furnished in a modern manner with isolated units of divans and
chairs, to assure some degree of privacy to individual conversational groups. Each
house has its own reference library.

Retrace Elm St.; L. from Elm St. on Round Hill Rd.

8. The *Clarke School for the Deaf* (*open by permission*), at the top of the

MASSACHUSETTS: ONE OF THE WORLD'S CENTERS OF LEARNING

THE educational opportunities that Massachusetts offers are surpassed by no other State. The laboratories of the Massachusetts Institute of Technology are ranked with the finest in the world. The administration and library building, shown on the same page with the photograph from the Institute's research laboratories, is situated on the Charles two miles below the Harvard buildings seen in the air view.

Contrasting these buildings, as well as Smith College and Andover Academy, with the little rural schoolhouse where Mary's lamb is said to have followed her to school, we see the extremes in the story of education in the State.

Massachusetts is rich in collections of fine art and in offerings of music, the two sometimes admirably combined. The Japanese Garden at the Museum of Fine Arts is only one of the Museum's rare exhibitions of foreign art. The court in the Isabella Stewart Gardner Museum is kept in colorful bloom all through the year, and on certain afternoons during the week concerts are given in the Tapestry Room. Likewise, Fogg Museum in Cambridge has an attractive interior court, where chorales are sung at Christmas time.

However, the popular concerts are those held outdoors — the orchestral concerts on the Charles River Esplanade, and the week of symphonies in the Berkshires.

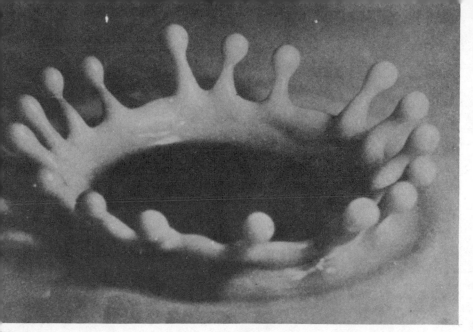

SPLASH OF A DROP OF MILK

Photograph, by Ultra-Rapid Camera, made at the Massachusetts Institute of Technology

THE MASSACHUSETTS INSTITUTE OF TECHNOLOGY, CAMBRIDGE

HARVARD COLLEGE FROM THE AIR

BULFINCH HALL, ANDOVER ACADEMY

SMITH COLLEGE QUADRANGLES, NORTHAMPTON

JAPANESE GARDEN, MUSEUM OF FINE ARTS, BOS

THE COURT OF THE ISABELLA STEWART GARDNER MUSEUM, BOSTON

THE COURT, FOGG ART MUSEUM, CAMBRIDGE

THE ESPLANADE SYMPHONY ORCHESTRA UNDER FIEDLER

THE LITTLE RED SCHOOLHOUSE, SUDBURY

hill, is a comparatively small but well-equipped institution, 70 years old and housing 150 pupils of both sexes from kindergarten to high-school age. Massachusetts pupils are paid for by the State. President of the Trustees is Mrs. Calvin Coolidge, who once studied in the teachers' training course.

Retrace Round Hill Rd.; R. from Round Hill Rd. on Elm St.; R. from Elm St. on Massasoit St.

9. *Calvin Coolidge's First Northampton Home (private)*, 21 Massasoit St., is a square two-family frame house with yellow clapboards, green blinds, two porches, and a small lawn, on a modest, tree-shaded residential street lined with similar houses.

Retrace Massasoit St.; R. from Massasoit St. on Elm St.

10. *Childs Park (privately owned, open; adm. free)* is a wooded beauty spot into which has been introduced practically every variety of New England wild flower.

L. from Elm St. on N. Elm St.; straight ahead from N. Elm St. on N. Main St.

11. *Look Park (open daily 7–10; first hour free, graduated charges after; pool 25¢; luncheonette)* was presented to Northampton by the widow of Frank Newhall Look, prophylactic toothbrush manufacturer, under a large endowment. The 125 acres, beautifully wooded and watered, contain an open-air Pompeiian swimming pool, an open-air theater, a deer park, picnic grounds, and a great variety of playing fields.

Retrace on N. Main St. and N. Elm St.; R. from N. Elm St. on Elm St.; R. from Elm St. on West St.

12. *Forbes Library (open weekdays 9–9; Sun. 2–6)*, a low granite building with brownstone trim, set on a wide lawn, is the city library. It contains *Portraits of President and Mrs. Coolidge*, by Howard Chandler Christy, an autographed photograph of *Marshal Foch*, the *Holland House Collection* of some 40 miniatures of English celebrities from Queen Elizabeth to Cromwell, which once adorned Holland House, the home of Charles James Fox, and the priceless *Judd Manuscript*, the chief source for the genealogy, manners, and customs of the entire Connecticut Valley in Colonial times.

Retrace on West St.; R. from West St. on Main St.; R. from Main St. on New South St.; L. from New South St. on High St.; R. from High St. on unmarked street ending in stone gates.

13. *The Beeches (private)*, facing the end of the street, is the home which Calvin Coolidge bought after retiring from the White House, and where he died. It is a large, many-gabled residence with gray-shingled walls and green trim, set in a fine grove of beeches with a view of the Holyoke Range.

Town: Alt. 262, pop. 1950, sett. 1673, incorp. 1723.

Railroad Stations: East Northfield for Central Vermont R.R. and B. & M. R.R.; Northfield for Central Vermont R.R.

Bus Stations: East Northfield, Northfield, and Mt. Hermon for Boston and Maine Transportation Co.

Accommodations: Four hotels.

Information: Northfield Hotel, off Highland Ave., E. Northfield.

NORTHFIELD is one of the most charming of the older rural communities. Overlooking the Connecticut River, it is crossed by Mill Brook and watered by more than a score of woodland brooks. The broad river meadows and the rolling plains rise to the wooded uplands. The main street of Northfield, home of Northfield Seminary, has a double arch of elms, fringing the chaste white frame dwellings so characteristic of many of the most attractive of old New England centers.

Northfield is one of the dozen Massachusetts municipalities which are internationally known, because for the past fifty years it has sent thousands of Protestant missionaries to remote corners of the globe.

In 1673 fourteen families moved into Northfield from Northampton and Hadley, but after two years of struggle with Indian raids they abandoned the settlement. In 1714, despite the dangers still apprehended from the French and Indian Wars, a permanent settlement was made.

Agriculture flourished, and to this was added apple-growing. In 1771, when the 'merino craze' swept New England, Northfield developed into a sheep-raising community. The town has ventured into the manufacture of brooms, cotton battings, and agricultural machinery, and the distilling of liquors. Market gardening, sheep raising, and apple-growing are the principal activities today.

In 1879 Dwight Lyman Moody established the Northfield Seminary for the daughters of farmers, and two years later, in the neighboring town of Gill, the Mount Hermon School for boys.

An equally celebrated Moody enterprise, closely allied with Mount Hermon, is the Student Volunteer Movement, established in 1886 in collaboration with the International Y.M.C.A., which results in the enlistment of many young men and women annually in foreign mission work.

The first American Youth Hostel was founded here in 1934. Separate sleeping quarters are provided for the boys and girls, with a common kitchen and recreation rooms. The young travelers carry their own sleeping sacks, but blankets are provided at the hostels. Each youth must present a Membership Pass, which costs a dollar for those under twenty-five years of age, two dollars for members over twenty-five, and three dollars for a family. Northfield was the first of several hundred towns in the United States which now recognize the cultural and educational benefits of youth hosteling.

TOUR — 9 m.

N. on Main St. (State 10) from the junction of State 63.

1. The *Old Janes House (private)* (L) is still occupied by descendants of the builders. Tradition has it that an underground tunnel connected it with the Young House, a white Colonial dwelling across the street, and it is said to have served as a station in the Underground Railway.

2. The *Captain Samuel Field House (open by permission)*, opposite a marker indicating the First Settlement, was built in 1784. The house has five enormous fireplaces and a large brick oven in the ell. The wainscoting is of virgin pine boards and the fine old doors have iron strap-hinges (H and L).

3. The *Old Dollard House (open by permission)* (R) is a restoration, but shows an arch under the massive chimney in the cellar. Sometimes such an arched tunnel was part of a secret chamber. The carving around the front door was taken from an old house in Factory Hollow near Greenfield.

4. The *Beehive (open as Ye Old Hunt Tavern)*, a big three-story house with verandas on the first and second floors, was for many years the village inn.

5. The *Old Pomeroy Place (private)* (L), owned by Northfield Schools, was restored by Elliot Speer, late principal of Mount Hermon, and presents a fine example of Colonial architecture.

R. from Main St. on the Schell Château Rd.

6. The *Schell Château (open)* (L), an annex of the Northfield Inn, built in 1890 by Robert Schell who originally intended it for an English country house.

Retrace on Schell Château Rd.; R. from Schell Château Rd. on Main St.

7. The *Home of the Rev. Dwight L. Moody (open)* is at the corner of the first road N. of West Northfield Rd. The son of a widowed mother, Moody lacked educational opportunities, but his driving ambition made him achieve financial success. In 1855, however, he was converted, renounced the world, and preached his way to fame. Conscious of his own meager opportunities and keenly sympathetic with those who yearned for an education, he founded Northfield Seminary and the Mount Hermon School.

8. *Northfield Seminary* (*open*) (R), established in 1879, occupies 1200 acres with 79 buildings accommodating over 500 women students. Its founder had been impressed with the hopelessness of the lot of the girls from the poorer homes after driving past a mountain cottage where a mother and two daughters were braiding palmetto straw hats in an effort to support a family whose father was a paralytic. All the Seminary students help with the housework and receive an education for about half the cost usual in other schools. Northfield Summer Conferences (*religious; open to public*) are held during the summer.

> *East Hall*, built in 1880 was the first building on the campus. The *Birthplace of D. L. Moody* and the house where he lived, as well as his *Grave* and that of his wife are on the campus grounds and may be visited by making arrangements at *Kernarden Hall*, the administration building. The beautiful *Chapel*, in Gothic style, a gift of Mrs. Russell Sage, and *Gould Hall*, given by Miss Helen Gould are two of the outstanding buildings on the campus. The *Auditorium* seats three thousand people.

Retrace on Main St. to junction with State 63; straight ahead on State 63.

9. The *Lookout*, a vantage-point high on the river terrace, offers an excellent view of the Connecticut River country with the towers of the *Mount Hermon Boys' School* (*see Tour 15A, Gill*) in the foreground.

N O R T O N . *Typical New England*

Town: Alt. 104, pop. 2925, sett. 1669, incorp. 1711.
Railroad Station: East Norton for N.Y., N.H. & H. R.R.
Accommodations: Inns and private boarding-houses.

NORTON is a pleasant small country town, well wooded and watered, which gives the general impression, no longer strictly correct, of a typical New England farming community. As it occupies a level plain, without hills of note, the landscape is not much diversified and makes no immediate or striking appeal. Norton is the sort of place, however, which grows upon the affections. In every direction there are agreeable walks, running now across open pastures, walled by the loose stones cleared from the fields by the first settlers, now past some small sawmill still in operation, now through pungent pines, and coming suddenly upon a pretty brook or delightful pond. These things the girls at Wheaton College have known for the past hundred years.

For Norton is distinctively a college town, the seat of Wheaton College, one of the pioneer schools for the education of women in this country. It is the only small independent college for women in Massachusetts which is neither co-educational nor affiliated with other institutions, with a limited enrollment of five hundred students in 1937, representing twenty-one States, Puerto Rico, and three foreign countries. The faculty is composed of both men and women. 'That they may have life and have it more abundantly' is the college motto.

Norton, originally a rural and agricultural village, took on its academic character with the founding of Wheaton Female Seminary, established by Judge Laban Wheaton in 1834 as a memorial to his daughter. Mary Lyon was its organizer, but left to found Mount Holyoke College after two years.

Jewelry has been manufactured in Norton since 1871, the first concern being established by W. A. Sturdy. The Barrowsville Bleachery has been in operation for over thirty years. These, along with the Talbot Wool Combing Company, the T. J. Holmes Company, manufacturers of atomizers, and the paper and wooden box factories, represent the industrial activity of the town today.

Norton for its size had an unusual amount of trouble with the powers of darkness. Beside Dora Leonard and Naomi Burt, town witches, old-timers tell a story from Colonial days about one Major George Leonard, a highfalutin fellow who sold himself soul and body to the Devil for gold. In 1716 His Satanic Majesty cashed in on his bargain, they say, whistling the Major's soul out of his body and then carrying his body off through the roof. Anyone who doesn't believe this can see with his own eyes the Devil's footprints on a rock below the eaves where Satan landed when he jumped off with his heavy burden. No one saw the corpse at the funeral, there being nothing but a log of wood in the box, to avert the townsfolks' suspicions.

TOUR — 12 m.

E. from State 140 on State 123 (Main St.)

1. *Wheaton College* is attractively placed on a campus of over 100 acres. It occupies 40 buildings, 15 of which are modern brick in the Georgian Colonial style of architecture, examples of restraint and usefulness, whose loveliness lies in their lines rather than in any external ornament. The extensive grounds include a beautiful strip of woods to the south, known as College Pines, and a body of water about two acres in extent. They are diversified by gardens, lawns, hedges, trees, and meadows, and contain athletic fields, concrete and clay tennis courts, and other equipment for outdoor sports.

> Among Wheaton College buildings are three designed by Cram and Ferguson. The *Chapel* (1917), the *Library* (1923), and *Everett Hall* (1926) are modern interpretations of Georgian Colonial style, in red New Hampshire brick with trim of limestone and white-painted wood. The architects are known also for their contemporary work based upon medieval precedent.

2. *House in the Pines*, a preparatory school for girls, was established in 1911, when Wheaton College was emerging from the old Wheaton Seminary and discontinuing its preparatory department. The school grounds, covering an area of 80 acres, have a great deal of natural beauty due to a variety of trees with pines predominating. Here are a beautiful outdoor theater with two old oaks and a hedge of pines; rose gardens; a lily pool surrounded by iris; Japanese cherry trees; the smoke bush, the lilacs, the lindens; and the arborvitae hedge that forms a screen for the athletic field. The school also has a string of saddle-horses.

R. from Main St. on Leonard St.; L. from Leonard St. on Plain St.

3. *King Philip's Cave*, near Becker's Farm on Great Rocky Hill, formed by the projection of one very large rock over another, is said to have been a favorite retreat of King Philip, on his fishing excursion to Winnicunnet Pond.

R. from Plain St. on Bay St.; L. from Bay St. on dirt road opposite Winnicunnet Pond.

4. *Winnicunnet Turkey Farm* (*open*), or the Rundge Turkey Farm, was formerly used for raising horses and was purchased from gypsies. It covers over 400 acres and is situated on Toad Island. Over 100,000 turkeys are raised annually. The flocks consume five tons of grain per day as food and rejoice in open-air roosts, on a triangular skeleton frame six feet high.

P I T T S F I E L D . *Power-Source and Playground*

City: Alt. 1038, pop. 47,516, sett. 1752, incorp. town 1761, city 1889.

Railroad Stations: Union Station, West St., for B. & A. R.R.

Bus Stations: 48 South St. for Greyhound, New England Transportation Co., Arrow, Interstate Busses Corp., Vermont Transit Lines, Berkshire Motor Coach Lines, Blue Way, Nutmeg Lines, and Peter Pan Bus Lines.

Accommodations: One first-class and three second-class hotels; numerous inns.

Information: Chamber of Commerce, 50 South St.; Automobile Club of Berkshire Co., 26 Bank Row.

IN THE shadow of Mount Greylock, high in the rolling Berkshires, Pittsfield opens the commercial gateway to western Massachusetts. Situated between the upper branches of the Housatonic River more than one thousand feet above sea level, the city is traversed by streams which for a hundred years or more have furnished power to factories producing such varied products as silk thread, mohair braid, tacks, metal goods, textiles, paper, and electrical machinery.

Today the city has a prosperous, tranquil look of general comfort and cultivation which makes it one of the most attractive industrial cities in the State. The homes of the well-to-do line its elm-shaded streets with substantial dignified residences and smooth lawns. From almost any point within the business and residential district there is a broad view of the rolling Berkshires, across the wide meadows and small lakes and elm-bordered streams of the plateau. The altitude of the city gives it a salubrious climate which makes it a favorite winter and summer playground for tourists and sportsmen.

There has been a change, however, in the character of the city's holiday population. In the latter part of the nineteenth century Pittsfield attracted a wealthy leisure class who resided solidly on spacious estates. The rambling old Maplewood Hotel, in the heart of the modern city, was a relic such as could not be matched short of Saratoga, with its long verandas and wide and spacious elm-shaded lawns, the latter dotted with seats, fountains, and urns.

But the great estates have been broken up into realty developments for smaller residences or business property, and the few that remain in the environs of Pittsfield have converted their stables into garages. The advent of the automobile has changed everything. The leisurely old-school ladies and gentlemen who once trotted sedately in victorias or runabouts along the city lanes are no more. Their modern successors now whirl in and out again in swift cars, and hotels, old and new, are conduits for a never-ending stream of summer and winter visitors. A great circle of the country round about is a motorists' paradise and Pittsfield is its hub. Nearly every owner of a car on the eastern seaboard and many from the Middle and the Far West at some time or other tour the Berkshires; and nearly everyone who visits the Berkshires calls at some time on Pittsfield.

The city's development from a small agricultural community to a thriving center of textile, paper, and electrical machinery manufacturing has paralleled the general development throughout the State. Its entire history is bound up with industrial progress.

Although Indian troubles and disputes with New York over the boundary of the State delayed its settlement until 1752, the plantation of Pontoosuck, as it was called, rapidly achieved agricultural prosperity and became a trading center for Berkshire communities. Two years later it had approximately two hundred inhabitants.

Pittsfield joined the eastern settlements in early protesting the domination of England. The town contained many wealthy Tories, but the majority of its citizens followed the Revolutionary leadership of Major John Brown and the Reverend Thomas Allen, the Fighting Parson, who mustered troops for the assault on Fort Ticonderoga led by his cousin, Ethan Allen. Heading the local Committee of Safety, this militant pastor organized the Berkshire Militia and led it to the Battle of Bennington. More than three months before the signing of the Declaration of Independence, Pittsfield renounced royal authority.

The little community, still predominantly agricultural, shared in the general depression which followed the Revolution; but while the farmers elsewhere were crushed by poverty, Pittsfield turned to industry. Although it seems certain that a majority of the townsfolk were in sympathy with the desperate rebellion of their neighbors under Daniel Shays in 1786, and although they treated the forty fellow citizens implicated in the rebellion with lenience, the hope of imminent prosperity deterred them from participating. Their hopes were justified: in 1801 Arthur Schofield, who had invented a wool-carding machine, opened a shop to manufacture his invention, and a few years later undertook the production of looms. The War of 1812 brought an abnormal demand for clothing and military supplies which definitely established the town as a manufacturing center. The consequent need for raw materials made sheep-raising an important affiliated industry. Later penetration by railroads connecting the town with New York and Boston made it the shipping distribution point for the whole district. Throughout the nineteenth century paper and shoes were among the most important products of its busy factories.

With the turn of the century came a change. The early isolation and independence fostered by Pittsfield's geographical situation were destroyed by an invasion of outside capital and a change of direction in its industrial activity. Pittsfield now began to change from a quiet self-insulated community to a unit integrated with the outer world and seething with business. Its population grew faster during the first decade of the new century than that of any Massachusetts city except New Bedford. This increase — no less than forty-seven per cent — created a serious housing problem which in turn attracted other outside capital. This was directed to housing construction and realty developments. The Tillotson Textile Plant; the General Electric Company; Eaton, Crane and Pike Company, famous manufacturers of stationery; foundries producing machinery for the textile and paper factories — all these and others contributed to make the development of Pittsfield a microcosm of what was going on in the entire country.

FOOT TOUR — 2.7 m.

E. from South St. on Bank Row.

1. In *City Hall Park*, the original village Green, was held in 1810 what is said to be the first cattle show in America. A marker memorializes that event, which was sponsored by Elkanan Watson, a famous patriot, friend of Washington, traveler, canal surveyor, biographer, and breeder of livestock. Watson stimulated the importation of merino sheep for

the textile mills of Pittsfield and encouraged agricultural improvement throughout New England.

A sundial marks the *Site of the Old Elm* beneath whose lofty branches stood such famous men as Holmes, Longfellow, Hawthorne, Melville, and Lafayette. On this spot soldiers of all wars were mustered and honored; old taverns and stores faced it on all sides, and historic houses, too. Here were held the Fourth of July celebrations, the cattle shows, and all the country gala days.

In 1790, when the destruction of the elm was planned to make way for a new meeting-house, Lucretia Williams, wife of a prominent lawyer in Pittsfield, stood guard over the tree, placing herself in front of it when the woodchopper came to cut it down. John Chandler Williams, whose former homestead, the Peace Party House, stands near-by, gave land to the town so that the park might remain an open space forever and the old elm be saved.

Such was the veneration in which the old elm was held by some of the citizens of Pittsfield that when at the age of 265 years, after being struck by lightning several times, it was so damaged that the axe had to be applied, there was actual weeping among those who witnessed its fall.

2. The *Berkshire Athenaeum* (*open weekdays* 9–9), 44 Bank Row, a Victorian Gothic structure of gray granite, has been noted as a public library and art repository for many years.

R. from Bank Row on East St.

3. The *Peace Party House* (*private*), southeast corner of Wendell Ave., erected in 1776, was the scene of a grand ball and feast in celebration of the signing of the Treaty of Paris in 1783. The Marquis de Lafayette was a guest here while on his tour in 1825. Though considerably altered, this white, three-story house, clapboarded, and gambrel roofed, still retains much of its original dignity.

Retrace on East St.

4. *St. Stephen's Episcopal Church*, next to the Parsonage Lot, is constructed of red granite in the Gothic manner.

R. from East St. on North St.

5. The *Old Cantonment Grounds*, opposite Linden St., were used during the War of 1812. The war brought to Pittsfield the manufacture of cloth, guns, and drums.

5a. The *Bulfinch Church* (1793), now in process of restoration for use by the New Thought Center, is located on Maplewood Ave., 0.1 *m.* east of North St.

Retrace North St.; R. from North St. on West St.

6. In *Crane Memorial Park*, in front of the Union Station, is a Marker in memory of the late Zenas Crane, a noted philanthropist.

Retrace West St.; R. from West St. on South St.

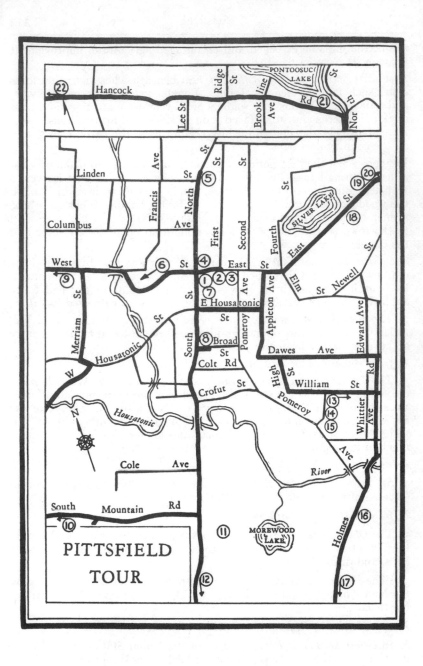

PITTSFIELD
TOUR

7. *Museum of Natural History and Art* (*open weekdays* 10–5; *Sun. and holidays* 2–5), 39 South St., is an adaptation of the Italian Renaissance style. The 'mineral room' is one of the most beautiful in the country. Ultra-violet rays are used to bring out the beauties of the collection.

Among the outstanding exhibits are: one of the two sledges used by Admiral Robert E. Peary when he discovered the North Pole, Nathaniel Hawthorne's desk, and (miraculously reconstructed?) the original 'one-hoss shay' which inspired Oliver Wendell Holmes's 'The Deacon's Masterpiece.' The art collection includes fine examples of the works of old masters and some excellent original Greek and Roman sculptures.

L. from South St. on Broad St.

8. The *Calvin Martin House* (*private*), 14 Broad St., removed here from its original site to make way for the Berkshire Museum, is a two-story frame building painted yellow with two inner chimneys. It is enriched by fluted Ionic pilasters and an elaborate cornice.

MOTOR TOUR — 32.5 *m.*

(Note: The Pittsfield Tour Map provides the tourist the means of covering this tour in smaller units)

W. from City Hall Park on West St.

9. *Fort Hill*, near Lake Onota, is the site of Fort Ashley, one of four early Colonial forts in Pittsfield. During the French and Indian wars there was a considerable settlement around the block-house, including many wigwams of friendly Indians.

The view of Lake Onota and the mountains beyond it, from this high point, is one of the most beautiful to be found in the Berkshire Hills country. The long sweep of the lake to the north draws the eye to the distant majestic height of Mt. Greylock almost 20 miles away.

PITTSFIELD MAP INDEX

Onota in the Indian language means 'Lake of the White Deer.' Legend relates that a pure albino doe used to come here to drink. No Indian's bow was ever drawn on her, for it was believed that she brought good luck to the valley. Should she be harmed, the pow-wows warned, disaster would befall the tribe. During the French and Indian wars a young French officer, hearing of the superstition, boasted that he would kill the white deer. He bribed an unsuspecting member of the tribe to show him the doe's watering-place, where he hid in ambush and made good his boast. The prophecy also was made good, however: the Frenchman met his death while trying to escape to Canada; the crops of the tribe failed and their prosperity waned, a plague came upon them, and they slowly dwindled away.

Retrace West St.; R. from West St. on Merriam St.; L. from Merriam St. on Woodleigh Ave.; R. from Woodleigh Ave. on West Housatonic St.; L. from West Housatonic St. on Barker Rd.; L. from Barker Rd. on South Mountain Rd.

10. *Walton Wild Acres Sanctuary* (*open to picnic parties; small fee*) is a tract of 83 acres of well-wooded land, established in 1929 as a bird and game sanctuary. The Izaak Walton League made it a semi-public recreation area, stocked the ponds with trout, built fireplaces and an outdoor pavilion, cleared away the underbrush, established trap-shooting ranges, and constructed a dam to enlarge Lake Holman.

R. from South Mountain Rd. on South St.

11. The *Pittsfield Country Club* (*open by invitation*), an 18-hole course, occupies a mansion known as Broad Hall, erected by Henry Van Schaack in 1785 and at one time owned by an uncle of Herman Melville. The cellar is said to have been one of the depots for the Underground Railroad. At the northeast corner of the club is Morewood Lake, sometimes known as Melville Lake, and called by Longfellow 'The Tear of Heaven.'

12. *South Mountain* (alt. 1870), is the highest point of land in Pittsfield, lying near the Lenox Line at the south end of the city and rising west of US 7 and US 20, just beyond the Pittsfield Country Club. A favorite resort for hikers, the mountain offers a view of the entire city. It is now largely owned by the Coolidge family, a member of which, Mrs. Elizabeth Sprague Coolidge, founder of the South Mountain Music Colony and Temple, sponsors a series of chamber music concerts given every Sunday during the summer months.

Retrace South St.; R. from South St. on East Housatonic St.; R. from East Housatonic St. on Appleton Ave.; L. from Appleton Ave. on Dawes Ave.; R. from Dawes Ave. on High St.; L. from High St. on William St.

13. The *Brattle House* (*open during summer; small fee for benefit of the National Memorial Foundation for army and navy memorial aid*), near Elm St., built in 1762, and now owned by a descendant of its builder, is the oldest house in Pittsfield, and is furnished with antiques of its period. It is set on a knoll surrounded by an apple orchard and ancient beech trees. It is a three-story red clapboarded, gambrel-roofed dwelling with an overhanging second story.

Straight ahead from William St. on Elm St.

14. *Wells's Tavern* (*private*), 847 Elm St., was one of several such places

of resort on the old stagecoach route to Springfield. It is a white clapboarded, two-story, hip-roofed house with a series of additions in the
rear. The old woodshed is a copy of the first frame house in Pittsfield.
The tavern contains portions of the original house, built by Solomon
Deming, the first white settler who came in on horseback through the
wilderness from Wethersfield, Connecticut, in the spring of 1752, bringing his wife, Sarah, on a pillion behind him.

15. The *Grave of Sarah Deming* (R), just inside the gate of the Old
East Park Cemetery, is indicated by a neat marble obelisk erected by
the city to its pioneer housewife.

Retrace Elm St.; L. from Elm St. on Holmes Rd.

16. *Holmesdale (private)*, just beyond junction with Pomeroy Ave., is
the former residence of Oliver Wendell Holmes. Here the physician
and poet spent seven seasons and wrote 'The Deacon's Masterpiece,'
'The New Eden,' and 'The Ploughman' on local themes. His favorite
refuge was the arbor formed by the low-hanging branches of a white
pine tree on a small knoll on the lawn. Only a glimpse of the house and
the famous *Holmes Pine* can be had from the road. Holmes did some of
his work in a little house on the hill across the road, now occupied by
Miss Hall's School for Girls.

17. *Arrowhead (private)*, a mile farther on Holmes Rd. at the top of the
hill, was the home of Herman Melville, where he wrote 'Moby Dick,'
'My Chimney and I,' 'Piazza Tales,' and 'October Mountain.'

*Retrace Holmes Rd.; L. from Holmes Rd. on Dawes Ave.; R. from Dawes
Ave. on Appleton Ave.; R. from Appleton Ave. on East St.*

18. The *General Electric Plant (open to visitors scientifically interested;
guide)* is fascinating to visit. The alternating current transformer invented by the late William Stanley was developed at the Pittsfield
Works of the General Electric Company. Recently, huge transformers for
Boulder Dam were constructed here.

Important electrical research is done here, requiring the services of internationally distinguished technicians and scientists. The most picturesque
feature of this research for the general public is the occasional display
of 'artificial lightning,' a series of huge blinding flashes occasioned by
testing the ability of electrical current to jump a long distance through
the air from two or more high steel towers unconnected by wire.

There were in 1890 about 1500 power stations throughout the country
operating on the alternating current system, with only two companies
producing the machines. The Stanley Electrical Manufacturing Company of Pittsfield was organized in 1907 into a corporation to supply
these stations first with transformers and later with generators, switch-
boards, and motors. The rapid growth of this corporation, which erected
a new plant in 1912 employing one sixth of Pittsfield's population, became a strain on the city's limited supply of capital, and threats of its
withdrawal from Pittsfield were a constant source of apprehension.

This disaster seemed imminent when, in 1930, the corporation was absorbed by the General Electric Company. The latter, however, to the great relief of the city, immediately announced that it had no intention of moving the plant away. On the contrary the bringing in of a new and practically unlimited supply of capital foreshadowed continued expansion.

L. from East St. on Merrill Rd.

19. The *Canoe Meadows* at Umkamet's Crossing, near the railroad bridge over the Housatonic River, were the site of an Indian fort and landing place for the Red Men in the ancient days when they came to visit the burial mounds of their ancestors — now obliterated by the march of progress and the overflow of the rivers.

R. from Merrill Rd. on Dalton Ave.

20. The *Government Mill* (*private*) is a branch of Crane & Co. of Dalton, manufacturers of paper for currency and United States bonds.

Retrace Dalton Ave.; R. from Dalton Ave. on Crane Ave.; R. from Crane Ave. on North St.

To the south from the crest of the hill on North St., a bird's-eye view of the entire city may be had. On the far side may be seen the *Bosquet Ski Run* (*small fee*), distinguishable in summer by the broad, bare swath curving down from the opposite mountain-top through the woods that clothe its slope.

L. from North St. on Hancock Rd.

21. *Pontoosuc Lake Park* (*picnicking grounds, public bathing; boats and fishing equipment for hire*), with its splendid white pines, is on the banks of Pontoosuc Lake, an Indian name meaning 'Place of Winter Deer.' Legend says that an Indian brave, while paddling across the lake to meet his sweetheart, was slain by a jealous suitor. The distracted maiden flung herself into the lake, following her lover to his watery grave. Even today, it is said, a spectral canoe with a shadowy paddler is sometimes seen to glide over the lake at midnight, darting from point to point. It is the frenzied lover searching for, but never finding, the drowned form of his betrothed.

L. from Hancock Rd. on Churchill St.; R. from Churchill St. on Shamrock Blvd.

22. The *Pittsfield State Forest* (*camping and picnicking*), covering 2127 acres, lies partly in Hancock and partly in Lanesborough. Several foot trails lead about the Forest, while the *Skyline Trail*, in process of being built, follows an ancient Indian hunting path along the crest of the Taconics, north to south. *Ghost Trail* and *Honwee Trail*, two ski trails, were recently constructed by the Civilian Conservation Corps, and plans are under way to provide facilities for all winter sports.

At the entrance to the camp area of the Civilian Conservation Corps is *Goodrich Cave*, forgotten for 40 years, its entrance blocked by boulders and a wash of sand and gravel. It was rediscovered by a worker on the 'Massachusetts Guide' and reopened, disclosing a large chamber beneath a shelf of limestone. Here, according to old inhabitants, a band of lawless youths used to hide for weeks, subsisting by raids on near-by farms, and making counterfeit half-dollars from stolen spoons, lead pipes, and quicksilver in a handmade mould.

Near-by is *Lulu Cascade*, a pretty fall of water on Lulu Brook.

High above the Cascades, on Honwee Mountain, is *Berry Pond*, the highest natural body of water in Massachusetts. Not far distant is a majestic view of the New York Taconics rising in the west with the Catskill Mountains on the horizon. The pond is the source of a brook which flows down the west side of the mountain through Goodrich Hollow, a secluded and lovely vale. Here, in May, are woods pink and white with mountain laurel; in June come the red and white azaleas; the deep wine-colored velvet of the September sumach is a color-theme for the gorgeous orchestration of later autumn.

P L Y M O U T H . *The Colony's First 'Main Street'*

Town: Alt. 29, pop. 13,183, sett. and incorp. 1620.

Railroad Station: Park Ave. for N.Y., N.II. & II. R.R.
Bus Station: Park Ave. for New England Transportation Co.

Accommodations: One hotel all year round; three during summer months; tourist houses.

Annual Events: Pilgrim's Progress; every Friday in August, march of Pilgrim descendants.

Information: Chamber of Commerce, Leyden St., opposite Post Office.

PLYMOUTH, its white beaches stretching for eighteen miles along the inner shore of Massachusetts Bay, is known as one of New England's famous shrines. Here the 'South Shore' is dotted with summer homes. Inland hummocky hills of tumbled pines are dotted with ponds and brooks running into Plymouth Harbor or Buzzard's Bay. Here, too, are bird sanctuaries and game preserves, the Myles Standish Forest, and the Town Forest. Erosion of the outer slopes of its coastal hills has left the boulders and bluffs of Manomet and lagoons and beaches of glistening white sand set against the sparkling blue sea.

Plymouth's main street is now a thoroughfare, bustling with shops and commerce as befits the county seat, but in many other ways, as a delightful bit of old New England, the town remains the same. (Even as late as 1840, Christmas, banned by the Pilgrim Fathers, was not observed. Newcomers who put wreaths in their windows were commented upon and called ''piscopals.') Ancient houses, few of them remodeled or modernized, line the ancient streets of the center, setting a tone which triumphs still over the outlying modern residential areas; and the old Pilgrim stock, though now in the minority, still dominates the community.

After the Civil War, the rise of manufacturing brought an influx of immigrants — German, French, Italian, and Portuguese — who now make up a quarter of the town. Today, with thirteen thousand people, the town has a score of mills, small factories, and ropeworks. As there is little good top soil, farming has not flourished, except poultry-raising, dairy farming, fancy stock breeding, and cranberry culture.

In the year 1620, the 'Mayflower,' bound for Virginia, was blown far north of her course and cast among the roaring breakers and dangerous shoals of Cape Cod. It anchored in what today is Provincetown Harbor, and finding that terrain unfriendly, about a month later the Pilgrims set sail for the mainland. They were tossed about by a storm and nearly wrecked, but at nightfall they landed on an island in Plymouth Harbor.

On December 21 (new style calendar), 1620, with seventeen men, occurred the 'Landing of the Pilgrims' at their first settlement. The legends surrounding the landing are picturesque, but seem to have little basis in substantiated fact.

The majority of the Pilgrims, indeed, remained aboard ship for the better part of a month until shelters could be erected ashore. Snow covered the decks of the vessel; exposure and insanitation increased, and sickness grew apace. Scurvy and ship fever raged, and juniper was burned aboard to dispel the noisome smells of death. Sometimes two or three died in a single day. By March nearly half the company was dead.

There was never actual starvation, for berries, wild fowl, and shellfish abounded; but great disaster befell the little community in their second year when the ship 'Fortune,' carrying over their entire yield of furs and produce, was captured by the French as a prize.

Early difficulties were not all material; the more important ones were spiritual. To the horror of the community, it was discovered that Lyford, their pastor, had been exiled from England as unfit for the ministry.

'The circumstances,' writes the good Governor Bradford, 'I forbear, for they would offend chaste ears to hear them related.'

Moreover, Lyford, along with one Oldham, was soon convicted at court of writing 'slanderous letters,' disparaging the Colony and the country. This gave great pain to the London Adventurers, who, to increase their revenues, depended on finding persons in England willing to go as colonists. Lyman and Oldham were exiled; Oldham, returning, was again deported, in the manner Thomas Morton recounts:

His exile was arranged after a solomne invention in this manner. A lane of mus-keteers was made and hee compelled in scorne to passe along betweene, and to receave a bob upon the bumme by every musketier. And then aboard a shallop and so conveyed to Wessaguscus shore.

Lyford was succeeded by 'one Mr. Rogers a young man for minister,' who within twelve months 'proving crazied in his brain, they were forced to be at further charge in sending him back after losing all the cost expended in bringing him over which was not small.'

Finally, the congregation secured the services of one Reverend Smith, a pastor who had been discarded by the Salem Colony; though it is related that he too was of odd temperament, even supposed by some to be insane.

Now Thomas Morton, a companion of Captain Wollaston, set up a rival trading colony near-by at what is now Wollaston, in Quincy. The staid Pilgrims were duly horrified by the 'Merrymount' revels, but Morton flourished in his wickedness like the green bay tree. He sold rum and guns; and with these to be got in exchange for their furs, the Indians practically refused to take any amount of the Plymouth wampum and trinkets. At last, however, Miles Standish proceeded to Merrymount, seized Morton prisoner, and deported him to England.

In spite of all such zeal, by 1642 the piety among the 'Pure and Un-spottyd Lambs of the Lord' of Plymouth seemed at a low ebb, and severe measures were taken to combat the powers of evil. For nearly fifty years there were but forty-eight freemen, all of whom had to be church members. They controlled all the affairs of the town, and it would have been hardly human if occasionally piety had not been made the handmaid of profit.

At the end of a century after the landing, Plymouth had a population of two thousand, comfortably supported by agriculture, navigation, and commerce. Already, too, settlers from the mother town had founded or were founding other prosperous communities in the environs, extending as far as Eastham on Cape Cod and the present city of Fall River near the Rhode Island Line. Whale-fishing, begun about 1690 and abandoned about 1840, occupied many of these daughter towns, notably Wareham and the Cape Cod towns.

By the turn of the nineteenth century, stagecoaches ran from Boston to Plymouth, and thence in various directions. Alongside the wharves were seventy-six ships, brigs, and schooners. By 1830 the population was nearly five thousand. A hundred ships engaged in coastwise trade and fishing, especially for cod and mackerel. Four vessels went whaling. The town had forty ships, five iron mills, two cotton mills, and three ropeworks. Among these was the Plymouth Cordage Company, which today is one of the largest in the world.

Honor was brought to the town by one of its most distinguished citizens, Dr. Charles Jackson, who was awarded twenty-five hundred francs by the French Academy of Science as the co-discoverer of etherization.

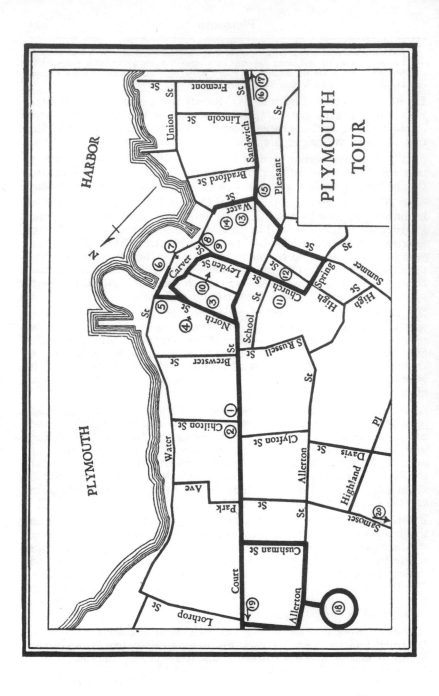

FOOT TOUR — 2.5 m.

NW. from Town Square on Main St.; straight ahead on Court St. (State 3).

1. The *Tabitha Plasket House* (*home of one of the earliest schools*) is located adjacent to Pilgrim Hall. It is said to have been built by Consider Howland, grandson of John Howland in 1722, but it has the appearance of having been built at a much later date — possibly 50 years. It is a large two-story white frame house, early Colonial, with four chimneys. Much of it is still intact, including the wide floor boards and H and L type hinges.

2. *Pilgrim Hall* (*open weekdays* 9–5, *Sun.* 12–5, *April–Nov.*), on the corner of Chilton St., is a granite building in the Greek revival style, dedicated to the memory of the Pilgrims. Erected in 1824, it has since been enlarged, and its Doric portico re-erected from plans by McKim, Mead and White. At the east end of the Hall is the famous painting 'The Landing of the Pilgrims' by Henry Sargent. On the north wall is the original of Robert F. Weir's 'Embarkation of the Pilgrims from Delft Haven.' From this study Weir produced the larger painting for the Capitol rotunda in Washington. Among historical articles in the Hall are: the patent of Plymouth Colony; the chairs of Elder Brewster and Governor Carver; the Peregrine White cradle, in which slept the first white child born in Massachusetts; the Bible of Governor Bradford, printed in Geneva in 1592.

Retrace Court St.; L. from Court St. on North St.

3. The *Lindens*, in front of the Public Library, were imported and planted in 1760 by Colonel George Watson.

4. The *Edward Winslow House* (*private*), on the corner of Winslow St., was built in 1754 by Edward Winslow, great-grandson of Governor Edward Winslow of the 'Mayflower' company, and brother of General John Winslow. Little is left of the original house, which in the 1890's was enlarged to manorial proportions with a formal garden added.

PLYMOUTH MAP INDEX

5. The *Pilgrim Mother Fountain*, at the corner of Water St., was erected as a tribute to the Pilgrim mothers, historically so much less vocal than the fathers, but certainly quite as deserving of admiration.

R. from North St. on Water St.

6. *Plymouth Rock*, with the date 1620 carved upon it, reposes under a magnificent granite portico of classical design. Two thirds of the rock is underground, and an iron fence protects the remainder from souvenir chippers. Historians have for the most part exploded the landing myth, but popular sentiment clings to the long-hallowed stepping-stone.

Retrace Water St.; L. from Water St. on North St.; L. from North St. on Carver St.

7. *Cole's Hill* was the scene of the secret night burials of those who died during the first year of the settlement. Corn was planted over their graves so that the Indians should not know how many of their number had perished. A sculptured sarcophagus now contains many of the exhumed bones. An imposing *Statue of Massasoit*, the Pilgrims' friend, crowns the hill.

R. from Carver St. on Leyden St.

8. The first houses erected by the Pilgrims stood on 'First St.' — now *Leyden St.* 'The Meersteads and Garden Plots' allotted to the early settlers, and on which the houses were built, sloped thence to the Town Brook — the 'very Sweet brook mentioned by the first explorers.'

9. Opposite the end of Carver St. is the *Site of the First 'Common House*,' marked by tablet. It was used as a shelter by the Pilgrims on their frequent trips to and from the 'Mayflower' before it sailed on the return voyage to England, April 15, 1621. Later it was used as a storehouse. In that house on February 27, 1621, the right of popular suffrage was exercised and Miles Standish was chosen Captain by popular vote.

10. The *House of the Rev. Nathaniel Leonard* (1734) (*private*), across from the Common House site, is an early white house with a rainbow roof.

Straight ahead into Town Square and Church St.

11. *Burial Hill* (*at head of Town Sq.*) was long used both as a place of defense and as a place of worship. On its summit are the sites of the *Watch-Tower* and *Old Fort*. The site of the *Old Powder House* on Burial Hill is marked by a small round brick house claimed to be a replica of the original.

12. The *Sites of Some of the First Houses* built in 1621 are along the south side of this square. These houses were started as common property but were finished by the people who were to occupy them: the Allertons, Winslows, Cookes, and others.

12a. The *Richard Sparrow House* (1640) (*open; adm. 25¢*), Summer St., corner of Spring St., is a restored house with red clapboards and shingles and early English diamond-shaped windows.

S. from Town Sq. on Market St.; R. from Market St. on Sandwich St.; L. from Sandwich St. on Water St.

13. *Brewster Gardens* provide a pleasant setting for the *Statue of the Pilgrim Maid*, dedicated to 'those intrepid English women whose courage and fortitude brought a new nation into being.' In Brewster Gardens are also the *Ship Anne Memorial* and the *Pilgrim Spring*, the latter a delightful spot to visit.

14. The *Antiquarian House* (*open weekdays* 10–5, *Sun.* 2–5; *closed in winter*), 126 Water St., was built in 1809, and is completely furnished in its period. The kitchen has century-old cookbooks, a children's playroom has old-fashioned dolls and toys, and there is an old-fashioned garden.

Retrace Water St.; L. from Water St. on Sandwich St.

15. The *John Howland House* (1666) (*open daily; adm.* 25¢) is opposite the southwesterly end of Water St. This two-and-a-half-story structure, painted red, with hip roof and central chimney, was restored in 1913.

16. The *William Harlow House* (*open summer, weekdays* 9–6, *Sun.* 2–5; *adm.* 25¢), 119 Sandwich St., was built in 1677 of timber taken from the Old Fort on Burial Hill. It is solidly constructed and clings close to the crest of a knoll; the smooth lines of the low gambrel roof melt into the slope of the ground from which it seems to have sprung. Overshadowing it is an ancient tree that was only a seedling when the house was already old. Recently this house has been acquired and authentically furnished in its own period by the Plymouth Antiquarian Society, which during the summer months keeps open house at the Harlow House and re-enacts the early domestic life of the Pilgrims. Flax grown in the garden at the rear of the house is harvested and prepared for spinning. Corn is planted by the school-children, who, following the old custom, place a herring in each hill.

L. from Sandwich St. into Winter St.

17. The *Kendall Holmes House* (*open, free*), Winter St., was built by William Harlow in 1666. It has been little changed. The old stairway and rooms on the lower floor as well as the chambers above preserve the original plan. There are open fireplaces and an old oven, and a great central chimney.

POINTS OF INTEREST IN THE ENVIRONS

18. The *National Monument to the Forefathers* is an immense and impressive memorial. The principal figure represents Faith, hand pointing to Heaven. At the base are four wings representing Morality, Law, Education, and Freedom. On the face of each wing are slabs of marble carved in bold relief to depict: the *Departure from Delft Haven*, the *Signing of the Compact*, the *Landing of the Pilgrims*, and the *Treaty with Massasoit*.

19. The *William Crowe House* (*not open*), about 3 miles north from the center, is claimed to be the oldest house in Plymouth, the rear portion dating to 1664. It is a two-story white house of early American design and typical Colonial simplicity.

20. The *Myles Standish State Forest* (8000 acres), one of the oldest in the State, was established in 1916 under the State Forest Commission. Picnic and camping areas (*small fee*), with individual fireplaces and tables, are open to the public on College, Charge, and Fearing Ponds.

P R O V I N C E T O W N . *Way Up Along*

Town: Alt. 11, pop. 4071, sett. shortly before 1700, incorp. 1727.

Railroad Station: N.Y., N.H. & H. R.R., Bradford St., east of Pilgrim Monument.

Bus Station: Same.

Piers: Town Wharf, Bay State S.S. Co., Monument Wharf, Commercial St., west of Town Wharf, Cape Cod S.S. Co. *Steel Pier.*

Local Bus: Busses run, Commercial St., length of town, supposedly every 20 minutes in summer time, fare 5¢, 25¢ sightseeing; no winter service.

Accommodations: Hotels and tourist homes. All rates higher in summer.

Swimming: All beaches private on Bay Side within limits of village center; public outside these limits.

HERE, where Cape Cod goes down to the sea with a last flourish of sandy beachland, nestles the best known and perhaps the most colorful of its old villages, Provincetown.

On the Cape, travelers have observed, 'They call a house a house, but a house with a shed is a village.' Provincetown, compact neighborhood of Portuguese fishermen, of artists and writers, and of old Yankee families, is by comparison a city. And its career from Old Colony days has had a touch of urbanity that sets it apart from its neighbor towns. Of interest historically as the first landing-place of the Pilgrims, the town has also been a center of whaling, an important fishing port, and in modern times the location of a famous art colony.

Much of the ancient flavor of Provincetown has been saved, especially in the old houses, the prim white cottages and staid Colonials that line its narrow streets, and in the bright gardens, the wharves, fish-sheds and vessels that still carry on with net and trawl.

The village is 'only two streets wide,' but for nearly four miles it skirts

the inner shore of the Cape; and from there out, Long Point extends like
a sandy finger crooked around the harbor. Here, at Long Point, is the
tip of Cape Cod, punctuated with a lighthouse. The remainder of the
township — broad dunelands reaching 'up-back' to the outer or Atlantic
shore — is called the Province Lands, and is owned by the Commonwealth.

The visitor who drives down the 122 miles from Boston, including the
65 miles on US 6 from the Cape Cod Canal, is well out to sea when he
reaches Provincetown — 55 miles from 'the mainland,' on a sandspit
where bedrock has never been found. Geologists say Provincetown
owes its very underpinnings to the sea, having been left here as Father
Neptune's own personal sandpile 30,000 years ago.

If so, the town has been acknowledging its debt ever since. Province-
towners say their village covers the waterfront — when the waterfront
is not covering it. 'The good God,' wrote Cotton Mather, after a visit
here, 'gives this people to suck of the abundance of the seas.' But the
seas, one might add, have been playing the town for a sucker from the
start — invading it, battering its stone breakwaters, sneaking up on it
to deliver a smashing southeaster against the bulkheads along its waterfront, in a hundred ways plotting to collect that 30,000-year debt. Sand,
wind, and tide are accessories before the fact, ever conspiring to fold
the dunes over upon the little village, to drive it into its own harbor.

Historically, Provincetown has had an ancient crow to pick with Plymouth.

'Plymouth Rock? That's the name of a chicken,' the proud old Cape
Cod Yankee will snort. 'The spot where the "Mayflower" people first
stepped on American soil is right here in Provincetown, and you ought
to freeze on to that fact in your guide book, for it's been rising three
hundred years now, and most off-Cape folks don't seem to know it yet!'
After falling 'amongst deangerous shoulds and roring breakers' off what
is now Chatham, the 'Mayflower' did indeed drop anchor in 'ye Cape-
harbor [Provincetown] wher they ridd in saftie,' November 11, 1620.
That same day the first party of Pilgrims came ashore in America, and
the ship lay at anchor five weeks here before her people decided to try
settlement at Plymouth.

Provincetown has placed a stone marker where those men climbed out
of their shallop, waded across the icy flats and 'fell upon their knees
& blessed ye God of heaven, who had brought them over ye vast &
furious ocean.' It has scattered other markers around too, to remind
the nation that the Pilgrims came here — *first*. There is even a great
stone tower for that purpose. And yet, Provincetown still has to tell
Americans from points west of the Cape Cod Canal that the 'stern and
rockbound coast,' across the Bay in Plymouth, was merely an after-
thought of the 'Mayflower' company! Provincetown has a great stone
tower. Plymouth has a poem.

Historians believe that before the Pilgrims came, Basques and other daring fishermen visited these shores; and there has long been the theory, without tangible support, that it was to Cape Cod the Norsemen sailed in their voyages of the early eleventh century. Gosnold, who sailed around the Cape in 1602, named the tip-end Cape Cod. Other explorers gave it other names, but 'Cape Cod' had clicked, and as Mather wrote, it is a name the Cape will never lose 'till the shoals of codfish be seen swimming on the highest hills.'

For nearly a century after the Pilgrims left, Provincetown drew a strange assortment of transients. The Indians — Pamets, of the tribe of Wampanoags — came here often, but had no permanent settlement. Provincetown was thus a sort of aboriginal Coney Island, where they gambled and drank with visiting fishermen. One imaginative historian writes of their 'bacchanalian carousals, which were continued sometimes for weeks with unrestrained license.'

In 1714 'the Province Town' was put under the jurisdiction of Truro, as a precinct. But pious, respectable Truro wanted no part of it, and after a long campaign, the horrified goodmen of that town succeeded in getting rid of the 'Poker Flats of Cape Cod,' as historian Shebnah Rich terms it. Provincetown was thus incorporated in 1727.

Deepwater whaling began at about that time, and the fleet grew rapidly. Provincetown and Truro took the lead. The whalemen and the Banks fishermen gave the Lower Cape a fair start toward prosperity in the latter half of the eighteenth century. At the same time the business of 'wrecking' was pursued with uncommon diligence.

Mooncussing and beachcombing — now synonyms meaning recovery of goods from the beach, chiefly cargoes drifting ashore from wrecked ships — were wreckers' work. This was a recognized means of livelihood — certainly recognized by the good citizens of 'Helltown,' as part of Provincetown came to be called, if not by the law. The legend of false lights hung out on moonless nights to lure unwary mariners of those days persists in the Cape's oral traditions. Rum-running and other smuggling were facilitated by long, deserted beaches, hidden from the village by the dunes.

About 1800 the Cape began making salt by evaporating sea water, and this discovery gave the fishery a new impetus. Provincetown became more prosperous and somewhat more respectable. A settlement grew up on Long Point itself, to be nearer the fishing. In lieu of lawns these people had patches of seaweed at their front doors, and children were cautioned against crossing the road at high tide.

Shortly before the Civil War the people at Long Point moved across-harbor to the main part of town. They loaded their houses, stores, church, and schoolhouse on scows and casks, and poled them across. The only structure one sees on the Point today is the lighthouse.

Fishing went on, however, and expanded, reaching a peak in the last quarter of the nineteenth century. A reporter for the *Chicago Tribune* visited the town in 1900, and wrote back, 'Fish is bartered at the grocery stores, shoe shops and bread stores for all the commodities of life.... The main business street is paved with rock cod. The women use the hind fin of the great halibut for brooms. Awnings shading the store fronts are made from the skin of the sportive porpoise. The bellrope in the church is made of eels, cunningly knotted by some old sailor. Over the altar was the picture of a whale. The collection plate was the top shell of a turtle. After the choir had sung "Pull for the Shore," the crew passed down the port aisle. Provincetown ladies trim their hats with red gills of the mackerel. Dog-fish often lie around the shore at low tide and bark and howl in a frightful manner.'

However, in the yellowed scrapbook in which this clipping was found, in Provincetown, is a notation by its one-time owner, 'A damned liar's description of Provincetown.'

Provincetown is still essentially a fishing village, and the majority of its people are fishermen and their families. They fish aboard the trawlers, the draggers, seiners and trapboats, and they work in the 'freezers' — fish-packing plants, of which there are five.

The industry, however, is long past its heyday, and many an old skipper who once hung out his sidelights and stood out for the Banks now hangs out a sign on his porch — 'Tourists Accommodated' — and sits down to wait for the summer people.

Beyond the first of June, they do not keep him waiting long. Artists at their easels begin to dot the wayside — and block the traffic; clicking typewriters join the nightly chorus of the crickets; and poets chirp from studio attics at all hours. These are Provincetown's trusty perennials — the yearly flowering of its 'art colony,' which, for all the confusion, has nevertheless produced many of the nation's foremost painters, playwrights, novelists and poets.

The founding of the Cape Cod School of Art here in 1901 by Charles W. Hawthorne was the real beginning of the art colony, though a few painters had visited the town before that. Hawthorne's own pictures of the Portuguese fisherpeople did much to build up the colony's prestige. Since his death in 1930, other schools have carried on, and the Provincetown Art Association's annual exhibit is an event of widespread interest.

Prominent painters who have been associated with the colony include, besides Hawthorne, Arthur Diehl, Heinrich Pfeiffer, Edwin W. Dickinson, Ross Moffett, Frederick Waugh, George Elmer Browne, Richard Miller, John Noble, Mrs. Max Bohm, John Frazier, Gerrit A. Beneker, Hans Hoffman, Jack Beauchamp, Karl Knaths, W. H. W. Bicknell, William Paxton, Tod Lindenmuth, John Whorf, Henry Hensche, Jerry Farnsworth, and Charles J. Martin. Among sculptors here have been William Zorach and William F. Boogar, Jr.

In 1915 the Provincetown Players gathered under the leadership of George Cram Cook. They later took a theater in New York City, where they carried on until 1922. Drama on Broadway, at the time they set themselves up, was stilted and heavily encrusted with outgrown traditions. The Players broke away from the timeworn formulae, offering plays with a fresh outlook, a new simplicity of method. The pioneering work done at that time has had a lasting influence, and has made the organization long remembered.

Among writers and dramatists who have lived in Provincetown are John Dos Passos, Susan Glaspell, Mary Heaton Vorse, Edmond Wilson, Harry Kemp, Frank Shay, George Cram Cook, Wilbur Daniel Steele, Max Eastman, and two winners of the Nobel Prize for literature, Eugene O'Neill and Sinclair Lewis.

Many of the artists and writers of reputation return each summer, and with them come large numbers of young unknowns. But to the old skipper of Provincetown who has retired from the sea and hung out his tourist sign, these are merely the forerunners of an even greater throng — the summer vacationers. By July 1 all is in full swing — the painters painting, the writers writing, tourists buying, and the traffic policemen perspiring.

On Labor Day the season ends. The Boston steamers whistle a last farewell, the 'accommodation' (street bus) is converted back into a fish truck, the dealer in 'Antiques' turns his sign around, the landlady cleans the cigarette butts out of the potted plant, and Provincetown settles down again to a 'nice quiet winter.'

'Summer people' are estimated at about 8000. Of the 4000 'year-round people,' at least three fourths are Portuguese — 'Azoreans' (from the Azores), 'Lisbons' (from the mother country), and a scattering of 'Bravas' (descendants of Cape Verde islanders who came over in the whaling days). The other 1000 are principally the 'old Yankee stock,' who have lost the town, politically, to the Portuguese; who deplore the influx of the 'off-Cape furriners'; and to whom a volume of genealogy is a piece of escape literature.

The Provincetown sea-food cuisine is justly famous. In these kitchens few fish are allowed to enter their third day ashore. The world knows many ways to cook a fish, and Provincetown claims to know an improvement on every one. To conventional recipes are added many methods of the Portuguese; and sea cooks have contributed their best inspirations.

Provincetown favorites are baked haddock, cooked Portuguese style with a sauce of tomatoes and spices; fresh mackerel, fried or baked in milk; tuna (horse mackerel) or sea catfish served *vinha d'alhos*, which involves a pickling process before frying; 'tinker' mackerel, which are baby fish pickled with a variety of spices, to be served cold or fried; and stuffed fish, baked. Favorites cooked English style include all manner of chowders, and such delicacies as sea-clam pie, broiled live lobster and salt-water scallops, sliced and fried or made into a creamy stew.

The Portuguese are fond of *linquiça*, a form of pork sausage, and of *toitas*, small pastries served at Christmas and other feast-days. These are stuffed with a sweet potato preparation, and fried in deep olive oil and coated with honey.

Beach plums grow in profusion at this end of the Cape, and housewives make the famous beach plum jelly. *Skully-jo*, once popular, is no longer made by any but a few Portuguese families. This is codfish or haddock cured in the sun, 'till it's hard enough to bend lead pipe around.' When fish was plentiful the Portuguese made barrels of it and the children carried it about in their pockets and chewed it instead of candy. It was said that 'the longer you chewed on a junk of skully-jo, the more you had.'

People at the Cape-end have always been willing warmers of the yarner's bench. Among them live many a legend and tall tale from seafaring days. There are still in Provincetown a few old-timers who can remember stories their own parents told them about the 'witch with red heels,' for example, who cruised in a cozy cabin inside a great whale. She played cards there with the Devil himself, and the stakes were the souls of luckless mariners whose vessels had run aground on Nauset shoals or the Peaked Hill Bars. To provide 'chips,' a light was hung from the flukes of the whale, and he would swim through the shoalest of the Cape waters.

There is the story, too, of the Whistling Whale, with a snore like a siren whistle, caused by an old iron embedded in his spout. Several times his whistling brought out the volunteer fire department. And when he was apprehended and finally harpooned — after weeks of serenading the town — some of the citizens declared they had become accustomed to the whistling, and were afraid they would never sleep again!

'Professor' George Washington Ready, town crier in 1886, one day solemnly deposed that he had seen a sea-serpent — not a common, run-of-the-mill sea-serpent, but a monstrous one, a reptile three hundred feet long and twelve feet in the beam, with three red eyes to port and three green eyes to starboard. The serpent came ashore, the Professor said, breathing sulphurous fumes and searing the beach-plum bushes at Herring Cove, undulated overland to Pasture Pond, and slowly went in, head first, never to be seen again! And the Professor made 'affidavy,' too, that he was 'not unduly excited by liquor or otherwise.'

Provincetown has too many such tales for space here, and the stuff of which these old yarns were spun would make a nautical glossary necessary equipment for the average listener of today. Even that would not clear up some of the local idiom. A ship bunk's mattress was a 'donkey's breakfast.' The 'apple-tree fleet' was the class of coasting schooners, with skippers who never sailed out of sight of the orchards alongshore. Molasses was 'Porty Reek long-lick,' or 'long-tailed sugar.'

FOOT TOUR — 3 *m.*

NE. from the Town Hall on Commercial St.

1. *Town Wharf*, a long, wide-timbered pier, is the heart of Provincetown's summer life. For many years it has been the landing stage of the daily Boston steamer in summer, and it is used by fishermen at all seasons.

The harbor view from this pier is a gay scene. Trawlers, seiners and draggers mingle with slim white yachts, low-lying cruisers and gray battleships. The short wharf on the left is littered with nets stretched to dry, lobster pots, kegs and coils of tarry rope. On the beach, artists are often at work, some singly, some in classes. Gulls wheel overhead, ever on watch for tidbits from the fishing boats.

Retrace Commercial St.; R. from Commercial St. on Ryder St.

2. A *Mayflower Memorial Tablet* near the Town Hall gives the wording of the Mayflower Compact, which was drawn up and signed in the cabin of that vessel while she lay at anchor in Provincetown Harbor. The names of the signers are appended.

3. The *Compact Memorial*, a large bas-relief by Cyrus F. Dallin, depicts the signing of the covenant. Fifteen by nine feet, it is set in a broad granite wall flanked by stone benches.

R. from Ryder St. on Bradford St.

4. Another *Mayflower Memorial Tablet*, at the junction of Bradford St. with the steep unmarked road leading to Pilgrim Monument, is in memory of 'the five "Mayflower" passengers who died at sea while the ship lay in Cape Cod Harbor.' The names include that of Dorothy Bradford, wife of the Governor.

L. from Bradford St. up the unmarked road to the Pilgrim Monument.

5. *Pilgrim Monument* (*open daily* 8–5, *Mar.* 1–*Nov.* 30; *closed in winter; adm.* 25¢) is constructed of gray granite, 252 feet high and 352 feet above sea level. It is visible many miles at sea. Storm signals are flown atop this hill from one of the steel towers of the U.S. Signal Service. The monument commemorates the landing of the Pilgrims at Provincetown, November 11, 1620, and the signing of the Compact. The view from the top is spectacular; to the north and east lies the open Altantic; to the west, across Cape Cod Bay, are Duxbury and Plymouth; to the south, the Cape, in bold relief, curves away in a tawny half-circle. The town below appears like a toy hamlet.

Retrace unmarked road; R. from unmarked road on Bradford St.; L. from Bradford St. on Ryder St.; R. from Ryder St. on Commercial St.

6. The *Town Hall* is a Victorian frame building housing art treasures, seafaring trophies and items of local interest. In the entrance hall are murals of Provincetown industries, by Ross Moffett. The offices on the

ground floor contain a painting, 'Provincetown Fishermen,' by Charles W. Hawthorne. In the same suite is Sir Thomas Lipton's $5000 gold and silver 'Fisherman's Cup,' won in 1907 by the schooner 'Rose Dorothea,' of Provincetown, Captain Costa. In the basement is an ancient horse-drawn fire pumper, with wide wheels, especially constructed a hundred years ago for use on the hard sand of the town beaches.

7. The *Church of the Redeemer* (Universalist) is a white frame edifice, with a steeple.

8. The *Historical Museum* (*open June–Oct.; adm.* 25¢), 230 Commercial St., a square brown Victorian building, houses an *Arctic Exhibit* contributed by Donald B. MacMillan, the Provincetown Arctic explorer, and also Indian relics, old glassware, ship models and whaling implements.

Straight ahead from Commercial St. into unmarked Tremont St., up Chip Hill.

9. The '*Norse Wall House*' (*private*), 15 Tremont St., is a small cottage built above an embedded wall (*not visible*) which is sometimes mentioned in support of the theory that the Norsemen came here. In 1853, Francis A. Paine began excavating for a cellar. At a depth of five feet (30 feet below the original level of the hill) a stone wall was encountered, three feet high and two feet wide, laid in shell-lime mortar. Later 'a hard earthen floor composed of peat, clay and fine white sand, hammered and pounded together,' was discovered, with the remains of a fireplace. These discoveries have been linked conjecturally to the visits of the Vikings to this country, where they saw the 'Wonder Strands' referred to in the three ancient Copenhagen manuscripts which tell of the early voyages from Scandinavia. In the vicinity of Provincetown there are no stones to be found of the size used in this wall. The Norse, it is said, carried such stones as ballast.

Retrace on Tremont St.; R. from Tremont St. on Commercial St.

10. The *Wharf Theater* is a remodeled gray-shingled fish shed on a harbor pier. A summer stock company plays here.

11. One of the oldest houses in Provincetown, the *Seth Nickerson House* (*open as hooked rug shop*), is at 72 Commercial St. The structure is estimated to be about 200 years old, and looks it, with its white clapboarded front, its shingled siding, its hip roof, broad central chimney and small-paned windows, around which climb rambler roses. When this house was built, the street did not exist and the residents of this district traveled to and from the village along the beach.

From this point on, prevailing features of the dwellings are gray-shingled walls, white picket fences, and gardens bright in summer with scarlet poppies, blue delphiniums and masses of white Easter lilies.

R. from Commercial St. on any of the lanes, all of which lead back to Bradford St.; two blocks back of Commercial St. and parallel to it; R. on Bradford St.

12. *Bradford Street* is the only other throughfare in Provincetown. The two streets run parallel, the length of the town, and all others are little more than interesting lanes.

MOTOR TOUR — 8 *m.*

W. from Town Hall on Commercial St.

13. The *Site of the Pilgrims' First Landing*, at the juncture of Commercial St. and Beach Highway, is marked by a bronze tablet on a low granite slab. To the left at a bend in the sandy isthmus, are *Wood End Light* and *Wood End Coast Guard Station* and at the tip-end, *Long Point Light*. Just outside, off Wood End, occurred one of the most horrible disasters of modern times, the sinking of the submarine 'S-4,' Dec. 17, 1927, when she breached under the bow of the coast guard destroyer 'Paulding' and went to the bottom with 40 men. Naval authorities were bitterly criticized on this occasion, both locally and throughout the country. A marked course off Wood End is still used as a proving ground for submarines, and .occasionally battleships come to anchor in the harbor. Provincetown is a lively scene when 'the fleet is in.'

R. from Commercial St. into Beach Highway.

14. *New Beach* was the location, a generation ago, of a colony of fishermen's shacks known as Hell Town. Its white shelving sand and its safe exposure on Cape Cod Bay make it now the finest bathing beach of the town. From here on the drive is one of unusual beauty, wild and desolate. The billowing sand dunes shift eternally, driven by gales that sweep in from the Atlantic. From time to time these sandhills have been planted by the Federal Government with scrub pine, beachgrass and other shrubs to stem their march. The co-operative bayberry grows wild. The cross-raftered poles which appear at intervals are spindle ranges used by the navy. In late afternoon the light over the dunelands is of many hues, sometimes a clear, soft golden-mauve, compounded of the slanting rays of the westerly sun, the tremendous open horizon, the sea air, the sage green of the grass, and the gold of the sand.

L. from Beach Highway on road marked, 'To Race Point Coast Guard Station.'

15. *Race Point Coast Guard Station* (*open to visitors at any daylight hour; drills Mon., Tues., and Fri.,* 9) becomes visible a long distance ahead, a two-story square white frame building with a red roof and a skeleton observation tower, standing upon a sandy bluff above the open waters of the Atlantic at one of the most dangerous spots to shipping on the eastern seaboard. It is a typical station, spotlessly clean, with a crew of ten men who do all the cooking and housework in addition to their seafaring duties. Chiefly interesting are the surfboats, 24 feet long. The shooting of the line for the breeches buoy may be seen at scheduled drills.

On the beach below the station is the wreck of the 'Spindler,' a rum-runner 125 feet long, which was cast ashore in 1922. A few years ago she stood high above the sand. Masts, riggings, even the bowsprit, are gone and the hull is deeply embedded now.

Retrace side road; L. from side road on Beach Highway; L. from Beach Highway on Bradford St.; R. from Bradford St. on Commercial St., un-marked, but evident as the last junction on Bradford St.

16. *Eugene O'Neill's Former Lodging* (*private*), 577 Commercial St., is the right-hand half (as one faces the dwelling) of the upper floor of a re-modeled sail loft with business offices on the first floor. Here the dramatist began his career. On the beams of the living-room of the apartment is written, 'Before the eyes can see, they must be incapable of tears.'

17. The *Church of St. Mary of the Harbor* (Episcopal) is a one-story, rambling frame structure, with a clapboarded front and gray-shingled sides. It has a small Mission bell. The simple and pleasing interior, with its alternating dark timbers and white plaster, and its white painted un-cushioned pews, is adorned with a small statue of Christ in cream-colored glazed terra-cotta. The figure stands upon a wooden cross beam, with arms outstretched, and is flanked by kneeling angels.

18. The *Figurehead House* (*private*) is a square yellow house with a ship's figurehead of a woman, surmounting the porch. The figurehead was found afloat in the Indian Ocean in Civil War days by Captain Ben Handy of Provincetown, who placed it where it is today.

19. The *Home of Commander Donald B. MacMillan* (*private*), 473 Commercial St., is a modern white frame house with a small lawn at the side and a large studio window in the north gable.

Q U I N C Y . *Iron Ships and Great Men*

City: Alt. 42, pop. 76,909, sett. 1625, incorp. town 1792, city 1888.

Railroad Stations: Atlantic off Hancock St.; Montclair off Montclair Ave.; Norfolk Downs on Newport Ave.; Quincy in Quincy Square; West Quincy on Willard St.; Wollaston on Beale St.; and Quincy Adams on Presidents Ave. for N.Y., N.H. & H. R.R.

Accommodations: Six hotels at reasonable rates.

Recreation: Swimming and bathing at Wollaston Beach on Quincy Shore Drive. Yachting at the Squantum and Wollaston Yacht Clubs (*adm. by invitation*).

Information: Chamber of Commerce, 1535 Hancock St.

QUINCY is one of the commercial centers of Massachusetts, known for its granite quarries, shipbuilding, machinery, and radio-transmitting stations WNAC and WAAB, part of the Yankee Network. Quincy owes much to the Italians, Jews, Finns, Scots, Greeks, and Syrians who came to work in the quarries and shipyards and who contributed generously toward the city's artistic, intellectual, and civic development. Thirty-two churches may be credited in part to a fund left to the Quincy churches by the King family to 'aid the breaking down of religious prejudice [in the belief] that a better understanding of the religious faith of one another is one of the most important movements in the world.'

In 1625 Thomas Morton, the 'pettifogger of Furnival's Inn,' as Governor Bradford contemptuously called him, arrived at Mount Wollaston and took part in establishing the settlement later to be known as Ma-re Mount or Merrymount. Morton traded with the Indians, taught them the use of firearms, and supplied them with liquor in exchange for furs, thus cutting in on the Plymouth trade. Bradford, further irked at Morton's celebration of May Day as a pagan feast and fearing that Morton's Merrymount would become a refuge for lawbreakers, dispatched Miles Standish and eight men from Plymouth, where a council was held, some members of which pressed for his execution. Instead, however, he was sent to England. Eighteen months later he returned to Merrymount, was again arrested, his house burned, and he himself again sent a prisoner to England. His 'Newe English Canaan,' published about 1637, gave excellent descriptions of New England scenery and bird and animal life, and scathingly exposed what he claimed to be the hypocritical pretenses to morality of the Pilgrims and Puritans.

Quincy was not separately incorporated till nearly one hundred and seventy years after the earliest settlements in this section. In 1789, while it was still the north precinct of Braintree, local consciousness was brought to a high pitch by the election of a native son, John Adams, to the Vice-Presidency of the United States. Eight years later, in 1797, he took the chair of President. His son, John Quincy Adams, was regarded as the finest diplomat in the foreign service. Later he, too, became President. When men with whom they had played as children were making history, Quincy's inhabitants felt it was high time to assert their right to an individual existence. The town was called Quincy in honor of Colonel John Quincy, an eminent and able citizen who had occupied Mount Wollaston.

Until 1830 the town was mainly a farming community, but from that date onward agriculture gave precedence to industry, a transition brought about by the expansion of the shoe trade, a natural outgrowth of the tanneries on the town brook; and by improved facilities for quarrying granite. Men had learned how to use iron instead of wooden wedges in splitting the rock.

In 1752 King's Chapel in Boston was built with Quincy granite. This sudden demand frightened the town fathers. Fearful of the supply of rock giving out, they passed an ordinance prohibiting the use of granite boulders for outside purposes. In spite of this, Quincy's trade in granite continued to expand until it was known the world over. In 1825 the Quincy quarries received a contract to supply the stone for the Bunker Hill Monument, and a railroad was built to convey the granite on horse-drawn wagons from the quarry to the wharf on the Neponset River.

In 1883 a little shop in Braintree Fore River experimented in marine engines. The business grew so fast that in 1884 it was forced to remove to Quincy Fore River. In 1913 it came into the possession of the Bethlehem Steel Corporation. During the world war thirty-six destroyers were built here. Today, as Quincy's main industrial unit it stands on a par with the greatest shipyards of the world, having built every conceivable type of vessel from the seven-masted schooner 'Thomas W. Lawson' to the giant airplane carrier 'Lexington.'

TOUR — 14 m.

NW. from the junction of the Southern Artery (State 3) on Hancock St.

1. *Adams and Son* (R), at the edge of Merrymount Park, near the corner of Fenno St., sculptor Bruce Wilder Saville (1893–   ), is a granite monument bearing a bronze bas-relief of John Adams and John Quincy Adams.

R. from Hancock St. on East Squantum St.; straight ahead on Dorchester St. which terminates in a rustic park, Chapel Rocks.

2. *Squaw Rock*, at the eastern end of the park, is the extremity of Squantum Peninsula. According to one tale, an Indian woman fell into the sea from the rock, which then became known as Squaw Rock and the whole district was called Squaw Tumble or Squan-Tum. Another account explains the name of the rock by the fact that it resembles an Indian profile, and states that Governor Winthrop named the region after Squanto, the Englishman's friend.

The ledges of the hill behind the rock are composed of 'Roxbury puddingstone,' an interesting conglomerate found in the environs of Boston.

Retrace Dorchester St. into East Squantum St.; L. from East Squantum St. on Quincy Shore Drive; R. from Quincy Shore Drive on Davis St.; R. from Davis St. on Muirhead St.

3. The *Colonel Josiah Quincy House* (*private*), 20 Muirhead St., was erected in 1770. This square yellow house with white block quoins and pillared portico was, until the middle of the 19th century, a gentleman's farmhouse, surrounded by rolling pasture. At the age of forty, Colonel Josiah Quincy (1709–1784) exchanged the career of successful shipbuilder for that of country gentleman. He was the father of Josiah Quincy, Jr., who horrified his parent by his defense of the British soldiers involved in

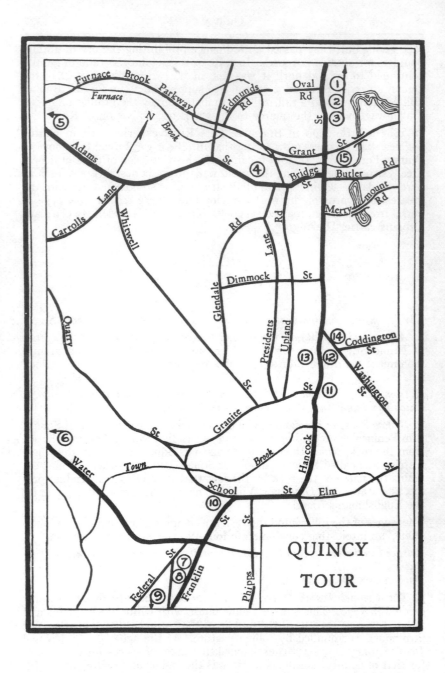

the Boston Massacre. The house was presently inherited by a third Josiah Quincy, who was successively Mayor of Boston, Congressman, and President of Harvard College.

Straight ahead from Muirhead St. into Beach St.; L. from Beach St. on Hancock St.; R. from Hancock St. on Bridge St.; straight ahead on Adams St.

4. The *Vassal-Adams Mansion* (R), (*open summer weekdays* 9–5; *adm.* 25¢), is a white clapboard Georgian Colonial house with five chimneys, and one brick end painted white. It was built in 1731, was the residence of Presidents John Adams and John Quincy Adams, and remained a private home of the Adams family until 1927.

L. from Adams St. on Furnace Brook Parkway; R. from Furnace Brook Parkway on Copeland St.

5. The *Granite Quarry,* across the tracks from the West Quincy R.R. Station, unmistakable by its high walls of stone detritus and its derricks, is the erstwhile center of New England's granite quarrying. The stone for Bunker Hill Monument came from here, as well as for countless buildings in Boston. This quarry is now only moderately active, as composition building materials have superseded natural granite.

Retrace on Copeland St.

6. The *Co-operative Market,* 32 Copeland St., founded over a quarter of a century ago by the Finnish residents of Quincy, transacts annually a business in excess of $100,000.

Copeland St. terminates in Water St.; R. from Water St. on Franklin St.

7. The *John Adams Birthplace (open weekdays* 9–6, *April* 19–*Nov.* 1; *adm.* 25¢), Adams Sq., is also a small red clapboard salt-box farmhouse built in 1681, enclosed by an ancient pole fence with turnstile, with small steep winding stairway, huge central chimney, and mammoth fireplace. One of the chambers has a false front at its fireplace, the entire panel from floor to ceiling swinging to reveal a space by the chimney large enough to hold a man in concealment. The central ceiling beams are hand-hewn. The inverted gunstock post used in the frame of the house distributes its weight equally. In the kitchen is the bole of the giant cedar tree which witnessed the notorious Merrymount revels.

QUINCY MAP INDEX

8. The *John Quincy Adams Birthplace* (*open weekdays* 9–6, *April* 19–*Nov.* 1; *adm.* 25¢), adjacent, built in 1716, is a red clapboard salt-box farmhouse with huge central chimney.

9. The *Abigail Adams Stone Cairn* (L), opposite 353 Franklin St., a duplicate of the Miles Standish Cairn, marks the spot on the summit of the hill where, during the Battle of Bunker Hill, Mrs. John Adams with her little son, John Quincy Adams, prayed for the safety of the Colonial soldiers.

Retrace on Franklin St.

10. The *Robert Burns Statue*, School and Franklin Sts., was erected by the Burns Memorial Association of Quincy to honor the poet who 'as a lover of Freedom and Democracy penned an ode to Washington.'

R. from Franklin St. into School St.; L. from School St. into Hancock St.

11. The *Granite Trust Building* (*tower open*) is Quincy's skyscraper.

12. The *Stone Temple, 'Church of the Presidents,'* 1266 Hancock St., now a Unitarian church, was built in 1828 of Quincy granite, and was designed by Alexander Parris in the style of the Greek revival. Its white colonnaded portico with pediment and the open cupola soften the severe mass of the structure. The name is derived from the fact that John Adams and John Quincy Adams worshiped and are buried here (*crypt open upon application to sexton*).

13. The *Old Cemetery*, opposite, dates from 1666, and is the burial place of many members of the Quincy and Adams families.

R. from Hancock St. into Washington St.

14. The *Crane Memorial Public Library*, at the corner of Coddington St., commissioned in 1880, is considered the best of H. H. Richardson's work in this field. The single low mass of the front is not broken by the gable over the entrance, and the stair turret is unemphasized. Romanesque to some degree, the design is also bold Richardsonian, with a notably original handling of fenestration, and the dominant Richardson theme — stress upon function and material — powerfully expressed.

Retrace Washington St.; R. from Washington St. on Hancock St.

15. The *Dorothy Quincy Mansion* (*open daily, April* 19–*Nov.* 1; *adm.* 25¢), 34 Butler Rd. (corner of Hancock St.), a spacious hip-roofed mansion built in 1706–09, was the birthplace and home of the spirited girl who became the wife of John Hancock. A feature of the house is a secret chamber which repeatedly afforded asylum to pursued Colonial troopers.

R E V E R E . *A Beach Beside a City*

City: Alt. 15, pop. 35,319, sett. about 1630, incorp. town 1871, city 1914

Railroad Station: Revere Center for B. & M. R.R.

Bus Stations: Revere Center and Point of Pines for Greyhound Bus Lines.

Accommodations: Several inns and overnight cabins on the Boulevard.

Swimming: The largest beach in New England; Ocean Pier Swimming Pool (*adm.* 50¢), Ocean Pier.

Dog Racing: Wonderland Park.

Information: Chamber of Commerce, Beach St.

REVERE is a city bordering a beach. Block after block stretch out the crowded habitations of those who from the Fourth of July till Labor Day will house or feed or amuse the vast throngs who cannot frequent expensive resorts and who take their sea air and their bright lights where they can afford it. The three-mile stretch of broad, sandy beach is one of the best in Massachusetts. Hundreds of amusement palaces line the promenade. On the sands, thousands of sun-bathers lounge and caper; thousands more frolic in the surf. Histrionic barkers cater to the carnival spirit of holiday throngs. High overhead, sinuous roller coasters stuffed with shrieking humanity dive into abysmal depths. And everywhere there is music — the swaying rhythm of the dance hall, the hoarse strains of the steam organ, the blaring syncopation of the loudspeaker, the unceasing beat of 'canned music.'

In view of its democratic present, the beginnings of Revere were distinctly aristocratic. Back in 1636, the town of Boston parceled off a surplus of undistributed land, part of which lay within the confines of what is now Revere. The first landowner of Revere was Sir Henry Vane, son of a Privy Councillor of England. Chosen Governor of the Massachusetts Bay Colony, he received an allotment of two hundred acres of Rumney Marsh, as Revere was then called. But his term of office was brief; handsome Harry Vane was a romantic idealist; his openly stated conviction that all creeds should have equal rights in New England appalled the clergy. Sir Harry sailed back to England and Rumney Marsh became the property of a dozen or so wealthy gentlemen who, for the most part, left it in the hands of tenants or servants.

The titles to these lands extended only to the beach. In 1812, in a lawsuit regarding the town's jurisdiction in the matter of digging clams at low tide when, the defense maintained, the floor of the ocean was exposed, the town won the case on the premise that 'if the sea rolled back to the Azores, it would do nothing more than expose undeveloped territory in the town of Chelsea.'

The necessity for reclaiming large areas of marsh and sea grass discouraged settlers, and until 1710, when the first church was erected at Rumney Marsh, community life in this locality progressed slowly.

For about a hundred years after 1739, when Chelsea separated from Boston, Rumney Marsh was the northern part of Chelsea. In 1852, Pullen Point broke away as the town of Winthrop. For the next twenty-five years North Chelsea was at a complete standstill; then, changing its name to Revere in honor of the famous patriot, it experienced a rebirth. The Narrow Gauge Railroad running out to its white sandy shore lifted Revere out of oblivion and gave it its place in the sun.

POINTS OF INTEREST

1. *Revere Beach* (*State bathhouse, moderate fee*), Revere Beach Parkway, is one of Boston's two Coney Islands.

2. The *Masonic Temple*, southeast corner of Eustis and Beach Sts., was originally *The Church of Christ in Rumney Marsh*, built in 1710. Its first pastor, the Rev. Thomas Cheever, was suspended from his ministry in a neighboring parish for breaking two of the Ten Commandments. At Rumney Marsh, however, he was greatly beloved for his championship of other sinners, and lived to the mellow age of 91, still eloquent in the pulpit and active in good works.

3. The *Hastings House* (*private*), southwest corner of Eustis and Beach Sts., was built in 1782, and preserves the flavor of a typical old New England farmstead. This effect is created in part by its rambling, weatherworn comfortable ells and gables; in part by its grass-grown yard shaded by old trees; and in part by the two huge clumps of very old lilac bushes at its front entrance.

4. The *Slade Spice Mill* (*open weekdays* 10–4), Revere Beach Parkway near Broadway, a small, red wooden building, was until 1934 a tidewater mill, and one of the old millstones is preserved within, and can still be turned. Spice has been ground here for over a century, and the visitor is greeted at once, on opening the door, by the pungent smell of mingled nutmeg, cinnamon, clove, pepper (red, white, and black), thyme, marjoram, and anise, much of which comes from the far-off Spice Isles of Java. A fine buff-colored dust permeates the air. The workers look healthy, however, and say that only white pepper makes them sneeze.

5. A *Granite Tablet*, corner of Revere Beach Parkway and Railroad St., commemorates the so-called Battle of Chelsea Creek, May 27, 1775. In the spring of 1775, the British, in need of fresh meat, food, and forage, overawed the farmers in and about Chelsea Creek into selling them such supplies. The Committee of Safety ordered the patriots of Chelsea and thereabouts to move back their cattle, sheep, and horses from the coast line. Hog and Noddle Islands (now East Boston) were at that time sep-

arated from each other and from the mainland by narrow sea inlets, easily forded at low tide. The patriots had just cleared off Hog Island, and were preparing to do likewise at Noddle Island when up Chelsea Creek to the east came the British schooner 'Diana' and opened fire upon the very damply 'embattled farmers.' Fortunately up came reinforcements, and at their head Israel Putnam, America's 'Cincinnatus of the Plow' who led his men out waist-deep into the water and returned the attack so vigorously that the British, after losing several men, abandoned their ship and rowed home in small boats. The 'Diana' was stripped and then burned by the Continentals, who could not use it themselves as the British were holding Boston Harbor. Chelsea Creek, though little more than a spirited skirmish, was of chief import because it seemed to be the first real American victory of the Revolution, and engendered in the ranks of the Continentals an invincible confidence.

S A L E M . *New England's Treasure-House*

City: Alt. 13, pop. 43,472, sett. 1626–28, incorp. town 1630, city 1836.
Railroad Stations: B. & M. R.R., Washington & Norman Sts.
Airport: Winter Island, U.S. Coast Guard base, private.
Bus Stations: Greyhound, at Harmon & Kimball's on Central St.
Piers: Salem Willows Pier, Salem Willows, launches to Marblehead and North Shore in summer. Congress St. Bridge, launch for Baker's Island (summer only).
Accommodations: Several hotels open year round, with no change in rates during tourist season.
Information: Hotel Hawthorne.

SALEM is one of the historic treasure-houses of New England. Here are the haunting shades, not only of Nathaniel Hawthorne, but also of every character Hawthorne created, of his old houses impregnated with supernatural influences, and of the eerie atmosphere that still lingers in the narrow streets which the master of delicate implications frequented. Here are the more robust memories of docks and wharves from which poured crude wealth in fish and ships' supplies, and into which, after many turnovers of cargo, flowed all the exotic treasure of the Indies and China. Here stored in old landmarks is the romance of swift clipper ships, of bellying sails, of masts stripped for the gale, of sailors' oaths and sailors' roaring chanteys, of ambition and avarice, of mansions built by merchant princes and delicate women nurtured in them.

Salem also possesses architectural treasures so numerous and so varied as to re-create in an almost complete synopsis the development of the Colonial architecture of New England. From the seventeenth-century house, accidentally beautiful in its expression of function, to the sophisticated maturity of Samuel McIntire's superb Federal mansions, eloquent expressions of each period are scattered throughout the city. Though chiefly concentrated about Washington Square, and on Essex, Federal, and Chestnut Streets, they occur sporadically throughout the old districts of Salem. McIntire, a native genius, labored here throughout his life; many of his superb houses retain their original beauty, and the dwellings of the great maritime period after his death partake of the dignity and delicacy of detail of the examples which he created. Salem cannot be neglected either by the student of the American tradition in architecture or by the lover of beautiful houses.

In 1626 Roger Conant and a group of emigrants from Cape Ann, after the failure of the Dorchester Company's fishing settlement there, chose this sheltered site to found a community where they might fish and farm, think their own thoughts, and hold their own religious opinions. They would have starved if Endecott with the advance guard of the Massachusetts Bay Company had not arrived in 1628. Endecott hung on in spite of famine and sickness. To Salem came John Winthrop with his fleet in 1630 to prospect before he went to Boston, and found that Salem had established a Congregational Church. The Conant and Endecott settlers soon became a united body, and the Conant group frequently represented Salem in the General Court.

Endecott and his followers had the faults of their strength and were often in opposition to the Boston group, who at one time disciplined the leader for cutting the cross from the British flag. This group had his friend Roger Williams banished from the Colony for preaching 'seditious' doctrines such as the freedom of conscience from civil control. Williams escaped deportation by fleeing from Salem. Probably Salem's weakness for Williams is one of the reasons why Harvard College was not located there, but at Cambridge.

When the Quakers came to Salem they were often in trouble because they represented extremes of opinion in the seventeenth century, but no Quaker was ever executed there. Unfortunately the same cannot be said of witches when belief in witchcraft spread from Europe to America.

In 1692, among the servants of the Reverend Samuel Parris was a West Indian slave named Tituba, with a talent for voodoo tales which she exercised not wisely but too well. Her auditors were young girls, and quite naturally Tituba's grisly tales scared them into fits. When bedtime came after a secret séance with Tituba they shuddered and screamed and saw things in dark corners. Examined by the village physician, they were declared bewitched. The little wretches accused Tituba and two unpopular old women. They were questioned with deep gravity; the tale was embroidered; Tituba and the others were charged with consorting with the Devil and sentenced to death.

For a year thereafter in Salem and neighboring towns, the witchcraft pestilence raged. Nineteen persons were hanged on Gallows Hill, and at least two died in prison. No one was safe. The saintly Mrs. Hale, wife of the Beverly minister, was accused. Even the wife of Governor Phips was suspected for sympathizing with a prisoner; but that finished the matter.

Agricultural pursuits predominated in early Salem. Slowly, however, during the seventeenth century, commerce and industry got a foothold. The protected harbor encouraged trade. By the beginning of the eighteenth century, shipbuilding and allied industries were thriving and extensive trade relations with the West Indies and European ports had been established. As its city seal, Salem adopted the motto, 'The wealth of the Indies to the uttermost gulf.'

The Revolutionary War turned seafaring Salem to privateering. The latter was profitable at first, but during the strict British blockade it proved ruinous. Moreover, at the close of the war England prohibited all relations with British controlled markets and Salem vessels were forced to rely on a meager coastwise trade.

Then the pendulum swung. The great Chinese market was discovered and Salem entered upon its career of maritime glory. In 1785 the stout ship 'Grand Turk' sailed out of Salem harbor, China-bound. Following her in rapid succession a fleet of thirty-four vessels were put into service between Salem and distant Cathay.

Rarely did they sail direct for the Orient. Around the Horn they went, with ports of call along the Northern Pacific Coast for valuable furs, and in the Hawaiian Islands for fresh supplies and sandalwood, before they set out to do their real trading in China. Then around the Cape of Good Hope and home, often touching at European ports. And all the way shrewd Yankee captains drove profitable bargains, often turning over their cargoes a dozen times. Profits of several hundred per cent were not uncommon. Huge wealth was piled up. Promotion was rapid. Wages were high. Often a captain had made his fortune and retired by the time he was thirty years of age. Many merchants in the Far East believed Salem to be a separate country of fabulous wealth.

The result of this rapid commercial development was a cultural expansion in the life of the city, and the growth of a romantic background peculiarly its own. Something of Oriental luxury and richness flowed into Yankee Salem. From Canton, the Dutch East Indies, from the Philippines and Mauritius, came rich and assorted cargoes of tea, chinaware, nankeens, silks, fans, feathers, embroidered shawls, coffee, spices, and with them glamorous tales of a different way of life in an ancient and fabulous country. Joseph Hergesheimer's novel 'Java Head' portrays this period of Salem's glory.

In 1812 the city was again seriously affected by a war and its ensuing depression. Before it could recover again, the Erie Canal was opened and New York entered the lists as a serious competitor in foreign and inland trade. Moreover, Salem Harbor was not deep enough for the new vessels of large draught.

From this period onward, Salem's position in the world of commerce slowly faded out, to be replaced by the growth of industry. In 1848 the Naumkeag Steam Cotton Mills were established, and after the Civil War numerous tanneries, paint, and shoe factories were founded. The great fire of 1914 destroyed a large part of the industrial district and many concerns moved to other towns; but Salem is still industrially active in the production of cotton goods, shoes, radio tubes, and games.

TOUR 1 — 2.3 m.

West from Washington Square on Essex St.

1. The *Gardner-White-Pingree House (property of the Essex Institute; open Wed. and Sat. afternoons or by appointment; fee 50¢)*, 128 Essex St., built in 1810, was among the last works of the architectural genius Samuel McIntire, and is conceded to be his finest work in brick. The house is square, with a low third story capped by a cornice and balustraded parapet. It has a symmetrical arrangement of marble-headed windows, a graceful elliptical porch, and the severity of the high façade is softened by broad bands of white marble at each floor level. The interior work is exceptionally fine.

McIntire, born in Salem in 1757, learned the trade of carpenter and joiner from his father, a successful housewright. His initiative and ambition made him the most highly skilled American woodcarver of his time. Permanent monuments to his memory are the finely wrought Federal houses of Salem, their uncompromising lines lightened and enriched by Palladian windows, porches with delicate fluted columns, and magnificent carved woodwork.

2. The *Essex Institute (open weekdays except holidays 9–5; adm. free)*, 132 Essex St., includes a library and a museum. The former contains the Ward China Library — probably the finest on China and the Chinese in the United States — logbooks and sea journals, and county and town histories. Exhibits in the museum consist of Colonial portraits and paintings, miniatures and silhouettes, and three period rooms, a kitchen typical of 1750 and a bedroom and a parlor of 1800.

The *John Ward House (property of the Essex Institute; open daily in summer except Sun. and holidays 9–5; adm. 25¢)* stands in the shady grounds to the rear of the main buildings of the Institute. It was built in 1684 with wide clapboards, a lean-to roof, and an overhanging second story. In the garden are reconstructions of an *Old Cobbler's Shop*, a '*Cent Shop*' and a *Weaving Room*.

3. The *Peabody Museum* (*open weekdays* 9–5; *Sundays* 2–5; *adm. free*), Essex St., was endowed by George Peabody as the permanent repository of a marine collection, including a circle of reflection presented by Napoleon to his navigation instructor; a sextant which served Livingstone in the mazes of the Congo; and ship models, nautical instruments, and whaling implements.

L. from Essex St. on Derby Square.

4. The *Old Town Hall* (*open* 9–5), opposite the Salem Five Cent Savings Bank, was built in 1816, and its ground floor was used as a market for more than one hundred years. Architecturally the hall is simple and dignified. Characterized by a gable roof with pedimental treatment accented by a fan window, the structure is interesting chiefly for its pleasant symmetrical arrangement of round-headed windows and door, with a Palladian window as the central feature.

Retrace Derby Sq.; L. from Derby Sq. on Essex St.

5. The *Witch House* (*open daily in summer* 9.30–5; *fee* 10¢), 310½ Essex St., once the residence of Judge Corwin of the notorious witchcraft trials, has, unfortunately, been altered by the addition of a modern drugstore in front; but the interior remains very much as it was in 1692.

6. The *Ropes Memorial* (*open Tues., Thurs., and Sat.* 2–5; *adm. to garden any day except Mon.; adm. free*), 318 Essex St., is a stately gambrel-roof building (1719) enclosed by a graceful wooden fence with carved posts. The upper slope of the roof is outlined by a railing. The house was owned and occupied by Judge Nathaniel Ropes (1726–74) and his descendants for four generations. It contains a rare and valuable collection of Canton, Nanking, and Fitzhue china and Irish glass.

7. The *Salem Athenaeum* (*adm. by invitation of a member*), 339 Essex St., contains, among other rare editions, the Kirwan Library, taken by a privateer from an English vessel and used as the basis for his studies by Nathaniel Bowditch, the famous mathematician and navigator, a native of Salem.

8. Behind a graceful wooden fence decorated with carved urns, at 393 Essex St., is the *Rev. Thomas Barnard House*, a large and delightful gambrel-roof dwelling with a pedimented doorway, and two great chimneys.

Retrace Essex St.; R. from Essex St. into Flint St.; L. from Flint St. into Chestnut St.

9. *Chestnut Street*, laid out in 1796, has been called one of the finest streets, architecturally, in America. Most of these Federal houses, among which are some designed by McIntire, are three-story, of mellow brick, with beautiful exterior detail of porches, columns, and Palladian windows. In the rear are charming gardens and picturesque buildings which form an

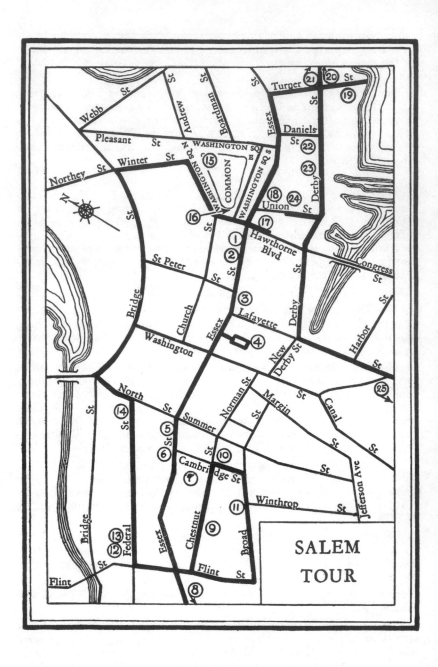

SALEM
TOUR

appropriate background. Almost every house deserves study. Among them, and selected almost at random, are the *Pickman–Shreve–Little House*, No. 27 (1816), with a classic porch below a Palladian window; the similar *Dodge–Shreve House*, No. 29 (1817), with balustraded hip roof, cornice set with modillions, and classic porch; the *Mack* and *Stone Houses*, No. 21 and No. 23 (1814–15), simple in detail but with elliptical colonnaded porches and keyed marble lintels.

10. *Hamilton Hall*, on the corner of Cambridge St., was designed by McIntire in 1805. Although somewhat altered, it retains some characteristic detail such as the five Palladian windows on the side, each with a paneled insert above containing a carved ornament. The famous McIntire eagle is preserved in the center panel.

R. from Chestnut St. into Cambridge St.; R. from Cambridge St. into Broad St.

11. The *Pickering House* (*private*) stands at the corner of Pickering and Broad Sts. Built in 1660 (altered), it is said to be the oldest house in Salem proper. The house has been extensively altered, and its medieval core is now veiled by excessive 'carpenter Gothic' work.

R. from Broad St. into Flint St.; R. from Flint St. into Federal.

12. The *Cook-Oliver House* (*private*), 142 Federal St., benefited greatly by that architectural tragedy, the destruction of the Elias Hasket Derby Mansion. After Derby's death, McIntire, who began this dwelling for Captain Samuel Cook in 1804, persuaded the Captain to buy the gateposts and much beautiful wood finish of the unoccupied Derby mansion. The fence, with its elaborate gateposts decorated with urns surmounted by the flame motif, is probably the best of McIntire's many delightful fences. The house is typical McIntire — square, three-story frame, hip roof, a heavy cornice with large dentils along the eaves, a horizontal band, vertically fluted, along the second floor line, finely wrought entablatures above the windows, and a porch and doorway

SALEM MAP INDEX

notable even among the many beautiful doorways of Salem for McIntire's free interpretation of the classic orders.

13. The *Assembly Hall* (*not open*), 138 Federal St., an historic McIntire building of 1782, has been remodeled for private use but the elaborate match-boarded façade, Ionic pilasters on the second story, and fanlight are unchanged. The porch, added later, is elaborately decorated with scrolls, festoons, and a heavy grapevine frieze.

14. The *Pierce–Nichols House* (*owned by Essex Institute*), 80 Federal St., is one of the most interesting houses, architecturally, in Salem. This magnificent dwelling, built in 1782, the first flower of McIntire's genius, has with its outbuildings been called one of the finest architectural groups executed in wood in the United States. The square, three-story exterior is of classic simplicity with a Doric pedimented porch and fluted Doric pilasters at the corners. Notable is the roof treatment with its balustraded parapet and belvedere. The urns on the gate-posts were carved out of solid blocks of wood by the hand of the master.

L. from Federal St. on North St.; R. from North St. into Bridge St.; R. from Bridge St. into Winter St.; R. from Winter St. into Washington Square.

15. The stately houses of Washington Square, surrounding Salem Common, perpetuate the charm and dignity of Salem's past. Included among many of architectural interest are the *Hosmer–Townsend–Waters House*, No. 80 (1795), by McIntire, known for its lovely, enclosed side porch and its hip roof rising to a massive central chimney; the *Boardman House*, No. 82 (1785), of beautiful proportion and detail, with an enclosed porch; the *Baldwin–Lyman House*, No. 92 (1818), with its symmetrical arrangement of great chimneys joined in pairs; and the distinguished hip-roofed *Andrew–Safford House*, 1818, which uses roof balustrades, heavy cornice, and fluted columns on a side portico for decoration, but centers its emphasis upon an elaborate Corinthian entrance porch below a Palladian window.

16. The *Statue of Roger Conant*, founder of the city, Washington Square and Brown St., was executed by Henry Hudson Kitson.

TOUR 2 — 4 m.

South from Washington Square into Hawthorne Boulevard.

17. The *Hawthorne Monument* by Bela Pratt, at the head of Hawthorne Boulevard, is appropriately placed near the scenes chiefly associated with Salem's great literary figure.

Retrace Hawthorne Blvd.; R. from Hawthorne Blvd. into Essex St.

18. The *Narbonne House* (*private*), 71 Essex St., stands almost opposite Washington Sq. E. Built before 1671, its steep pitched roof and great central chimney proclaim its period. The Dutch door of the lean-to was formerly the entrance to a 'Cent Shop,' as described by Hawthorne.

R. from Essex St. into Turner St.

19. The *House of the Seven Gables* (*open daily* 10–5; *fee* 25¢), 54 Turner St., is, as the supposed setting of Hawthorne's novel by that name, perhaps the most celebrated spot in all historic Salem. Unfortunately for sentiment, there is some grave doubt whether this house is actually the one described by Hawthorne. There is even more doubt as to how much of the building is authentic. It was certainly greatly restored in 1910, and it has been said that a good deal of imagination went into the restoration. Its present appearance is weather-beaten and rambling, with seven gables, huge chimneys, a lean-to, and a second-story overhang adorned with pendrils; it shows strong medieval influence. It was probably built in about 1668.

The House of the Seven Gables is one of three 17th-century dwellings clustered about a garden, the others being the *Hathaway House* (*parlor and kitchen open; included in the original fee*), built in 1682 and, with its overhanging second story and small diamond-paned windows, beautifully preserved; and the *Retire Becket House* (*open during summer as teahouse*), built in 1655.

Retrace Turner St.; R. from Turner St. into Derby St. Straight ahead into Fort Ave.; R. from Fort Ave. into Winter Island Road.

20. The *J. C. B. Smith Swimming Pool* is a large and inviting salt-water cove made by damming the head of Cat Cove.

R. around swimming pool to Winter Island.

21. The *U.S. Coast Guard Air Station* (*open 3 to sundown on weekdays; 1 until sundown on Sat. and Sun.; guide*) is a modern, completely equipped depot, which includes airplane hangars.

Retrace Winter Island Rd.; L. from Winter Island Rd. into Fort Ave.; straight ahead into Derby St.

22. The *Richard Derby House* (*open daily* 9–5; *fee* 20¢), 168 Derby St., built in 1762 and now owned by the Society for the Preservation of New England Antiquities, is the oldest brick house in Salem. Except for its gambrel roof, it is American Georgian in style, with dentiled cornice, pedimented doorway, and four-end chimneys joined in pairs. From its small-paned windows, the first of the line of merchant princes could watch his vessels unloading almost in his dooryard, or follow with his glass their topsails receding beyond the horizon.

23. The old *Custom House*, 178 Derby St., built in 1819, where Nathaniel Hawthorne once dreamed over his ledgers, looks down along the granite finger of *Derby Wharf* that once beckoned home the vessels of the Derby family but which now points only to a harbor empty of ships. In architecture it is akin to the Federal dwellings of Salem. The Palladian window above the Ionic, balustraded portico, the round-headed first-floor windows, the balustraded parapet, and the cupola are the outstanding architectural features. Surmounting the parapet rail is a carved eagle.

R. from Derby St. into Union St.

.24. Hawthorne's Birthplace (private), 27 Union St., is a gambrel-roofed house built before the witchcraft year, 1692. It is said that the author was born (1804) in the left-hand chamber of the second story. In the shadows of the old house he spent a shy, solitary boyhood. Though he was city port surveyor in 1846, he was a mystic and a recluse by nature and entirely unfitted by an abnormal sensitiveness for his duties at the Custom House. He realized that actualities must be insisted on in America, but his genius reached its full fruition only when he turned to romantic fiction. Three volumes of short stories, besides 'The Scarlet Letter,' 'The House of Seven Gables,' 'The Blithedale Romance,' and 'The Marble Faun,' are works of major significance. He created one of the best sustained prose styles in American literature.

Retrace Union St.; R. from Union St. on Derby St.; L. from Derby on Lafayette St. (State 1A); L. from State 1A into Clifton Ave.

25. *Forest River Park* overlooks the harbor and sea, almost at the city limits. Three acres of this park are devoted to *Pioneers' Village* (*open until dusk, adults 25¢, children 15¢*), an accurate reproduction of typical units of a Puritan community of about 1630, ranging from dugouts and primitive cabins to the 'Governor's Fayre House' with its huge central chimney and vast fireplace. Here can be seen the village life in epitome: a blacksmith's forge, a saw-pit, a brick kiln, as well as the grim whipping-post and stocks; in the garden are the same flowers and herbs that grew in the dooryards of the pioneers.

Below are briefly listed other buildings in Salem worth a visit for their architectural significance.

'The Studio'	1826	2 & 4 Chestnut St.
Mansfield-Bolles House	1810	8 Chestnut St.
Hodges-Peele-West	1804	12 Chestnut St.
Goss-Osgood House	1810	15 Chestnut St.
Hawthorne's Residence	1846–1847	18 Chestnut St.
Peabody-Rantoul House	1810	19 Chestnut St.
Mack and Stone Houses about	1814	21 & 23 Chestnut St.
Hoffman-Simpson House about	1827	26 Chestnut St.
Hodges-Webb-Meek House before	1802	81 Essex St.
Col. Benjamin Pickman House	1743	165 Essex St. Rear
Lindall-Gibbs-Osgood House	1773	314 Essex St.
Cabot-Endicott-Low House	1748	365 Essex St.
Salem Public Library		370 Essex St.
Wheatland House before	1773	374 Essex St.
Peabody-Silsbee House	1797	380 Essex St.
Stearns House (East India Inn)	1776	384 Essex St.
Captain Edward Allen House	1780	125 Derby St.
Home for Aged Women (Benjamin W. Crowninshield House) (Samuel McIntire)	1810	180 Derby St.
County Commissioners Building		Federal St.
City Hall (eagle by McIntire)		93 Washington St.
Railroad Station	1847	Washington & Derby Sts.
Bertram Home for Aged Men (Colonel George Peabody House)	1818	29 Washington Sq.
Silsbee-Mott House	1818	35 Washington Sq.

S O M E R V I L L E . *Traditions of Trade*

City: Alt. 41, pop. 100,773, sett. 1630, incorp. town 1842, city 1871.

Railroad Stations: North Somerville, off Broadway near Boston Ave.; Somerville, Park St.; Somerville Junction, 114 Central St.; for B. & M. R.R.

Accommodations: One hotel.

Information: Chamber of Commerce, 59 Union Square.

ONE of the independent municipal spokes radiating from the Boston hub, Somerville is a type of the many industrial-residential communities that press upon the borders of the capital of the Commonwealth and which, proud of their own identity, have stood their ground against annexation to Boston. The city is the center of a network of highways reaching all New England, and its railroad facilities are unusually good.

Although part of Charlestown until 1842, Somerville has had a past that is distinctly its own. Traditions of trade dominated the early settlers. For the early Somervillite, there was little of the frivolous diversion of concern about one's neighbor's conduct and beliefs so characteristic of his Boston neighbor.

About the beginning of the nineteenth century, Somerville took on distinct individuality. The building of the Cambridge and Charlestown bridges to Boston had established the city as an important outpost on the direct route from Boston to the north; but it was the opening of the Middlesex Canal through Somerville in 1803 that gave impetus to its industrial development. By 1822 the canal had been outmoded by the turnpikes, and by 1835 Somerville was a regular stopping-place on the new Boston and Lowell Railroad.

With such transportation advantages, it was not long before the town entered upon an era of expansion. Three-fourths of the meat-packing of the Commonwealth is carried on in the six packing-houses of the city. In the order of their importance, other leading industries are: slaughtering, bakery products, confectionery, foundry and machine-shop products, beverages, structural iron and steel, printing, automobile assembling, coffee-roasting, furniture making, and household and photographic equipment.

Because of its definitely residential character, self-rule is prized in Somerville. It is this love for self-government that gives the city its vigor and its virility.

MOTOR TOUR — 12.2 *m.*

N. from Union Square into Bow St., straight ahead into Summer St.

1. *St. Catherine's Church*, 183 Summer St., designed by Maginnis and Walsh and executed in 1892 in gray brick with white marble trim, shows the influence of the Byzantine style of northern Italy, and of the Gothic. It has been termed by authorities one of the most beautiful churches in America. The basement is treated as a crypt, its arched vaulted ceiling supported by heavy piers.

Retrace Summer St.; L. from Summer St. into Washington St.

2. The *James Miller Tablet* stands at the spot where James Miller, aged 65, was slain by the British retreating from Concord and Lexington, April 19, 1775. 'I am too old to run,' he said.

L. from Washington St. into Medford St.; L. from Medford St. into Prospect Hill Ave. to junction of Munroe St.

3. The *Prospect Hill Tablet* commemorates the raising, Jan. 1, 1776, of the first American flag of 13 stripes. It was unfurled here over the main American fortress covering the siege of Boston, where the British were entrapped, except for egress by sea, for 11 months.

R. from Prospect Hill Ave. into Munroe St.

4. The *Memorial Tower* crowns the site of the fortress (*Point* 3). At the base of the tower are five small tablets, one of which reads: 'The flower of the British army, prisoners of war who surrendered at Saratoga, were quartered on this hill from November 7, 1777, to October 15, 1778.' They numbered about 4000 men, of whom half were Hessians. The winter was very cold, firewood was scarce, and hardship was extreme.

L. from Monroe St. into Walnut St.; R. from Walnut St. into Aldersey St.; R. from Aldersey St. into Vinal Ave.; R. from Vinal Ave. into Highland Ave.

5. At Central Hill Park is a *Civil War Monument*, the work of Augustus Lukeman, depicting an angel as bodyguard for a marching soldier. Adjoining it, directly in front of the Public Library, is a simpler *Spanish War Monument*, by Raymond Porter, in which the treatment of both soldier and sailor are markedly realistic. This monument includes commemoration of Americans in the Boxer Revolt in China in 1900, being one of the few to do so.

6. The *Public Library* (*open weekdays* 9–9), 35 Highland Ave., contains in its central hall a full-size copy of the frieze of the Parthenon at Athens. As was the case in the original, the frieze has been tinted in blues and greens. Of note, also in the entrance hall, is a bas-relief portrait of Sam Walter Foss, author of the poem, 'The House by the Side of the Road,' and former librarian (1898–1911).

Retrace on Highland Ave.; R. from Highland Ave. into Sycamore St.

7. The *Oliver Tufts House* (*private*), 78 Sycamore St., was originally built on Barberry Lane (Highland Ave.) by Peter Tufts, grandson of the Peter Tufts who emigrated to America in 1646, and who operated a ferry from Charlestown to Malden. The house was the headquarters of General Lee of the American Army during the siege of Boston. Some 50 years later Charlotte Cushman, the noted Boston actress, spent her childhood holidays at 'Uncle Oliver's Farm.'

R. from Sycamore St. into Broadway.

8. *Ploughed Hill* is the site of a celebrated and distressing incident of social history, the burning by an anti-Catholic mob in 1834 of the Ursuline Convent. Broadway below the hill, traversed at this point, was in 1775 a narrow neck of land enclosed on two sides by water. It was the last hostile territory crossed by the British on their retreat from Concord and Lexington, before they plunged into present-day Charlestown, then held by them. Here was also the start of the Middlesex Canal.

L. from Broadway into Union St.; L. from Union St. into Mystic Ave.; R. from Mystic Ave. into Middlesex Ave.

9. The *Ford Motor Plant* (*visitors by permission*), Middlesex Ave., corner of Fellsway, is a model assembly unit of the Ford system, capacity 300 cars daily.

10. A *Marker* at junction of Middlesex Ave. and Fellsway indicates where Governor John Winthrop built a bark of 36 tons, named 'The Blessing of the Bay,' which was launched July 4, 1631. This was probably the first vessel built in Massachusetts.

Sharp (*L.*) *from Middlesex Ave. into Fellsway; R. from Fellsway into Puritan Rd.*

11. The *Site of Ten Hills Farm*, now covered with modern residences, extended from Shore Drive to the Fellsway. Here Governor Winthrop spent his first winter in America, afterward maintaining a town house in Boston, but frequently visiting his country estate, of which he was very fond.

L. from Puritan Rd. into Shore Drive; L. from Shore Drive into Mystic Ave.; R. from Mystic Ave. into Temple St.; R. from Temple St. into Broadway.

12. The *Magoun House* (*private*), 438 Broadway, is a two-and-a-half-story gray wooden dwelling, remarkable for its delicate arched fanlight, one of the best Colonial specimens remaining in Greater Boston. In this house the first printing press in Somerville was operated.

13. The *Old Powder House* (L) (*not open*), facing Powder House Square, a circular field-stone structure 40 feet high, with cone-shaped shingled roof, was a storm-center of Revolutionary history. Here, on September 1, 1774, General Gage seized the 250 half-barrels of gunpowder stored in it, thereby provoking the Great Assembly of the following day on Cam-

bridge Common, when thousands of patriots met ready to fight at once if called upon. Judicious counsel postponed the event till the following April at Lexington. In 1775 this Powder House became the magazine of the American army besieging Boston. The structure was built in 1703 as a gristmill.

SOUTH HADLEY. *Milk, Butter, and Ideas*

Town: Alt. 260, pop. 6838, sett. about 1659, incorp. 1753.
Transportation: Busses to Holyoke, Granby, Belchertown.
Accommodations: Two inns open all year round; one in summer only.
Information: College Inn and Book Shop Inn, South Hadley Center.

SOUTH HADLEY is a farming and college community on the Connecticut River below the low foothills of the Holyoke range of mountains, which give variety to the town's northern horizon. It is characterized by shaded streets, broad lawns, and quiet homes, and in the outskirts by elm-bordered sunny pastures, on which farms produce milk and butter for near-by manufacturing districts.

Early development was slow. The first meeting house, begun in 1732 and still standing, took five years to complete, owing to a violent controversy as to its site, during which the opposing parties several times removed structural timbers from the frame and hid them. The first minister was presently dismissed, but took no notice of his removal, and eventually had to be forcibly ejected from the pulpit with a handkerchief stuffed in his mouth, to prevent him from praying en route.

The local Indians, the Norwottucks, were peaceable, but the cruelties of invading tribes in the Connecticut Valley, especially at Deerfield, were never far out of mind, and the South Hadleyites did not feel safe until the Norwottucks were reduced to begging at scattered farmhouses for food or cider.

The Revolution found South Hadley active in the patriot cause. In 1774 the citizens voted to 'chuse four men to inspect the District about drinking East India tee.' Two shillings a day were voted 'for training men to go at a minute's warning.'

After the Revolution the town became interested both in manufactures and in the development of river navigation by means of locks and canals. By 1831 a map of the town shows at South Hadley Falls, a sawmill, a gristmill, a button factory, two paper mills, a tannery, and a large popular tavern. The leading industry continues to be paper-making, on a moderate scale, but farming is a close second. A large Irish immigration in the 1840's revived the town's agricultural interests. French-Canadians followed, taking to the mills, and there are smaller colonies of German and Polish descent.

For the past century, however, South Hadley has been best known as the seat of Mount Holyoke College for women, the oldest of the seven leading colleges for women in New England, and the mother of five colleges at home and five abroad, notably Mills College in California and the International Institute at Madrid. It has now (1937) one thousand students. Courses in the liberal arts are chiefly emphasized, but the curriculum includes also excellent courses in science.

Mary Lyon, founder of the college, was born in 1797 on a farm in near-by Buckland, and began teaching at the age of seventeen. She early displayed a scholarship remarkable for those times, as well as earnest convictions relating to the betterment of her sex through intellectual development. While she was teaching at Ipswich in the early 1830's she envisaged a permanent seminary for the thorough education of young women of moderate means. Her organization of Wheaton Seminary in 1834 (*see NORTON*) was the first step toward her goal. In 1837 Mount Holyoke opened its doors as a seminary with Mary Lyon as principal and with eighty students, who filled its four-story brick building to capacity. Co-operative management of the dormitories was an immediate feature which still exists, the students giving one hour's service each day to their household tasks, with the primary purpose of furthering training and self-reliance in household arts. In 1893 a new charter was issued to Mount Holyoke College. From 1900 to 1936, its President was Mary Emma Woolley, best known to the general public as an American delegate to the International Disarmament Conference at Geneva, the first time in history that any woman other than a reigning ruler has been admitted to participation in such an international conference.

MOTOR TOUR — 7 *m*.

N. from the village green on Woodbridge St. (State 116).

1. The *Skinner Museum* (*open daily 2-5, free*) occupies a small former church across the road from the beautiful Skinner estate (*private*), with its white house hidden behind formal evergreen trees. An *Historical Museum* is housed in the church, which, without its present spire, was the Congregational meeting house of Prescott, purchased and moved to its present site during preparations for the flooding of the town of Prescott by the waters of the Quabbin Reservoir.

Retrace State 116 through South Hadley Center.

2. The *Mount Holyoke College Campus* of 270 acres, spreading over a naturally beautiful terrain, includes *Prospect Hill*, an athletic field, tennis courts, ample lawns and farm lands, and two small lakes for canoeing, swimming, and skating. At the *Pageant Field*, an open-air auditorium, is held the annual May Day Festival.

The lecture halls and dormitories, mainly of red brick in Tudor style, are widely spaced on vivid greensward under fine trees. Outstanding are *Mary Lyon Hall*, which contains the administrative offices, and *Dwight Memorial Art Building* (*open weekdays* 9–5, *Sundays* 12–1; *adm. free*), housing a complete collection of the noted engravings of Elbridge Kingsley (1842–1918). The *Talcott Arboretum* consists of plant houses, a palm house, a horticultural economics house, and a house for aquatics. The *Playshop Laboratory* is a small, completely equipped modern experimental theater. *Mary Lyon's Tombstone* on the campus bears her memorable statement: 'There is nothing in the universe that I fear, except that I may not know my duty, or may fail to do it.'

Retrace State 116 to village green; L. from State 116 on State 63.

3. The *Pass of Thermopylae*, well named, is a narrow rock-bound passage through the foot of Mt. Holyoke near the Connecticut River. Early settlers laboriously constructed it by pouring water on the rock in winter and raking away the frozen gravel that split off.

R. from State 63 on Mt. Holyoke Rd.

4. *Titan's Piazza*, a volcanic bluff of columnar formation, has been classified as one of the world's major natural phenomena. A short distance from this bluff fossil footprints have been found.

5. The *Devil's Football* is a magnetic boulder weighing 300 tons. Geological authorities agree that it was carried here from Sunderland or Deerfield during the glacial period. Its name is derived from the popular legend that Satan kicked it from the Devil's Garden at Amherst Notch several miles away.

R. from Mt. Holyoke Rd. on toll road (small fee).

6. *Mt. Holyoke* (alt. 995), from which the college takes its name, is a huge wooded mass of trap rock of exceptional beauty, which rises high above the Connecticut River; and from the top, on a clear day, it is possible to see a distance of 70 miles. The hotel on its summit is the third to stand there. In the first one, in 1825, the town planned to entertain Lafayette with a choice of Jamaica rum, St. Croix rum, Holland gin, brandy, cognac, or cherry cordial. Unluckily the Marquis was late in his tour schedule, and had to pass directly through the town without pausing for these refreshments.

SPRINGFIELD

The Metropolis of Western Massachusetts

City: Alt. 69, pop. 149,642, sett. 1636, incorp. town 1641, city 1852.

Railroad Station: Union Station, Lyman & Liberty Sts., for N.Y., N.H. & H. R.R., B. & M. R.R., and B. & A. R.R.

Accommodations: Seven hotels.

Information: Chamber of Commerce, 134 Chestnut St.; Automobile Club, 140 Chestnut St.; A.L.A., 1387 Main St.

SPRINGFIELD, the metropolis of western Massachusetts, lies on the east bank of the Connecticut River, holding a strategic position in the traffic of the New England states with New York and the West. Its situation on a series of terraces and in gently rolling country produces an effect of spacious leisure, and imposing architecture and tree-shaded lawns, parks, and boulevards give it an atmosphere of dignity, substance, and comfort. Its diversified industries, superior transportation facilities, large merchandising establishments, and fine residential sections make it an important center of industry, commerce, and finance; and its notable interest in music and the other arts make it an outstanding cultural center.

In 1636 a dozen families made their way to the inviting valley where the Agawam River joins the Connecticut. Their livestock inflicted so much damage on the cornfields of the Indians that they were forced to abandon the settlement. They moved on across the Connecticut River, to a barren terrain demanding heart-breaking labor and promising little reward for toil.

Fortunately, the leader of the group was stout-hearted William Pynchon. With such vigor did he build up the new settlement that even after a board had been elected determination of program and policy was left in his hands. His leadership was not questioned until 1650, when he published a theological work. The Puritan Fathers detected in the book germs of heresy. To protect the community from infection they administered the antitoxin of denunciation. The services of Pynchon were soon forgotten; he was badgered on all sides, and finally returned to England. His son, John, remained and assumed the management of the town.

In the next year the Springfield community indulged in a witch hunt — a sport more exciting than the battle against heresy. Hugh Parsons was a dyspeptic, of choleric disposition which had not endeared him to his neighbors. His wife was subject to periodic fits, probably epileptic. But such an explanation of their eccentricities was too simple, and the savants of the occult brought charges of witchcraft against the couple. Not a few good people were disappointed when the court acquitted the pair.

Twenty peaceful and constructive years followed. In 1675, however, King Philip declared war on the Colony, and Springfield did not escape. The town was almost totally burned. The townspeople pushed reconstruction, building on a larger scale.

Early in the eighteenth century the citizens of Springfield made the river a capital asset. They erected sawmills and gristmills and took their first step away from a complete agricultural economy. The large clay deposits were utilized in the manufacture of brick.

Acute financial depression resulted from the Revolutionary War; farmer and mill-owner were bogged in a morass of debt. Thousands banded themselves together under Daniel Shays, and for six months tramped up and down western Massachusetts in an attempt to prevent the convening of the courts and the entering of judgments against debtors. Although their cause won numerous sympathizers, it failed. Springfield became Shays's Waterloo when an attempt to capture the United States Arsenal was frustrated.

The manufacture of metal goods was given an impetus in 1794 by the passage of a bill in Congress establishing the United States Armory at Springfield. The advent of the railroad, about 1835, stimulated business. At that time the town already had seventy-three mechanic shops, six cotton mills, four printing offices, thirteen warehouses, two card factories, two forges, one rifle factory, one powder mill, six sawmills, four grist mills, three tanneries, two jewelers' tool factories, one sword factory, and one spool factory.

Developments in the manufacture of textiles brought French-Canadians, English, and Scots. Skilled artisans of all races were attracted by the openings in the machine shops. Irish, Italian, Swedish, and German labor was plentiful. Long hours and meager wages were the lot of those whose labor enriched the town. But aside from the general agitation that accompanied the crisis of 1830, there was no real organization of labor until after the Civil War.

The year 1824 marked the founding of the *Springfield Republican* by Samuel Bowles. The excellent style of this journal, under the editorship of Dr. J. G. Holland, and the liberal philosophy of its editorials, made the paper almost a national institution. The first newspaper in Springfield, however, was the *Massachusetts Gazette and General Advertiser*, published in 1782, which failed to survive, posting this notice: 'Those gentlemen who engaged for their papers in grain are once more requested to make immediate payment, as the printers are in much want of that article.' Other papers published during this period were the *Hampshire Chronicle*, the *Hampshire Herald*, and the *Federal Spy*.

In 1847 John Brown of Akron opened the warehouse of Brown and Perkins, wool merchants. The business enjoyed a fair degree of prosperity, but John Brown was absent from business the greater part of the time, his real enthusiasm being centered in the Abolitionist movement. Said Emerson, 'If he kept sheep, it was with a royal mind. And if he traded in wool, he was a merchant prince, not in the amount of wealth, but in the protection of the interests confided to him.' He organized the United States League of Gileadites, which assisted fugitive slaves to escape.

Shortly after his arrival in Springfield, John Brown was visited by Frederick Douglass, Negro orator and scholar, who found him living in a cottage near the shacks occupied by Negroes. 'Plain as was the house on the outside,' wrote Douglass, 'the inside was plainer. Its furniture would have satisfied a Spartan. There was an element of plainness about it which almost suggested destitution.... The meal was such as a man might relish after following the plow all day, or performing a forced march of a dozen miles over a rough road in frosty weather.' John Brown lived in Springfield for two years, and during this time hundreds of runaway slaves were harbored in the town, then were passed along to the next station of the Underground Railway.

The termination of the war once more allowed the free flow of commerce. An expanding market aided in Springfield's prosperity. Factories were rebuilt and enlarged, the population swelled. Simultaneously labor took its first organized steps toward improving working and living conditions. Following the example of the horse car drivers, who in 1861 had established a benevolent association, which was forced by a threatened wage reduction to transform itself into a trade union, workers in many industries began to wage a united battle for the eight-hour day. In 1864 cigarmakers, stonecutters, pianoforte-makers, blacksmiths, carpenters, and tailors were organized to secure higher wages and shorter hours. The Massachusetts Legislature investigated the possibilities of regulating and limiting hours of labor, and eventually the eight-hour day became a reality. In the later 1880's all the trade unions in the city participated in the formation of the Central Labor Union. To Bishop N. Saltus, first president of this federation, belongs a chief share of the credit for its vigorous development.

Since 1890, such large industries have been established as the Van Norman Tool and Machine Company, the United States Envelope Company, the Fiberloid Company, the Westinghouse Electric and Manufacturing Company, and the Milton Bradley Company, makers of toys, games, and school supplies. Motorcycles have been manufactured here since the beginning of the century. On the West Springfield side of the river numerous industries have located. The Gilbert and Barker Company makes gasoline pumps and oil-burners. Matches, packaging machinery, radios, magnetos, hot-water heaters, air-conditioning equipment, and forgings are also manufactured here.

Between 1910 and 1920 the population increased 117 per cent. Of the present residents of Springfield, about one-fourth are foreign-born. The largest racial group is the Irish, which numbers nearly 6000. The Italians follow with about 4500, Russians with 3800, French-Canadians with

3700, and Poles with 2400. Scotland, England, Sweden, and Germany each contribute about 1000 to the foreign-born population.

The high percentage of skilled workers among the population has been a strong influence in the social and political life of the city. The general housing situation, for example, is considerably better in Springfield than in most industrial cities of its size. The civic life is heightened by the social clubs, singing societies, and physical culture centers of the various racial groups.

A flood in 1927 caused considerable loss when the Connecticut River overflowed its banks; but it can hardly be compared to the catastrophe of 1936, when the worst flood in the history of New England inflicted untold suffering on Springfield and caused property losses amounting to millions of dollars. Only efficient organization, prompt action, and many deeds of heroism prevented wholesale loss of human life.

FOOT TOUR — 1.5 *m.*

NW. from State St. (US 20) on Main St.; L. from Main St. into Court Square Green.

1. The *First Church of Christ* (Congregational), near the midpoint of the Green in Court Square, was designed in 1819 by Isaac Damon, the fourth structure of the First Parish. Commissioned to design a church 'with a decent plain front' he achieved a building adorned by a portico with Doric columns, triangular pediment, and decorated frieze, and topped by a cupola of three members — none, unfortunately, of open design.

2. The *Hampden County Courthouse* was built in 1871 after the design of H. H. Richardson, and showed his individualistic adaptation of late Gothic, powerfully handled to express modern function. Remodeling in 1906 has changed the mass and composition and virtually destroyed the Richardsonian elements.

3. The *Springfield Municipal Group,* on the north side of the Square, consists of an administration building, an auditorium, and a 300-foot campanile (*open Mon.–Fri.* 9–11, 2–4; *Sat.* 9–11), with an illuminated clock and a carillon of 12 bells. It was designed by Pell and Corbett and dedicated in 1913. The view from the observatory platform (*elevator*) offers a view of the city against a background of mountain peaks. The group is an impressive civic monument, imposing in its proportions, its classic detail and in the identical Corinthian porticoes which dignify the front of both buildings.

Retrace on Court Square; R. from Court Square Green into Main St.; L. from Main St. into State St.; R. from State St. into Maple St.

4. The *Colony Club,* 50 Maple St., is the former home of the late D. B. Wesson, manufacturer of firearms. The walls are of pink Milford granite;

the interior is finished in woods of native and tropical origin, variegated marbles, and satin wall coverings.

L. from Maple St. on Cemetery Ave.

5. In the *Springfield Cemetery* is a bronze relief by Saint-Gaudens representing J. G. Holland, author and associate editor of the *Springfield Republican*.

Retrace Cemetery Ave.; R. from Cemetery Ave. on Maple St.; straight ahead on Chestnut St.

6. In Merrick Park, corner of State St., is *The Puritan*, by Saint-Gaudens.

R. from Chestnut St. into first drive.

7. The *Springfield Museum of Fine Arts* (*open weekdays except Mon.* 1–4.30; *Sun.* 2–5), erected in 1933, is of steel with limestone facing, by Tilton and Githens, architects.

8. The *George Walter Vincent Smith Art Museum* (*open weekdays except Mon.* 1–5; *Sun.* 2–5) was designed in 1895, in the Italian Renaissance style, by Renwick, Aspinwall, Renwick and Walter T. Owen. In addition to paintings, it contains an especially fine collection of Chinese porcelain and cloisonné enamels.

9. The *Museum of Natural History* (*open weekdays except Mon.* 1–4.30, *Sun.* 2 5), with limestone facing, was recently rebuilt from the brick museum erected in 1899. It is by Tilton and Githens, and corresponds in style to the new Museum of Fine Arts. Groups of mammals and birds are mounted in reproductions of their natural habitat. An American Indian group illustrates the manufacture of soapstone bowls.

10. The *William Pynchon Memorial Building* (*open weekdays except Mon.* 1–4.30, *Sun.* 2–5) of Georgian Colonial architecture, was designed by Gardner, Payne, and Gardner, architects, and completed in 1927.

Retrace driveway; R. from driveway into Chestnut St.

11. *Christ Church Cathedral* (Episcopal) (*open*) was built in 1876. The pulpit and lectern were carved by Kirchmayer. The windows are by Butler and Payne and by Kemp and Kemp. A window by La Farge pictures 'Mary and Magdala at the Tomb.'

Retrace on Chestnut St.; L. from Chestnut St. into State St.

12. The *City Library* (*open weekdays* 9–9; *Sun.* 2–6), erected in 1912, is built of Vermont marble in the Italian Renaissance style; it was designed by Edward L. Tilton. Open stacks give patrons direct access to the books.

13. The *Church of the Unity* (Unitarian-Universalist), opposite the City Library, was designed by H. H. Richardson. It is notable for its stained-glass windows by Louis Tiffany, a rose window, and 14 memorial windows which include 'Heosphorus the Light-Bearer' by Edward Simmons, 'The Family' by Will H. Low, and 'Rebecca at the Well' by La Farge.

The competition for the Church of the Unity was H. H. Richardson's first real opportunity. The English parish church type was the model set, but the architect's interest already centered upon function. His adapta-

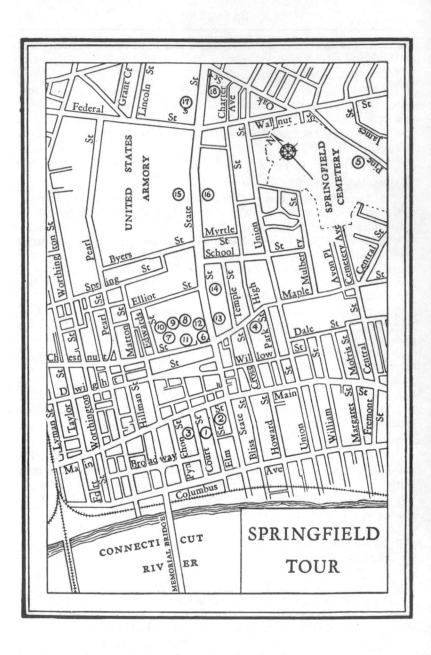

SPRINGFIELD

TOUR

tion of medieval precedent, fumbling though it was, gave promise of his later brilliance. The proportion and harmony of the interior detail are noteworthy, and the focalization of interest upon the east end of a non-ritualistic church is handled with rare mastery.

14. The *Classical High School* (*open*), opposite Elliot St., of yellow brick, was designed by Hartwell and Richardson. It contains a mural painting, 'The Light of Education,' by Robert Reid.

15. The *U.S. Armory and Arsenal* (*open by permission*) occupies a site selected by George Washington and Colonel David Mason of Boston. It was established by Congress in 1794, and the first muskets were manufactured here in 1795. The Civil War brought a great influx of workmen and in 1864 over 3000 men were employed turning out 1000 rifles a day. The Springfield rifle is still made here. Henry Wadsworth Longfellow stopped at the Arsenal on his honeymoon; his wife noticed the resemblance of the tiers of stacked arms to the pipes of an organ, and Longfellow afterward wrote 'The Arsenal at Springfield.'

The *Museum* (*open weekdays except Sat.* 8.30–12, 1–4.30) has an excellent collection of small arms. Of especial importance is the old Blanchard lathe, an invention for turning gunstocks.

16. The *High School of Commerce* (*open*), opposite the Arsenal, is of Tudor style and was designed by Kirkham and Parlett. It contains a mural 'Beside the Still Waters' painted by Paul Connoyer.

17. The *Site of the Crucial Battle of Shays's Rebellion* is marked by a large boulder on Benton Lawn, between St. James Ave. and Federal St. Here the United States soldiers, commanded by General Shepard of Westfield, repulsed Shays's attack on the stores in the Springfield Arsenal in 1786. On the same Green is an *Old Brownstone Milestone* bearing Masonic symbols erected by Joseph Wait of Brookfield in 1763 after he had lost his way in a blizzard at this parting of the Bay Path and Chicopee Road.

18. *St. Peter's Episcopal Church* (*open*), Buckingham St. near State St., is of Gothic design, with murals painted by Arthur S. Smith in the style of the 14th century.

SPRINGFIELD MAP INDEX

MOTOR TOUR — 16 *m.*

SW. from Main St. on State St.; L. from State St. on Columbus Ave. (*US* 5).

19. *Forest Park* (*open to motorists, low speed rate*) is a woodland area of 800 acres. Small ponds contain rare varieties of lotus and water lilies which bloom in July. Porter Lake is a haunt of several species of wild ducks and herons. There are trails, bowling greens, a paddle pool, tennis courts, botanical gardens, and a rose garden. A large *Zoo* (*open daily* 10–7) contains many species of animal life, while at the *Trailside Museum*, a branch of the Springfield Natural History Museum, are exhibits of flora and fauna. An exhibition of sandstone slabs shows fossil footprints of dinosaurs quarried in the Connecticut Valley near Holyoke.

20. *Pecousic Villa*, on a terrace near Longhill St., is the former home of the late Everett H. Barney, skate manufacturer, by whom a large part of Forest Park was bequeathed and endowed to the city of Springfield.

21. The *Site of King Philip's Stockade* and the vantage-point from which King Philip is said to have directed and observed the burning of Springfield in 1675 is in Forest Park. The drive, planted with rhododendrons, swings out on a terrace overlooking the Connecticut River.

L. from Columbus Ave. through South Main Entrance of Forest Park; traverse Forest Park northwesterly; R. from Forest Park into Sumner Ave.

22. *Trinity Methodist Episcopal Church*, opposite Oakland Ave., is part of a connecting group of buildings of Gothic architecture designed by Allen and Collins, including a community house with its gymnasium, swimming pool and playrooms, an auditorium with well equipped stage, and other facilities. It is surmounted by a tower containing a carillon of 61 bells. The church contains a series of 24 stained-glass windows representing historic personages with the theme 'The Light of Christ in the Life of Civilization,' depicting Lindbergh, Streseman, Kellogg, Briand, and others.

L. from Sumner Ave. on Oakland St.

23. The *All Saints' Episcopal Church* is a copy of the All Saints' Church in Springfield, England, from which came William Pynchon, founder of the city.

L. from Oakland St. on Allen St.

24. The *Drop Forge Plant* of the United States Armory (*open by permission*), known as the 'Watershops,' borders on Massasoit Lake.

R. from Allen St. on Hickory St.

25. *Massasoit Lake* or *Watershops Pond* (*swimming, boating, canoeing*) was formed by damming the Mill River to provide power for the Armory.

26. *Springfield College* is also known as International Y.M.C.A. College. Founded in 1885 by the Rev. David A. Reed, it was first known as the

School of Christian Workers. It is widely known for training in physical education and for boys' work, with graduates in nearly every part of the world. It was at this college that Professor James Naismith is said to have invented the game of basketball in the winter of 1891. Across Massasoit Lake in a grove is the Freshman Day Camp known as the *Pueblo of the Seven Fires (open by arrangement)*, a roomy lodge for camp work and nature study. Designed like the pueblos in the Southwest, it is decorated with murals in Indian symbolism painted by the Indian artist Wo Peen (Louis Gonzaleus of Santa Fé), also a few murals by Bear Heart (Herman Stoldt).

27. The *House of Professor Edgar M. Robinson (private)*, near Cross Town Boulevard, is a strange architectural whimsy. Straight lines were disregarded when its bricks, stones, and slates were fashioned into house and garage, and oddest of all are the large pictures of bears, birds, and snakes painted on gable ends and edges, the work of Ernest Thompson Seton.

L. from Hickory St. on Wilbraham Rd.

28. *American International College* (co-educational), between College and Amaron Sts., was chartered in Lowell, Mass., in 1885, where it was known as the French Protestant College. Moving to Springfield in 1888, it became known in 1894 as the French-American College, and in 1905 the name was changed to its present form. Most of the buildings are of red brick with light gray granite pillars and trim, in the Georgian Colonial style.

R. from Wilbraham Rd. on Amaron St.; R. from Amaron St. on State St.

29. *Massachusetts Mutual Life Insurance Company Building (open weekdays 9-4; apply front door for guide)* is in the Georgian Colonial style, and was built in 1926.

L. from State St. on Alton St.

30. *Blunt Park* is a grove with picnic tables and fireplaces, rustic shelters, and nature trails.

T A U N T O N . *Largest City for its Size*

City: Alt. 37, pop. 37,355, sett. 1638, incorp. town 1639, city 1864.

Railroad Stations: Central Depot, corner of Cohannet and Washington Sts., for N.Y., N.H. & H. R.R.; Whittenton Station, Whittenton St. (flag stop).

Bus Stations: City Square for Eastern Mass. Street Ry. and Greyhound Line.

Accommodations: Six hotels.

Information: Chamber of Commerce, 35 Summer St.

ABOUT the Green, an elm-fringed rectangle, is concentrated the business and civic life of Taunton; but for fifty square miles the city stretches out in fertile acres, broken by rocky outcrops and dotted by quiet residential sections and factories. Not excluding Greater Boston, Taunton is the largest city in point of area in Massachusetts. Its manufactures include textile machinery and products, machine drills and tools, marine engines, electrical specialties, minor hardware, silver jewelry, Britannia metalware and pewterware, stoves, stove linings, ceramic products, leather novelties, and medicines. But it has plenty of elbow room, and that is why despite its busy manufactures the city has an air of tranquil leisure and placidity.

Records are somewhat at variance as to the actual first settlers of Taunton. The city's seal, however, adopted January 1, 1865, bears on a central shield the figure of a woman negotiating with Indians, and above the shield the inscription ('Æneid,' I, 364), '*Dux Femina Facti*' (A Woman was the Leader of the Things Accomplished). This commemorates an early proprietor, Elizabeth Poole, in whose hands tradition places a jackknife and a peck of beans, regarded as symbolic of industry and agriculture.

The story of Taunton's 'Things Accomplished' dates back to the fisheries in Mill River, which had long been visited by the Indian tribes, and from which the first white settlers obtained their livelihood. It is quite possible that the stories of the fabulous herring-runs in April of each year, when the fish swarmed up the Cohannet and Taunton Rivers to spawn, attracted many of the first colonists. With the building of mills and the consequent pollution of the river waters the herring-runs diminished — a cause of bitter controversy between the fishermen and the early mill operators.

Some ten years after her alleged purchase of Cohannet, Elizabeth Poole formed a joint-stock company capitalized at six hundred pounds for the manufacture of bar iron; and in 1652 the town of Taunton imported three men from Braintree to assist in the erection of an iron bloomery, believed to be the first successful one in America, two previous ones in Quincy and Braintree having failed. The manufacture of bar iron and ironware was for many years one of the town's principal industries. During a scarcity of specie at the time of King Philip's War, when there were few Bank of England notes in circulation and no paper money had as yet been issued in Massachusetts, bar iron manufactured in Taunton became an accepted medium of exchange.

As early as 1684 the townsfolk replied to demands of Governor Andros for poll and property taxes that they did not 'feel free to raise money on the inhabitants without their own assent in assembly.' For transmitting this message the town clerk was fined twenty marks and held in jail for three months. On his release, however, his fellow townsmen presented him with one hundred acres of land.

In October, 1774, a Liberty Pole, 112 feet tall, was erected on the Green, bearing a Union Jack lettered with the words 'Liberty and Union; Union and Liberty'; and nailed to the pole was a bold declaration of the rights of the colonists as free and independent people. The claim is advanced locally that Taunton Green, and not Faneuil Hall in Boston, was the true 'Cradle of American Liberty.'

In 1699 the building of the first shipyard launched Taunton on its way to fame as a seaport. A lively coasting trade was soon built up. Small sloops and shallops of ten and twenty tons, laden with brick, hollow ware, and iron, sailed to Providence, Newport, and New York. As early as 1800 there was remonstrance against the construction of a bridge below the Weir because of the fact that sixteen coasting vessels were berthed above the Weir, which had, in the past year, freighted out 3,000,000 bricks, 800 tons of ironware, and 700 tons of nails. By the first decade of the nineteenth century the name 'Taunton' was painted on the sterns of more ships than that of any other New England coastal town. The first multimasted schooners along the coast were Taunton-built and owned.

After the Revolution, industries sprang up overnight, more than two hundred of them in the first half of the century. Among the more prominent were the manufacture of iron, bricks, cotton, paper, and boxboards. The Taunton Manufacturing Company, an early industrial syndicate, was organized in 1823 for rolling copper and iron and the manufacture of cotton and wool. Reed and Barton founded an extensive silverware and plated-ware works in 1824. Isaac Babbitt, the inventor of babbitt metal, and John Crossman in 1824 produced the first Britannia ware, used in inkstands, shaving boxes, and mirror frames. The Taunton Locomotive Company, which claims to be the first to manufacture locomotives in New England, began in 1846 and in 1883 added printing presses. The Weir Stove Company, now the Glenwood Range Company, one of the largest producers of stoves in the country, erected its first buildings in 1879. The Rogers Silverware Company, which enjoys an international reputation for fine silver, was incorporated in Taunton in 1883.

POINTS OF INTEREST

1. *General Cobb Boulder*, Taunton Green. At the September, 1786, term of the Common Pleas Court an armed mob in sympathy with Shays's Rebellion approached the courthouse and demanded that the court be not held. General Cobb, one of the justices, appeared on the steps and shouted: 'Away with your whining. I will hold this court if I hold it in blood; I will sit as a judge or die as a general.' The mob dispersed, but at the October sitting of the Supreme Court they assembled again. This time they found General Cobb ready for them with 400 men and a loaded cannon on the courthouse lawn. The General declared: 'If you want those papers, come and take them; but pass that line and I fire, and the blood

be on your own head.' This was the last instance of armed resistance in Bristol County.

2. The *Memorial to Elizabeth Poole* in Mt. Pleasant Cemetery, Crocker St., was erected by the women of Taunton.

3. A *Giant Oak Tree*, White St. and Somerset Ave., is known as King Philip's Oak, and is believed to be more than 400 years old.

4. The *Glenwood Range Company* (*showroom only open*), West Water St., also called the Weir Stove Company, is one of the largest manufacturing companies of its kind in the United States.

5. The *Old Colony Historical Society* (*open Mon.–Fri.* 10–12 *and* 1–4; *adm.* 25¢), 66 Church Green, occupies the Old Bristol Academy building, designed in 1852 by Richard Upjohn, a New York architect. This was formerly one of the country's leading educational institutions. The field-piece used by the militia to disperse the rioters during Shays's Rebellion is here, together with much local historical material, portraits, military uniforms, swords, and guns.

6. A *Statue of Robert Treat Paine*, one of the signers of the Declaration of Independence, designed by Richard E. Brooks, stands on Summer Street. Paine, a native of Boston, studied law and was admitted to the bar in 1757. He moved to Taunton and married Sally Cobb of Attleboro. From 1773 to 1778 he was a member of the Massachusetts General Court, and served as a delegate to the Continental Congress in Philadelphia.

7. The *Meeting House* on Spring St., transitional in plan between the meeting house and church styles of architecture, was designed by Charles Bulfinch about 1789 and completed in 1793. Showing typical contemporary design in the belfry and spire, the church is interesting as a step in Bulfinch's development of the façade with projecting porch, and for the cupola belfry characteristic of his work.

W A L T H A M . *City of Five-Score Industries*

City: Alt. 48, pop. 40,557, sett. 1634, incorp. town 1738, city 1884.

Railroad Stations: Waltham North Station, off Lexington St., and Waltham Station, off Carter St., for B. & M. R.R.

Bus Stations: 66 Main St. for Greyhound Lines; 509 Moody St. for Berkshire Motor Coach.

Accommodations: Two hotels at reasonable rates.

Information: Chamber of Commerce, 657 Main St.

WALTHAM, the home of the world's largest watch factory, is a prosperous manufacturing city situated near the headwaters of the Charles River, nine miles west of Boston. Rugged and picturesque eminences skirt the northern and western limits of the city; wild forest growth, thriftily cultivated farm acreage, and well-kept estates, all watered by ponds, brooks, and rivers, diversify the pleasant scene. The thickly settled part of the city is built upon an undulating plain, surrounded by hills and bisected by the Charles River, which divides it into the North Side and the South Side, connected by a series of substantial bridges. The river itself is the central artery of the city life. Not only has it contributed natural beauty; it has also supplied excellent facilities for manufacturing and has been a dominant factor in Waltham's prosperity.

In 1738, after much agitation and considerable disagreement, the West Precinct of Watertown was incorporated as the township of Waltham, a name which means Forest Home, *walt* signifying a forest or wood, and *ham* a dwelling or home. As an outlying part of Watertown the growth of Waltham had been slow, but immediately following its birth as a separate town it began to thrive agriculturally, and so continued until, about the beginning of the nineteenth century, agriculture yielded to industry.

In 1813 the Boston Manufacturing Company was organized. This company established a factory which was the first in America to manufacture raw cotton into finished cloth, carrying out the complete process under one roof. The enterprise prospered, and with it the town. In 1819 other mills arose, added to the original plant, and a bleachery was set up where cloth could be bleached by a chemical process.

There now sprang up various other manufacturing enterprises: an iron foundry; a laboratory where some of the first experiments were made with petroleum products; a factory for the manufacture of crayons, the invention of an ingenious citizen.

More important was the establishment in 1854 of the American Waltham Watch Company, which manufactured the first machine-made watches in the United States. This enterprise more than any other advanced the progress of Waltham, and extended its name over the civilized world.

At the present time there are one hundred and twenty-five industries engaged in the manufacture of such other diverse articles as knit goods, furniture, canoes, enamelware, plumbing supplies, paper, silk goods, silk screen art goods, traffic signs, vermin exterminators, salesbooks, shoes, batteries, and oil-burners.

Until about 1840 the population was entirely of native English stock, but with the change from a strictly agricultural community to a rapidly expanding industrial town, a supply of cheap labor became necessary. Accordingly such racial elements as the French, Irish, Poles, Russians, Jews, and Italians were brought into the town, with the ultimate result that of the present population about two-thirds are of foreign derivation.

POINTS OF INTEREST

1. The *Waltham Public Library* (*open weekdays* 9–9), 735 Main St. (1915), is the work of Leland and Loring, and is a charming contemporary adaptation of the late Georgian style. In the Sears Room is a permanent collection of Woodburyana, the gift of the Misses Sears. Charles H. Woodbury, born in Lynn in 1864, is one of America's noted marine artists.

2. *Theodore Lyman House* (*private*), Lyman St., screened by tall trees, is attractively situated on the shore of Lyman Pond. This manorial structure, with two-story wings and hip roof, was built in 1798 from designs by Samuel McIntire. Like all his work, it shows strong Adam influence and is one of the few houses designed by McIntire outside of Salem. The severity of its masses is relieved by Ionic pilasters, roof balustrades, and much fine detail in the Adam manner. The east wing is an addition, and the house was altered in 1882.

3. The *Old Mansion House* (*adm.* 10¢), Beaver St., stands on the hill of the Girl Scouts' Reservation, overlooking a maze of thick arborvitae, copied from the famous one made for Cardinal Wolsey at Hampton Court, England, in the sixteenth century.

4. The *Walter E. Fernald School* (*open Wed. and Thurs.* 2–5) (also known as the Massachusetts School for the Feeble-Minded), Trapelo Rd., founded in 1848, is one of the oldest State institutions of its kind in the country, and was named for its first superintendent, a noted psychiatrist. It houses about 2000 mental defectives. Education goes through the first five grades and includes the following subjects: sense training, physical training, music, dramatics, domestic science, and industrial training. The latter includes dressmaking, knitting, and beauty-parlor training for girls, and repair work, printing, and manual training for boys.

5. The *Governor Christopher Gore House* (*open as tearoom, adm.* 25¢), stands on Gore St., near Main St., behind an old stone wall, set back in a widespread lawn dotted with trees. As rebuilt between 1799 and 1804 it may be the work of Charles Bulfinch. It is among the comparatively few New England houses which exemplify the projecting elliptical salon derived from French influence. The main building with its two long low wings — about 200 feet in length — uses the salon as the focal point of the garden front. The façade of the entrance front is characterized by a triple arched doorway, and the long roof is surrounded by an eaves balustrade illustrating the use, new at the time, of long solid panels with baluster openings only above the windows.

6. The buildings of the former *Boston Manufacturing Company*, between Elm and Moody Sts., which went into receivership in 1929, are now occupied by several separate concerns. Here the No. 1 Mill (1813), now a shoe factory, still stands on the banks of the Charles, the first mill in the

country in which all operations for making cotton were carried on under one roof.

In 1811 Francis Cabot Lowell of Boston journeyed to Manchester, England, to study the cotton industry there. Although he was not allowed to make drawings of equipment, he successfully and ingeniously designed similar machinery from sheer memory. On his return he chose Waltham (1813) for the site of the Boston Manufacturing Company, which assumed at once an important place in American industry. At the height of its prosperity it had over 2000 looms with a daily capacity of 30 miles of cotton fabrics.

7. The red-brick buildings of the *Waltham Watch Company* (*open daily* 10–3), Crescent St., are also on the banks of the Charles River. In 1849 Aaron Dennison, one of the founders of the Dennison Manufacturing Company, and Edward Howard, who had previously tried to interest the former in making steam engines, established a partnership for the manufacture of watches by machinery, the first attempt of the sort in America. Although there were industrial watch centers in Europe, in America the various parts were still produced by hand and assembled by single artisans. Dennison went to England; he also studied Eli Whitney's new methods as applied to the factory production of rifles with interchangeable parts; finally, after four years of labor and study, he and Howard were successful in designing and building a machine to create watch movements. In 1868 American companies began to manufacture other parts, such as dials, jewels, and hands. Such is the intricacy of the manufacture of watches that some of the fine parts have to be handled in wax and assembled under a microscope.

8. *Perrine Quality Product Corporation* (*open*), 55 Rumford Ave., manufactured the batteries taken to Little America by Admiral Richard E. Byrd on his first trip.

9. The building of the *Middlesex College of Medicine and Surgery* (*open*) (chartered in 1850; moved to Waltham in 1928), South St., is an astonishing piece of architecture, styled as a Gothic castle and fashioned of varicolored stones. Towers and cone-topped turrets rise high above the main body of the structure, while the rear is guarded by a high stone wall typical of those which surround ancient European castles. Stone stairways lead from the ground to the battlements above. From here a superb view reveals the industrial section of the city, flanked by a residential belt more and more sparsely settled toward the broad flat lowland fields and woods raggedly split by the upper reaches of the Charles River.

10. *Prospect Hill Park*, Prospect Hill Rd., off Main St., a large wooded public reservation, is covered with 'small pines, oaks, and maples. It has two summits, one of which is the highest point in Greater Boston next to Great Blue Hill.

11. The *City Hall*, designed by Kilham, Hopkins and Greeley and built in 1925, is a fine contemporary adaptation of Georgian Colonial design.

W A T E R T O W N . *Cradle of the Town Meeting*

Town: Alt. 20, pop. 35,827, sett. 1630, incorp. 1630.

Railroad Station: Union Market Station, Market St., for B. & M. R.R.

Bus Station: Watertown Square, for Greyhound, Victoria Coach, and Black Hawk Lines. B. & W. Lines are part of the National Trailways connecting the east and west coasts.

Accommodations: Rooming and boarding-houses. A few overnight tourist places.

WATERTOWN presents an example of a vigorous community cramped within boundaries no longer adequate to normal expansion. The original boundary included, besides the present town, the whole of Waltham and Weston, parts of Belmont and Cambridge, and the greater part of Lincoln. Disagreement over the location of a meeting house led to the secession of one faction to form Weston, and an argument relating to a schoolhouse caused the origin of Waltham. Now Watertown is compressed into an area of approximately four square miles surrounding the falls of the Charles River.

It is a town in which the natural processes of growth maintain a wavering balance between the residential and industrial sections, and between racial groups. About one third of the inhabitants are descendants of American-born parents; a little less than one half are native born of foreign or mixed parentage, and about one sixth are foreign born. In all, thirty-five nations are represented, chief groups being the Irish, Italians, Canadians, English, and Armenians.

Though in material aspects resembling the rest of the Boston Metropolitan area, Watertown is distinguished by its spiritual fidelity to the past. Outwardly there is no semblance between these streets thickly lined with dwellings, stores, office-buildings, and factories and the cluster of primitive lean-tos scattered along the Charles River. Inwardly, the early Watertown spirit of impatience with prescribed forms and of self-determination and self-expression in government exists both in the citizens' attitude and in the political symbol, the representative town meeting, which is still used.

The history of Watertown dates from 1630, when Governor Winthrop's fleet arrived in Massachusetts Bay with a thousand souls on board. The flagship 'Arbella' carried Lady Arbella Johnson and her husband, Sir Richard Saltonstall and his motherless children, the Reverend George Phillips, the Reverend Mr. Wilson, and others.

Exhausted, ill, and weakened by privations and disease, the company rested for a short while in Charlestown. Then they split into two congregations and signed two church convenants. One group removed to Boston with the Reverend Mr. Wilson; the other, numbering more than one hundred families, followed the Reverend Mr. Phillips, to make the first inland settlement of the Bay Colony. The colonists sailed up the Charles River to the fertile lands about Gerry's Landing, now in Cambridge, where they built their first homesteads. Because it was so well watered, they named the region Watertown.

The falls of the Charles contributed natural water-power suitable for industrial development. Shortly after the settlement was established a mill and dam were built by Thomas Mayhew and Elder Edward How. In the nineteenth century the same source furnished power to the mills and factories making soap, candles, paper, tan bark, cotton warp, and cotton-sail duck for the merchant fleets of Salem and Boston. A laundry and a dye-house prospered beside the river, and an ice company was established. During this period the beauty of the Charles attracted many Boston merchants, who established pretentious estates on its shores.

Immediately after the Revolutionary War, during the era of depreciated currency and high taxes, when many Boston fortunes vanished, the citizens of Watertown remained secure, their capital firmly invested in land.

A tremendous impetus was given to industrial development in 1816 by the choice of a site on the Charles River at Watertown for the United States Arsenal. During the Civil War the Walker and Pratt Company of Watertown supplied the Union with ammunition and gun-carriage castings. By 1875, the population had increased to approximately six thousand, but there it hung until the opening of the Cambridge subway, in 1909, brought a flood of newcomers and gave fresh impetus to the town's industries.

The founders' democratic and liberal spirit predetermined the character of the community's institutions and conduct. Three men initiated a democracy of government which has been consistently followed. They were John Oldham, an exile from the Plymouth Colony, Sir Richard Saltonstall, and the Reverend George Phillips. Oldham realized the mistakes that had been made in Plymouth — lack of democratic spirit, absentee control by proprietors resident in England, and the aristocratic pretensions of a few citizens. He was determined that these mistakes should not be repeated in Watertown. The first Board of Selectmen was elected in August, 1634; to Watertown goes the honor of having the first such board in New England.

Under the Reverend Mr. Phillips and his successor the early church was as democratic as the town meeting. For this reason the Watertown church was constantly under fire. That there were no Quaker hangings in Watertown was a matter of deep concern to those neighboring congregations who regarded themselves as God's appointed representatives. It was still more distressing to the pious that Watertown was completely free of supernatural affliction when surrounding communities were having an epidemic of witches and highly satisfactory persecutions. Neighboring churches finally became so concerned that the Reverend Mr. Gibbs, then pastor of the Watertown church, was invited to visit Salem Village and attend the witch trials there, no doubt in the hope that Watertown might be educated to know a witch when it saw one. The spectacle at Salem Village was most convincing and Mr. Gibbs returned perplexed and grieved; but Satan continued to ignore Watertown.

During the pre-Revolutionary decade the town was aflame with revolt against British tyranny. Boston was full of Tories, and many Whigs fled to Watertown for refuge. Among these was Printer Edes, publisher of the inflammatory *Boston Gazette and Country Journal*, which sent out political news of a strong Whig bias all over the country. Setting up his shop near the bridge of Watertown, Edes worked there unmolested for more than a year, printing and distributing his subversive literature.

About the middle of the next century a citizen of Watertown, Benjamin Robbins Curtis, then an associate justice of the Supreme Court, gave the dissenting opinion in the Dred Scott Case. Later, when Congress impeached Andrew Johnson, Curtis secured the President's acquittal.

Though it flowered late, Watertown had a period of distinguished culture. Early in the nineteenth century the Reverend Convers Francis's study became headquarters for the Transcendentalists. Here Ralph Waldo Emerson, Margaret Fuller, Theodore Parker, and others met to talk with him and his sister Lydia Maria Francis, whose published works include an Indian romance, an epic poem, a cookbook, 'The Frugal Housewife,' and 'The Progress of Religious Ideas Through Successive Ages.' With her husband, Dr. Child, she joined the anti-slavery movement.

Another native of Watertown, Charles Pratt (1830–91), founded Pratt Institute in Brooklyn, New York. In Watertown, also, James Russell Lowell courted Maria White. Here Celia Thaxter wrote poetry which was popular in its day. Ellen Robbins painted china coveted by the most stylish cupboards of New England, and Harriet Hosmer achieved a place in sculpture. Watertown was also the home of Anne Whitney, who wrote undistinguished poetry until she was forty years of age and then became a sculptor. Her statue of Samuel Adams stands in Adams Square, Boston; her 'Charles Sumner' is in Cambridge; and best known is her 'Leif Ericson' on Commonwealth Avenue.

TOUR — 6.5 *m.*

NE. from Watertown Square on Mt. Auburn St.

1. A stone tablet, corner of Mt. Auburn and Marshall Sts., identifies the *Site Where the Provincial Congress Sat in* 1775.

L. from Mt. Auburn St. on Marshall St.

2. *Marshall Fowle House (open on request)*, 28 Marshall St., was recently

purchased by the Watertown Historical Society. In this large rectangular building of clapboarding, painted yellow and fronted by a small lawn, Mercy Warren entertained General Washington. Here, it is claimed, General Warren spent his last night before the Battle of Bunker Hill. Better established, however, is the claim of the Hunt House, demolished May 1935, which was across the river, off Galen St. Here General Warren boarded for a time. In her diary Mrs. Betsy Hunt Palmer wrote: 'He was a handsome man and wore a tie wig, he had a fine color in his face and light blue eyes. He dined with us and while at dinner said, "Come, my little girl, drink a glass of wine with me for the last time, for I am going on the hill tomorrow and I shall never come off!"'

R. from Marshall St. on Spring St.; straight ahead on Common St.; R. from Common St. on Belmont St.

3. The *Oakley Country Club* (*open by permission*), 410 Belmont St., which was built as a summer residence for Harrison Gray Otis in 1700, is owned by a private club. The house contains a circular stair and one of the few remaining oval rooms in New England. Beneath the floor of the huge beamed kitchen is a dry well believed to have been used as a hiding-place from the Indians.

R. from Belmont St. on Arlington St.

4. The *Old Cemetery*, Grove St. at Coolidge Square, dates back to 1642. Here are the graves of the Coolidges and the Garfields, ancestors of two Presidents.

R. from Arlington St. on Mt. Auburn St.; L. from Mt. Auburn St. on School St.; L. from School St. on Arsenal St.

5. *U.S. Arsenal* (*not open to the public*). During the World War the Arsenal was enlarged by $24,000,000 worth of new buildings devoted to the manufacture of ordnance, employing over 3000 persons.

Retrace on Arsenal St.; L. from Arsenal St. on School St.; straight ahead on Charles River Rd.; R. from Charles River Rd. on Irving St.; R. from Irving St. on Riverside St.

6. *Perkins Institution and Massachusetts School for the Blind* (*open weekdays; free*) was founded in 1829, opened in South Boston in 1832, and removed to Watertown in 1912. Its first director was Dr. Samuel Gridley Howe, assisted by his wife Julia Ward Howe, the abolitionist, best known now as the author of 'The Battle-Hymn of the Republic.' Helen Keller spent part of a year here.

The grounds, 35 acres, form a park on a terraced knoll overlooking the Charles River. The buildings, in Tudor-Gothic style, are grouped about four garden closes. A tower above the Charles stands out boldly against the sky, offering an excellent view of the river and adjacent sections of Cambridge and Newton. A *Museum* (*open weekdays* 9–5; *Sat.* 9–12) contains exhibits of fish, birds, reptiles, minerals, and plants.

General education from kindergarten through high school is offered, with emphasis upon arts and crafts. A Braille library of 25,000 volumes is used in the school, with free circulation among the adult blind of New England. Training courses for teachers of the blind, offered in conjunction with Harvard University, draw students from all parts of the world.

Retrace Riverside St.; L. from Riverside St. on Irving St.; R. from Irving St. to Charles River Rd.

7. Overlooking the river stands a bronze statue of *Sir Richard Saltonstall* by Henry Hudson Kitson. A bronze plaque on the left wing of the base shows in bas-relief the historic exchange of a bass for a 'biscuit cake' — the friendly first meeting of Roger Clap and the local Indians, an episode also depicted on the Town Seal. On the right wing a similar plaque depicts the Rev. Phillips's protest against 'Taxation without Representation.' On the river bank near-by is the spot where Roger Clap landed with a party from Nantasket on board the 'Mary and John.'

Here also is the site of one of the first bridges in New England, now replaced by a modern structure spanning the Charles River. Close by was the ancient ford approached by the 'Old Mill Road' from Cambridge. One hundred rods above the ford and 100 rods below it were weirs to protect the fisheries.

Straight ahead to Watertown Square; straight ahead across Watertown Square into Main St.

8. The *Abijah White House* (*occasionally open on request*), 249 Main St., is largely a restoration. In this beautiful square Colonial house of pink brick overgrown with ivy and surrounded by shrubbery, with its four great chimneys and handsome porch with granite steps, was born Maria White, who later became Mrs. James Russell Lowell.

9. The *Celia Thaxter House* (*private*) is diagonally opposite at 262 Main St. An oblong house of faded yellow clapboards with a hip roof, the one-time residence of the poet, stands in a small neat yard enclosed by an iron picket fence.

10. The *Captain Abraham Browne House* (*open; adm.* 15¢), 562 Main St. The weather-beaten house, behind its green hedge and shadowing pines, is largely a restoration; but the original part, built in 1663, and its chimney, remains. Its three-part casement windows are claimed to be the only ones extant in New England. In the kitchen an old fireplace is fitted with the original utensils, great pots, roasting spit, crane, ladles and other equipment.

L. from Main St. on Gore St.

11. The beautiful *Governor Christopher Gore Estate* is bisected by the Watertown-Waltham line (*see WALTHAM*).

WELLESLEY . *Town of Schools — and a College*

Town: Alt. 140, pop. 13,376, sett. 1660, incorp. 1881.

Railroad Stations: Wellesley Farms, off Glen Rd.; Wellesley Hills, 335 Washington St.; Wellesley, foot of Grove St. at Wellesley Square, for B. & A. R.R.

Accommodations: One hotel at reasonable rates.

Water Sports: Canoeing, boating, swimming, and bathing in Lake Waban and Lake Morse.

Information: Public Library, Town Hall Building.

WELLESLEY is chiefly known as the seat of Wellesley College. Its proximity to Boston, however, its convenient rural atmosphere, pleasant homes, the beauty of the college campus, the delightful drives, and hills which offer charming vistas at every turn, combine to make Wellesley a most attractive residential town. Though it is by no means a manufacturing center, several industrial establishments are situated here. As long ago as 1704 a sawmill was set up. Later on paper mills, hosiery mills, in 1880 a shoddy mill, a shoe factory, a paint factory, and a chemical factory developed. At present the industries of the town are the making of electrical machinery, hosiery, and shoddy. For the most part, however, Wellesley comprises farms and residences.

The name Wellesley is an adaptation of the family name of Samuel Welles, a Harvard graduate and son of a graduate of Yale, who in 1763 established his home here, within the limits of the town of Natick. In 1881, Samuel Welles's grandson-in-law, H. Hollis Hunnewell, bought the vast Welles estate from the several heirs who then owned it, and gave to it the name of Wellesley.

The first white settler to establish himself in this region was Andrew Dewing, who erected a garrison house in 1660. In the spring of 1881 a petition was granted whereby the settlement became a separate town. That it was poor compared with other communities is clear from the absence of fine old houses of the Colonial period. The farmers, who comprised nearly the whole population, did not cultivate large tracts of ground, but depended chiefly upon a sale of wood, bark, hoop-poles, and fagots to supply them with the necessities they could not raise. About the middle of the nineteenth century, however, the town took a new lease of life. In 1883 sidewalks were laid, a watering cart was put into service, and a fire department was organized. A board of health was established in 1889.

About this same time the town was given its present trend by the foundation in 1871 of a Female Seminary, later to be Wellesley College. Henry Fowle Durant, the founder, was a resident of Hanover, New

Hampshire, and a graduate of Harvard. His purpose in creating the Seminary was not only to offer young women opportunities for education equivalent to those provided for men, but also 'to establish an institution for the greater glory of God.' On August 18, 1871, the cornerstone of the first building was laid by Mrs. Durant. On September 8, 1875, the school, now officially Wellesley College, opened its doors to three hundred and fourteen students. Two hundred were turned away for lack of room. The main building contained the first laboratories for scientific investigation made available for women in the United States.

The college offers the baccalaureate degree of A.B., the graduate degree of M.A., and the degree of M.S. in Hygiene and Physical Education. It is neither sectional nor sectarian. Although Christian in influence and instruction, it makes no distinctions of race or faith. About seventy per cent of the students have homes outside New England and represent the nations of the world. The enrollment averages about fifteen hundred students. Wellesley contributes toward the support of the American School of Classical Studies in Athens and in Rome, the Marine Biological Laboratory at Woods Hole, and the Women's Table at the Zoological Station in Naples.

As usually happens when a college occupies a town, preparatory schools cluster about it. In Wellesley, Dana Hall, a girls' preparatory school, opened its doors to thirty students four years after the founding of the college. It now has (1937) an enrollment of about one hundred and sixty-five. Pine Manor, a junior college, established in 1911, has (1937) some one hundred and fifty students. Ten Acre (1910), a school for younger girls, with an enrollment of seventy pupils, is also well known.

The town has many names with important historical, scientific, and literary associations. Isaac Spoge, illustrator of Grey's 'Botany,' a friend and collaborator of Audubon, was a resident of Wellesley. Alexander Graham Bell lived here at the time of his invention of the telephone. Dr. W. T. C. Morton, co-discoverer of the use of ether in surgery, was a member of the community. Agnes Edwards Rothery and Katharine Lee Bates, writers, were graduates of Wellesley College.

TOUR — 11.2 m.

W. from Wellesley Square on Central St.

1. The *Wellesley College Campus* embraces 400 acres of undulating hills covered with velvety greensward and shady groves.

A disastrous fire in 1914 destroyed the old College Hall, the laboratories, classrooms, offices, auditorium, and dormitories housing 216 students. The halls of science, dormitories, recreation center, lecture halls, and administration building which replace them have been so fitted to the rolling contours of the campus that they seem an integral part of its beauty.

> The architecture of the new Wellesley is a modern adaptation of the Gothic, and is probably at its best in *Hetty H. R. Green Hall*, the Administration building. To the left of the fine entrance is a large reception hall known as the 'blue lounge' because of its predominant color — the deep, rich Wellesley blue. At the ends of the room are murals painted by Albert Herter and given by Caroline Hazard, Wellesley's fifth president, in memory of the poet Katharine Lee Bates, an alumna. The murals were inspired by Miss Bates's best-known poem, 'America the Beautiful.'

> *Sage Hall*, a large modern brick building, is devoted to the biological sciences, botany and zoology. It borders on a courtyard enclosed by fourteen botany greenhouses and the Zoology Vivarium.

> The *Whitin Observatory* (*open only on special occasions*) is a low, white building surmounted by two small revolving domes. It contains an attractive study hall and several smaller study rooms; at the farther end of the building is a dimly lighted room with two telescopes trained on the heavens.

> The *Houghton Memorial Chapel* shows the Gothic influence.

> The *Farnsworth Art Museum* (*open during the college year, weekdays,* 8–5.30; *Sun.* 2–5) contains exceptionally fine Italian and Siamese paintings, and specimens of Egyptian materials and lace, as well as representations of contemporary art.

> *Tower Court* is the largest dormitory in the campus. Near-by are *Severance, Crawford*, and *Claflin Halls*. The latter contains carved figures on the balcony above the Great Hall representing the Mad Hatter, the Red Queen, the March Hare, and the Red King, and once in each college generation the students in Claflin give an 'Alice in Wonderland' skit.

> *Alumnae Hall* (1925), designed by Cram and Ferguson, contains a spacious white-paneled ballroom and a theater with a seating capacity of 1500. It is late Tudor in style, with some early Renaissance detail in parts of the building.

> The *Library*, erected through the generosity of Andrew Carnegie, has a collection of about 155,000 volumes. The entrance is through heavy bronze doors designed by Evelyn Beatrice Longman.

L. from Central St. into Pond Rd.

2. *Lake Waban* is the scene of many of Wellesley College student outdoor activities. Here are held crew practice and the races; here the students row about or paddle canoes; here in mid-May is held Float Night, when the sloping shores form a natural amphitheater from which to enjoy the moonlit pageant.

3. The *Welles House* (*private*), corner of Washington St., is a two-story frame structure with four large chimneys. Built in 1763, it was once the home of Samuel Welles, in whose honor the town was named.

L. from Pond Rd. into Washington St.

4. The *Hunnewell Gardens*, on the grounds of the Hunnewell Mansion (1852), were laid out in the Italian style, and cover six terraces rising 400 feet above the level of Lake Waban. These gardens contain over two acres of shrubs and flowers of great variety and beauty.

5. A tablet on a *Boulder* beside the door of the town library reads: 'Here lived W. T. G. Morton. He gave the world the use of ether in surgery. A.D. 1846.' The historic *Wellesley Buttonwood Tree* figures ironically in the story of one of humanity's greatest benefactors. On this tree, which

formerly stood on the southerly side of Washington St., east of Wellesley Square, Dr. Morton was hanged in effigy as an expression of the popular resentment of his fellow townsmen at his failure to pay his bills.

R. from Washington St. into Wellesley Ave.

6. *Babson Institute*, founded in 1919, aims to provide a thorough and practical training in business fundamentals, business ethics, and executive control. From a humble beginning in a single residence, the Institute now consists of 12 large brick buildings of Colonial design situated in Babson Park — a tract of 135 acres covering one of the highest points of land in Wellesley.

> In the *Coleman Map Building* (*open weekdays throughout the year*, 8–5; *Sat. Sun. and holidays* 2–6, *between April* 19 *and last Sun. in Oct.*), the largest building on the campus of Babson Institute, is being erected a large relief map of the United States. This map is built on a spherical surface in exact proportion to the actual curvature of the earth. It is 63 feet long (east and west) by 46 feet in width (north and south), and covers an area of 3000 square feet. When completed this map will show in proportional relief the exact topographical elevations of the country.

L. from Wellesley Ave. into Brookside Rd.; R. from Brookside Rd. into Oakland St.

7. The *Ware House* (1720) (*private*), at corner of Oakland St. and Brookside Rd., is a two-story structure with clapboarded walls and slate roof, extensively remodeled, but retaining the old beams, corner posts, wall paneling, and wide pine floor boarding.

L. from Oakland St. into Hunnewell St.; L. from Hunnewell St. into Cedar St. '

8. The *Slack House* (*private*), corner of Cedar and Walnut Sts., is a two-story white house built before 1775 as a place of refuge for the family of Benjamin Slack of Roxbury. Despite alterations the Slack house still retains much of its initial character, and contains the old Dutch oven, fireplaces, and some of the original beams.

W E Y M O U T H . *Aggregate of Villages*

Town: Alt. 42, pop. 21,748, sett. 1630, incorp. 1635.

Railroad Stations: Weymouth Station, Commercial St., Weymouth Heights Station, North St., East Weymouth Station, Station St., and South Weymouth Station, Pond St., for N.Y., N.H. & H. R.R.

Accommodations: Two hotels at reasonable rates.

Water Sports: Whitman Pond, Weymouth Great Pond for canoeing, Hingham

Bay for motor boat trips and sailing. Wessaguset Yacht Club (*adm. by invitation*), and King Cove Yacht Club (*adm. by invitation*).

Riding: Weymouth Pond Bridle Trail, Pine Grove Park, Cedar Park, and Massasoit Trail. Horses may be hired at sections near these paths.

Information: Tufts Library, 60 Washington St.

WEYMOUTH is an aggregate of a half-dozen villages, each composed of a compact industrial center surrounded by its own residential section and outlying fields. At Weymouth Landing the appearance is still that of a seaport, for here on the tidal Fore River are the old wharves. Toward South Weymouth lies a great pine grove, an oasis of quiet, possibly two square miles in extent.

For nearly two hundred years Weymouth, the second settlement in Massachusetts, was a fishing and agricultural community with productive farms and celebrated dairies. Gradually mills polluted the waters and prevented the fish from ascending to the ponds; there was no more fishing; the source of fertilizer was cut off, and this had a deleterious effect upon the farms.

As early as 1697 a tannery was established. In 1853 James Sylvester Clapp founded the Clapp Shoe Company, which for four generations has remained in the same family. Clapp's native shrewdness brought about the transition from outmoded processes and materials to the then recently developed use of French kid and patent kid in the manufacture of shoes; and his organization was a pioneer in the replacement of steam power by electricity. Later came the Stetson Shoe Company, an additional source of civic prosperity.

In 1771 iron ore was found in the ponds of the town, and the manufacture of iron commodities, especially nails, was begun. Weymouth also possessed a hammock factory, a fireworks factory, established in 1850, and a heel factory. Today, next to shoemaking, granite-quarrying and electric power production are most important.

TOUR — 23 m.

N. from Weymouth Square on Commercial St.

1. The *Samuel Arnold House* (*private*), 75 Commercial St. (old number 17, still on the house), built about 1803, was later known as the Cowing House. Samuel Arnold was the son of a prominent tavern-keeper who then lived opposite. This large brick mansion with white stone trim is the only 'three-decker' among the old houses of Weymouth.

L. from Commercial St. into Church St.; L. from Church St. into North St. (Weymouth Heights); L. from North St. into Bridge St.

2. The *Abigail Adams Birthplace* (1740) (*private*), 450 Bridge St. Only a portion remains of the original dwelling where Abigail Smith Adams, daughter of a Weymouth clergyman and later the wife of President John Adams, was born.

R. from Bridge St. into Birchbrow Ave. (North Weymouth); L. from Birchbrow Ave. into Babcock Ave.

3. At *King's Cove* the ships 'Charity' and 'Swan' landed in 1622 with the first Weymouth colonists. The nascent community, obliged to hang a young man who had committed a crime against the Indians yet unable to spare the offender's muscle, solved the dilemma by hanging an innocent bedridden comrade (whether with or without the martyr's consent is not quite clear), thus tricking the savages and saving an able-bodied citizen. The town historian denies that this heinous act was really committed, but true or not, the original story is embedded in Butler's 'Hudibras,' where it delighted England, ever a bit critical of the peccadilloes of her colonies.

Retrace on Babcock Ave.; R. from Babcock Ave. into Birchbrow Ave.; R. from Birchbrow Ave. into Bridge St.

4. The *Power Plant of the Edison Electric Illuminating Company* (*open on application*), on the westerly bank of the Fore River, designed by Stone and Webster, supplies Greater Boston and other Massachusetts towns with electricity. The enclosed corridor outside the building is 180 feet high. It conveys 1000 tons of coal daily, which are never touched by hand from the time of unloading until, after passing through the roaring furnaces of the interior, they return as ashes. The burning furnaces may be inspected through a heavy shield of blue glass. The interior of the plant is immaculate in white glazed brick and polished brass.

Retrace on Bridge St.; R. from Bridge St. into North St.; straight ahead from North St. into Commercial St.; L. from Commercial St. into first unmarked road after Church St.

5. The *Emery House* (*private*), crowning the summit of King Oak Hill, resembles on a small scale, Mt. Vernon, George Washington's Virginia home.

Retrace unmarked road; L. from unmarked road on Commercial St.; straight ahead from Commercial St. into Middle St.

6. The *Town Hall* is a modern structure, influenced by the Old State House in Boston. The British Lion and Unicorn of the east gable in Boston are replaced on the gable here by a large sundial of terra cotta.

Adjoining, and fronting the high school, is the finely imaginative *Memorial of All Wars*, an open-air auditorium.

R. from Middle St. into Essex St.; R. from Essex St. into unmarked road, almost opposite Spring St., best traversed by foot, although passable by car.

7. *House Rock*, a boulder as large as a small house, sometimes referred to as the Weymouth Sphinx, stands up commandingly upon two heavy

stone prongs, between which a low arch affords room for a small person to crawl through under the boulder. The faintly discernible profile in its side has been variously considered to resemble the Egyptian Sphinx and Queen Victoria. This is the largest boulder left in Massachusetts by the glaciers.

Retrace on unmarked road; L. from unmarked road into Essex St.; L. from Essex St. into Middle St.; R. from Middle St. into Charles St.

8. The *Clapp Shoe Company* (*visitors not allowed*), a four-story gray building away from any industrial center, has an old-time air of native independent enterprise. Through the windows may be seen workers in denim or leather aprons, the traditional dress of the guild.

L. from Charles St. into Lake St.; straight ahead from Lake St. into Shawmut St.; R. from Shawmut St. into Pleasant St. (East Weymouth); L. from Pleasant St. on Washington St. (State 3).

9. The *Old Toll House* (*private*), 1284 Washington St., a one-story stone building with a red-shingled roof, was built in 1800 by Bela Pratt, a Revolutionary patriot and ancestor of the famous sculptor.

Retrace Washington St.; L. from Washington St. into Pleasant St.; L. from Pleasant St. into Pine St.

10. *Mt. Hope Cemetery and Bird Sanctuary*, at the junction of Pine and Elm Sts., is a happy symbol of life in death. To the elms within are attached bird-houses, recalling Bryant's wish:

> 'The oriole should build and tell
> His love-tale close beside my cell.'

R. from Pine St. into Elm St. (L. if the visitor's car has entered the cemetery and retraced); L. from Elm St. into Pleasant St.; R. from Pleasant St. into Park Ave.

11. The *Old Indian Trail*, a delightful wooded walk of a mile or more, begins inconspicuously before the front door of 76 Park Ave.

Retrace on Park Ave.; R. from Park Ave. into Pleasant St.

12. The *Fogg Library* (*open weekdays except Wed. 2–6*), Columbian Square, South Weymouth, houses the splendid collections of the Weymouth Historical Society. Dedicated in 1898, it is a two-story structure in the Italian Renaissance style, of Weymouth seam-faced granite.

Owned by one of the members of the Society, but not on exhibition, is a small Confederate flag which has a pleasant history concerning a fiery little Barbara Fritchie of Warrentown, Virginia, and Captain James L. Bates of Weymouth.

On the lawn of the library is an Indian corn-mill, a bowl a foot in diameter hollowed in a granite block.

WILLIAMSTOWN

Buckwheat, Barley, and Gentlemen

Town: Alt. 603, pop. 4,272, sett. 1749, incorp. 1765.

Railroad Station: Williamstown Station, lower end of Cole Ave., for B. & M. R.R.

Bus Station: Drugstore, Williamstown Center, for Berkshire Street Ry. Co.

Accommodations: Inns, tourist houses, and two hotels, one open summers only.

Information: Williams Inn.

WILLIAMSTOWN lies in a valley among encircling hills. Into it lead winding roads which thread the wild and lovely hill country, coming suddenly upon fields of corn, buckwheat, and barley, the outskirts of this serene and dignified college town.

For more than a hundred years after the Pilgrims had settled at Plymouth, little was known of this remote corner of northwestern Massachusetts, cut off by the high mountain wall of the Hoosacs. It could be reached only by the old Mohawk warpath through the Taconic hills, along which came the Indians of the Five Tribes to spread terror through the settlements.

The destiny of Williamstown was decided in 1755 when, before leaving for the French and Indian War, Colonel Ephraim Williams penned a clause in his will leaving a bequest to be used toward the establishment and support of 'a Free School forever in the township west of Fort Massachusetts, called West Hoosac, provided it be given the name of Williamstown.'

Six weeks later Colonel Williams, at the head of his troops, was killed. Not till 1790 was the free school started. Three years later it was given a charter as Williams College, and Dr. Fitch, its first president, met with a faculty made up of four members. In those days, church and college were closely interbound. Students were required to attend chapel every morning and church on Sundays, and there were frequent extra meetings for prayer at noon and in the evenings. Yet despite these holy activities the student body was far from sanctified. Morning chapel often found the Bible nailed to the pulpit, and once it is even rumored to have been burnt. In vain the pious teachers labored with revivals and prayer to dispel the Devil.

Nevertheless, despite the repeated onslaughts of Satan, both town and college continued to grow. After the Civil War, many fine sections of land were purchased by people of wealth for use as summer residences. The college buildings increased in number and in beauty of architecture.

Spring Street was opened and, with its banks, offices, theater, police court, and new Colonial post-office, became the center of civic activity.

At the present time, as always, the town's outstanding institution is Williams College. Williams has been known by long tradition as 'the college of gentlemen,' a spirit created by its first president. In keeping with this aspiration for quality rather than size the college has remained small and has quietly turned its efforts toward culture rather than ostentation.

TOUR — 20 m.

N. from State 2 *into US* 7.

1. A monument at the junction of US 7 and State 2 marks the *Site of the West Hoosac Blockhouse* of 1756, otherwise known as Fort Hoosac.

2. The *Robert Hawkins House* (*open during summer as Cozy Inn*), also known as the Old Well Sweep House, corner of Simonds and North Hoosac Rd., was built in 1765. It is a one-and-a-half-story white clapboarded structure with dormer windows, massive central chimney, and a large enclosed porch. The old well sweep with field-stone masonry still stands on one side of the lawn.

3. The *River Bend Tavern* (*private*), opposite, was built in 1750 by Colonel Simonds and opened under his genial hospitality. Rye and Indian bread and beans for the Revolutionary soldiers were baked in the huge stone ovens of this old house.

R. from US 7 *into Sand Springs Rd.*

4. The *Sand Springs* (*visitors welcome*), enclosed by an aluminum fence, form a sparkling pool. The spring flows up naturally through 3000 feet of sand and gravel, and had been used for hundreds of years before the coming of the white man. As early as 1800 a log hut was built to accommodate those who wished to bathe. Today the waters are used in the manufacture of ginger ale as well as for medicinal purposes.

Retrace Sand Spring Rd.; L. from Sand Spring Rd. into US 7; *L. from US* 7 *into State* 2.

5. *Williams College Campus* covers an area of approximately 350 acres and is valued with its buildings at $5,000,000. Williams College takes its architectural theme from the work of Cram and Ferguson, who between 1912 and 1928 designed the auditorium known as *Chapin Hall*, the *Library*, and three dormitories. All are of red New Hampshire brick with limestone trim, and all belong in the English Georgian phase of the architects' work.

> It is told that in 1806 five young students met, in a retired spot, to pray for a mission to heathens. During a storm which suddenly broke, they fled to shelter beneath a near-by haystack. The odd *Haystack Monument*, with its pedestal support-

ing a huge marble world outlined with five continents, marks the spot, and the granting of their prayer. *Mission Park*, the field in which they met, is now a part of the college, and commemorates the birthplace of the first American Foreign Mission.

The most striking building on the campus is the *Thompson Memorial Chapel* (1905), which stands on a high embankment at the right, a massive structure of fine-grained limestone in English Gothic, from which to a height of 120 feet rises a magnificent square tower with four pinnacles. *Chapin Hall*, with an imposing façade of Corinthian columns, contains the Trustees' Room and a spacious auditorium seating over 1300 people, with a large electric organ of unusual size and beautiful tone. Within, the considerable decorative detail of carved woodwork, especially the massive pillars of teak from Burma, are worth inspecting.

Three separate large buildings house the laboratories of chemistry, biology, and physics.

Other noted campus buildings are *West College* (1790), a plain four-story brick building, the first one built by the college and now a dormitory; the *President's House*, an oblong two-story white frame dwelling of the early Federal period, with a roof-rail and a doorway above which is a delicate fan-light; and the *Van Rensselaer Manor House*, now the home of Sigma Phi Fraternity, but formerly the late Georgian residence in Albany of Stephen Van Rensselaer, last of the Dutch patroons, projector of the Erie Canal, and founder of Rensselaer Polytechnic Institute at Troy, N.Y. Van Rensselaer cast the deciding vote in Congress for the election of John Quincy Adams as President, by closing his eyes, praying to God, opening them, and finding Adams's name printed on a ballot at his feet. When the demolition of the house was ordered at Albany, Williamstown acquired it and brought it here, owing to Van Rensselaer's close friendship with Amos Eaton, an early professor at Williams who had surveyed the route of the Erie Canal.

At *Jesup Hall* the Williams Little Theater presents three programs of one-act plays each year. The Cap and Bells, another college dramatic organization, puts on two elaborate productions annually.

6. The *Green River Mansion* (*private*), 0.8 *m.* E. of the junction with US 7, was built in 1772 by Captain Smedley of the North Williamstown militia. Colonel Benedict Arnold stopped at this house on the evening of May 6, 1775, and gave Captain Smedley's wife three pounds to bake a batch of rye and Indian bread for the soldiers at Fort Ticonderoga.

Retrace on State 2; L. from State 2 into State 43; L. from State 43 on country road at Sweats Corner.

7. The *Hopper* (*reached by footpath*) is a huge hollow in the Mt. Greylock Reservation resembling a vast grain hopper, shadowed by the tall peaks of Mts. Greylock, Fitch, and Williams, with Prospect Mountain serving as a giant plug in the north end of the cavity. New paths developed by the Civilian Conservation Corps are *Hopper Trail* to Greylock summit, *Money Brook Trail* up Mt. Williams and Mt. Fitch, connecting with the main Appalachian Trail (*see Tour* 9).

8. On Money Brook Trail is *Money Brook Falls*, one of the highest in the Berkshires, with a sheer descent of about 80 feet, and 200 to 300 feet of cascades. Near-by is a cave where, tradition has it, Pine Tree Shillings were counterfeited in Colonial days, thus giving the brook its name.

9. In the Williamstown area of the reservation lie *Goodell Hollow*, a favorite skiing place, and *Deer Hill*, a spruce-clad mountain spur where deer 'yard-up' in considerable numbers during the winter months.

Retrace on country road; L. from country road into State 43; *R. from State* 43 *into US* 7.

10. A footpath (L) at the junction of US 7 and State 2 over Phelps Knoll on the eastern slope of Petersburg Mountain leads to *McMaster's Cave,* from the entrance of which is a descent of 250 feet underground.

L. from US 7 *into State* 2.

11. The *Taconic Trail* climbs 1200 feet in a distance of 3 miles.

Retrace State 2; *L. from State* 2 *into US* 7.

12. At *Flora's Glen Brook* a trail leads (L) into *Flora's Glen,* where William Cullen Bryant, while a student at Williams College, is said to have gained inspiration for the lighter passages in 'Thanatopsis.'

13. The *Capes to the Berkshires Bridle Trail* (*see Tour* 12) starts from its western end in the northern section of Williamstown.

W O B U R N . *Home of a Yankee Count*

City: Alt. 83, pop. 19,695, sett. 1640, incorp. town 1642, city 1888.

Railroad Stations: Cross Street, Woburn Highlands, Woburn, Central Square, North Woburn, Montvale, and Walnut Hill for Boston and Maine Railroad.

Accommodations: Limited to boarding and rooming houses.

Information: Public Library, 45 Pleasant St.

THE territory of Woburn is diversified by detached hills and rounded knobs, streams, valleys, ravines, and glens. The city has both a residential and an industrial aspect. Foreign immigration, bringing in Roman Catholic and Greek Orthodox groups, broke down the sectarian homogeneity of the town and for a while upset the Protestant town fathers; but religious differences settled down in time, and the permanent effect was merely to give the community a somewhat cosmopolitan cast, the population now consisting very largely of native-born Irish, Italians, Swedes, and Greeks.

In 1636, six years after Charlestown was founded, its residents began to feel crowded and the town fathers selected Woburn for more land for their farms.

In the latter part of the eighteenth century two incidents occurred in the domestic life of the community which caused a pleasurable agitation among the decorous citizens. One was the case of Ichabod Richardson, who was seized by the British while on board a privateer and kept a prisoner for about seven years. His wife, convinced that her husband was dead, married Josiah Richardson. Upon his release the prisoner came home to find his family under another man's roof. The matter was adjusted by the good wife's returning to the bed and board of her first husband. A more realistic transaction of about the same date was the barter by one Simeon Reed of his wife to James Butters of Wilmington for a yoke of oxen.

The building of the Middlesex Canal in 1803 played a major part in the town's economic development. During the first half of the nineteenth century, Woburn rapidly changed to an industrial community, with shoe-manufacturing and leather-tanning predominating. In the ten years before the Civil War the increased demand for unskilled and semi-skilled cheap labor led to an influx of foreign races. By 1865, there were twenty-one tanning and currying establishments and four factories for the manufacture of patent and enameled leather. Later, machinery, glue, chemicals, and foundry products were added to the list. Before the crisis of 1929 there were fifty-three manufacturing establishments with more than two thousand employees, more than fifty per cent being leather or shoe companies.

TOUR — 6 m.

W. from City Square; on Pleasant St.

1. The *Winn Memorial* (*Woburn Public*) *Library* (about 1877) was the first of H. H. Richardson's remarkable series of libraries. The architect did not achieve in this plan the complete mastery of his profession he was soon to show; yet the boldness of planning to fit functional needs, the simplicity, the symmetrical design which maintained delicate balance, the vivid carving — all these notably displayed in the stark wing — atone for his failure to merge all the units into one harmonious whole. In the tower is a so-called 'Antique Kitchen' (*open upon application*, 9–5 *except Sun. and holidays*), a curious potpourri of mineral and ornithological collections.

2. The *Statue of Count Rumford* stands in front of the Library. Benjamin Thompson (1753–1814) was a native of Woburn, an expatriate, a noted scientist, statesman, philanthropist, economist, and military leader. His birthplace (*see below*) is usually visited by distinguished foreign scientists who come to America, and was one of the first places sought by Anton Lang, the Christus of the Oberammergau Players, when he was here. This statue, revealing a typical shrewd Yankee face and wiry figure, the latter fashionably garbed in military court dress, is a replica of one by Casper Zumbusch which stands in the English Gardens at Munich.

Thompson was a boyhood friend of Woburn's other celebrity, Loammi Baldwin, the engineer. Together they tramped ten miles daily each way to Harvard College. At fourteen Thompson's scientific knowledge enabled him to calculate a solar eclipse within four seconds of accuracy, and during his years of apprenticeship to a storekeeper in Salem he was always busy with chemical and mechanical experiments. At eighteen he removed to Concord, New Hampshire (then called Rumford). Here at nineteen he married the widow of Colonel Benjamin Rolfe, a woman whose wealth and influence helped to further his career.

Suspected of Tory sympathies prior to the Revolution, Thompson migrated (1776) to England and thence to Bavaria, countries which shared thereafter the fruits of his versatile genius. In 1791 he was created a count of the Holy Roman Empire, and chose his title to accord with the name of his wife's home town. He finally returned to England and presented to the Royal Society his most important scientific theory, that heat was a form of motion. Late in life he married again, this time the widow of the scientist Lavoisier.

L. from Pleasant St. on Woburn Parkway.

3. *Horn Pond Mountain* (*off Woburn Parkway*) must be ascended by footpath. East from the summit are the charming small lakes of the Mystic Valley, the Boston Customhouse Tower, and the Blue Hills.

Retrace Woburn Parkway; from Woburn Parkway on Pleasant St. to City Sq.

4. The *Hiker's Monument*, a very masculine bronze, is the work of a woman, Theo Alice Ruggles Kitson, first wife of H. H. Kitson, the sculptor. At the left corner, across from this statue, is a unique souvenir, a *Ventilator Cowl from the United States Ship Maine*, retrieved from Havana Harbor some time after the explosion of 1898 which precipitated the Spanish War. Its battered hood is green with sea stain, and its base is covered with coquina, the marine shell growth of West Indian waters. Preserved from further wear of elements by a glass case, it is a visible embodiment of the tragically ambiguous slogan: 'Remember the Maine.'

L. from City Square into Park St.

5. The *Ancient Burying Ground*, junction of Park and Center Sts., dates from 1642, and contains the graves of ancestors of Presidents Pierce, Garfield, Cleveland and Benjamin Harrison. The quaintest inscription is that of Mrs. Elizabeth Cotton:

> If a virgin marry, she hath not sinned;
> Nevertheless she shall have trouble in the flesh;
> But he that giveth her not in marriage doth better;
> She is happier if she so abide.

Retrace Park St.; L. from Park St. on Main St.

6. The *Old Middlesex Canal Channel* borders both sides of the highway near the railroad tracks. This canal, some 25 miles long, ran from the present city of Somerville to Lowell. It was opened in 1803, the work chiefly of Loammi Baldwin, more popularly known as the promoter of the famous Baldwin apple. Passenger and freight boats were drawn by horse or mule plodding along a 'tow-path.'

L. from Main St. into Elm St.

7. The *Baldwin Mansion* (*private*), still occupied by Loammi's descendants, has been subjected to many alterations since its erection in 1661, and retains little of its original character. Remodeled in 1800, it now stands, three-story square, with white pilasters at the corners and an elaborate doorway. In the fields are two aged Baldwin apple trees, sprung from the first parent.

8. *Count Rumford's Birthplace* (*open weekdays* 9–5; *adm. free*), 90 Elm St., a modest buff-colored frame house, with a combination of gambrel and lean-to roofs, was erected in 1714 by the Count's grandfather, plain Mr. Thompson. The future count lived here only during his babyhood; his family soon removing to another Woburn residence. Within the house is a steep stairway with two turns, which is enclosed by an unplastered brick wall. The white paneling in the various rooms, however, indicates greater prosperity. On the first floor hangs an oil copy of the Gainsborough portrait of 'The Count,' of which the original is at Harvard University. Rumford was the only Yankee painted by Gainsborough. It is interesting to compare the avid youthful grace and charm here revealed with the severe maturity in the statue before the Library.

> Upstairs, the chief object of interest is one of the original Rumford Roasters. As a scientist, Rumford was especially interested in heat, and this is one of the first fireless cookers marketed. In effect, it is a cylindrical iron oven which when heated retained its heat a long time.

> The garden at the rear of the house perpetuates the Count's fondness, among several less gentle tastes, for flowers. The cannon in the yard was captured from the British in Portland Harbor in the War of 1812, and its position is a comment, probably unconsciously ironic, on the Count's Tory sympathies. Another irony, equally unconscious and far more amazing, was the invitation to him from President Adams to return and command West Point. Wisely, Rumford remained abroad. He died and was buried in France.

W O R C E S T E R . *Heart of the Commonwealth*

City: Alt. 492, pop. 190,471, sett. 1673, town 1722, incorp. 1780, city 1848.

Railroad Station: Union Station, Washington Square, for B. & A., B. & M., and N.Y., N.H. & H. R.R.

Bus Stations: 92 Franklin St. for Greyhound; 3 Salem Square for B. & W., Washington Square for New England Lines; 60 Foster St. for Prescott Short Line, Berkshire; 72 Franklin St. for Great Eastern; 203 Front St. for I.R.T.

Accommodations: Eighteen hotels.

Information: Chamber of Commerce, 32 Franklin St.; A.A.A., Bancroft Hotel Building; Young Men's Christian Association, 766 Main St.

WORCESTER is favored in appearance by its terrain. Hills break its surface everywhere, even in the core of the city, and rescue it from monotony. Zoning and city planning have co-operated to increase its variety and beauty. Factories are counterbalanced by municipal parks.

'Heart of the Commonwealth' is the emblem engraved upon the municipal seal. The claim is not only geographical but industrial. Excellent facilities for transport, diversified manufactures, and flourishing mercantile establishments give the city a central position and a vital function in the life of New England.

To the visitor the first impression of the mid-State metropolis will be one of tremendous activity, commercial and industrial. This impression will, however, soon be supplemented by a realization that Worcester is equally a cultural center, interested in the arts, in higher learning, and in historical research.

The old Worcester halls were the scene of dramatic, musical and civic events unsurpassed in New England. Here Fanny Kemble, Bernhardt ('la divine Sarah'), Joe Jefferson, Edwin Booth, the beautiful Lily Langtry, and Charlotte Cushman were seen in never-to-be-forgotten rôles. Here the lovely Parepa-Rosa and the daring Lola Montez danced. Here Patti and Jenny Lind sang, Rubinstein played his own compositions, and Ole Bull enthralled the city with the tones he evoked from his violin. Here appeared many celebrities, the spectacular Victoria Woodhull, Dickens, P. T. Barnum, Thackeray, Kossuth, Deborah Sampson, the Revolutionary Amazon, and Abraham Lincoln. Here Emerson spoke for abolition and, six years later, Frederick Douglass and John Brown lectured passionately on the same subject. Here shortly after John Brown's death, Thoreau appeared with an address on the martyr to emancipation. In 1854 'The Angel Gabriel' (J. S. Orr) fanatically attacked the Papacy. Here Matthew Arnold complained of having been served cold oysters at luncheon. Here was exhibited in 1818 Columbus, the first elephant seen in America, and here the amazing P. T. Barnum gravely produced an ancient colored woman who he declared was George Washington's nurse — 161 years old!

In Mechanics Hall were held for many years Worcester's famous Musical Festivals, which are still a noteworthy annual event, held now in the Memorial Auditorium.

Worcester is the home of six institutions of learning: Clark University, Holy Cross College, Teachers' College, Worcester Academy, Worcester Polytechnic Institute, and Assumption College.

A brief list of outstanding Worcester names with their major contributions to civilization would include Ichabod Washburn, wire-drawing processes and wire forms; William A. Wheeler, metal machine tools; Thomas E. Daniels, power planing machine; H. H. Biglow, leather heeling machine; George Crompton, looms. Not to be omitted, also, is the name of J. C. Stoddard, inventor of a steam calliope, which he played in an excursion from Worcester to Fitchburg in 1856, greatly startling the citizens along the way.

At the time of the building of the Blackstone Canal (1828), laborers came over in great numbers from Southern Ireland and were followed in 1845 by many of their countrymen during the Potato Famine in Ireland. Many French-Canadian workers came to Worcester after the Civil War, and today they and their descendants number some thirty thousand. Beginning 1868, the demand for skilled engineers and craftsmen attracted many Swedish immigrants. It is estimated that in 1935 one fifth of the population was of Swedish descent. At the close of the nineteenth century began an influx of Poles, Jews, Lithuanians, Italians, Greeks, Armenians, Syrians, and Albanians, which terminated only with the outbreak of the World War. The Negroes also form a definite group. Such divergent racial strains have brought to the city cultural backgrounds which differ widely. This has had the effect of giving Worcester a cosmopolitan stamp, preserved by fraternal organizations, singing societies and athletic associations of the various groups.

In 1674 Daniel Gookin visited the Nipmuck Indians with the Apostle Eliot. Eight years later he returned as the leader of a small group. But in 1702, Queen Anne's War drove out the little band of settlers just as they were about to enjoy the fruits of their labors. In 1713, at the close of the war, one of the refugees, Jonas Rice, returned to Worcester, and the home he built marked the beginning of the permanent settlement. Within five years two hundred people had established themselves here. The rumblings of the next half century, which were to culminate in the Revolutionary War, found a responsive echo here, and the town ultimately set up its own Patriot's Committee. The patriot publisher, Isaiah Thomas, escaped from the Boston Tories to Worcester with his printing press, and here in a hospitable environment continued printing his paper, *The Massachusetts Spy*. The broadsides and pamphlets which poured from his presses had much to do with consolidating the various revolutionary elements throughout New England.

In 1786, the courthouse was besieged by impoverished farmers, a major demonstration of Shays's short-lived rebellion, frustrated by Chief Justice Artemas Ward (*see No. 16, Motor Tour, below*). Significant also was the action of a Worcester lower court in 1791 in a case involving the rights of a Negro slave. The court decided that the clause in the Bill of Rights stating that 'all men are born free and equal' was applicable.

Textile manufacture started in 1789 when the first piece of corduroy came off a Worcester loom. In 1789 a factory (Worcester Cotton Manufactory) was organized, but this attempt proved premature owing to the primitive stage of mechanical development. Cotton goods could still be imported from England far more cheaply. Domestic paper, however, found a ready market. The city became a manufacturing center after the advent of steam power. Then, in 1828, the Blackstone Canal was opened, the first step toward making Worcester the greatest industrial city in the United States not on a natural waterway.

In the issue of the *National Aegis* for August 31, 1814, Worcester frankly regretted that President Madison was not destroyed along with the Capital in the burning of Washington. With similar vigor of conviction, the city entered upon the national scene in 1848 when its delegate to the Whig Convention, Charles Allen, later Chief Justice of the Supreme Court of the Commonwealth, threw a Free Soil meeting at Worcester into an uproar by announcing at the conclusion of the debate on slavery, 'We declare the Whig Party of the Union this day dissolved.'

Hardly had the tumult ceased when the Rev. George Allen, his brother, proposed the memorable resolution, 'Resolved: that Massachusetts wears no chains and spurns all bribes; that Massachusetts goes now and will ever go for free soil and for free men, for free lips and a free press, for a free land and a free world.' This action resulted in the formation of the Free Soil Party in Massachusetts, which paved the way for Lincoln and the Republican Party.

For the women of Massachusetts the anti-slavery movement opened up a new sphere of activity. They willingly undertook to carry on much of the necessary organizational work. Their success led them to feel confident that it was in their power to render public service of an even wider scope. Accordingly the Woman's Rights Convention, which launched the Equal Suffrage Movement, was held at Worcester in 1850.

Quick to see the rise to the challenge of the Kansas-Nebraska Bill, Eli Thayer called a meeting in Worcester out of which was organized the Massachusetts Emigrant Aid Company, designed to settle Kansas with Northerners. Due in part to the activities of this committee, Kansas was admitted to the Union as a free state in 1861.

Worcester witnessed, during the fifty years after the Civil War, the growth of four major industries. A decade prior to the war Ichabod Washburn had improved the process of manufacturing wire, specializing in the manufacture of piano wire. Today the giant plants of the American Steel and Wire Company employ 6000 persons. Their 200,000 wire products include ordinary nails, as well as platinum wire valued at $1000 per pound, and the heaviest cable in the country.

The invention of a fancy loom in 1837 by William Crompton, then a resident of Taunton, revolutionized the textile industry. The Crompton Loom Works, later established by him in Worcester, carried on a successful business for well over a half century, finally consolidating with the Knowles Loom Works. Today it is a 26-acre plant.

In 1875 F. B. Norton made a modest start at producing grinding wheels by the vitrified process. Today the Norton Grinding Company supplies a world-wide market and has several plants in Europe.

The first practical machine for making envelopes was invented by Russell Hawes of Worcester in 1852, and numerous improvements on the machine were made later. After a number of consolidations the giant United States Envelope Company emerged at the turn of the century, controlling some sixty per cent of the envelope production of the country.

Although these four industries dominate the city's industrial life, there are nearly 1000 other manufacturing units, the products including shoes, slippers, rugs, leather belting, paper-making and textile-making machinery, crankshafts, valentines, Pullman coaches, and screws. In 1929, the peak year, these manufactures were valued at $216,000,000.

FOOT TOUR — 2 m.

N. from Franklin St. on Main St.

1. *City Hall (open)*, erected in 1898 from plans by Richard Howland Hunt, is designed in a modified Italian Renaissance style. The Florentine campanile towers rise 205 feet. Within, on the main stairway, given by Worcester, England, hang the helmets and breastplates of two of Cromwell's soldiers who fell at the battle of Worcester. A *Bronze Star* set in the sidewalk marks the spot where Isaiah Thomas stood on July 14, 1776, and read, for the first time to a New England audience, the Declaration of Independence.

Through the City Hall onto the Common.

2. *Worcester Common* today comprises a scant five acres of the twenty acres set aside in 1669 by the proprietors for use as a training field, and to accommodate a meeting house and school building. From 1800 a *clock* made by Abel Stowell of Worcester kept time in the steeple of the meeting house, and the equipment was completed in 1802 by the purchase of a bell weighing nearly a ton from the foundry of Revere and Sons, Boston. There was not always a spirit of co-ordination between the dials of the clock and the clapper of the bell, for the latter went periodically on striking sprees that lasted until the arrival of its official guardian, or, more often, until the mechanism ran down. In 1888 the bell was moved to the New Old South Church at the corner of Main and Wellington Sts.

3. A *Hidden Graveyard* lies in the area between Salem Square and the Bigelow shaft. In it are the graves of several hundred citizens buried between 1730 and 1795. In 1854 the headstones were recorded, laid flat on the graves, and the whole area covered with earth and seeded.

R. from Salem Square into Franklin St.; R. from Franklin St. into Main St.; L. from Main St. into Pearl St.; R. from Pearl St. into Chestnut St.

4. The *Worcester Horticultural Society (open)*, corner of Elm St. was organized in 1840. The building is designed in the Renaissance style. From June 1 to October 1 weekly flower shows (*free*) are held on Thursday afternoons and evenings. There are also a November Chrysanthemum Show and a March Spring Show (*both free*).

R. from Chestnut St. into Elm St.; L. from Elm St. into Main St.; L. from Main St. into State St.

5. The *Natural History Society* (*open*), corner of Harvard St., contains some teeth and bone fragments found at Northborough in 1884. Harvard College scientists pronounced them mastodon bones, the only specimens of their kind found in New England.

Retrace State St.; L. from State St. into Main St.; L. from Main St. at Lincoln Square into Salisbury St.

6. The *Municipal War Memorial Auditorium* (*open*), occupies the entire block between Highland, Salisbury, and Harvard Sts. and Institute Rd., and is located at the north end of the Square. It was erected by the City of Worcester in 1933, from plans by Lucius Briggs and Frederick Hirons. Built of Indiana limestone with a base of granite, it is of modified classic design and monumental in proportion. The colonnade at the front of the structure is reached by a wide terrace and a flight of stone steps. Bronze lighting fixtures and great windows ornamented with bronze decorate the principal façade. The World War Memorial Flagstaff, from which the flag, floodlighted at night, is never lowered, rises 90 feet from a base of bronze and granite, directly opposite the Auditorium.

7. The *Worcester Historical Society* (*open* 2–5, *Tues., Wed., Thurs., Fri., Sat.*), 39 Salisbury St., founded in 1875, has in its collection a typewriter invented by Charles Thurber in 1843, workable, but too slow for commercial success. Another relic is a huge iron link, part of the chain that was stretched across the Hudson River at West Point in 1778, thus preventing the British in New York and Albany from joining forces.

L. from Salisbury St. into Tuckerman St.

8. The *Worcester Art Museum* (*open daily* 9–5; *Sun.* 2–5), 55 Salisbury St., of modified classic design, was founded in 1896 by Stephen Salisbury III. A sequence of galleries traces the entire history of the fine arts in both the eastern and western hemispheres from prehistoric times to the present.

Works of Hogarth, Gainsborough, Raeburn, Reynolds, Romney, and Mingard, genre pictures by the Dutch painters, and Venetian carnival scenes by Canaletto and Guardi are exhibited in *Gallery XIII*. In the French collection are 'The Card Player' by Cézanne and 'Girl on a Balcony' and 'The Promenade' by Henri Matisse. There are also two paintings by Claude Monet, 'Waterloo Bridge' and 'Water Lilies,' and works by Derain, Picasso, and others. Portraits by Gilbert, Sully, Peal, Copley, and Inman, landscapes by the Hudson River School, and various works by Earl, Eakin, Whistler, Sargent, Homer, Blakelock, Fuller, Hassam, Hunt, Inness, Metcalf, and Wyant are on display.

Stained-glass exhibits include two windows from the Chapel of Borsham House (English) about 1400, a 13th century window from Strasbourg, a fragment from a window in Chartres Cathedral (13th century French) and the 'Peacock Window' by John La Farge. Among the representative

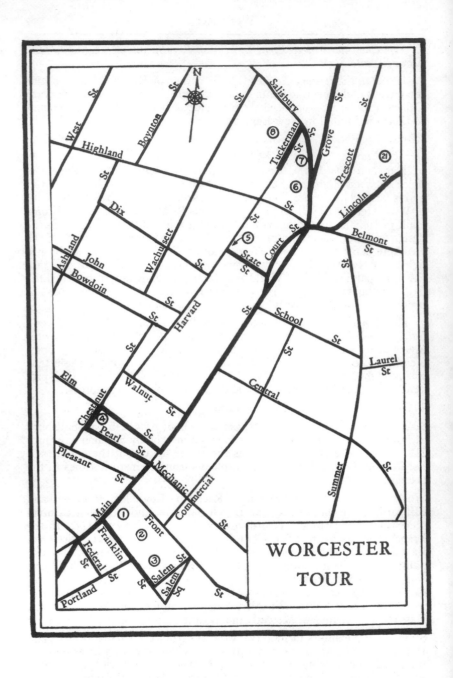

WORCESTER
TOUR

pieces of Eastern art is a collection of Japanese prints showing the work of such masters as Hiroshige and Hokusai. The evolution of American furniture is traced through Chippendale, Sheraton, and Adam.

MOTOR TOUR 1 — 8 m.

S. from Franklin Square on Southbridge St.

9. *Holy Cross College* (*open*), on Mt. St. James, towers high above the city. It was founded in 1843 by the Rt. Rev. Benedict Joseph Fenwick, second Bishop of Boston, and is the oldest Catholic college in New England. The avowed purpose of the founders was 'the advancement of the arts, the cultivation of the sciences, and the promotion of patriotism, morality, virtue, and religion.'

> *Fenwick Hall*, the Administration Building, and also the oldest one, is capped by two stately towers. *St. Joseph's Memorial Chapel* (1923), the *Dinand Memorial Library* (1927), and *Kimball Hall* (1935) were designed by Maginnis and Walsh, and exemplify the masterly adaptation of the Georgian and French Renaissance styles to modern function. The Library contains 100,000 volumes and a *Museum* with a notable collection of Jesuit writings. Kimball includes the dining hall and a little theater. Below the college spreads *Fitton Field*, the athletic field, with a *Stadium* seating 20,000.

Retrace Southbridge St.; L. from Southbridge St. into Cambridge St.; R. from Cambridge St. into Richards St.; R. from Richards St. into Main St.; L. from Main St. into Maywood St.

10. *Clark University* (*open*), opposite University Park, was founded in 1887 by the gift of Jonas Gilman Clark. At first the institution was devoted wholly to post-graduate work, Dr. Granville Stanley Hall, as president, receiving the first students in the fall of 1889. Special provision was made in Mr. Clark's will for the establishment of an undergraduate division which was opened in 1902 under a separate president, Caroll D. Wright.

While offering a four-year course leading to the A.B. degree, Clark is still favorably known for its graduate work, approximately a quarter of the student body being enrolled for advanced study. Under Dr. Hall the psychology department was famed throughout the world; Dr. Wallace W. Atwood, President of the University, has elevated the Graduate School of Geography to a similar position of eminence.

WORCESTER MAP INDEX

The University is situated on a tract of eight acres, bounded by Main, Woodland, Maywood, and Downing Sts. The original building — *Jonas G. Clark Hall*—faces Main St. and is still the heart of the University. The *Library* at the corner of Main and Downing Sts. is a more modern structure housing 154,000 volumes and, in a separate wing usually known as the *Geography Building*, the Graduate School of Geography.

R. from Maywood St. into Park Ave.; L. from Park Ave. into Chandler St.

11. *Worcester State Teachers' College*, 486 Chandler St., was opened in 1874. From 1915–1937 it admitted women students only. In 1937 it again became co-educational. E. Harlow Russell, principal from 1874 to 1909, made this institution a co-pioneer with Clark University in the study of child psychology. In 1917 the Department of Hygiene and Psychology founded the *American Journal of School Hygiene*, issued monthly since then.

R. from Chandler St. into May St.; R. from May St. into Pleasant St.; L. from Pleasant St. on Highland St.

12. *Elm Park*, part of the Elm Park System, was (1854) one of the first purchases of land for park purposes made with public funds in the United States. The corner of Highland St. near the Kennedy Memorial was the unofficial starting line in the days of snow racing. The sides of the avenue were lined with family sleighs and pungs, and the whole city turned out to watch the thrilling impromptu races. Finally traffic congestion compelled the city to ban the races on the 'Boulevard' and set off an official sleigh race track elsewhere — which was little used.

L. from Highland St. into Park Ave.; R. from Park Ave. into Salisbury St.

13. *Worcester Polytechnic Institute*, familiarly known as Worcester Tech., was founded in 1865, by John Boynton of Templeton and from its beginning has ranked as one of the leading technical schools of the country.

It has several large and well equipped buildings: the *Salisbury Laboratories* of Physics and Chemistry, the *Washburn Shops*, laboratories for civil mechanical engineering, the power laboratory, the foundry, an electrical engineering laboratory, and an experimental hydraulic plant (in Holden). It was the first school in the country to establish workshops as an adjunct to the training of engineers. *Institute Park*, directly opposite, was given to the city by Stephen Salisbury. In the park is a *Reproduction of the So-Called Norse Mill* at Newport, R.I. (*see also Tour 15B, CHESHIRE*).

Retrace on Salisbury St.

14. The *American Antiquarian Society* (*open Mon.–Fri. except holidays, 9–5*) was founded in 1812 by Isaiah Thomas. Its collection of printed Americana and manuscripts is considered one of the most valuable and complete in the country; and its files of newspapers are without rival.

15. The *Site of the Birthplace of George Bancroft*, early American historian, founder of the Naval Academy and Minister Plenipotentiary to Great Britain (1846–49), is indicated, opposite Massachusetts Ave. by a small boulder bearing a bronze Tablet.

L. from Salisbury St. into Massachusetts Ave.

16. The *Trumbull Mansion* (*private*), 6 Massachusetts Ave., was originally located at Trumbull Sq., and was the Second Court House of Worcester. Up its steps marched Judge Artemas Ward through the ranks of Daniel Shays's army. Refused entrance, he opened and adjourned court in the United States Arms Hotel.

R. from Massachusetts Ave. into first unmarked street after Metcalf St.

17. *Bancroft Tower*, a battlemented stone structure, offers the finest observation point in the city.

Retrace on Massachusetts Ave.; R. from Massachusetts Ave. into Salisbury St.; L. from Salisbury St. into Park Ave.; straight ahead into Grove St.; straight ahead into West Boylston St.

18. The *John Woodman Higgins Armory* (*open weekdays* 7-6), maintained by the Worcester Pressed Steel Co., is designed after the castle of Prince Eugene Hohenwefen at Salzburg, Austria. To the right is the *Medieval Wing*, where silent rows of armor-clad figures stand surrounded by their banners and arms, while at the far end of the hall three mounted knights are poised in medieval pageantry. Behind the mounted figures hangs a Gobelin tapestry that once adorned the palace of Louis XIV. The *Higgins Collection of Armor and Mail* is unsurpassed in Massachusetts.

19. *Assumption College*, founded in 1904, is conducted by the Augustinian Fathers of the Assumption. Emphasis is laid on religious instruction and moral guidance. Situated on a hill in Greendale, the college overlooks one of the most beautiful sections of the city. The main building in the form of a T serves the High School Department, and a large wing built in 1926 is occupied by the College.

20. The *Pullman–Standard Car Co. Plant* (*open*), just beyond, are producers of steam and electric railway cars. Osgood Bradley of Worcester designed the first railroad coach in 1833, and this twenty-passenger affair was first used on the Boston–Worcester railroad. It is claimed that the modern Pullman sleeper was made possible by another Worcester invention — the hinge that operates the upper berth.

Retrace on W. Boylston St.; straight ahead into Grove St. which bears L.

21. The *North Works of the American Steel and Wire Co.* (*open by special permission*) is at 94 Grove St. This was the original plant of Washburn and Moen, pioneers in the drawn wire industry. Nearly opposite the office entrance at No. 183 on the corner of Faraday St., is a *Museum* with exhibits tracing the development of the industry.

MOTOR TOUR 2 — 10 *m.*

N. from Lincoln Square on Lincoln St.

22. The *Home of Timothy Paine* (*private*), known as 'Paine the Tory,' is at 140 Lincoln St. Appointed Mandamus Councillor, he was forced by the patriots in 1774 publicly to resign his post. John Adams, some twenty years after his teaching term in Worcester, was a dinner guest in Timothy Paine's home when his host offered a toast to 'the King.' At a nod from Adams, the embarrassed patriots joined in His Majesty's health. Mr. Adams then — so the story runs — offered a toast 'to the Devil.' Consternation reigned; no one knew what to do, when Mrs. Paine, smiling, remarked to her husband, 'My dear, as the gentleman has been so kind as to drink to our king, let us by no means refuse to drink to his.'

23. *Burncoat Park*, L. beyond Brittan Sq., is a 50-acre recreational reservation with skating and ice hockey in winter.

24. *Green Hill Park* (*open*), opposite Burncoat Park, is named for Andrew H. Green, a Worcester native who later became known as the 'Father of Greater New York' through his efforts in making civic and public improvements in that city. His birthplace, the *Mansion*, has been well preserved, and its grounds and gardens have been kept in much their original condition. Herds of elk and bison are pastured within the reservation. At the northern end is an 18-hole *Municipal Golf Course*. There are also bowling greens, archery butts, and provisions for tobogganing and skiing in winter.

R. from Lincoln St. into Lake Ave.

25. *Lake Quinsigamond* (*recreational parks, boat liveries*), a favorite resort for the Indians, was known by them as the 'Place of Long Fishes,' and the earliest settlements of Worcester bore that name. Bordered on the east and west by the hills of Shrewsbury and Worcester, it stretches nearly nine miles, broken by several causeways and bridges. For many years this waterway made Worcester prominent as the home of leading oarsmen, best known of whom, perhaps, is Edward Ten Eyck, the first American to win the Diamond Sculls trophy at Henley, England. National and college regattas are occasionally held here, and in late years it has been the course for Olympic try-out finals.

26. *Lake Bridge*, at the junction of Lake Ave. and Belmont St., was constructed in 1920, and is an important link in the Boston–Worcester Turnpike (*State* 9, *see Tour* 8). It is said that originally local Indians constructed at this point a grapevine cat-walk crossing which saved them many miles as they made their summer pilgrimages to the sea coast. White men later spanned this narrow gap with a floating bridge buoyed up by logs and casks.

27. On each side of Lake Avenue lies *Lake Park* (*municipal bath houses, good beach, tennis courts, playgrounds*).

R. from Lake Ave. into Park Drive.

28. *Davis Tower* (*open occasionally*), the gift of a former Mayor to the city, offers a fine view of the lake. On the Tower is a bronze tablet recounting the story of Samuel Lenorson. In 1690 the Lenorson family came to the new settlement of Quinsigamond, and built their cabin near the present Davis Tower. In the autumn of 1695 young Samuel, the only son, then 12 years old, was stolen by Indians. Nothing was heard from him until the spring of 1697, when, after the sack of Haverhill, Mrs. Hannah Dustin and her nurse, Mary Neff, were brought to an island at the junction of the Merrimack and Contoocook Rivers as captives. Here they met the Lenorson boy. The three captives killed ten of the savages and escaped to Haverhill. The General Court voted that Samuel be paid £12, 10s. for 'the just slaughter of so many of the Barbarians.'

Straight ahead on Hamilton St.; R. from Hamilton St. into Grafton St.; L. from Grafton St. into Providence St.

29. *Worcester Academy* (*open*), 81 Providence St., was founded under the auspices of the Baptist denomination and incorporated in 1834 as the Worcester County Manual Labor High School. The original plant comprised a tract of 60 acres of land and buildings on Main St. About 1860 it was sold and in 1870 the school moved to Union Hill. The general principles laid down by the founders were: 'That the instruction should be of the first order; that strict moral and religious character should be attained; and that every facility should be afforded for productive labor, to the end that education should be good, but not expensive.'

The *Kingsley Laboratories* (1897–98) are a group of seven buildings with individual lecture-rooms, stock-rooms, and laboratories for elementary and advanced chemistry, elementary and advanced physics, physiography, zoology, botany, meteorology, anatomy, and physiology. *Adams Hall* is the dining hall. The *Gymnasium* (1915) contains a swimming-pool and an indoor track. *Gage Hall*, now a dormitory, is the oldest building. The *Warner Memorial Theater* (1929) was given by Mr. and Mrs. Harry Warner of New York, in memory of their son, Lewis. It contains a stage and a complete up-to-date motion-picture equipment.

Retrace Providence St., straight ahead on Grafton St.

30. To the left of the New Union Station is the *Old Union Station*, built in 1875. It was proposed to raze it when the new one was built, but a committee of local and other architects pleaded for the preservation of its tower. This Victorian Gothic structure with its ornate campanile was designed by Ware and Van Brunt. It is one of many monuments in this perverse style by the designer of Harvard's Memorial Hall.

III. HIGH ROADS AND LOW ROADS

The tours which follow cover every city, town, and village in the State. If laid end to end they would stretch from Boston to San Francisco, but no traveler, it is hoped, will attempt to lay them end to end, or even to follow them in their entirety. Accordingly, the tours have been so arranged that you may choose the most direct route, if you are in a hurry. If you have more time, a plenitude of more devious routes and side trips awaits you.

Tours with a number only (as Tour 1) in general follow express highways. Tours with a number followed by a letter (as Tour 1A) are alternate routes, beginning or ending at an express highway. Although less direct, they are often more interesting.

Unlike Gaul, the tours are divided into two parts: Those that run North to South (and they bear odd numbers); and those that go East to West (and they bear even numbers). There are more odd-numbered tours, because there are more North to South routes.

Side trips off the main road are indicated by smaller type, indented. Side trips always begin and come back to the same point on the tour, so that the through mileage is not affected. Very long tours are divided into convenient sections, with continuous mileage. The mileage will vary, you will find, according to whether you are driving in the sun or the rain, on a deserted highway or along a road crowded with traffic, in a luxurious next-year's model with brand-new tires, or in a late '29 with tires worn to a whisper.

Why follow a tour, anyway? Be your own gypsy, running along a main tour until you get tired of it, then branching off on a side trip, and instead of returning to the main route, doubling back on another road. The Tour Map on pages 408, 409 will help you to abandon all rules and directions and to make up your own tours; and to assist you, addresses have been given for points of interest whenever possible. If you get lost, consult the State Map in the pocket at the back. If you are still lost, never mind. It's fun being lost in Massachusetts.

Tours beginning or ending at State Lines have indicated in parentheses the nearest large city on the same route in the adjoining State.

For those who prefer to tour by train, railroad lines servicing each area are given at the head of each tour. Or for those who flee this mechanized age, there are foot tours and a 400-mile bridle trail. The only tour, by the way, which was not carefully checked on the road is the Capes to the Berkshires Bridle Trail (Tour 12). There are no horses who can write in Massachusetts.

Space prohibited telling the same story twice, no matter how good. And some of the cities and towns were described at too great a length to fit comfortably on a tour. Please use the index! It's an excellent one, made to consult in a hurry.

T O U R   1 : *From* NEW HAMPSHIRE STATE LINE (*Portsmouth*) *to* RHODE ISLAND STATE LINE (*Providence*), 77.9 *m.*, US 1.

Via (*sec. a*) Salisbury, Newburyport, Georgetown, Topsfield, Boxford, Lynnfield, Saugus, Malden, Everett, Somerville, Cambridge, Boston; (*sec. b*) Walpole, North Attleborough.

B. & M. R.R. and N.Y., N.H. & H. R.R. parallel the route at intervals.

Good hard-surfaced road, mostly three- and four-lane.

Sec. a. NEW HAMPSHIRE STATE LINE to BOSTON 41.3 m.

US 1, the most direct route between Portsmouth, N.H., and Pawtucket, R.I., enters Massachusetts as a concrete road winding through a pleasant countryside bordered by farm land and open fields. South of Newbury-port, it is still locally called the Newburyport Turnpike. Built in 1804 as a stagecoach road between Newburyport and Boston, the Turnpike, sometimes called the 'airline route,' is unusual among Massachusetts highways in that in 35 miles it deviates only 83 feet from a straight line. From Newburyport it runs through rolling country up and down the glacial hills of Topsfield and Danvers. At Lynnfield it levels out as it passes Suntaug Lake, swings around its only curve between the red rock outcrops of Saugus.

US 1 crosses the N.H. Line 15 *m.* south of Portsmouth, N.H.

SALISBURY, 2.3 *m.* (town, alt. 15, pop. 2,245, sett. 1638, incorp. 1640). The *Quaker Whipping Stone* in the tiny triangular Green marks the site of Major Robert Pike's championship of three Quaker women whipped at the tail of an ox-cart, a story told in Whittier's poem 'How the Women Went from Dover.' The stone originally served as the stepping-stone of the Quaker Meeting House in Salisbury, erected in 1752.

A marker at the north end of the Square indicates the *Site of the Betsy Gerrish House*, within whose narrow walls a session of the General Court squeezed itself in 1757, when the community was a 'shire town' and the only settlement north of the Merrimack River.

Two hundred yards to the right of the Square on the road marked *To State* 110 is the Green known as *Potlid Square*, where the women of Salisbury melted down their pewter pots to make bullets in the cause of liberty. Settlers from Newbury, Massachusetts, and from Salisbury, England, took their part in early frays with the Indians, trying at the same time to build up the fishing industry, the manufacture of oak staves, and shipbuilding. The woolen industry, introduced into Salisbury in 1812, was soon transferred to Amesbury and neighboring towns.

> Left from Salisbury Square on State 1A is the *Old Burying Ground* at the junction of State 1A and Beach Rd. In this cemetery, laid out in 1639, may be seen large flat stones known as 'wolf slabs,' placed on the graves to protect them from hungry wolves.

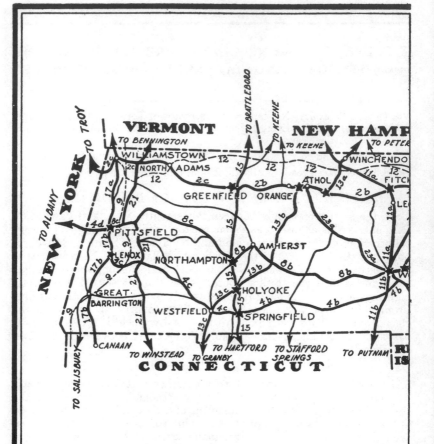

KEY TO
MASSACHUSETTS TOURS

•

See Table of Contents

Main Tours . . . . a   b   c

Side Tours . . . .

Bridle Trails 12

Appalachian Foot Trails 9

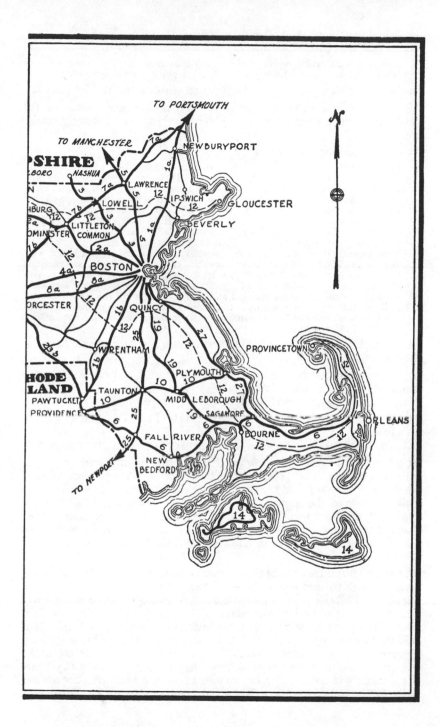

Salisbury Beach (public bathing facilities, salt-water swimming pool, amusement and recreational equipment), 2.1 m. on State 1A, is a popular summer resort.

At 2.4 *m.* is a sign pointing to the junction with State 110 (*see Tour* 7).

Along the smooth three-lane concrete way, no vestiges remain of the dark forest which once menaced the very dooryards of the early settlement.

At 4.2 *m.* is the junction with First St.

Left on First St. is the original settlement, the Ring's Island section. Only the sharply rising bank (L) and the tiny creek (R), 0.1 *m.*, mark the *Fish Flakes* and *Shipyards* of early days. Up the steep slope were once wheeled barrows of fish, brought in from Labrador and Chaleur Bays, to be spread in the sun on drying racks or 'flakes.' The *Site of the Old Ferry Slip*, 0.2 *m.*, on the bank of the Merrimack River, is revealed by rotting timbers still visible at the water's edge. At 0.3 *m.* on a little dirt road stands the *Nathan Dole House (seen by arrangement)*, an ancient dwelling built in 1680. Edna St. Vincent Millay once made her home here. Near-by is the *Marches Tavern (private)* built in 1690 by John March who, as early as 1687, operated the ferry connecting the settlement with Newbury and the near-by port towns. From the tavern, looking seaward are seen *Indian Shell Heaps* now barely visible as green mounds across the marshes. These accumulations of broken clam shells and fish and animal bones mark the spot where the Indians gathered for generations in the summer months to fish in the Merrimack before they returned at the approach of winter to the protection and comparative warmth of the woods.

At 4.3 *m.* US 1 rises to the bridge and crosses the Merrimack River at the Newburyport City Line.

At 4.8 *m.* a glimpse is caught (L) of the rear wall and the squat stone frame of the *Old County Jail* (1744) (*private*) within whose grim walls during the Revolution British privateersmen were shackled to the floor.

At 4.8 *m.* is the junction (R) with State 125 (*Tour* 7A) and (L) State 1A (*Tour* 1A).

Left, State 1A leads to the center of NEWBURYPORT (*see NEWBURYPORT*).

At 8.5 *m.* US 1 crosses the *Parker River*, at this point a narrow stream running between vivid green marshes. At 9.1 *m.* the aged buildings of (*Governor*) *Dummer Academy (campus open; buildings by permission)* are visible (R) from the highway. This boarding-school was established in 1762 and among the clapboarded dormitories that have been added through the years is the tiny original schoolhouse. One story high, with a little belfry, it is more than reminiscent of the 'little red schoolhouse' of rural New England.

The architectural treasure of the campus is the *Governor Dummer Mansion* (*private*), now the headmaster's house, built in 1715 and shaded by arching elms. This charming building is an outstanding example of the early Georgian Colonial period; the detail of the doorway is unusually fine. The mansion has for some reason an unusual number of phantoms. It is said that when August has two full moons, on the night of the first moon Governor Dummer rides a white charger up the broad staircase as he did on the night of his grand housewarming in 1715. For many years the kitchen was haunted by the smiling ghost of a child peeping always through the same doorway. Not until her bones were discovered in a mouldering box in the cellar and given proper burial did the little apparition vanish. It is also averred that the ghost of an English officer who was killed in a duel on the lawn occasionally reappears in powdered wig, embroidered cloak, sword and all.

At 12.3 *m.* is the intersection with State 133.

Right on this road is GEORGETOWN, 4.9 *m.* (town, alt. 74, pop. 2009, sett. 1639, incorp. 1838), offspring of the mother town of Rowley, and one of the last settlements in Essex County. The story goes that grants in this district were held in abeyance by Ezekiel Rogers, head of the Rowley Company, so that his friend, Oliver Cromwell, might find refuge if his efforts to dethrone Charles I should be unsuccessful.

The *Brocklebank House* (*open, free*) about 0.4 *m.* from the Common on State 133, was built in 1670. This attractive gambrel-roof dwelling was once the home of Captain Samuel Brocklebank who was killed in King Philip's War. The old sign of the White Horse Tavern, 1773, swings in front of it.

Left from the Center on State 97, 1.1 *m.*, is an oiled road (R) which leads through an attractive wood to the summit of *Baldpate Hill* (alt. 312), one of the highest points in Essex County.

At 1.2 *m.* is *Baldpate Inn* (*open*). The rambling old structure, with its seven outside doors, is the setting of Earl Derr Biggers's drama, 'Seven Keys to Baldpate.'

At 17.3 *m.* is the intersection with State 97.

Right, State 97 leads to TOPSFIELD, 0.5 *m.* (town, alt. 85, pop. 1113, sett. about 1635, incorp. 1648). The village green is the center of this unspoiled New England community. The *Public Library* (*open Wed. and Sat.*, 3–5) contains a series of murals of historic scenes by Harold Kellogg, its architect. Quiet Topsfield was something of a boom bonanza town in early Colonial times. As early as 1648 bog iron was dug, to be smelted at the Boxford Iron Works, and excitement ran high when a copper vein was struck on the Endicott grant. Mining the ore proved unprofitable, however, and agriculture continued to be the mainstay of the town.

On a lane to the right, opposite the end of the Green, stands the *Choate House* (*private*), a white frame structure, set on a grassy terrace above a shaded lawn fenced with graceful ball-topped posts. It has a hip-roof with a parapet, and four corner chimneys. The front doorway is unusually fine with a fanlight and a Doric portico.

Just beyond in a field adjacent to the old white church, overlooking quiet meadows and ringed by woods, stands the *Parson Capen House* (*open summer months; adm.* 10¢). Built in 1683, it is an outstanding example of the medieval tradition that dominated 17th-century Colonial architecture. In this house is found the simple plan of the massive central chimney, the overhang and lean-to. The overhang of the second story occurs in the front and the third or attic floor overhangs at the end. The front overhang is supported by heavy hewn brackets on either side of the front door and the end overhangs with similar brackets in the center. The only features of ornamentation are the heavy pendrils at the ends of the overhangs and the elaborate broken lines of the chimney. It is in these features that its Elizabethan heritage is betrayed. The lean-to of this house was built as a part of the original structure. The Metropolitan Museum of New York City has reproduced the kitchen for its American Wing. The furnishings are of the period in which the house was built and include a chair-table, a wooden trough, wooden plates and mugs. The brick oven is within a fireplace eight and a half feet wide.

North on State 97, at 1.1 *m.*, is *Pine Grove Cemetery*, which contains old stones some of which date back to 1663. Here are buried the ancestors of Joseph Smith, founder of the Mormon Church.

At 3.2 *m.* is the *Perley-Hale-Perkins House*, built in 1760 by Major Asa Perkins.

The old house, forlorn but still lovely with its weather-beaten frame, its lean-to roof and central chimney, stands vacant and deserted in a neglected yard where one huge elm guards the door.

At 3.5 *m.* is the intersection of State 97 with Depot St.

Left on Depot St. at 5.4 *m.* is BOXFORD (town, alt. 95, pop. 726, sett. 1645, incorp. 1694), occupying an unspoiled stretch in an area with low rolling hills, woods and large lakes. So healthful is the air that the town physician in 1855 is said to have remarked with some regret that he might as well practice in heaven.

The single melodramatic episode in Boxford's peaceful history was the Ames murder trial which in 1769 attracted widespread attention. John Adams, who later became President of the United States, served successfully as attorney for the defense. This trial was perhaps the only one in New England at which the ordeal by touch was employed — a test based on an ancient superstition that the wounds of a corpse would bleed if the murderer touched the body.

Left of the Green is the *First Congregational Church*, a charming white meeting house with its long row of horsestalls still standing. On the other side of Depot St. stands *Journey's End* (*open by permission in summer*). A miniature sand village built in this garden, 'Boxford in the Eighties,' inspired G. Stanley Hall to write 'The Story of a Sand Pile,' a book that made a distinct contribution to the modern playground movement.

At 17.7 *m.* (L) US 1 passes the *Topsfield Fair Grounds.*

At 19.7 *m.* the *Old Milestones* have *B* (Boston) and *P* (Portland) cut deep into the granite. At 21.4 *m.* is the junction with State 62 (*see Tour 1C*). On the southwest corner of the junction (R) is the *Danvers State Hospital for the Insane* (*special visiting hours for groups interested*).

The 'Pike' at 23.2 *m.* continues past pine groves and *Puritan Lawn Memorial Park*, and at 25.7 *m. Suntaug Lake.*

At 25.9 *m.* the road cuts through the *Site of the Old Civil War Training Ground.*

SOUTH LYNNFIELD, 26.3 *m.* (alt. 77, Lynnfield), is a crossroad village at the junction with State 128.

Right from South Lynnfield on State 128 at 0.4 *m.* is the intersection with Summer St. To the right, Summer St. leads past *Pilling's Pond*, 1.8 *m.*

LYNNFIELD, 3 *m.* (town, alt. 90, pop. 1896, sett. 1638–39, incorp. 1814), is set high on a plateau. The winding reaches of the Ipswich and Saugus Rivers provide boating, fishing, and swimming. Many people employed in near-by industrial centers make Lynnfield their home.

At 27.5 *m.* lies the *Lynn Reservoir*; and at 28.7 *m.* US 1 skirts the 580-acre *Breakheart Reservation*, a State-owned tract with trails, picnic grounds, lookouts, and parking spaces constructed by the Civilian Conservation Corps.

At 28.7 *m.* is the intersection with Lynn Fells Parkway.

Right on the Parkway at 1.2 *m.* is the intersection with Howard St. At No. 7 is the *Scotch Boardman House* (*open by permission*), once the home of 'King' Nanepashemet. This house, built in 1651, was used as quarters for Scottish prisoners captured by Cromwell at the Battle of Dunbar. The captives were brought to Saugus to labor seven years in New England as indentured servants in the iron works. Owing to frequent boundary changes the dwelling has at various times stood in two counties and four towns. The original boundary between Lynn and Boston ran through the middle of the front door, which for many years bore the letters *B* and *L* on its respective halves. With its sagging roof-line, its lean-to roof reaching almost to the ground, the broken line of its central chimney, its second-story overhang and weather-beaten walls, it is an excellent example of the early American period.

At 30.1 *m.* is the intersection of US 1 and Main St.

Left on Main St. is SAUGUS, 0.7 *m.* (town, alt. 20, pop. 15,076, sett. 1630, incorp. 1815).

Close by, on Central St., is the *Old Ironworks House (private)*. This restored example of 17th-century American architecture was built in 1643 by Farmer Thomas Dexter, one of the original owners of the iron works. The house, one of the most delightful in the county, has diamond-paned casements, steep gables, batten doors and an immense central chimney with a buttress-like extension about 12 feet down the lean-to roof. Ornamental drops suspend from the second-story overhang. The house has been greatly altered, many additions having been made in recent years. Among these distortions of the original structure are the odd-shaped carved ornaments attached to the peak of the gables.

The interior shows the original exposed timbers of English oak, some of them at least two feet square and ornamentally carved. It is said that the builder, never dreaming of the vast forests in this country, brought these timbers with him from England for the frame of his house. The fireplaces in the kitchen and living room are at least 12 feet wide and still contain pot hooks and cranes supposed to have been made at the near-by forge.

The *Site of the Forge*, directly across the road, is marked by a tablet, while near-by are grass-grown cinder banks, relics of the years when the plant was in operation. Bog iron ore was common in the vicinity of Saugus. There was also plentiful oak timber for charcoal. John Winthrop, Jr., ever alert to commercial possibilities, formed a company of capitalists in England in 1641 and two years later sailed for America with a group of skilled iron workers. In 1645, under the management of Richard Leader, the plant had an output of eight to ten tons a week, and within a few years it had achieved a surplus for export.

It is claimed that among the articles turned out were the first dies in America for coining money and the first fire engine, as well as kettles, anchors, cranes, and bar and wrought iron for blacksmiths. Restlessness of the iron workers and difficulties with the backers ruined the enterprise, however, and Scottish prisoners sent out as indentured servants in 1654 proved less amenable than the paid workers. At the breakup of Hammersmith, as Saugus was then called, the more skilled of the scattered workers set up forges and bloomeries throughout New England.

Except for this venture, Saugus was largely agricultural through the first two centuries of its existence. Several factories which opened in the 19th century turned out a variety of products — snuff, chocolate, nails, and shoes — but industry declined, and the town is today a purely suburban community.

The *Old Indian Trail*, 32.2 *m.*, is indicated by a marker and a granite milestone (R). Over this trail, according to tradition, William, Richard, and Ralph Sprague, the first white men to pass through this region, journeyed on their way from Salem (Naumkeag) to Charlestown (Mishawam) in 1629.

At 32.4 *m.* is the intersection with Salem St.

Right, this street leads to MALDEN, 1.5 *m.* (*see MALDEN*).

US 1 follows Broadway through a thickly populated district and at 34.5 *m.* is EVERETT (*see EVERETT*).

At 34.8 *m.* is the junction with the Revere Beach Parkway, State 1A (*see Tour 1A*).

At 36.4 *m.*, at the junction with State 28 (*see Tour* 5), US 1 becomes the Northern Artery, one of the great traffic thoroughfares leading into Boston.

At 38.0 *m.* is the junction with Somerville Ave.

Right on Somerville Ave. is SOMERVILLE, 0.5 *m.* (*see SOMERVILLE*).

Between Somerville and Cambridge, US 1 passes through an industrialized area noted for its meat-packing plants.

At 39 *m.* is the intersection with Memorial Drive, leading along the Charles River past the buildings of the *Massachusetts Institute of Technology*, 40.1 *m.* in Cambridge (*see CAMBRIDGE*).

Right here on Massachusetts Ave. is CAMBRIDGE, 1.0 *m.* (*see CAMBRIDGE*).

At 41.2 *m.* is the Cottage Farm Bridge over the Charles River, the Boston City Line. US 1 turns left and crosses the Cottage Farm Bridge to Commonwealth Ave., 41.3 *m.*

Left on Commonwealth Ave. is BOSTON, 2.5 *m.* (*see BOSTON*).

Sec. b. BOSTON to RHODE ISLAND STATE LINE, 36.6 *m.*

South of Boston at 1.5 *m.*, US 1 bears left, enters the beautiful Jamaicaway, and skirts *Jamaica Pond* (*see BOSTON*).

At the traffic circle, 3.6 *m.*, where State 3 (*see Tour* 27), State 28 (*see Tour* 19) and State 138 (*see Tour* 25) branch left, the route follows (R) a four-lane bituminous-asphalt highway, passing the *Arnold Arboretum* at 4.5 *m.* (*see BOSTON*).

At 7.9 *m.* is the junction with State 109 (*see Tour* 1D).

At 9.2 *m.* US 1 passes over *Mother Brook*, dug prior to 1640, which connects the Charles and Neponset Rivers, making Boston an island.

At 9.6 *m.* is the intersection with State 1A (*see Tour* 1B). Curving, rising and dipping, and occasionally flanked by steep embankments, US 1 threads its way through alternating woodlands and open fields.

At 17.0 *m.* is the junction with Moose Hill Rd.

Left on this road is the entrance to the *Moose Hill Bird Sanctuary*, 2.0 *m.* (Town of Sharon), covering the highest land in the town and crowned by an *Observation Tower*. The sanctuary is in charge of the Massachusetts Audubon Society and comprises over 2000 acres.

At 21.1 *m.* is the intersection with Water St.

Right on this street is SOUTH WALPOLE, 0.2 *m.* (alt. 220, Walpole, *see Tour* 1B). Here, on the corner of Neponset and Washington Sts., stands *Fuller's Tavern* (*open*), a rambling frame building, with great shade trees, and a pleasant small lawn with a row of hitching posts. This inn, built in 1807 and restored in 1927, was once a famous halfway house between Boston and Providence.

At 29.3 *m.* US 1, State 1A (*see Tour* 1B) and N. Washington St. meet at a square

Right on N. Washington St., is the *Woodcock House* (*private*) (No. 362). In 1669 John Woodcock made the first permanent settlement in the North Purchase — now North Attleborough — and established a tavern which during its 170 years of service, 1670–1840, was visited by George Washington, General Lafayette and

Daniel Webster. In its earliest days the hostel served as a link in the chain of garrisons stretching from Boston to Rhode Island. Woodcock, an Indian fighter of repute, killed many Indians and survived seven wounds received at their hands. Vengeance was reaped by the Indians, however, who killed his son, Nathaniel, and placed his scalp on a stick in the old Burying Ground opposite the tavern.

NORTH ATTLEBOROUGH, 0.8 *m.* (town, alt. 183, pop. 10,202, sett. 1669, incorp. 1887) was originally a part of Attleborough. The town's industrial development started in 1780 with the establishment of a jewelry shop by 'the Frenchman,' reputed to be a nobleman incognito. It was not until 1807, however, that the first jewelry manufacturing company was organized.

The *North Attleborough Historical Society Headquarters* (*open 3d Tues. of each month*, 2–5), 224 Washington St., is a two-and-a-half-story clapboarded house with slate roof. The barn, adjacent, contains a number of historical relics.

At 1.8 *m.* State 1A rejoins US 1.

At 36.6 *m.* US 1 traverses an old stone bridge and crosses the Rhode Island Line 2 miles north of Pawtucket, R.I.

T O U R 1 A : *From* NEWBURYPORT *to* EVERETT, 38.4 *m.*, State 1A.

Via Newbury, Rowley, Ipswich, Essex, Hamilton, Wenham, Beverly, Manchester, Gloucester, Rockport, Salem, Peabody, Marblehead, Swampscott, Lynn, Nahant, Revere, Winthrop, Chelsea, Everett.

B. & M. R.R. (Eastern Div.) parallels route.

Macadam roadbed; open all year; traffic heavy near Boston.

Accommodations: Chiefly hotels in larger cities and tourist homes in villages.

STATE 1A, south of Newburyport, parallels the coastline rather closely.

As High St. it branches south from its junction with US 1 (*see Tour 1*) in Newburyport (*see NEWBURYPORT*), running through a residential district.

At 0.6 *m.* is the *Swett–Ilsley House* (1670) (*open by arrangement*), which was enlarged, and later became the Blue Anchor Tavern.

At 1.5 *m.* is NEWBURY (town, alt. 40, pop. 1576, sett. and incorp. 1635). The *Upper Green* lies almost opposite the entrance to the Plum Island Rd. As the townsfolk gradually moved back from the Parker River side, they centered their homes in the vicinity of this strip of grassy land.

The *Coffin House* (*open June–Oct.*, 2–5; *adm.* 25¢), 0.2 *m.* north of the Center, was built about 1653 and later enlarged. It is a well-preserved example of 17th-century architecture. The part played by the Coffins in the town's development has been traced by Joshua Coffin in his 'History of Newbury, Newburyport, and West Newbury from 1635 to 1845.'

The old *Noyes Homestead*, on Parker St., 0.2 *m.* from the Green, was built by the Rev. James Noyes, teacher, about 1646. Additions to the original pitched-roof structure with a central chimney have not destroyed its charm.

The *Short House* (*open June–Oct.*, 2–5; *adm.* 25¢), on State 1A, near Plum Island Rd., with a fine doorway and brick gable ends, was built sometime between 1717 and 1733.

> Left from Newbury Upper Green, a marked road leads across a broad stretch of marsh, its level reaches broken by high conical stacks of salt hay piled on staddles, to *Plum Island* (*parking facilities*), 2.7 *m.* Through the marsh meanders the salt stream of the Plum Island River, bright blue against a background of tawny sand dunes. Right of this road the sands stretch unbroken for 10 miles to the *Brown Bird Sanctuary* at Ipswich.

The *Jackman–Willett House* (*open June–Oct.*, 2–5; *adm.* 25¢), 3.7 *m.*, a short distance north of the lower Green, was built in 1696, on the site of the original burying ground of 'Ould Newberry.'

NEWBURY OLD TOWN, 4 *m.* (alt. 40). Here on the lower Green the townsfolk used to gather when Newbury vessels arrived from trading along the coast or with the West Indies. Limestone discovered near-by in 1697 for many years provided a valuable export. Newbury Old Town's industries have long since been surrendered to Newburyport, and life here has resumed its leisurely and tranquil air.

Near-by (W.) is *Oldtown Hill* (alt. 180), from the summit of which is a sweeping view (E.) of the Atlantic coastline and rolling hills. In the sides of the hill near its base are several *Dugouts* where the settlers endured the bitter winter of 1635. Thatched saplings were stuck in the ground outside as windbreaks.

South of Newbury, State 1A winds between orchards and fields and across stretches of salt marsh.

At 7.8 *m.* the *Platts–Bradstreet House* (*open in summer; adm.* 25¢), headquarters of the Rowley Historical Society, overlooks a small village green. This two-and-a-half-story frame house was constructed about 1660.

ROWLEY, 8.2 *m.* (town, alt. 59, pop. 1495, sett. 1638, incorp. 1639), is the center of a peaceful agricultural area. On *Rowley Common* in 1813 the 'Country's Wonder,' a 90-ton vessel, was built, and afterward hauled to the river (1.5 *m.*) by 100 yoke of oxen, while bystanders refreshed themselves from a well into which had been poured a full barrel of Jamaica rum. Shipbuilding here was begun in 1780, and continued for nearly a century.

Near-by stands the *Public Library* (*open*) housing a good collection of local birds.

At 8.7 *m.* is the junction with State 133.

> Right on this road, 0.4 *m.*, is the *Clarke House* (1671), now in disrepair, but still picturesque with its lean-to roof and overhanging second story. (Open on request.)

At 11.3 *m.* in Ipswich is the junction with Linebrook Rd. and High St.

> 1. Right on Linebrook Rd., 0.7 *m.*, is the *Burnham-Harte House* (1640) (*Ye Olde*

Burnham Inn, open as summer tearoom). one of the best-known 17th-century houses of New England, which through successive reconstructions has lost its typical exterior mass. The rooms within, on five levels, retain such original features as a nine-foot fireplace, hand-hewn joists, and 'frog-leg' hinges. The living-room has been copied for the American Wing of the Metropolitan Museum of Art, and in 1937 the parlor and an upstairs chamber were removed and sent to the Metropolitan. Copies of these have replaced the originals.

2. Left on High St., the worn slate stones of the *Old North Burial Yard* straggle up the slope of Town Hill. Many of the pioneers are buried here; the oldest legible stone is dated 1634.

At 0.2 *m.* on elm-lined High St. is (L) the *Waldo Caldwell House*, built before 1650, which has small-paned windows with old glass.

The *Rogers Manse* (*open by permission*) at 0.4 *m.*, a gracious example of early 18th-century architecture, contains elaborate paneling and a wide staircase with beautifully turned balusters.

High St. is lined with tall elms, and on days when the wind blows strong from the east it brings through the shaded streets the throb of surf on far-off Ipswich Bar. This sound calls to mind the legend of Harry Main, a smuggler and pirate of the old days, who, so runs the tale, was chained to the Bar and condemned to coil a rope of sand till Doomsday. When the moaning of the bar is heard, the old folks still say, 'Harry growls at his work today.'

High St. becomes East St. at N. Main St.

The *Norton Corbett House* (*private*), 0.5 *m.*, 8 East St., little changed since it was built, before 1650. has a lean-to roof and massive central chimney.

At 0.7 *m.* the *Hovey House* (*private*), also with lean-to roof and large central chimney, faces County St. In 1655 this house was occupied by Jeffrey Snelling, the Town Whipper.

Left from East St. on County St. to Green St.; left on this to No. 8 (L), the *Burley House* (*private*), built before 1688 and now falling into decay.

Green St. crosses the Ipswich River and enters Turkey Shore Rd. Here, directly opposite the bridge, stands the *Emerson House* (*open daily in summer; adm. 25¢*) on a grassy terrace. Built in 1640, and now belonging to the Society for the Preservation of New England Antiquities, it has an overhanging second story, steep roof, and large central chimney.

IPSWICH, 11.7 *m.* (town, alt. 30, pop. 6217, sett. 1633, incorp. 1634), first known as Agawam, was settled by a group of 12 pioneers, among whom were three or more 'gentlemen' who apparently set the tone for this community; for this remote frontier village was a cultural center of the 17th century. Anne Bradstreet, the poet, and Nathaniel Ward, witty author of 'The Simple Cobler of Aggawam,' lived here.

The *Rebellion Tablet* marks the spot where in 1687 the townsfolk, led by John Wise, gathered nearly 100 years before the Revolution in angry protest against the oppression of Governor Andros.

On the North Green stood the First Parish Church, built in 1635. Deep in the rock beside the present Congregational building (1847) is a cloven hoofprint left, legend says, by the Devil.

Lacemaking, the first industry here, was supplanted by tanning and shoemaking, and later by machine knitting. The small parts of the knitting machines were said to have been secreted in pots of Yorkshire butter and brought to Ipswich in defiance of English export regulations.

The *Choate Bridge*, built 1764, of rough-hewn granite blocks, spans the amber water of the Ipswich River. From here are visible the stark red-brick buildings of the *Ipswich Mills*, an important hosiery plant till 1927, when it was closed and its equipment sold to the Soviet Union. Several small industries now occupy the building. Digging and marketing clams supports many of the residents.

The square, three-story *John Heard House* (*not open*, 1937), on State 1A, built in the late 18th century by the father of Capt. Augustine Heard of the China sea trade, is now owned by the local historical society.

Opposite is the *Whipple House* (*adm.* 25¢), built about 1640, with over-hanging gable end, massive central chimney and long sweep lean-to roof. The well-preserved, age-darkened timbers are exposed in the low-ceiled rooms of the structure — one of the few existent with hand-carved shadow mouldings in every room. The house is furnished almost entirely with originals.

The *South Church* (1748), with white columned portico and an exterior of classic simplicity, overlooks the South Green.

> 1. Left from the South Green on County Rd. to the *Town Wharf*, 0.7 *m.* (*boats for hire to Plum Island*, 7 *m.*, *and Brown Bird Sanctuary*).
>
> 2. Left from South Green on Argilla Rd. is *Ipswich Beach* (*parking fee; limited bathhouse facilities; three small restaurants*), 4.5 *m.*, an unspoiled stretch of shore line and sand dunes.

At 12.5 *m.* is the junction with State 121.

> Left on State 121 through hills to sea level. The *John Wise House* (*open on request*), 3.5 *m.*, built in 1701, has a long roof and central chimney, and was the home of a minister honored for his vehement defense of victims of the witchcraft frenzy, and even more for his denunciation of the Taxation Edict of 1687.
>
> At 4.6 *m.* is ESSEX (town, alt. 27, pop. 1486, sett. 1634, incorp. 1819). A thin stream of tidewater divides the township of Essex, spinning out from the shuttle of the village, the strongest thread in a web of creeks and channels woven through miles of salt marsh. The clammers' flat-bottomed dories slide along on the stream, bringing their catches for roadside vendors to fry and sell to tourists on the cause-way joining the two halves of the town.
>
> Annually in May or June, the river is barred with a net, leaving an opening large enough to permit some of the alewives to continue upstream to spawn. The others, baffled by the net, pack the stream solidly and are ladled into barrels. The town owns the alewife rights, and sells them each year to the highest bidder.
>
> The *First Congregational Church* (1792–93, remodeled 1842) has one of the last three bells cast by Paul Revere.
>
> The gracious old *Universalist Meeting House* (1836) looks down on the *Shipyards* (1668). The yards have launched many types of vessels, from small 'Chebacco Boats' of the old-time Cape Ann fishermen to modern schooners, trawlers, yachts, and freighters. Tradition says that the first boat was built by a Burnham in the garret of an ancient house, and that it was necessary to cut away the windows in order to launch her.

State 1A, here the Old Bay Rd., winds through farms, woods, and fine estates.

HAMILTON, 16 *m.* (town, alt. 52, pop. 2235, sett. 1638, incorp. 1793), named for Alexander Hamilton, spurned an offer from a newer town to buy its name.

Mary Abigail Dodge (pseudonym, Gail Hamilton), a writer romantically devoted to the memory of Alexander Hamilton, is said to have asked to be buried under the pine trees outside her house, and she is supposed to have had the habit of rising from that dark resting-place to stand, a white-shrouded figure, in her own bedroom window. The pine trees still remain, but if gravestones may be believed, Mary Abigail Dodge is decently interred in Hamilton Cemetery.

The *First Congregational Church*, with a congregation formed in 1714, has a square tower surmounted by a steeple, and two Ionic columns at its entrance.

The *Town Hall* of Hamilton is a white frame building with a well-proportioned cupola.

Beside the church is the *Covered Wagon House (private)*, from which in December, 1787, departed the first covered wagon to leave Massachusetts for the Northwest Territory. The Rev. Manasseh Cutler (1742–1823), Yale graduate and Hamilton's second pastor, was the moving force in this emigration. He was sent to Congress to secure land for the Ohio Company, of which he was one of the founders.

On the corner of Farms Rd. and State 1A is the old *Brown House (private)*, with lean-to roof and small-paned casement windows, fine doorways, and large central chimney.

Right on Farms Rd. at 0.4 *m.* to the *Black Brook Plantation (open)*, a large demonstration forest owned by Harvard University (*see CAMBRIDGE*).

On Bridge St., 0.2 *m.* E. of the Center, is the *Oldest House (private)* in the town, built in 1680; it has an overhanging second story with carved pendrils. Wings added in later years show three distinct periods of architecture.

The polo field stretching along the highway at 16.6 *m.* belongs to the *Myopia Hunt Club*, so named when established in 1882, because all the founders happened to be near-sighted. An annual event on Labor Day is a combined horse-show, polo match, and steeplechase.

At 17.1 *m.*, at the corner of Asbury St., is the *Hamilton-Wenham Community House*, presented to these towns by the Mandell family as a memorial to a son killed in the World War. A bronze statue of young Samuel Mandell by Anna Coleman Ladd stands on the stone-flagged porch.

Right on Asbury St. 1 *m.* to the picnic ground and Methodist camp-meeting place, *Asbury Grove*.

At 17.8 *m.* is the junction with Larch Row.

Left on this road, 0.2 *m.* to the *Lowe-Pickering House*, built before 1680 and restored in 1924; it has been considerably altered, but has fine paneling, the original broad floor boards, old hinges, and box locks, and a small archway in the rear with linen-fold carving. Its large main chimney contains a smoke-house, and wood-ash and soap-making arches. Near the house are 13 magnificent English lindens said to have been planted by Alexander Hamilton to symbolize the 13 original Colonies.

At WENHAM, 18.1 *m.* (town, alt. 56, pop. 1196, sett. 1635, incorp. 1643), on the Green is the frame *First Church* (1843), a favorite with artists. The interior has been restored, and the pulpit is a copy made from the wood of the original pulpit. John Fiske, the first pastor (1644) of the parish, was described by Cotton Mather as ranking 'among the most famous preachers in primitive New England.' A dissenter, he is said to have hidden in a cellar in England for six months before he came to Massachusetts.

The second dwelling along the Green beyond the church is the *Henry Hobbs House* (*private*), built in 1747, with a gambrel roof, paneled wainscoting, exposed beams, H-L hinges, eight fireplaces, and a brick oven. Here once lived the Tory Nathaniel Brown, whom representatives of the Marblehead Company attempted unsuccessfully to tar and feather.

Almost opposite is the restored *Claflin-Richards House* (*open 1-5; adm. 25¢; adm. in morning by application at the Tabby-Cat Tea House, opposite*). This house (1664) with huge serpentine braces, said to be the only ones in New England, contains an international collection of 1000 dolls. A *Shoe Shop* (*open June-Sept.*) stands in the rear. In 1860 there were over 80 such shops in Wenham.

At 18.7 *m.* is *Wenham Lake*, remembered as the scene of Whittier's poem, 'The Witch of Wenham.' A boulder by the lake shore marks the site of Peters Hill, upon which the Rev. Hugh Peters of Salem preached the first sermon in the new settlement, choosing the text 'In Enon near to Salem, for there was much water there.' In the days of the clipper ships, ice from Wenham Lake was exported as far as India.

State 1A runs through flat fields covered with suburban homes.

At 19.5 *m.* is NORTH BEVERLY (alt. 69). In this vicinity is Grover St., named for the family of a Beverly citizen of long ago who in punishmer ᴣ for some mysterious crime was haunted by troops of black cats.

This region was part of the 1000-acre grant allotted to the 'Old Planters,' among whom was Roger Conant. In 1668 the Bass River settlement, incorporated as the town of Beverly, was maliciously dubbed 'Beggarly' by the Salem autocrats whom the planters had flouted.

The *Scruggs-Rayment House* (*private*), 64 Dodge St. (State 1A), built before 1683, has been altered so much that its original lines have been lost.

At 20.2 *m.* is the junction with Conant St.

> Right on Conant St. is the *Second Church*, built in 1714.

Beside the fire station, at 20.5 *m.* on the corner of Cabot St., is a tablet marking the birth of an American industry, the *Site of the First Cotton Mill*, built 1789. The jenny of the mill spun 60 threads at once, and the carding machine carded 40 lbs. of cotton a day. Nineteenth-century Beverly specialized in shoemaking, silversmithing, and the manufacture of britannia ware.

> Right on Conant St. is the *Conant House* (*private*), at No. 634, built on land given

by Roger Conant to his son Exercise in 1666. It is much altered, but the original steeply pitched roof and central chimney are visible through the trees.

The many-gabled' *Balch House*, 21.2 *m.*, is the home of another of the old planters. Incorporated in the quaint dwelling with its steep pitch roof and gables is the hut built in 1638 by John Balch, one of the first settlers of Beverly, and a member of Roger Conant's company of pioneers.

At 21.3 *m.* is the junction with Balch St.

Right on this street and L. on McKay St. to the plant of the *United Shoe Machinery Corporation* (*open to genuinely interested persons*), the largest industry in Beverly and the largest of its kind in the world. All of the machinery is owned by the corporation and leased to shoe factories on a royalty basis.

McKay St. continues to the Bass River, on whose banks the 'Old Planters' landed; near its mouth are *Salter's Point* and *Dock Lane*, early the centers of town activities. John Winthrop, Jr., in 1638 established a salt works at the point; at the foot of the lane vessels were built for the coastwise trade soon developed for salt fish and local products. This trade in time extended to South America and Europe.

At 22 *m.* is BEVERLY (city, alt. 26, pop. 25,871, sett. about 1626, incorp. town, 1668, city, 1894). From the modern business section, it is hard to visualize the post-Revolutionary decades when the merchant princes of Beverly were sending their vessels to sea and the fisheries aided by Federal subsidies were flourishing; when rich cargoes from Africa and the Spice Islands scented the air of the waterfront.

The first letter of marque in the United States was issued to the local schooner 'Hannah,' commissioned by George Washington and said to be the first vessel to fly the Continental flag.

The basis of the *Salem Athenaeum* (*see SALEM*) was a collection of more than 100 scientific volumes captured from a British vessel off the Irish coast and brought to America as the Kirwan Library. This collection played a vital part in developing the mathematical genius of Nathaniel Bowditch.

The original building of the *First Church* on Cabot St. was erected in 1656. During the last days of the witchcraft hysteria of 1693, Mistress Hale, exemplary wife of the Beverly minister, was among the accused. Her case was dismissed, and shortly after that the witch trials were abandoned altogether.

At 115 Cabot St. is the *Historical House* (*open daily in summer; on Sat. the rest of the year; 10–4; adm. free*), a stately building erected in 1781 by John Cabot, now containing a collection of relics.

Beverly is at the junction with State 62 (*see Tour 1C*).

At 22.6 *m.* is the junction with State 127.

Left on State 127 is the North Shore Drive, which follows the rocky edge of the harbor to *Independence Park*, 0.5 *m.*, *Dane Street Beach* (*public*), and *Lyon's Park*, 0.9 *m.* Here, as in the Montserrat section, granite hills, heavily wooded, are monopolized by pretentious estates.

The *Old Woodbury Tavern* (*still a hotel*), 1.4 *m.*, was built in 1690 and remodeled in 1933. This building, with pitch roof and massive central chimney, has lost much of its charm through the addition of an outdoor dining-room.

PRIDE'S CROSSING, 3.8 *m.* (alt. 57, City of Beverly), a residential village, is noted for its fine summer homes.

BEVERLY FARMS, 4.5 *m.* (alt. 21, City of Beverly), was the summer home of Oliver Wendell Holmes, poet and novelist, and of his son, the late Justice Holmes. State 127 runs along between estates half concealed behind their field-stone walls, and the rocky rim of the bay.

At 6.2 *m.* is the junction with Harbor St. which leads (R) to *Tuck's Point Beach* (*picnicking and bathing*), 0.5 *m.*

MANCHESTER, 7 *m.* (town, alt. 14, pop. 2509, sett. 1626–27, incorp. 1645), is a sleepy village clustering about its Green; its frame church (1809) is surmounted by an unusual tower. The first settlers were two fishermen who established themselves at Kettle Cove when the Cape Ann Colony broke up in 1626. The little Salem community was known as Jeffrey's Creek. It throve as a fishing village, but by the middle of the 19th century Boston merchants had already begun to transform it into a fashionable resort.

Opposite the town library is the *Trask House* (*open July–Aug.*, 3–5), headquarters of the local historical society. The *Major Israel Forster House* (*private*), 0.1 *m.* south of the Center on State 127, is a fine building of the Post-Colonial type, with a Captain's Walk. On the front door is the original knocker, inscribed 'I. Forster, 1804.'

Towering over Friend Court about 0.5 *m.* north of the Center on School St., is wooded Powder House Hill. On its summit is the red-brick *Powder House*, used during the War of 1812 for storing ammunition.

GLOUCESTER, 15 *m.* (*see GLOUCESTER and ROCKPORT, CAPE ANN*).

At 24 *m.* is SALEM (*see SALEM*).

Right from Salem on State 128, at the corner of Bridge and Winter Sts., a marked highway leads (R) to PEABODY, 2.2 *m.*

The industrial section of the city is one of the largest leather-processing districts of the world, with 37 tanneries (1934). Tanning was done here before the Revolution, and by 1855 it was carried on in 27 plants; the town had also 24 currying shops. As early as 1638 glassmaking was started by Ananias Conklin, who manufactured coarse lamps and squat, heavy bottles.

The *Peabody Institute*, Main St., contains a general library, a fine reference library and a commodious auditorium. It was founded in 1852 by the philanthropist George Peabody, in whose honor the city changed its name in 1868. This man, born February 18, 1795, came of poor parents, and his formal education was limited to that provided by the public schools. Later, going to London, he became a business man and finally a great banker. He declined a baronetcy offered by Queen Victoria, accepting instead (a charming and typically democratic gesture) the Queen's gift of a miniature of herself, now on exhibition in the auditorium. When the death of George Peabody occurred in England in 1869, a funeral service was held for him in Westminster Abbey, and the man-of-war 'Monarch' of the Queen's Navy, convoyed by French and English warships, bore his remains back to the United States for burial.

Right from the square on Central St. 0.9 *m.* to Andover St. (State 114); left here to an old dwelling, 1.8 *m.*, with a sign proclaiming it the summer home of Elias Hasket Derby, bought and remodeled by him in 1776 and officially known as the *Eppes-Derby-Endicott-Osborn House* (*seen by courtesy of tenant*). Horse-chestnut trees stand in a sentinel row across the lawn.

St. Joseph's Juniorate (*Oak Hill*) (*grounds open*), at 2.4 *m.* on Andover St., is housed in a building designed by Samuel McIntire (1800). Although somewhat altered, the three-story hip-roof mansion retains such distinctive McIntire touches as window heads ornamented by carved eagles, a front porch with dignified Ionic columns and pilasters, and a doorway finely carved by hand. The interior contains exceptionally fine woodwork on the stairway, mantels, and elsewhere. The Juniorate is conducted by the Xaverian Brothers as a college preparatory school, especially for those who intend to join the brotherhood. Three of the finest rooms have been removed to the Boston Museum of Fine Arts.

State 1A continues south through residential and business areas. At 27.4 *m.* is the junction with Vinnin Square.

Left on Vinnin Square past the *General John Glover Inn* (1781) and straight ahead on Tedesco St., on Humphrey St., on Pleasant St., and (R) on Washington St. is MARBLEHEAD, 3 *m.* (*see MARBLEHEAD*).

SWAMPSCOTT, 28.8 *m.* (town, alt. 127, pop. 10,480, sett. 1629, incorp. 1852), a summer resort and fashionable residential suburb of Boston, was settled as an outpost of Saugus. The first white settler was Francis Ingalls, who erected a tannery in 1632.

The spot was from the beginning noted for its fine fishing; lobsters were picked up at low tide, and the sunken ledges offshore teemed with cod. The beaches offered a convenient place to land the catches, and it is said that piles of frozen cod used to be stacked like cordwood near where the Swampscott Club now stands. Although there was a ready sale for fish, and farmers from inland drove their wagons to Swampscott to trade geese, eggs, butter, and cheese for the yield of the sea, the fishermen were always wretchedly poor.

On Paradise Rd. (State 1A), 0.1 *m.* northeast of the Center, is the *Mary Baker Eddy House* (*open daily* 10 12, *Sun.* 2 5; *adm.* 25¢), where the founder of Christian Science began her demonstrations of healing in 1866. By that year the metamorphosis from poverty-stricken fishing village to luxurious resort was well under way. In 1815 'Farmer' Phillips had taken in the first 'summer boarders.' A few years later 'Aunt Betsey' Blaney was obtaining the scandalous price of $3 a week for room and board. The first summer hotel was built in 1835. When the farmer owning the land adjoining was offered $400 an acre for it, he ran to get the deed before the 'city man' should come to his senses.

The *Humphrey House (now a candy shop)*, 0.2 *m.*, northeast of the Center on Paradise Rd., was built between 1635 and 1640. It has an overhanging second story, and contains interesting relics. John Humphrey, a wealthy English lawyer, was treasurer of the Dorchester Adventurers and later a magistrate of the Bay Colony and member of the first Board of Overseers of Harvard. His wife, Lady Susan, was a daughter of the Earl of Lincoln and a sister of the ill-fated Lady Arbella for whom Governor Winthrop's ship was named. Mr. Humphrey and his wife came to settle in Swampscott in 1634; but, unhappy on the frontier and homesick for the brilliant life they had left, they soon sold their house and grant and took ship for England. According to Winthrop's 'Journal,' several passengers on this vessel spoke slightingly of God's Province of Massachusetts Bay and almost immediately a storm descended upon them. A shipwreck was averted only by earnest prayers.

The Humphrey House and land were soon purchased by Lady Deborah Moody. Lady Deborah appears to have had a mind of her own, for she almost immediately became involved in a religious controversy and was banished from Swampscott for 'maintaining that the baptism of infants was unwarranted and sinful.' She departed to Long Island, where she became a person of great influence in the Dutch Colony.

Left from the Center on Burrill St., to the junction with Humphrey St.; left here past *Blaney's Beach* to the junction with Puritan Rd., 0.7 *m.*, at the corner of which is the Town Fish House, where bronzed fishermen sit mending and drying their nets.

Puritan Rd. continues past *Whale's Beach*, 1.3 *m.*, and on through the estates on exclusive Little's Point to *White Court* (*private*), once the summer White House of Calvin Coolidge.

At 29.8 *m.* is LYNN (*see LYNN*).

Left from Lynn on Nahant St. and right on Nahant Rd. to the narrow isthmus of *Long Beach*, 0.4 *m.*, where Longfellow and Emerson once walked together. It was at Nahant that Longfellow wrote 'The Golden Legend' and part of 'Hiawatha.' Here also Professor Louis Agassiz wrote 'Journey Through Brazil' and John Lothrop Motley began work on his 'Rise of the Dutch Republic.'

A bridle path follows the beach, gay on a warm day with gay-suited bathers, to LITTLE NAHANT (alt. 46), 2.1 *m.* A road (L) makes a complete circle of Little Nahant. A spread of ocean, several beaches, and the city of Lynn in the background form an impressive panorama.

Nahant Rd. continues along *Short Beach*, passing (L) the *U.S. Coast Guard Station*, 2.5 *m.*, where visitors are permitted to inspect the various life-saving devices. Off Short Beach (also popular with bathers) lies (L) *Egg Rock*, the reputed home of a sea serpent 'as big round as a wine pipe and 15 fathoms or more in length.'

Bearing (L) from Short Beach up the hill, Nahant Rd. runs through an *Avenue of Elms* planted by Frederic Tudor, the 'Ice King,' about 1825.

NAHANT, 3.7 *m.* (town, alt. 90, pop. 1748, sett. 1630, incorp. 1853). Nahant is a high rocky isle once covered with trees, where the lonely haywards of early days guarded hedges and fences against damage by cattle and strays. Nahant and Little Nahant were sold in 1730 by the Indian Chief Poquanum to a Lynn farmer, Thomas Dexter, for a suit of clothes, two stone pestles, and a jew's-harp.

Here in 1802 Joseph Johnson erected a tavern called *The Castle*, and informed 'the public in general and valetudinarians and sportsmen in particular' that he was 'furnished with every good thing to cheer the heart, to brace the frame, or to pamper the appetite.' The success of this venture and the establishment of steamboat service to Boston in 1817 caused Nahant to develop rapidly as a fashionable watering place.

Off Nahant Rd., south of the Center, is a public footpath winding down to the sea, along which are views of the coastline and some odd rock formations. The *estate of the late Senator Henry Cabot Lodge* (*private*) is on Cliff St.

On Swallow's Cave Rd. fled fugitive Indians during King Philip's War, to *Swallow's Cave* (*private property*), a natural recess in the rocky shore. Victims of the witchcraft persecution also took refuge here.

Right from Swallow's Cave Rd. on Vernon St. is the junction with Cliff St. (later Willow); left here to the links of the *Nahant Golf Club*, 1.6 *m.* (*adm. by invitation*). On the grounds is *Bear Pond*, into which John Breed, an early settler, is said to have been chased by a bear and where he stayed until rescued.

At 1.9 *m.* is *Fort Ruckman* (*closed to visitors*), a unit of the coastal defense; here are stationed electrically operated barbette guns designed to protect Boston Harbor.

State 1A southwest of Lynn passes through a congested shoe factory district, and at 31.8 *m.* crosses the *General C. R. Edwards Memorial Bridge* (1936) over the Saugus River.

POINT OF PINES (alt. 8, City of Revere), 32 *m.* is a summer colony at the north end of Revere Beach.

At 34.5 *m.* is a rotary traffic circle (Beach St.).

1. Right from the traffic circle on Beach St. is REVERE, 0.9 *m.* (*see REVERE*).

2. Left from the traffic circle Route C1 provides an express route to BOSTON through the *Sumner Tunnel* (*toll* 15¢ *per car*).

3. Left from the traffic circle on Beach St. to the Revere Beach Parkway, 0.5 *m.*; right here to Eliot Circle, 0.9 *m.*; right from the circle on Winthrop Parkway; right on Revere St. at 1.9 *m.*

At 2.4 *m.* (R) is *Fort Banks Government Reservation* (*open by permission*), the key fort in the intricate network of Boston Harbor defense. Spacious mounded lawns conceal artillery and winding subterranean passages stored with ordnance.

At 2.5 *m.* on Revere St. is the junction with Shirley St. on which (L) is the *Deane Winthrop House* (*open Tues., Wed., Fri., 2–5; adm.* 10¢), a pitched-roof, two-story frame building with central chimney, built in 1637, by Captain William Pierce, a skipper of the 'Mayflower.' Purchased in 1647 by Deane Winthrop, it contains the Winthrop family relics, a collection of portraits, and objects of historical significance.

Straight ahead from Revere St. on Winthrop St. to WINTHROP, 3 *m.* (town, alt. 36, pop. 17,001, sett. 1635, incorp. 1852), named for Governor Winthrop. The region first appears in the records as Pullen Point because fishermen passing through the channel now called Shirley Gut were forced to land and pull their boats against the strong current.

Straight ahead from the village on Winthrop St. to Washington St., 0.3 *m.*; left here to Shirley St., 0.9 *m.*; right on Shirley St. at 1 *m.* is the junction with Moore St. on which (L) is Shore Drive, where flood tides in winter and early spring, whipped by northeasters, hurl spray 40 feet or so in the air against the sea wall.

At 1.2 *m.* on Shirley St., left on Terrace Ave., which becomes Harbor View Ave., to the summit of *Great Head*, 0.4 *m.*, a drumlin rising 105 feet above the sea.

POINT SHIRLEY (alt. 17, Town of Winthrop) (*fishing; deep-sea fishing trips; yacht races*) is at 1.9 *m.* on Shirley St. A small settlement at Shirley Point, named for the Royal Governor, came into being in 1753 as a fishing enterprise. This failed, however, and the buildings were used to shelter Boston victims of the smallpox epidemic of 1765, and later yet by a party of Acadian refugees.

Tafts Inn (*open*), Tafts Ave., is on the site of the original Taft House. This hostelry, renowned for its fish and game dinners, was headquarters for the Atlantic Club, attended by Longfellow, Emerson, James Russell Lowell, Oliver Wendell Holmes, and other men of prominence. The *Reed House* (1753), 7 Siren St., is a two-story house erected by a group of men who sought a co-operative livelihood from the sea. The *John Hancock House* (*open by arrangement*), 49 Siren St., is a two-story, red-brick house with two chimneys; it was built in 1756 as the summer home of the wealthy Boston merchant.

State 1A follows the Revere Beach Parkway.

At 37.1 *m.* is the junction with Washington Ave.

Left on Washington Ave. is CHELSEA, 0.9 *m.* (*see CHELSEA*).

At 38.4 *m.* is EVERETT (*see EVERETT*) and the junction with US 1 (*see Tour* 1).

T O U R 1 B : *From* DEDHAM *to* NORTH ATTLEBOROUGH, 20.8 *m.*, State 1A.

Via Norwood, Walpole, Norfolk, Wrentham, and Plainville.

N.Y., N.H. & H. R.R. parallels the route at intervals.

Macadam and concrete highway, mostly three-lane. Passable year round.

STATE 1A runs through country of predominantly rural character. Winding country roads afford delightful side trips. At the southern end, the region is more sparsely settled.

State 1A branches right from US 1 (*see Tour* 1) 0.9 *m.* south of the Boston city limits on the Jamaicaway.

DEDHAM, 0.1 *m.* (*see DEDHAM*).

State 1A passes through a residential area that gradually thins out to scattered groups of houses.

NORWOOD, 4.1 *m.* (town, alt. 149, pop. 15,574, sett. 1678, incorp. 1872), is a residential and manufacturing town which has attracted a number of immigrants, chiefly Canadians, Irish, and Scandinavians; these form approximately one-third of the population and are in general employed in book printing, sheepskin-tanning, and the production of roofing. The section comprising the present town was purchased from the Indian Chicataubot about 1630.

Manasseh Cutler, later famous as a preacher and for his connection with the Ohio Land Company, taught school here and married the daughter of the local pastor. Frank G. Allen, who came to Norwood at the age of 22 as an employee of the tanning mill and eventually became president of the company, was elected Governor of the Commonwealth, 1929–30. Norwood is unusual in that it has a town manager.

The *Norwood Memorial Municipal Building*, an impressive structure of Gothic design. It has a 170-foot tower containing 52 bells. On the lawn is a German field-gun captured during the World War.

The massive tower of *Saint Catherine's*, a gray-brick church on Nahatan St., is also designed in the Gothic style.

The *Day House* (*open Sun.* 3–5; *other days by application*), 93 Day St., headquarters of the Norwood Historical Society, is built of light brown stuccoed brick with exposed timbers in the English manner.

The *Morrill Memorial Library*, corner of Beacon and Walpole Sts., is a building of gray stone in the Romanesque style. On the lawn is a *Boulder* bearing the following inscription:

Near this spot
Capt. Aaron Guild
On April 19, 1775
Left plow in furrow, oxen standing
And departing for Lexington
Arrived in time to fire upon
The retreating British.

The *Plimpton Press* (*open on request* — 10 A.M. *preferred; guide furnished*), Lenox St., extending over several blocks, is housed in a mammoth red frame building, dominated by a large bell-tower. This press is capable of producing over 50,000 volumes a day.

On Washington St. is the *Norwood Press* (*open by permission; mornings preferred; guide provided*). This attractive red-brick, ivy-covered plant, with its clock-tower and landscaped setting, is also capable of tremendous daily output.

The *Dean Chickering House* (*private*) (R), 101 Walpole St., built in 1806, is a splendid type of post-Colonial farmhouse, with solid construction, slightly pitched roof, wide clapboards painted white, cheerful green shutters, and neatly terraced lawn.

Walpole St. (State 1A), once known as Roebuck Rd., later as Sawmill Rd., was part of an early stagecoach route between Boston and Providence, R.I. Over it marched Colonial soldiers in King Philip's War and in the War of the Revolution. At 5.5 *m.* in front of the Ellis Home (R), on the banks of Ellis Pond, is the old *Five-Mile Elm*, as it was known to stage-drivers, who often used trees as milestones.

State 1A continues through fairly open and sparsely settled country.

At 7.2 *m.* is the *Norfolk Agricultural School* (*open; guides*), a large yellow building fronted by small flower beds and flanked by greenhouses. The school maintains a farm of 40 acres for scientific agricultural experiments as well as for the practical instruction of nearly 200 students.

At 7.9 *m.* State 1A crosses Neponset River near the site of the King's Bridge. During King Philip's War a company of troopers on their way to Attleboro were, while crossing the old bridge, terrified by an eclipse of the moon in which they imagined they saw Indians and dripping scalps.

WALPOLE, 8.5 *m.* (town, alt. 155, pop. 7449, sett. 1659, incorp. 1724), was named for Sir Robert Walpole, English statesman. Situated on the Neponset River, it was well supplied with water-power, and a number of factories sprang up, turning out cotton goods, cassimeres, satinets, nails, farming implements, and paper. Today manufactures include building papers, shingles, roofing materials, and hospital supplies — cotton, gauze, and paper. A handicraft shop, *Homespun*, at Lewis Farm, home of George A. Plimpton, uses Colonial methods in the making of cloth from the wool of its own cheviot sheep.

In front of the Town Hall is an *Old Milestone* dated 1740.

The new brick Colonial *Blackburn Memorial Building* (*indoor pool, tennis courts*), on Stone St., is part of an extensive Memorial Park. The *Memorial Park Bridge* was dedicated in 1924, on the 200th anniversary of the incorporation of the town, in honor of the Revolutionary soldiers, sailors, and nurses of Walpole.

On the corner of Diamond and East Sts. is the *Catholic Church*, built of red brick with yellow trim in the Renaissance style. Near-by on East St. appears the unique plant of the *Walpole Woodworkers* (*open*), a company specializing in rustic woodwork.

> Left from Walpole Center on East St. is the *Castle* (*private*), 1.2 *m.*, built in 1898 by Isaac Newton Lewis, a small stone edifice with a battlemented tower now surrounded by woods and a gladioli farm.
>
> At 1.5 *m.* is a small triangular park with a *Drinking Fountain* honoring Bradford Lewis, a civic benefactor; and a *Horse and Rider*, on a granite pedestal, dedicated to the memory of Lieutenant Barachiah Lewis (1663–1710).

South of Walpole Center, State 1A traverses a thickly wooded stretch of largely undeveloped country.

At 11.4 *m.* is the junction with Winter St.

> Right on Winter St. at 1.2 *m.* is the *Norfolk Prison Colony* (*open by pass; restricted visiting hours; guides*). Willow trees line the road, which passes between fields tilled by convicts under an honor system. The pleasant fields and the entrance with its spreading lawn and gay beds of flowers are in sharp contrast to the grim gateway, the concrete wall topped by electrically charged wire, and the watchtowers and floodlights. Established in 1927 to relieve the congestion in the antiquated Charlestown Prison, the Norfolk Prison Colony is conducted in accordance with modern principles of penology, attempting to rehabilitate social misfits and those who have turned to crime because they lacked vocational training. Psychiatrists and other experts try to develop the inmates' interests and skills in intramural social and occupational centers. The criminal records and intelligence levels of the men are studied before they are placed in groups of about 50. Each group is housed in a separate dwelling under a resident officer. This permits intimate acquaintance with the inmates as individuals. The colony has an advisory council of prisoners, which co-operates with the administration on all local matters except those involving penal offences — thus giving the men a measure of responsibility in the affairs of the institution and encouraging them to become responsible citizens.

At 13 *m.* is the junction with State 115.

> Right on State 115 is NORFOLK, 2.4 *m.* (town, alt. 218, pop. 2073, sett. 1795, incorp. 1870), an agricultural town centering about the Grange. Once the domain of the Neponset Indians, this area was claimed by the sachem Philip as part of his kingdom. The General Court, however, ignored the title in its expansion of the Dedham settlement in 1635–36.
>
> At 4.3 *m.* (R) is the *Mass. Fish and Game Preserve* (*open by pass*).

At 13.6 *m.* is *Weber Duck Inn*, a roadhouse famous for its pure white ducks raised on the grounds, for its own use and for wholesale and retail markets. When viewed from above, these birds appear like a large blanket of snow and have been picturesquely referred to as the 'snow glaciers of Wrentham.'

WRENTHAM, 15.2 *m.* (town, alt. 254, pop. 4160, sett. 1669, incorp. 1673), originally a part of Dedham, was named for Wrentham, England.

During King Philip's War, just before the burning of the town by the Indians, the entire population fled to Dedham. At the beginning of the 19th century, the town underwent industrial development with the establishment of several woolen and cotton mills. The manufacture of straw hats, started in 1798 by Mrs. Naomi Whipple, and the making of jewelry were expanded, several factories being opened. A tap and die company has a national market today. The development of the town as a summer resort has materially aided its present prosperity.

At the village center stands a granite stone marking the site of the *First Meeting House* (1684).

    1. Right from Wrentham on State 140 at 0.4 *m.* is the junction with a dirt road; right on this road is Emerald St.; at 0.7 *m.* on Emerald St. is (L) the *Wrentham State School for Feebleminded Children.* Established in 1907 by the Massachusetts Legislature, this co-educational institution provides vocational training.

    2. Left from Wrentham on State 140 at 0.1 *m.* is the junction with Taunton St.; right on Taunton St. to a private way at 0.2 *m.*; right on this way at 1.3 *m.* is the *Pumping Station.* Around the station is a recreational ground suitable for picnics. The underbrush has been cleared under the towering pines.

At 19.3 *m.* (R) is the *Captain John Cheever House* (*private*), a substantial white frame building built about 1800, with a fine old door with pilasters and an ornamental pediment.

PLAINVILLE, 19.9 *m.* (town, alt. 207, pop. 1606, sett. 1661, incorp. 1905), a small manufacturing town, was once called the 'world's largest specialty jewelry manufacturing center,' now sadly crippled by unemployment. The farmers in the outlying areas specialize in dairy products, hay, potatoes, and berries.

The *Benjamin Slack House* (R), at the Center, a rambling frame structure painted yellow, was erected in 1726, and is claimed by the town to be the oldest building in New England housing a public library. It was erected by a local landowner by whose name the town was originally known (Slackville).

The *Whitfield Cheever House* (1807), corner of West Bacon and Warren Sts., has an ell at the rear containing a fireplace with a brick oven large enough to hold a huge iron kettle used for hog-scalding and soap-making. East of the house a path leads from West Bacon St. through woods to the *Angle Tree Monument* in 'Mary Sayle's pasture.' This is a slate shaft 7 feet tall erected about 1640 near the North Attleborough Line. A circle at the top on the north side of the shaft carries the words 'Massachusetts Colony,' and one on the south side bears the inscription 'Plymouth Colony.' According to a tradition, when the line dividing Massachusetts Bay and Plymouth Colonies was first established at the Angle Tree, the following warning was posted on it: 'Beyond this line Roger Williams may not goe.'

At 20.8 *m.* is the junction of US 1 (*see Tour 1*).

T O U R   1 C :   *From* BEVERLY *to* UXBRIDGE, 66.3 *m.*, State 62 and 126.

Via Danvers, Middleton, North Reading, Wilmington, Bedford, Carlisle, Concord, Wayland, Framingham, Ashland, Hopkinton, Holliston, Sherborn, Milford, Hopedale, and Mendon.

B. & M. R.R. and the B. & A. Division of the N.Y.C. Lines parallel the route.

State 62 is mostly macadam in good condition, with the exception of the North Reading-Bedford area. Many curves and dangerous intersections require extreme caution on both routes. Inadvisable for winter touring.

STATE 62–126 runs through rolling farm country, with residential suburbs in the northern part.

West of its junction with State 1A (*see Tour 1A*) in Beverly, State 62 passes the huge plant (R) of the *United Shoe Machinery Corporation* (*adm. by pass obtained at office*), 0.3 *m.*, the largest and most completely equipped factory of its kind in the world. Its buildings cover 25 acres of floor space, and have six miles of aisle and 43 designing rooms. About 500 types of shoe machinery are made and over 125,000 different machine parts are kept in stock to be leased, with a royalty on each pair of shoes, to factories all over the world.

At 2.7 *m.* is a junction with Conant St.

Left on Conant St. is DANVERS, 0.9 *m.* (town, alt. 51, pop. 12,957, sett. 1636, incorp. 1757).

Settlers came here from Salem in search of farm lands and the place was first called Salem Village. In 1688, Cotton Mather hastened to Danvers to attend a witchcraft trial, and preached a sermon which so inflamed the villagers that in 1692, when 10 young girls accused a Negro nurse, Danvers became the center of witchcraft hysteria that caused 200 arrests and 20 deaths before public sanity was restored.

Seventeen emigrants from Danvers joined the covered wagon caravan to Marietta, Ohio, in 1787. About this time Zerubbabel Porter, a tanner, wishing to dispose of surplus leather, developed a commercial shoe factory. In the year 1833 Nathan Read made a machine for cutting nails, and in 1843 Gilbert Tapley started the manufacture of carpets. Two panics, a severe fire in 1845, and the Civil War caused an industrial decline.

Today Danvers, a pleasant residential community, has leather, shoe, crayon, lamp, and chemical factories.

In the *Town Hall* are *Murals*, done as part of a Federal project under the Emergency Relief Administration, depicting episodes in the town's history.

A boulder on the lawn of the Danvers Saving Bank at the edge of Danvers Square marks the *Site of the Encampment of Arnold's Forces* on their march to Quebec in 1775.

The *Page House* (*open Mon., Wed., and Sat.* 2–5; *adm.* 25¢), 11 Page St., built in 1754, is an attractive dwelling with gambrel roof and dormer windows. This house was the scene of the amusing incident related in Lucy Larcom's poem 'The Gambrel Roof,' concerning a rebellious wife who retorted to her patriotic husband's edict that British taxed tea should not be served beneath his roof, by staging a tea-party on the roof.

In the *Historical Society Headquarters* (*open*), adjacent to the Page House, are 18th-century portraits, old china, pottery, and pewter, including the baptismal bowl and communion tankard of the First Church.

The *Peabody Institute*, on Sylvan St., which joins Elm St. at the Town Hall, is a distinguished building of the Classic revival, Palladian type, set on a wide lawn.

1. Left from Danvers on High St. 0.9 *m.*, is the *Samuel Fowler House* (*open July and Aug.*; *adm.* 15¢), built in 1809 and owned by the Society for the Preservation of New England Antiquities. The exterior is little changed; within is imported scenic wallpaper designed by Jean Zuber of France, the first artist (1829) to print continuous rolls in color.

Left from High St. to Liberty St.; here are remnants of the yards in which the privateers 'Harlequin' and 'Jupiter' were built during the Revolution.

2. Right from Danvers on Holten St. 0.7 *m.*, to the junction with Pine St.; left here to the *Rebecca Nurse House* (R), 0.9 *m.* (*open daily* 9–5; *adm.* 25¢), built in 1636. The aged Rebecca Nurse was executed as a witch at the height of the witchcraft hysteria, stoutly protesting her innocence till the last. Her grave in the family burial ground is marked by a tablet bearing the names of the courageous friends who dared to testify in her behalf.

At 1.6 *m.* on Holten St. is the *Judge Samuel Holten House* (*open*), 171 Holten St., owned by the D.A.R. This dwelling with steep-pitched roof and central chimney has two oddly placed ells, but later additions are in harmony with the original structure, which was built in 1670; it stands on a pleasant, tree-shaded, sloping lawn.

On Centre St., a continuation of Holten St., at 1.9 *m.*, a sign indicates the *Site of the Church of Salem Village*, whose pastor's children, overexcited by the tales of their West Indian nurse, old Tituba, started the witchcraft epidemic.

Right from Centre St. at the Training Ground on Ingersoll St. 0.4 *m.* to the *Endicott Estate* (*private*). In a formal garden stretching back from the road stands the *Garden House*, created by the genius of Samuel McIntire in 1793, a delicate little structure showing the Palladian influence in its formality, pilasters, cornice, and decorative detail. The roof, with a typical McIntire urn at each corner, supports, astride its ridgepole, two bold life-size figures carved from wood — a milkmaid and a reaper — that contrast with the conventionally sculptured figures in the garden below. In this spot Elias Hasket Derby took his tea when the house was part of his Peabody summer residence.

At 3.7 *m.* on State 62 is the junction with Summer St.

Right on Summer St. 0.3 *m.*, under tall elms, is the weathered, gambrel-roof *James Putnam House* (*now a roadhouse*), home of an eminent pre-Revolutionary lawyer. Near-by is *Oak Knoll* (*private*), where the poet Whittier lived from 1876 until his death in 1892. On the lawn are wild flowers, transplanted by Whittier, and a spruce that Oliver Wendell Holmes named 'the poet's pagoda.' Adjacent to the Whittier place is *St. John's Preparatory School*, 0.7 *m.*, founded by the Order of St. Francis Xavier, with an enrollment of 450.

At 5 *m.* is the junction with US 1 (*see Tour* 1), a dangerous intersection.

On the corner stands the *Birthplace Of Israel Putnam* (1718–1790) (*open as a teahouse*), built in 1648. The older part of the house has a plain peaked roof and end chimney; a gambrel-roof addition, now the main part of the house, was built in 1744. General Putnam at Bunker Hill gave the famous command: 'Don't fire until you see the whites of their eyes.'

Diagonally across the Turnpike, 5.1 *m.*, on a high hill, with red-brick buildings resembling a Victorian castle, is the *State Hospital For The*

Insane (open by permission), built 1874. The institution has facilities for over 2000 patients.

At 5.7 *m.* the buildings and extensive experimental grounds of the *Essex County Agricultural School (open)*, lie on both sides of the road.

At 6.7 *m.* is the junction with East St.

> Right on East St. 0.5 *m.* to the *Colonel Benjamin Peabody House (private)*, a three-story gambrel-roof structure with dormer windows. Between spreading trees is seen, over the front door, a gilded eagle, and on the barn a full-rigged ship serves as a weathervane.

MIDDLETON, 8 *m.* (town, alt. 95, pop. 1975, sett. 1659, incorp. 1727), is surrounded by pine-covered hills, divided by the winding Ipswich River. *The Essex County Sanatorium* (State 62), is one of the leading tuberculosis hospitals in the eastern United States.

About half a mile northeast of the Center on State 62 is the *Middleton Congregational Church*, a white building with tall slender spire, standing on the site of the original church. Middleton has had only one congregation since the General Court permitted 'Will's Hill Men' to incorporate a town composed of outlying sections of neighboring towns.

Will's Hill *(inaccessible)* was named for a friendly Indian, whose lookout over the distant mountains is still known as 'Old Will's Easy Chair.'

Middleton's company of Minutemen arrived too late to join in the Battle of Lexington, but old Tom Fuller rode after the retreating British, blazing away at their backs. The British, in grim compliment to his marksmanship, nicknamed him 'Death on the White Horse.'

Winding on through the beautiful wooded country, State 62 follows the leisurely course of the Ipswich River.

NORTH READING, 12.5 *m.* (town, alt. 80, pop. 2321, sett. 1651, incorp. 1853), after a brief era of shoe-manufacturing is now predominantly agricultural. Facing the town square is the *Stagecoach Tavern (now a general store and private house)*, built in 1812 by Ebenezer Damon, when this was a halfway stop between Salem and Lowell, and between Boston and Haverhill. The tavern had 21 rooms, 7 fireplaces, 51 windows, 7 stairways, and 7 main doorways. Though North Reading for a time had hope of becoming a boot-and-shoe-manufacturing center, its present population, which is partly Canadian, is chiefly engaged in truck farming.

> Right from the Center, on Haverhill St. 0.5 *m.* to the junction with a private road; right here 0.2 *m.* to the *Gowing House*. The ell was part of a blockhouse erected by Sergeant George Flint for protection against Indians in the early 1650's.
>
> *Willow Lane Farm*, at 0.8 *m.* on Haverhill St., has a two-story, white clapboarded, hip-roof house, formerly the home of George F. Root, author of Civil War songs, among them 'Tramp, Tramp, Tramp, the Boys are Marching.' Here he composed 'The Battle Cry of Freedom' and 'Just Before the Battle, Mother.' His daughter, Clara Louise Burnham, a novelist, describes the brook running through the farm in a novel, 'No Gentlemen.'

At 14.3 *m.* is the junction with State 28 *(see Tour 5)*, which unites with State 62 to 14.5 *m.*, where State 28 bears right.

At 16.1 *m.* on State 62 is the *Site Of The Old Mill*, where Silas Brown manufactured boards used in flannel-stretching.

At 16.9 *m.* is the *Pearson Tavern (private)*, 344 Salem St., a well-preserved two-story house, built 1730. This white clapboarded structure, with two wings and two inner brick chimneys, was maintained as a tavern, prior to 1850, by Aaron Pearson, Jr., a son of the Major Aaron Pearson who commanded the Massachusetts troops during the War of 1812.

> Right on Andover St. at 0.5 *m.* at the rear of No. 116 is the *Devil's Den*. Tradition states that on the threshold of this cave lies buried some of Captain Kidd's treasure, guarded by the ghost of a Negro. One morning about a century ago, so the story runs, residents of the old Harnden House, corner Salem and Woburn Sts., saw a wagon proceeding toward the Den. The driver was a stranger in town. Beside him was seated a Negro. In the afternoon the conveyance returned, empty except for its driver, who was never seen thereafter. Supposedly the Negro was murdered after having assisted in concealing the treasure, and it is presumed to be his ghost which haunts the environs of the cave. Any attempt to dig up the treasure is futile, for the spectral guardian drags the chest out of the cave into the fields until the fortune-seekers are gone, after which he returns with it and continues his vigil.

At 17.1 *m.* stands the *Ford-Blanchard House (private)*, 300 Salem St., built in 1720 by Cadwalader Ford, a captain in the Colonial army. Subsequently this two-and-a-half-story gabled mansion with an added wing belonged to the Blanchard family, who were identified with the hop-raising industry. Across from the Ford-Blanchard House is the house, enclosed by a white picket fence, built by Caleb S. Harriman on the *Site Of The Hop Brokerage House*. Members of the Blanchard family were (1806–1837) the brokers for sixteen and a half million pounds of hops raised in the uplands of Wilmington.

WILMINGTON, 18.4 *m.* (town, alt. 100, pop. 4493, sett. 1639, incorp. 1730), was named in honor of Lord Wilmington, a member of the British Privy Council.

> Left from Wilmington on Wildwood St. 1.1 *m.* is the junction with Woburn St.; right here to the *Sheldon House (private)* 1.2 *m.*, once the abode of Asa G. Sheldon, author of 'Asa G. Sheldon, Wilmington Farmer,' who in 1835 cut down Pemberton Hill in Boston and removed the earth by oxcart.

At 22.5 *m.* is the junction with US 3 (*see Tour* 3). Between this point and 22.9 *m.*, US 3 and State 62 are united. At 22.9 *m.* State 62 branches left and continues between pine groves, hay fields, and apple orchards.

At 26.3 *m.* is the junction with Old Billerica Rd.

> Right on this road 0.8 *m.* to (R) the *Bacon House (private)*, a two-and-a-half-story dwelling built in 1682. It has a cement-covered central chimney and clapboarded siding painted red. A well sweep is still in use. This house commands a view of the Shawsheen Valley, and was occupied by the same family for six generations.

At 26.8 *m.* is the junction with Page Rd.

> Left on Page Rd. 0.1 *m.*, at the corner of Shawsheen Rd. (L) is the *Kendrick House (private)*, sometimes called the Shawsheen Tavern, built on what is said to be the site of an old Indian trading post. This two-and-a-half-story yellow frame house still preserves the socket where a flag was inserted to signal the stagecoach to stop for passengers.

At 27 *m.* (R), as the highway swings left, is the *Page House*, built in 1687. This two-and-a-half-story light gray dwelling now has a front porch and a black-topped white chimney; it serves as the home for the foreman of the Page estate, which runs east along State 62.

BEDFORD, 28 *m.* (town, alt. 118, pop. 3186, sett. about 1640, incorp. 1729), was first settled around the Shawsheen House, an Indian trading post. In the Town Hall is the Bedford Flag, designed in England between 1660 and 1670, and carried by Nathaniel Page, 3d, when on April 19, 1775, responding to the call sent out by the Massachusetts Committee of Safety, he left his wife and her newborn child in the Page house (*see above*) and hurried to join the Minutemen.

On State 62 (R) is the *Stearns House* (*private*), built 1790, a yellow mansion with green door and shutters, white window casements, quoined corners, and a large inner chimney. Dentil moldings grace the well-executed white door-frame. This is the home of William Stearns Davis, author of 'Gilman of Redford,' a story of Revolutionary times with its setting in this town.

1. Right from Bedford on Springs Rd. is the *United States Hospital for Veterans* (*open Tues., Thurs., Sat., Sun. and all holidays; guides provided* 2–4) 1 *m.*, opened in 1928. The brick buildings are surrounded by smooth lawns and bright flower-beds. At 2.8 *m.* on Springs Rd. is (R) the *Convent of St. Thérèse of Liésieux*, opened in 1929, where young women are trained as missionaries. Adjacent is the *Maryvale Seminary* of the Maryknoll Fathers.

2. Right from Bedford on North Rd. (State 4) 0.8 *m.* is (R) the *Lane House* (*private*), sometimes called the 'House on the Hill.' This fine old house, built in 1660, is a one-and-a-half-story white clapboarded structure with a central chimney.

At 1.4 *m.* on North Rd. is the junction with Dudley Rd.; left here 0.4 *m.* is the junction with a private road (*permission needed to enter*). From here a footpath leads to the *Two Brothers Boulders* on the banks of the Concord River, twin rocks bearing the names of Dudley and Winthrop, respectively, dated 1638. Here Governor Winthrop and Deputy Governor Dudley met in 1639 to settle the boundaries of their grants.

North Rd. continues to Bedford Springs, 1.5 *m.*, where (R) is the *Old Garrison House* (*private*), erected in 1664 and used in 1775. It is a two-and-a-half-story weather-beaten dwelling of the salt-box type, with a central chimney. Near-by is *Bedford Springs* (*hotel accommodations, horseback riding*). In 1856 Dr. William R. Hayden purchased 300 acres of wooded land about the spring, built a summer hotel, a factory for the production of a patent medicine, a mile or more of lovely woodland bridle paths, and a small artificial lake.

3. Turn right from Bedford on State 25, crossing the Concord River at 2.2 *m.*, to CARLISLE, 4.5 *m.* (town, alt. 220, pop. 688, sett. about 1650, incorp. 1805), named for the Scottish birthplace of James Adams, a refugee, who, banished by Oliver Cromwell for political offenses, became the first settler of the district. About 1850 the farmers successfully objected to vegetation-killing fumes from a local copper-smelter. Present inhabitants engage in dairying, orchardry, truck-gardening, and poultry-raising.

The *Old Wheat Tavern* (*private*) on Westford St. (R) (State 25) facing the town Green, was originally a station on the post road between Boston and Vermont. The tavern proper is an undistinguished two-and-a-half-story white frame building with a red-brick facing on the left side. A nondescript porch with six columns is the only reminder of its former function.

Right from the Center on Westford St. to Curve St. at 1.5 *m.*; right on Curve St., a dirt road, 1.8 *m.*, is *Railtree Hill* (alt. 400), the base of which is marked by a sand pit near a farm. Here are the *Carlisle Pines*, a majestic grove now owned by the State. An effort is being made to save these trees, some of which are believed to be more than 150 years old.

State 62 continues its way through woodland and farming country and past *Sleepy Hollow Cemetery* (*see CONCORD*).

In CONCORD, 32.4 *m.* (*see CONCORD*), is the junction with State 126, Lexington Rd.; left on State 126.

At 33.7 *m.* is the junction with State 2 (*see Tour 2*).

State 126 traverses the *Walden State Reservation*, 33.8 *m.* (*bathing, boating, fishing, hiking*). On the north shore of Walden pond, opposite the highway, visitors add stones to a cairn which marks the lonely and beautiful *Spot Where Thoreau Built His Cabin* in 1845. This dwelling, measuring 10 by 12 feet, in which the philosopher wrote and studied for two years, had a garret, a closet, two large windows, and a brick fire-place; it cost only $28.12½, since Thoreau built it himself, cutting and hewing trees for the frame with a borrowed axe. The house was used at times as a link in the Underground Railway. Near-by is the beanfield described in Thoreau's writings.

At WAYLAND, 40 *m.* (town, alt. 120, pop. 3346, sett. about 1638, incorp. 1780), is the junction with US 20 (*see Tour 4*).

State 126 continues south following the line of the old Connecticut Path, a former stagecoach route.

At 43.1 *m.* State 126 passes *Cochituate Lake* (L), a large body of water surrounded by hardwood trees and towering evergreens.

At 45.7 *m.* is the junction with State 9 (*see Tour 8*).

FRAMINGHAM, 47.2 *m.* (town, alt. 189, pop. 22,651, sett. 1650, incorp. 1700), for 35 years after its settlement had indefinite boundaries and organization, and was generally known as Danforth's Farms. Near here were villages of Praying Indians, engaged in farming and cattle-raising, and having their own churches and civil government. By 1700 Framingham had about 70 families, including refugees from the witch-craft persecution in Salem Village (now Danvers).

Crispus Attucks, a mulatto resident of the town, was a member — some historians say a leader — of the mob that attacked the King's soldiers in Boston on March 5, 1770, in the famous Boston Massacre; he was one of the five who were killed.

After 1800 the water-power of the Sudbury River, flowing through the town, was increasingly used for manufacturing purposes. In 1837 the New England Worsted Company moved its machinery here from Lowell and other industrial enterprises were started. Many of the original factories are now out of existence, but shoes, paper and rubber products, and carpets are produced at present. The Dennison Paper Manufacturing Company, the dominant industry, has an industrial partnership plan and well-managed welfare activities. Surrounding farms now engage in market-gardening and fruit-growing.

Right from Framingham on State 135 3.2 *m.* to the junction with Main St., on which 0.3 *m.* (R) is ASHLAND (town, alt. 188, pop. 2497, sett. about 1750, incorp. 1846). The original settlers were attracted to the region by its fertile valleys. Water-power furnished by the Sudbury River was gradually put to use, and by the time Ashland was incorporated it was a flourishing mill community. After 1872, when the city of Boston obtained control of the Sudbury River and deflected it for part of its water supply, only a few small factories remained in operation.

In 1750 Sir Harry Frankland, descendant of Oliver Cromwell, friend of the Earl of Chesterfield, and for some years a Crown official in Boston, built a manor-house in Ashland, planting an orchard and arranging a garden filled with ornamental trees imported from England. While on a visit to Marblehead he saw a beautiful young girl, Agnes Surriage, scrubbing the floor of a tavern, took a fancy to her, and carried her away to Boston to receive a polite education. Finding that she was snubbed by Boston society, he brought her to Hopkinton, where they lived very happily. They traveled a great deal, and Agnes's beauty and grace aroused ardent admiration in all the gay capitals of Europe, where Puritan snobbery was happily absent. In 1755, during a visit to Lisbon, Portugal, the pair were caught in an earthquake; this apparently caused Sir Henry to think on his latter end, for he came back to America a changed man, and married Agnes Surriage. He died in 1768. In 1775 Lady Agnes was suspected, rightly or wrongly, of Tory sympathies, and felt it best to sail for England. Her career was not yet ended, however, for after a decent interval she married another titled gentleman. Ashland's cherished story has been told in 'Agnes,' a poem by Oliver Wendell Holmes; in 'Brampton Sketches,' by Mary B. Claflin, a native of Hopkinton and wife of Governor Claflin; in 'Old Town Folk,' by Harriet Beecher Stowe; and in 'Agnes Surriage,' a novel by Edwin L. Bynner.

On the lawn of the *Public Library*, Front St., is a cannon of the type used for coastal defense in the early 1800's. The *Ashland Historical Society Headquarters* (*open by appointment*), in the basement of this building, has a collection of Colonial furnishings and papers of importance in local history.

The *Gay House* (*private*), 2 Myrtle St., is a two-and-a-half-story white house built in 1743. The heavy growth of young fir trees on the lawn bordering the walk completely hides the front from view. In the rear the lawn slopes down to a millpond which in bygone days created power for a near-by paper plant.

The *Warren Telechron Company Plant* (*private*), on the corner of Railroad Ave. and State 135, a pioneer in the manufacture of electric clocks, is the basic industry of Ashland and its neighborhood.

At 4.2 *m.* on State 135 is the junction with Franklin Rd. where (R) is a marker inscribed 'The Bay Path'; this route extended from Plymouth to the North Shore past the Praying Indian Town, Magunkquog (Ashland) where, governed by Pomhaman, the Indians maintained a flourishing community for 15 years. On Magunka Hill, the site of the early settlement, the Indians planted corn, received their education from a teacher named Job, and worshiped the white man's God.

A resident of the town who collects local Indian artifacts was much puzzled by some oval bits of granite, shaped presumably by the aborigines. He related that having read somewhere that the Indians used oval stones for fishing-bait, he determined to test the stones and theory by fishing with the pebbles in Boston Harbor; in a few hours (or so he claims) he had caught six cod on the same line, the fish successively swallowing the stone and expelling it through their gills.

At 5.7 *m.* is *Lucky Rock Manor*, a farm marked by a wooden sign. From here the Boston Marathon starts each year at noon on the 19th of April. For many years its starting-point was in Ashland, but a recent checkup showed that the original Marathon of ancient Greece covered 26 miles, 385 yards, and the route was altered. Clarence De Mar, a middle-aged printer of Melrose, and seven times a winner of the Marathon, is now a teacher in New Hampshire, but comes to Boston each year to run along the road that brought him fame. In 1936 Tarzan Brown, a Narragansett Indian of Rhode Island, was the winner; in 1937, Walter Young of Canada.

HOPKINTON, 6.8 *m.* (town, alt. 439, pop. 2616, sett. about 1715, incorp. 1744), was named for Edward Hopkins, Governor of Connecticut. The first settlers were from surrounding villages and leased the land from Harvard College, executor of Hopkins's estate. This town is the birthplace of Daniel Shays (1747–1825), leader of Shays's Rebellion; of Lee Claflin (1791–1871), one of the founders of Boston University and founder of Claflin University in South Carolina. Pegged shoes were first made by Joseph Walker in 1818. Walker's invention changed the making of shoes throughout New England.

Facing the town Common is the *Valentine Tavern* (about 1750) (*private*), a two-and-a-half-story rambling structure of cut stone and gray clapboards, with a modern shingled roof; Washington, Lafayette, and Daniel Webster are said to have lodged here.

Hopkinton Academy, 21 Church St., was one of the scenes of Henry Ward Beecher's abortive efforts to become a school teacher. According to a local legend, his pupils on one occasion tossed him from a window into the snow. This house originally stood on the corner but a few years ago was removed to its present site and extensively modernized.

In Mt. Auburn Cemetery on Mayhew St., in the northeast corner adjacent to the town vault, is the *Grave of the Unknown Indian*. For many years the residents were surprised to find this grave decorated on Memorial Day. One citizen secreted himself to watch for the donor, but though he came earlier each succeeding year, the grave was always decorated before he arrived. After the death of an elderly lady, the floral tribute ceased.

Left from the Center on Ash St. at 1 *m.* is the *Elijah Fitch House* (*closed*); around this two-and-a-half-story, weather-beaten house cluster many romantic tales of runaway slaves and hairbreadth escapes in the days of the Underground Railroad.

State 126 passes the south shore of *Lake Waushakum*, 48.3 *m.*, and the entrance to the *Workmen's Circle Camp* (R), 49.6 *m.*

On the western outskirts of EAST HOLLISTON, 52.1 *m.* (alt. 260), is the junction with State 16.

Left from the junction on State 16 is SHERBORN, 3.5 *m.* (town, alt. 175, pop. 994, sett. 1652, incorp. 1674), supposed to have been the site of an Indian settlement. Many Indian artifacts have been found here. The hand-manufacturing of shoes, the willow-weaving, and the whip-making of the 19th century are gone. Apple cider remains an important product.

Right from the village on Maple St., 0.9 *m.*, in a rural section, is the *Buttonballs House* (*private*), a two-story frame structure, named for the large sycamore trees surrounding it. The building itself is of uncertain age, though the ell is known to have been built in 1722. The main part of the structure remains as it was in 1778, with brick fireplace, brick ovens, a smoke-closet, hand-hewn oak timbers, and hand-wrought nails.

HOLLISTON, at 52.9 *m.* (town, alt. 198, pop. 2925, sett. about 1659, incorp. 1724), was named for Thomas Hollis, an early benefactor of Harvard College; though essentially an agricultural community, quite surrounded by wooded upland and open meadows, it has two shoe factories.

An extraordinary event in the history of Holliston was its visitation by a strange plague which, between 1752 and 1754, devastated the district, carrying off more than an eighth of its population. The nature of the disease was never fully determined, nor why it did not spread beyond the borders of one small town.

Winthrop Pond, off Winthrop St., a delightful body of water enclosed by wooded banks, is stocked with trout and perch. On the east side of the pond rises *Mt. Goulding,* offering a view of the neighboring villages, forested hills, and tranquil countryside.

At 58.3 *m.* is the junction with State 109 (*see Tour 1D*).

MILFORD, 59.4 *m.* (town, alt. 257, pop. 15,008, sett. 1662, incorp. 1780), is a modern industrial town. Early in its history it became economically independent. By 1819 small boot shops, employing from two to ten men and boys, were marketing their product in Boston and Providence, and by 1870 the town had two of the largest boot factories in the United States. The Milford Branch of the Boston and Albany Railroad, built in 1845, accelerated industrial expansion. After 1900, however, local footwear production declined, and only three factories remain.

About the middle of the 19th century, the Rev. Patrick Cuddahy discovered pink granite here and opened the first quarry. Stone from local quarries was used in the Boston Public Library, the Corcoran Art Gallery in Washington, and the Grand Central and Pennsylvania Stations in New York.

The *Irish Round Tower* is in the Catholic Cemetery on State 85. This 60-foot high, well-proportioned granite structure rising candlelike from a sturdy base was erected by the discoverer of Milford's granite.

At 60.1 *m.* is the junction with State 140 (*see Tour 23B*).

At 60.7 *m.* is the junction with Hopedale St.

Right on Hopedale St. 0.3 *m.* is HOPEDALE (town, alt. 240, pop. 3068, sett. 1660, incorp. 1886). Originally in Mendon, the land comprising Hopedale was purchased in 1841 for the establishment of a communistic religious community, by a joint-stock company under the leadership of Adin Ballou, Universalist minister and a relative of Hosea Ballou. Called the Hopedale Fraternal Community, it paid for the education of its children and made its own streets, though taxes were paid to Milford. E. D. Draper succeeded Adin Ballou as president of the community, bought up three-fourths of the joint stock, and finally demanded and achieved the dissolution of the experiment. The Draper family manufactured textile machinery and supplies, and the Draper Corporation, a leader in its field, still owns many of the houses in the northern part of the town. In the small park is the *Statue of Adin Ballou.* Right of the statue is a large flagstone in one end of which is embedded an old-fashioned iron boot-scraper, the doorstep of the house (1700) of Elder John Jones. This house served as the first church in Hopedale.

On Hopedale St. is the *Hopedale Community House,* gift of the Draper family; it has an auditorium and recreational facilities.

At 62.3 *m.* on State 126 is MENDON (town, alt. 420, pop. 1265, sett. 1660, incorp. 1667), originally Quinshepauge, named for Mendon, England. It was the second town formed in the county, and was one of the first to suffer attack in King Philip's War. The inhabitants were ordered by the General Court not to abandon the settlement; they disregarded the order and the town was burned. Mendon, unsympathetic with

Shays's Rebellion, helped quell the uprising. The town has remained essentially agricultural in its economy.

In the park stands the *Founders Memorial* on the *Site of Mendon's first Meeting House*. Here are also two milestones, the larger reading '37 miles from Boston T.H. 1785,' the other '38 miles to Boston 1772.'

The small, one-story, brick *Mendon Historical Society Building* (*open*), near-by, served as a bank from 1820 to 1826. In it are Indian relics, and a collection of old newspapers, photographs, and pictures.

On Main St. is the *Old Mendon Tavern* (*private*), a two-story house where Washington did *not* spend the night (*see NORTH UXBRIDGE, Tour 23 for the story*).

Opposite the Town Hall on the Common is the *Abraham Staples Elm*, said to have been a large tree when the first settlers came to Mendon.

On State 126 (R), adjoining the *Mendon Airport*, stands the fine old *Jonathan Russell House* (*open by arrangement*), built by one of the commissioners who negotiated the Treaty of Ghent.

> Left from Mendon on the Blackstone Rd. 0.7 *m*. is the *Austin Taft House* (1720). A granite boulder at 1.4 *m*. commemorates the *Site of the Massacre* (1675) in which several persons were killed by the Nipmucks at the beginning of King Philip's War.

At 66.3 *m*. is UXBRIDGE (*see Tour 23*), at the junction with State 122 (*see Tour 23*).

T O U R   1 D : *From* BOSTON *to* MILFORD, 20.5 *m*., State 109.

Via Boston, Dedham, Westwood, Dover, Medfield, Millis, Medway, and Milford.

N.Y., N.H. & H. R.R. services the area.

Hard-surfaced road; passable all year.

STATE 109 passes through several pleasant residential villages in a semi-agricultural area, with dense woodlands at frequent intervals, branches west from US 1, 7.9 *m*. south of Boston, crosses the Charles River, and passes through a countryside of neat homes and well-kept estates.

At 2.7 *m*. is the junction with a macadam road.

> Right on this road at 0.5 *m*. is the main entrance (L) to *Ottershaw Farm* (*private*), formerly *Dunroving*, the estate of General Clarence R. Edwards of the 26th (Yankee) Division.

The *Town Pound*, 3 *m*. (L), marks the location of the first grant of land in Westwood, made to the Rev. John Allen in 1639. The Pound was built in 1700 by Lieutenant Joseph Colburn. A low stone wall surrounds a gnarled oak, on the trunk of which is nailed the original sign, its wording almost obliterated. There is still a pound-keeper, elected yearly, but his duties are now those of a minister without portfolio.

At 3.7 *m.* is the junction with Dover Rd.

> Right on Dover Rd. is the junction with Carby St. Right on Carby St. is the entrance to *Scoutland, Inc.*, 0.3 *m.*, a 1300-acre reservation, which with about 41 cabins forms a 'city' for Scouts. To this non-sectarian camp journey Scouts from all over the world, with the climax of activities each autumn. Just inside the entrance is the rangers' cabin (*private*); next is the superintendent's cabin. Both are of log construction, chinked with clay. A short distance in is the *Trading Post*, a two-story square tower of broad stone with a bell, resembling a California Mission. It is possible to drive through the reservation over a narrow rough road bordered by a second-growth forest; but the drive is for hardy souls only.

WESTWOOD, 4 *m.* (town, alt. 102, pop. 2537, sett. 1640, incorp. 1897), from its earliest settlement as the Clapboardtree Parish of Dedham has been occupied by those who loved the land. Today, however, agriculture is largely the hobby of retired business men.

At 4.7 *m.*, on the Green at the junction with Pond St., crowning a low knoll and shaded by a stately elm, is the *Clapboardtree Meeting House* (1731), a two-and-a-half-story white clapboarded structure with dark green blinds. The clapboards graduate in breadth from about 1½ inches at the base to the usual 4½ inches at the roof. The squat steeple has a well-proportioned belfry.

At 4.8 *m.*, opposite 948 High St., is the *Baker Homestead* (*private*), one of three houses to receive the Better Homes of America award in 1928 for excellence in design, equipment, construction, and grounds. Here in 1798 at the age of 12, Betsey Metcalf Baker, so taken with a beautiful bonnet one of her girl friends had received from England that she was determined to have one for herself, devised a method of splitting and braiding straw. Soon she was making hats for her friends; but because she considered it irreligious to patent her process, she realized little money from her device, which soon caused the development of one of the leading industries in the East.

At 5 *m.* (R), plainly visible from the road, is *Oven's Mouth*, also known as Devil's Mouth. It is said to have been used by Indians as a bake oven and as an arsenal — presumably at different times.

At 7 *m.* is the junction with Walpole St.

> Right on Walpole St. is DOVER, 3.2 *m.* (town, alt. 156, pop. 1305, sett. about 1635, incorp. 1784). In the Center is the *Town House*, of brick topped by a graceful spire. The *Dover Church* on Springdale Ave., built in 1839, contains a Paul Revere bell.
>
> Southwest of the Center, Springfield Ave. passes over *Trout Brook*, which rises in Great Spring, the north source of the Neponset River. It is known to old-timers as Tubwreck Brook, from an episode jovially chronicled by a local historian: 'One spring when the brook was unusually swollen, Captain James Tisdale attempted to sail down the stream in a half hogshead to gather flood cranberries. The tub became unmanageable, and capsized. Captain Tisdale's friends made much of this event. A quantity of ship bread together with some other articles as might be

washed ashore from the wreck of a merchant ship were left at his door, and the neighbors gathered and celebrated his rescue from the wreck. An original poem telling this story was repeated for many years around Dover fireplaces.'

The *Sawin Memorial Building* (*open*) right from the Center on Dedham St., is the headquarters of the Dover Historical Society, a two-story red-brick structure erected in 1905. The *Miller Caryl House* (R) (1777) (*open*), also on Dedham St. near Park Ave., was once the parsonage of a beloved pastor of the parish.

Continuing S., State 109 passes through wooded countryside.

At 9.2 *m.* (R) is the *Peak House* (1680) (*open*). With an extraordinarily high-peaked roof that explains its name, small leaded casements with diamond-shaped panes, and one small door, it must have been the envy of humbler householders when Seth Clark, receiving indemnity from the Colonial government for the burning of his first home by King Philip's Indians in 1676, is said to have built this house on its site. Another story says that this was Seth's original house, spared by the Indians in return for a keg of cider.

MEDFIELD, 9.7 *m.* (town, alt. 179, pop. 4162, sett. and incorp. 1651). During King Philip's War more than half the village was burned to the ground. It was soon rebuilt. When Norfolk County was formed in 1793, Medfield citizens successfully objected to their town's becoming the county seat, on the ground that visiting the courtroom would be detrimental to the industrious habits of the townspeople. Most of the original farms have been transformed into residential estates. Opposite the Town Hall is the Public Library, in which are the headquarters of the *Medfield Historical Society* (*open to the public*).

The *Unitarian Church*, North St., is an excellent example of Georgian Colonial architecture with its square clock-tower, belfry, and tall slender spire.

1. Right from Medfield on State 27 (North St.), which becomes Harding St., is the junction with Hospital Rd. Left on Hospital Rd. at 1.5 *m.* is an old square boarded well with an oaken bucket hanging under its dilapidated red roof, one of the few still seen in Massachusetts.

2. Left from Medfield on State 27 at 0.8 *m.* is an *Old Gristmill* built about 1705. At 1.4 *m.* (L) is a large formal garden enclosed by stone posts and a clipped hedge. Spilling over into dooryard, farmyard, and onto the long low farmhouse itself is an amazing *Collection of Bronze and Iron Eagles* from all over the world.

At 11.8 *m.* is the junction with Dover Rd.

Right on Dover Rd. at 1 *m.* is the transmitting station of the *Westinghouse Radio Station* (*open* 9–10.30; *adm. free*). Opened in 1931, its control-room contains some of the finest equipment in the world.

Directly opposite is the *Willis House*. At the rear stand 15 of the original 50 *King Philip's Trees*, supposed to have witnessed the celebration of the Nipmuck Indians after the burning of Medfield in 1676.

At 12.7 *m.* is the junction with State 115.

Right on State 115 is MILLIS, 0.2 *m.* (town, alt. 167, pop. 2098, sett. 1657, incorp. 1885), on the west bank of the winding Charles, named in honor of Lansing Millis.

On the Common (R) is the *Church of Christ*, Congregational, founded in 1714, a white clapboarded building with a large green central door and a squat tower surmounted by an unpainted shingled steeple with a clock.

The *Dinglehole*, northwest of the Center on Union St., is a pit formerly filled with water, where Puritans heard the ringing of the bell that summoned the witches to their evil rites and saw on moonlight nights a headless man keeping vigil.

Straight ahead from Millis on State 115 are *Boggestowe Pond*, 1.4 *m.*, and the *Site of the Old Gristmill*. On the crest of a hill about 100 yards (R) from the road is an *Old Windmill*.

Southwest from Millis, State 109 skirts the *Black Swamps* (R and L).

At 15.4 *m.* is the junction with Holliston St.

Left on Holliston St. is MEDWAY, 1 *m.* (town, alt. 184, pop. 3268, sett. 1657, incorp. 1713), a quiet manufacturing center on the north bank of the Charles, surrounded by meadowlands and wooded hills. The town lands were set off in 1713, but their seclusion from the rest of the Commonwealth is revealed by Medway's reluctance to send representatives to the General Court for 13 years. In 1763, however, the first known census in Massachusetts was taken here, and during the Revolutionary War the town took an active part in boycotting British goods.

Shoe, needle, and textile factories remain of a long list of plants formerly including straw bonnet-making, carpet-weaving, organ-building, and an important bell foundry, one of the oldest in the United States.

State 109 continues over *Drybridge Hill*, reputed to be the highest point of land between Boston and Worcester.

At 16.8 *m.* on the corner of Franklin St. (L) is the *Old Parish House* (1817–1913), now the home of the *Medway Historical Society* (*open*).

At 20.5 *m.* is the junction with State 126 (*see Tour 1C*) 1 *m.* east of Milford.

T O U R　2 :　*From* BOSTON *to* NEW YORK LINE　(*Troy*), 148 *m.*, State 2 (*The Mohawk Trail*).

Via (*sec. a*) Cambridge, Arlington, Belmont, Lexington, Lincoln, Concord, Maynard, Acton, Littleton, Ayer, Shirley, Lunenburg, and Fitchburg; (*sec. b*) Westminster, Gardner, Hubbardston, Templeton, Phillipston, Athol, Royalston, Orange, Wendell, Erving, Montague, Gill, and Greenfield; (*sec. c*) Shelburne, Colrain, Buckland, Charlemont, Heath, Rowe, Monroe, Florida, North Adams, and Williamstown.

B. & M. R.R. parallels route throughout.

Hard-surfaced road three lanes wide near Boston. Western end very hilly, and dangerous in winter season. Passable except during heavy snowstorms.

Sec. a. BOSTON to FITCHBURG, 48.2 *m.*

BETWEEN Boston and Fitchburg State 2 runs through country closely connected with Colonial and Revolutionary history.

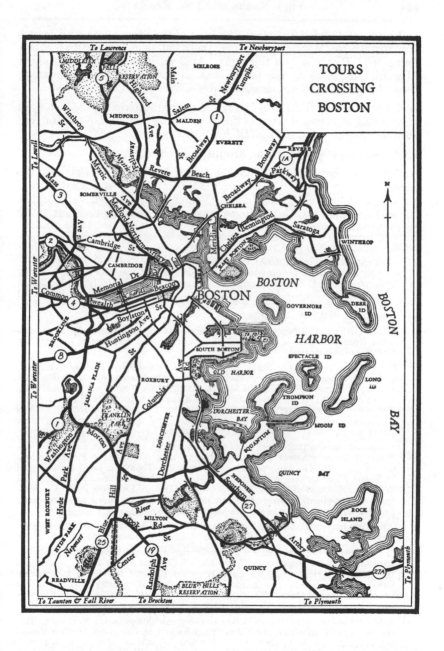

TOURS
CROSSING
BOSTON

In Boston State 2 follows Beacon St. west of the State House and crosses Harvard Bridge (Massachusetts Ave.), with buildings of the *Massachusetts Institute of Technology* on the right. At 2 *m.* it turns left and follows Memorial Drive along the north bank of the Charles River, running through CAMBRIDGE (*see CAMBRIDGE*).

At 4.4 *m.* is the old *Weld Boat House,* closely connected with the history of crew-racing at Harvard. Across the river are the buildings of the *Harvard Business School* (*see CAMBRIDGE*).

At 4.7 *m.* State 2 turns left on Mount Auburn St.

At 5.3 *m.* on the corner of Elmwood Ave. is *Elmwood* (*private*), once the home of James Russell Lowell (*see CAMBRIDGE*). At 5.3 *m.* State 2 turns right into Fresh Pond Parkway, which crosses *Lowell Park*, and at 6.5 *m.* turns right on *Alewife Brook Boulevard Extension*; then left at 7.2 *m.* into the Concord Turnpike.

At 8.3 *m.* is the junction with Pleasant St.

1. Right on Pleasant St. to ARLINGTON, 1 *m.* (*see ARLINGTON*).

2. Left on Pleasant St. on which No. 338 is the *Abraham Hill House* (*private*), built 1693, a plain buff clapboarded dwelling that was reputedly the birthplace of Zachariah Hill's five Minutemen sons and was a haven for patriots on that April day when the countryside rallied to Concord's aid. In it are two cannonballs fired at the Battle of Lexington.

BELMONT, 1 *m.* (town, alt. 39, pop. 24,831, sett. 1636, incorp. 1859), derives its name from the estate of John P. Cushing, the heaviest taxpayer at the time the town was incorporated.

On Pleasant St. near the Public Library is the *Site of Roger Wellington's House* (1636). Shaking the dust of Sir Richard Saltonstall's Watertown Plantation from his feet, Wellington broke ground in the Pequossette Plantation. He was soon joined by others, for the fertile soil lent itself readily to agriculture and dairying. The year 1859 was noted for the first Strawberry Festival — destined to become an annual event of such popularity that in 1863 about 2000 people gathered under the spreading elms on Pleasant St. to feast on the luscious berries.

Improved transportation facilities brought a change in the town's interests. No longer do its greenhouses and truck-gardens send produce to the Boston market, nor do pure-bred Holsteins pasture on open fields. Today the fields are occupied by homes whose owners work either in Boston or in the factories of Watertown and Waltham. Because of the increased population the town meeting form of government was modified in 1926, Belmont being divided into seven precincts, each precinct electing its representatives to the town meeting.

Anne Whitney, sculptor of the statue of Leif Ericson in Boston, was a resident of Belmont.

On the lawn of the Town Hall is a *Cannon*, removed from the U.S. Frigate 'Constitution' in 1931. Opposite the Town Hall on Concord Ave. is a brick building in the Colonial style housing the publicly owned Belmont Municipal Light Company, which purchases power from Cambridge and distributes it at one of the lowest rates in the State.

Pleasant St. continues to a junction with Trapelo Rd., 1.9 *m.*; right on this road 2.2 *m.* is the legendary scene of beaver-trapping expeditions by the Norsemen. This region was a favorite haunt of James Russell Lowell, and his poem, 'Beaver Brook' was dedicated to it; another poem, 'The Oak,' is said to refer to the Waverley Oaks growing in the reservation. The poet called the Waverley Oaks section 'one of the loveliest spots in the world.' Mill St. leads right 0.3 *m.* from the Reservation to Wellington Hill, where in 1824 Lafayette stopped to drink cider with Jeduthan Wellington, who had fought under him at Dorchester Heights.

State 2 continues on the Concord Highway over a long hill covered by a new realty development and small farms.

At 12 *m.* is the junction with Waltham St.

Right on Waltham St. to LEXINGTON, 1.2 *m.* (*see LEXINGTON*).

State 2 now crosses *Hobbs Pond*, part of the Cambridge water system.

At 14.5 *m.* is the junction with Lexington Rd.

Left on Lexington Rd. is the *Flint House* (*private*) 1.1 *m.* (R), built before 1653 by Thomas Flint, one of the first settlers to come here from Concord. The house retains its original front, but two additions have been made to the rear. It is a two-and-a-half-story frame structure with two inside chimneys.

LINCOLN, 1.6 *m.* (town, alt. 208, pop. 1573, sett. about 1650, incorp. 1754), is a beautiful residential and farming town, named for Lincoln, England. West from Lincoln 0.5 *m.* on Sandy Pond Rd. is the *House of Julian de Cordova* (*open Sat. 2–4; adm. free*), a copy of a Spanish castle. Construction was started in 1882 and completed in 1900. The house contains over 500 pictures, a few by old Spanish masters; many tapestries, chiefly Chinese; and a large collection of Chinese and Japanese objects. The estate covers 25 acres including part of a lake, a tower with a superb view, and a children's park. The museum is endowed and will pass to the town at Mr. De Cordova's death.

At 15.7 *m.* is the junction with Bedford Rd.

Right on Bedford Rd. at 0.9 *m.* is the junction with North Great Rd. (State 2A), which follows the line of march taken by the British on their way to Concord in April, 1775. Josiah Nelson, a Lincoln Minuteman, lived near this road. Hearing the approach of the troops, he rushed out to battle single-handed and was slashed on the head by the sword of a British soldier. Pausing only to staunch the wound, he hastened to Bedford to give the alarm. Lincoln believes that this was the first blood spilled in the War for Independence.

Right on North Great Rd. 1.4 *m.* is the spot where Paul Revere was captured in 1775. At this point on the then Old Concord Rd., the 'midnight ride' ended when Revere and his companions, William Dawes of Boston and Dr. Samuel Prescott of Concord, were halted by a British patrol. Dawes turned back and made his escape. Prescott jumped a stone wall, and following a path known to him, regained the highway at a point further down the road and gave the alarm at Concord. Revere was caught by the patrol and carried back to Lexington. There he was released and at once joined Hancock and Adams.

State 2 at 17 *m.* makes a wide circle (L), by-passing Concord Center.

Right (straight ahead) on Cambridge turnpike is CONCORD, 1.5 *m.* (*see CONCORD*).

At 20.2 *m.* is the junction with State 62.

Left on State 62 is MAYNARD, 4.3 *m.* (town, alt. 176, pop. 7107, sett. 1638, incorp. 1871), a hill town of unusual beauty. Maynard was early concerned with manufacturing, particularly with woolen products, highly profitable from the beginning. Amory Maynard, from whom the town took its name, founded the original textile mill, out of which has grown the present immense American Woolen Company.

A legend from the days when the settlement was known as Assabet Peninsula, asserts that a tinker, who frequently plied his trade in the homes of the settlers, suddenly disappeared without leaving a trace. Shortly thereafter persons passing the river meadows swore they heard him at work and that the sounds followed them for some distance. At last an old lady, a resident of that district, died. Just why this should have been a matter of import to the vanished tinker, the legend does not explain; but all the oldest inhabitants know that the phantom sound accompanied the old lady's body to the grave and was heard no more.

At 60 Main St. is the plant of the *United Co-operative Society*. Started in 1907 by mill workers of the lowest economic strata, this society is one of the most successful consumer enterprises in the United States, handling almost half a million dollars' worth of business in 1935. Of especial interest are the sanitary, attractive, and efficiently managed stores of the society.

At the corner of Main and Walnut Sts. is the *Site of the First Mill of the American Woolen Company*, built in 1846. The buildings of this huge mill border Main and Walnut Sts. for several blocks.

South from Maynard 0.9 *m.* on Parker St. is the junction, Four Corners; right here on Great Rd. 0.2 *m.* to No. 178, the *Thompson* or *Eveleth House (private)*, formerly a tavern known as the American House. It is a well-preserved, two-and-a-half-story, white frame structure with a large central chimney.

At *Gulf Meadow* in the rear of the house at 36 Great Rd., 1.2 *m.*, have been found a number of Indian hatchets and 'banner stones.'

Parker St. continues south to a junction with Marlboro Rd., 1.6 *m.*; right on Marlboro Rd. 0.3 *m.* is Puffer Rd., on which at 0.6 *m.* is (R) the *Puffer Place* or *Pratt House (private)*, a modest structure with central chimney. Here lived the Rev. Reuben 'Pigeon' Puffer, Harvard 1778, whose hobby was the netting of pigeons on his grounds, whence he got his name. Later Ephraim Pratt, who attained the age (or so he claimed) of 116, lived here. When 94 years old he dickered with a farmer to board him for the rest of his life for $120. The farmer probably thought he was driving a shrewd bargain, but he had not counted on Ephraim's tenacity. In the end the centenarian had paid about $5 a year.

The *Concord Reformatory (visited by permission)*, at 21.2 *m.*, has a group of brick granite-trimmed buildings, surrounded by a high brick wall. The attractive lawn and flower beds near the road contrast sharply with the drab, iron-shuttered windows of the inner buildings. Blacksmithing, plumbing, printing, carpentry, and other trades are taught to the inmates, the products being sold to other institutions. Outside the walls is a 190-acre farm tilled by the more trusted inmates.

State 2 continues its winding way through a pleasant countryside with rambling farmhouses and short stretches of dense woodland.

At 23.5 *m.* is the junction with Brook St.

Left on Brook St. 0.2 *m.* (R) is the *Estate of Dr. W. J. Middleton (open)*, a private bird sanctuary, through which courses a brook stocked with trout.

At 0.4 *m.* is the junction of Brook and Main Sts.; left on Main St. at 1 *m.* is ACTON (town, alt. 150, pop. 2635, sett. about 1680, incorp. 1735), originally a settlement of Praying Indians. The town was granted in 1643 to a Mr. Wheeler and called Concord Village. The Fitchburg Railroad, built through the town in 1844, started a period of industrial development that was arrested in 1862 when a fire destroyed the Center. Today there are three small factories manufacturing woolen goods, radio cabinets, and metal products.

The *Acton Memorial Library* on Main St. is a brick building with brownstone trimmings. The solid freestone arched entrance is enriched with mouldings and carved spandrels. Above the brick fireplace of the reading room is the inscription: 'This building a gift to his native town by William Allen Wilde.'

Continuing south, Main St. becomes High St. At 2.5 *m.* (L) is the *Faulkner Homestead (private)*, atop a small hill. This two-and-a-half-story white frame house with central chimney, on the site of the early Garrison House, was the house of Colonel Winthrop Faulkner of Revolutionary War fame. The exact date of its construction is not known.

State 2 follows the shore (L) of *Lake Nagog* (Ind. 'Many Waters') 25.6 *m.* (*fishing; picnicking*). The lake provides part of Concord's water supply.

A square granite slab at 26.8 *m.* (L) marks the *Site of the Mary Shepard House*, built in 1676. At 15 years of age, Mary, while doing lookout duty on Quagana Hill, was captured by the Indians; her brothers, Abraham and Isaac, were killed. Mary was taken to Lancaster, where in the dead of night she removed a saddle from under the head of a sleeping Indian, mounted a horse, and escaped.

At 26.9 *m.*, corner of Great Rd. and Shaker Lane, is a *Stone Post* marking the northeast corner of Nashoba, the original site of Littleton. Nashoba ('Hill that Shakes') was the sixth Indian Praying Town in the State. The Indians believed that on a certain occasion they had seen the hill vibrate and heard it rumble.

LITTLETON COMMON, 28.5 *m.*, is at the junction with State 110 (*see Tour 7*) and State 119 (*see Tour 2A*).

LITTLETON CENTER, 29.2 *m.* (town, alt. 230, pop. 1530, sett. about 1686, incorp. 1715), is in one of the 14 towns of the Nashoba Health District, which aims by inter-town co-operation to protect against disease and to provide more complete public health facilities. This district specializes in poultry and dairy products and has some of the finest apple orchards in the State.

The *Reuben Hoar Library* (*open evenings*), a small yellow-brick structure, contains Colonial relics — spinning wheels, dishes, silverware.

The *Old Tory House* (*open*), on State 2, is a two-and-a-half-story white frame house with small-paned windows and several additions in the rear. Just prior to the Revolution, when patriotic sentiment was running high, it was the home of the Rev. Daniel Rogers, who was visited by a squad of soldiers determined to make him declare himself. When their knocking was not answered, they shot through the closed door, the bullets lodging in the staircase. The bullet-riddled door is preserved in the historical collection in the Houghton Memorial Building.

State 2, now a narrow road, winds through a rolling countryside of small farms and large tracts of uncultivated land.

At 33.5 *m.* is the junction with a country road.

> Right on this road to *Snake Hill*, 1.5 *m.*, where years ago lived Prudence Shedd, a lady who achieved considerable fame as a rattlesnake-hunter.

At 34.2 *m.* State 110 (*see Tour 7*) branches left.

AYER, 35.2 *m.* (town, alt. 232, pop. 3861, sett. about 1668, incorp. 1871), was named in honor of James C. Ayer, a patent-medicine manufacturer of Lowell who extended financial aid to the town.

The *Public Library*, on State 2, houses a small collection of shards of

Nashoba Indian pottery, old paper currency, a service flag, and Fort Stevens's first papers.

> 1. Right from Ayer on Washington St. 0.8 *m.* is *Nonacoicus Park*, which offers a magnificent panoramic view.
>
> 2. Left (straight ahead) from Ayer on West Main St. 1.2 *m.* is *Fort Devens*, established in 1917 as a training-camp.

At 35.9 *m.* is the junction with State 111 (Groton Rd.).

> Right on State 111 at 0.5 *m.* is a dirt road (L) leading to the *Ayer State Game Farm* (*open*), 1.8 *m.*, where Chinese pheasants are raised for release in suitable covers. Five hundred eggs were brought from China in 1933. The breeding has been difficult but successful.

At 38.4 *m.* is the junction with Center Rd.; on the northwest corner is *Bull Run Tavern* (*open*), built in 1789, a two-and-a-half-story building with a long low covered porch. It has been painted red, with white trim. It contains many pieces of old furniture and Colonial relics. Just west on State 2 (R) is the *Revolutionary Tavern* (*private*), a faded white frame house with a central chimney, built before 1747 by Obadiah Sawtell, a delegate to the Provincial Congress.

> Left from State 2 on Center Rd. at 0.7 *m.* (R) is the *Stephen Stone Homestead* (*open as tearoom, May* 15–*Sept.* 15), a white two-and-a-half-story early Colonial house with green blinds and adjoining woodshed and barn (1796). Set 25 feet from the road, with an old white well in front, it is shaded by three maples.
>
> SHIRLEY, 1 *m.* (town, alt. 283, pop. 2548, sett. about 1720, incorp. 1753). On the north side of the Common is the *Home of the Rev. Seth Chandler* (*private*), where Ralph Waldo Emerson was often a guest. It is a broad two-and-a-half-story house with a pitch roof, ell, and central chimney. The philosopher's room and its furnishings have been kept intact by the present owner.
>
> SHIRLEY VILLAGE, 3.1 *m.* (Town of Shirley), was named for Provincial Governor William Shirley. In 1871 a Shaker community sprang up. At first the townspeople looked askance on the members, but eventually they accepted them. Oliver Holden, author of many hymns, was born in Shirley September 18, 1765. His 'Coronation,' long a favorite, was used as a battle hymn during the Civil War. Opposite 14 Leominster Rd. is the *Site of the Birthplace of Sarah* (*Edgarton*) *Mayo* (1819–48), poet and author, editor of the *Ladies' Repository* and the *Rose of Sharon*. A footpath through the pine grove (*left of the Administration Building*) leads to the *Holy Hill of the Shakers* where this sect congregated twice a year for religious services.

State 2 becomes more winding, and passes through alternate woods and open meadows.

LUNENBERG, 43.8 *m.* (town, alt. 377, pop. 2124, sett. 1721, incorp. 1728). Although attempts have been made to change the agricultural complexion of the town, Lunenberg is still a quiet farming community with many spacious summer residences on the outskirts. Some mulberry trees remain from an attempt at sericulture. Luther Burbank, the horticulturist, in this town perfected the potato known as the Red Rose.

The *Ritter Memorial Library* has a fine collection of Lunenberg Bibles (*not for public inspection*) and a Bible donated to the town by John Hancock in 1772. The historic room also houses several objects resembling carved ivories; they were made by George Gilchrist, a Lunenberger, from meat bones when he was in Libby Prison during the Civil War.

The *Cushing House* (1728), 0.2 *m*. west of State 2 on Lancaster Ave., is a large two-and-a-half-story white frame dwelling easily identified by a row of seven tall trees in front. Here, in 1820, William Greenough printed the Polyglot Bibles,which include not only the Old and New Testaments, but also the 12 books of the Apocrypha, attributed to the Greeks. The old horse who furnished the power for the printing shop is said to have been given Christian burial in recognition of his distinguished contribution toward spreading the Word of God. The house was at one time the home of Luther Cushing, author of the 'Manual of Parliamentary Practice' (1844), which, little changed, still guides Americans in the conduct of public meetings.

> Left from Lunenberg 2 *m*. on Lancaster Ave. is the *Houghton Homestead*, an example of shrewd Yankee ingenuity with its 'tax-exemption' roof, which slopes to one story in the rear, thus avoiding the tax imposed on two-story houses.

At 45.3 *m*., near the junction with State 13, is a fine view of the city of Fitchburg with Mt. Wachusett in the distance.

Between Lunenberg and Fitchburg the road runs through an industrial and residential area.

At 47.8 *m*. is the junction with State 12 (*see Tour* 11), which offers a detour around the business area.

FITCHBURG, 48.2 *m*. (*see FITCHBURG*).

Sec. b. FITCHBURG to GREENFIELD, 49.3 *m*. State 2.

Between Fitchburg and Greenfield, State 2 passes through a pleasant rural countryside, increasingly hilly as it approaches the foothills of the Berkshires.

At 1.5 *m*. is the junction with State 12 (R) (*see Tour* 11).

The old *Warner House* (*private*), 4.7 *m*., known also as the Valley House, was a stagecoach stop on the Boston–Brattleboro route; it had a large marquee under which passengers alighted. The house was also a station on the Underground Railway and slaves were hidden in a hole behind the chimney, reached by a small door at the head of the cellar stairs. This house was occupied for a time by Olin L. Warner (1844–96), the sculptor, whose works include statues of William Lloyd Garrison and General Devens, and the two bronze doors of the Library of Congress.

From *Round Meadow Pond*, 6.2 *m*., is a fine view of *Mt. Wachusett* (alt. 2000) (*see Tour* 11A).

WESTMINSTER, 7.2 *m*. (town, alt. 724, pop. 1965, sett. 1737, incorp. 1759), was a part of grants made by the Legislature to the veterans of the Narragansett War. One of the earliest settlers, Abner Holden, describes the land and life: 'A howling wilderness it was, where no man dwelt; the hideous yells of wolves, the shrieks of owls, the gobbling of turkeys, and the barking of foxes, was all the music we enjoyed; no friend to visit, no soul in the adjoining towns — all a dreary waste, exposed to a thousand difficulties.'

During the 19th century Westminster became a lively industrial community, but tanning and the manufacture of cotton cloth, bricks, chairs, and paper have been replaced by lumbering and dairying; in the village is a cracker factory that at one time caused Westminster to be called 'Cracker Town.'

At the Center is the junction with State 64 (see *Tour* 11A).

SOUTH GARDNER, 11 *m.* (alt. 1027), has a huge *Wooden Chair* at the depot facing the railroad tracks to advertise Gardner's leading industry. This is believed to be the largest chair ever made.

1. Right from South Gardner on State 68 is GARDNER, 1.8 *m.* (city, alt. 1030, pop. 20,397, sett. 1764, incorp. town, 1785, city 1923). Manufacturing displaced agriculture in importance here after 1805, when James M. Comee established the first Gardner chair factory in his home. Comee introduced the use of flags for chair seats; Elijah Putnam, a graduate apprentice, in 1832 began to manufacture chairs with cane seats, following a sample brought from the Connecticut State Prison by one of his workmen. Later on the inventive genius of Levi Heywood revolutionized the whole industry, and Philander Derby in 1844 made a fortune by designing the Boston rocker, known to comfort-lovers throughout America, and demoded only when increasingly cramped living quarters made it impracticable. On Park St. is *Crystal Lake* (*outdoor and indoor swimming pools*).

Right from the Center on a side road is the *Gardner State Colony* (*open to students; guide*), 'a farm for the able-bodied and quiet chronically insane.'

2. Left from South Gardner on State 68 is HUBBARDSTON, 6 *m.* (town, alt. 980, pop. 1000, sett. 1737, incorp. 1775), named for Thomas Hubbard, a proprietor who promised to provide window glass for the first meeting house if the district was named for him.

A fifth of the population of this agricultural community is Finnish. The farmers specialize in poultry-raising and are developing blueberry and strawberry patches. During its existence, the town has had a number of small factories, including a woolen mill, but the last was closed in 1933.

The first settlers, and for some time the only ones, were Eleazer Brown and his wife, whose 60 acre farm was granted on the condition that 'he or his heirs keep a house thereon for the entertainment of travelers, for a space of seven years.' A party of distinguished travelers found the 'inn' exceedingly primitive; one of them, asking at dinner for a clean plate after a first course of hasty pudding, was annoyed when Mrs. Brown merely dipped his plate in water and returned it wet. He asked her to wipe it, which she did; his satisfaction was dampened later when a companion informed him that the dish-towel used was the hostess's 'shortgown.'

About 1790 an apple tree of uncertain stock was found on a rocky hillside pasture bearing apples of unusually fine flavor; this, the parent tree of the Hubbardston Nonesuch apple, which gained a wide market, was blown down in 1895.

About the time the apple was drawing public attention to Hubbardston, the town was attracting less pleasant notice through the activities of a native rascal, Ephraim Grimes, a convicted counterfeiter, as his cropped ear indicated. Grimes had no shame about this deformity; it is said that in Canada he once went into a store and asked the price of enough ribbon to reach 'from ear to ear.' When told 'a few cents,' he cried, 'Begin to measure off! I have one ear here and they have the other in Worcester.' Old Grimes, as he came to be called, is the hero of the poem of that name, sung to the tune of 'Auld Lang Syne.'

On Main St. is the *Jonas G. Clark Memorial Library*, named for a Hubbardston man who was founder of Clark University in Worcester. Near-by is the home in which Clark was born, Feb. 1, 1815.

At 13 *m.* (L) is a *Brick Kiln.*

TEMPLETON, 16 *m.* (town, alt. 964, pop. 4302, sett. 1751, incorp. 1762). Abundant water-power enabled the early settlers to start first a sawmill, then a corn mill, and finally factories producing lumber, chairs, furniture, and other products. At one time Templeton specialized in raising greenhouse cucumbers.

Opposite the Common is *Landlords' Inn,* a huge structure dismantled in 1935 and now standing as a melancholy reminder of an unsuccessful philanthropic venture. It was built at a cost of $150,000 by Moses Richardson, and was turned over by him to the Templeton Improvement Society.

At 19.1 *m.* is the junction with US 202 (R) (*see Tour* 13).

At 20 *m.* is the junction with an improved road.

> Left on this road is PHILLIPSTON, 1.5 *m.* (town, alt. 914, pop. 423, sett. 1751, incorp. 1814), which is in that part of the grant known as Narragansett Number Six organized as the town of Templeton. When Templeton was subdivided this part was named Gerry, in honor of Elbridge Gerry, Governor of Massachusetts 1810–11 and Vice-President of the United States during the administration of James Madison. Gerry's political actions caused the town to change to the present name, which honors William Phillips, for 12 successive terms Lieutenant-Governor of the State. Sawmills were early of importance. In 1837 Phillipston produced large quantities of cotton and woolen goods and palmleaf hats. Although some lumbering is still carried on, farming, dairying, market-gardening, poultry-raising, and fruit-growing are the chief occupations.
>
> Left of the small Common stands the Congregational Church (1785) with its old *Horse Shed,* the only one of its kind in this part of the State. Perched on a windy hilltop where snowdrifts are deep in winter, it was made large to provide ample hitching facilities and also to allow sleighs to be turned around inside.

At 24 *m.* is the junction with State 32 (*see Tour* 23), which runs south to New London, Conn.

ATHOL, 26 *m.* (town, alt. 550, pop. 10,751, sett. 1735, incorp. 1762), was named by John Murray, one of the leading proprietors, who thought that the scenery resembled that about Blair Castle, the home of the Scottish Duke of Atholl. Later it transpired that he, John Murray, was none other than the duke's son. Athol, like many other New England towns, was originally a farming community, but in the 19th century became somewhat industrialized, with factories producing scythes, cotton, and paper. It now has 34 industries employing over 2000 people and manufacturing products ranging from furnaces to cigars, toys, and thread.

A large factory on Royalston Rd., making precision tools, was founded (1868) by Leroy S. Starrett, who invented many of the products, including the American meat chopper.

> Right from Athol on Royalston Rd. 4.8 *m.* to *Doane's Falls,* 200 ft. high (*reached by trail*).
>
> ROYALSTON, 6.8 *m.* (town, alt. 817, pop. 841, sett. 1762, incorp. 1765), has devoted itself entirely to agriculture except for one short period when toy manufacturing was attempted. Early Royalston had a firm belief in God's personal attention in its affairs; when in 1769 15-year-old Katurah Babcock was struck dead by lightning, her fate was held up as an example of divine punishment for non-attendance at church. In 1845 two other children met the same fate on the same spot, an event that made the village unpopular as a place of residence.

The heavy hand of Providence was also seen when the lands of Isaac Royal, a Tory for whom the town was named, seemed to resist cultivation after their owner fled to England. 'The scythe refused to cut Tory grass, and the oxen to plough Tory soil.'

At 26.5 *m.* is the junction with a road.

Right on this road is a farmhouse, 1.9 *m.* (L); on a high hill back of it is a marker designating the *Site of the Sentinel Elm*, and the *Site of a Garrison* occupied by Ezekiel Wallingford, who on the night of August 17, 1746, thinking he heard bears in his cornfield, was lured out, surrounded, scalped, and killed by Indians. The sentinel elm, used as a lookout by both Indians and Colonists, was destroyed by a storm in 1933.

At 28 *m.* is the junction with US 202 (L) (*see Tour* 13).

ORANGE, 30.7 *m.* (town, alt. 505, pop. 5383, sett. about 1746, incorp. 1810), was named in honor of William, Prince of Orange. On the banks of a rapid river, the town was destined to become a manufacturing center. Among the industries here are the Rodney Hunt Machine Company, founded in 1840, and the Minute Tapioca Company.

Orange attracted national attention by the unveiling of a war memorial dedicated to peace, portraying a veteran explaining to a child the futility of war. On the base of the group, sculptored by Joseph P. Pollia of New York, aided by sketches by the Rev. Wallace G. Fiske of Orange, is the inscription, 'It Shall Not Be Again.'

At 32 *m.* is the junction with State 78 (*see Tour* 2B).

At 33.5 *m.* is a junction with a hard-surfaced road.

Left on this road across Miller's River and through woodland that is part of the *Wendell State Forest* is WENDELL, 5 *m.* (town, alt. 500, pop. 397, sett. 1754, incorp. 1781), named in honor of Judge Oliver Wendell of Boston. By 1810 the town reached its maximum population of 983. There are two stories to account for the name of the tiny near-by settlement of *Mormon Hollow;* according to one it was named because the settlers were people who had left a Mormon caravan passing through the town on its way West, and according to the other because settlers already there embraced Mormonism and left to join a colony of the Latter-Day Saints.

At 34 *m.* are the *State Proving Grounds*, where acres of red and white pine seedlings are raised for reforestation purposes.

At 34.5 *m.* the hills of Wendell rise blue in the distance (L), and 50 feet below the road is Miller's River. The river, according to legend, was named for a young man who was drowned in this stream in sight of his sweetheart and her Indian guide, when his canoe struck a cake of ice.

At 35 *m.* across the river (L) is the Orange section of the *Wendell State Forest* (*see above*). The bridge crossing the river at the Erving paper mill was destroyed by the 1936 floods.

ERVING, 36 *m.* (town, alt. 474, pop. 1283, sett. 1801, incorp. 1838). The town land was sold to John Erving of Boston in 1752, but the earliest known settler was Colonel Asaph White, who arrived in 1801. Most of the inhabitants gain their livelihood in near-by towns or in home industries, chief among which are a tool factory, two paper mills, and a heel firm that is subsidiary of the United Shoe Machinery Corporation.

At 38.5 *m.* is FARLEY (alt. 540, Town of Erving). About 0.2 *m.* left from the village and with an entrance visible from the highway is *Barndoor Cave*, which cuts through 50 feet of rock and emerges on top of the cliff. It receives its name from the size of the entrance.

At 40.5 *m.* is the junction with State 2A.

Left on State 2A across Miller's River to MILLER'S FALLS (alt. 292), 0.9 *m.*, a manufacturing settlement lying in both Erving and Montague Towns. South from Miller's Falls on a road paralleling railroad tracks is *Green Pond* (R) (*bathing and boating*) 1.9 *m.*, and *Lake Pleasant* (L) 2 *m.*, the town reservoir, once the sacred lake of the local Indians.

At 41.9 *m.* State 2 crosses the Connecticut River on the *French King Bridge*, a magnificent structure about 750 feet in length, named for *French King Rock*, visible in midstream. From its height of 140 feet the bridge commands a fine view of the river valley and of the surrounding countryside.

State 2, here called French King Highway, follows the Connecticut River and provides views of wide sweep at frequent intervals.

The *Old Red House*, 45.4 *m.* (*tearoom*), built in 1736, contains a small collection of Indian relics.

At 44.9 *m.* is RIVERSIDE (alt. 85, Town of Gill). In 1676, 180 colonists under the leadership of Captain Turner surprised and destroyed 300 savages who were encamped here. Farming is the chief occupation, with dairying and truck-gardening yielding the best livelihood.

1. Right from Riverside in a narrow valley is GILL, 3.3 *m.* (town, alt. 233, pop. 995, sett. 1776, incorp. 1793), a community of small homes with neat lawns.

2. Left from Riverside across the Connecticut River on a *Suspension Bridge* is TURNER'S FALLS, 0.6 *m.* (Town of Montague, alt. 185, pop. 7967, sett. 1715, incorp. 1775), built on a series of terraces rising above the Connecticut River to a height of 100 feet. Captain Elisha Mack here built the first dam on the Connecticut River.

The ice jam preceding the 1936 flood swept away three bridges within a few miles of this place. One of these, on top of which ran the tracks of the Boston and Maine Railroad, was the longest covered wooden bridge left in the State.

In the *Carnegie Library* (*open* 2–9), corner of State 2A and Avenue A, is a fine collection of Indian relics.

1. Right from Turner's Falls on Avenue A to MONTAGUE CITY, 1.9 *m.* (alt. 164, Montague). One of the largest hydro-electric generating stations in New England completed in 1918 is at this point. It generates two-thirds of the electricity sold by western Massachusetts companies. There is a large fishing-tackle manufacturing plant here.

2. Left from Turner's Falls, State 2A parallels the Connecticut River. Indian encampments were common along these fishing grounds. At 1.3 *m.* is *Mayo's Point*, from which is a splendid view of the river and the encircling hills.

State 2 crosses the Falls River at 45.6 *m.*

GREENFIELD, 49.3 *m.* (town, alt. 204, pop. 15,903, sett. 1686, incorp. 1753), with its wide, elm-shaded streets, is one of the most beautiful towns in western Massachusetts. Originally part of Deerfield, Greenfield took its name from the fertile valley it occupies. Although still a prosperous agricultural town, specializing in poultry, tobacco, onions, and dairy products, it has become an industrial center. In 1792, the Locks and Canal Company began to use Cheapside, at the mouth of the Deerfield River, as a landing place. Early in the 19th century the first cutlery factory in America was established in Greenfield, but later it was moved to Turner's Falls. Today there are 30 manufacturing plants here, with diversified products.

The *Potter House* (*private*), corner Main and High Sts., has been described in *Country Life* (1937) as an 'Ionic columned Greek temple.' The house shows the extent to which the Greek Revival was carried in American architecture.

St. James' Church (Episcopal), corner of Federal and Church Sts., was built in 1847 and reproduces the Church of St. Mary the Virgin, in South Milford, Yorkshire, England. The church, parish house, and sexton's house are connected by cloisters surrounding a garden close.

The *Greenfield Historical Society* (*open* 10-6) has its headquarters in the brick Devlin House at the corner of Church and Union Sts. An oar about 25 feet long, of the type formerly used in steering a boat plying the Connecticut River, is an exhibit.

About 0.5 *m.* southeast of the Center off US 5 is *Rocky Mountain Park*, a rugged area of high ridges, wooded copses, and glens occupying the high land west of the Connecticut River.

At Greenfield is the junction with US 5 (*see Tour* 15).

> North from Greenfield on Conway St. to the *North Parish*, once the Center of Greenfield. At 4.4 *m.* is a junction with a road that leads left across Glen Brook to a fork at 4.8 *m.*; left at this fork through the Greenfield Water Works Reservation and then right is the *Eunice Williams Monument* (*see DEERFIELD*), 5.1 *m.* Just beyond this, spanning Green River, is the only *Covered Bridge* remaining in Greenfield.

Sec. c. GREENFIELD to NEW YORK LINE, 50.5 *m.* State 2.

Between Greenfield and the New York Line, State 2, the Mohawk Trail makes a gradual climb over the Hoosac Range, descends abruptly into the Hoosac Valley, and then crosses the Taconic Mountains into New York State. Along the route is some of the most beautiful scenery in Massachusetts.

West of Greenfield State 2 climbs Greenfield Mountain. To the east is a view of the placid town, encircled by the winding Connecticut and its three tributaries, the Green River, the Deerfield River, and the Falls River.

On *Shelburne Summit*, 3.4 *m.*, alt. 1170, is a Tower (*picnic grounds; adm.* 10¢) that overlooks Greenfield. New Hampshire and Vermont peaks are visible from this point.

SHELBURNE, 6.9 *m.* (town, alt. 700, pop. 1606, sett. 1756-60, incorp. 1768), was once known as Deerfield Pasture or Deerfield Northwest. About 1756 several families settled near Shelburne Falls, but left at the time of the French and Indian Wars. About 1760 a permanent settlement was made and the town was named for the second Earl of Shelburne. In 1849 the manufacturing of cutlery was started; it remains the important local industry. The first Yale locks were made here by Linus Yale in 1851.

West of Shelburne, where the Deerfield River 200 feet below parallels the road, and the precipitous bank of the stream rises several hundred feet, the route offers a series of magnificent views.

SHELBURNE FALLS, 10.8 *m.* (alt. 252, Towns of Shelburne and Buckland), is unusual in that it is bisected by the Deerfield River, which is the township line between Shelburne and Buckland; so that Shelburne Falls is actually the governmental center of two townships.

The *Salmon Falls*, on the Deerfield River, named for the quantities of salmon formerly caught here, have three distinct cataracts with pot-holes at the foot.

Right of the bridge crossing the Deerfield River is an old *Trolley Bridge*, now used by pedestrians; it is decorated in summer with flowers and shrubbery.

Right from Shelburne Falls on State 112, is LYONSVILLE, 5.4 *m.* (alt. 570, Town of Colrain). In the village cemetery a *Boulder* commemorates Amasa and Rhoda Shippee, who in 1812 raised the first United States flag to fly over an American schoolhouse. Left from Lyonsville are two old covered bridges. FOUNDRY VILLAGE, 5.8 *m.* (alt. 600, Colrain), contains one of the town's two iron foundries. The village received its name because of these two foundries, which produced cast iron here during the early 19th century.

COLRAIN, 6.9 *m.* (town, alt. 620, pop. 1554, sett. 1735, incorp. 1761), settled originally by Scotch-Irish from northern Ireland, was presumably named for Lord Coleraine, an Irish peer. About 1818 the beginning of manufacturing brought an influx of French-Canadians, who erected a Roman Catholic church, conducting services in French. Only recently the transition to English was made by a priest who spoke both languages.

Sheep-raising was an important industry until the Civil War. A small cider mill and two mills manufacturing absorbent gauze constitute the present industries. From the village, State 112 bears sharply left. At 8 *m.* the *Harp Elm*, formed like a gigantic lyre, stands at the entrance of the North River Cemetery.

A Stone, 8.8 *m.*, marks the *Site of Fort Morrison*, a defense against the Indians and French from 1754 to 1763.

At 9.7 *m.* is the junction with a country road; left on this road is the *Colrain State Forest*, 1244 acres, with some of the oldest surviving forest growth in the State.

At 12.1 *m.* on State 2 is the junction with State 112.

Left on State 112 is BUCKLAND, 3.4 *m.* (town, alt. 492, pop. 1540, sett. 1779, incorp. 1794). None of the early mills using water-power supplied by the Clesson River now remain. Despite the broken and stony surface of the land, the inhabitants depend on agriculture, and there are some noted apple orchards and large dairies.

The *Baron Rudduck House* (*private*), built in 1796, is a fine example of the architecture of its period; it contains an unusually fine collection of pewter. Near-by is the *Mary Lyon House* (*open*), built 1818, a three-story building that has been covered with stucco. In this house is a room furnished as it was 100 years ago when Mary Lyon, later founder of Mount Holyoke College (*see SOUTH HADLEY*), conducted a private school here.

The *Site of the Birthplace of Mary Lyon,* marked by a bronze tablet, may be reached at 5 *m.* on a circuitous dirt road in the southeast section of the town.

CHARLEMONT, 19.3 *m.* (town, alt. 555, pop. 923, sett. about 1742, incorp. 1765), was first known as Boston Township No. 1, then as Chickley's Town, and later as Charley Mount. Except for a few small industries and sawmills in the past and a woodworking factory, now in operation, the town activities have been agricultural. Dairying, fruit- and vegetable-growing, and bee keeping are the main sources of income. Some seasonal income is derived from maple sugar groves.

North from Charlemont on an improved road is a fork at 2.4 *m.*

1. Left from the fork is the abandoned village of DAVIS (alt. 1340, Rowe), 3.9 *m.* Here is an iron pyrite mine, operated from 1882 to 1910. A large community sprang up in the vicinity, but today the cellar holes of 150 buildings are the only evidence of the settlement. Copper still colors the waters of Mill Brook, which flows through the mine. At the lower end of the mill pond is a building that was formerly the *Shop of the Giant Blacksmith Newall,* who reputedly cured by the laying on of hands.

2. Right from the fork on a road that runs through wooded mountainous country is HEATH, 5 *m.* (town, alt. 1665, pop. 368, sett. 1765, incorp. 1785), named for William Heath, a major general in the Continental Army. At one time staves and barrels were extensively manufactured, but Heath has always been and still is a farming community. At the Center is a small triangular Green surrounded by a group of buildings. The *Old Town House* (1835) has been restored and is maintained by the Heath Historical Society.

At 19.9 *m.* (L) an old *Covered Bridge* spans the Deerfield River.

The *Warner* or *Rice House (private)* at 20 *m.* was the boyhood home of the author, Charles Dudley Warner, who described the town in his autobiography, 'Being a Boy.' It contains timbers hewn and squared by its builder, Captain Moses Rice, earliest white settler of Charlemont, killed by Indians in 1775. Large shade trees lining the approach cast their shadows on the many-paned windows of the weathered gray two-story house.

At 21.5 *m.* is the junction with an unnumbered road.

Right on this road, which parallels the Deerfield River, is ZOAR, 2.1 *m.* (alt. 623, Charlemont). Here the road crosses *Pelham Brook* and comes to a fork.

1. Right at this fork, higher into the hills to ROWE, 3 *m.* (town, alt. 1360, pop. 277, sett. 1762, incorp. 1785), named in honor of John Rowe, a wealthy merchant of Boston. Rowe was early the site of many industries whose owners were attracted by the water-power. In 1850 wooden bowls, especially designed for washing gold, were made here and shipped to California. All of these industries are now gone, and today the townsfolk are engaged in agriculture and cattle-raising.

a. Right from Rowe on Sibley Rd. is the base of *Adams Mountain* (alt. 2140), 0.5 *m.* A *Tower* on the summit *(reached by footpath)* provides a splendid panorama of New Hampshire, Vermont, and New York.

b. Left from Rowe on Whitingham Rd. is a junction with another road, 1.1 *m.*: left on this to a footpath, 1.5 *m.*, leading to *Pulpit Rock* (alt. 954) 2.3 *m.*, a geological phenomenon resembling an old-fashioned canopied pulpit.

c. Straight ahead from Rowe on Main Rd. is *Pelham Lake (summer cottages),* 1.4 *m.*

2. Left from the fork at Zoar on a dirt road paralleling the Deerfield River.

At 1.2 *m.* the road crosses a bridge and continues along the rapidly flowing river flanked on both sides by high hills.

At 4.4 *m.* is the village of HOOSAC TUNNEL (alt. 745, Florida). The Boston and Maine Railroad tracks pass through the village before entering the *Hoosac Tunnel*, about 0.5 *m.* west. This 25,000-foot tunnel was completed in 1875, after 24 years of work; it cost 195 lives and $20,000,000. Right of the east entrance to the tunnel is a footpath leading a short distance to the *Twin Cascades*, 40 and 90 feet high; these are among the most beautiful of Berkshire waterfalls.

At 11. *m.* is the village of MONROE BRIDGE (alt. 1040, Monroe).

Left from the village on a road that rises 600 feet in a half mile.

Left at 13.8 *m.*; right at 14 *m.* is *Monroe State Forest* (*camping, fireplaces*), a hilly 4117-acre region of spruce growth. *Spruce Hill* (alt. 2700) is an observation point in the west part of the reservation (*reached by marked trails*).

At 15.4 *m.* is the junction with a dirt road; right here is MONROE, 1.5 *m.* (town, alt. 1860, pop. 240, sett. about 1800, incorp. 1822), named in honor of the then President of the United States. Agriculture remained the town's chief occupation until 1886, when a paper mill, utilizing the surrounding forest of spruce and poplar, was erected. Twenty years ago the mill property was purchased by the New England Power Co., and subsequent development of power led to the formation of the Deerfield Glassine Company, which manufactures a material similar to cellophane. In this industry is centered the life of the village of Monroe Bridge (*see above*).

West of the junction with the Monroe Rd., the main route crosses *Dunbar Brook*, at a point where the water drops over large boulders and flows through a deep gorge.

From Dunbar Brook the road ascends a steep hill, and at 16.3 *m.* passes through a grove rough with boulders and lovely with the white birches.

At 17.6 *m.* is a parking space (*leave cars here or drive* 0.2 *m. on a wood road to a high-tension tower*); from the tower a trail runs 0.25 *m.* through the woods to an *Observation Platform*, from which there is a panorama of the Deerfield River Valley.

At 20 *m.* is the village of FLORIDA and the junction with State 2 (*see below*).

At 21.7 *m.* State 2 crosses the Deerfield River and runs through *Mohawk Park* (*tourist cabins*). On a knoll (L) is a large *Statue of a Mohawk Indian*, facing east with upraised arms. At the foot of the knoll is the *Wishing Well*, a pool bordered by several rocks, each bearing the name and order of a lodge of the Red Men of America, who built the statue and the well.

Following the course of the Cold River, State 2 enters the *Mohawk Trail State Forest*, 22.6 *m.* (*skiing in winter, swimming, picnicking, camping; small fee for log cabins*), of 5371 acres, including a Sky Trail and a Ski Slalom. The Mohawk Trail was blazed through the mountains by Mohawk Indians traveling between New York State and Massachusetts.

State 2 continues west; on the left are high cliffs and on the right is *Cold River* (*picnic grounds at intervals*). At 26.2 *m.* is a junction with Black Brook Rd.

Left on this road is the junction with a good gravel road, 1.8 *m.*; right on this is the *Savoy Mountain State Forest* (*camping*) of 10,433 acres, including a game preserve and reaching at its highest point an elevation of 2500 feet.

From *Tannery Falls Park* (*picnic ground*), 2.6 *m.*, a half-mile trail descends through the woods beside a brook which has deeply entrenched itself in a rocky gorge. The stream makes several dips over solid rock, then a total drop of 150 feet to a clear pool. Geological action has caused many large fragments of rock to be tipped on end, so that the pathway along the brook is far from smooth and the waters wander off here and there in erratic rills and miniature cascades. The Civilian Conservation Corps has made it possible to approach the very edge of the gorge, in many places hitherto inaccessible.

At 3.8 *m.* on the gravel road is the junction with a road; left on this road is *Balance Rock*, a huge boulder of granite gneiss.

State 2 crosses the Cold River, 26.3 *m.*, and begins to climb over Hoosac Mountain. In six miles the ascent is over 1200 feet. Mountains rise sharply from the farther bank (L), and (R) the road is flanked by a high rocky wall; it passes through this narrow defile and emerges into a stretch of wooded country.

As the road ascends, the trees (R) are less dense, permitting views across Deerfield River valley to the mountains beyond.

At 29.5 *m.* is FLORIDA (town, alt. 2180, pop. 405, sett. 1783, incorp. 1805). The opening of the Mohawk Trail motor route in 1915 made catering to automobile tourists an important industry. References to Florida are found in Washington Gladden's 'From the Hub to the Hudson' and Nathaniel Hawthorne's 'Ride Toward Charlemont.'

> 1. Right from Florida is a road descending sharply to the mouth of the Hoosac Tunnel 1.5 *m.* (*see above*).
>
> 2. Right from Florida a road leads to the *Monroe State Forest* (*see above*).

The Mohawk Trail west of Florida passes through a shallow valley.

At 31.1 *m.* is the *Elk's Monument* (R), a chunk of blue-gray granite surmounted by a bronze elk, erected in 1923 by the Elks of Massachusetts in memory of their members who died in the World War.

Whitcomb Summit, 31.2 *m.* (alt. 2110) with a 65-foot observation tower, offers a view that includes a bit of four States, Massachusetts, New Hampshire, Vermont, and New York. East is Mt. Monadnock in New Hampshire; north are the Green Mountains of Vermont; south are the rounded Berkshires; and west is Greylock, topped by a beacon, with the city of North Adams at its foot.

> Right from Whitcomb Summit on a path that leads (300 feet) to *Moore's Summit* (alt. 2250), the highest point along the Mohawk Trail.

State 2 now descends into a valley; at 33.2 *m.* is the junction with Shaft Rd.

> Left on this road is the tiny settlement at the *Central Shaft* of the Hoosac Tunnel, 1.5 *m.* The shaft, bored straight down over 1000 feet to assist in construction work, was maintained as a vent for smoke, from the steam engine before the tunnel was electrified in 1911, and is still part of the tunnel ventilating system.

At 33.8 *m.* is the *Western Summit* (alt. 2020), of the mountain, disclosing Mt. Greylock in all its majesty.

Here the road drops rapidly (*keep cars in second*). The *Hairpin Turn* (alt. 1650), 34.6 *m.*, is a sharp cutback on an outcropping ledge.

At 37.3 *m.* is a junction with a dirt road.

> Left on this road is *Windsor Pond* (*bathing, boating, fishing*).

At 37.6 *m.* (R) is the junction with State 8 (*see Tour* 21).

State 2 enters a textile section crowded with mills and humble dwellings.

At 38.5 *m.* is NORTH ADAMS (city, pop. 22,085, sett. about 1767, incorp. town 1878, city 1895). To the visitor arriving from points east, whether by automobile on the famous Mohawk Trail, or by train through the equally famous Hoosac Tunnel, this little mill city bursts suddenly into view in a setting of striking mountainous beauty. On the west is Mt. Greylock, 3505 feet high, and on the east is Hoosac Mountain.

Fort Massachusetts (*see below*) was the scene of numerous attacks by roaming tribes of Indians led by French officers. It was besieged and burned by a combined force of 900 French and Indians in 1746. Rebuilt, it successfully repelled a second attack, and the beginnings of a village were attempted in 1765 by a group of Connecticut Congregationalists. They did not remain long, however; either their hearts or their energies failed them. A company of Quakers from Rhode Island, with more determination, followed and built up a permanent settlement on the northern outskirts of East Hoosac, incorporated in 1778 as the town of Adams. A century later North Adams was set off and became a town by itself. The building of the Hoosac Tunnel (*see above*), with its northern terminal at North Adams, was a most important element in the development of the town.

Woolens, cotton goods, silk and rayon goods, shoes, and radio and electrical supplies arc today produced in the plants of the city. French-Canadian groups attracted about 1840 by the textile industry and Italian and Jewish groups drawn in after the completion of the Hoosac Tunnel still conduct church services in their native languages, and in the French parochial schools classes are carried on in the mother tongue.

At the Center is the junction with State 8 (L) (*see Tour* 21).

At 39.6 *m.* is the junction with Marion Ave.

Left, at the end of Marion Ave., is the *Cascade*, which makes an abrupt plunge of about 40 feet into the abyss below. The *Trail* leads along Notch Brook into a deep gorge between the hills. Above the Cascades is a reservoir serving North Adams.

At 39.7 *m.* is the junction with Notch Rd. (*to be opened Aug.*, 1937).

Left, this road leads to the *Top of Mt. Greylock.* As it climbs it affords an awesome view down into the Notch, a vast crevice extending to the narrow opening between Mt. Williams and Ragged Mountain known as the Bellows Pipe. During winter storms the north wind roars through this opening so loudly that it can be plainly heard in the city below. The Indians believed it to be the angry voice of Manitou.

At 40.5 *m.* is a *Replica of Old Fort Massachusetts* (built in 1745) (*open summer months*) (*see above, NORTH ADAMS*). This was the westernmost of a chain of four forts built by Massachusetts Bay Colony to guard against attacks by the French and Indians, and also to stop the Dutch settlers from creeping up the Hoosic River from the Hudson and claiming the land of Berkshire County.

At 41.4 *m.* the Appalachian Trail (*see Tour* 9) crosses State 2.

At 43.7 *m.* is WILLIAMSTOWN (*see WILLIAMSTOWN*).

State 2 swings left on US 7 (*see Tour* 17) to a junction, then right, and begins the ascent of the Taconic Trail, which rises 1200 feet for three miles and passes the *Lawrence Hopkins Memorial Forest*, a branch of the Northeast Forest Experiment Station of the U.S. Department of Agriculture.

At 50.5 *m.* State 2 crosses the New York Line about 30 *m.* east of Troy, N.Y.

T O U R   2 A :   *From* NEW HAMPSHIRE LINE (*Peterboro*) *to* LITTLETON, 28.4 *m.*, State 119.

Via Ashby, Townsend, Pepperell, and Groton.

B. & M. R.R. services the area.

Hard-surfaced but narrow roadbed; hazardous in bad weather.

STATE 119 crosses the Massachusetts Line 15 *m.* southeast of Peterboro, N.H.

Watatic Pond, 3.3 *m.*, the source of the Souhegan River, is at the foot of densely wooded hills. On the summit of *Mt. Watatic* (alt. 1847) (*reached by foot trail*) is a heap of stones marking a former Indian lookout. Eternal misfortune is the lot of the visitor — according to an old Indian legend — who fails to add a stone to this cairn.

State 119, bordered by evergreens, birches, maples, and oak, winds among the foothills of· the White Mountains, with here and there well-tilled farms bounded by old stone walls.

ASHBY, 6.4 *m.* (town, alt. 900, pop. 957, sett. about 1676, incorp. 1767), is in a typical New England rural town, noteworthy for its fine orchards and for the profusion of mountain laurel covering the wayside with pink blossoms in the late spring.

The *First Parish Church*, 1809, is an example of Federal church architecture, notable for the charm of its triple door, its main cornice, and its well-proportioned belfry tower.

In *Willard Brook State Forest*, 8.3 *m.* (*camp sites, outdoor swimming-pool, groves, fireplaces, fishing, hiking trails*), *Willard Brook*, a swift stream of clear water, takes a sheer drop of 20 feet into a natural rock basin or trap and is known at this point as *Trap's Falls*. The brook, stocked by the State with trout, is open for fishing in season.

State 119 at 9.4 *m.* has been walled along by retaining granite blocks hewn from near-by hills.

WEST TOWNSEND, 11.2 *m.*, (alt. 330), is a small village. The *Tavern* (*open*), erected in 1774, was a stagecoach station on the route between Boston and Keene, N.H. The Colonial exterior and the low-beamed rooms remain unchanged.

TOWNSEND, 13.2 *m*. (town, alt. 295, pop. 1942, sett. 1676, incorp. 1732), was named for Charles Townshend, English Secretary of State until 1730 and opponent of the Tories. In 1733 gristmills and sawmills were erected, and these later became cooperage plants utilizing the timber from the ample forests about the town.

Near the Spaulding Memorial High School, on Main St., is an *Octagonal Brick House* (*private*), a type of architecture which has no legitimate parentage, all the more conspicuous in homogeneous Massachusetts.

TOWNSEND HARBOR, 14.9 *m*. (alt. 270, Town of Townsend), is on the Squannacook River. Right of the Center, on the river bank, is *Spaulding's Gristmill* (*open; small fee*), owned by the Society for the Preservation of New England Antiquities. It has been carefully preserved, with the ancient wooden and wrought-iron machinery intact. The *Old Cooper Shop* (*closed*) across the road was one of the first in New England. The *Conant House* (*open*) across the river was erected about 1744 and later enlarged for a tavern. It exhibits a stenciled dado, and hinged partitions between the parlors. The bridge spanning the stream at this point was destroyed in the flood of 1936.

At 16.9 *m*. is a junction with State 113.

Left on State 113 is (R) a granite marker, 0.7 *m*., inscribed: 'After the surrender of Burgoyne at Saratoga in 1777, certain British officers, prisoners of war, quartered in this vicinity but released upon parole, were permitted to enjoy, in all their military finery, a "trysting place" at this spot.'

PEPPERELL, 2.5 *m*. (town, alt. 195, pop. 3004, sett. 1720, incorp. 1753), a rural town, was named for Sir William Pepperell, hero of the Battle of Louisburg.

On the Main St. side of the burying ground is the *Grave of Prudence Wright*. During the Revolutionary War, Mrs. Wright, with several other women, while patrolling the road near the old covered bridge in North Pepperell to prevent Tories with messages for the British from reaching Boston, captured Leonard Whiting, of Hollis, N.H., with a dispatch concealed in his boots. They guarded their prisoner until the authorities arrived, and sent the treasonable papers to the Committee of Safety at Cambridge.

Between Pepperell and Groton, State 119 threads its way through a countryside of meadow and thick woods, and at 19.6 *m*. enters a part of Groton called *Paper Mill Village*, because of the paper industry established here in 1841.

GROTON. 21.2 *m*. (town, alt. 300, pop. 2534, sett. 1655, incorp. 1655), was probably named for the ancestral home of John Winthrop's family. It was destroyed by the Indians during King Philip's War and abandoned by the settlers. Later rebuilt, it was successfully defended against Indians in 1694; but in 1707 several residents were killed and a number of children were carried off.

According to legend one John Chamberlain of Groton killed Paugus, chief of the Pequawkets. Years later a young Indian, fully armed, entered the village and inquired for him. Chamberlain, then an old man, was at work in his sawmill. Warned by the tavern-keeper, who (rightly or wrongly) suspected that it was the son of Paugus come to avenge his father's death, the old man surprised the young brave, killed him, and buried his body in the mill brook, which was thereafter called Paugus Brook.

In the Old Burying Ground on Hollis St., which dates from about 1678, weather-beaten headstones rise starkly on a green knoll. Here is the *Grave of Captain Job Shattuck*, Revolutionary War veteran, who participated in Shays's Rebellion and was tried for high treason. He was convicted and sentenced to be hanged, but was twice reprieved and finally pardoned.

Opposite the Town Hall is *Governor Boutwell House* (*private; open by special permission*), built 1851, and visited by General U. S. Grant. It is a well-preserved frame mansion painted yellow, with green shutters. George Sewall Boutwell (1818–1905), prominent politically, was an organizer of the Republican Party, Governor of Massachusetts, and Secretary of the Treasury under Grant. Adjoining the Boutwell House is the former *Home of Dr. Samuel Abbot Green* (1830–1918), superintendent of the Boston Dispensary, Overseer of Harvard College, and Mayor of Boston, and the *Home of Abbott Lawrence* (1792–1855), Minister to Great Britain in 1849 and donor of the Lawrence Scientific School to Harvard University.

The *First Parish Meeting House* (Unitarian), 0.3 *m.* southeast of the Center on State 119, erected in 1755, was remodeled and partially turned around in 1839, and restored about 1916. The utmost care was taken to preserve the form and atmosphere of the New England meeting house. It is a white wooden church typical of its period, with two massive columns supporting the pediment front. Its delicate, slender spire, capped by a gilded ball and cock weathervane, rests on an inverted cone atop a belfry shuttered by wooden blinds. Behind these hangs its bell, cast by the Paul Revere foundry in 1819. The church faces the town Common, where the Minutemen assembled on the morning of April 19, 1775.

Opposite is the *Dix House* (*private*). The brick part of the house was built about 1767, and was used at one time as a general store. The ground floor of the wooden section, built about 1782, was at first open and served as a horse shed, while the upper floor was utilized as barristers' chambers.

Right from Groton, State 11 passes through verdant countryside to *Groton School*, 1.5 *m.*, with boarding accommodations for about 200 boys. This distinguished secondary school was established in 1884 on a 90-acre farm by the Rev. Endicott Peabody, who 'wanted an Episcopal School where the Headmaster, as in England, was also pastor; where the traditions of the Episcopal Church as a teaching church would be carried on; and where parents could send their sons knowing that those sons would receive religious training side by side with secular teaching.' The school is today as nearly like an English 'public school' as any American school can be. Its rural campus is crossed by tranquil loops of the Nashua River. The spire of the Gothic chapel dominates the countryside. A roster of distinguished Groton alumni includes President Franklin D. Roosevelt; Richard Whitney, president

OLD HOUSES AND
OLD CHURCHES

THE Benjamin Abbott House in Andover is the kind of homestead that most residents of Massachusetts like to think of as typical of their State. These early houses and taverns had oddly friendly exteriors; they were well proportioned, carefully made, and adapted to the harsh New England climate. The pictures that follow show you some of them and also some of the churches which were the necessary focus for almost every village Green.

Early Massachusetts had few really large houses that could be compared with the mansions of the South, for they seemed an extravagance to the cautious New Englander. For an example of unusual opulence, we refer you to the Governor Gore House in Waltham.

NJAMIN ABBOT HOUSE, ANDOVER

PARSON CAPEN HOUSE, TOPSFIELD

OLD SHIP CHURCH, HINGHAM

CAPE COD COTTAGE: JOHN KENRICK HOUSE, ORLEANS

WOODEN QUOINS, WINSLOW HOUSE, MARSHFIELD

MONROE TAVERN, LEXINGTON

FAIRBANKS HOUSE, DEDHAM

OLD CHURCH IN CONCORD

SPARROW HOUSE, PLYMOUTH

GOVERNOR GORE HOUSE, WALTHAM

of the New York Stock Exchange; Lincoln McVeagh, president of the Dial Press and Minister to Greece; Ellery Sedgwick, editor of the *Atlantic Monthly*.

At 21.8 *m.* is a small Green with a tablet commemorating Colonel William Prescott, commander of the American forces at the Battle of Bunker Hill, who was born on February 20, 1726, near the spot.

At 22.1 *m.* is the *Groton Inn Golf Club* (*public;* 9 *holes*). When the club-house, built in 1776, was remodeled some years ago, richly carved wood paneling was found under the plaster in one of the rooms.

LITTLETON COMMON, 28.4 *m.*, is at the junction with State 2 (*see Tour* 2) and State 110 (*see Tour* 7).

T O U R   2 B :   *From* ORANGE *to* NEW HAMPSHIRE LINE (*Keene*), 9.6 *m.*, State 78.

Via Warwick.

Hard-surfaced roadbed; passable most of the year.

STATE 78, branching north from WEST ORANGE on State 2 (*see Tour* 2), is an attractive route through a hilly, forested region.

At 2.5 *m.* is the junction with a road.

> Left on this road, at the end of which is another road leading right to *Lake Moore*, 4.8 *m.* (*bathing, fishing*), a body of pellucid water encircled by hills. (State 78 may be regained by retracing or by continuing north 1.8 *m.*)

At 5.8 *m.* is the junction with a road.

> Left on this road to the *Warwick State Forest*, 1 *m.* (*hunting permits to holders of State licenses*).

WARWICK, 6.2 *m.* (town, alt. 940, pop. 565, sett. about 1739, incorp. 1763). For services in the campaign of 1690 against Canada certain British soldiers were granted four townships, one of them Warwick. Settlers were offered as high as 30 pounds sterling to settle Warwick, then known as Gardner's Canada.

The *Capes to the Berkshires Bridle Trail* (*see Tour* 12) passes through the village. Northwest looms *Mt. Grace* (alt. 1620), with the Telephone Trail. In the early days, Mrs. Rowlandson of Lancaster, with her infant daughter Grace, was captured by Indians. On the march to Canada the baby died, and is said to have been buried by her mother's hands at the foot of the mountain that now bears her name.

> Right from the Center, then left at 1.5 *m.* to *Mallard Hill* (alt. 1340) and the *Asa Conant House*, 3.5 *m.* When Daniel Shays and his company of 300 men were fleeing from General Lincoln, half of them took refuge during a blizzard in this house.

State 78 here commences a descent into a deep gorge known as the Gulf, by a series of hairpin curves between high banks.

At 6.6 *m.* is the start of the *Snowshoe Trail* circling Mt. Grace, and also the *Novice Ski Trail.*

At 7.3 *m.* are *State Picnic Grounds* (*nominal charge for use of table and fireplaces*), a cleared pine grove with a charming brook, spanned by rustic bridges, meandering through it. In the center is a marker with an inscription 'Zilphia Smith' and an old overgrown cellar hole. Here formerly lived Zilphia Smith, an aged recluse, seen only on her rare visits to the village store. She had retreated to this spot when jilted on the eve of her marriage.

At 7.4 *m.* is the *Professional Ski Trail*, one of the fastest and first of its kind in the State, dropping 1000 feet in one mile.

At 9.6 *m.* State 78 crosses the New Hampshire Line about 5 *m.* south of Winchester, N.H.

T O U R   3 :   *From* BOSTON *to* NEW HAMPSHIRE (*Concord*), 36.1 *m.,* US 3.

Via Boston, Cambridge, Arlington, Winchester, Woburn, Burlington, Billerica, Lowell, Tewksbury, Tyngsborough, and Dunstable.

B. & M. R. R. parallels this route; N.Y., N.H. & H. R.R. also services Lowell.

Two-lane or three-lane macadam road, with many curves.

ONE of the main routes between Boston and central New Hampshire, US 3 traverses a rolling countryside of meadowland edged by patches of wood, and of small, well-tilled farms surrounded by grazing lands. The only large city is Lowell, a textile center. Between Lowell and the New Hampshire Line, US 3 parallels the Merrimack River.

West from the State House, Boston, on Beacon St. (*see Tour* 4) to Kenmore Square, 1.7 *m.*; right on Commonwealth Ave. to Cottage Farm Bridge and the junction with US 1 (*see Tour* 1), 2.5 *m.*; right over bridge and left along the Charles River on Memorial Drive (*see Tour* 2).

At 4.5 *m.* is Harvard Square, Cambridge (*see CAMBRIDGE*).

Between Cambridge and Arlington, US 3 (Massachusetts Ave.) passes through a densely populated area, and at 8.1 *m.* reaches the center of ARLINGTON (*see ARLINGTON*).

North of Arlington US 3 cuts through a prosperous residential section bordered on one side by the Mystic Lakes.

At 9.3 *m.* on a triangular plot is a large tablet indicating the *Reservation of the Squaw Sachem*, a woman leader of the Nipmuck Indians. In 1639 she sold all the land of her people saving only this, 'the ground west of the two great ponds called the Mystic Ponds, for Indians to plant and hunt upon and the weare above for the Indians to fish at.' In exchange she received clothing and trinkets.

At 10.4 *m.* is the junction with Church St.

> Right on Church St. is WINCHESTER, 0.9 *m.* (town, alt. 22, pop. 13,371, sett. 1640, incorp. 1850), called successively Woburn Gates, South Woburn, and Black Horse Village. Its present name came from Colonel Winchester, a Watertown business man who presented his municipal namesake with $3000. Edward Converse, called 'the Father of Winchester,' erected a gristmill utilizing the power of the Aberjona River.
>
> On the site of this mill was built in 1839 a plant housing various enterprises, among them those of Joel Whitney and Amos Whittemore. Whitney built machinery for making veneers; Whittemore introduced machinery for pegging shoes, an innovation that forced him to raise the wages of his women binders because of the hostility to machine production felt by his competitors, the old-fashioned shoemakers. The plant was bought by the United Shoe Machinery Corporation in 1929.
>
> By 1860 three tanneries were in operation, and by the end of the century the manufacture of leather had become important. The Mackey Metallic Fastener Corporation, established in 1893, absorbed in time by the United Shoe Machinery Corporation, attracted many workers, causing a building boom. Today the town is largely residential, and only a few long-established factories continue to operate, producing leather uppers, gelatine, watch hands, and felt products.
>
> A prominent resident was Edwin Ginn, who founded the great schoolbook-publishing house and made a million-dollar gift with which was created the World Peace Foundation. Another resident was Samuel McCall, editor, author of biographies of Thaddeus Stevens and Thomas B. Reed, and Governor of Massachusetts (1916–19).
>
> The *Winchester Public Library*, Washington St. and Mystic Valley Parkway, a structure of stone and half timber, built in 1930, houses a small museum.
>
> North of the Center 1.4 *m.* on Washington St., at the corner of Forest St., a marker identifies the *John Harvard Land* (*see CAMBRIDGE*).

Between Winchester and Woburn, US 3 runs through a section where shrubs, vegetables, and flowers are grown for the market in colorful acres dotted with greenhouses.

At 11.4 *m.* is the junction with State 128.

> Right on State 128 is WOBURN, 1.6 *m.* (*see WOBURN*).

North of Woburn, US 3 traverses gently sloping hills and broad fertile acres.

BURLINGTON, 15.2 *m.* (town, alt. 123, pop. 2146, sett. 1641, incorp. 1799), is an agricultural community. The *Marion Tavern* (*open*), on Center St., a low, rambling, white house with a large gray barn, was known in coaching days as the Half-Way House.

Left on Bedford St. a short distance are the *Old Burying Ground*, a peaceful spot where nodding goldenrod and lazy creeping vines mask the weather-beaten slabs in summer, and the *Old Meeting House*, built in 1732, now the Church of Christ. It has been remodeled, but the oaken interior remains. A sign says: 'Its walls were shaken by the firing of artillery during the siege of Boston, the muskets clattered in the aisle when the men brought their arms and accotrments (*sic*) to meetings.'

At 18.1 *m.* is PINEHURST PARK, a summer recreation spot.

BILLERICA, 20.8 *m.* (town, alt. 126, pop. 6650, sett. 1637, incorp. 1655), is an agricultural village with some woolen industries and the *Billerica Car Shops* of the Boston and Maine Railroad, employing from 2000 to 3000 men. Apples, cherries, and strawberries are an important part of the agriculture, intensively developed by the Polish settlers.

Billerica, home of the Wamesit tribe, and one of the Praying Indian towns, was originally called Shawsheen, the Indian name. It was later named for Billericay, in Essex, England. Many settlers were massacred in the French and Indian Wars. There is a story that during one of the alarms, when neighboring women and children were left under the protection of one man in the home of Warren Dutton, Mary Lane urged the man to shoot at what appeared to be a stump near the house. When he refused, she took the gun and shot. The stump fell over — a dead Indian.

At 22 *m.* US 3 crosses the Concord River.

At 22.9 *m.* is the junction with Chelmsford Rd.

> Left on this road at 0.4 *m.* stands the *Manning Manse* (*open as tearoom*). This long, rambling two-and-a-half-story house was built by Ensign Sam Manning in 1696 for a tavern. Here each year is held the reunion of the Manning Family Associates, a nation-wide organization.

At 23.4 *m.* US 3 crosses the Middlesex Canal, one of the country's oldest commercial canals, no longer used but for 40 years a busy waterway (*see Tour 1C, WILMINGTON*).

The *Billerica Town Line* is crossed at 24.1 *m.* An ancient State law compels the selectmen, once every five years, to walk the entire boundary line between Billerica and adjacent towns, an action called 'walking the line.' Between Billerica and Lowell, US 3 passes flourishing truck-gardens and attractive homesteads.

LOWELL, 27 *m.* (*see LOWELL*), is at the junction with State 110 (*see Tour 7*).

> Right from Lowell on State 38 is TEWKSBURY, 4.9 *m.* (town, alt. 105, pop. 6563, sett. 1637, incorp. 1734), probably named for Tewksbury, England. The original proprietors devoted much attention to laying out bridle paths (then called *bridal* paths) in order to attend church; many of the present roads follow the crooked courses of these old lanes.
>
> The *Rev. Sampson Spaulding Homestead* (1735) (*private*), East St., a good example of Colonial Georgian architecture, has two and a half stories and stands in attractive surroundings.
>
> In the *Old Center Burying Ground* on East St., 0.2 *m.* east of the Center, is a stone to Lieutenant William Kitteredge, who died at the age of 92, which carries this inscription:
>> 'He's gone at length, how many grieve
>> Whom he did generously relieve.
>> But O how shocking he expire
>> Amidst the flames of raging fire!
>> Yet all who sleep in Christ are blessed
>> What ever way they are undress'd.'

St. Joseph's Juniorate (private), 32.9 *m.*, is the house of studies of the Marist Brothers. On the grounds is the *Jonathan Tyng House*, built in 1674, for a time the most northerly house in the Colony; it served as an outpost of a near-by garrison erected for protection from the Indians. Imported delft-blue tiles, hand-wrought stair rails, and paneling ornament the interior. In the attic are slave pens and a slave bell.

TYNGSBOROUGH, 34.3 *m.* (town, alt. 112, pop. 1331, sett. before 1661, incorp. 1809), is a residential and farming town on the banks of the Merrimack River, named for the Tyng family, whose coat of arms became its official seal.

South of the Center on US 3 is the *Robert Brinley Mansion (private)*, built in 1803 for 'Sir' Robert and 'Lady' Brinley, who succeeded the Tyngs as town leaders; the house was famous for its hospitality. Near-by is the *Nathaniel Brinley Mansion (private)*, a stately three-story edifice built before 1779 on a high rise of land. It is surmounted by a tall cupola, and on both sides are spacious two-story verandas, added later.

1. Right from Tyngsborough on State 113 is *Tyngsborough Bridge*, 1.8 *m.*, a modern structure spanning the Merrimack River. The western approach is 10 feet higher than the eastern.

At 2.2 *m.* on State 113 is the junction with two roads.

a. Right here on Island Rd. is *Tyng's Island*, 2.2 *m.*, a 65-acre tract formerly owned by the Merrimack Indians; the flood of 1936 uncovered many Indian relics here.

b. Left from the junction on a side road that meets Sherbourne Ave., on which (R) is the *Littlehale Homestead*, 0.3 *m.*, which is associated with a tragedy of a kind common in early Colonial days. Mrs. Littlehale, hunting her two little sons, who had failed to return when sent to find the cows, saw Indians and ran for help. When she returned the Indians were gone; she never saw her children again.

2. Left from Tyngsborough on State 113, along which are beautiful views of the sparkling Merrimack and Nashua Rivers.

The summit of *Negro Hill*, 2.2 *m.*, covered with juniper, can be reached only by those willing to break their own trail. The hilltop is the supposed burial place of John Blood's Negro servant. During an illness Blood called an Indian medicine man to prescribe for him, but suspecting the remedy offered him, John tested it on the Negro — whose prompt demise confirmed his master's fears.

DUNSTABLE, 3.5 *m.* (town, alt. 190, pop. 419, sett. 1656, incorp. 1673), a farming hamlet named for the English birthplace of Mary Tyng, mother of Jonathan Tyng. (Dunstable is derived from 'dun,' a *hilly place*, and 'staple,' a *mart*.)

The fur trade, timber, and the stretches of fertile soil in the Merrimack and Nashua River Valleys, early attracted settlers from around Boston. Dunstable's development was retarded by the Indian wars, which raged here for 50 years without cessation; and the families lived in garrisons.

A poem, 'The Ballad of Captain John Lovewell's Fight at Pequawket,' relates the chief incidents of two expeditions from the town.

At 35.4 *m.* is a junction with Farewell St.

Right on Farewell St. is the *Nathaniel Lawrence House (private)*, 0.5 *m.* (R), a two-story frame Colonial building with two end chimneys. Built in 1775 for the Rev. Nathaniel Lawrence, one of the town's early pastors, it is a fine example of 18th century architecture. The *Oliver Farewell Homestead (private)*, 0.8 *m.* (R), built in 1750, has an 'L' ground plan unusual for that time.

At 36.1 *m.*, US 3 crosses the New Hampshire Line 5 *m.* south of Nashua, N.H.

T O U R   4 :   *From* BOSTON *to* NEW YORK STATE LINE,
144.3 *m.*, US 20.

Via (*sec. a*) Watertown, Newton, Waltham, Weston, Wayland, Sudbury, Marl-
borough, Hudson, Northborough, Shrewsbury; (*sec. b*) Worcester, Charlton,
Sturbridge, Southbridge, Brimfield, Wales, Palmer, Wilbraham, Ludlow,
Springfield; (*sec. c*) West Springfield, Westfield, Russell, Huntington, Chester,
Tyringham, Lee, Lenox; (*sec. d*) Pittsfield, Hancock.

The B. & A. R.R. and the N.Y., N.H. & H. R.R. parallel the road at intervals.

The road is hard-surfaced throughout, but narrow and in poor condition in
some of the rural sections; open at all seasons.

Sec. a. BOSTON to JUNCTION WITH STATE 9, 35.2 m.

BETWEEN Boston and Waltham, US 20 traverses a heavily congested
area. In some places between Boston and Worcester the route follows
the Upper Post Rd., an alternate to the first or Old Post Rd. between
Boston and Hartford, Conn. Many historic taverns still offer hospitality
to the traveler. The countryside, dotted with farms and orchards, is
beautiful, especially in the spring and fall.

US 20 follows Beacon St. west from the State House in Boston to Kenmore Square, 1.7 *m.*; thence along Commonwealth Ave. to Brighton
Ave., 3.2 *m.*

ALLSTON, 3.8 *m.* (City of Boston), is a residential and industrial
suburb.

At 5.1 *m.* US 20 crosses the Charles River, and at 5.7 *m.* (R) passes the
U.S. Arsenal (see WATERTOWN).

At 6.4 *m.* is WATERTOWN (*see WATERTOWN*).

> Left from Watertown Square on Galen St. to NEWTON line, 0.7 *m.* (*see NEW-
> TON*).

US 20 passes through sparsely settled sections and reaches WALTHAM,
10.2 *m.* (*see WALTHAM*).

West of Waltham US 20 runs through a hilly, heavily wooded countryside with fine estates.

At 11.4 *m.* is the junction with Summer St.

> Left on Summer St. is the *Norumbega Tower*, 1.3 *m.*, a massive stone structure
> built by E. N. Horsford, a Harvard professor who made a fortune out of acid
> phosphate sold under a proprietary name. He spent considerable time and money
> in a vain attempt to establish his contention that Norumbega, the city mentioned
> in the 'Saga of Eric the Red,' was here; Eric's son, Leif Ericson, may have visited
> the shores of the present State of Massachusetts, though there is little proof of
> this. The panoramic view from the tower makes it well worth a visit.

At 12.2 *m.* on US 20 is the junction of Wellesley St. (L) and the Upper

Rd., known here as the Boston Post Rd. (R), which is an alternate at this point to US 20.

1. Left on Wellesley St. is the *Oliver Robbins House* (*private*), on the northwest corner of Chestnut and Wellesley Sts., 1.2 *m.* It was occupied by Thomas Allen in 1698, and later by Thomas Rand and his son, who fought at Lexington and Concord. It is a fine example of an early Colonial dwelling, with a large red-brick chimney.

At 1.4 *m.* on Wellesley St. are the entrance gates of the *Regis College for Women*, a parochial college, administered by the Sisters of St. Joseph. The 170-acre campus is markedly beautiful.

2. Right on the Boston Post Rd. to WESTON, 0.3 *m.* (town, alt. 199, pop. 3848, sett. about 1642, incorp. 1712), in what was originally the 'more westerly' precinct of Watertown. During the Revolution there was a beacon light on Sanderson's Hill. Weston became a thriving agricultural and industrial center owing to its situation on a main thoroughfare, but about 1840 its industries left for neighboring cities, and today it is chiefly a residential section.

The town counts among its noted sons the Rev. Edmund Hamilton Sears, who wrote 'It Came Upon the Midnight Clear'; Carlton Stevens Coon, author of 'The Flesh of the Wild Ox' and other books; and Arthur Train, lawyer and writer, who found much of the background for 'Puritan's Progress' in Weston. Gertrude Fiske, well-known portrait painter, makes her home here.

At the *Free Outdoor Swimming Pool* (15¢ *fee for non-residents*), corner of Old Boston Post Rd. and US 20, instruction in swimming and life-saving is available from July 1 through the summer.

The *Weston Public Library* (*open Mon., Wed., Fri., and Sat. 2–9, Tues. and Thurs. 2–5.30*), corner School St. and Boston Post Rd., an attractive brick building, houses a small collection of fine Japanese ivories.

The *Artemas Ward House* (*private*), corner of Concord Rd. and the Post Rd. (R), was built in 1785 by two brothers named Easton and sold about four years later to Artemas Ward, son of General Ward of Revolutionary fame. Set 100 feet from the road on a hill, with beautiful terraced lawns and gravel driveway, it is a broad gable house with white clapboards, fine dentil mouldings in the cornice, and a shingled roof. A gabled portico with dentil moulding sets it apart from its more modern neighbors.

The *Elisha Jones Place*, or Golden Ball Tavern (*private*), 662 Boston Post Rd., was built in 1751 by Colonel Jones, and was the headquarters of the Tories during the Revolutionary War. It is a two-and-one-half-story mansion with two wings. At this house, John How, a British spy sent out in 1775 by General Gage to report on rebel ammunition stored on the Worcester Road, was discovered. Though he escaped and reached Worcester, the Weston patriots so aroused the countryside that How reported to Gage that any attempt at the movement of troops in that direction would result in certain defeat — with the result that Lexington was chosen for the British line of march.

North from Weston 1.7 *m.* on Concord Rd. is *Weston College* (Jesuit), where men are prepared for active religious and intellectual apostolates. The college buildings are on an elevation, from which there is a good view of the surrounding hills and valleys. The campus includes a nine-hole golf course, three tennis courts, a good ball field, handball courts, and extensive landscaped grounds.

WAYLAND, 15.8 *m.* (town, alt. 140, pop. 3346, sett. 1638, incorp. 1835), was named for Francis Wayland, clergyman and president of Brown University (1827–55). He was instrumental in establishing here in 1848 a *Free Library* claimed by a boulder on the Green to be the first free library in Massachusetts. Shoemaking and the harvesting of meadow grass were once important in the town; today market-gardening is the chief occupation.

The *Unitarian Church,* completed in 1815, derives its design from the work of Sir Christopher Wren. It is well proportioned and has a charming tower belfry with a Paul Revere bell.

Right from Wayland on the Old Sudbury Rd. at 1.1 *m.* is the *Home of Lydia Child* (*private*), a charming house of clapboards painted black, with two brick inside chimneys. Dormer windows with small, square panes light the upper story. Lydia Child, author and abolitionist, gave up her work as editor of the *Juvenile Miscellany,* the first American periodical for children, to follow William Lloyd Garrison in his anti-slavery crusade.

At 18.6 *m.* is the junction with Concord Rd.

Right on Concord Rd. at 0.1 *m.* is the *Goodnow Library,* opened in 1863. It contains some old manuscripts, diaries, and papers.

At 0.4 *m.* on Concord Rd. is the *Israel Brown House* (*private*) built in 1725. Prior to the Civil War this house served as a station on the Underground Railroad for slaves escaping to Canada. Brown used a stake wagon with a false bottom to carry the refugees to the next station at Lancaster; though suspected and often stopped, he was never apprehended. The house is a three-story hip-roof building with white clapboards. The slaves were secreted in a portion of the cellar reached from a trap door near the fireplace.

At 0.5 *m.* is a junction with a short private road; right on this road is the *Wadsworth Monument,* a granite shaft erected in 1852. When Marlborough was fired by the Indians in March, 1676, Lieutenant Curtis of Sudbury led a party in a surprise night attack. The leader of the Indians, Metus, was killed. A month later Captain Wadsworth of Milton arrived to assist Marlborough and discovered that the Indians had moved on to Sudbury. After augmenting his forces, Wadsworth marched to Sudbury and was ambushed near the base of Green Hill. After fighting his way to the top, he maintained a stout defense, but toward evening King Philip routed the Colonials by setting fire to the woods. In the ensuing battle only 14 Englishmen escaped. Captain Wadsworth and 28 of his men were killed, and they are buried beneath this monument.

The *Goulding House* (*open*) (R), 0.6 *m.* is a restored two-story center-chimney dwelling built about 1690. Set well back from the highway on a gentle grade, with an orchard forming a charming background, and a well sweep and bucket in front, this house forms a pleasing picture. Some of the rooms have walls covered with matched boarding. The massive beams are exposed, displaying the fine flooring above. Wrought-iron hardware and large brick fireplaces indicate the age of the house.

At 1.5 *m.* is SUDBURY (town, alt. 165, pop. 1638, sett. 1638, incorp. 1639). Land here was originally granted in 1637 on petition to the residents of Watertown, but most of the actual settlers came directly from England. Their names appear on the passenger list of the 'Confidence,' which sailed from Southampton April 24, 1638.

At the outbreak of the Revolution, Sudbury had a population of 2160 inhabitants, the highest in its history, about 500 of whom saw active service in the war. The list of officers from this town in the Continental Army includes a brigadier general, colonels, majors, adjutants, surgeons, 24 captains, and 29 lieutenants. In the 19th century, Sudbury lost much of its territory to new towns; its industries died and were not replaced. Today, its nurseries, carnation greenhouses, and vegetable farms furnish the chief occupations.

Northeast from Sudbury at 0.6 *m.* is *Whitehall,* the estate of Ralph Adams Cram, distinguished architect. On the grounds Mr. Cram built his *St. Elizabeth's Chapel,* a small stone structure in the French Provincial style, with antique reredos.

At 21 *m.* a tablet marks the *Site of the Parmenter Garrison House,* built before 1686. The carpenters building the Wayside Inn (*see below*) took refuge here during an Indian attack.

At 21.1 *m.* is a junction with the Old Boston Post Rd., again an alternate to US 20.

Right on this road 0.3 *m.* is the *Wayside Inn* (*guide; adm.* 25¢), the core of which was built by Samuel Howe in 1686, and immortalized by Longfellow in 'Tales of a Wayside Inn' (1862). It is now owned by Henry Ford, who added a two-story wing on the north end and restored some of the original appearance of the ordinary by authentic furnishings. He also placed here a number of objects of historical significance.

When the Inn was first opened to the public, it was known as Howe Tavern, but after 1746, when Colonel Ezekiel Howe put up a new sign, it became known as the Red Horse Tavern. The original structure had four rooms on the ground floor in addition to a kitchen ell, four sleeping-chambers on the second floor, and an unfinished attic; it is now a three-story gambrel-roofed building with two brick inner chimneys. The west wing, including a dining-room on the ground floor and a ballroom above, was added in 1800. The grounds are entered through wrought-iron gates, and the old Red Horse sign, suspended on a bracket, bears the names of some of the former owners.

Lyman Howe, the last proprietor of the Howe line (d. 1861), is thus described by Longfellow:

> 'Grave in his aspect and attire;
> A man of ancient pedigree,
> A justice of the Peace was he,
> Known in all Sudbury as "The Squire."'

The Inn has entertained many distinguished guests, including Washington, Lafayette, General Knox, President Coolidge, Thomas Edison, and Harvey Firestone. Longfellow visited it but twice, and the friends he represents as exchanging tales before the old hearth were actually never simultaneously assembled here.

At 0.4 *m.* on the Post Rd. is the *Redstone Schoolhouse,* a small red frame building set in a grove of pines. A tablet on a huge boulder near it says that the old schoolhouse is the one immortalized in 'Mary Had a Little Lamb' (*see Tour 11, STERLING*). This claim, however, is disputed. At 0.5 *m.* on the Boston Post Rd. is a *Gristmill* (*open; free*), the property of Mr. Ford. It is a three-story structure built of native field-stone, with a gable roof. The field is dotted with old discarded millstones. The great water wheel turns daily to grind the corn and other grains sold chiefly to visitors.

Between Sudbury and Marlborough US 20 passes through a pleasant countryside, predominantly orchard land.

MARLBOROUGH, 25.9 *m.* (city, alt. 386, pop. 15,781, sett. 1657, incorp. town 1660, city 1890), was the site of an Indian plantation called Okammakamefit. The English knew this area as Whipsufferage. Later it was part of Sudbury Town.

Although Marlborough was one of John Eliot's Praying Indian towns, where the Indians had been converted to Christianity, it was attacked during King Philip's War. The following account is given by a Mr. Packard: 'On the Sabbath, when Mr. Brimmead was in sermon, March 20, 1676, the worshipping assembly was suddenly dispersed by an outcry of Indians at the door. The confusion of the first moment was instantly increased by a fire from the enemy: but the God whom they worshipped shielded their lives and limbs, excepting the arm of one Moses Newton, who was carrying an elderly and infirm woman to a place of safety. In a few minutes they were sheltered in their fort, with the mutual feelings peculiar to such a scene.'

At one time Marlborough ranked fifth in national production of shoes. Today its manufactures include paper boxes, wire goods, shoe machinery, metal products, oil-burners and cosmetics. Marlborough's several racial groups have been attracted to the town by the opportunities offered in various trades.

On the corner of Maple and Valley Sts. is the *Dennison Factory* (*open by permission*), which specializes in the manufacture of paper boxes, paper novelties, and office accessories. This is a branch, established in 1925, of the Dennison Manufacturing Company of Framingham (*see Tour 1C*). Several hundred workers are employed in this modern structure of concrete and steel.

At 277 Main St., headquarters of the American Legion and the Grand Army of the Republic, is the *John Brown Bell*, taken by Marlborough soldiers from the engine house at Harper's Ferry in 1861, and hidden by a loyalist in Williamsport, Md., until 1892, when it was brought to Marlborough.

Right from Marlborough on State 85 is *Fort Meadow Reservoir*, 1.6 *m.* (*boating, bathing*). Its waters are used by mills for wool-cleansing, and its shores are occupied by summer camps. Local historians believe the reservoir is on the site of an Indian fort.

At 3.5 *m.* on State 85 is HUDSON (town, alt. 211, pop. 8495, sett. 1699, incorp. 1866), first known as the Mills, then as Feltonville; it received its present name when Charles Hudson agreed to give $500 as the foundation for a library if the change was made. In 1816 Daniel Stratton began the manufacture of shoes here. Francis Brigham, introducing machinery in 1835 and utilizing the water-power of the Assabet River, made this industry the most important in the town; in the course of time dye factories, tanneries, machine shops, box factories, and cloth mills made their appearance. George Houghton started manufacturing shoes in his home, but in time with the aid of machinery had an important factory. These industries eventually drew large numbers of Portuguese, French, Greek, Russian, Jewish, and Italian workers. On July 4, 1894, boys setting off firecrackers behind a shoe factory started a fire that destroyed about 40 buildings, chiefly factories; the area was rebuilt, the factories acquiring the modern equipment of which they had long been in need.

At 26.9 *m.* is the *Williams Inn Club* (L), formerly the Williams Tavern. The original tavern, built in 1662, was burned by Indians in 1676; the present building was built in the following year. Many famous guests, including Washington and Lafayette, have stopped here. The walls of the two lower stories are of brick painted white, the walls of the upper story are covered with scalloped white shingles. Four columns support the three-story porch.

US 20 turns right and follows Lakeside Ave. past *Lake William*, 27 *m.*

At 29.4 *m.* is a marker giving directions for a five-minute walk to the *Monument and Grave of Mary Goodnow*. On August 18, 1707, Mary Goodnow and a friend, Mrs. Fay, left the garrison to gather herbs near Stirrup Brook. They were surprised by a small band of Indians; Mary, who was lame, was caught in flight, slain, and scalped, her body being left beside the path.

NORTHBOROUGH, 31.7 *m.* (town, alt. 303, pop. 2396, sett. about 1672, incorp. 1775), is a town that was once part of Marlborough. Market-gardening and fruit-raising are carried on extensively in the area. In 1884 teeth and other remains of a huge animal were uncovered in the lower part of the town; these were identified as those of a mastodon and are now in the Museum of the Worcester Natural History Society (*see WORCESTER*).

West of the town hall on Church St. is the Triangular Green, on which is the *Old Congregational Church* (1808) with a bell from the Paul Revere foundry, cast in 1809. Behind the church is the *Old Cemetery*, opened in 1750, containing the *Grave of Rabbi Judah Monis* (1683–1764), for 40 years Professor of Hebrew at Harvard University and one of the first prominent orthodox Jews to embrace Christianity in North America.

US 20 runs through a prosperous country of poultry farms, market-gardens, and fruit orchards as neat and gaily colored as a patchwork quilt.

At 33 *m.* is the junction with the Old Boston Post Rd. and the Southwest cut-off.

> Right on this road at 2.3 *m.* is the *Artemas Ward Homestead* (*open; free*). Ward, first Commander-in-Chief of the Continental Army, later became Chief Justice of the Court of Common Pleas. The estate is now the property of Harvard University, and the house, largely unaltered, contains the Ward family furnishings, including the desk used by the General while in command of the Continental Army. It is a two-and-a-half-story gray-shingled house with two front entrances and two red brick chimneys. In front of the house are two hitching posts, a gray picket fence, and an old sycamore tree. Across the street is *Dean Park* (*swimming pool*), site of the birthplace of Artemas Ward. The park was a gift from Charles A. Dean to the town.

> SHREWSBURY, 3.2 *m.* (town, alt. 671, pop. 7144, sett. 1722, incorp. 1727), named for Charles Talbot, Duke of Shrewsbury. Its lack of water-power and inaccessibility to outside markets precluded the development of industries. Agriculture, therefore, has remained the chief occupation. Luther Goddard, a Baptist preacher born in the town, is said to have been the first watchmaker in America. He followed watchmaking purely as an avocation, and on Sundays after his sermon he was accustomed to collect any faulty timepieces among his parishioners and return them the following Sunday in good repair.

> The *Howe Memorial Library* (L) on Main St. contains books and papers of the Ward family.

> Just west of the Town Hall is the Common, near which in Colonial days were the stocks and whipping-post required by law. The first person sent to these stocks was their manufacturer. His only payment for making them was the remittance of a fine for some previous misconduct.

> At 4.1 *m.* on the Old Boston Post Rd. is the junction with a side road. Right on this road at 0.8 *m.* is the *State Rifle Range*, marked by an old-fashioned cannon and a flagpole.

US 20 west of 33 *m.* is known as the Southwest Cutoff, a three-lane express highway passing few points of interest and avoiding large communities.

At 35 *m.* is the junction with State 9 (*see Tour 8*).

Sec. b. JUNCTION STATE 9 *to SPRINGFIELD*, US 20, 57.3 *m.*

Between the junction of State 9 and Springfield, US 20 traverses a pleasant countryside broken by low hills sloping gently into the Connecticut Valley.

At 8 *m.* are the drying beds and fountain sprays of the *Worcester Purification Works*, where the Imhoff system is used, the sludge being separated by the 'digestive' system.

US 20 skirts the city of Worcester; at 13.6 *m.* is the junction with State 12 (*see Tour* 11).

At 19.9 *m.* is a junction with an improved road.

Left on this road is CHARLTON, 0.8 *m.* (town, alt. 925, pop. 2366, sett. about 1735, incorp. 1755), named for Sir Francis Charlton, a Privy Councillor of England. Since 1789 the population has increased by only 286, and the Puritan tradition still dominates the community. Agriculture is still the chief means of livelihood. Factories and mills have operated at intervals, but the lack of abundant waterpower has always hindered any permanent industrial development.

On the Common is a *Memorial to William Thomas Green Morton* (1819–68) (*see BOSTON*), given by the dentists of America to honor the man whose experiments with ether first made possible anesthesia during surgical operations. A dentist, he started the experiments to enable him to extract deep roots of teeth, working with Dr. Charles T. Jackson, a dentist. Dr. Morton did his first tooth extraction with ether on September 30, 1846, and a month later gave a public demonstration, administering ether at the Massachusetts General Hospital for a major operation. Dr. Morton was born in Charlton.

The *Masonic Home*, north of the Center on a broad hill, is one of the finest of fraternal homes for the aged in New England. It was originally built for a hotel.

On Main St., just south of the Center, the old Burying Ground (1750), now called Bay Path Cemetery, contains three *Photograph Stones* — headstones provided with small glass-covered niches in which were placed daguerreotypes of the deceased. Once the vogue, few of these curious stones now remain.
Here also is the '*Grizzly' Adams Headstone*, beneath which one of P. T. Barnum's bear-tamers was buried after a disastrous encounter with Bruin. The great showman himself ordered the stone, and had it decorated with a carved bas-relief of Grizzly Adams in buckskins, standing with one hand resting trustfully on the shoulder of a bear — presumably not the one that did away with him.

East of the Cemetery near Dudley Rd. is *Mugget Hill* (*no road*), crowned with 'mowings.'

CHARLTON CITY, 20.9 *m.* (Town of Charlton), contains two woolen mills.

At 26.6 *m.* is the junction with State 15.

Left on State 15 at 0.3 *m.* is the junction with State 131; left on 131 is STURBRIDGE, 0.5 *m.* (town, alt. 622, pop. 1918, sett. about 1729, incorp. 1738), visited by Englishmen as early as 1633, but not settled for nearly a century. Dairying, sheep-raising, and orchard culture were the main occupations until the water-power attracted industries including tanneries, a shoe factory, a cotton mill, and an auger and bit factory.

On the edge of the Common is the *Hyde Library* (*open Wed.* 2–4; *Sat.* 2–4; 6–9), with a copper dome and semi-circular entrance. Here are Indian relics collected by Levi B. Chase. Opposite is the *Old Cemetery*, enclosed by a stone wall that was built by four companies of Revolutionary Soldiers from Sturbridge — each company building one side.

1. Straight ahead from Sturbridge is SOUTHBRIDGE, 4.2 *m*. (town, alt. 518, pop. 15,786, sett. 1730, incorp. 1816), a manufacturing community lying in a valley. More than half the inhabitants are French-Canadians, who maintain their native customs and language. The first factory was built to make cotton yarns but was changed to a woolen mill. There are now a number of mills and factories.

The *Wells Museum* (*open weekdays* 9–4; *adm.* 25¢), 176 Main St., is a private collection of early American and English, Spanish and Central European articles. The museum contains old pottery, andirons, guns, clocks, and Colonial utensils.

The *American Optical Company* (*open by permission*) on Mechanic St., 0.2 *m*. east of the Center, employing 3200 people, is the most important business in the town. In the building is a *Museum* (*open during business hours*), in connection with the laboratories where Dr. Edgar Tillyer, an outstanding optical expert in the country, carries on experiments.

South of Southbridge, State 131 is a fine scenic route passing through the Quine-baug Valley. At 9.8 *m*. it crosses the Connecticut line, 10 *m*. north of Putnam, Conn.

2. Right from Sturbridge on State 15, at 5.4 *m*. is the junction with a side road; right on this road 1.2 *m*. is the *Site of the Abandoned Tantiusque Lead Mine.* In 1633 John Oldham and Samuel Hall, on a scouting expedition from Plymouth, encountered some Indians whose faces were blackened with graphite. Inquiry revealed that this came from 'Black Hill,' and the visit of the two scouts to this spot is the first recorded entrance of white men into Worcester County. In 1638 John Winthrop, Jr., purchased a tract here, four miles square, the deed for which is now in the Winthrop Collection of the American Antiquarian Society of Worcester. Winthrop's attempt at mining the graphite did not meet with success, however, inasmuch as the vein proved to run almost perpendicular and the difficulty of extracting the ore was too great. From that time until early in this century there have been spasmodic attempts to work the mines. The region is honeycombed with shafts and tunnels, and the various workings are plainly discernible. Caution should be used in exploring, as the undergrowth has obscured some of the veins and open pits. Discarded machinery serves to identify the site.

At **27.7** *m*. (L) is the plant of the *Snell Manufacturing Company* (*private*), the oldest auger and bit factory in the country. Tools manufactured here were used in building the U.S. Frigate 'Constitution' ('Old Ironsides'); a new set of tools was presented to the Navy by the company at the time the old ship was refitted.

In FISKDALE, **28.2** *m*. (Town of Sturbridge), on US 20 east of the Center, is the *Shrine of Saint Anne*, containing a relic of the saint brought here in 1892. Today clustered about her statue are canes, crutches, and broken casts left by the afflicted who believe they have been restored to health by her gracious intercession. About a hill on the grounds are the 14 Stations of the Cross with 49 steps leading to a cross on the summit.

1. Right from Fiskdale on Brookfield Rd. at 0.2 *m*. (L) is the *Abner Allen House,* a long, low, one-and-a-half-story structure built in 1735 and still occupied by the Allen family, whose ancestor, Moses Allen, built the first gristmill in the village. At 1 *m*. on Brookfield Rd. can be seen (L) below the highway the long sloping roof and a side of the *Salt-Box House* (*private*), built in 1750.

2. Left from Fiskdale on Holland Rd. is the *Shumway House* (*private*), 1.7 *m*., known also as the old Palmer Place. The house itself is in poor condition. The paneling from the old parlor, a corner cupboard with cloverleaf shelves, and several paneled doors have been taken to furnish the Fiskdale Room of the Boston Museum of Fine Arts.

Between Sturbridge and Brimfield, US 20 crosses rolling farm country.

On both sides of the road the fields slope gradually to the base of the distant hills.

At 30.7 *m*. is the junction with a road in EAST BRIMFIELD.

Right on this dirt road is *Little Alum Pond*, 1.3 *m*. (*picnic grove, refreshment stand, boating, bathing, and fishing*).

At 5.1 *m*. is the *Birthplace of Thaddeus Fairbanks* (*private*), inventor of the platform scale.

At 33 *m*. is the junction with an improved road.

Left on this road is *Holland Pond* (*picnicking, boating, fishing*).

HOLLAND, 4.1 *m*. (town, alt. 700, pop. 201, sett. 1725, incorp. 1835), was settled by Joseph Blodgett and named in honor of Lord Holland, the father of Charles James Fox. Destruction of a textile mill by lightning in 1851 ended a brief period of manufacture, and agriculture resumed its importance.

At 5.4 *m*. is the causeway across the *Holland Reservoir* (*bathing, fishing, boating*), formerly called Lake Massaconnet, a name made by combining abbreviations of Massachusetts and Connecticut.

At 34 *m*. is BRIMFIELD, (town, alt. 660, pop. 892, sett. about 1706, incorp. 1731). The village, with its white Colonial church overlooking the village Green, and street lined with closely planted elms, is on the old stagecoach route. Its few industries did not survive the introduction of mass production.

1. Left from Brimfield, State 19 follows Wales Brook, skirting the southern part of the Brimfield State Forest, with the summits of Mt. Pisgah and Mt. Hitchcock visible to the west.

WALES, 4.4 *m*. (town, alt. 890, pop. 382, sett. about 1726, incorp. 1775), is surrounded by woodlands, market-gardens, and dairy farms. Originally incorporated as South Brimfield, the town in 1828 was renamed for James Lawrence Wales, in acknowledgment of a $2000 legacy. A number of cloth mills and sawmills used the small streams for water-power in the early days. The only manufacturing plant at the present time is a small textile mill.

Dominating the village is an old-fashioned New England hotel with a wide porch extending across its breadth, on which a row of inviting chairs offers a vantage-point for observing the leisurely goings and comings of the townsfolk.

Left from *Lake George* (Wales Pond) (*fishing, hunting, picnicking*), south of the Center, a dirt road crosses Veineke Brook at 1 *m*. This brook flows south 0.5 *m*. into *Veineke Pond*. On its shores (*inaccessible by car*) are the *Cellar Holes* of an old Hessian village established by Veineke, one of the Hessian soldiers taken prisoner at the surrender of Burgoyne's army in 1777.

2. Right from Brimfield on Warren Rd. (*see marker*) at 2 *m*. is the junction with a mountain road; left on this mountain road (25¢ toll) is *Steerage Rock*, a huge boulder used as a landmark by Indians and travelers on the Bay Path during the colonization of the Connecticut Valley. It was said to be a favorite camping-place for King Philip; from here he could watch the villages in the valley below.

At 39.7 *m*. is the junction with West Warren Rd.

Right on this road is WEST BRIMFIELD, 3 *m*. (Town of Brimfield). Here is the *Captain Nicholas House* (*private*), an old brick building used for quarters by the Hessian soldiers who marched from Saratoga to Boston in 1777.

At 41.1 *m*. is the junction (L) with State 32 (*see Tour 23A*).

PALMER, 42.2 *m*. (town, alt. 332, pop. 9437, sett. 1716, incorp. 1775, was known as the Elbow Tract until its incorporation, when it was named for

Chief Justice Palmer. It has developed industries producing cotton piece-goods, wire, wire cables, screen cloth, pinion rod and pinion wire, culverts, paper boxes, hotel service wagons, casters for tables, and hospital screens.

At Palmer is the junction (R) with State 32 (*see Tour 23A*).

At 43.4 *m.* US 20 crosses the Quaboag River. A pile of stones (L) in the middle of the river is the *Remains of Scott's Bridge*, built in Colonial days and used by General Washington on his way to Boston in 1775.

At 47.2 *m.* is a junction with a side road.

Right on this road 0.2 *m.* is an *Old Covered Bridge* spanning the Chicopee River. Built in 1852, this bridge is the last of its kind in Hampden County.

NORTH WILBRAHAM, 47.4 *m.* (town, alt. 240, pop. 2969, sett. 1730, incorp. 1763), is a trading-village and the political center of Wilbraham. The first settlement, made by Nathaniel Hitchcock, was farther south in a section called Outward Commons. In 1741 the region was set aside as the Fourth Precinct of Springfield.

The *Public Library* (*open*) in the Town Hall has an exhibit of Indian relics.

Left from North Wilbraham on a hard-surfaced road is WILBRAHAM, 2.1 *m.*, (alt. 285) the geographical center of the township.

Wilbraham Academy, founded in 1817 as Wesleyan Academy in Newmarket, N.H., was moved eight years later to Wilbraham, and occupies the group of brick buildings on the hill (and L). In 1911 it became a college preparatory school for boys after having been a co-educational institution for 94 years. The school is on the site of the first settlement of the town. Near the academy is the brownstone Methodist Church, and beyond is a frame dwelling (*private*), the *Original Church* building. The gable end toward the street, the unusually large windows on the first floor, and the Gothic arched moldings over the windows on the second floor are reminders of the original use of the building.

On Dipping Hole Rd. is '*Peggy's Dipping Hole*,' so-called because on a certain winter Sabbath morning one 'Miss Peggy,' who was riding to church on horseback, broke through the ice and was 'dipped' in the freezing water.

1. Left from Wilbraham is a mountain road to the *Lookout Tower*, 1 *m.*, on the summit of Wilbraham Mountain, affording a view of the Connecticut River Valley and the Mt. Holyoke Range.

2. Straight ahead from Wilbraham at 0.5 *m.* is the junction with an improved road; right on this road at 1 *m.* is the *State Game Farm* (*open*), established in 1912. This 160-acre farm raised 8200 ring-neck pheasants in 1935, and in recent years has specialized in the propagation of pheasants for stocking natural coverts throughout the State.

At 51.1 *m.*, in the Indian Orchard section of Springfield, is the junction with State 21.

Right on State 21, at 0.9 *m.* the Chicopee River is crossed. The *Ludlow Manufacturing Associates* (*private*) have one of the largest jute-manufacturing plants in the world, stretching along the north bank of the Chicopee River at the bridge. Local industries have centered about this group of manufacturers. In an early decade of the 19th century the Boston Flax Mills were purchased and brought to Ludlow. Between 1889 and 1906 ten new mills, a power house, and machine shops were erected. Since 1920, however, there has been some decrease in business owing to the removal of industry to southern towns. In 1935 so many buildings were unoccupied that several were razed.

LUDLOW, 1.2 *m*. (town, alt. 239, pop. 8569, sett. about 1751, incorp. 1775), originally known as Stony Hill, a district of Springfield, was separately incorporated because of the difficulty of crossing the Chicopee River, dividing the two communities. Water-power encouraged the establishment of sawmills, for a time an important industry.

The *Hubbard Memorial Library* (*open*) has a small exhibit of local relics.

At 1.6 *m*. is the junction with Joy St.; left to the end of Joy St., where an unmarked street (L) leads to a path between the last two houses (R). This path affords the best approach to *Indian Leap*, a high rocky cliff on the bank of the Chicopee River. During King Philip's War, Roaring Thunder and a band of his warriors leaped from the cliff to escape pursuit. Roaring Thunder waited until the last of his men had plunged into the river, to escape or perish; then he followed.

At 2.6 *m*. State 21 passes *Haviland Pond* (*bathing and fishing*).

LUDLOW CENTER, 4.1 *m*. (Town of Ludlow), is the geographical center of a town that once included a prosperous glass works and chair factory.

Between Wilbraham and Springfield, US 20 passes a group of ponds that provide various recreational facilities, then traverses a thickly populated section, and at 57.8 *m*. reaches SPRINGFIELD (see *SPRINGFIELD*).

The junction of State and Columbus Sts. in the heart of the city is the junction of US 20 and US 5 (*see Tour* 15) and State 116 (*see Tour* 15*B*).

Sec. c. SPRINGFIELD to JUNCTION WITH US 7, US 20, 51.8 m.

Between Springfield and the junction of US 7, US 20, the Jacob's Ladder Trail, crosses the beautiful lower Berkshire Hills.

At 0.3 *m*. US 20 crosses the Connecticut River on the *Hampden County Memorial Bridge.*

WEST SPRINGFIELD, 2 *m*. (town, alt. 103, pop. 17,118, sett. about 1660, incorp. 1774), has a subsidiary of one of the oil corporations, a large paper manufacturing plant, a glazed paper establishment, the Boston and Albany Railroad repair shops, and chemical, machine, and other factories. Large market-gardens flourish in Riverdale, and some dairying is carried on west of the town. The Eastern States Exposition is held here.

The *Common* was the camp site of three Revolutionary War armies under the respective commands of Generals Amherst, Burgoyne, and Riedesel. the latter in charge of the German mercenaries. Later it was the drill ground of Captain Luke Day's insurgents during Shays's Rebellion.

The *First Congregational Church* (1800) on Orthodox Hill, now the Masonic Temple, is designed in the manner of Christopher Wren, with less modification than is usual in New England.

The *Day House* (*open Tues., Thurs., Sat.; adm.* 10¢), north of the Common, built in 1754, is a historical museum maintained by the Ramapogue Historical Society. It is a two-story brick building with a lean-to at the rear. Furnishings of an early period are to be found in the rooms, each of which has an enormous fireplace.

At the Center is the junction with State 5A (*see Tour* 15*D*).

At 3.9 *m.* is the junction with Churchill Rd. (L), the entrance to *Mittineague Park* (*athletic fields; picnicking*).

At 5 *m.* the country is more open, with nurseries and tobacco fields occupying most of the land between the scattered houses. At 5.4 *m.* the road enters a cut through trap rock, an extension of Mt. Tom Range.

At 7.5 *m.* US 20 crosses the Westfield River, tributary of the Connecticut, furnishing water-power for many industries.

At 8.5 *m.* US 20 crosses the Little River; just north of this point the first settlers built a fort. The last Indian raid in this region occurred in 1820.

At 9.4 *m.* is WESTFIELD (city, alt. 154, pop. 18,788, sett. about 1660, incorp. town 1669, city 1920). The first road was cut through in 1668 and travel increased so rapidly that four years later Captain Aaron Cook opened a tavern here.

The *Westfield Athenaeum* (*open weekdays*, 9–9; *Sun.* 2–6), corner of Elm and Court Sts., overlooking the Green, is an attractive brick building with limestone trim, housing the library. On the upper floor is the *Edwin Smith Historical Museum*, which consists of a large hall divided into two parts, the one containing a well-furnished Colonial kitchen brought from Connecticut, and the other a living-room of a typical New England home of the late 18th century; among the exhibits in the latter are women's costumes and a number of dolls. The *Jasper Rand Art Museum*, in an adjoining room, holds continuous exhibitions of the works of well-known American artists.

The *State Teachers' College*, on Court St., established in 1844, is the second oldest institution of its kind in the State. The imposing three-story building of red brick stands on a three-acre campus.

At 10.2 *m.* is the junction with Smith Ave.

Left on Smith Ave. 0.1 *m.* in front of the Westfield High School is *Grandmother's Garden*, planted with nearly all known herbs and with old-fashioned flowers.

At 14.2 *m.* is the entrance (L) to *Tekoa Park* (*picnic facilities*). Directly opposite, across the Westfield River, is *Mt. Tekoa* (alt. 1211), a rugged, dome-shaped peak of solid rock.

WORONOCO, 15.5 *m.* (alt. 255, Town of Russell), is best known as the home of the *Strathmore Paper Company Plant* (*open by permission*), across the river. The village is at the junction with State 17 (*see Tour 4A*).

At 17.9 *m.* is RUSSELL (town, alt. 266, pop. 1283, sett. 1782, incorp. 1792). Here in 1858 the Chapin and Gould Paper Mills were established. These paper mills, with those in Woronoco and Westfield, are the chief support of the area.

HUNTINGTON, 22 *m.* (town, alt. 381, pop. 1345, sett. 1769, incorp. 1775), at first called Norwich, was later named for Charles F. Huntington. The town was barely a year old when it organized a military company and began to store ammunition. The townsfolk displayed little sympathy with Shays's Rebellion, and a group of rebels stormed the town, seizing John Kirkland, captain of the local militia.

In the early days the townspeople raised corn, rye, oats, and potatoes, and in their homes carried on the manufacture of cotton and woolen cloth for the market. Potatoes, ensilage, and dairy and poultry products are now the chief sources of income.

The *Murrayfield Grammar School* on the Worthing Rd. houses a historic bell stolen by Union soldiers from New Orleans during the Civil War.

At 22.1 *m.* is the junction with Old US 20 (*see Tour 4B*).

Boulder Park (*camping, swimming, picnicking*), 24.1 *m.* (L), deriving its name from a huge rock by the roadside, is in the Chester-Blandford State Forest (*hunting and fishing by permit*).

At 25.3 *m.* is a *Tourist Camp* (*fireplaces, spring*).

At 26.2 *m.* is the junction with a road.

> Left on this road through the forest along Sanderson Brook to a sign pointing to beautiful *Sanderson Brook Falls*, 1.1 *m.*, 100 feet high.

At 28.8 *m.* is the *Cortland Grinding Wheels Corporation Plant* (*open by permission*), one of the largest manufacturers of emery wheels in the country.

Beyond the factory is a *Fountain*, a water spout at the end of the town water main, which in winter freezes to a glittering mosque-like dome 50 to 60 feet high.

CHESTER, 28.9 *m.* (town, alt. 601, pop. 1363, sett. 1760, incorp. 1765), was incorporated as Murrayfield, in honor of John Murray, treasurer of the proprietors. Ten years later the citizens voted to change the name, apparently as a result of his Tory sympathies. When Murray left the country in 1778, he was forbidden to return.

Agriculture, including the production of maple sugar from 1800 trees, and the mining of mica, emery, and corundum have been the chief occupations of the people. The granite quarries are less important than formerly.

The advent of the railroad here drew the population away from Chester Center (*see Tour 4B*).

The *Hamilton Memorial Library* (*open Tues. and Fri.* 3–8.30) has a large collection of minerals.

Beyond (W) the *Town Hall* is a high promontory called *Big Rock*, providing a good view; here are the entrances to some of the old emery mines. The *Hamilton Emery and Corundum Company Plant* (*open by permission*), Middlefield Rd., is one of the oldest and most important manufacturers of emery in the country. It also refines Turkish and Naxos ore.

> Right from Chester on Middlefield Rd. to a trail at 1.3 *m.*; left on this to the summit of *Mt. Gobble* (alt. 1600). The ascent is facilitated at intervals by a stairway.

At 29.2 *m.* is a junction with a dirt road.

> Left on the road across a small bridge is a parking space. Up a hillside path about 1000 feet is the old *Wright Emery Mine*, with a horizontal shaft running through 900 feet of rock. The mine is flooded to a depth of a few inches most of the year.

Near-by are several other emery mines and a mica mine (*guides advised for exploration*).

At 31.5 *m*. is the blue-gray quarry region — home of Becket's early industry. Blocks of this colorful stone are seen along the highway.

At 32.5 *m*. is the foot of *Jacob's Ladder*; the climbing highway opens up many vistas of beautiful mountain country.

At 33.1 *m*. on a small plateau lies *Bonny Rigg Four Corners* (alt. 1400), a famous old stagecoach crossroads from which State 8 (*see Tour* 21) runs right.

US 20 rises steadily by a series of steep hills, passing many small clearings in the woods (*deer-hunting in season; picnic tables, parking places*).

At 34.9 *m*. is *Jacob's Well* (R) a wayside spring dating from ox-cart days. Near the top of the Ladder new forests of white pine are slowly restoring the richness of the woodland, damaged by an ice storm in 1920.

At 35.4 *m*. (alt. 2100), at the summit of the pass (*picnic and camping*), is a wooden *Tower* (*fee* 10¢) affording an extensive view.

At 37.4 *m*. is the junction with a side road.

Right on this road is the summer colony of *Ted Shawn's Dancing Group*, 1 *m*. (*performances open to public one day each week*), near Jacob's Dream.

US 20 drops gradually down into a marshy valley where lies *Shaw Pond* (*camping*); along its western bank, off State 8, is a thriving cottage colony.

At 38.6 *m*. is the junction (L) with State 8 (*see Tour* 21).

At 39.8 *m*. US 20 passes through the cutaway embankment of the 'Huckleberry Line' of the Berkshire Street Railway, and continues through wild country the chief crop of which was once huckleberries.

US 20 skirts the hill-banked shores of *Greenwater Pond* and traverses a narrow plain flanked by partly cleared mountain slopes.

At 42.1 *m*. is a junction with a dirt road.

Left on this road is *Upper Goose Pond* (*excellent fishing*).

Here is visible (R) a distant mountain range, with October Mountain the most prominent peak.

EAST LEE, 44.5 *m*. (alt. 940), was formerly a prosperous mill village, utilizing water-power from Greenwater Brook.

At 45.7 *m*. is the junction with State 102 and an unnumbered road.

1. Left on this unnumbered road, through the 'hidden vale of Tyringham,' at 3.4 *m*., built of stone and wood, with tapering towers, in landscaped gardens, is the *Home of the Sculptor, Henry Hudson Kitson*.

Across the valley at 4.4 *m*. (R) are visible the wooded slopes of Mt. Horeb, on which is *Fernside*, a former Shaker community. The meetings of the Shakers, inaugurated in 1784, led to the establishment of the colony in 1792. On the summit of Mt. Horeb they met in a rudely fenced yard containing bare wooden seats. It is said that true Shakers believed that there was an invisible tabernacle here in the midst of a beautiful garden where all kinds of fruit grew in abundance.

TYRINGHAM, 5.1 *m.* (town, alt. 900, pop. 243, sett. 1735, incorp. 1762), originally known as 'No. 1' of four townships granted in 1735, was bought from the Stockbridge Indians. It was named Tyringham at the suggestion of Lord Howe, who owned an estate in Tyringham, England. Maple sugar-making was learned here from the Indians. A paper mill was built in 1832, and the manufacture of hand rakes began even earlier.

At the Center is a brick smokestack beside the brook, all that remains of a flourishing paper mill of the 1850's.

Samuel Clemens (Mark Twain) lived in Tyringham during the summer of 1903, and presented the *Library* with a complete set of his books.

2. Left from US 20, State 102 crosses the Housatonic River at 0.2 *m.* and swings through an Italian colony. The *American Legion Park*, 0.3 *m.* (R), is a civic recreational field built on the site of a horse-racing track and park.

Straight ahead rises the long, lofty ridge of Beartown Mountain, for years the home of a hermit known as Beartown Beebe, whose weather predictions were published in many metropolitan dailies. The lowlands along the highway are called the Hoplands because of wild hops that grow beside the brooks and river. In these two regions several local skirmishes occurred in 1787 during Shays's Rebellion. On one occasion dummy cannon made of logs and mounted on ox-cart wheels were used by loyal militiamen to frighten Shays's rebels.

SOUTH LEE, 2.4 *m.* (alt. 844), lies beside the Housatonic River at the foot of high, forest-covered hills and mountains. Spanning the river is a *Covered Bridge.* Left from South Lee 0.5 *m.* on a dirt road are the scientifically constructed *Beartown Mountain Ski Trails*, in a section of the Beartown Mountain State Forest (*see Tour 4A*).

US 20, northwest of East Lee, parallels the Housatonic and threads its way among the fertile fields and rich farms.

LEE, 46.6 *m.* (town, alt. 888, pop. 4178, sett. 1760, incorp. 1777), named for General Charles Lee, later notorious for his treason to Washington, is a prosperous paper manufacturing town. Because of its abundant water power, three mills had been built by 1821; the Smith Paper Company, one of the first to use wood pulp, greatly reduced the price of newsprint. This company in 1913 began to manufacture India Bible paper, up to that time exclusively a British product. It is said that one half of the paper used in cigarettes during the World War was made in Lee.

The slender-spired *Congregational Church*, built in 1857, has walls and ceilings decorated by an itinerant German painter in true fresco. The white marble *Public Library* occupies the site of the log house where the original settlers held their first town meetings.

On Orchard St. is the entrance to *Ferncliff*, an evergreen-crowned eminence, on the northwest slope of which is *Peter's Cave*, where Peter Wilcox, Jr., condemned to die for his participation in Shays's Rebellion, hid for a time. He was captured, but was eventually pardoned.

Left from the village on West Park St., across the river, at 0.4 *m.*, a road runs left to the *Lime and Marble Quarries* that supplied marble for the Capitol at Washington, D.C., and for the Philadelphia City Hall. The small mill near-by has cut thousands of headstones for the graves of soldiers buried in Arlington Cemetery.

At 48 *m.*, where US 20 swings sharply across the railroad tracks and the river, is the entrance to the *Lee Paper Mills* (*open by permission*), established in 1808.

At 48.3 *m.* US 20 turns sharply right, ascends a steep hill, and passes charming *Laurel Lake* (*bathing, fishing*), 49.2 *m.* Back of the lake to the northwest amid forested green hills is *The Mount*, home of Mrs. Edith Wharton, the novelist. Henry James was a frequent guest here.

US 20 here gives glimpses of *Mt. Stockbridge* and *Mt. Baldhead* (L); far across Lake Mahkeenac (L), 49.9 *m.*, is the red-roofed castle-like villa in which Andrew Carnegie was living when he died in 1919. It is now a Jesuit novitiate, *Shadowbrook*.

LENOX, 51.8 *m.* (*see Tour* 17), is at the junction with US 7 (*see Tour* 17), with which US 20 unites, to PITTSFIELD, 58.4 *m.* (*see PITTSFIELD*).

Sec. d. PITTSFIELD to NEW YORK LINE, US 20, 7.8 m.

West of Pittsfield, US 20 crosses the Taconic Range.

At 3.4 *m.* is a splendid view of the mountains (N). Prominent in the group is the *'Ope of Promise* (*see HANCOCK, Tour* 17, *sec. a*), a knob-like peak on Tower Mountain. On this the spirits of dead Shakers were supposed to dwell.

The *Old Shaker Colony*, 4.7 *m.*, was established between 1780 and 1790. At the *Community House and Handicraft Shop* (*open May* 1–*Oct.* 1) the handicrafts are still cultivated, though less than a dozen members remain of a once large and prosperous community. There is a circular stone barn here.

The *Summit House* (alt. 1480) and an *Observation Tower* are at 6 *m.*

At 7.1 *m.* on *Lebanon Mountain* (alt. 1400) is a turnout from which there is a view of open fields, and in the distance the wooded tops of the New York Berkshires. In the heart of the valley are a group of buildings of the Lebanon (N.Y.) Shaker Village (L). The *Lebanon School for Boys* occupies a group of buildings formerly owned by a Shaker Community in New York State.

At 7.8 *m.* US 20 crosses the New York Line, 25 *m.* east of Albany, N.Y.

T O U R   4 A : *From* WORONOCO *to* GREAT BARRINGTON, 31 *m.*, State 23.

Via Blandford, Otis, and Monterey.

Road hard-surfaced and hilly. To be avoided in times of heavy snow, although usually passable for those familiar with it.

THE KNOX TRAIL (State 23), over which General Knox brought cannon from Fort Ticonderoga for General Washington's siege of Boston, is a section of the old stage road between Boston and Albany. It climbs

1500 feet in the first five miles, passing through woodlands and farming country. The scenery is especially delightful about the third week in June, when the mountain laurel is in bloom (*see Tour* 4).

State 23 branches west from US 20 at WORONOCO (alt. 255), and climbs steadily through a narrow valley, down which tumbles Potash Brook in a succession of little cascades. The *Old Milestone*, 1.9 *m.* (L), marked the stage road.

A little *Old Toll Gate House* (*private*) is at 4.2 *m.* The *Laurel Hill Stock Farm*, 4.8 *m.*, is famous for the Morgan horses which it breeds.

At 5.2 *m.* is the *Site of an Old Kaolin Mine*.

BLANDFORD, 5.8 *m.* (alt. 1440, town pop. 469, sett. 1735, incorp. 1741), settled by a Scotch-Irish group from Hopkinton, was at first called Glasgow, and the people of Glasgow, Scotland, offered the town a bell if the name were retained. Provincial Governor Shirley, who arrived from England on the ship 'Blandford,' denied the petition of the inhabitants and gave the town its present name.

About 1807, Amos M. Collins convinced the farmers that they should turn from the cultivation of grain and wool to the production of butter and cheese. He proposed to purchase the cows himself, sell them to the farmers, and accept payment in cheese. The venture was so successful that within a short time Blandford became one of the richest towns in the Berkshires. There is still a considerable output of dairy products, but orchardry has superseded dairy farming to some extent.

> Right from Blandford on North Blandford Rd. is NORTH BLANDFORD, 3.5 *m.* (alt. 1360). L. from North Blandford at 1.5 *m.* is *Long Pond.* The wild and rugged country surrounding this pond was used as the setting for many scenes in 'Tarzan' and in 'The Littlest Rebel,' with Shirley Temple.

Between Blandford and Otis, State 23 traverses a heavily wooded country with mountain laurel growing wild on both sides of the road.

At 11.5 *m.* is the junction with a dirt road.

> Right on this road is *Winnicut Lake*, 1 *m.* (*cottages, boating, bathing, fishing*), in which is a small rock island with a cave.

At 12.0 *m.* is the junction with a marked road.

> Left on this road is the *Otis Reservoir*, 0.5 *m.* (*bathing, fishing*). The *Falls on Otis Reservoir Brook*, an outlet of the reservoir and a tributary of the West Branch Farmington River, are visible at 2.1 *m.* The road continues to the *Tolland State Forest* (*see Tour* 13).

At 15.3 *m.*, set well back from the road, is the *John Davison House* (*private*), a belated example of New England Georgian architecture, built in 1787. The original pine paneling in the living-room has been restored to its satin finish.

OTIS, 15.8 *m.* (town, alt. 1240, pop. 415, sett. 1735, incorp. 1778), is at the junction with State 8 (*see Tour* 21). The town was named for Harrison Gray Otis, then Speaker of the House of Representatives. In the early 19th century the town had gristmills, tanneries, and forges; but today poultry-raising is the chief source of income.

St. Paul's Episcopal Church, built in 1828, has windows containing the old wavy glass. Adjoining is the *Squire Filley House* (*open on request*), a well-preserved brick house built in 1800. The imported wall paper in the living-room depicts the Coliseum at Rome, Italian olive groves, pastorals, and a marine sunset in full color.

In 1933, the Burgoyne Trail Association opened the first *Nudist Colony* (*no visitors*) in the Berkshires, founded in the belief that physical and mental health, a relaxing of nervous tension, a normal attitude toward sex, and a spiritual re-creation are fostered by properly regulated nudism.

At 17.6 *m.* is the main entrance to the *Otis State Forest*.

> Left on this road is *Upper Spectacle Pond*, 0.8 *m.*, an excellent picnic and camping area of about 30 acres, heavily stocked with trout from the State Fish Hatcheries.

At 19.4 *m.* is WEST OTIS (alt. 1390).

> 1. Left from West Otis on an unnumbered road is *Morley Brook*, at 1.1 *m.* A trail follows the bank of the brook to *Gilder Pond*, 1.6 *m.*, privately owned by Richard Watson Gilder, poet and fishing companion of ex-President Grover Cleveland. While fishing with his friend, Mr. Cleveland was approached by a game warden who demanded to see his fish. He had one bass which did not meet the required length, and he was fined ten dollars at the Great Barrington District Court. The poet paid the fine.
>
> 2. Right from West Otis on an improved road is the old *Rake Shop Dam*, confining the headwaters of Hop Brook, 2.3 *m.*, the sole remnant of the original industry of wooden rake-making.

At 20.2 *m.* (L) are the waters of *Piedmont Pond*, famous in summer for a mass of pink and white and gold water-lilies which with their dark-green pads almost cover its placid surface.

*Fine villas and cottages border the highway and in the distance (R) at 21.9 *m.* appears *Lake Garfield* (*boating, fishing, camping*). The approach to a summer cottage, at 22 *m.* (R), is flanked on each side by a pair of remarkably fine silver spruces.

MONTEREY, 23.1 *m.* (town, alt. 1200, pop. 325, sett. 1739, incorp. 1847), formerly a district of Tyringham, was named for the American victory of the Mexican War.

> Right from Monterey on an improved road is a fork at 0.7 *m.;* right here to a *Dam*, 0.9 *m.*, at the foot of Lake Garfield. The densely wooded shores of the lake are lined with masses of laurel.

At 25.5 *m.*, State 23 begins the descent of a long decline known as *Three-Mile Hill* (alt. 1160).

At 25.6 *m.* is the junction with a side road.

> Right on this road is the *Beartown State Forest*, 0.4 *m.* (*see LEE, Tour* 4), embracing 7714 acres (*picnic groves, foot and ski trails, fishing, bathing, hunting*). *Mt. Wilcox* (alt. 2155), the highest point in the area, will have a fire tower erected upon its summit. A thousand-acre tract has been set aside as a bird and game preserve.

At 27.5 *m.* is a junction with Lake Buel road.

> Left on this road at 1.2 *m.* is *Lake Buel* (*fishing*), the terminus of a *Bicycle Trail* from Canaan, Conn.

At 2.4 *m.* is the Center of the village of HARTSVILLE (alt. 920, Town of New Marlborough).

1. Left from Hartsville across the Konkapot River is a *Picnic Area* at 0.5 *m.* The Konkapot furnishes some of the finest trout-fishing in Berkshire County.

2. Left from Hartsville, on the second road (L), is the *Federal Fish Hatchery*, 0.5 *m.*, for breeding trout.

3. Right from Hartsville is a junction with a road (L) at 1 *m.* which leads south to MILL RIVER, at 4.7 *m.* (town, alt. 720, pop. 921, sett. 1738, incorp. 1775), seat of the Town of New Marlborough. Manufactures of gunpowder and paper were at one time important industries. Just below, on the Konkapot River was a mill, the second in the United States, where paper was made from straw. At the old Carroll Paper Mill, newsprint was made during the Civil War period for the *New York Tribune.* Dairy products are today shipped in large quantities to New York.

South from Mill River the road parallels the Konkapot River. At 6.1 *m.* is a road (L) leading to the *Umpachenee Falls*, 0.2 *m.*, descending a stairlike rock formation for 0.5 *m.*

The road continues south, and at 9 *m.* a path (L through a field leads to the entrance of *Cat Hole Cave*, over 400 feet deep, with several levels which may be reached by rough wooden ladders.

4. Straight ahead from Hartsville is NEW MARLBOROUGH, 3.5 *m.* (alt. 1380), formerly a station on the famous Red Bird Stagecoach Line. Here stands a *Monument to Elihu Burrit*, the 'Learned blacksmith.'

At 4.9 *m.* the road bears left and reaches the village of SOUTHFIELD at 7.7 *m.* (alt. 1220, Town of New Marlborough).

Rock Ledge, sometimes called Cook's Ledge (*accessible by motor*), 0.2 *m.* southeast of Southfield, affords a sweeping view. *Tipping Rock*, 0.4 *m.* southwest of Southfield, is a 40-ton boulder so delicately balanced that a pressure of the hand will sway but not dislodge it.

Straight ahead from Southfield the road (marked Norfolk, Conn.) continues southward up hill and down dale through forest and farm country. At 11.9 *m.* is the junction with a road (R.) which leads to CAMPBELL'S FALLS, 12.4 *m.*, in a State Reservation. This cataract, one of the most impressive and picturesque in the Berkshire region, was little known until recently. The Whiting River pours over a split-rock ledge in a spectacular drop of 80 feet, and then rushes on, foaming and swirling, through a deep gulch in the evergreen woods. A trail leads along the river bank from Canaan to Clayton, Conn., a distance of about 8 *m.*

At 28.6 *m.* is a junction with *Wildcat Foot Trail*, a branch of the Appalachian Trail (*see Tour* 9) which leads (L) to another section of the *Beartown State Forest* (*see above*), 2 *m.*, and (R) to top of Warner Mountain.

At 29.1 *m.* is an entrance (L) to *East Mountain State Forest Ski Trails* and *Great Barrington Sport Center*.

State 23 traverses hilly, pastoral country and at 31 *m.* reaches the junction with US 7 (*see Tour* 17).

T O U R   4 B : *From* HUNTINGTON *to* HINSDALE, 20.7 *m.*,
Sky Line Trail.

Via Chester Center and Middlefield.
Mostly hard-surfaced road; not recommended for winter or early spring.

THE SKY LINE TRAIL runs through heavily wooded and hilly country across the central Berkshire Hills. There are few points of interest
on this route, but the scenery is unusually attractive, especially during
the latter part of June, when mountain laurel is in bloom.
'Old US 20' branches northwest from US 20 about 0.1 *m.* west of the
Green in Huntington. At 1.3 *m.* the Sky Line Trail turns right and
abruptly ascends from the Valley of Roaring Brook to a plateau of
rolling hills at an altitude of 1500 feet.
CHESTER CENTER, 5.2 *m.* (alt. 601, Town of Chester), is the old
town center entirely cut off now from the modern center, Chester Village
(*see Tour* 4), by a high range of hills. The *Congregational Church* (L)
contains parts of the first church, which was located a little to the north
of the present site. The *De Wolf House* (*private*), probably the oldest
house in the town, is a fine Colonial type and was built about 1770.

> Right from the Center a dirt road passes through the valley of Day Brook. On a
> hillside at 1 *m.*, is *Hiram's Tomb*. Hiram Smith and his sister are buried in an
> enormous glacial boulder about 30 feet in diameter, a natural rock sepulchre. The
> vault is sealed with fragments of the granite chipped off in cutting out the tomb.
> It is recorded that Hiram had a horror of being buried in the ground and had this
> tomb made during the last years of his life. He willed enough money to have a
> highway leading to the entrance of his tomb kept in repair, but the trustee of this
> fund diverted the money to his own use, so the tomb is now in the midst of a hem-
> lock forest and difficult to find. The seeker must go on foot through briar, brush,
> and swamp to reach this unique mausoleum.

At 7 *m.*, from the top of the hill, is a grand view on both sides of the
highway: the beacon of Gobble Mountain (L) with the Berkshire peaks
beyond, and the Central Massachusetts hills and Mt. Monadnock in
New Hampshire.
The Sky Line Trail continues its climb, to level land atop a range of
hills. At 8.1 *m.* (R) is a *Fire Tower* from the summit of which is one of
the best views of a mountain area, extending north to Mt. Greylock
and east to Mt. Monadnock.
At 9.8 *m.* (L) is the *George Bell House* (*private*), once the headquarters
of Shays's insurgents.
At 10.3 *m.* is the junction with a country road (R).

> Right on this road at 2 *m.* are the *Glendale Falls*, a series of rapids and cascades, on
> Glendale Brook as it enters the Middle Branch of the Westfield River.

At 10.7 *m.*, the junction of the Huntington–Middlefield route with the

Chester–Middlefield Rd., stands (R) the *Harold Pease House* (*open*), an old dwelling formerly a tavern. The original diamond pattern of the old barroom floor is still plainly visible in the living room.

MIDDLEFIELD, 11.9 *m*. (town, alt. 918, pop. 220, sett. about 1780, incorp. 1783). Many of the settlers migrated from Connecticut and Pennsylvania after the Revolutionary War, impoverished by their losses at the hands of both the British and the Indians. Most of the inhabitants were loyal patriots and expelled a number of Tories. For some time after 1794 woolen goods were made in the homes of residents; later several mills and fulling houses were established. The demand for wool encouraged the raising of Saxony sheep, an occupation that flourished for a long period. In 1874 and 1901, great floods caused considerable loss; the town declined in prosperity and its factories removed to other sites. Cattle-raising thus assumed a new importance, and Middlefield became a beef-producing center.

The *Middlefield Fair Grounds* are located in the village on a high plateau. Here the Highland Agricultural Society, in existence since 1857, holds its annual fair and cattle show early in September.

One mile west of the Center (*no direct road*) is the *Site of the Dam* that once furnished power for the woolen mills in the valley below. The barrier broke in 1874 and again in 1901, causing so much damage the second time that the owners were not allowed to rebuild it. A great jagged hole in the middle of the old wall recalls the double catastrophe.

At 16 *m*. is the *Peru State Forest* (*camping grounds, fireplaces, tables, swimming*), a 1974-acre recreational area ideal for hiking and camping. From the camp grounds a foot trail northwest ascends *Garnet Hill*, from which may be obtained a remarkably fine view of the surrounding forests.

At 20.7 *m*. is the junction with State 8 (*see Tour* 21) about 0.8 *m*. south of Hinsdale.

T O U R　5 :　*From* BOSTON *to* NEW HAMPSHIRE LINE (*Salem*) 31.6 *m*., State 28.

Via Somerville, Medford, Stoneham, Melrose, Reading, Wakefield, Andover, North Andover, Lawrence, and Methuen.

B. & M. R.R. (Haverhill Division) parallels this route throughout.

Macadam and concrete roads; heavily traveled.

NORTH from Boston, State 28 passes along landscaped boulevards through an industrial and heavily settled area. The countryside gradually becomes more open, and the cities give way to rolling farmlands and residential towns.

West from the State House, Boston, on Beacon St. to Massachusetts Ave.; right on Massachusetts Ave. to junction with US 1 (*see Tour* 1), State 2, and State 28, at 2 *m.*; right on State 28, passing *Massachusetts Institute of Technology* (L) (*see CAMBRIDGE*).

At 4.5 *m.* is the junction with Somerville Ave.

Left on Somerville Ave. is SOMERVILLE, 0.5 *m.* (*see SOMERVILLE*).

At 6.5 *m.* US 1 (*see Tour* 1) branches right.

At 7.6 *m.*, at the junction of Fellsway West and East, is the *Immaculate Conception Convent*, awarded the Parker Medal for its architecture.

At 8.7 *m.* are Roosevelt Circle and the junction with Forest St.

Left on Forest St. is MEDFORD, 0.7 *m.* (*see MEDFORD*).

Between Medford and Stoneham, State 28 cuts through a section of Middlesex Fells. The *Old Man of the Fells*, 9.3 *m.*, is a rock formation with realistic profile, especially when thatched with snow.

At 11.3 *m.* on State 28 is the junction with South St.

Right on South St. is *Spot Pond*, one of the important distributing reservoirs of the Metropolitan System in the beautiful *Middlesex Fells Reservation*.

At 0.4 *m.* is the *Fells Zoo*, containing a large collection of wild animals.

STONEHAM, 12.2 *m.* (town, alt. 147, pop. 10,841, sett. 1645, incorp. 1725), was settled as part of Charlestown. Unsuited for farming, the town early developed small industries, such as shoemaking in private homes. Of the many factories into which these home industries expanded, only two large ones remain. Stoneham has become a residential suburb of Boston.

On the corner of Central and Pleasant Sts. is a house bearing a sign stating that it was built in 1826 on Summer St. as the first *Town House*, and in 1833 was moved by 40 yoke of oxen across a frozen meadow to its present site.

1. Left from Stoneham on Maple St. to Park St., 0.2 *m.*, which leads left to South Marble St., 0.6 *m.*, at the end of which, 1.3 *m.*, is a footpath running to the summit of *Bear Hill* (alt. 280). This hill was visited in 1632 by Governor Winthrop and an exploring party, who ate a meal on a rock near its base. They dubbed it *Cheese Rock* because they discovered that the Governor's aide had supplied them with cheese but no bread. From the *Observatory Tower* on a clear day there is a wide view, including the waters of the Atlantic.

2. Right from Stoneham on Franklin St. at 2.1 *m.* is the junction with Main St.; right on Main St. is MELROSE, 3 *m.* (city, alt. 55, pop. 24,256, sett. about 1629, incorp. town 1850, city 1899). Formerly a part of Malden, this district was known locally as the North End or North Malden.

The Boston and Maine Railroad, opened in 1845, was an important factor in increasing the population and in developing Melrose as a residential center. Chiefly a suburban city, Melrose manufactures a brand of 'Boston Baked Beans' sold from coast to coast.

Native of Melrose and a graduate of its public schools was Geraldine Farrar (b. 1883), dramatic soprano, member of the Metropolitan Opera Company.

Walter Emerson (d. 1895), cornetist, during most of his lifetime was a resident of Melrose.

Along the Lynn Falls *Fellsway* is *Sewall Woods Park*, the gift of the heirs of Judge Samuel Sewall, the abolitionist. It was a condition of the gift that the park remain wooded with uncut trees.

Left from Melrose on Grove St. at 0.3 *m.* is the junction with Lebanon St.; left on Lebanon St. to Laurel St. at 0.4 *m.*; right on Laurel St. at 1.4 *m.* is *Mt. Hood Park.* An *Observatory* provides a view ranging from New Hampshire's hills to the ocean horizon. Tradition states that upon this summit the Wampanoag Indians lighted signals fires by which they communicated with other tribes as far away as Mt. Wachusett.

The *Mt. Hood Reservation* (*municipal golf course; bath house, beach at Low Pond*), holds an annual Winter Carnival sponsored by the National Ski Association.

At 15.3 *m.* is READING (town, alt. 107, pop. 10,703, sett. 1639, incorp. 1644). The English title to the lands comprising Lynn and Reading was confirmed by the heirs of Wenepoykin, the deceased sachem of Lynn, for whose tribesmen this had been a favorite hunting ground.

Shoemaking and furniture-making prospered until the Civil War, when the loss of the Southern market and the increasing competition of mass production combined to ruin this business. Other factories grew up, however, for a great variety of products, but almost all are now idle. Today the town is chiefly residential.

The *Old South Church* (1818), on the Common, is a stately reproduction of the original church on this site.

On Washington St. near State 28 is the *Parker Tavern* (*open Sun. aft. 3–6, May–Oct.; guide; adm. free*), built 1694. During the Revolution the old place served as quarters for Colonel Campbell, a British officer captured at Boston Harbor in 1776. British officers taken in the War of 1812 were held here as 'guests.'

The *Reading Inn*, 633 Main St., is noted for its baked bean suppers. Beantown was the ancient nickname of Reading, and the coach which operated between Boston and Reading was called the Bean Pot.

The *Octagonal House* (*open*), 21 Pleasant St., has a novel interior arrangement.

Right from Reading on State 129 is the junction with Bay State Rd. at 1.4 *m.*; left 0.3 *m.* on this road is *Camp Curtis Guild*, the State Rifle Range, one of the best equipped camps in this section and site of the annual New England championship matches.

State 129 parallels the wooded shores of beautiful *Lake Quannapowitt* (*every form of fresh-water sport*), and turns right to WAKEFIELD, 2.9 *m.* (town, alt. 88, pop. 16,494, sett. 1639, incorp. 1812), named for one of its leading citizens, Cyrus Wakefield, who on Water St. established the first *Rattan Factory* in the world.

The *Beebe Memorial Library*, 1923, is one of the many public buildings designed by Cram and Ferguson. Their work here reflects late English Georgian influence. The building is constructed of red New Hampshire brick with limestone trim.

The *Hartshorne House* (*open 2.30–5*), 41 Church St., a restored dwelling (1663) is furnished with authentic Colonial furnishings.

On Prospect St., between Cedar St. and Fairmont Ave., is the *Emerson House* (*private*). Its exterior is plain, but details of the interior are wide board floors.

pegged, instead of nailed; beautiful paneling; hand-hewn beams pinned with wooden dowels; hand-wrought thumb-latches and H and L hinges; and early kitchen equipment, including a Dutch oven, cranes, and a spit.

Straight ahead from Wakefield on Main St., 3.5 *m*. are *Crystal Lake*, a local reservoir, and *Hart's Hill Reservation*, a natural park. Near-by stands a *Fire Tower* from the top of which on a clear day are visible the blue Atlantic, the misty Berkshires, and the wooded hills of New Hampshire.

At 3.6 *m*. on Main St. is the junction with Green St.; left here to Oak St. at 4.1 *m*., leading left to Nahant St. at 5 *m*.; right on Nahant St. to the *Wakesaw Reservation*, the name a combination of 'Wakefield' and 'Saugus,' 5.3 *m*., a State park of 600 acres with bridle paths and footpaths.

At 19.1 *m*. is the junction with State 62 (*see Tour* 1C).

At 21.3 *m*. on State 28 is a junction with State 125.

Right on State 125 0.4 *m*. to the *Harold Parker State Forest*, 2800 acres (*foot trails and picnic areas; hunting and fishing; small fee for use of fireplaces and wood*).

At 24.4 *m*. in Andover are the buildings of *Phillips Andover Academy* for boys, oldest incorporated school in the United States, established in 1778 by Samuel Phillips, Harvard graduate (1771), with the co-operation of his family. The school has today (1937) 650 students, a faculty of 70, and nearly 100 buildings.

The Phillips family, with William Bartlett and Moses Brown of Newburyport and John Noyes of Salem, also founded here Andover Theological Seminary, now situated in Newton. The Academy and the Seminary drew Lowells and Quincys from Massachusetts, Washingtons and Lees from Virginia. Eminent graduates have been Samuel F. B. Morse, Oliver Wendell Holmes, Josiah Quincy, and George Herbert Palmer.

On the corner of Phillips and Main Sts. is the *Phillips Academy Archaeology Museum* (*open weekdays* 9-5, *Sun.* 1-5; *adm. free*).

Pearson Hall (R), built in 1818 and then known as Bartlett Chapel, one-time center of the Theological Seminary, was also designed by Bulfinch. Its cupola is typical of his work. The half-windows which are placed in a long series between the arch-topped windows of the first story and the rectangular windows of the second story, designed to bring light to the chapel galleries and the library, are an unusual feature. *Bulfinch Hall* (1818) is named for its architect. The building shows Bulfinch characteristics, especially in the pediment on the projecting central section and the beautifully proportioned cupola. The interior has been altered, but the exterior remains much as it was when a Phillips graduate, Oliver Wendell Holmes, described it in his poem 'The School Boy.'

The *Phelps House* (*private*), on Main St., is attributed to Bulfinch. It is a two-story building with hip roof, balustraded parapet, Ionic portico, and central Palladian window. Elizabeth Stuart Phelps Ward, the novelist, lived here during her father's seminary professorship.

On the campus, directly opposite the Phelps House, is an *Armillary Sphere* in the Assyrian style, designed by Paul Manship. The *Memorial Tower* with its carillon of 37 bells was dedicated to Academy men who died in the World War. The *Oliver Wendell Holmes Library*, in Georgian style, decorated with murals, houses the Charles H. Forbes group of 'Virgiliana,' over 100 volumes, and Holmes's collection of first editions. On Chapel St. (R) are the red brick *Academy Chapel* and the *Elm Arch* shading the path across the campus to Salem St.

Phillips Inn, also on Chapel St., harmonizes architecturally with the surrounding buildings and is furnished with Colonial pieces, old engravings, and Currier and Ives prints. Behind the inn is the gambrel-roofed stone *Stowe House* (1828). Remodeled in 1852, it became the residence of Harriet Beecher Stowe, author of 'Uncle Tom's Cabin.' 'Dred' was written in the study on the lower floor. She is buried in near-by Chapel Cemetery beside the son she mourned in 'Only a Year.'

Also on Chapel St. is the *Addison Gallery of American Art* (*open weekdays 9–5; Sun. 2.30–5; free*). Completed in 1931, this Georgian style building houses an excellent·collection of American paintings, including works by Ryder, Sully,.Copley, Sargent, Whistler, John Marin, Preston Dickinson, and Thayer. There is also a fine collection of American silver, furniture, models of famous American ships, prints, and sculpture.

On Chapel St. (R), is *George Washington Hall*, administrative center of the Academy, named to commemorate the friendship of General Washington with its founder. Left from here are the blue of *Rabbit's Pond* (*skating and boating*) and the 150-acre tract of the *Moncrieff Cochran Bird Sanctuary* beyond.

ANDOVER, 25 *m.* (town, alt. 92, pop. 10,542, sett. about 1642, incorp. 1646), was purchased from the Indians about 1643 by John Woodbridge, for £6 and a coat. Known as Cochichewick (Indian, 'Place of the Great Cascade'), it was named Andover for the English home of early settlers.

Powder mills built during and after the Revolution were operated by Samuel Phillips until they were destroyed by explosions. Then Phillips established a paper mill and Abraham Marland commenced the manufacture of woolen cloth; flannel-weaving was begun, the first flax products mills in the country opened. Mulberry trees were planted to furnish food for silkworms in a futile attempt to produce silk. Present industries are the making of rubber and woolen goods.

From the Center, where ancient elms cast their shadows across smooth lawns and stately residences, to the summit of the Hill, dignified by Phillips Academy, Andover displays the serenity of a cultured tradition.

The *Andover Historical Society House* (*open Tues. and Sat. 3–5; adm. free*) on Main St., built in 1819, has 19th-century furnishings.

The *America House* (*private*), 147 Main St., makes up in interest what it lacks in architectural beauty, for it was here that Samuel F. Smith when but 24 wrote the words of 'America.'

The 25-acre campus and the buildings of *Abbot Academy*, named for Mrs. Nehemiah Abbot, wife of the Steward of the Commons at Phillips Academy, are close to State 28 on School St. Founded in 1829, this was the earliest incorporated school for girls in New England. The first building on the extreme left is the *John Esther Art Gallery* (1907), containing a small collection of oils, bronzes, and engravings.

At the *Samaritan House* (*private*), on Main St., identified by its hip roof, elliptical porch, and Corinthian columns, Harriet Beecher Stowe wrote the 'Key to Uncle Tom's Cabin.'

The *Isaac Abbot Tavern* (*private*), 70 Elm St., was probably built in 1740.

Left from Andover Square on Central St. to the junction with Andover St. at 0.9 *m.*; left on Andover St., where on the corner of Argilla Rd. is the *Benjamin Abbot Homestead*, 1.1 *m.* (*owned by the Society for the Preservation of New England Antiquities; not yet open to visitors*). Erected in 1685, it is said to be the oldest house in town. The walls, dark and weathered, the lean-to roof with pilastered central chimney, the ridgepole sagging under the weight of years, link it in age with the gigantic elm tree in the yard.

At 26.2 *m.* is SHAWSHEEN (alt. 40, Town of Andover), formerly a company village, planned by William Wood, president of the American Woolen Company, to embody architectural beauty, efficient operation, and pleasant working conditions for mill employees.

Right from Shawsheen on State 133 is the junction with Andover St. 2 *m.*; right on Andover St. to NORTH ANDOVER CENTRE, 2.1 *m.* (town, alt. 53, pop. 7164, sett. before 1644, incorp. 1885), the oldest section of historic Andover. The Davis and Furber Machine Co., textile machinery manufacturers, and the M. T. Stevens and Sons Co. Mills are leading industries.

East of the Common is the *Kittredge Memorial*, commemorating the family of Thomas Kittredge, surgeon of the 1st Regiment in the Revolutionary War. The *Kittredge Mansion* (1784) (*private*), just north of the Green at 114 Academy Rd., is a three-story dwelling with a belvedere and two large chimneys.

At 148 Osgood St., which branches from Massachusetts Ave. at the end of the Green, is the gambrel-roofed *Phillips Mansion* (*private*), built in 1752 by Samuel Phillips, one of the founders of Phillips Academy, Andover. The house, with fields behind it, is set on a wide lawn in the shade of tall trees.

Just opposite stands the white *Bradstreet House* with a central chimney and lean-to roof. The house was built in 1667 by Governor Bradstreet, whose wife was Anne Dudley Bradstreet, the Colonial poet, who as an 18-year-old girl came over in the 'Arbella,' leaving a life of ease for the hardships of the pioneer settlement.

On Great Pond Rd., within sound of the Paul Revere Bell in the *North Parish Church*, is *Cochichewick Lake* (*no swimming; boating and fishing by permit*), half hidden among the rolling hills.

At 28.7 *m.* is the junction with Essex St.

Right on Essex St. into LAWRENCE, 0.7 *m.* (*see LAWRENCE*).

At 29.6 *m.* is the large plant of the *Arlington Mills* (*see LAWRENCE*).

METHUEN, 30.6 *m.* (town, alt. 105, pop. 21,073, sett. about 1642, incorp. 1725), formerly in Haverhill, was named for Lord Paul Methuen, an English official of pre-Revolutionary days. Industrial development began after the Civil War; today the local products are diversified and of considerable value.

The *Spicket River Bridge*, 0.2 *m.* south of the Center on State 28, has cruciform-slotted square stone towers (R) and round towers (L).

About 0.4 *m.* east of the Center, off Charles St., is *Daddy Frye's Hill*,

topped by the gray-stone towers of *Tenney Castle* and the battlemented
walls of the Searles estate. During the 19th century, Mark and Nathaniel
Gorrill, brothers, courted and were rejected by the same girl. They
became hermits, never speaking to each other, though they continued
to live in their homestead on Daddy Frye's Hill near the Castle. Recently a townsman said he had dreamed of hidden treasure in a wall;
the place was searched, and in the cellar of one of the Castle's towers
was found $20,000 in bonds, presumably hidden by the brothers.

The *Nevins Memorial Hall and Library (open weekdays except holidays
1.30–9)*, 0.3 *m.* north of the Center, built in 1888 of mellow brick, with
cloistered portico and stained-glass windows, was designed by Samuel
J. F. Thayer.

At 31.1 *m.* are the stables of the large *Vacation Farm for Horses*, given
to the Massachusetts Society for the Prevention of Cruelty to Animals
by Harriet F. Nevins. Race-horses recuperate here between seasons,
and dray-horses rest from years of labor.

At 31.6 *m.*, State 28 crosses the New Hampshire Line, about 25 *m.* south
of Manchester, N.H.

T O U R   6 : *From* ORLEANS *to* RHODE ISLAND LINE
(*Providence*) 87.6 *m.*, US 6.

Via Brewster, Dennis, Yarmouth, Barnstable, Sandwich, Bourne, Wareham,
Rochester, Marion, Mattapoisett, Fairhaven, New Bedford, Dartmouth, Westport, Fall River, Swansea, and Seekonk.

N.Y., N.H. & H. R.R. services this area.

Hard-surfaced road, concrete and asphalt paving.

US 6 on this part of the Cape skirts the shore of Cape Cod Bay, running
through white dunes, pine woods, and cranberry bogs that only occasionally allow a view of the gray or blue of the water. West of the Cape
it cuts south to skirt the west shore of Buzzard's Bay.

ORLEANS (town, alt. 35, pop. 1425, sett. 1693, incorp. 1797) was
presumably named for Louis Philippe, Duke of Orleans, who visited
New England in 1797. The settlers were engaged in shipping, shell
fisheries, and salt works. Windmills and surf mills were used to pump
the sea water for the latter into vats on the shore.

Orleans, like other coast towns, suffered during the War of 1812, but
immediately afterward had a return of prosperity and the number of
salt works increased to 50, cod fisheries developed, and the fields, fertilized by horseshoe crabs and seaweed, were cultivated. Even manu-

facturing, represented by a shirt and overalls factory, was attempted, and lasted till about 1900. Catering to tourists is now the most profitable occupation.

Orleans was the setting for Joseph C. Lincoln's novel 'Mr. Pratt'; Thoreau gave excellent descriptions of it in 'Cape Cod'; and Elizabeth Reynard has preserved local folklore in 'The Narrow Land.'

In Orleans on US 6 is the *Site of Jeremiah's Gutter*, the first Cape Cod Canal. In 1717, the water had a free sweep through this cut, enabling a whaleboat to pass from the bay to the ocean.

    1. Right from Orleans on Rock Harbor Rd. at 0.3 *m.* is the junction with Skaket Rd., left on which at 1.2 *m.* is the *Linnell House* (1855), on Rock Harbor Rd., built by Captain Eben Linnell, skipper and tea trader renowned for a record trip from the Thames to Hong Kong in 83 days. The design of his home was based on a country house in southern France that the Captain had noted on one of his many voyages; he added the traditional widow's walk.

    At the end of Rock Harbor Rd. is the *Town Landing*, 1.1 *m.* This is the *Site of the Battle of Orleans*, in which, in December, 1814, Orleans militia repulsed a British landing party.

    2. Left from Orleans to *Nauset Beach*, 3.3 *m.*, where one quiet Sunday morning in July, 1918, a submarine rose suddenly offshore and bombarded a tug and three coal barges, firing 147 shots in a little more than an hour. The aviation base at Chatham was notified, but all the flyers were away playing baseball; one plane arrived eventually and dropped monkey-wrenches on the spot where the submarine had been. There is still no explanation why a 'German' submarine should have wasted 147 shots on empty coal barges when the town lay at its mercy.

At 0.9 *m.* is *Higgins Tavern (private)*, a gray two-and-a-half-story inn with red trim, once a stagecoach station. Thoreau once spent a night here before hiking the 30 miles to Provincetown. The old ballroom has in recent years been used as a summer theater by the Drama Guild of Orleans.

At 2.8 *m.* is the *Roland C. Nickerson Park (cabins, tent sites; trout and salmon fishing).* This 1727-acre tract was the first park in Massachusetts to be administered by the State Conservation Commission.

BREWSTER, 5.7 *m.* (town, alt. 116, pop. 715, sett. 1656, incorp. 1803), was named for William Brewster of Plymouth Colony. Fortunes made at sea in the early 19th century brought wealth to the town and built luxurious homes.

The *Captain Elijah Cobb House* (1800), off US 6, 0.2 *m.* west of the Center, is a yellow two-story late Georgian house surmounted by a widow's walk. The stirring life of Captain Cobb, a wealthy shipmaster, is told in 'The Memoirs of a Cape Cod Skipper.'

The *Joseph C. Lincoln Birthplace* (1870–   ), 0.3 *m.* north of the Center, is a small one-and-a-half-story white clapboarded house. Mr. Lincoln has used Brewster as a setting for many of his stories. The writer's father was the last of a long line of sea captains.

At 8.2 *m.* are the two *Dillingham Houses* (1660), one of the salt-box type, with small enclosed old-fashioned gardens.

At 9.4 *m.* is the junction with a road.

Right on this road is the site of *Sears' Folly*, 0.8 *m.* John Sears in 1776 constructed what is said to have been the first vat on Cape Cod for making salt by solar evaporation of sea water. He began by using a vat 100 feet in diameter and 10 feet high, with rafters over it, and shutters so contrived as to cover the vat when it rained and expose it to the rays of the sun on fair days. Local people called it Sears' Folly, but in time this invention built up a two-million-dollar business.

DENNIS, 12.2 *m.* (town, alt. 160, pop. 2017, sett. 1639, incorp. 1793), originally in Yarmouth, was named for the Rev. Josiah Dennis, pastor of the first meeting house. Important in the fishing and coasting trade, Dennis in 1837 had 150 skippers sailing from American ports. It also had salt works.

About 1816 cranberry culture was started at North Dennis, by a native who noticed that wild cranberries grew best when a light sand covering had been blown over them. Sand overlay is now an essential part of the cultivation of these berries.

At Dennis are the *Cape Playhouse* and *Cape Cinema.* The Playhouse was once a Colonial meeting house in Barnstable; and the Cinema, one of the smallest in America, has Rockwell Kent murals and a façade copied from that of the Congregational Church in Centerville. Many celebrated actors have appeared in the theater in try-outs of plays that became Broadway hits. The two buildings, located on a 27-acre farm, are surrounded by flower gardens and landscaped woodlands.

Left from Dennis on an improved road to *Scargo Hill*, 0.6 *m.*, topped by *Tobey Tower*, affording an expansive view of Cape Cod Bay, and the Atlantic, with Cape Cod, a narrow arm between them.

YARMOUTH, 16.3 *m.* (town, alt. 24, pop. 2095, sett.-incorp. 1639), is known for its elm-shaded streets. Yarmouth's history is typical of that of the Cape in general, and after the confusion of the Revolutionary War, like other Cape towns, it struggled to adapt itself to new conditions. A large share of the ships which New England sent in response to alluring opportunities offered by the Napoleonic Wars were commanded and sailed by men from Cape Cod, with those of Yarmouth in the forefront. The years between 1815 and 1855 saw the zenith of its prosperity, with great activity both ashore and afloat. Just before the Civil War, however, the glory of the American merchant marine began to fade, the fishing business tended to become concentrated in Gloucester, Boston, and Provincetown, and the Yarmouth fleet, like those of the other Cape towns, gradually went out of existence.

Captain Asa Eldridge of Yarmouth, one of the famous Cape skippers, made a memorable racing voyage across the Atlantic in the clipper 'Red Jacket.'

At the Center cn US 6 the *Thacher House* (*open as antique shop*), bears the date 1680 on its large square chimney.

BARNSTABLE, 19.8 *m.* (town, alt. 40, pop. 8037, sett. 1637, incorp. 1639), was settled by the Rev. Joseph Hull and Thomas Dimmock, with their band of followers. The pioneers were undoubtedly attracted by the great marshes that yielded an abundance of salt hay for their cattle.

A trading establishment set up in 1700 developed into a commercial exchange dealing in codfish caught on the Grand Banks and rum and molasses made in the West Indies. By 1800 Barnstable was prospering from a general coasting trade and the Northwest fur trade. The town, now a popular summer resort, is the county seat for all Cape Cod.

The *Sturgis Library* (1645), on US 6, a good example of the old Cape Cod style house, is one of the oldest library buildings in the United States.

On a small triangular Green at the Junction of US 6 and Rendezvous Lane is the *Site of the Liberty Pole*, erected in Revolutionary days. When the pole disappeared, Aunt 'Nabby' Freeman, a defiant Tory who had publicly threatened 'straightway to heave that dead tree up,' was tarred and feathered and ridden from town astride a wooden rail.

At 21.1 *m.* is *Sacrament Rock*, a large boulder with bronze tablet, inscribed: 'Here the settlers received their first sacrament in 1639, and held their first town meeting.'

The *Coach House* (1640) at 21.2 *m.*, is a good example of the salt-box type house; this building, gay with Cape Cod blue trim, has never been structurally altered.

At 22.2 *m.* is the junction with Oak St.

Left on this road to the summit of *Shoot Flying Hill*, 0.7 *m.*, from which there is a clear view of *Sandy Neck* (N.), 7 *m.*, of marshes and sand, one of the Cape's most beautiful dune formations.

At 24 *m.* is WEST BARNSTABLE (alt. 42).

Left from West Barnstable on State 49 at 0.8 *m.* is a white *Congregational Church* (1717), believed to be the oldest structure in the country belonging to this denomination.

At 27.4 *m*, is the junction with a side road.

Left on this road to the *State Game Farm*, where pheasants are propagated.

At 28 *m.* is the junction with a side road.

Left on this road to 1.3 *m.* to the *State Fish Hatchery*, a swamp and marsh area utilized especially for the propagation of trout.

SANDWICH, 31.2 *m.* (town, alt. 15, pop. 1516, sett. 1637, incorp. 1639), named for the town in England, was the first place on the Cape to be settled. From 1825 to 1888 it was famous for its beautifully colored glass made from a secret formula, now lost. The first pressed and the first lace glass in America were made here. At present cranberry culture is the chief occupation.

The *Sandwich Historical Museum* (*open Wed.* 2–5; *adm.* 25¢), at Main St. and Tupper Rd., a two-and-a-half-story building, houses relics related to the early history of the town, including a notable collection of Sandwich glass.

The *Congregational Church*, corner of Water and Main Sts., with its beautiful spire, is a favorite subject for painters.

The *Hoxie House* (*open; adm.* 25¢), in a lane near Shawme Lake, at the head of School St., is of the salt-box type, with thick hand-hewn timbers and recessed windows. A brick in the original chimney was dated 1637, establishing the house as one of the first erected by the 'ten men of Saugus.'

The *Daniel Webster Inn* on Main St. is a rambling old building with several ells. It contains the room regularly occupied by Daniel Webster when he stopped here on fishing and hunting trips.

On Main St. is the entrance to the *Shawme State Forest Reservation* (*tenting, picnicking*).

At SAGAMORE, 33.6 *m.* (alt. 18, town of Bourne), US 6 crosses *Sagamore Bridge*, spanning the *Cape Cod Canal*. It is the longer twin of the Bourne Bridge (*see Tour* 19).

The Cape Cod Canal is an 8-mile-long cut connecting Cape Cod Bay and Buzzards Bay, and providing a shorter and safer passage from Boston to Long Island Sound. When present work on the channel is completed, it will be 32 feet deep and 500 feet wide. The tidal current here runs 4–7 miles an hour, and traffic moves alternately east and west. This route was used as a waterway by the Indians who portaged from Scusset Creek to Manomet River. In 1627 Governor Bradford and the Plymouth Colony established a trading-post at the mouth of the Scusset Creek, where they exchanged commodities with the Dutch traders from New York. In 1697 the General Court of Massachusetts ordered a report made on the possibilities of a canal.

In 1914, the canal, started in 1909 and built by the Boston, Cape Cod, and New York Canal Company, was opened. In 1927, it was purchased by the Federal Government for $11,500,000. Over 10,000,000 tons, gross, of shipping pass through the canal annually.

At 38 *m.* US 6 passes under the Bourne Bridge (*see Tour* 19), similar to the one at Sagamore but shorter.

At 38.2 *m.* is the junction with State 28 (*see Tour* 19).

At 39.6 *m.* US 6 crosses the Buttermilk Bay Bridge.

At 40 *m.* is the junction with Onset Rd.

Left on this road, which crosses Onset Bay Bridge, in ONSET, 1.9 *m.* (alt. 23 town of Wareham), a delightful summer resort attracting a summer colony and several thousand visitors every season. Here 50 years ago was one of the first Spiritualist colonies on the Atlantic Coast.

At 42.7 *m.* is the junction with the White Island Rd.

Right on this dirt road to a *Massachusetts Experimental Station*, 0.4 *m.*, concerned chiefly with the cultivation of cranberries.

At 42.8 *m.* US 6 crosses the Agawam River, up which herring annually fight their way (*see Tour* 19).

At 42.9 *m.* State 28 (*see Tour* 19) branches right.

WAREHAM, 45 *m.* (town, alt. 8, pop. 6047, sett. 1678, incorp. 1739), engaged first in whaling, then, following the Revolution, in shipbuilding, of which the Cape Cod Shipbuilding Corporation on the Wareham River is the only remnant; it is now the center of the cranberry industry. Nail manufacturing and the shellfish business — particularly the oyster — are important additional sources of income.

During the War of 1812 Wareham was attacked, some ships were burned, and a cotton factory at Wankinko Dam was partly destroyed.

The *Benjamin Fearing House* (*private*), Main St., part of it 300 years old, is a weather-beaten two-and-a-half-story dwelling.

The *Tremont Nail Factory* (*visited by permission*), ¼ *m.* northwest of the house, more than a century old, is still in operation.

At 49.3 *m.* is the junction with State 105 and Front St.

    1. Right on State 105 is ROCHESTER, 3.2 *m.* (town, alt. 140, pop. 1229, sett. about 1638, incorp. 1686). First known as Sippician, the town was named Rochester for the English home of some of its settlers. At that time, it included the harbors on Buzzards Bay now belonging to the towns of Mattapoisett and Marion, and had a thriving coastal trade.

    The *Congregational Church* at the Center was erected in 1837. It is of wood, painted white, with a graceful spire.

    2. Left on Front St. is MARION, 0.6 *m.* (town, alt. 29, pop. 1867, sett. 1679, incorp. 1852). Marion was set off from Rochester and named for General Francis Marion, southern Revolutionary hero. The usual small industries developed here, replacing agriculture, but these in turn were overshadowed by marine activities. Ships were built for 150 years, the last vessel leaving the ways in 1878.

    Tabor Academy (1877), Front St., ranks high among the smaller private preparatory schools that contribute to the educational prestige of Massachusetts.

The Radio Corporation of America's giant *Wireless Station* at 49.5 *m.* receives and transmits messages to ships in coastal and transatlantic shipping services.

At 50 *m.* is the *Holmes Memorial Woods* (*free camp sites*), an unusually attractive place, maintained by the town.

At 50.3 *m.* is junction with Converse Rd.

    Left on Converse Rd. is the *Nye Homestead* (*private*), built between 1750 and 1760 and since then slightly altered, with the original old doors with hand-wrought latches; its hand-hewn timbers and framework are still fastened together with treenails and hand-forged nails.

At 53.6 *m.* is a junction with an improved road.

    Left on this road is MATTAPOISETT (Indian, 'Place of Rest'), 1.3 *m.* (town, alt. 9, pop. 1682, sett. 1750, incorp. 1857), now a summer resort, but once busy with shipbuilding, salt-manufacture, and whaling.

    The post-office, corner of Cannon and Main Sts., bears a plaque inscribed: 'Francis Davis Millet, born Mattapoisett — Nov. 3, 1846. Drummer Boy — War Correspondent — Author — Illustrator. Went down on the *Titanic* April 15, 1912.' The building was Millet's birthplace.

    Shipyard Park is the site of Jonathan Holmes's shipyard, where, in 1878, the last whaler of Mattapoisett, the 'Wanderer,' was built. The mizzenmast of this ship serves as a flagpole in the park. Many of the whalers flying pennants from New Bedford were built here.

Mattapoisett Harbor, south of the Center, is a rendezvous for the New York Yacht Club and the Eastern Yacht Club; upon their arrival and during their annual cruise (*Aug.* 10–18), special events are planned in the town.

At 55.8 *m.* on the Mattapoisett River is the *Mattapoisett Herring Weir*. Thousands of visitors come to this spot each spring to watch the annual run. (*See AGAWAM RIVER, Tour* 19.)

FAIRHAVEN, 60 *m.* (town, alt. 45, pop. 11,005, sett. 1660, incorp. 1812), was originally known as Sconticut, the name of the Indian tribe formerly living here, and separated from New Bedford in 1812. Whaling was important and, in 1858, 48 whaling vessels were owned locally. Shipbuilding and allied industries were also pursued; and there are still four boatyards actively engaged in the overhauling, repairing, and refitting of pleasure craft.

William Bradford (1823–92), marine artist and descendant of the first Pilgrim governor of Plymouth, was born here. A member of the National Academy of Design, his paintings have hung in the private apartments of Queen Victoria of England and in the London Royal Academy. He twice accompanied Arctic exploration expeditions.

The group of buildings comprising the *Unitarian Memorial Church* was dedicated in 1904. The church proper is an adaptation of the then prevalent Early English perpendicular Gothic, while the *Parish House* and *Parsonage* are imitations of a later phase of the style.

The *Millicent Library*, completed in 1893, was designed by Charles Brigham of Boston. A not too masterful adaptation of the Italian Renaissance, its style was obviously influenced by the already famous, but not yet completed, Boston Public Library building. The library was given to Fairhaven in memory of Millicent Rogers, whose father, Henry H. Rogers, gave the town many public buildings.

The *Fairhaven Academy* (*open by appointment*), on Main St., built 1798, has a beautiful old fanlight over the front door, and old wide pine floor boards in the bottom story. One of the schoolrooms, in its original state, has the old benches and desks for pupils, a raised platform at the side for the teacher, and a hand-made school bell.

The *Coggeshall Memorial Building* (*open weekdays* 9–5, *Sun.* 2–5), at 6 Cherry St., was given to the Colonial Club in 1916. The museum contains etchings, engravings, and Colonial furnishings.

At 60.6 *m.* US 6 crosses Acushnet River.

NEW BEDFORD, 61.2 *m.* (*see NEW BEDFORD*), is at the junction with State 140 (*see Tour* 23*B*).

At 63.7 *m.* is the junction with Slocum Rd.

Left on Slocum Rd. at 2.3 *m.* is the junction with Elm St.; left on this road is PADANARAM, 4 *m.* (town of Dartmouth, alt. 240, pop. 9424, sett. 1650, incorp. 1664), named for Dartmouth, England, to which the 'Mayflower' went for repairs after having set sail from Southampton.

During King Philip's War the town was practically annihilated. It was rebuilt, and received an influx of tradesmen and mechanics when whaling developed in

Bedford village; Portuguese arriving about 1870 on a whale ship were the nucleus of a Portuguese colony. Though the town, near the end of the 19th century, became temporarily popular as a summer resort, it is now largely dependent on farming and dairying.

Right from Padanaram at the traffic light on Bridge St., over the Apponaganset River is the junction with Smith's Neck Rd. at 4.4 *m.*; left on this road which parallels Apponaganset Bay, where yachts ride at anchor. At 7.3 *m.* (traffic lights) is the entrance to the *Colonel E. H. R. Green Estate* (*open*), on whose beach is the old whaler 'Charles W. Morgan,' embedded in the sand and protected by a cement wall; this ship is said to have sailed more miles and taken more whales than did any other of its kind.

At 7.7 *m.* is the junction with Little River Rd.; (R) on this road is RUSSELL'S MILLS (town of Dartmouth). Here is (R) the *Puppet Theater*, oldest marionette theater in the United States.

Right on Russell's Factory Rd. is the *Friends' Meeting House*, 13.3 *m.*, on the bank of the Paskamansett River. This large, square, unpainted two-and-a-half-story building, erected 1790, has records of meetings of the local society as early as Aug., 1699. Meetings are still held here in summer.

At 15.6 *m.* is the junction with Elm St. (*see above*).

WESTPORT MILLS, 67.6 *m.* (alt. 60, town of Westport), a small village, is built around the textile-manufacturing company from which it derives its name. The first mill was built in 1812.

Left from the village on an improved road is CENTRAL VILLAGE, 7.6 *m.* (town of Westport, alt. 140, pop. 4335, sett. 1670, incorp. 1787). In 1652 the land here, then in the town of Dartmouth, was purchased from the Indians by Miles Standish and several others. The first settlement was made 18 years later, many settlers being members of the Society of Friends. They established their right to their own religious forms and beliefs, but when the town was devastated during King Philip's War the Plymouth Court declared this was 'an evidence of the wrath of the Almighty against the people for their neglect to worship in the Puritan faith.'

Clifford Ashley, the marine artist, lives near Westport Point on Drift Rd.

The *Friends' Meeting House* at the Center was moved to its present site in 1840. In the meeting house yard stands a granite *Memorial to Captain Paul Cuffee* (1759–1817), son of a freed Negro slave; Captain Cuffee, a Friend, amassed a fortune at sea and won important civil rights for his race when he successfully refused to pay the personal property tax, basing his refusal on his lack of citizenship rights; he was the first Negro to be granted all privileges enjoyed by white men in Massachusetts. At one time he attempted to form a colony for Negro slaves in Sierra Leone.

Straight ahead from Central Village on West Beach Rd. to *Horseneck Beach*, 6.4 *m.* (*sections privately owned, but open for small fee*), a hard sandy beach extending for about 1.5 *m.* along Horseneck Beach Rd. to *East Beach*, a part of Horseneck. From this drive the Elizabeth Islands and the gay-hued cliffs of Gay Head are visible.

At 75 *m.* is FALL RIVER (*see FALL RIVER*), which is at the junction with State 138 (*see Tour 25*).

At 76.5 *m.* US 6 crosses Taunton River and continues through open country.

At 78.8 *m.* is the junction with Gardner's Neck Rd., a tarred highway.

Right on this road at 0.4 *m.* is the junction with Main St.; (R) on Main St. is SWANSEA, 0.7 *m.* (town, alt. 120, pop. 4327, sett. 1632, incorp. 1668), a part of Old Rehoboth until the Baptists in 1667 under Obadiah Holmes, who had settled in Rehoboth 1649, created a separate town. It is memorable as the place where the first blood was shed (1675) in King Philip's War, during the course of which the town was a place of assembly for the Massachusetts troops. At one time, shipbuilding played an important part in its growth. The town is now essentially agricultural.

The *Cape Codder*, a house at Swansea Village near Gray's corner, is said to be about 250 years old. Although considerably modernized, it still retains its original mammoth central chimney and traces of its early architectural lines. Used at one time as the Town Hall, it is now the property of Christ Church (Episcopal).

Abram's Rock is reached through the land at the rear of the house. The legend is that an Indian, called Abram by the white people, deserted his tribe and sought refuge in the town. Captured by the Indians, he was given the choice of 'death at the stake or three leaps from the top of the rock to the ground below.' The first and second leaps were safely made, but the third proved fatal.

At 83.4 *m.* is the *First Baptist Church* (L) established 1663 when John Myles, a Welsh Baptist and one of Cromwell's Tryers, fleeing the intolerance of Charles II's reign, took his congregation to Rehoboth. Here they were allowed to remain on condition that they establish their meeting place at a considerable distance from that of the standing order.

At 86.9 *m.* is a junction with a paved road.

Right on this road is SEEKONK, 1 *m.* (town, alt. 140, pop. 5011, sett. 1636, incorp. 1812). The name (Indian, 'Black Goose') indicates an abundance of these birds prior to the coming of the white men. In 1862 a part of the town was set aside as East Providence, reducing the area and leaving a population of but 800. There is now one factory, making tennis racquets and croquet sets.

At 87.6 *m.* US 6 crosses the Rhode Island Line about 5 *m.* southeast of Providence, R.I.

T O U R   6 A : *From* ORLEANS *to* PROVINCETOWN, 28.4 *m.*, US 6.

Via Eastham, Wellfleet, Truro.

Cape Cod Division of N.Y., N.H., & H. R.R. parallels route.

Hard-surfaced road, but curves make fast driving unsafe; open except during heavy blizzards in January and February.

NORTH of Orleans, US 6 is shaded by locust trees; all along the route are views of far-reaching yellow dunes freckled with patches of coarse grass and clumps of bayberry; of exquisite small lakes cupped in piney hollows; of hamlets still retaining much of their ancient charm.

At 2.1 *m.* is the junction with a packed sand road.

Right on this road at its end, 0.2 *m.*, is an *Old Indian Burying Ground*, on a knoll overlooking Nauset Inlet. The skeletons of seven Indians were discovered here in 1935.

At 3.2 *m.* is EASTHAM (town, alt. 36, pop. 606, sett. 1644, incorp. 1651), explored in 1606 by Champlain, who anchored his ship off Chatham.

Dangerous shoals kept the French from settling here, just as they deterred the Pilgrims 14 years later. In 1644, however, 49 persons from Plymouth returned and formed the village of Nausett.

The worst foes were not Indians, but crows and blackbirds. These pests caused so much damage to crops that a 1667 ordinance demanded that each householder kill 12 blackbirds or three crows a year, and one of 1695 ordered that no bachelor be allowed to marry who had failed to kill his quota.

After the Revolution fishing and coastwise trading flourished. Whales and blackfish (members of the whale family) were sometimes driven ashore by storms and captured. In 1662 the town agreed that part of the proceeds from the sale of each whale should go to the support of the clergy. Thoreau, remarking that the support of the clergy was thus left to Providence, added, 'For my part, if I were a minister, I would rather trust to the bowels of the billows, on the back side of the Cape, to cast up a whale for me, than the generosity of many a country parish I know.'

After the middle of the 19th century fishing and shipping were of less importance than agriculture. A feature of this period was the Methodist camp-meeting. On a 10-acre tract set aside for this purpose, more than 5000 listeners congregated, some of them coming from as far as Boston.

On Samoset Rd. 0.1 m. west of the Center is an *Old Windmill* (1793), one of few remaining on the Cape, and restored by a Works Progress Administration Project in 1936. On Saturday afternoons, if there is a 'likely' breeze, Miller John G. Fulcher, who operated the mill 40 years ago as a regular business enterprise, still grinds a couple of bags of corn for the entertainment of visitors. The mill is an octagonal, gray-shingled tower, tapering as it rises, and topped by a conical cap out of which the drive shaft extends, bearing the great fan of four arms. Originally a long timber went from the cap down to a large cartwheel, which rolled in a path around the mill site, pulled by a yoke of oxen — or when oxen were not available the neighbors were called to give the miller a hand. This part of Eastham Mill is missing, and Miller John now calls in the assistance of a motor car to 'swing her head into the wind' by a cable.

The *Prince Hurd House* (*private*), also on Samoset Rd., built about 1750, was formerly known as Tom Crosby's Tavern. It has a taproom where 23 men of the British frigate 'Spencer' were taken prisoner during the War of 1812.

> Right from Eastham on Nauset Rd. is the *Nauset Coast Guard Station*, 2 m. From the dunes here is a beautiful view of the ocean and long stretches of fine sandy beach. The spot has a long history of stranded vessels, heroic rescues, and tragic drownings.

At 4.2 m. is the *Grave of Freeman Hatch* (1820–89) with the confident epitaph: 'In 1852 he became famous making the astonishing passage in the clipper ship Northern Light from Frisco to Boston in 76 days, 6 hours, an achievement won by no other mortal before or since.'

US 6 continues through a region of low, widespread salt-water marshes, high cliffs, beaches, sand dunes, and forests of scrub pine.

SOUTH WELLFLEET, 9.5 *m*. (alt. 26), is a small village.

1. Right 0.8 *m*. from the village on a hard sand road are concrete foundations, the mass of rotting timbers, and half-buried cables that are the *Remains of the First Transatlantic Wireless Station in the United States*, which was put into operation by Marconi, Jan. 19, 1901. This point offers one of the finest views of the outer shore of the Cape.

2. Left from the village on a hard sand road is PLEASANT POINT, 1 *m*., a cluster of cottages on Blackfish Creek. Across the Creek, about 0.5 *m*., is the barren mound of Lieutenant's Island, a favorite haunt of duck-hunters that was visited every season by Grover Cleveland.

At 11.1 *m*. (L) is an *Observation Tower* (*open* 9–5, *April–Oct.*).

At 12.8 *m*. is the junction with a hard-surfaced road.

Right 2.4 *m*. on this delightful winding road to *Cahoon's Hollow Coast Guard Station*, featured in certain works of fiction. A cluster of small buildings houses the life-saving boats, breeches buoy, equipment, and crew. A beautiful sandy beach stretches for miles in both directions; the vast sweep of the ocean is broken only by the occasional smoke of liners, the squat rig of a fisherman or a yacht's sails.

According to a local story, a young girl, Goodie Hallet, was stoned out of early Eastham, having borne an illegitimate child to Black Sam Bellamy, a notorious pirate, and taken possession of a shack on Wellfleet Beach. Goodie, it is said, bartered her soul to the Devil in exchange for her lover's drowned body. The Devil apparently kept his bargain, for in April, 1717, Bellamy and his crew were shipwrecked off the Back Shore near Goodie's Hut.

WELLFLEET, 13.2 *m*. (town, alt. 5, pop. 948, sett. before 1724, incorp. 1763), was formerly in the Billingsgate section of Eastham. Whaling and oystering were the principal sources of wealth until the British blockade of Revolutionary days brought all industry to a standstill. Although the community became destitute, it was revealed through court records that Colonel Elisha Doane, the town's wealthiest man, reaped a fortune by trafficking with the enemy.

After the Revolution, Wellfleet traders regained prosperity by barter with England and France, until the Embargo Act of 1807 again interrupted business. In 1850 Wellfleet, with a fleet of 30 vessels, was second only to Gloucester as a cod and mackerel port. From 1830 to 1870 the town enjoyed a virtual monopoly of oystering in New England. The town still derives some income from fishing, but the main source is the tourist trade.

Memorial Hall, a good example of the simple early 19th century New England church, has an open octagonal cupola. Directly in front of the hall, on a granite boulder, is the *Pilgrim Memorial Tablet*, commemorating the expedition of a group of Pilgrims who on Dec. 6 and 7, 1620, explored Wellfleet Harbor in the 'Mayflower's' shallop before going on to Plymouth.

Also at the Center is *Belvernon*, the home of Captain Lorenzo Dow Baker, modestly engaged for several years in coastwise shipping trade in his 85-ton schooner the 'Telegraph.' While loading bamboo in the West Indies he decided to take a few bananas back to the States. The new fruit caused a sensation. This exploit was the nucleus out of which the United Fruit Company (est. 1899) was to grow. Captain Baker became managing director of the Jamaica division of the firm. It was a decided case of 'local boy makes good.' 'Cap'n Baker' in his palmy days continued to take an interest in the town of his birth.

Left from Wellfleet on Holbrook Ave. is the *Old Cemetery*, 0.5 *m.*, from which, across a narrow inlet, is seen *Great Island*. Here recent excavations have revealed the ruins of a building that was about 100 feet long, with a stockade of planking caulked with clay. A number of knives, forks, spoons, clay pipes, nails, pewter buttons, and an English coin dated 1723 have been found. The place may have been a trading-post of the Dutch East India Company.

Threading its course among the dunes, US 6 at 16.7 *m.* reaches the junction with a two-lane tar-surfaced road.

Left on this road is the village of SOUTH TRURO, 2 *m.*, in which is the *Old Methodist Church*, 1851. It has not been used in recent years, and looks lonely and forlorn on its high barren dunes.

The dunes of South Truro are unusually fine specimens of drumlins, lenticular mounds of unstratified clay, sand, and pebbles deposited by receding masses of ice of the glacial period.

TRURO, 18.1 *m.* (town, alt. 12, pop. 541, sett. 1700, incorp. 1709) (*golf, tennis, bathing, motor-boating, sailing, clam digging*), 'the wrist of the bended arm of Massachusetts,' was settled by the Pamet Proprietors, organized about 1689.

As at Eastham, schools of blackfish stranded on the sandflats provided an early source of income. Soon Truro men took to boats, and, armed with harpoons, helped to initiate the whaling industry. Edicts in 1711 and 1713 forbidding the exhaustion of the sparse timber in the process of extracting lime from shell beds left by Indians, restricting the grazing of cattle, and requiring the planting of beach grass, indicate early concern for the harbors, which began to silt up just at a time when the decline of shore fishing made larger boats necessary. Attempts to save the anchorages proved ineffectual. The year 1850 marked the peak of expansion with a population of 2051 and a fleet of 111 vessels. From then on, marine disasters, with attendant property loss and business failure, sealed Truro's industrial fate.

The close of the Civil War, to which Truro contributed the services of over 200 men, marked a further decline. Offshore weirs superseded the whalers and codfish boats, cheaper sources of supply abroad ruined a thriving salt business, and farming without extensive fertilization was unprofitable.

With its harbors obliterated and its population dwindled to 541 persons, half of them of Portuguese descent, Truro has attracted a colony of artists and writers who have found its quiet simplicity and freedom from crowds a congenial environment for creative work.

No other spot on the Cape is richer in folklore and piquant legend than Truro. Here was the famous Lyars' Bench, utilized for the sole purpose of telling tall stories. The local electrical inspector vouches for a yarn

,about a sea captain before whose stubborn ire the whole village cowered: all except his daughter, who, apparently a chip off the old block, was determined to have modern improvements in the home. The inspector swears he was called in the night the Captain died and found the house in darkness. And the explanation is given in a locally concocted limerick:

> There was an old sea dog named ——
> Who stood six foot four in his shoes;
> He damned all things modern,
> Swore they weren't Cape-Coddern
> The new-fangled he'd roundly abuse.
>
> He lived with his daughter, Miss ——
> Who yearned 'lectric lighting to use;
> She won the long fight
> But he died the same night,
> And his passing soul blew out the fuse!

In Truro, too, they have a refreshing point of view on the 'summer people.' The 'natives' publish sporadically a small paper. One of the anecdotes printed in an issue of not too ancient date says that an affable lady visitor was being carried from the railway station to her destination by the local carter. She tried diligently but without success to make conversation by commenting on the weather, the landscape, and the road. Finally she remarked, 'What a lot of quaint people one sees around here!'

That drew a response. 'Yes, mam,' said the carter, 'but most of 'em go home after Labor Day.'

The *Hill of the Churches* is at 18.5 m. In 1826 the Methodists built a chapel on a high hill above the village 'to be nearer to God and as a landmark for fishermen.' The dome of the cupola is in the fascinating shape of a mandarin hat. The next year the 'orthodox' chose the top of the same hill for the site of a large church, long to be known as the Bell Meeting House because of a legend which claims that the bell is still mysteriously rung in the deserted building.

NORTH TRURO, 21.9 m. (alt. 10).

At the beach end of Depot Rd. is the *Bayberry Candle Place (open)*, looking like an old sail loft, sheathed with weather-beaten gray shingles. Here bayberry candles are dipped by hand for the summer trade.

On the beach is the *Fish-Freezing Plant (open to visitors)*, formerly a cooperative enterprise, a large frame building surrounded by grass-green sheds used for storing traps. The freezer is able to freeze everything — except the smell of fish. In the storage rooms, tiers of horizontal frosted pipes hold trays of mackerel, whiting, and herring taken in the weirs a few hundred yards offshore. A temperature of five degrees below zero is maintained, and 30,000 pounds of fish have been shipped in one day.

Near-by offshore is a tall, skeletal landing stage for the trawlers, well buttressed with rocks and concrete. From this the fish are brought across the shallows by pulley and bucket.

Right from North Truro 1.5 *m.* to the circular white tower of *Cape Cod*, or *Highland Light* (*open daily* 10–12, 2–4), built in 1797 on a clay cliff just south of one of the most dangerous bars on the Atlantic coast. The top of the 66-foot tower is 140 feet above the sea, and contains a powerful revolving white light. Adjoining it are the high steel towers of the *Radio Beacon*, whose signal, 'Quack,' is known to all mariners in North Atlantic waters. In a low hut facing the tower is the *U.S. Naval Compass Station*, which supplies ships at sea with their bearings. On the edge of the cliff are two enormous megaphones — electrically operated *Foghorns*.

South of the station is a large *Stone Tower*, on the estate of a railroad official. It is one of the towers of the old Fitchburg Station in Boston, and Cape Cod storms have not yet washed the soot of 80 years from the granite battlement.

At 24.4 *m.* is a junction with a sand road.

Right on this road is Pilgrim Heights, 0.7 *m.* Here is *Pilgrim Spring*, where the settlers drank their first New England water.

From the heights can be seen to the northwest *Peaked Hill Bar*, which vies with Hatteras as a ship graveyard.

At 28.4 *m.* is PROVINCETOWN (*see PROVINCETOWN*).

T O U R 7 : *From* NEW HAMPSHIRE LINE (*Seabrook*) *to* WORCESTER, 75.2 *m.*, State 110 and State 70.

Via Amesbury, Merrimac, Haverhill, Lawrence, Lowell, Dracut, Chelmsford, Westford, Littleton, Harvard, Boxborough, Bolton, Stow, Lancaster, Clinton, Berlin, and Boylston.

B. & M. R.R. parallels the route.

Hard-surfaced roadbed throughout.

Sec. a. NEW HAMPSHIRE LINE to LOWELL, 33.1 *m.*

STATE 110 crosses the New Hampshire Line about 15 *m.* south of Portsmouth, N.H., and cuts inland along the winding banks of the Merrimack River, running through a farming area sprinkled with hamlets.

At 2.8 *m.* is the junction with Elm St. (unmarked).

1. Right on Elm St. at 0.4 *m.* is the square white *Rocky Hill Meeting House*, built in 1785. The exterior is notable for its doorway and numerous windows with small square panes. In the interior are a high pulpit, square pews, and a 'whispering gallery,' an acoustic phenomenon.

At 0.8 *m.* is the junction with Monroe St.; right on this to a lane at 1.2 *m.*, the entrance to the *Amesbury Country Club* (*public; greens fee $1 weekdays, $1.50 Sun.*). On a knoll in a pasture to the south is the white, domed *Powder House* used during the War of 1812.

At 4.1 *m.* is the junction with Main St.

1. Left on Main St. at 0.1 *m.*, the *Macy-Colby House* (1654) (apply 273 Main St.), 259 Main St., a 17th-century structure with central chimney and long sloping

roof, put together with wooden pegs, was the home of Thomas Macy and Anthony Colby. Macy was exiled in 1655 for sheltering Quakers during a rainstorm, an incident described in Whittier's poem 'The Exile.'

The *Squire Bagley Homestead* (*adm.* 25¢), 277 Main St., 0.2 *m.*, was twice occupied by Mary Baker Eddy, founder of Christian Science. In 1868 she lived here with the squire's daughter, and in 1869 she here completed the manuscript of 'Comments on the Scriptures.'

Alliance Park, 0.4 *m.*, is a small tree-shaded spot on the banks of the Merrimack River at its junction with the Powow, the center of a large shipbuilding region in the late 1700's. The park is the site of the building in 1777 of the 'Alliance,' a ship commanded by John Paul Jones.

2. Right on Main St. at 0.1 *m.* at the south corner of the high-school yard is a granite reproduction of the old wooden well described in Whittier's poem 'The Captain's Well.' A three-panel relief shows Captain Valentine Bagley, hero of the poem. On the school lawn is the *Doughboy Statue*, the work of Leonard Craske. It depicts with vigor and sensitivity an American soldier on the march.

AMESBURY, 0.5 *m.* (town, alt. 90, pop. 10,514, sett. 1654, incorp. 1668), at the foot of Lake Gardner in the shadow of rounded glacial hills, is a community of quiet streets of elm-shaded, neat white houses behind picket fences; and, in the northeast section, of abandoned factories.

Amesbury was an important shipbuilding center before steam supplanted the clipper ships of 1850. The manufacture of hats is today the town's single important industry.

The Powow River, a small stream, flows beneath the streets and buildings of Amesbury Square to its junction with the Merrimack.

The *Whittier House* (*open weekdays*, 10–5; *adm.* 25¢), corner of Pickard and Friend Sts., is a simple white frame dwelling behind a neat picket fence. John Greenleaf Whittier lived in Amesbury 56 years; most of his poems were written here, and the desk he worked at, as well as other interesting relics, are in this house.

The *Friends Meeting House* (1851), Greenleaf St., is a plain frame structure in which Whittier's pew is marked.

Straight ahead from Bartlett Sq. on Main St. to Market Square 0.7 *m.*

1. Right on Elm St. to Congress St., 0.6 *m.*; left on this to *Osgood House* (*private*), 15 Congress St., built in 1650 but much altered. From the tiny garret window under the lean-to roof the elderly owner is said to have dropped a prowling Indian with a charge from his long-barreled firearm.

2. Left from Market Square on High St., 0.1 *m.*; right on Powow St. is the summit of Powow Hill and *Victoria Park*, 1.1 *m.* with a panoramic view.

At 4.2 *m.* left, is Union Cemetery, in which is the *Grave of Whittier*.

At 5.1 *m.* is the junction with a dirt road.

Left on this road is a shrub-concealed boulder marking the *Site of the Home of Susanna Martin*, better known as Goody Martin, a famous Amesbury witch, tried, convicted, and sentenced to hang at Salem in 1693. The story goes that on the scaffold she uttered incantations which caused the rope to wriggle and dance about so that the hangman could not tie the knot, till a crow, flying overhead, cawed down the advice to try a noose of willow withe. When this was done, the execution was successfully completed.

Amesbury was especially favored by the powers of darkness. Goody Whitcher was another town witch, whose loom kept banging day and night even after she was dead. In the early days people strolling late at night through the quiet streets of the town often met a headless man walking along and carrying his head under his arm. In the early years, too, Barrow Hill was the scene of witches' routs. Late at night the light of their fires could be plainly seen on its top, as shadowy forms danced and sailed around its summit in the eerie glare.

At 6.1 *m.* is the *Challis Hill Farmhouse* (*open by arrangement*) (about 1660), a white frame structure with a red roof, and a secret trapdoor formerly used for refuge from Indians.

South of Amesbury the route gains altitude, allowing a widening view of the rolling country.

At 6.9 *m.* is the junction with a dirt road.

Right on this road a short distance to *Lake Attitash* (*swimming*), one of Whittier's favorite haunts.

MERRIMAC (Indian, 'Swift Waters'), 8.1 *m.* (town, alt. 105, pop. 2209, sett. 1638, incorp. 1876), lies in the midst of a region where the river of ice left many traces of its passage. With the exception of two level plains, the region is sharply rolling, a series of drumlins (lenticular glacial mounds), many of them too steep for cultivation.

The *Sawyer Home* (*open by arrangement*), 0.1 *m.* east from the Center on State 110, a two-and-a-half-story frame structure, built 1750, contains furniture and utensils used during the middle of the 19th century.

The *Pilgrim Congregational Church*, Church St., organized in 1726, has a Corinthian arched portico and, in the rear, old horse stalls.

Left from Merrimac on School St. is MERRIMACPORT, 2 *m.* (town of Merrimac). Vessels for West Indian and coastwise trade were built here before 1700. Trade with Newburyport was carried on, 'gundalows' — long, square-ended barges — being poled up and down the winding Merrimack, carrying hogshead staves and local produce in exchange for molasses.

At 9.7 *m.* is the junction with Amesbury Line Rd.

Left on Amesbury Line Rd. at No. 29 is the *Mary Ingalls Birthplace*, 1.3 *m.* Mary, born 1786, was celebrated in Whittier's poem 'The Countess' as the first girl born in the United States to marry a title. The house is located in Rocks Village, which has a beautiful setting on the Merrimack River.

At 10.6 *m.* are the *Whittier Birthplace* (*open 10–sunset; adm.* 10¢) and the *Whittier Family Monument*. The simple white house (1668) with steep pitched roof and massive central chimney, is shielded from the highway by a screen of trees, and has in the back an orchard; in the front is a lawn descending to Whittier Brook. The interior is furnished as it was in the days when the Quaker poet, in this peaceful and secluded house, immortalized the 'barefoot boy with cheek of tan.'

At 14.3 *m.* is HAVERHILL (*see HAVERHILL*). Here is the junction with State 125 (*see Tour 7A*).

Southwest of Haverhill, State 110 follows the broad river flowing between wooded banks. The trees show the effects of the 1936 flood, which covered many of them halfway up with a black sticky tar.

At 22.7 *m.* is the Center of LAWRENCE (*see LAWRENCE*).

At 23.4 *m.* is the junction with State 28 (*see Tour 5*).

At 33.1 *m.* is LOWELL (*see LOWELL*).

Right from Lowell on Bridge St. is DRACUT, 1.7 *m.* (town, alt. 100, pop. 6500, sett. 1664, incorp. 1702), a pleasant farming and manufacturing town. This region was once the capital of the Pawtucket tribe of Indians, whose chief, Passaconaway, was friendly to the white men. Samuel Varnum was the earliest settler, and the town was named for his native town in England. Dracut suffered several attacks during King Philip's War, and a tale of female heroism centers in the Old Garrison House, over 200 years old and now in Lowell. An alarm had called the soldiers away, and this house, occupied only by a woman and several children, was left unguarded. A band of Indians crept toward it. Catching sight of them and realizing the danger, the woman hurriedly dressed herself in a soldier's uniform and patrolled the house as though on guard. After a time she went in and reappeared, this time in a colonel's coat and hat. The Indians, deceived into thinking the house was thoroughly garrisoned, stole away in silence.

An early settler about whom a romantic aura gathered was a citizen of France, the son of a marquis, who called himself simply Louis Ansart. He was an engineer whose special work was the casting of cannon. When Lafayette visited this country in 1825 he visited Ansart, and the Frenchman's presence in Dracut is said to have drawn thither a large French population.

The *Congregational Church*, corner of Bridge and Arlington Sts., is an odd-looking clapboard structure, painted yellow, with an open belfry and unique steeple. Originally a conservative building, its present bizarre appearance is due to additions made in 1895.

Sec. b. LOWELL to WORCESTER, 42.1 m.

Between Lowell and Clinton, State 110 passes through the Nashoba Valley, an important apple-growing region, especially attractive during the summer months, when colorful orchards vie with old houses in interest.

At 0.7 m. is the junction with US 3 (*see Tour 3*).

At 2.6 m. the road crosses the old *Middlesex Canal* (*see Tour 1C*).

CHELMSFORD, 4.3 m. (town, alt. 149, pop. 7595, sett. 1633, incorp. 1655), was settled by people from Concord and Woburn, and named for Chelmsford in Essex, England. It was represented at the Battle of Bunker Hill, and one of its citizens, Joseph Spalding, is said to have thus described firing the first shot. 'I fired the shot ahead of time and General Putnam rushed up and struck me for violating orders. I suppose I deserved it, but I was anxious to get another shot at Gage's men ever since our affair at Concord. The blow from Old Put hit me on the head, made a hole in my hat, and left me a scar.' The hat with the hole in it was preserved in the Emerson House, Spalding's home, until that building was destroyed by fire.

Local mills and factories in the early 19th century produced lumber, corn, powder, and cotton cloth; the textile factory later produced woolen cloth. An iron foundry was erected to manufacture the bog ore, mined as early as 1656. Ice harvesting and granite quarrying have also been important to the town's prosperity.

The *Fiske House* (*private*) at the corner of Littleton and Billerica Sts., is a white clapboarded structure, built 1790, with brick ends, now painted white, and four end chimneys. The doors have fanlights. Originally a tavern, its bar and early furnishings have been preserved.

Facing the Common is the *Unitarian Church* of the First Congregational Society, which was organized in Wenham, 1644. The edifice (1840), the fourth on this site, has a red-brick base, white wood front, clapboarded sides, and a steeple with an open belfry and a four-faced clock. The first pastor of this church was the Rev. John Fiske, who came from Wenham in 1655, bringing with him most of his flock. He was the author of the 'Chelmsford Catechism,' the only known copy of which is in the Lenox collection of the New York Public Library. On the title-page of the 88-page pamphlet is: 'The Watering of the Olive Plant in Christ's Garden, Or a Short Catechism of our Chelmsford children Enlarged by the three-fold Appendix by John Fiske, Pastor of the Church of Christ at Chelmsford in New England.... Printed by Samuel Green at Cambridge in New England, 1657.' The catechism occupies 9 pages; the remaining 72 being devoted to the 'threefold Appendix.'

Adjacent to a school is the *Deacon Otis Adams House* (*private*), where in 1866 a school for the deaf, using the purely oral method, was established. One of the pupils, Mabel Hubbard, became the wife of Alexander Graham Bell; it is said that from his study of the vibrations of speech that enable deaf children to read lips came the inspiration for the telephone.

The *Spaulding House* (*private*), corner of North and Dalton Rds., was once the home of Colonel Simeon Spaulding, a member of the Provincial Congress in 1775. This two-and-a-half-story white frame house with its large central chimney has been subjected to mid-Victorian renovations; garish ornaments and oddly cut decorations in wood have been attached to its gables and slopes at every possible point.

Left from Chelmsford on Acton Rd., 2 *m.*, is SOUTH CHELMSFORD (alt. 220). Here in 1835 Ezekial Byam manufactured lucifer matches that had to be scratched on sandpaper and were sold at 25¢ a hundred. Byam later purchased the patent rights for the Chapin-Phillips matches, and went into business near the junction of the roads leading to the Center, thus giving the spot its name of *Brimstone Corner*. The business was moved to Boston in 1848. Byam's Matches, which became nationally famous, were advertised by this verse:

> For quickness and sureness the public will find,
> These matches will leave all others behind;
> Without further remarks we invite you to try 'em,
> Remember all good that are signed by ——
> E. Byam.

At 8.5 *m.* on State 110 is the junction with Boston Rd.

Right on Boston Rd. which leads through long stretches of apple orchards interspersed with fine birch groves, is WESTFORD, 1.3 *m.* (town, alt. 160, pop. 3789, sett. 1653, incorp. 1729), the scene of the Nashoba Apple Blossom Festival in which, in 1935, thirty-eight towns participated with an attendance of some 50,000 persons. The present town comprises about 20,000 acres of land, chiefly hills and valleys of glacial origin. The soil of its hills contains the slowly disintegrating feldspar rocks brought from Canada by the glacial sea, which yield the vital plant element, potassium, in just the right proportion for the growth of trees and fruits.

The *Old Fletcher Tavern* (1713) (open April–Sept.) faces the Town Green on Fletcher Hamlin Circle. This fine structure is one of the most carefully preserved in Massachusetts. The clapboards are a creamy white and the blinds, which adorn the windows and door, are green. The roof is slate and the brick chimneys are painted white. The old oven in one of the fireplaces, where for over 200 years the Saturday rite of baking beans has been observed, is sure to delight even the most enthusiastic supporter of modern culinary methods. It was at this inn that Daniel Webster courted Grace Fletcher.

LITTLETON, 11.4 *m.* (*see Tour* 2). Here is the junction with State 119 (*see Tour* 2A) and State 2 (*see Tour* 2), which unites with State 110 to 17.1 *m.*, where State 110 branches left.

HARVARD, 20.8 *m.* (town, alt. 390, pop. 952, sett. 1704, incorp. 1732), was named in honor of John Harvard, first patron of Harvard University. It has always been an agricultural community, although at various times there have been industrial activities. In 1783 a group of townspeople opened a 'silver mine' near Oak Hill, but the silver was nonexistent. Horticulture is now the chief occupation, apples and peaches being grown in large quantities.

The *Library* (*open daily except Sun. and holidays* 2–6), bordering the Common, is a one-and-a-half-story red-brick building with a brownstone foundation; in it is the private library started about 1793 by the Rev. William Emerson, father of Ralph Waldo Emerson.

1. Left from Harvard on the Old Littleton Rd. to Oak Hill Rd., 1.2 *m.*; left on this to the entrance of the *Harvard Astronomical Observatory* (*open*), 0.4 *m.* A 61-inch reflecting telescope, equipped for spectroscopic and solar work, several smaller reflector and refractor telescopes, and a number of special cameras are part of the equipment. The plates made here are filed at Harvard University (*see CAMBRIDGE*). A narrow footpath leads from the entrance through a tunnel of young evergreens to a seven-story tower, from which is revealed a magnificent vista of rolling hills.

2. Left from Harvard on State 111 to the junction with a side road at 3.2 *m.*; left on this road, which ascends by a crooked route, to BOXBOROUGH, 4 *m.* (town, alt. 235, pop. 404, sett. 1680, incorp. 1783), so named because of the original square form of the township. The community devotes itself mainly to the production of small fruits and dairy products for the Boston market.

At 21.7 *m.* is the junction with a road marked 'Fruitlands.'

Right on this road 1 *m.* to the entrance of the *Wayside Museums, Inc.* (*guides; adm.* 10 ¢, *open summer daily exc. Mon.* 12.30 *to* 6.30). Three buildings stand close together on the hillside. In the center is *Fruitlands*, the farmhouse of Bronson Alcott's New Eden. This community lasted only a few months, though established in 1843 as the nucleus of a new social order in which neither man nor beast should be exploited. Following this principle, the Con-Sociate Family adopted vegetarianism, eschewed the use of wool (obtained by depriving sheep of their covering), cotton (the product of slave labor), and leather; to provide garments other than linen for the members mulberry trees were planted as a beginning of sericulture, before it was understood that silk was obtained by the exploitation of silkworms. The Con-Sociates even attempted to pull their plows, compromising on this point only when the planting season was far advanced with little ground ready for seed. Practical difficulties were so great that the experiment ended before there was an opportunity to demonstrate the high spiritual principles on which it was started.

Fruitlands is now a transcendentalist museum, containing not only articles used by the Con-Sociate Family but also many pictures and relics of leaders in this significant philosophical movement. The house, very old and dilapidated at the time of the experiment, has been carefully restored, and the Colonial kitchen, in ruins in 1843, has been rebuilt to hold some of the mementoes; in renovating and refurnishing the place, Miss Sears has been aided by 'Transcendental Wild Oats,' Louisa May Alcott's record of her father's venture, in which she took part as a child. The visitor may see the fireplaces where the Alcott 'little women' hung their stockings at Christmas time, and Louisa's attic bedroom where she used to lie awake and listen to the rain. Two old mulberry trees, survivals of the abortive experiment in silkworms, stand near the house.

Equally interesting is the square, prim *Shaker House* near-by, moved here from the old Shaker community several miles away (*see below*). To this house in June, 1781, came Mother Ann Lee, founder of the American branch of the United Society of Believers in Christ's Second Appearing, known as Shakers because of the rhythmic movement that was an essential part of the sect's ceremonies. The community was communistic and celibate, believing in spirit communications, but had a practical core manifesting itself in agricultural and industrial activity that was very successful and in the contrivance of ingenious labor-saving devices. The sect is fast dying out, and Miss Sears has collected all available relics — furniture, homemade costumes, implements, and documents — in the Square House. Many of the garments are displayed on life-sized wax figures posed in natural positions about the house.

The third building in the group is the *Indian Museum*, which contains a small, carefully selected collection of Indian relics from many parts of the country. The main part of this museum is an old schoolhouse that has been veneered with bricks from the former Town Hall of Lancaster.

The gray clapboarded *Henry Willard House* (1687) (*open on application*), 23.3 *m.*, has a black-shingled roof, and an exceptionally large chimney. Originally a half-timber house with brick filling between the framing, the walls have since been covered over with clapboards. In the house is a hooked rug depicting it as it was before the porch was added.

The *Marshall Place* (*date uncertain*) (*private*), at 23.9 *m.*, an ancient three-story gabled dwelling with unpainted weather-beaten clapboards on the front and shingles on the sides, is enclosed by a fence of small branches; in the rear is a huge old barn and on the front lawn stands a gigantic old sycamore.

At 25.7 *m.* is the junction with State 117.

1. Left on State 117.

At 1.5 *m.* is the junction with Lancaster Rd.; right on this 0.5 *m.* to the *Wilder Mansion* (1687) (*private*), a beautiful two-story structure. The roof of the main building and those of the one-story adjoining wings have balustraded roof railings. Octagonal granite pillars connected by iron chains enclose the terraced and landscaped lawn.

BOLTON, 2.4 *m.* (town, alt., 380, pop. 739, sett. 1682, incorp. 1738), early had a lime kiln, two potash and a pearl ash works, a comb factory, two brickyards, a cooper's shop, and a tannery with which was associated a chain of shoemaking shops. Removal of industries to larger centers left fruit, milk, and poultry as the chief products, though hand-made ostrich-feather dusters are manufactured here by George T. Beckner, a former missionary to South Africa; one of his best customers is the Pullman Car Company.

The *Country Manor* (*a hotel*), 0.2 *m.* west of the village on Main St., was erected in 1740 by General Amory Holman. This dignified mansion with its white columns and balcony stands on a hill and is surrounded by beautiful gardens; it was the scene of lively activity in the days when General Holman operated a stage line on the Boston Post Rd. The barns and sheds that formerly housed the horses and coaches still stand opposite the library.

The *Godings House* (*private*), 0.3 *m.* on Main St., is reputed to be a remodeled block-house of Indian days; it has vertical boards on the walls, 18-inch floor boards, wooden latches and bolts on the doors, and portholes in the walls.

Right from State 117 at 7.2 *m.* is *Spindle Hill* (alt. 400 — *footpath*), rugged and somewhat forbidding, with moss-covered boulders and rocks, there is, however, a wide view of the countryside.

STOW, 8.1 *m.* (town, alt. 330, pop. 1190, sett. 1681, incorp. 1683), named for John Stow, a close friend of Simon Bradstreet, Governor of Massachusetts, was raided by Indians in King Philip's War and then resettled. Raising hops, silkworm culture, milling, and minor manufacturing have been engaged in temporarily; today only a woolen mill and a box factory are the chief non-agricultural activities.

Stow has a legend concerning William Goffe, the regicide (*see HADLEY, Tour 8, sec. b*). It is said that with a price of £100 upon his head, his death was reported by his friends in Hadley, while he came to Stow as 'John Green,' and spent his remaining years here in peace. As substantiation the town presents a sworn affidavit that the grave of 'John Green' was opened in 1930, and no skull was found among the bones — the implication being that the head had been sent to England for the reward.

2. Right from State 110 on State 117, 0.2 *m.*, are *Twin Elm Trees* connected, Siamese-like, by a cross-limb a few feet above the ground.

At 1.5 *m.* State 117 passes the *Beaman Oak*, estimated by State Foresters to be about 700 years old, and believed to be the largest oak in Massachusetts.

At 1.8 *m.* is a junction with a crossroad.

a. Right on this road is the junction with a road marked, 'Shirley'; right on this to a junction with a second dirt road and the *Brick Tavern (open)*, 5.1 *m.*, built 1804, as a stagecoach house and later owned by the Shakers. During the Shaker ownership William Dean Howells stayed here and wrote 'The Undiscovered Country.' Directly across the road is a small wooden building once a *Shaker Hospital*, having a room with a closet said to have been used by the Shakers for disciplinary purposes. Latched on the outside, the door to the closet contains a heart-shaped aperture through which recalcitrant members were watched or fed.

Left on the dirt road by the tavern to a narrow dirt road at 6 *m.*; right on this at 6.3 *m.* is *Fort Pond* (*bathing, boating, fishing; small fee*), an island fort built here during the Indian War.

b. Left on the side road, opposite the one marked 'Shirley,' under ancient elms to LANCASTER, 2.8 *m.* (town, alt. 277, pop. 2590, sett. 1643, incorp. 1653). When the town fathers applied for permission to name the town Prescott in honor of a popular local blacksmith, the General Court decided: 'Whereas no town of the Colonies had as yet been named for any Governor; and whereas it were unseemly that a blacksmith be honored ahead of his betters, the name Prescott could not be permitted.' If this was a hint, the town evaded it by naming itself for Lancaster, England.

The settlement was destroyed during King Philip's War and was attacked again in 1696 and 1704. Manufacturing industries in the surrounding area were lost to neighboring towns, and Lancaster became a residential community.

Many years ago a Lancasterman, Jonathan Wilder, courted a girl in vain; later, having lost the wife who was his second choice, he renewed his first suit. Refused again, he married another girl. Wife number two died, and once more Jonathan renewed his early suit. This time he was accepted. His wife, now middle-aged, bore him a son, then twins, and finally triplets. At least that is the story; he would better have let well enough alone.

Facing the Common is the *Old Meeting House* ('The Lancaster Church'), of brick laid in Flemish bond. Designed by Charles Bulfinch in 1816, it is probably the finest of his many beautiful churches.. The façade with its arched portico and the beautifully proportioned cupola, surrounded by Roman Ionic columns which support a nicely balanced entablature, are especially noteworthy. The church reflects the beginning of Greek influence upon American architecture.

In the days of Bride Cake Plain (Old Lancaster — origin of name unknown) a feud occurred between two men who held adjoining pews in the church; one of them erected a 'spite-fence' between the pews to such a height that his devotions should not be disturbed by the sight of his hated neighbor. Church authorities, however, ruled that the screen was un-Christian and ordered it removed.

Luther Burbank, the 'plant wizard,' was born (1849) in Lancaster in a frame house which later became the ell of a more imposing brick structure. Henry Ford purchased the ell and removed it to Dearborn, Mich.

The *Thayer Bird Museum* (*open Mon. Wed. Sat. 8–4*), 3.8 *m.*, housing a fine collection of North American birds, was willed to the Harvard University Museum of Comparative Zoology by Colonel John E. Thayer. Although many specimens were removed to Cambridge, most of the collection is here.

At 4.1 *m.* on George Hill, a marker indicates *Rowlandson Rock*, where Mary Rowlandson and her Indian captors spent the first night after the sacking of the town. The account written by Mrs. Rowlandson of her adventures during the seven weeks of her captivity gives an intimate description of Indian life (*see Warwick, Tour 2B*).

At 29.1 *m.* is the junction with State 70; straight on State 70.

CLINTON, 29.4 *m.* (town, alt., 328, pop. 12,373, sett. 1654, incorp. 1850), has shallow soil and a hilly terrain that discourage farming. Clinton developed as an industrial community. Its prosperity, however, declined somewhat with the closing of the Lancaster Cotton Mills in 1930 and the Bigelow Sandford Carpet Company in 1933.

The *Holder Memorial Building*, opposite 209 Church St., dedicated 1904, is of red brick laid in Flemish bond, with granite bases, pedestals, terracotta columns and pilasters, and copper mouldings.

On Green St. stands the huge plant of the *Lancaster Mills* (*not open to visitors*) incorporated in 1844. At one time the company employed 2600 operatives, and was the largest producer of ginghams in the world. Its weaving room covered one and a third acres. Several small industries now occupy sections of the plant.

At 30 *m.* is the junction with State 62.

Left on State 62 is BERLIN, 3.7 *m.* (town, alt. 326, pop. 1091, sett. 1665, incorp. 1784), an agricultural community in spite of unfavorable soil conditions. There are a few profitable orchards and dairies.

At 30.6 *m.* on State 70 are *Wachusett Dam and Reservoir*. The dam, 114 feet high, has a promenade on the top 971 feet long. The reservoir, eight-and-a-half miles long and two miles wide at its widest point, has a maximum depth of 129 feet and impounds about 62 billion gallons of water.

BOYLSTON, 35.1 *m.* (town, alt. 300, pop. 1361, sett. 1705, incorp. 1786), a quiet residential village in a town originally part of Lancaster and Shrewsbury, was named for the Boylston family of Boston and Roxbury; a member of this family gave a pulpit Bible, communion cups, bell, and a generous sum of money to the church. In 1896 the construction of the Wachusett Reservoir, which covers 2700 acres of town land, forced many residents to move away.

At 37.4 *m.* a tree-lined driveway (R) leads up to the former *Home of John B. Gough* (*private*), temperance advocate and reformer, who captivated audiences all over the country, between 1842 and 1886, by his impassioned eloquence, and the funny stories with which he interlarded his serious appeals for personal abstinence.

State 70 enters a suburban residential area and at 42.1 *m*. reaches the Center of WORCESTER (*see WORCESTER*), where it meets State 9 (*see Tour* 8), State 12 (*see Tour* 11), and State 122 (*see Tour* 23).

T O U R   7 A :   *From*   NEWBURYPORT   *to*   HAVERHILL, 12.5 *m*., State 125.

Via West Newbury and Groveland.

Excellent macadam highways; winding, but little traffic.

STATE 125 is an alternate route between Newburyport and Haverhill, making a wide loop through unspoiled countryside south of the Merrimack River. Towns along it date from the early 17th century, stemming from the parent communities of Newbury and Rowley, and though they are not quite so rich in historic sites as the towns along the seaboard, they have a quiet charm that is fast disappearing in the more thickly settled parts of the State. The rolling country has exceptional beauty, with open pastures, fertile acres of orchard and tillage, and miles of forest; with glimpses of the Merrimack, here very wide and not marred by the stark factory buildings of its upper reaches.

State 125 branches west from US 1 (*see Tour* 1) in Newburyport.

Between Newburyport and West Newbury, State 125 dips and rises over the rounded hills to reveal pleasant vistas of fields, narrow valleys, reedy swampland, and rows of neatly kept houses backed by fertile meadows and open country.

At 3.3 *m*. the road crosses a loop of the Artichoke River and a reedy marsh which has been set aside as a *Bird Sanctuary* (*marked by signs*).

At 4 *m*. is the intersection with Garden St.

> Left on this road which forks right at 1.7 *m*. Here, on the left, a sign declares: 'The Only Indian Killed in West Newbury was Shot by Hananiah Ordway.' Right at the fork to the *Cherry Hill Nurseries*, 2.1 *m*., which ship their products all over the world; in their seasons the peonies, dahlias, lilacs, and other flowering plants make a beautiful display.

At 4.7 *m*. the House of the Angel Guardian, a Catholic institution for orphaned boys, sits on the lower slope of *Pipestave Hill*, a glacial drumlin once forested with hardwoods, but now covered with grass and ground pine. On this hill, as early as 1685, staves were cut for use in making wine casks and molasses hogsheads, articles of export to Europe and the West Indies.

WEST NEWBURY, 5.7 *m*. (town, alt. 180, pop. 1475, sett. 1635, incorp. 1819), an agricultural town, spreads over a series of high well-watered hills. Before the spectacular growth of Newburyport, which increasingly monopolized foreign commerce, ocean-going vessels ascended the Merrimack as far as Haverhill; but with the building of the Chain Bridge in the early 19th century the river was closed to ships. West Newbury relapsed into an agricultural calm, and there are no traces today of the comb factory started by Enoch Noyes in 1770 or of the small shoe manufactories that once flourished here. Two college presidents were born in the town in the early 19th century, Cornelius Conway Felton of Harvard and Leonard Woods of Bowdoin.

The *Training Field*, Main St. (State 125), with its World War Boulder, is surrounded by houses overarched by elms.

At 6.8 *m.* is the intersection with Church St.

Right on Church St. at 0.9 *m.* is *Rocks Bridge*, which spans the Merrimack. At this point the river sweeps into a wide course, its broad expanse ruffled by the swift current, between banks on which a few scattered farmhouses and the clustered buildings of tiny Rock Village at the far side of the bridge create a charming pastoral scene. Purple loosestrife blooms in profusion during July and August along the river edge. The only blemish, a grim reminder of the disastrous spring floods of 1936, is the high-water mark of dried black scum high among the branches of the trees.

This section of State 125 is bordered by woods and fields with streams that can be whipped for trout, and covers where it is still possible to flush a pheasant.

The *George Thomas Savory House* (*open to the public; adm.* 25¢), 8.8 *m.* standing in the shade of two giant elms, was built in 1826, and still has dignity and charm despite the addition of a mansard roof which has partially hidden the four original chimneys. Rural scenes are depicted on the plaster walls of the interior, done at the time the house was built, by an artist and inventor, Rufus Porter, of Boxford.

GROVELAND, 9.7 *m.* (town, alt. 47, pop. 2219, sett. about 1639, incorp. 1850), is a quiet suburban village. In its early years the town depended on the power supplied by the Merrimack River for its economic life. The industries of the early years, however, and the later manufacture of woolens and flannels were gradually absorbed by the neighboring city of Haverhill. The town is unique in Massachusetts in having a government by three selectmen but no town hall.

Facing the Common is the Congregational Church (1727), in the belfry of which hangs a *Paul Revere Bell*, engraved with the somber but apparently popular reminder, since it was so often used: 'The living to the church I call, and to the grave I summon all.'

At 10 *m.* State 125 crosses *Groveland Bridge* over the Merrimack River (Haverhill City Line). In the flood of 1936 this bridge stood staunch while furious waters battered it with houses, trees, and all sorts of débris from the upper river.

State 125 joins State 110 (*see Tour 7*) in HAVERHILL (*see HAVERHILL*) at 12.5 *m.*

Via (*sec. a*) Brookline, Needham, Wellesley, Natick, Framingham, South-borough, Westborough, Worcester; (*sec. b*) Leicester, Spencer, East Brookfield, North Brookfield, Brookfield, West Brookfield, Warren, Ware, Amherst, Hadley, Northampton, Westhampton; (*sec. c*) Williamsburg, Goshen, Cummington, Windsor and Dalton.

B. & A. R.R. parallels this route.

Hard-surfaced road; heavily traveled; western section hilly and slippery during wet weather.

Sec. a. BOSTON to WORCESTER, 38.1 m.

BETWEEN Boston and Worcester, State 9, called the Worcester Turn-pike, is an express route avoiding all town centers. Laid out by Isaiah Thomas of Worcester and opened in 1809, it was a toll road until 1835. The Turnpike curves as it passes ponds and reservoirs, but for long stretches it is as straight as a surveyor's line, running through open country with little scenic interest.

West of Boston (Copley Square) State 9 follows Huntington Ave.

At 2.3 *m.* is BROOKLINE (*see BROOKLINE*).

At 7.1 *m.* is the junction with State 128.

Left on State 128; right (straight ahead) on Highland Ave. when State 128 branches left at the overpass; the *William Carter Plant*, Mill No. 1, 2.5 *m.*, is the chief industry of the town and one of the largest knitting mills in the country. During the Civil War the manufacture of knit goods, introduced by Jonathan Avery, became an important economic factor in the community. In recent years the Carter Company has been pioneering in the production of rayon and other synthetic materials.

At 2.9 *m.* is the junction with Rosemary St. Right on this is *Rosemary Lake*, a small body of water popular with local sportsmen (*sandy beach and toboggan slide*).

On Highland Ave. is NEEDHAM, 3.3 *m.* (town, alt. 169, pop. 11,838, sett. 1680–94, incorp. 1711). On April 16, 1680, the Dedham Company of Watertown purchased a large tract of land from an Indian, part of which, with some of Dedham, was incorporated as Needham. Between 1714 and 1789 the town was active in road- and bridge-building; before 1720 a few sawmills and corn mills were operated, but farming was the chief occupation. The town is now a residential suburb.

Right from Needham on Great Plain Ave. is the junction with Nehoiden St.; on this is the *Fuller House*, 0.6 *m.* (*private*), 220 Nehoiden St., a trim and attractive white clapboarded dwelling (1754).

At 1.1 *m.*, on the corner of Nehoiden St. and Central Ave., is the *Townsend House* (*private*), a three-story square, yellow clapboarded dwelling. For over 100 years it was the home of the town pastors.

Left on Central Ave. 0.5 *m.* to the *Gay House* (*private*), 1196 Central Ave., a simple little two-story white house, built in the early 1700's. The chimney in the rear is that of the first kitchen. The planks of the living-room floor are over 20 inches wide.

West of the junction with Central Ave. on Great Plain Ave. is (L.) *Babson Park*, 1.9 *m.*, devoted to semi-business interests, but containing charming wooded drives. Visible near the entrance are the towers of *Radio Station WORL* (*open daily*, 7 *to sunset*). The *Stone Bird Sanctuary* and the *Woodlot Library* (*open*) are 0.7 *m.* from the entrance, the latter a one-story white frame dwelling housing more than 200 stuffed birds native to this area.

WELLESLEY HILLS, 10.5 *m.* (alt. 140). Here is a *Stone Clock-tower* of a modified Colonial design faintly suggestive of the Campanile at Venice. A shaft of granite masonry is topped by an open wood belfry.

Left from Wellesley Hills on Washington St. is WELLESLEY, 1 *m.* (*see WELLES-LEY*).

At 15.2 *m.* is the junction with State 27.

Left on State 27 is NATICK, 1.5 *m.* (town, alt. 158, pop. 14,394, sett. 1718, in-corp. 1781), granted to John Eliot in 1650 as a plantation for his Praying Indians. It was a self-governing community for more than half a century; when white settlers appeared the Indians were crowded out. It was a farming settlement until the 19th century. Industries at the present time are two shoe factories, a baseball factory, a paper-box factory, and a saw and tool manufacturing plant.

On the Park St. side of the Common a boulder memorial marks the *Henry Wilson Tree*, planted by him in 1857. Henry Wilson 'the Natick cobbler,' was born in New Hampshire in 1812 and was known as Jeremiah Jones Colbaith until he was 21, when he had his name changed by an act of the Legislature; he came to Natick in 1833 as a cobbler's apprentice. He entered politics and gained considerable attention by his anti-slavery oratory, and served as U.S. Senator 1855–73 and as Vice-President of the United States 1873–75.

Left from Natick on Union St.; at the intersection of Eliot and Pleasant Sts. in SOUTH NATICK, 1.8 *m.* (alt. 119), is a boulder on the *Site of the Indian Meeting House* (1651), used by John Eliot. Across the street is the *Natick Historical Society Headquarters* (*open Wed. and Sat.* 2.30–5.30), a two-story, red-brick building with broad windows. Field stone is laid in a pattern in the first-story walls. The build-ing holds many articles of historic value, and is surrounded by extensive grounds bordered by old trees and an iron fence. Within this enclosure is the *Site of an In-dian Burying Ground*. Here also is a *Monument to Eliot*, a granite shaft with a cross on one side and an open Bible on the other.

Opposite the Library, on Pleasant St., is the old *Stowe House* (*private*), built in 1816. The gabled two-and-a-half-story white clapboarded structure with an end chimney and a field-stone foundation is well preserved. An old carriage lamp on the wall by the door, and blue spruce trees on both sides of the walk, date back to the boyhood days of Professor Calvin Stowe, the Horace Holyoke of 'Old Town Folks,' written by his wife, Harriet Beecher Stowe. On a granite block at the entrance to the driveway is a slate tablet marking the *Grave of Takwambait*, an Indian disciple of Eliot.

The *Charles River* (*swimming and canoeing*) is spanned at Pleasant St. by a new stone bridge with modern lamp-posts and iron handrails, occupying the *Site of the Old Indian Bridge* used in 1650 by the Praying Indians of Natick.

At 17.6 *m.* is the junction of State 9 and State 126 (*see Tour 1C*).

The *Commonwealth of Massachusetts Muster Field*, at the junction, is a tract of several hundred acres used since Revolutionary days.

FRAMINGHAM CENTER, 19 *m.* (alt. 199), is the old village of the township. The governmental center has now been shifted to Framing-ham (*see Tour 1C*).

On Oak St., opposite the Common, is the *Framingham Memorial Library* (*open Mon., Wed., and Fri.* 9–9; *Tues. and Sat.* 9–6). This structure was built in 1872–73 in memory of the citizens of Framingham who served in the Civil War.

Facing the Common at the corner of Grove and Vernon Sts. is the *Old Stone Academy Building* (*open by appointment*), built in 1837 and now the home of the Framingham Historical and Natural History Society.

The *Framingham State Teachers' College*, on Maynard Rd., is the oldest normal school in the country, having been founded one year before Craftsbury Academy in Vermont. Originally opened in Lexington in 1839, the institution was moved to Framingham in 1853.

On a tiny Common in the center of Buckminster Square, at the junction of Main, Maple, and Curve Sts. and Union Ave., is the *Revolutionary War Memorial*, a bronze statue of a Minuteman loading a musket from a powder horn. On the corner is a roughhewn *Milestone* set up in 1768 when this village was on the 'Connecticut Path.' Near-by, on Main St., is the *Church Hill Cemetery*, containing the grave of Peter Salem, the Negro slave (*see LEICESTER, Tour 8, sec. b*).

    1. Left from Framingham on Main St., straight ahead on Union Ave. to the junction with Mt. Wayte Ave.; right here to the corner of Chatauqua Ave. where a boulder marks the *Site of the Thomas Eames House*, burned by Indians during King Philip's War. Eames's wife and five of their children were slain; the remaining four children were taken captive.

    2. Right from Framingham on Vernon St.; left on Grove St. 1 *m.* to the corner of Belknap Rd., where is the *Pike-Haven Homestead* (*private*), a two-and-a-half-story gambrel-roof, clapboarded structure, now painted red and surrounded by spreading elms and slender poplars; built by Jeremiah Pike in 1693, it has housed eight generations of his descendants.

    Right from Grove St. on Belknap Rd.; left on Edgell Rd. to a path at 3.7 *m.* which leads left to Nobscot Hill (alt. 600) and the ruins of a lookout built by the Indian Tantamous, called Old Jethro, who settled here about 1640 with his family. In 1675 he allied himself with the Praying Indians against King Philip, but he scorned Christianity. When the English confiscated his lands and insisted that the Natick Indians stay within prescribed limits, he was infuriated. Joining King Philip's band, he participated in the massacres, till he was tricked into delivering himself to the English at Dover, N.H.; he was tried and hanged in Boston, September 26, 1676, and his family was sold into slavery.

    Among the Indian remains in the town are the underground granaries and the sweating pits; the former are circular holes about 5 feet deep and from 3 to 16 feet across, usually in the side of a knoll. The sweating pit near Farm Pond is a circular hole about 4 feet deep; small stones placed on its bottom were heated and water poured over them, making steam. The Indians used this steam as a purification bath before tribal ceremonies.

West of Framingham State 9 passes through sections of the Metropolitan Water Works Reservoir System. At 22.6 *m.* is the *Sudbury Reservoir.*

At 23.5 *m.* is the junction with State 85.

    Right on State 85 is SOUTHBOROUGH, 1.1 *m.* (town, alt. 314, pop. 2109, sett. 1660, incorp. 1727). The settlement of Richard Newton and his family was the nucleus of the community. When there were about 50 families here, the area was separated from Marlborough and incorporated.

    Although the town was primarily concerned with farming, manufacturing flourished during the 19th century, producing boots, shoes, and cotton and woolen goods. The factories gradually disappeared, and when the Metropolitan Water Commission took over 1200 acres of land, and Stony Brook became a Metropolitan Aqueduct, the last of the mills was abandoned. The remaining acreage is now devoted to the production of milk or fruit. Thousands of pine trees planted on the watershed add beauty as well as revenue to the district.

St. Mark's Episcopal Church, a beautiful edifice of multi-colored stone with a slate roof, has a tablet commemorating its founder and builder, Joseph Burnett of Southborough.

Deerfoot Farms (open), on Deerfoot Rd. was founded in 1847 by Dr. Joseph Burnett, a pioneer in scientific farming and an early importer of Jersey cattle.

At **27.3 *m*.** is the junction with State 30.

Left on State 30 is WESTBOROUGH, 1.5 *m*. (town, alt. 298, pop. 6073, sett. about 1675, incorp. 1717), originally granted by the General Court to several individual proprietors in return for services to the colony. Among these grants was one of 500 acres, made in 1659, to Charles Chauncy, second president of Harvard College, but revoked in 1660, when it was found to be a section of the Marlborough grant of that year. The Westborough section was called Chauncy until it was separated from Marlborough and became the hundredth town incorporated in the State.

Westborough's agricultural character was changed by the busy Boston–Worcester Turnpike, a stagecoach route after 1810; its industrial character was firmly established when the Boston and Albany Railroad was run through the village in 1835. Boots and shoes were the principal manufactures, but straw goods, particularly straw hats, and sleighs and tools were produced in quantities.

Left from Westborough on Main St. to the junction with Ruggles St.; left on this to Eli Whitney St.; right on the second street to the *Site of the Birthplace of Eli Whitney* (1765–1825), 1.3 *m*. (*open; adm.* 10¢). The site of the home of the inventor of the cotton gin is marked by a boulder.

On Ruggles St. about 0.1 *m*. south of Eli Whitney St., a marker says: 'An Indian trail prior to 1630 crossed here. The Old Connecticut Path.' On *Jack Straw Hill*, back of the marker, Jack Straw, a Christian Indian who held much of this section built his cabin. Jack Straw, believed to have been the first Massachusetts Indian converted by the white men, was one of two Indians taken to London by Sir Walter Raleigh and presented to Queen Elizabeth.

At **27.9 *m*.** is the junction with Lyman St.

Right on Lyman St. to *Chauncy Lake*, 0.4 *m*. (*fishing, bathing, boating, dancing, and picnicking*), on the rescinded grant of Harvard's second president.

To the southwest is *Hoccomocco Pond*, named by the Indians after an evil spirit. This was the scene of the activities of one Tom Cook, a highwayman, born in Westborough in 1738, who used to rob the well-to-do and give to the poor. The wealthy are said to have paid this local Robin Hood large sums annually for immunity from his depredations. Though there seems to have been an engaging side to Tom's character, he seems incontrovertibly to have been the original racketeer.

At **31.2 *m*.** State 9 overpasses US 20 (*see Tour 4*) at traffic cloverleaf.

At **35.8 *m*.** is *White City Park*, a large amusement area (*fee*) on the Shrewsbury bank of Lake Quinsigamond (*annual regattas, boat races, picnic grounds*).

At **38.2 *m*.** is WORCESTER (*see WORCESTER*). Here is the junction with State 122 (*see Tour 23*), State 12 (*see Tour 11*), and State 70 (*see Tour 7*).

Sec. b. WORCESTER to NORTHAMPTON, 56.3 *m.*

West from Lincoln Square in Worcester, State 9 passes *Elm Park*, 1 *m.*

LEICESTER, 7.4 *m.* (town, alt. 1009, pop. 4426, sett. 1713, incorp. 1722), now a manufacturing and residential community, offered hospitality to Quakers and Anabaptists when they were persecuted elsewhere.

Since 1786 the town's history has been identified with the woolen trades. By 1890 approximately one fourth of the cards, both hand and machine, used in the United States were produced here, and 10 woolen mills, of which only two have survived, were established. Present manufactures now include cards and shuttles, children's games, advertising literature, and flannel cloth.

The *Stone Walls* of the Winslow Farms on Winslow Ave., off Paxton St., varying in width from 2 to 20 feet, are relics of privately subsidized relief work. During the panic of 1873 Mrs. Edward Flint, then owner of the farm, hired the unemployed of the town to clear her fields of stone and build these walls.

> Left from Leicester on Rochdale Rd.; left at 1.2 *m.* on a side road to the *Site of the Shack of Peter Salem*, 1.4 *m.* Salem, a Negro slave, killed the British officer, Major Pitcairn, in the Battle of Bunker Hill. After the War he came to Leicester, where he built a crude hut and lived in poverty until, in his old age, he was taken to the poorhouse in Framingham, where he died.

At 11.5 *m.* are the modern and sanitary *Sibley Dairy Farms (open)*, containing one of the best Jersey herds in the East. On the crest of Moose Hill, left of the Farms, is the *Sibley Mansion (closed)*, product of another private effort at relief, in 1898–99. All building supplies were purchased through local merchants, and the work was performed by unemployed workmen of the town.

SPENCER, 12.4 *m.* (town, alt. 860, pop. 6487, sett. 1721, incorp. 1775), named for Lieutenant-Governor Spencer Phipps, instrumental in securing the town's district status, has been a manufacturing town since 1810; its most important activity began in 1811 when Josiah and Nathaniel Green began making shoes sewed with thread. Boot and shoe production, at present confined to two large firms, and the allied manufactures of slippers and heels, form the major industrial interest of the town. The Alta Crest Farms, producing dairy products, owns one of the largest herds of pure-bred Ayrshire cattle in America; and the Treadwell Farm is nationally known for the breeding of poultry, particularly Rhode Island Reds.

The *Richard Sugden Public Library (open daily, 2–8)*, Pleasant St., is a brick building with brown stone trim, housing the *Spencer Museum* founded in 1874. This has a collection of Indian relics and historical objects.

> Left from Spencer on Maple St.; right at 1.2 *m.* on the first dirt road to a *Cobblestone Monument* in front of the cellar hole of the old *Howe Homestead*, 2.2 *m.*, where Elias Howe, Jr. (1819–67), who first patented the lock-stitch sewing machine, was born. This site is now a part of *Howe Memorial Park (fishing, picnicking)*.

At 12.9 *m.*, in front of the West Main St. School, is the *Howe Monument*, dedicated May 19, 1910, in honor of Elias Howe, Jr., his uncle William Howe, originator of the Howe truss-type bridge, and Tyler Howe, inventor of the spring bed.

At 15.9 *m.* is EAST BROOKFIELD (town, alt. 621, pop. 945, sett. 1664, incorp. 1920), the youngest town in the State. The vicinity was inhabited by the Quabaug Indians, who were visited in 1655 by John Eliot, apostle to the Indians.

Lake Lashaway (*fishing, boating, swimming, picnicking; skating, hockey, ice-boating in winter*) stretches north from the main highway in the village into North Brookfield; its wooded shores, once inhabited by Indians, are a popular resort.

At 16.4 *m.* is the junction with State 67, a part of the Old Post Rd. skirting the former Great Swamp.

> Right on State 67 at 0.4 *m.*, on the Drake Farm, in a one-room wayside stand, is the carefully mounted *Drake Collection of Indian Relics* (*open; adm. free*), containing 119 specimens. Most of these artifacts were found within 10 miles of this farm.

> Left on State 67 at 0.8 *m.* (*dirt road*) are several milestones set out when Benjamin Franklin was Deputy Postmaster-General of the Colonies, the longest unbroken line of them known.

> At 4.2 *m.* on State 67 is NORTH BROOKFIELD (town, alt. 960, pop. 3186, sett. 1664, incorp. 1812), agricultural till its incorporation, when manufacturing began, first with tanning, then shoemaking. Today the leading manufactured products are rubber goods and asbestos matting. Farming, however, is still important, with dairying, poultry-raising, and orchardry predominating. The setting of George M. Cohan's play 'Fifty Miles from Boston' is thought to be here.

At 18.2 *m.* is the junction with a dirt road.

> Left on this road to *Lake Quabaug* (*fishing, boating, camping*). It is annually stocked by the State with bass, bluegills, and white perch.

BROOKFIELD, 10.2 *m.* (town, alt. 706, pop. 1309, sett. 1664, incorp. 1718), was originally called Quabaug. The territory surrounding Brookfield was granted by the General Court to residents of Ipswich in 1660. Brookfield was the most important township in the county until about 1810. Although there was a large boot and shoe industry here in the 19th century, the two factories remaining in the town produce electric wire and gummed papers. The main occupation is dairying, and the region is known for its Jersey herds.

The *Merrick Library* (*open weekdays* 2–5, *Sun.* 3.30–8), built of stone, at the northeast corner of the Common, houses the French writing desk of Louis XVI and Marie Antoinette, a gift to William Draper in 1863 from the Marquis Bernard De Marigny.

The *Brookfield Inn* (*open*), on State 9, with low ceilings, a taproom, and a sign dated '1771,' still has the atmosphere of an ancient hostelry.

On West Main St. opposite the Inn is the *Chapin House* (*private*), built in 1797. Its doors and windows are among the finest of their period in New England.

In the village cemetery on State 9 is the *Grave of Joshua Spooner*, whose epitaph states that he was

> 'murdered by three soldiers of the Revolution,
> Ross, Brooks, and Buchanan,
> at the instigation of his wife, Bathsheba.'

This event, which took place March 1, 1778, was one of Worcester County's grisliest tragedies, culminating in the hanging of Mrs. Spooner and the three soldiers. The execution proved a gala event for Worcester, with a long sermon full of sulphurous fumes preceding the grisly climax and a terrific thunderstorm illuminating the path to the gallows.

At 20.3 *m.* a marker records: 'Brookfield — settled in 1660 by men from Ipswich on Indian land called Quabaug. Attacked by Indians 1675, one garrison house defended to the last. Reoccupied 12 years later.' Massasoit is supposed to have died in the Quabaug settlement in 1662. The highway here follows the Quabaug River, which in the springtime is a vast lake spreading over miles of lowland, and in August is a narrow stream twisting in and out among the hummocks, and forming strange geometric figures on the green table of the meadow.

WEST BROOKFIELD, 22 *m.* (town, alt. 604, pop. 1258, sett. 1664, incorp. 1848), first section of the original Brookfield grant to be settled, was, prior to 1789, the most important section. Of the various industries that have been in the town, only one, a yeast manufactory, remains. Farming and dairying are the principal means of livelihood.

In the two-story *Brick Building* on Main St., Isaiah Thomas in 1798 edited the first newspaper of the Brookfields. Four years later Ebenezer Merriam & Co. acquired the paper and conducted a general printing business for 60 years. The sons of Ebenezer Merriam opened a printing shop in Springfield and published Noah Webster's dictionary.

> Right approaching Common on Foster Hill Rd. is a huge *Boulder*, from which George Whitefield preached, in 1741, to more than 5000 people.
> At 0.7 *m. Indian Rock* is clearly visible. This natural breastwork was used by the warriors of King Philip, August 2, 3, and 4, 1675, when they directed their fire on 'one garrison house defended to the last.' The *Fortified House Site* is marked.

At 23.2 *m.* is the junction with State 19.

> Left on State 19 at 0.5 *m.* are evergreens planted in the gravel bank of a high cut; originally they spelled in green letters: 'Keep your roadsides clean.' Besides adding beauty to the road, these trees prevent soil erosion.
> At 1.7 *m.* is the junction with Washington St., part of the *Old Bay Path* traversed in 1759 by Lord Jeffrey Amherst with over 10,000 men on the way to join Wolfe at Quebec. General Burgoyne traveled over the same route after his surrender at Saratoga, and General Washington used it earlier on his way to Cambridge. At 0.3 *m.* on this road is a *Franklin Milestone* reading '71 miles from Boston,' and just beyond in the yard of a house is a tall *elm* (1750) under which Washington is said to have stopped in 1775.
> At 2.5 *m.* on this road is WARREN (town, alt. 609, pop. 3662, sett. 1664, incorp. 1742), called Squabaug ('Red-Water Place') by the Indians. This town was incorporated as Western and renamed in 1834 in honor of General Joseph Warren, author of the 'Suffolk Resolutions' and Revolutionary hero, killed at Bunker Hill, 1775. An outpost frontier town, it was heavily garrisoned against Indian attacks.

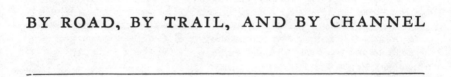

BY ROAD, BY TRAIL, AND BY CHANNEL

IN MASSACHUSETTS, whether you tour by land or by sea, by car, by boat, or on foot, there are continually agreeable vistas and close-ups that confront you. A few such are included here: seascape and landscape, city and farm, winter and summer. The memory of such scenes as these must have heartened many a Massachusetts man when crossing the Western Plains or sailing the China Seas.

STREET IN MARBLEHEAD

BOSTON FROM THE AIR

HARVARD BUILDINGS ON THE CHARLES, CAMBRI

WINDMILL, CAPE COD

MARBLEHEAD HARBOR

LIGHTHOUSE, CAPE COD

CONNECTICUT VALLEY, NEAR NORTHAMPTON

LEXINGTON GREEN

MEMORIAL TOWER, TOP OF MT. GREYLOCK

A story is told of a Mrs. Mark, who, frightened by lurking Indians while her husband was away and the garrison unmanned, put on her husband's clothes, shouldered a musket, and marched up and down in front of her home crying 'All's well! All's well!' at intervals till the Indians disappeared.

Warren's industrial activity, at its height in the 19th century, has declined. Nathan Read, a native of Warren, is said to have constructed and in 1789 successfully operated a steamboat. He also invented a nail machine now in general use.

Right from the village on the West Warren Rd. about 0.5 m. is a place described as the *Site of the Wooden Truss Bridge Invented by William Howe* of Spencer. To the south is *Mark's Mountain* (*no direct road*), a favorite hunting-ground of the Indians; a primitive stone fireplace was found here.

At 26.4 m. is the *Rock House*, formed by large fragments dropped from an overhanging ledge; it is frequently used by picnic parties.

At 27.5 m. as State 9 enters the Ware River Valley, is the junction (R) with State 32 (*see Tour 23A*), which unites briefly with State 9.

WARE, 28.8 m. (town, alt. 488, pop. 7727, sett. about 1717, incorp. 1775), was called Nenameseck ('Fishing Weir') by the Indians, a name applied also to the river, where salmon were caught. The town seal represents an Indian standing, spear in hand, above a roughly constructed weir.

The town supported Shays's Rebellion, and Captain Jacob Cummings's home here was a supply depot. At the beginning of the 19th century, sawmills and gristmills and a textile mill were opened in the Ware River Valley.

Grenville Park (*amphitheater; baseball field, tennis courts, picnicking*), between Church St. and the Ware River, was established to preserve the rustic beauty of the area.

From the river bank is visible the upper side of the dam, the setting of the 'Legend of Nenameseck.' White Dove, an Indian girl, was betrothed to Gray Eagle; his rival, the Squirrel, ambushed him, but was himself killed in the encounter. The Council, deceived by false testimony, found Gray Eagle guilty, and bound and set him in a canoe above the falls. While the tribe watched for his destruction, White Dove leaped into the fragile craft, and together the lovers were swept over the falls to their death on the rocks below.

State 32 (*see Tour 23A*) branches left at the western end of Ware.

WARE CENTER, 30.7 m. (alt. 481, town of Ware), was the original Center of the town. In the late 18th century it had eight taverns in which public affairs were really settled, though they were officially ratified at town meetings in the meeting house; even the formal sessions were at times adjourned to a tavern to enable the participants, fortified by cider and applejack, to continue their arguments in the taprooms.

The *Meeting House*, 1820, was the work of Isaac Damon. It is simple and dignified, and its interest centers in the Ionic portico and in the cupola topped by a dome and surrounded by an open balustrade.

The old *Gould Tavern* (18th century), two stories, with a hip roof, stands on a low bank surrounded by overhanging trees. L-shaped in plan, the front and east sides look much alike, each having a center door with flanking windows and a fanlight and five windows in the second story.

At 33.4 *m.* is the *Quabbin Park Cemetery* established by the Commonwealth for the bodies disinterred when the Quabbin Reservoir was built.

At 34.5 *m.* is the junction with an improved road.

Right on this road is the dam of the Quabbin Reservoir, constructed (1937) in the Swift River Valley, inundating the towns of Enfield, Greenwich, and Prescott. It has 177 miles of shore line, surrounding 39 square miles, with a maximum depth of 150 feet and a storage capacity of 415 billion gallons. The water will flow by gravity into Wachusett Reservoir, through Quabbin Aqueduct, a 24.6 mile tunnel through solid rock.

At 39.4 *m.* is the junction with US 202 (*see Tour* 13).

At 40.9 *m.* the road passes a group of *Ponds* (*swimming, boating, fishing*).

At 42.3 *m.* is a beautiful path (R) along a brook to *Holland Glen*, a park developed by the Belchertown Historical Society.

At 48.8 *m.* is AMHERST (*see AMHERST*) (alt. 249) and the junction with State 116 (*see Tour* 15B).

At 50 *m.* is a view of the Mt. Holyoke Range and the summit-houses on Mt. Tom and Mt. Holyoke.

HADLEY, 53.3 *m.* (town, alt. 129, pop. 2711, sett. 1659, incorp. 1661), named for Hadley or Hadleigh, England, former home of its founders, was settled in 1659 by John Webster and the Rev. John Russell, who had left Connecticut because of religious dissension.

Hadley indulged in a bit of witch-baiting. In 1683 Mary Webster, accused of bewitching and murdering Deacon Philip Smith, was 'hung till nearly dead,' taken down, and buried in the snow. In spite of this she survived, and died several years later from natural causes.

Broom corn, introduced here in 1797 by Levi Dickinson, had by 1850 become an important product.

The *Hadley Farm Museum* (*open Wed., Sat., Sun. 2–5; adm. free*), is an old barn (1782), with a large well-sweep in front of it, and a Colonial doorway with a pediment resembling the bonnet tops of highboys or secretaries. The museum contains a large collection of farm implements that trace the evolution of farming in the Connecticut Valley; it also has early vehicles, and a number of old household articles.

Adjacent to the Town Hall on State 63 (Middle St.) is the *First Congregational Church* (1808), with a Wren-type spire surmounted by a weathercock brought from England in 1752. Over the large double door at the front is a semicircular fanlight, the whole framed by beautifully carved trim. The church has a silver communion service and cups of odd design, presented to the parish in 1724, and a pewter platter of unrecorded age. Several of the original pews are still in use.

The ancient *Allen Tavern* (*open*) on Middle St. (18th century), contains many old relics and pieces of furniture. This large white Colonial house is notable for its row of seven windows on the main façade and its gable end, which has two more windows and a large door. At the rear an ell connects the structure with an old-fashioned carriage house.

A stone marker north of the Center on the east side of West St. identifies the *Site of the House of the Rev. John Russell.* Edmund Whalley and William Goffe, members of the High Court of Justice established by the Commons which condemned Charles I to death, fled to America when the monarchy was restored and Charles II issued warrants for the arrest of his father's 'murderers.' Landing in Boston in 1660 and learning that royal officers were hunting them, they hurried on to Connecticut; finding no safety there, they came in 1664 to Hadley, where they were hidden and protected by Mr. Russell for fifteen years. There is a tradition that Goffe, whose identity was not known locally, was of much service to the settlement, giving the alarm before a surprise attack by King Philip's warriors and leading the confused townsmen in a successful defense. Goffe's end is unknown, but Whalley died in the Russell house, and bones supposedly his were found in the cellar many years later. (*See STOW, Tour 7.*)

On West St. 0.2 *m.* beyond the site of the Russell house is the *Porter House* (1713), the oldest dwelling in Hadley, a white two-and-a-half-story house with gabled roof, large central chimney, an elaborate two-leaf Colonial doorway, with beautiful paneling surmounted by a highboy scroll.

A large white quartz boulder (L.) opposite the Porter house indicates the *Site of the Birthplace of Major General 'Fighting Joe' Hooker*, of Civil War fame, born November 3, 1814.

1. Right from Hadley on State 63 is (L) the *Bishop Huntington House* (*apply to caretaker*), 2.2 *m.* This house, built in 1753 and standing in a beautiful grove of elms, rock maples, and hemlocks, was for many years the summer home of Frederick Dan Huntington (1819–1904), a native of Hadley and the first bishop of the Episcopal Diocese of Central New York. Surrounded by a split-rail fence, this large three-story gambrel-roof structure has (L) a kitchen ell, woodshed, and carriage house, in a long low line connecting it with a newer and smaller house of simple Colonial style. Beyond the house are the waters of the Connecticut and the roofs and steeples of Hatfield.

At 3.2 *m.* on State 63 is NORTH HADLEY (alt. 130, Town of Hadley). Opposite the church a farm road leads through fields to the *Site of an Indian Fort* on a bluff overlooking the banks of the Connecticut River; several Indian skeletons have been discovered here.

2. Left from Hadley on State 63 at 1.1. *m.* the Fort River is spanned by a concrete bridge. At 1.6 *m.* a farm road leads right to a bluff overlooking the Fort River, which was also the *Site of an Indian Fort.* At 2.4 *m.* State 63 enters a stretch of woodland, at the beginning of which are (R. and L.) the *Remnants of a Ditch* dug by the early settlers as part of the boundary of a sheep pasture, neither stones nor wood being available at that time for the building of fences. This ditch can be traced in a wide circle around the foot of Mount Holyoke, but is conspicuous at this point.

At 54.5 *m.* the road crosses the Connecticut River.

In NORTHAMPTON, 56.3 *m.* (*see NORTHAMPTON*) (alt. 145), is the junction with US 5 (*see Tour 15*) and State 10 (*see Tour 15C*).

Left from Northampton on State 66 at 8.2 *m.* is the junction with a road; right is WESTHAMPTON, 9.6 *m.* (town, alt. 460, pop. 405, sett. 1762, incorp. 1778).

The western part of Northampton was set off as Westhampton in 1778. In 1765 a lead mine, partly owned by Ethan Allen, was opened, and is said to have furnished lead for Revolutionary War bullets. Natural resources led to the establishment of grist and lumber mills, and many of the attempted manufactures were connected with the natural resource of timber: chairs, boxes, potash, and firewood. A brass foundry was also in operation at one time. Today dairying, farming, and lumbering are the chief occupations.

The *Sylvester Judd House* (1816) is at the Westhampton Village. Sylvester was the first town clerk, one-time publisher of the *Hampshire Gazette*, and author of a 'History of Hadley.'

South of the village 0.2 *m.* is the *Hale House* (R.). Here lived the Rev. Enoch Hale (1753–1837), brother of Nathan Hale, for 57 years minister of the town. He was author of a spelling book, now a literary curiosity, written according to the then advanced ideas of adapting style and content to the understanding of the child. Later his daughters conducted a school in the house.

Right from the village on an improved road is *Pine Island Lake*, 2.3 *m.*, an increasingly popular location for summer residences.

Sec. c. NORTHAMPTON to JUNCTION with US 7, 43.9 *m.*

State 9 branches right from Main St. on Elm St. in Northampton, and passes through a level fertile farming land.

At HAYDENVILLE, 6.2 *m.* (alt. 439, town of Williamsburg), cloth-covered buttons are believed to have been first manufactured by machinery.

On State 9, 0.2 *m.* west of the Center, is the *Hayden House* (*private*), home of Governor Hayden, a white-painted, dignified brick dwelling, built about 1800. Set 50 feet back from the road and surrounded by elms, this mansion has four massive fluted Doric pillars and a carved door.

State 9 continues through a narrow valley.

WILLIAMSBURG, 8.3 *m.* (town, alt. 500, pop. 1859, sett. 1735, incorp. 1771), was once in Hatfield Town. The earliest settler was for 17 years without a close neighbor. By the end of the 18th century many small factories had been opened here, utilizing the abundant water-power and producing leather, cotton, and woolen goods, shoes, buttons, pens, penholders, hardware, woodwork, and ironware. In 1874 a dam, built nine years before about three miles above the village, burst, releasing a raging flood that drowned 136 people, washed out the entire industrial section of this town, and seriously damaged neighboring communities. The local mills were not rebuilt; today only a few very small factories are in operation.

The *Meekins Library* is an attractive building of gray granite given by Stephen Meekins, a farmer, who made $40,000 in raising sheep. He intended leaving this sum for a monument but was persuaded to use it for a library. Another town benefactor was Dr. Daniel Collins, long a familiar figure as he made his rounds on his horse, his saddlebags bulging not only with medicines but often with food and garments for the poor. He established the Collins Fund for the benefit of needy local students.

At 8.7 *m.* is the junction with State 143 (*see Tour 8A*).

At 9.2 *m.* is SEARSVILLE (alt. 700, town of Williamsburg), a small village.

At 9.7 *m.* is the junction with a dirt road.

Left on this road at 0.1 *m.* is a fork.

1. Left from the fork through a pasture is *Rhena's Cave,* 0.5 *m.*, a mass of rock with several apertures. According to legend, the beautiful Rhena Meekins, sister of Stephen, donor of the library, lived here as a recluse after her parents forbade her to marry the man she loved.

2. Right from the fork is *Silas Snow Farm,* 0.3 *m.*, part of the tract received by Samuel Barber from King George II by a deed still extant. Interesting geologic formations on this land are studied by students of Smith and Amherst Colleges· the bricks used in building the Governor Hayden House in Haydenville (*see above*) were made here. A path from the house leads through the pasture 0.5 *m.* to *Burgoyne's Cave.* Here, according to legend, Burgoyne took shelter from a rainstorm as he was being taken to prison after the Battle of Saratoga.

At 12 *m.* is the junction with a side road.

Right on this road at 0.1 *m.* is the junction with a dirt road. Left on the second dirt road and right at 0.1 *m.* on a path through open fields, then through the woods to *Packard Falls.*

Straight ahead on the main side road at 0.6 *m.* is a path; left here through the woods to the *Devil's Den,* a rocky gorge (*guide needed for difficult descent to Mill River bed*) with beautiful granite walls green with moss, and deep pools.

At 13.3 *m.* is the *Whale Inn* (*open in summer*), built and occupied by three generations of Putneys. The old plastering and wide floor boards, lovely paneling, and huge hearthstones from the near-by ledges of Goshen schist are well preserved. In the center of the broken pediment over the front door is a whale, a modern addition. The Whale Inn was christened by the late Arthur Warner of Florence, Massachusetts, who said he had always heard that

The Whale, he swam around the ocean
And landed Jonah up in Goshen.

GOSHEN, 13.7 *m.* (town, alt. 1460, pop. 257, sett. 1761, incorp. 1781), is in a dairying community that derives profit also from poultry-raising, lumbering, and maple-sugaring.

Right from Goshen on West Shore Rd. to *Highland Lake,* 0.3 *m.* (*boating, fishing, swimming*).

At 14.1 *m.* is the junction with Ashfield Rd.

Right on this road to the entrance at 0.1 *m.* of the *Daughters of the American Revolution State Forest* (*picnic grove*); right at 1.1 *m.* on a trail to *Moore's Hill* (alt. 1713), a rounded elevation from which is an unobstructed panorama of the countryside.

At 14.5 *m.* (R) is the *Snake House;* in front of it are two boulders banded with veins of contrasting stone that resemble snakes.

LITHIA, 16 *m.* (town of Goshen), is a tiny village. North of the Center on State 112 is *Mountain Rest,* a summer resort with several buildings, including a community hall and playroom for children, and with facilities for outdoor sports. While the general public is accommodated, preference is given to missionaries of all denominations who are home on furlough.

SWIFT RIVER, 17.8 *m.* (alt. 1090, town of Cummington) junction of the Swift River with a branch of the Westfield River; west of the village, State 9 meanders through the Westfield Valley, which occasionally widens into broad stretches of farmland.

CUMMINGTON, 20.7 *m.* (town, alt. 1050, pop. 610, sett. 1762, incorp. 1779), was named for Colonel Cummings, purchaser of the land. Cotton and woolen mills, paper mills, tanneries, and other factories flourished here for a while in the early 19th century and then dwindled away.

A *Covered Bridge,* 50 feet north of the Square, is one of the few remaining in Massachusetts.

At 21.4 *m.* is the junction with a marked road.

Left on this road at 0.4 *m.* is a fork.

1. Left from here 0.6 *m.* is the *Playhouse in the Hills,* also known as the Music Box, where music, sculpture, painting, writing, and dancing are taught as creative expression rather than professions. Founded in 1922 by Katherine Frazier, it is in the original Center of Cummington and includes among its buildings the parsonage of the first Cummington church. A monument on Playhouse property marks the *Site of the Birthplace of William Cullen Bryant* (1794–1878).

2. Right from the fork 1.6 *m.* is (L) the *Bryant Homestead* (*open Mon., Wed., Fri.* 2.30–5, *June* 15–*Sept.* 15), a beautiful two-and-a-half-story Dutch Colonial house of white clapboards with a wing on each side. Originally a one-and-a-half-story dwelling, the main structure was elevated in 1856 and a new lower floor was added. The smaller wing was used by Bryant as a library and study.

At 22.6 *m.*, marked by a white wooden sign set about 15 feet from the bridge, is the brook of Bryant's poem, 'The Rivulet.'

At 26.1 *m.* is WEST CUMMINGTON (alt. 1200).

Right from West Cummington a marked road follows the East Branch of the Westfield River; at 2.8 *m.* is the junction with a dirt road; right here to another road at 3.3 *m.*; right here to the *Windsor State Forest.* A foot trail leads to an *Observation Point* in the northwest corner of the area near the Westfield River.

The motor road leads past a swimming pool to a parking space about 300 feet from the head of the *Windsor Jambs.* This cascade, part of Boundary Brook, is viewed from the top of rock cliffs reached by several foot trails. At one point the waters take a sudden drop of about 50 feet between walls of solid jagged rock, and rush on over boulders and ledges.

At 27.4 *m.* is EAST WINDSOR (alt. 1320). At the Center in the gorge beside Walker Brook is (R) an old *Red Mill* that for many years turned out lollypop sticks and butchers' skewers.

State 9, winding between the stony brook (L) and the steep side of the mountain (R), ascends by abrupt grades to a plateau.

WINDSOR, 32.3 *m.* (town, alt. 2030, pop. 412, sett. 1767, incorp. 1771), originally called Gageborough for the Governor, General Thomas Gage, changed its name, presumably for patriotic reasons.

Right in the Center is a four-story *Observation Tower* (*open*), from which is a comprehensive view of the mountain country, including Greylock.

Right from Windsor on an improved road is a *State Camping Site*, 3 *m.*, in the Savoy State Forest, a detached area some distance from the main forest (*see Tour* 2).

West of Windsor, State 9 descends again into a valley. The downgrade unfolds a magnificent view, framed by forests of spruce, of the distant Taconic Mountain Range west of Pittsfield.

At 36.2 *m.* is the junction with a marked road lined with maples.

Left sharply on this road to the *Falls of Wahconah Brook*, 0.5 *m.*, which in three leaps descend about 80 feet and then wind through evergreen woods to join the East Branch of the *Housatonic River*. The brook's name comes from a legend: Wahconah, a young Mohawk girl, was courted by Nessacus, a handsome young warrior of an enemy tribe, and by his rival Yonnongah, a war-hardened Mohawk. Wahconah loved Nessacus, but her father insisted on leaving the decision to the Great Spirit. Below the falls in the middle of the stream rose a rock, dividing the river into two channels. A canoe with Wahconah aboard was to be launched above the rock, and guided by the Great Spirit either to the side of the stream where Nessacus waited or to the other side and Yonnongah. Although the Mohawk, on the night before the trial, sank rocks in the river bed to divert the current to his side, the canoe floated to Nessacus and brought him a happy bride.

The *Flintstone Farm* (R), 36.6 *m.*, distinguished by its large red barns, has been cultivated since 1819 by the Crane family of paper-makers. Champion shorthorn cattle are bred on this farm and experiments in the breeding of Belgian horses and Berkshire swine are conducted.

At 38.4 *m.* is the junction with a road.

Right on this road to the *Wizard's Glen*, 1.3 *m.*, a narrow valley enclosed by steep hills covered far up their sides with mammoth flint rocks. There is a tradition that Indian priests offered human sacrifices in this dim glen to the spirits of evil.

At 38.8 *m.* is the junction with State 8 (*see Tour* 21); between this point and 41.2 *m.* State 8 and State 9 are united.

DALTON, 39.5 *m.* (town, alt. 1199, pop. 4282, sett. 1755, incorp. 1784), originally granted to Colonel Oliver Partridge and others, was known as the Ashuelot Equivalent.

The *Crane Paper Mills* were established here in 1801. Although a woolen mill was built some 13 years later by the Rev. Isaiah Weston, the manufacture of paper, controlled by the Cranes, the Carsons, and the Westons, has remained the chief industry. The Crane mills have manufactured currency paper for the Federal Government since 1846, and now supply a world market.

The *Crane Museum* (*open daily*, 2–5), maintained by the Crane Paper Company, was the rag-room of the Stone Mill, built in 1844. It has a complete collection of exhibits showing the history and progress of the mills and of the paper industry in general.

State 9 parallels the East Branch of the *Housatonic River*, passing several Crane mills.

At 41.2 *m.* State 8 (*see Tour* 21) branches right.

At 43.9 *m.* is the junction with US 7 (*see Tour* 17), 2 *m.* north of Pittsfield.

TOUR 8 A : *From* WILLIAMSBURG *to* HINSDALE, 25.7
m., State 143.

Via Chesterfield, Worthington, and Peru.
Rolled gravel roadbed; very steep at times; poor in winter.

STATE 143, bordered in June by masses of pink and white laurel, passes
over high hills affording excellent views. Heavy growths of spruce and
birch line both sides for long stretches. The valleys are narrow and the
road descends and ascends steeply.

West of Williamsburg (alt. 494) on State 9 (*see Tour* 8), State 143 begins
a hilly and winding climb.

CHESTERFIELD, 6.3 *m.* (town, alt. 1440, pop. 445, sett. about 1760,
incorp. 1762), originally called New Hingham, was eventually named for
the polished Earl of Chesterfield. Farming and cattle-raising have been
the most prominent economic activities from the beginning, while the
forests have always encouraged the lumber trade.

West of Chesterfield, State 143 drops about 600 feet in 2 miles.

At 8.6 *m.* is WEST CHESTERFIELD (alt. 795, Town of Chesterfield)
on the East Branch of the Westfield River. A small lumber mill here is
the only appreciable industry in the town.

> Left from West Chesterfield on an improved road following the river is *Chester-
> field Gorge*, 1 *m.*, 1000 feet long and 30 feet deep. The long grooves in the walls
> were made by glacial action. In the gorge a gift shop, run by an old-time Yankee,
> has many odd labor-saving devices and machines invented and made by the owner.

West of West Chesterfield, the road climbs steadily.

At 12.8 *m.* is WORTHINGTON CORNERS (alt. 1500, Town of Worthington).

> Left from Worthington Corners on State 112 is WORTHINGTON CENTER,
> 0.7 *m.* (town, alt. 1460, pop. 530, sett. 1764, incorp. 1768), a community engaged
> in dairy farming. In season the maple sugar industry provides an additional
> source of revenue.
>
> At 2.7 *m.* on State 112 is the junction with a dirt road; left here 0.5 *m.* to *Indian
> Oven*, a natural formation in a large rock, said to have been used by the Indians for
> baking.
>
> At 5.6 *m.* on State 112 is the village of SOUTH WORTHINGTON (town of Worth-
> ington). Left across the bridge here on a country road is the junction with another
> road at 0.2 *m.*; left here to the *Birthplace of the Rev. Russell H. Conwell (open)*,
> 0.4 *m.*, a red-painted farmhouse, maintained much as it was in the early days of
> the educator who founded Temple University in Philadelphia. The main part of
> the building dates back to about 1800; the veranda and kitchen are recent addi-
> tions.
>
> About 5.8 *m.* on State 112 is *South Worthington Cascade*, a gentle but beautiful falls
> with a 50-foot drop.

Northwest of Worthington Corners, State 143 passes between several
beautiful estates as it rises to a higher level.

At 14.6 *m.* is the entrance to the *Worthington State Forest*, a 412-acre tract of natural woodland (*picnicking facilities*), with shaded walks and many points of scenic beauty.

WEST WORTHINGTON, 17 *m.* (alt. 1300, Town of Worthington). *West Worthington Falls*, 0.4 *m.* south on Huntington Rd. makes a 75-foot plunge down a tree-bordered gorge. In summer there is only a sparkling rivulet falling over bare rocks into the chasm, but in floodtime there is a roaring torrent.

PERU, 21 *m.* (town, alt. 2295, pop. 151, sett. 1767, incorp. 1771), the highest village in the State, is perched on the summit of the Green Mt. Range. First called Partridgefield, it was incorporated 1806 under its present name on the suggestion of the Rev. John Leland 'because,' he said, 'it is like the Peru of South America, a mountain town, and if no gold or silver mines are under her rocks, she favors hard money and begins with a P.'

In former days the poor of Peru were disposed of at auction. In 1807 'Abagail Thayer was bid off by Shadrach Pierce at 90 cents a week for victualizing'; she was auctioned for nearly 30 successive years. The last of the old-time 'Pooh-Bahs' of the hill towns of the Berkshires was Frank Creamer, a shrewd and entertaining public auctioneer. He was known as the 'Mayor' of Peru, holding all important town offices, while his wife held most of the minor ones.

Because of the condition of the roads, church services are held here only from May until November, and school opens in August and is closed from Christmas until March. A few families hold to an old New England custom of 'storing up for the winter,' and in the fall buy a whole winter's supply of groceries.

Self-sufficiency and the ability to solve their own problems are two characteristics held in high esteem by the townspeople. Back in 1799, Charles Ford moved into Peru with a horse and cart, a yoke of oxen, and one hog. Since the hog had to walk, it became footsore and caused much delay. A shoemaker by trade, Mr. Ford had leather and tools with him, so he sat down by the roadside, then and there made boots of sole leather for the hog, fastened them on, and neither he nor his traveling companion encountered further difficulty.

The most exciting day for Peru is the second of March, town-meeting day, the pivot around which the town revolves all year. All the townspeople, young and old, and even Peru voters living in other towns and cities during the winter, turn out for this event. At times the intensity of feeling almost creates a feud — though there has never been any serious disturbance — as the contest continues, not between the regular parties, Democrats and Republicans, but between those on one side in local affairs and those on the other.

State 143 continues west, and begins its descent of a long hill through pleasant wooded country.

The *Ashmere Reservoir*, named by William Cullen Bryant, is passed at 23.2 *m.*

At 25.7 *m.* is HINSDALE (*see Tour* 21) at the junction with State 8 (*see Tour* 21).

T O U R 9 : *From* VERMONT STATE LINE (*Stamford*) *to* CONNECTICUT STATE LINE (*Salisbury*), 86 *m.* (Appalachian Foot Trail).

Via Clarksburg, North Adams, Adams, New Ashford, Cheshire, Dalton, Washington, Tyringham, Monterey, New Marlborough, Sheffield, Egremont, and Mt. Washington.
B. & M., B. & A., and N.Y., N.H. & H. R.R.'s service this area.

THE Massachusetts section of the *Appalachian Trail* runs north and south through Berkshire County from Vermont to Connecticut. Wild mountain scenery provides natural grandeur, thrilling beauty, and exciting climbs.

Leaving the Vermont border, the trail runs from its connection with the Long Trail of that State to Blackinton, and continues south over an abandoned trolley line beside State 2 (*see Tour* 2). Through North Adams and Adams the varied route passes over or near such picturesque points as *Jones's Nose* (alt. 3000), *Mount Greylock* (alt. 3505), the *Hopper* (alt. 1000), and *Bellows' Pipe* (alt. 2700).

In Cheshire the route joins with State 8 (*see Tour* 21), where a marker tells of the famous Cheshire Cheese, 1235 pounds in weight, sent in 1801 to President Jefferson.

The Trail runs through Dalton and there strikes the junction of State 8 (*see Tour* 21) and State 9 (*see Tour* 8). From here it continues across the Housatonic River, passes over the peak of *Warner Mountain* (alt. 1835), descends to the Pittsfield–Becket road, and enters Washington Town. A short distance farther south the trail ascends *Bald Top* (alt. 2200), and runs through the October Mountain State Forest. It skirts the north and east shores of *Finerty Lake* and passes by a steep climb over the summit of *Becket Mountain* (alt. 2200), to reach US 20, Jacob's Ladder Highway (*see Tour* 4). The slopes in this vicinity have been cleared to provide a ski trail for winter use.

On through the *Beartown State Forest* the Trail crosses a stream, with a swimming-pool (R), passes below the summit of *Mt. Wilcox*, and enters the *Swann State Forest*. From here the route runs in a southerly direction through continuous scenic splendor, traversing the towns of Great Barrington, Sheffield, and Egremont. It climbs *June Mountain* (alt. 1140), descends to cross the Housatonic River and the Housatonic Valley, and rises again to the crest of *Jug End* (alt. 1600) and the summit of *Mt. Everett* (alt. 2624), where an observation tower provides a spectacular view of the countryside in all directions. From here the Trail passes *Guilder Pond* (alt. 2100), the highest in the State, and reaches *Sage's Ravine* on the Mass.–Conn. Line.

T O U R   1 0 : *From* PLYMOUTH *to* RHODE ISLAND STATE LINE (*E. Providence*), 39.4 *m.*, US 44.

Via Carver, Plympton, Middleborough, Lakeville, Raynham, Taunton, Rehoboth.
N.Y., N.H. & H. R.R. services this area.
Hard-surfaced road.

US 44 passes mainly through a rural countryside watered by numerous lakes and rivers. The open character of the country offers extensive views from the summits of the low hills.

West from PLYMOUTH (*see PLYMOUTH*), US 44 follows the old King's Highway, one of the first legally established roads in America. It winds past pleasant farms, and runs between acres of cranberry bogs.

NORTH CARVER, 8.2 *m.* (Town of Carver, alt. 114, pop. 1559, sett. 1660, incorp. 1790), a peaceful farming community, was named for John Carver, first governor of Plymouth Colony.

The Green is the *Site of King Philip's Spring*, now filled in, where Indians, returning from the attack on Chiltonville during King Philip's War (1675–76), are said to have stopped to wash the blood of the settlers from their hands. Opposite the Green is the *Sturtevant Home* (*private*) (L.) (built about 1750), a weather-beaten gambrel-roofed house with a lean-to.

Right from North Carver on State 58, a fair tar road leads past cranberry bogs and beautiful pine groves to PLYMPTON, 2.6 *m.* (town, alt. 79, pop. 558, sett. 1662, incorp. 1707). Because of its geographic propinquity to Plymouth, it was named for Plympton, a borough near Plymouth, England. Industries were born, lived for a brief span, and died; a casting factory turned out cannon and cannonballs used in the Revolution. A factory making boxes for farm produce is the only one still in operation.

Left on Elm St. is the *Deborah Sampson House* (*private*), 0.4 *m.*, an unpainted Cape Cod cottage, once occupied during her early childhood by Deborah Sampson, who as 'Robert Shurtleff' served in the Revolutionary War. Deborah was born in Plympton in 1760. Owing to the defection of her father and the poverty of her mother she was forced to live with families in Plympton and Middleborough until she was 18. About this time she left home and became a school teacher in Holden, where, the story goes, she fell in love with David Potter, who was having difficulty with the authorities of the Continental Army due to desertion. Deborah

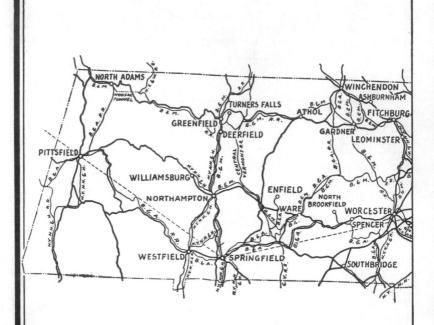

TRANSPORTATION MAP
OF MASSACHUSETTS

— • —

LEGEND

AIRWAYS   ----------------

BUS LINES   ——————

RAILROADS   ——————

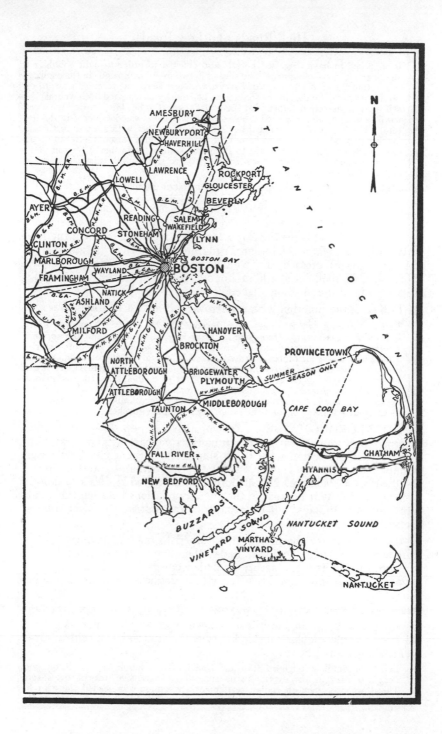

is supposed to have disguised herself and enlisted in order to fight shoulder to shoulder with her young man. She served in two major campaigns in the company of Captain Webb of Holden. At Tarrytown, New York, she received a sword cut on the head and a bullet in the shoulder. The plucky girl treated both wounds herself to avoid detection and carried the bullet the rest of her life. During the Yorktown campaign she contracted a fever and her disguise was discovered in the hospital. The doctor did not reveal her secret but sent her with a letter to General Washington, who gave her an honorable discharge and a personal letter of appreciation. She was married in 1784 to Benjamin Gannett, a farmer of Sharon. During Washington's presidency she was invited to the capital. She also received lands and a pension from Congress.

Straight ahead from Plympton on a hard-surfaced unnumbered road to junction with State 106, 5.1 *m.*; left here to *Wolf Rock*, 5.6 *m.*, 200 yds. off road (L). Here in the early days of the Colony a little band of eight people, including two women and small children, fought off a fierce pack of wolves.

At 14.5 *m.* on US 44 is the *Wading Place*, identified thus: 'Site of the Ford or Wading Place where the Indian Trail from Plymouth to "Middleberry" (Middleborough) crossed the Nemasket River. When the Town was established in 1669 its southern boundary was described as extending "Six mile from the Wading Place."'

At 14.6 *m.* is the junction with a narrow road near a factory.

Left on this road, which crosses the old wooden bridge over the Nemasket River, is *Hand Rock*, 0.5 *m.* (*footpath from the bridge*), so-called because of the apparent imprint of a human hand carved upon it by some unknown sculptor. During King Philip's War an Indian mounted this rock, which was opposite the Old Fort on the farther bank of the river, at least 155 rods distant. With taunts and gestures he tried to provoke an attack. After thoughtful deliberation, the commander lent his highly prized gun to a crack marksman, Isaac Howland, who killed the heckler with a single shot. This was considered a remarkable feat for that time, as the Indian was far beyond the range of an ordinary musket.

MIDDLEBOROUGH, 15.3 *m.* (town, alt. 110, pop. 8865, sett. 1660, incorp. 1669), was known to the Indians as Nemasket. The first white men to visit the region were three shipwrecked Frenchmen, who were promptly taken by the Indians as slaves. Children and grandchildren of the Pilgrims settled here. Middleborough was spared in the early months of King Philip's War because of the friendly relations between the inhabitants and the Indians, but eventually it was destroyed. After the war the settlers returned and rebuilt it.

In the 19th century the inhabitants turned to manufacturing products from straw hats to fire engines. Today there are more than 40 industries in the town, and its manufactures include ice bags, heating pads, hospital supplies, caskets, fire apparatus, and metal products. Five firms produce shoes.

The Church of Our Savior, Center St., was designed in 1898 by Cram, Goodhue, and Ferguson, architects known especially for their ecclesiastical work. Perpendicular Gothic in style, the church has a central tower and shallow transepts.

Left from Middleborough on State 105 LAKEVILLE, 3.9 *m.* (town, alt. 94, pop. 1443, sett. 1717, incorp. 1853), a name suggestive of extensive areas of cool waters. This town was once an Indian settlement. Sassamon was deeded the area by King Philip's brother-in-law. In 1674 Sassamon revealed Philip's war plans to the

English. Branded as a traitor, he was subsequently murdered, allegedly by three of his race, whose execution by the English precipitated the war prematurely, thus causing Philip's final defeat. The Indians continued to make their homes about the picturesque ponds of Lakeville until the year 1930, which marked the death of Charlotte Mitchell, a half-breed, the last of a once powerful and numerous tribe. Although small industries have flourished and died, the town has always been essentially agricultural.

Pond Cemetery, on the shore of Assawampsett Pond, left from the center on State 18, 1.2 *m.*, contains many Indian graves.

At 17.3 *m.* is the junction with State 28 (*see Tour* 19).

At 23.7 *m.* is the junction with State 104.

Right on State 104 is RAYNHAM, 1.2 *m.* (town, alt. 51, pop. 2208, sett. 1652, incorp. 1731), a farming and poultry-raising community, originally the east precinct of Taunton, and named in honor of Lord Townshend of Rainham, England. The settlement was left unharmed during the Indian War inasmuch as the local forge had provided King Philip with tools and repaired his weapons. The earlier settlers, however, had suffered much at the hands of the Indians, and several of their number had been massacred. The victims were interred at *Squawbetty*, a burial ground on the west bank of the Taunton River, now so thickly overgrown with brush that it is difficult to get to it.

On State 104, 0.4 *m.* south of the Center, is the *Site of an Iron Forge* locally claimed to be the first in America, established by the Leonard family in 1652 and operated by them for more than a century. Other early industries were shipbuilding, shoe manufacturing, lumbering, and flour-milling. The only industries now surviving are a rivet works and a bleachery.

West of the intersection with State 104, US 44 enters a thickly settled, highly industrialized area.

TAUNTON, 24.8 *m.* (*see TAUNTON*).

In Taunton Center US 44 crosses State 138 (*see Tour* 25) and State 140 (*see Tour* 23B) (*Rotary Traffic, US* 44, *R*).

US 44 proceeds southwest, traversing a rural area.

At 31.8 *m.* is *Anawan Rock* (L), 150 yards from the highway. This huge conglomerate, about 80 feet long by 25 feet high, marks the site of the last major incident of King Philip's War, the surrender of Anawan, the bravest of Philip's generals, to Captain Church in 1676. Near the southeast end is an angular opening, like a room, with its sides nearly perpendicular, where Anawan and his men are said to have encamped.

At 33.4 *m.* at the crossroads stands the *Anawan House*, a typical old New England stage hostelry and inn.

1. Right from Anawan House on a side road 1.3 *m.*; right here on a dirt road to 2.2 *m.*; left uphill to the *Rehoboth State Forest*, 3 *m.* Great Meadow Hill (alt. 265) is a State park for picnicking and camping, reforested with white pines and spruce. A *Fire Tower* on the hilltop (*observer on duty here daily from Mar. to Nov.*) offers a magnificent view of the rolling hilly countryside, partly forested and dotted with lakes and streams.

2. Left from the inn on the side road 0.8 *m.*; right here to REHOBOTH (Hebrew: 'Enlargement'), 1.3 *m.* (town, alt. 256, pop. 2777, sett. 1636, incorp. 1645). Although the first settlers were Plymouth Congregationalists, Baptists were permitted to reside in Rehoboth if they were peaceable. A Baptist Church, the fourth in America, was founded in 1663, but owing to a violent disagreement with the Congregational brethren, it moved to Swansea. The town was the scene of bloody

fighting during King Philip's War, when all the garrison houses were destroyed. The iron industry began early in the 18th century and included the production of cast-iron plows. Today only a porcelain enamel company remains.

Goff Memorial Hall on Bay State Rd., a one-and-a-half-story brick structure given to the town by Darius and Lyman Goff, serves as an auditorium, public library, and museum. In the museum is an old Scotch sword. During the French and Indian Wars, it was used by a Mr. Davidson, who is said to have answered an opponent's plea for quarter with 'Halves is all I can give!' — and forthwith proceeded to demonstrate.

US 44, after passing through wooded country thickly dotted with boulders, traverses a rural section and reaches the Rhode Island Line at 39.4 *m.*

T O U R   1 1 : *From* NEW HAMPSHIRE LINE (*Fitzwilliam*) *to* CONNECTICUT LINE (*Thompson*), 65.5 *m.*, State 12.

Via Winchendon, Ashburnham, Fitchburg, Leominster, Sterling, West Boylston, Worcester, Auburn, Oxford, Webster, and Dudley.

B. & A. R.R. and N.Y., N.H. & H. R.R. parallel the southern part of this route; B. & M. R.R. services the northern area.

Hard-surfaced roadbed; open all year.

Sec. a. NEW HAMPSHIRE LINE to WORCESTER, 44.4 *m.*

BETWEEN the New Hampshire State Line and Worcester, State 12 traverses a hilly farming country with widely separated cities.

State 12 crosses the Massachusetts State Line about 20 *m.* south of Keene, New Hampshire.

WINCHENDON, 3.3 *m.* (town, alt. 992, pop. 6603, sett. 1753, incorp. 1764), at the junction with US 202 (*see Tour* 13), is known as the 'Toy Town.' First known as Ipswich Canada, it received its present name of an old English town at its incorporation. The woodenware industry dates from 1827. Toys became the chief product and Winchendon was one of the leading toy-manufacturing towns. Educational toys have been a specialty.

At 4 *m.* on State 12 stands a huge *Rocking Horse*, Winchendon's sign, symbolic of its chief industry.

ASHBURNHAM, 11.4 *m.* (town, alt. 1037, pop. 2051; sett. 1736, incorp. 1765), was founded upon seven grants of land: the Starr Grant given to the heirs of Dr. Thomas Starr, an army surgeon in the Pequot War; the Cambridge Grant (1734), to the town of Cambridge as compensation for maintaining a bridge across the Charles between Brighton and Cambridge; the Lexington Grant, sold in 1757 to 7 German immigrants and thereafter known as Dutch Farms; the Bluefield Grant, to three men for erecting an inn on the Northfield Rd.; the Converse Grant, to the heirs of Major James Converse of Woburn in recognition of services to the Colony; the Rolfe Grant, to the heirs of the Rev. Benjamin Rolfe of Haverhill, slain by the Indians in 1708; and the most important (1735), the Dorchester Canada, or Township Grant of six square miles divided among descendants of 60 soldiers from Dorchester who fought in the Canadian expedition of 1690.

Because of the town's rocky surface, large-scale agriculture has never been profitable, but dairying and fruit-growing are carried on. Of small industries the most important was, and still is, the manufacture of furniture from local timber.

Cushing Academy, a co-educational preparatory school, was founded by Thomas Parkman Cushing in 1874.

At 18.9 *m.* is the junction with State 2 (*see Tour* 2).

FITCHBURG, 21 *m.* (*see FITCHBURG*).

LEOMINSTER, 24.6 *m.* (city, alt. 409, pop. 21,894, sett. 1653, incorp. town 1740, city 1915), was originally a part of Lancaster Town (*see Tour* 7). In the first 50 years of its existence it had some manufacturing activity, and today less than one-fifth of its land area is devoted to agricultural pursuits, which center in orcharding and dairying. Combs were made as early as 1770, and by 1845 there were 24 factories producing them. As a substitute for the horn originally used, viscoloid has been developed. The du Pont Viscoloid Company is the most important industry in the town.

Once 75 per cent of the Nation's piano-cases were made here, but in 1935 this activity ceased. In that year but 67 industrial plants remained, turning out such diverse products as furniture, toys, combs, buttons, worsted dress fabrics, wool yarn, dress ornaments, paper, and paper boxes.

On the Common is an old *Indian Mortar*, a block of stone rudely hollowed out, about 18 inches in diameter and 8 inches in depth.

The *Public Library Museum* (*open* 9–9) contains a facsimile of a hornbook used by the Pilgrim Fathers; tools made by the early settlers; a hand reel for winding yarn from a spinning wheel; wool card, shutters, and bobbins from hand looms; a sausage-filler made about 1790, and a number of books printed in Leominster between 1796 and 1813.

STERLING, 31.5 *m.* (town, alt. 500, pop. 1556, sett. 1720, incorp. 1781), was named for Lord Stirling.

In the domestic factory stage the chief industry was chair-making. Baltimore chairs became famous, and were shipped to the West Indies and to the Southern States for use on the cotton plantations, where they were called 'Yankee Sticks.' Clocks, hats, shirts, patterns, pottery, cider and vinegar, textiles, tannery products, and emery wheels were also made at various times. In 1828 Silas Lamson, a native, patented the crooked scythe snathes and started a business still carried on in Shelburne Falls. During the Civil War, Silas Stuart, another native, invented a machine for the manufacture of sewing-machine needles. The first standardized paper patterns for dressmaking were designed here in 1863 by Ebenezer Butterick, a tailor and shirtmaker. The shirt patterns met with such instant success that patterns for children's and women's clothes were added. Butterick Patterns and eventually *The Delineator*, a women's magazine, developed from this invention.

The town is now mainly agricultural, with fruit-growing predominant.

The *Sterling Cattle Show*, established in 1857, is held on the Common every fall.

Left from Sterling on the Redstone Hill Rd., from which there is a fine view, is the junction with a road at 1.3 *m.*; which leads (R) to the *Mary Sawyer House* (*open by permission*), the home of Mary's Little Lamb.

The story runs that Mary and her father found two newborn lambs in the barn. One was so weak that Mary took it into the house and nursed it. The lamb became a pet and followed Mary about the farm. One day he followed her to school and Mary hid him beneath her desk. When she was called to the front for spelling class, the lamb followed her sedately down the aisle, to the amusement of the pupils, if not of the teacher.

The schoolhouse has been removed to South Sudbury (*see Tour* 4) by Henry Ford. The story has the distinction of being the first rhyme recorded by a phonograph. When the first record was made, Mr. Edison was asked to 'say something' into the machine. The first words that came to him were the verses of 'Mary Had a Little Lamb,' said to have been written by John Rowlstone, a resident of Sterling at the time Mary Sawyer lived there. New Hampshire, however, insists that the lamb and Mary belong to it.

At 36.2 *m.* State 12 crosses the Metropolitan Reservoir by a causeway.

WEST BOYLSTON, 37.1 *m.* (town, alt. 495, pop. 2158, sett. 1642, incorp. 1808). Its 600 settlers were at first mainly engaged in agriculture but water-power, furnished by the Nashua, Quinnepoxet, and Still-water Rivers, eventually stimulated the building of textile mills and the manufacture of boots and shoes. In 1895 many manufacturing sites and extensive farmlands were purchased for the creation of the Wachusett Reservoir, which was completed in 1905. This hindered the industrial development of the town, now primarily a residential community.

Robert Bailey Thomas (1766–1846), originator of the *Old Farmer's Almanac*; Erastus Bigelow (1814–79), inventor of the power carpet loom; and Thomas Keyes, Jr., were born in West Boylston. Keyes invented an orrery, an instrument to illustrate the movement of the solar system, and also a stop-motion machine used in warping cloth.

At 43.6 *m.* is the junction with State 122A (*see Tour 11A*).

WORCESTER, 44.4 *m.* (*see WORCESTER*), is at the junction with State 9 (*see Tour* 8), State 122 (*see Tour* 23), and State 70 (*see Tour* 7).

Sec. b. WORCESTER to CONNECTICUT LINE, 21.1 *m.*

South of Worcester, State 12 runs through a thinly settled area.

At 5.4 *m.* is STONEVILLE (alt. 564, Town of Auburn).

Left from Stoneville on a road skirting *Dunn Pond* is AUBURN, 0.8 *m.* (town, alt. 560, pop. 6535, sett. 1714, incorp. 1837), at first named Ward, for Artemas Ward, popular Revolutionary officer. Confusion between the words Ward and Ware caused the change in 1837 to the present name, probably suggested by Goldsmith's line, 'Sweet Auburn, loveliest village of the plain.'

Agriculture, the original occupation, was supplanted by industry that died out as the town became a residential suburb of Worcester.

At 8.4 *m.* is the junction with US 20 (*see Tour* 4).

At 10.5 *m.* is the junction with a dirt road.

Right on this road at 0.8 *m.* is the *Birthplace of Clara Barton* (*adm.* 25¢). Clara Barton (1821–1912), the organizer of the American National Red Cross, was a teacher in New Jersey, working to popularize free schools. At the outbreak of the Civil War she went to the aid of the suffering soldiers. She labored in person on the battlefield, carrying her own supplies and never leaving the scene until all the wounded and dead had been removed or cared for. She also established search for the missing and helped to identify and mark the graves of the dead. In 1866–67 she lectured on incidents of the war. She went to Europe in 1869 for her health, and thus was in Switzerland at the outbreak of the Franco-Prussian War. The day after the fall of the Commune she entered Paris and remained there eight months, creating work for the women of the town which kept 1200 from beggary and clothed 30 thousand.

She went to Geneva in 1869 as a member of the International Committee of Relief for the Care of the War Wounded. At that time there was no American organization, and it was several years before she was able by her sole efforts to overcome the indifference and actual hostility of American officialdom. Her biographer, William E. Barton, says: 'The history of the American Red Cross cannot be written apart from its founder, Clara Barton . . . her voice almost alone pleaded for it. [After its organization] she was its animating spirit, its voice, its soul.'

Clara Barton helped in the work of the Red Crescent in Turkey in 1896 and distributed relief funds among the sufferers in Armenia. She did personal field work during the Spanish-American War. She received decorations from ten leading countries of the world and published several books including 'The History of the Red Cross.'

At 11.9 *m.* is a cemetery containing the *Grave of Clara Barton*.

OXFORD, 13.3 *m.* (town, alt. 516, pop. 4249, sett. 1687, incorp. 1693), named for Oxford, England, is on land purchased from the Nipmucks in 1681. The first attempted settlements made by French Huguenots were abandoned owing to Indian depredations. Permanent settlement was made by the English in 1713.

Manufacturing began to supplant agriculture in 1811 when Samuel Slater opened a spinning mill. Though a diversity of products such as scythes, nails, hoes, chaises, harnesses, chain, and bricks have been made in the town, the textile industry alone has persisted to the present. The *Larned Memorial Library* (1904) has a stained-glass window depicting the Pilgrims embarking at Delft Haven.

The *Church* just beyond the Town Hall, built in 1792, and remodeled in 1840 to accommodate stores on the first floor, was the first house of worship erected in America by the Universalists, after a profession of faith had been drawn up. The society still treasures the pulpit from which Hosea Ballou preached.

Left from Oxford on Sutton Ave. is the 30-acre *Oxford State Forest*, **2.7 m**. From the *Fire Tower* (810 ft.), there is an excellent view.

At 14.7 *m*. a tablet on a granite monument states that the long flat stone next to it is the *Chimney Stone* against which the Johnson children had their brains dashed out by Indians.

At 15 *m*. is the junction with a road.

Right on this road at 0.6 *m*. is the *Old Maanexit Ford*, pointed out by a marker. This was the post route established in 1672 for monthly service between Boston and New York.

At 17.5 *m*. is EAST VILLAGE (alt. 478, Town of Webster).

Left (straight ahead) from East Village on State 193 at 0.9 *m*. is the junction with a road (L) on which, at 0.2 *m*., is *Beacon Park* (*open*) on the shores of Lake Webster, the site of a village of the Nipmuck Praying Indians, established by John Eliot (*see Tour* 8) and Daniel Gookin in 1674. The Indians believed that the islands in the lake were the abiding-places of benevolent spirits. Lake Webster's Indian name is *Chargoggagogmanchaugagogchaubunagungamaug*.

WEBSTER, 18.7 *m*. (town, alt. 458, pop. 13,837, sett. about 1713, incorp. 1832), was named for Daniel Webster. Industrialization began when Samuel Slater in 1811 set up a cotton mill, which proved so successful that four years later five more mills were erected. New industries were attracted by the completion of the Norwich and Worcester Railroad in 1840. Today textile and shoe industries are first in importance.

On George St. is a *Burying-Ground* in which the graves are marked with field-stones; large ones indicate old men, small ones, young men.

At 19 *m*. on State 12, one of the buildings of the Steven Linen Mills is claimed to be the *First Linen Mill* in America.

At 19.2 *m*. is the junction with State 197.

Right on State 197 is the junction with a road (R), 1.1 *m*., on which is DUDLEY, 2.3 *m*. (town, alt. 453, pop. 4568, sett. 1714, incorp. 1732). Resident Indians gave four acres of land for the church, and in return special pews were reserved for them. Manufacturing began here in 1812, and has continued an important factor in town development.

The *Black Tavern* (*open*), at the Center, built in 1803–04, was originally a stage-coach stop between Hartford and Boston, and is now the home of the Rev. Charles L. Goodell, author of 'Black Tavern Tales,' a collection of stories and legends of Dudley.

Left from the Center at 1.5 *m*. is a dirt road leading (L) to a fork at 1.6 *m*.; straight ahead here leads to the *Durfee Farm* (*open*) (R), at 2.1 *m*. The land was deeded to Elijah Gore in 1738, and the house was probably erected about that time. An excellent example of Colonial farmhouse, it has a massive central chimney with fireplace on both sides, old hand-hewn oak timbers fastened together by hand-hewn wooden pins instead of nails, hand-wrought door hinges and latches, and wide white pine paneling. On this farm is a pink *Granite Monument* placed on its present site in 1650 to mark the boundary between the territory of the whites and Indians. Because the stone is so near the Connecticut Line, some authorities believe that it may have marked an ancient boundary between the two states.

At 21.1 *m*. State 12 crosses the Connecticut State Line, about 10 *m*. north of Putnam, Conn.

TOUR 11 A : *From* WESTMINSTER *to* WORCESTER, 23.7 *m.*, State 64, 31, 122A.

Via Princeton and Holden.

B. & M. R.R. services part of this area.

Road hard-surfaced throughout.

THIS route, winding through hill country, has delightful farm and woodland vistas.

Branching southeast from State 2 (*see Tour* 2) at Westminster, State 64 at 2.8 *m.* passes *Wachusett Pond* (R), which is in the Fitchburg water-supply system. From this point, a hard-surfaced road runs (R) to *Mt. Wachusett* (*see below*).

At 3.8 *m.*, right, a short distance off the road, is *Redemption Rock.* Here Mary Rowlandson of Lancaster (*see Tour* 7), who was taken captive during an Indian raid on that town, was ransomed in the spring of 1675.

At 6.4 *m.* is EAST PRINCETON (alt. 730), at the junction with State 31; right on State 31 PRINCETON, 9.4 *m.* (town, alt. 949, pop. 717, sett. 1743, incorp. 1771), an agricultural community, was named for the Rev. Thomas Prince, associate pastor of Old South Church in Boston, 1718. In 1793 the town had several gristmills and sawmills, a fulling mill, and a cloth mill.

Colonial Princeton was the scene of an unsolved mystery — the disappearance of Lucy Keyes, the Lost Child of Wachusett. In 1755 the five-year-old daughter of Robert Keyes was following her sisters along a trail to Wachusett Pond, to get sand for cleaning the family pewter. The older girls sent her home. When they returned, Lucy had not arrived. Frantic searching parties found nothing but a few broken twigs at one point on the trail. Years later, a party of fur trappers returning from northern Vermont reported that in an Indian camp they had found a 'white squaw' whose only English was an unintelligible phrase containing the word 'Wachusett.' She was happily married and refused to leave the tribe. Still later, the mystery was revived by the dying statement of John (Tilly) Littlejohn, a neighbor who had led one of the searching parties, who confessed quarreling with Robert Keyes and killing his daughter for revenge. Little credence was given to this explanation because Tilly's mind was obviously unsound and his story contained chronological errors.

In the *Goodnow Memorial Building* (*open*) is an historical museum, containing an old spinning wheel, an ancient Bible, and three antique cradles, including the one in which little Lucy Keyes once slept.

Right from Princeton on an unnumbered road that ascends a steep hill, curving left at 3.4 *m.*; at this point, straight ahead on a path, and left at 0.6 *m.* to *Balanced Rock* 1.2 *m.*

From the junction with the side route the road (from here one-way) continues to the top of *Mt. Wachusett*, 5 *m.* (alt. 2018), which is in a 3000-acre State Forest Reservation. Along the route are observation points. Standing well above the surrounding hills, Wachusett from its summit provides a panoramic view that, on clear days, includes the Customhouse Tower in Boston, Mt. Greylock, and the Presidential Range in New Hampshire. The hotel at the summit is maintained by the State.

From the summit the Sky Line Foot Trail runs north 22 *m.* to *Watatic Mountain* (alt. 1840), on the New Hampshire Line.

At 14.7 *m.* is a *Watering Trough*, all that remains of the once prosperous mill settlement of QUINAPOXET.

HOLDEN, 17.3 *m.* (town, alt. 855, pop. 3914, sett. 1723, incorp. 1741), is in a town once known as the 'North Half' of Worcester; at its incorporation, it was named for Samuel Holden, a London merchant whose philanthropies aided the Colonies. As in many other rural towns of the State, there were some small industries in early days, including a brickyard, two potash works, and several sawmills and gristmills. During the first part of the 19th century, the town's woolen mills had an extensive market; the competition from mills in States with lower wage levels has closed all but one. Truck-gardening, fruit-growing, and poultry-raising are the principal agricultural pursuits.

Holden was the home of Captain Webb in whose company a descendant of Governor Bradford, Deborah Sampson, disguised as a young man, served during the Revolution (*see Tour* 10).

At the Center is the junction with State 122A; left on State 122A at 23.7 *m.* is the junction with State 12 (*see Tour* 11) at the northern edge of Worcester.

T O U R   12 :   *From* PROVINCETOWN *to* WILLIAMSTOWN. 400 *m.*, the CAPES TO THE BERKSHIRES BRIDLE TRAIL.

Via Truro, Wellfleet, Eastham, Orleans, Dennis, Yarmouth, Barnstable, Sandwich, Bourne, Plymouth, Kingston, Milton, Canton, Sharon, Medfield, Sherborn, Framingham, Groton, Rowe, and Adams.

Trail marked by white and orange spots painted on trees, rocks, and other objects at road and trail intersections.

THE *Capes to the Berkshires Bridle Trail* is the first established unit in a proposed network of bridle and hiking trails that will eventually form a vast system of trails throughout the length and breadth of Massachusetts, making accessible many out-of-the-way beauty spots in the State.

Enthusiastic horsemen and other sportsmen initiated the idea in 1933. The problem of connecting the scattered local trails of the State into through trails was undertaken by the Forest and Park Association, a private organization, working in co-operation with public and other private organizations.

In addition to making accessible remote points not reached by motor roads, the Trail will meet the bridle trails of New Hampshire and Vermont. It runs through several State Forests. At Groton a branch leads to Rockport on Cape Ann.

TOUR 13 : *From* NEW HAMPSHIRE LINE (*Rindge*) *to* CONNECTICUT LINE (*Granby*) 83.7 *m.*, US 202.

Via (*sec. a*) Winchendon, Templeton; (*sec. b*) New Salem, Shutesbury, Pelham, Prescott, Belchertown, Enfield, Granby, South Hadley, and Holyoke; (*sec. c*) Montgomery, Westfield, Southwick, Granville, Tolland.

B. & M. and B. & A. R.R.'s for northern towns; B. & A. R.R. for south central section; N.Y., N.H. & H. R.R. for southern towns in this area.

Hard-surfaced road throughout.

Sec. a. NEW HAMPSHIRE STATE LINE to ATHOL, 22.3 m.

US 202 crosses the State diagonally, traversing hill country, at one time heavily wooded and now covered with a second growth of hardwood and evergreens. Only a few scattered settlements break the woodland.

US 202 crosses the New Hampshire Line 15 *m.* south of Peterboro, N.H.

WINCHENDON SPRINGS, 1.5 *m.* (alt. 1020, Town of Winchendon), is a small village, with *Chalybeate Spring* (a short distance to the east), formerly valued by the Indians for its medicinal quality.

WINCHENDON, 3.7 *m.* (*see Tour* 11), the 'Toy Town,' is at the junction with State 12 (*see Tour* 11).

US 202 follows the winding course of Miller's River.

BALDWINSVILLE, 10.4 *m.* (alt. 900, Town of Templeton), a small village, was named for Deacon Jonathan Baldwin, a wealthy settler responsible for the early development of manufacturing.

When the *First Baptist Church* was moved to its present site, the process of removal extended over a period of days, and on Saturday night the structure was straddling the railroad tracks. Because the elders of the congregation sternly banned labor on the Lord's Day, the schedule of the railroad had to be canceled for that day.

1. Left of the Center on South Main St., 0.5 *m.*, are the *Bryant House* (1780) and the *Jonathan Baldwin House.* The former was the tavern and home of Captain Eden Baldwin, son of Jonathan Baldwin. Captain Eden, a man of literary tastes, is remembered for his 'Diary of Christopher Columbus Baldwin,' his experiences day by day as he traveled about the vicinity during the early part of the last century.

2. Left from the Center on Bridge St., at 0.6 *m.*, is the entrance to *Baldwinsville Cottages* for crippled and handicapped children. Incorporated in 1882, it was a pioneer institution in giving the best possible care and training to unfortunate children. Financed by individual gifts and by the State, the institution now has five large buildings with accommodation for 135 pupils.

At 13.8 *m.* is the junction with State 2 (*see Tour* 2) which US 202 follows west to 22.3 *m.*

Sec. b. JUNCTION WITH STATE 2 to HOLYOKE, 40.2 *m.*

Between State 2 and Holyoke, US 202 is called the Daniel Shays Highway, because this region was the center of many activities of Shays's Rebellion. For about 20 *m.* it skirts the Quabbin Reservoir.

South of its junction with State 2 (*see Tour* 2) in ATHOL, US 202 at 0.4 *m.* passes a, *Covered Bridge* over Eagleville Pond Brook.

At 1.4 *m.* is *Lake Rohunta* (*small fees*), a summer and camping resort.

At 3.8 *m.* is the junction with a road marked North New Salem.

Right on this road is NORTH NEW SALEM, 1.2 *m.* Adjacent to the green is the *Curtis House* (*private*), built in 1775 and used for many years as a tavern on an old stage road. The building is a familiar two-and-a-half-story gabled-roof type with nine windows in front. It has a simple front entrance with a six-paneled 'Christian' door (*see Tour* 21, *Cheshire*). In the center of the house is a huge oven. Above this, on the second floor in a small room fugitive slaves were secreted until they could be taken to the next station north on the Underground Railway.

Left from the Green a road leads up a hill, enters the forest, and at 1.1 *m.* reaches the point where there is a footpath (R) into the woods. This terminates at *Bear's Den and Falls* on the middle branch of the Swift River. The waters cascade through a rocky gorge, some 50 feet in depth, several falls occurring before the river makes a sharp bend to continue its journey through the dim forest over huge boulders.

Just beyond the bend, the rock fragments are so thickly piled as to cause a jam, which tumbles the water about and tosses it over in a series of leaping, splashing little falls. Three caves in the cliff (L), once inhabited by bears, give this spot its name. A few yards downstream, a three-sided high stone wall built into the side slope suggests that once a mill of some sort used the power from these falls. Legend says that here King Philip held a council of war prior to his attack on Hatfield in 1675, and that the place was used by the Indians as a meeting-place, that they celebrated their victories on the cliffs above the falls, with feasting and dancing, and that they retreated here when outnumbered.

US 202 continues through wooded country with fine views of the hills (L).

NEW SALEM, 7.5 *m.* (town, alt. 1030, pop. 443, sett. 1737, incorp. 1753), was named for Salem, because the original proprietors were residents of that town. After the Revolution, agriculture and lumbering flourished, and by 1820 New Salem had a population of 2146. Stagecoaches running between Brattleboro and Worcester made the town a center of trade. With the building of railroads, however, it was gradually isolated, and its population decreased rapidly. At present fruit-growing and the cultivation of raspberries comprise the principal occupations. Miss Sophia B.

Packard and Miss Harriet E. Giles, natives of New Salem, in 1881 organized the Spelman Seminary for Negro girls in Atlanta, Ga.

The route south of New Salem will be changed somewhat when the Quabbin Reservoir occupies the valley.

At 12.8 *m.* is a junction with a road marked *Shutesbury.*

Right on this road, which winds up a steep hill, is a *Stone Wall*, 0.9 *m.* (L), partly in ruins, that formerly enclosed the town pound. During the early days of the Revolution, the local minister, Rev. Abraham Hill, who entertained pronounced Tory sentiments, was incarcerated in the pound and fed on dried herring, tossed to him over the wall, a diet guaranteed to reduce almost any brand of political ardor.

SHUTESBURY, 1.3 *m.* (town, alt. 1000, pop. 239, sett. 1735, incorp. 1761), in what was originally part of a grant called Roadtown, was named for Samuel Shute, one-time Governor of the Bay Colony. Sawmills and agriculture furnished the chief means of livelihood for many years. Basket-making, one of the earliest industries, still survives and is carried on as a monopoly by the Pratt family.

At the Center is the old burying ground in which repose the remains of 'Granther Pratt' (1686–1800), a Shutesbury Methuselah who, if tombstones do not lie, actually saw the turning-points of three centuries! He is buried in the west cemetery under a white marble shaft bearing the following tribute:

> 'He was remarkable, cheerful in his disposition and temperate in his habits. He swung a scythe 101 consecutive years and mounted a horse without assistance at the age of 110.'

The general store adjoins the *Site of the Birthplace of Ithamar Conkey* (born 1815), who wrote the music for the hymn, 'In the Cross of Christ I Glory.'

Right from the village 4.9 *m.* is *Lake Wyola* (*excellent fishing, picnicking, boating, and swimming*).

PELHAM, 17.1 *m.* (town, alt. 800, pop. 504, sett. 1738, incorp. 1743), is a small agricultural community set high between ranges of forest-crowned hills. Originally settled by Colonel Stoddard of Northampton, the grant was purchased by a group of Scotch Presbyterians from Worcester, who called the new settlement Lisburn. At its incorporation it was named for Lord Pelham, then traveling in the Colony. Agriculture has never flourished here owing to the hilly country and rocky soil. The cleared land is used largely for pasturage and blueberry-raising. The chief source of income is lumbering and stone quarrying.

Pelham was the home of Daniel Shays. Shays's Rebellion was the result of the post-Revolutionary depression, in which currency deflation and high taxes caused an epidemic of mortgage foreclosures. Sporadic attempts were made by armed mobs in various parts of the State to prevent the courts from meeting to give the foreclosure orders. Discontent was particularly strong in this part of the State and Shays succeeded in organizing an army that at one time numbered 1900 men. After preventing the sitting of the Supreme Court in Springfield in 1786, Shays attempted to capture the arsenal, but failed and was forced to retreat to Pelham. His *Encampment Site* is in the southern part of the village. Shortly afterward Shays was pursued to Petersham by a large force from Boston under General Benjamin Lincoln. The rebels, outnumbered and poorly armed, were dispersed; and Shays took refuge in Vermont. He was pardoned in 1788 and died in 1825 at Sparta, N.Y.

1. Right from the village on an unnumbered road is the *Orient Springs Picnic Grounds*, 3.5 *m.*, at the base of Mt. Orient. From here a footpath leads up the mountain to a *Sulphur Spring*, well known in the middle of the last century.

2. Left from the village on an unnumbered road past *Swift River Falls*, 2.1 *m.*, is PRESCOTT, 3.7 *m.* (town, alt. 1120, pop. 18, sett. 1742, incorp. 1822), one of the towns to be inundated upon the completion of Quabbin Reservoir. This agricultural community was given its name in honor of Colonel William Prescott, commander at the Battle of Bunker Hill. In the 19th century the village produced lumber, grist, cider, cheese, matches, packing-boxes and carriages, quarried soapstone, and wove palmleaf hats. In 1876 pure Italian bees, especially queens, bred by James Wood, commanded a national market. All landmarks of this busy past will soon be buried beneath the waters of the Swift River.

South of Pelham, US 202 passes over *Pine Hill* (alt. 720), 17.5 *m.*, with an excellent view of the Swift River Valley.

Right from here on a good foot trail is *Mt. Lincoln* (alt. 1220).

At 24.7 *m.* is a junction with State 9 (*see Tour* 8).

BELCHERTOWN, 25.7 *m.* (town, alt. 476, pop. 3863, sett. 1731, incorp. 1761), was named for Jonathan Belcher, late Governor of the Province. *Holland Glen* honors a native son, J. G. Holland, poet, novelist, historian, editor of the *Springfield Republican*, and author of a 'History of Western Massachusetts.' At one time the manufacture of sleighs, wagons, and carriages was important, but now most of the town people are engaged in dairy farming and the growing of the McIntosh apple.

On South Main St. is the *Clapp Memorial Library* (L), founded in 1882 by a $40,000 bequest of John Francis Clapp, a native. Built in the form of a Latin cross, the Library has two stained-glass memorial windows. One of these, a copy of Domenichino's painting in the Paris Louvre, represents Music; the other symbolizes Literature.

The *Stone House* (*open Wed.* 3–5, *adm.* 25¢), 0.1 *m.* south of the Center on US 202, built in 1827, is occupied by the Belchertown Historical Association. Adjoining it is the *Carriage Shed Annex*, donated by Henry Ford, containing early farm implements, spinning wheels and looms, and vehicles formerly made in Belchertown.

Left from Belchertown on State 21 is ENFIELD, 3.5 *m.* (town, alt. 417, pop. 495, sett. about 1742, incorp. 1816), most of which will be inundated in the course of the Metropolitan Water Development.

Belchertown State School, 26.3 *m.*, cares for over 1300 mentally deficient children. Dr. George E. McPherson, superintendent, is well known not only for his professional work, but also for his work in bird-banding.

At 29.9 *m.* is the junction with a side road.

Right on this road at 0.1 *m.* is the large rectangular three-story granite building of *St. Hyacinthe's Seminary*, a Franciscan institution for the training of men for the priesthood to serve Polish congregations of the Roman Catholic Church. The windows are plain, but the doorways are in the Gothic manner, and the portico has a large Gothic arch flanked by two small ones. The building is set on a double terrace lined with formal evergreens. The rugged Holyoke Range makes a beautiful background, and the monastery faces on *Forge Pond*.

US 202 continues through farmland on both sides.

At 30.1 *m.* are visible the saw-tooth peaks of the Holyoke Range which resulted from tilting after the traprock and sandstone sheets were broken into blocks. The peak (extreme L) with a hotel on its summit is *Mt. Holyoke.* This and succeeding summits are known as the *Seven Sisters.* The *Wind Gap* was deepened and widened in the past when a branch of the Connecticut River flowed through it. A large mountain to the right of the Wind Gap is *Mt. Norwattuck.* An overhanging ledge on the southern slope of this eminence is called *Shays's Horse-Shed,* because some of Shays's troops stabled their horses here the night after their defeat at Springfield.

GRANBY, 31.4 *m.* (town, alt. 250, pop. 956, sett. 1727, incorp. 1768), is an attractive residential village, named for the Marquis of Granby, a popular English military leader of pre-Revolutionary days. Sporadic attempts to industrialize the community have met with little success, and today there are no traces of the distilleries, wool, and satinet factories that flourished briefly in the 19th century. A farm that once supplied clinics and hospitals with cancerous mice, guinea pigs, and rabbits for experimental purposes has likewise passed into oblivion.

At 32.5 *m.* is the junction with West St.

Right, West St. passes over *Cold Hill,* 1.5 *m.* (alt. 380), from which is a fine view across the Connecticut Valley. Straight ahead is majestic *Mt. Tom* (with observatory); the buildings of Mount Holyoke College, looking as though they were at the foot of the mountain, are separated from it by the Connecticut River. The Holyoke Range is far to the rear (R). To the left of Mt. Tom is the city of Holyoke with hills in the background. The river cannot be seen, but the stacks of manufacturing plants along its banks trace its course between the clustered roofs of residential sections. The old Smith College hymn gives very well the feeling of the scene:

'And where the hills with purple shadows
Eternal vigil keep,
Above the happy river meadows
In golden haze asleep...'

SOUTH HADLEY FALLS, 36.5 *m.* (*see SOUTH HADLEY*), is at the junction with State 116 (*see Tour 15B*).

From Canal St. on the east bank of the Connecticut River, are traces of the oldest canal in the State, used, before the dam was built, to take river boats around the rapids. Instead of using locks to reach the upper level, the boats were loaded onto a wagon with large wheels that ran up an inclined plane. The city seal of Holyoke shows a sketch of this device.

At 37.9 *m.* is the Connecticut River. From the bridge is a fine view of the *Holyoke Dam* (R). For the history of this dam, see HOLYOKE.

US 202, bearing right at the end of the bridge, passes several paper mills and crosses two of the three canals.

At 38.4 *m.* State 116 (*see Tour 15B*) branches left.

At 40.2 *m.* is HOLYOKE (*see HOLYOKE*).

Here is the junction with US 5 (*see Tour 15*).

Sec. c. HOLYOKE to CONNECTICUT LINE, 21.2 *m.*

This section of US 202 crosses a mountain range with wooded slopes to a typical Connecticut Valley farming country in which tobacco-raising and dairying are among the principal industries.

US 202 continues south through the outskirts of Holyoke; at 5.8 *m.* are *Hampton Ponds.*

At 8.9 *m.* is the junction with State 10 (*see Tour 15C*) and at 10.9 *m.* is the junction with Pochassic St.

> Right on Pochassic St. at 0.3 *m.* is Montgomery St.; right on this street, which rises steadily through a region of hills ranging in height from 400 to 1400 feet; at 6.5 *m.* (R) is a clear view of Mt. Holyoke and the Holyoke Range.
>
> MONTGOMERY, 6.9 *m.* (town, alt. 332, pop. 174, sett. before 1767, incorp. 1780), was named in honor of General Richard Montgomery. The exact date of its early settlement is unknown, but on a beam in the Kelso barn is the inscription 'M.M. 1744'; it is known that Ephraim Avery brought his family here in 1767. According to a tale, the Rev. Seth Noble, the first pastor of the *Congregational Church* (1797), was so inordinately fond of the hymn 'Bangor' and called for it so frequently that his congregation first protested and then dismissed him in 1806. He went to a settlement in that part of Massachusetts that later became the State of Maine and after its incorporation represented his town in the legislature. Evidently the clergyman's favorite hymn was more appreciated in Maine, for it gave the name to the town: Bangor.
>
> At 10.5 *m.* on Montgomery St. is the junction with a road (*impassable in bad weather*) that winds through dense woods to *Hockhouse Mountain*, 2.5 *m.*, whose cliffs rise sheer to a height of 150 feet. A natural ledge trail, by which the face of the cliff can be scaled, leads along a wall of rock. During summer the widespread forests show the dark green of pines, junipers, hemlocks, and cedars; in the autumn, the hardwood trees set a higher key with their flaming red, yellow, green, gold, and russet.

WESTFIELD, 11.2 *m.* (*see Tour 4*), is a prosperous business and cultural center at the junction with US 20 (*see Tour 4*).

At 14.6 *m.* is the *Captain David Fowler House* (*open*) built 1747, now known as Old English House. In its center are the remains of a dark room, built of brick, for protection in the event of Indian attack. Parts of the central chimney are still standing.

SOUTHWICK, 17.1 *m.* (town, alt. 260, pop. 1540, sett. 1770, incorp. 1775), was named for an English village. The chief products of this agricultural town are tobacco and potatoes. During the winter, ice is harvested in large quantities on the Congamond Lakes, east of the village.

> Right from Southwick, State 57 runs through a beautiful *Gorge* 4 *m. Sodom Mountain* (alt. 1126), a rocky ledge, rises (L) abruptly from the roadside and the waters of *Munn Brook* (R) barely visible from the highway, are heard gurgling and splashing about the foot of the ledge. The gorge is thickly wooded with hemlock and deciduous trees.
>
> State 57 winds up the mountain-side with wooded banks rising abruptly (R) and mounded hilltops (L). GRANVILLE CENTER, 6.6 *m.* (alt. 720, pop. 704, sett. 1736, incorp. 1775, town of Granville), situated on the old Massasoit Indian Trail, which followed the Little River Gorge, was settled by Springfield folk. On Liberty Hill stands the *Liberty Pole*, symbol of the town's Revolutionary enthusiasm. Shays's Rebellion found many sympathizers here, and a local official was held captive by the rebels. Another captive was a deacon, who prayed so hard

that he converted the rebels to his idea of marching to Springfield and surrendering. Today the town is chiefly engaged in the manufacture of toys.

The *Granville Community Building*, 7.7 *m.*, is a recent structure in neo-classic style. The building has a portico with six Greek Ionic columns. A fanlight over the front portico relieves the severity of the façade. At each end of the structure is a porte-cochere supported by four columns. Ancient maple trees line the roadside at the bottom of the sloping lawn.

East of the Community Building, 0.1 *m.* on State 57, is a beautiful two-story white frame residence with identical front, north and east sides, and elaborate center entrance and many windows. Fine cornices and graceful fanlights add to the dignity of the structure, which is enhanced by elm and maple trees set at irregular intervals on the sloping lawn.

At 7.8 *m.* is the junction with a dirt road; right on this road, which crosses *Trumble Brook*, the outlet of a lovely little pond, to a foot trail at 1.7 *m.* that leads to the *Fire Tower* on Sweetman Mountain. The road continues through hilly wooded country to the junction with a road (R) at 3.6 *m.* on which at 4 *m.* is a view of the *Cobble Mountain Reservoir*. This road follows the banks of the reservoir and crosses the *Cobble Mountain Dam*, an unusually high earth structure. This dam impounds water not only for the city of Springfield, but also for power development. A right turn at 4.5 *m.* leads over a shoulder of Cobble Mountain to an open space at 5.9 *m.* where (L) is the so-called *Surge Chamber*, a cylindrical metal tube rising to a height of 207 feet, designed to absorb back pressure in the water tunnels when the gates are closed. The gorge of the Westfield Little River far below stretches to the eastward, while a high hill rises directly opposite.

The little brick building at the base of the Surge Chamber houses only the valve machinery, the power plant itself being in the bottom of the gorge near the river bank and accessible only by a long and circuitous road.

State 57 winds through hill country to WEST GRANVILLE (alt. 1200, town of Granville), 12 *m.* A fine two-story square brick Colonial house having a low roof and four chimneys is between the church and the new brick schoolhouse.

At 12.9 *m.* on State 57 is the junction with a road (L) running into the *Granville State Forest*, 0.6 *m.*, covering 4582 acres (*tenting, camping, picnicking*). A number of pleasant trails wind along Hubbard River discovering several ponds. This forest has more rolling terrain than most of the western Massachusetts forests.

Along State 57 at 13.1 *m.* are beautiful beds of mountain laurel.

TOLLAND, 15.8 *m.* (town, alt. 1540, pop. 141, sett. about 1750, incorp. 1810), named for a town in Wales, has always been an agricultural community. Cattle-raising and dairying are the chief occupations. Many years ago an attempt was made to grow tobacco, and, while the effort was not a failure, the results seemed not to justify continuance.

At 16.7 *m.* a foot trail (R) leaves State 57 and leads by Noyes Pond to Noyes Mountain (alt. 1700), 3.5 *m.* From the *Fire Tower* at the summit a striking view of the countryside is obtained.

At 17.3 *m.* on State 57 is a junction with an unnumbered road; right on this road is *Noyes Pond*, 2.4 *m.* (*State controlled; fishing*). On the southern shores are the camps and game preserve of the exclusive *Tunxis Club* (*private*).

At 17.8 *m.* is a junction with a dirt road.

Right on this road are the scattered homes of the descendants of the Congamuck Indians, a racial strain so mixed now with white and Negro blood that the Federal Government no longer officially considers the people Indians.

At 19.3 *m.* is a junction with dirt road.

Left on this road are the *Congamond Lakes*, a series of narrow sheets of water about 3 *m.* in length.

The *Roger Moore House* (*private*), 20.4 *m.* (L), erected in 1736, is a two-and-a-half-story, gabled house with a central chimney.

At 21.2 *m.* US 202 crosses the Connecticut Line, 8 *m.* north of Granby, Conn.

T O U R   1 4 :   NEW BEDFORD—MARTHA'S VINEYARD — NANTUCKET, 100 *m.*

Steamship Service: New Bedford, Martha's Vineyard & Nantucket Steamboat Line, Front St.; From New Bedford to Woods Hole, 1¼ hours, 75¢; to Oak Bluffs, 2 hrs., $1.10; to Nantucket, 4½ hrs., $2.20 — round trip, $4.10.   Car Transportation $5–$8. Sailings every 3 hrs. in summer (approximately). Special excursion rates.   Winter sailings.

Airplane Service (*summer only*): Seacoast Air Transport Co. From New Bedford to Edgartown $4.50; from New Bedford to Nantucket, 40 min. $7.50.

Sightseeing busses at each port.   Hard-surfaced roads encircling islands.

Sec. a. NEW BEDFORD to MARTHA'S VINEYARD, 20 *m.*

LEAVING the wharf in New Bedford, the steamer swings out into the lower Acushnet River and heads southeast toward Buzzard's Bay, passing between *Fort Phoenix* (L), of Revolutionary fame, in Fairhaven (*see Tour* 6) and the more modern *Fort Rodman* (R) at the southern extremity of New Bedford (*see NEW BEDFORD*). To the right of Fort Rodman can be seen Round Hill, the estate of the late Colonel E. H. R. Green, where the old whaler, 'Charles W. Morgan,' rests at her final mooring.

The low-lying ELIZABETH ISLANDS (*see GOSNOLD*) loom up ahead in Buzzard's Bay, pass to the right as the vessel enters Woods Hole Channel, a narrow passage between the northernmost of the islands and the mainland of Cape Cod.   On rare occasions, heavy tide-runs force the steamers to use *Quick's Hole*, a passage farther south.

The ELIZABETH ISLANDS (*mostly privately owned*), a long fringe stretching out into Buzzard's Bay from the Falmouth shore, reached only by small boat, constitute GOSNOLD (town, alt. 10, pop. 129, sett. 1641, incorp. 1864), named for Bartholomew Gosnold, who, in 1602, settled temporarily on the island of Cuttyhunk.   In 1641, Thomas Mayhew was given authority to 'plant' upon the islands, and some generations later they were included in the Lordship and Manor of Martha's Vineyard.

There are no public roads, with the exception of a quarter-of-a-mile stretch of State road on the island of Cuttyhunk. To see the primitive loveliness of this archipelago and the beauty of its isolated summer estates, it is necessary to follow lanes and bypaths afoot.

Transportation to Cuttyhunk can be secured by a small launch which leaves New Bedford daily, weather permitting (75¢ *round trip*). One and a half miles left of the motor-boat landing is the *U.S. Coast Guard Station*, and about a half-mile in the opposite direction are the magnificent buildings and grounds of the *William M. Wood Estate* which covers more than a third of the entire area of the isle.

Tarpaulin Cove, on the east shore of Naushon Island, has been a haven for pilots and pirates, and was the last port of call for Captain Kidd. The *French Watering Place*, a little southeast of Tarpaulin Cove, was so named because of the French privateers who swarmed in Vineyard Sound. During the Revolution, British foraging expeditions cleared the island of livestock, and during the War of 1812, Naushon was used by them as a naval base. The geologist finds Naushon one of the best places to study the features of the great terminal moraine.

PENIKESE ISLAND was given in 1873, to Professor Louis Agassiz with an endowment fund of $50,000 to establish a game sanctuary and a school of natural history. In 1907, the State acquired the island and established a leper colony, which was later abandoned.

The first port of call is WOODS HOLE (*see Tour 19A*), home port of the famed ketch 'Atlantis.' (*Transportation of motor cars from this point should be arranged for in advance.*)

Continuing through the channel, the vessel enters Vineyard Sound, where the water is usually slightly rougher, and approaches the island of Martha's Vineyard, rounding the sandy shelving headlands that surround Oak Bluffs and that give the island a deceptive appearance of bulk.

MARTHA'S VINEYARD, a triangular isle off the elbow of Cape Cod, measures less than 20 miles from east to west and 10 from north to south, with its highest point 311 feet above the sea. Leif Ericson may have been an early visitor, but Bartholomew Gosnold, in 1602, was the first known white man to visit it. The island was permanently settled in 1642, and in the 18th century became a whaling center. It was part of the original New York Grant until 1692, when it was ceded to Massachusetts, forming, with the Elizabeth Islands, Dukes County.

Martha's Vineyard has been summarized by Walter Prichard Eaton as 'a land of old towns, new cottages, high cliffs, white sails, green fairway, salt water, wild fowl and the steady pull of an ocean breeze.' Few islands are 'so many things to many men' as this. From the bare ridge of Indian Hill (260 ft.) to south and east stretches a level plain of dwarf forest-top without a sign of civilization; to the west the land rolls away hilly and broken by rocky outcrops and tree-filled ravines. Northward lies the blue of the Sound with the faint tracery of the Elizabeth Islands on the far horizon. Yet down in the heart of Oak Bluffs the little cottages are set so close and at such extraordinary angles that a motor car can hardly make its way safely at more than ten miles an hour. Again in Edgartown there is gracious spacing in the comfortable small eastward-looking houses with their silvered shingles and picket fences and lilac hedges. Then out beyond on the Island are the isolated small farms, the salt ponds and lonely beaches, the pines and yellow sandbars, the high bluffs and heavy surf on the south and placid small harbors on the north, with the extraordinary colored clay cliffs of Gay Head at the southwestern tip.

Sec. b. OAK BLUFFS — EDGARTOWN — GAY HEAD — VINE-YARD HAVEN, 48 m.

OAK BLUFFS (town, alt. 10, pop. 1657, sett. 1642, incorp. 1880), an attractive village greatly increases its population in the summer. The Algonquin name for this tract of land was Ogkeshkuppe ('Damp Thicket'), but the earliest English name, given in 1646 by Thomas Mayhew, the first proprietor, was Easternmost Chop of Holmes' Hole. Mayhew granted it to John Dagget. There is a story, not vouched for, however, that Dagget's son Joseph married the daughter of a local Indian sachem and as a dowry received practically all the land comprising the present town.

At the Center is the *Methodist Tabernacle* (R) surrounded by tiny, ornate cottages. Summer campmeetings have been held in the village since 1835.

The *East Chop Lighthouse* (1869), on the north tip of Oak Bluffs, stands on a cliff 75 feet above the sea.

A short walk south across *Farm Pond* (R) leads to the *Norton House* (1752), held together by stout wooden pegs except where modern restoration has required the use of nails and metal fastenings.

Broad, tarred Edgartown Rd. runs south from Oak Bluffs through HARTSVILLE, a hamlet named for a family that has for generations maintained summer homes here.

The road continues between white sand dunes, covered with coarse grass in summer, on a narrow strip of land bounded for many miles (R) by *Sengekontacket Pond* (Indian, *'Salty Waters'*), and (L) by the Nantucket Sound, with the open Atlantic beyond it, shining blue and calm, or green-gray and turbulent, according to the weather. The pond has several inlets permitting the tidal ebb and flow that keeps it stocked with shellfish. The island affords delightful swimming off its white sandy beaches.

EDGARTOWN, 5 m. (town, alt. 10, pop. 1399, sett. 1642, incorp. 1671), was first called Nunnepog (Indian, *'Fresh Pond'*), and, when incorporated, was named for Edgar, son of James II.

At early island elections corn and beans were used as ballots. 'The freeman shall use Indian corn and Beans, the corn to manifest Election, the Beanes Contrary' — which explains the phrase 'to corn a man.'

In the 18th century Edgartown was the prosperous home port of Arctic whaling vessels, and in a typical year of the 19th century men were busy refining whale oil and making candles, while the women turned out 15,000 pairs of socks, 3000 pairs of mittens, and 600 wigs.

West at the upper end of the village into Cooke St., the oldest street on this island, is the *Edgartown Cemetery* (R), with headstones dating from 1670, inscribed with curious epitaphs. Also on this street are some of the oldest houses in Martha's Vineyard, including (R) the *Thomas Cooke House* (*open*), built in 1766, now the headquarters of the Dukes County Historical Society.

At the east end of Cooke St., left into Water St., is the *Public Library*, which houses a collection of paintings and etchings done by famous artists, and an exhibit of bronze statuary.

Water St. continues to *Edgartown Harbor Light*, where the route turns into Pease's Point Way, which crosses Edgartown Rd. and becomes the Takemmy Trail, passing through Edgartown Plains.

The *Martha's Vineyard State Forest*, along the Takemmy Trail, covers a wooded area of 4473 acres. A short distance west of the State Forest, at a cut-off (L), stands a pile of rocks enclosed by an iron railing, a *Memorial to the Rev. Thomas Mayhew*, son of Governor Mayhew, whose labors won many converts among the Indians. Departing for England in 1668, Mr. Mayhew here bade farewell to his Indian friends. He was lost at sea, and the Indians henceforward placed a rock on the spot when they passed.

WEST TISBURY, 13 *m.* (town, alt. 10, pop. 282, sett. 1669, incorp. 1861), named for the English birthplace of Governor Thomas Mayhew, was first known as *Tackhum-Min-Eyi* or *Takemmy* (Indian, '*The Place Where One Goes to Grind Corn*').

In its youth the town had saltworks on the shore, smokehouses on the hills where fat herring were cured and prepared for market, brickworks, and a lumber trade. But it has now placidly settled down to farming, fishing, and the cultivation of the summer tourist trade.

It is said that every wild flower known to eastern Massachusetts has been found in the town, the Tea Lane section alone yielding over 700 varieties. Glacial boulders and hills of unconsolidated drift appear in the midst of fresh-water springs and ponds, one of which is one and a half miles long. Many Algonquin names still survive; among these is *Manitouwattootan* ('*Christiantown*'), applied in 1659 to a reservation for the Praying Indians that is now an almost deserted village.

In the village is *Music Street*, so named because, after one family acquired a piano, all the others on the street followed suit.

The route swings past the Congregational Church and shortly reaches the junction with an unimproved road.

Left at this intersection, then right at the first fork is the *Experience Mayhew House* (*private*), a typical frame dwelling of the Cape Cod type, the oldest house in the town. To the south, white-capped combers of the Atlantic pound the hard-packed white sands of *South Beach*, rarely patronized by swimmers because of the heavy undertow.

Abel's Hill Cemetery (R.) on the main highway contains lichen-covered tombstones bearing many odd epitaphs.

From *Stone Wall Beach*, 15 m., NO MAN'S LAND, a tiny island lying eight miles offshore, is visible on clear days.

This island is reached only by small boat or airplane. The one family on the island is completely isolated when bad weather and raging surf make these means of communication impossible. On the island are huge rocks of unusual formation, one of which is known as *Devil's Bed and Pillow*. Many Indian remains have been found, including a kind of workshop for the manufacture of arrowheads and other stone implements. A boulder on the shore bears the figure 1004 in eroded marks that have caused some authorities to think that Leif Ericson may have visited this spot almost 600 years before the arrival of Bartholomew Gosnold.

A short distance west of Stone Wall Beach is *Beetle Bung Corner*.

Left here on a road that crosses *Nashaquitsa Pond*.

GAY HEAD (town, alt. 185, pop. 158, sett. 1669, incorp. 1870) is one of the two towns in Massachusetts which are still mainly occupied by people of Indian descent. A paradoxical situation occurred in 1711, when the Society for Propagating the Gospel purchased the lands at Gay Head for the sole use of the Indians, their original proprietors. In the early days fishing, whaling, and agriculture furnished the chief source of revenue which, at its best, was scanty. Labor in the cranberry bogs and the sale of bowls and jars fashioned from the colored clays of the cliffs now are the chief present source of livelihood.

The road passes the tip of *Black Brook*, where at certain seasons the headless ghost of a man supposedly murdered here is said to appear as a warning to the spectator that his own end is approaching. The omen always comes true, old-timers say.

A road continues to *Gay Head Light*, built in 1799, rebuilt in 1859. It contains 1003 prisms of cut and polished crystal glass, and flashes every ten seconds, three white beams and one red.

Below the lighthouse a *Cliff* (60 ft.) drops straight down to the waters of Vineyard Sound. Composed of variegated vertical strata of clay ranging from white, blue, orange, and red, to tan, the precipice, in the rays of the late afternoon sun, presents a gorgeous reflection, best appreciated from offshore. (*Small boats will make special trips for the sunset hours.*)

Beetle Bung Rd., running straight ahead from Beetle Bung Corner, with clipped wooded sides as in English rural lanes, shortly joins North Rd.

Left turn here 0.5 ·· the old-fashioned fishing village of MENEMSHA (Town of Chilmark, alt. 140, pop. 253, sett. 1671, incorp. 1714), where the air is permeated by the smell of lobster bait being ripened in the sun. The regions now known as Chilmark, Tisbury, and Elizabeth Island were granted in 1671 by patent, under the name of Tisbury Manor, to Thomas Mayhew, Sr., with the privileges of feudal lordship, as in the medieval manorial system. The settlers were considered tenants, and required, in spite of their protests, to pay quit-rents. Mayhew, Jr., sold his privileges to Governor Dungan in 1685, and was appointed steward, a position in which he continued for 25 years.

At the end of the road is *Menemsha Pond*, which was connected with Menemsha Bight by the Government several decades ago to provide a harbor for the fishermen. Along the shores of this artificial salt-water pond are numerous shacks of fishermen.

North of Beetle Bung Rd., North Rd. runs by *Peaked Hill* (alt. 311) (R), a high point on the island. Left, almost opposite Peaked Hill, is an early home now gray with age, formerly the *Home of Captain George Claghorne*, designer and builder of the U.S. Frigate '*Constitution*.' Adjacent, *Roaring Brook* runs through an abandoned brickyard. Here is an ancient *Aqueduct*, of rude construction, that once carried water from the brook.

North Rd. passes between *Indian Hill* (alt. 261) (L), *picnicking*, and (R) *Brandy Brow Place* (*private*), which takes its name from a former salt-box house on the site in which the island's supply of brandy was hidden during a British raid of the Revolutionary War.

Along the North Rd. are many large trees, bent almost to the ground. Tradition has it that when the Indians inhabited this section, they bent small oaks over and pinned them down to mark a trail.

On the outskirts of Vineyard Haven, North Rd. passes beautiful *Tashmoo Lake* (L), the largest fresh-water body on the island. Legend relates that an Indian, on a journey through the deep forest, had been told by his mother, a seeress, that the end of his trip would be marked by beautiful springs of pure water. When he came to the lake, he knelt down, drank out of a snow-white shell his mother had given him, and gave the water his name.

VINEYARD HAVEN, Town of Tisbury, 43 *m.* (alt. 20, pop. 1822, sett. 1660, incorp. 1671), is a rapidly developing summer resort. Agriculture, whaling, fishing, and salt-making were the early industries of the township, which extends to the south shore of the island and has a bay. During the Revolution this harbor was a refuge for many of the British men-of-war. In 1775 the people erected a Liberty Pole on Manter's Hill. A captain of the British ship 'Unicorn' desired this pole, and one of the selectmen, not daring to refuse, set a price on it; but his daughter, Polly Daggett, and her two friends, Parnel Manter and Maria Allen, decided to destroy the pole rather than let it be made a spar on a British ship. To his fury the captain was obliged to sail away without his prize.

In 1778 Tisbury was ravaged by Major-General Grey in a raid described by a contemporary: 'They caryed off and Destroyed all the corn and Roots two miles around Homses Hole Harbour; Dug up the Ground everywhere to search for goods the people hid, even so Curious were they in searching as to Disturb the ashes of the Dead. Many houses were all Riffled and their Windows were all broke.' Grey departed September 14, having been in the harbor only four days; he had destroyed one brig and cargo, one schooner and cargo, four vessels with several boats, 23 whaleboats, and two saltworks, and he took with him 388 stands of guns, 1000 pounds sterling, 300 oxen, and 10,000 sheep. This left the people greatly impoverished, and, during the severe cold of the following winter, they would have suffered for food had not a northeast blizzard driven a school of sea bass into Lagoon Pond. People from every part of the island cut tons of frozen fish out of the ice, which saved many of them from starvation.

'Bum-boating' was early established in Tisbury. A bum-boat was to the coasting vessel what the pack-peddler was to the country housewife. To the sailor, the boat might be called a 'floating dittybox,' where he could find every blessed thing he wanted.

A fire in 1883 ravaged an area of 40 acres, destroying many historic houses filled with family treasures.

The HISTORICAL BUILDING (L), on Main St., owned by the Sea Coast Defense Chapter of the D.A.R., contains many interesting relics of the early settlers.

> Left from Vineyard Haven on Huzzelton's Head, a bold bluff, stands (L) the *Haunted House* (*boarded up*). Here during the Revolution lived Daggett, a Tory, who was often visited by British officers. Two of them came one day to bid him good-bye after having seized a Falmouth pilot to take them over the shoals to Nantucket. Friends of the captured pilot, learning of the visit, crossed to the island in whaleboats, surrounded the house, and took the officers prisoner; on their return to Falmouth, they were in an excellent position to dicker for the return of their friend, the pilot.

Branching right from Main St., Harbor Rd. passes the *Marine Hospital* (R) and leads back to OAK BLUFFS, 48 *m.*

Sec. c. MARTHA'S VINEYARD to NANTUCKET, 15 m.

Leaving Martha's Vineyard, the vessel follows a southeast course through Nantucket Sound and enters the great bay made by the north shore of Nantucket Island and its small sister islands.

NANTUCKET (Island) is named from the Indian *Nanticut*, meaning 'The Far Away Land.' The island is approximately 14 miles long and has an average width of three and a half miles. Nantucket is an experience. The steamer rounds Brant Point Light and comes suddenly on 'the little gray town in the sea,' a town today full of visitors all summer long; its cobbled lanes and bypaths are bright with summer frocks, polo shirts and white ducks, striped shorts and gay 'bras'; its beaches are covered with brown throngs and dots of color; yet the little gray town has not lost its sense of the past, the days when it was the great whaling port of the world and only simple folk in homespun or oilskins trod its crooked paths from house and warehouse, cooper shops and rigger shops to the quays and back again. The old cobblestoned streets, the comfortable homes and well-kept estates, the open moors swept by the salt breezes of the ocean, the stately trees still entitle the island to its Indian name *Canopache* ('The Place of Peace').

Nantucket was included in the royal grant to the Plymouth Company in 1621. In 1641 the island was purchased by Thomas Mayhew, who in 1659 sold nine tenths of it to nine other people. Because of the Puritan severity in Amesbury and Salisbury, people from those towns, accompanied by Peter Folger of Martha's Vineyard, emigrated to Nantucket in June, 1661. From 1660 to 1692, when it was ceded to Massachusetts, the island belonged to the Province of New York.

Farming, fishing, and sheep-raising provided the settlers with a livelihood, but the farms were soon exhausted and the people turned to whaling. In 1768 the town possessed 125 whaling ships, and the whale oil was exported directly to England in Nantucket vessels. The town, the pioneer in whaling, was eventually displaced by New Bedford with which it shares honors in Herman Melville's 'Moby Dick.'

During the Revolution, caught between the British warships and Continental privateers, the people suffered severely. Over 1600 men were lost, and very few ships survived the blockade. The fleet was gradually rebuilt, and Nantucket again became a thriving port; in 1779 the town was raided by eight British vessels, with staggering property damage.

Between 1797 and 1812 shipbuilding and nail and wool manufacturing developed. In the War of 1812, 11 Nantucket vessels were captured by the British. By 1830 Nantucket rated third among the commercial towns of Massachusetts in spite of the fact that the whaling fleet had by 1812 dwindled to 40 ships.

Sec. d. NANTUCKET — SIASCONSET — NANTUCKET, 17 m.

NANTUCKET, 0.1 m. (town, alt. 12, pop. 3495, sett. 1641, incorp. 1687), also takes its name from the Indian Nanticut.

At the head of Steamboat Wharf, the docking point, stands (L) the *Art Gallery* (*open*), where the works of the many famous summer colonists are exhibited.

Straight ahead on Broad St.

The *Whaling Museum* (*open weekdays*, 9.30–5.30, *Sun.* 2–6; *adm.* 25¢) is an old brick structure built in 1847, for use as a sperm-candle factory. It now contains many relics of the whaling era.

R. from Broad St. on Center St.; L. from Center St. on West Chester St.

On Sunset Hill (R) is the *Oldest House* (*open* 9.30–5.30; *adm.* 25¢), also known as the Jethro Coffin House. Built in 1686, it is a two-story frame structure of compact proportions with shingled walls. On the face of its massive central chimney is a raised brickwork ornament, horseshoe in shape, to discourage witches from entering.

L. from West Chester St. on New Lane; R. from New Lane on Madaket Rd.

A *Drinking Fountain* here bears a tablet honoring Abiah Folger Franklin, Benjamin Franklin's mother, born in a house near-by.

Retrace Madaket Rd.; R. from Madaket Rd. on Saratoga St.; L. from Saratoga St. on Vestal St.

The *Maria Mitchell House* (1790) (*open weekdays*, 10–12 *and* 2–5; *adm.* 25¢), 1 Vestal St., is the birthplace (1818) of the famous astronomer and discoverer of the comet named in her honor. The long wooden latch on the front door is made from a bit of mahogany from a wrecked ship. In the rear is a small *Observatory*, and across the street is a scientific library with Mitchell relics.

R. from Vestal St. on New Dollar Lane; L. from New Dollar Lane on Prospect St.

The *Old Mill* (*open* 11.30–5.30; *adm.* 25¢), built in 1746, stands conspicuously on a hill. The great spar and wheel stretch out behind, and are so fixed that the arms of the mill can revolve only when the wind is due west. The corn meal ground here is in great demand. In the days of the whalers, homecoming vessels were first sighted from this hill, and the families of men at sea spent many anxious hours scanning the horizon for approaching sails.

L. from Prospect St. on South Mill St.; R. from South Mill St. on Lyons St.; L. from Lyons St. on Fair St.

The *Friends' Meeting House* (*open*), corner of Moore's Lane (L), built 1838, has the Quaker simplicity of hard benches, bare floors, and candles on the walls. Adjoining is the *Nantucket Historical Society Building* (*open in summer* 9–5; *adm.* 25¢).

R. from Fair St. on Main St.

At the head of Straight Wharf (1723) is the *Rotch Market* (1772), two red-brick buildings that were originally the warehouses of William Rotch, but later the Pacific Club, a rendezvous of the old whaling captains.

Retrace Fair St. to Main St.; L. from Main St. on Orange St.

SIASCONSET ('Sconset), 8 *m.* (alt. 18), is the Newport of Nantucket. Its greatest charm lies in its grassy lanes and low, picturesque cottages hemmed in with little white fences and gay with bright-hued flower gardens. Many of them have the blue shutters that, tradition says, were reserved by unwritten law in the past for the houses of captains and first mates.

Just left of the bus-stand, near the bluffs, is a sign pointing out over the ocean: 'To Spain and Portugal, 3000 miles.' The nearer waters below are dotted with fishing smacks bobbing up and down in quest of shimmering cargo; in the distance the great black hulls of merchantmen and the sharp prows of ocean liners plow through the furrows of the open sea.

> Left from 'Sconset a walk of about 1.5 *m.* along the cliffs leads to *Sankaty Head Light*, built 1850. A climb of 75 steps to the walk of the light is rewarded by a view of the neighboring moors and the ocean.

East of 'Sconset, a road runs through POLPIS. It leads through undulating moors with enchanting vistas of the harbor and of small ponds. *Altar Rock* (alt. 102), one of Saul's Hills, is the highest point of land on the island, and provides a grand panorama of moor and blinding-white beaches, framed by the blue-gray rim of the ocean.

TOUR 15 : *From* VERMONT LINE (*Guilford*) *to* CONNECTICUT LINE (*Thompsonville*), 55 *m.*, US 5.

Via Bernardston, Greenfield, Deerfield, Whately, Hatfield, Northampton, Holyoke, West Springfield, Springfield, and Longmeadow.

B. & M. R.R. services area from Springfield north; N.Y., N.H. & H. and B. & M. R.R.'s service southern area.

Road is hard-surfaced throughout.

US 5 passes through the Connecticut Valley connecting important cities along the river. North of Deerfield is rolling country, with mountain ranges visible in the distance; south of Deerfield, US 5, closely paralleling the Connecticut River, travels through flat country rimmed by the foothills of the Berkshires (R) and the central highlands (L).

US 5 crosses the Vermont State Line 10 *m.* south of Brattleboro, Vt.

At 0.6 *m.* is the junction with an unnumbered road.

Right 4.5 *m.* on this road, which parallels Shattuck Brook, is LEYDEN (town, alt. 940, pop, 253, sett. 1738, incorp. 1784), named for Leyden, Holland, where the Pilgrims sought refuge for a time.

Although exceedingly hilly, this area contains much excellent farmland and is especially suited to dairying. Stone quarried in the town was used for the bridge across the Connecticut River, but lack of transportation facilities limits quarrying as a source of income.

In the last decade of the 18th century, William Dorrell came to Leyden and began to teach a philosophy of life founded on doctrines of free love and the unalterable sanctity of life, animal as well as human. He gained followers who joined him in religious demonstrations that shocked the community until the order was extinguished by Ezekiel Foster in 1800. Dorrell continued to live in Leyden until, at the age of 94, he starved himself to death, declaring he had lived long enough.

At 3.1 *m.* is a marker designating the *Site of Burke Fort* (1738) where 50 persons took shelter during the French and Indian War. After the raid on Deerfield in 1704, the Indians crossed the waterfalls near the village on a crude log bridge; one of the women captives, unable to keep her footing, fell into the rapids and was dashed to death.

BERNARDSTON, 4.7 *m.* (town, alt. 353, pop. 975, sett. 1738, incorp. 1762), was formerly called Falls Fight Township, owing to an encounter in 1676 between the settlers and the Indians. The name was shortened to Fall Town and later changed to Bernardstown, in honor of Sir Francis Barnard, Provincial Governor of Massachusetts under George III. Four forts were built about 1736, and the first 24 years after the settlement were spent in intermittent warfare. Dairy farming is at present the chief means of livelihood, though there have been attempts at industrial development.

In Bernardston is the junction with State 10 (*see Tour 15A*).

At the center of GREENFIELD, 11.5 *m.* (*see Tour* 2), is the junction with State 2, the Mohawk Trail (*see Tour* 2).

At 14.3 *m.* is DEERFIELD (*see DEERFIELD*).

SOUTH DEERFIELD, 19.6 *m.* (alt. 204), is at the junction with State 116 (*see Tour* 15*B*). In front of the Deerfield High School 0.4 *m.*, north of the center on US 5, runs *Bloody Brook*, scene of a massacre on Sept. 18, 1675. Captain Lathrop and 84 men had been sent to Deerfield to convoy harvested grain to Hadley in 17 wagons furnished and driven by Deerfield people. Ambushed while fording a sluggish brook, 63, including Captain Lathrop and all the teamsters, were killed by the Indians. A common grave 200 feet south of the monument is marked by a flat slab.

South of Deerfield, US 5 passes through a tobacco-growing district. On both sides of the highway stretch wide fields which, in spring, look like velvety blue-green carpets. On them are tobacco barns, easily recognized because their sides, instead of being solid, are equipped with ventilating shutters that permit the air to circulate freely through the drying leaves.

At 22.1 *m.* is a junction with an unnumbered road.

Right on this road across Mill River, 0.2 *m.* to a crossroad at 0.3 *m.*

1. Left on this road is WHATELY, 0.4 *m.* (town, alt. 183, pop. 1133, sett. 1672, incorp. 1771), named by Governor Hutchinson for Thomas Whately of England. Although primarily an agricultural community, a variety of articles have been made here from time to time, including machinist tools, brooms, spinning wheels, and pottery. Today, the chief products are tobacco and onions.

2. Right on this road is *Whately Glen Park* (*privately owned; nominal fee*), 3 *m.*, a charming spot in a deep ravine down which flows Roaring Brook. On the east bank is the *Old Man of the Glen*, a rock bearing a striking resemblance to a human face. Another natural wonder is a waterfall 25 feet high, known as the *Maiden's Plunge*.

At 27.4 *m.* is WEST HATFIELD (alt. 120).

Left from West Hatfield is HATFIELD, 2 *m.* (town, alt. 160, pop. 2433, sett. 1661, incorp. 1670). The year 1675 witnessed an attack here by about 800 Indians, who were repulsed after great slaughter. A captive squaw alleged to have divulged the plans of the Indians was thrown by her tribe to savage dogs who tore her limb from limb. In 1677 the town suffered another attack. Twelve inhabitants were killed and many were taken captive; in the winter of 1677–78, Stephen Jennings and Benjamin Waite of Hadley paddled to Quebec, where, with the aid of Governor Frontenac and a ransom of £200, they secured the release of their wives and children, captured by the Indians in this attack.

The *Sophia Smith Homestead* (*open*), 75 Main St., built in 1790, was the birthplace (1796) and home of the founder of Smith College (*see NORTHAMPTON*). In 1915 the Alumnae Association purchased the frame two-story dwelling and the class of 1896 restored and refurnished it. Sophia Smith's uncle, Oliver Smith, left an immense fortune to the 'Smith Charities.' The probate hearing, at which the will was unsuccessfully contested by relatives, brought Rufus Choate and Daniel Webster together as opposing lawyers.

Other educators associated with Hatfield were Colonel Ephraim Williams (1715), founder of Williams College (*see WILLIAMSTOWN*), the Rev. Jonathan Dickinson (1688), first president of the institution that later became Princeton University, and Elisha Williams, president of Yale (1726–39).

The chief crop produced in the town is onions, with tobacco a close second. The consolidation of tobacco companies, with their consequent control over the price of raw products, has caused many former tobacco farmers to turn to potato-raising.

NORTHAMPTON, 31.4 *m.* (*see NORTHAMPTON*), is at the junction with State 9 (*see Tour* 8) and State 10 (*see Tour* 15C).

At 33 *m.* US 5 runs in open country, affording a fine view of *Mt. Holyoke* and *Mt. Tom*, separated by the Connecticut River. Oxbow Lake at 33.3 *m.* was formed by a change in the channel of the Connecticut.

At 35.8 *m.*, *Smith's Ferry*, is the *Holyoke Canoe Club*, a recreational center for water sports, baseball and tennis. Opposite is the entrance to the *Mt. Tom Reservation* (*see HOLYOKE*).

US 5 follows Northampton St., a residential thoroughfare.

At 39.6 *m.* is HOLYOKE (*see HOLYOKE*), the junction with US 202 (*see Tour* 13).

At 46.7 *m.* on *Meeting House Hill* (R) at the junction with State 5A (*see Tour* 15D), is *White Church*, now the Masonic Temple, in the tower of which hangs a Revere bell.

In WEST SPRINGFIELD, 48.8 *m.* (*see Tour* 4), is the junction with US 20 (*see Tour* 4).

At 49.1 *m.* US 5 crosses the *Hampden County Memorial Bridge* over the Connecticut River.

In SPRINGFIELD, 49.9 *m.* (*see SPRINGFIELD*), is the junction with State 116 (*see Tour* 15B) and US 20 (*see Tour* 4).

At 50.3 *m.* is the junction with State 83.

Left on State 83 is EAST LONGMEADOW, 4.3 *m.* (town, alt. 237, pop. 3375, sett. about 1740, incorp. 1894). Fertile soil here has lent itself to market gardening, poultry farming, and the development of apple orchards. At the sheds, bordering the railroad west of the center, the local sandstone is cut according to specifications. For more than a century after 1740, East Longmeadow quarried a sandstone, sometimes called 'brownstone,' for export. As many as 20 carloads a day were shipped. Of recent years, however, Indiana limestone has superseded sandstone as a building material so that very little is now cut.

Right from the center, Shaker Rd. leads over the Connecticut Line to the *Connecticut Prison Farm*, 3 *m.* The buildings were originally occupied by Shakers.

At 5.5 *m.* on State 83 is an *Abandoned Quarry* now filled with water and popular as a swimming hole.

At 5.9 *m.* is the junction with an unnumbered road; left here to HAMPDEN, 10 *m.* (town, alt. 300, pop. 854, sett. about 1741, incorp. 1878), an isolated community cut off from the rest of the world by lack of roads. A good yarn is that of Kibbe's shirt. An alarm being raised on the Sabbath Day that Indians were coming, Kibbe ran into the woods to get his cow. He took his gun with him, although hunting was forbidden on the Lord's Day. Not long after he entered the woods, two shots were heard; he, knowing that he was in danger of punishment for Sabbath-breaking, came running out of the woods yelling, 'Indians! Indians!' The searchers saw no savages, but at his request they examined Kibbe's shirt. There were two holes in the shirt, but none in Kibbe. He finally confessed that he had been tempted by Satan to shoot at some handy game and had then made holes in his own shirt to escape punishment. Old-timers say that this was the only actual (*sic!*) Indian alarm in Hampden history.

The demand for a light tobacco has destroyed the market which Hampden formerly had for its dark crop. Dairying and market gardening are now the chief occupations.

Anice Terhune, wife of Albert Payson Terhune, is a daughter of Hampden. Her novels, 'The Boarder Up at Em's' and 'Eyes of the Village,' contain characters said to be local townspeople. Thornton Burgess, author of stories for children, owns an estate here. Opposite the Town Hall is a general store, where lively discussions are carried on during the winter months when the farmers feel the need of warming up around the comfortable stove before beginning the cold drive home.

US 5 here traverses the long fertile plain bordering the east bank of the Connecticut River and follows Longmeadow St., wide and elm-shaded, bordered by homes.

LONGMEADOW, 52.6 *m.* (town, alt. 55, pop. 5105, sett. 1644, incorp. 1783), the 'long meddowe' purchased from the Indians in 1636, rapidly became a substantial settlement. During King Philip's War, after months of confinement in their homes, a party ventured out to attend worship in the parent community at Springfield. On their way they were attacked by Indians, who killed some, wounded others, and took a few captive.

In 1709 there was a general removal to the more elevated section of the town owing to frequent inundations by the Connecticut River. Longmeadow was the first town in the State incorporated after the recognition of American independence. At the close of the War of 1812, so lively was the expression of happiness over the cessation of hostilities that the church bell cracked of its own pealing. The natural beauty of this town has been enhanced by skillful landscaping, and the once quiet farming community is now a delightful residential and social center.

Local genealogical records are unusually complete because, it is said, Jabez Colton carried a notebook and inkhorn with him wherever he went.

William Sheldon, who died in 1874, was a courtly local gentleman of the old school who devoted himself successively to the mysteries of the Scriptures, Spiritualism, Magnetism, and the Od forces. His records, replete with impressive statistics, tell how his odic apparatus, charged with mystic power, arrested an epidemic of cholera in the South, and also the Russian plague.

Aaron Burt, a local hermit of the past, occasionally made ceremonious trips to the village, dressed in sheepskin like a prophet of old, and followed by a bullock, a heifer, a sheep, a cow, and a pig — all adorned with ribbons. He was a pious fellow after his own lights, and, when attending worship, frequently broke out into song to the confusion of the congregation; the 'Indian Philosopher,' far from a hymn, appears to have been his favorite. At other times he rose and, taking the service out of the mouth of the flustered minister, delivered a stentorian harangue denouncing the sins of his generation.

At *Storrs Parsonage* (*open July–Aug.*), 697 Longmeadow St., owned by the Longmeadow Historical Society, is a fine collection of Colonial furniture. Just off Longmeadow St. is the *Municipal Swimming Pool*, from the outlet of which flows a pretty brook through a rustic glen, popular with lovers and picnickers.

At No. 674 Longmeadow St. is the house where *Eleazar Williams* (1787–1858), who called himself the 'Lost Prince,' received his education. Williams's strong resemblance to the Bourbons of France gave rise to the supposition that he was the missing Dauphin, Louis XVII, a rumor to which Eleazar apparently felt little aversion. His story forms the basis of three novels highly popular in their day.

At 55 *m.* US 5 crosses the Connecticut State Line, 20.4 *m.* north of Hartford, Conn.

T O U R 1 5 A : *From* NEW HAMPSHIRE LINE (*Hinsdale*) *to* BERNARDSTON, 8.5 *m.*, State 10.

Via Northfield.
B. & M. R.R. parallels the route.
Hard-surfaced road.

THIS section of State 10 passes through a part of the Connecticut Valley characterized by broad meadows stretching out to rolling hills and heavily wooded uplands.

State 10 crosses the New Hampshire Line 4 *m.* south of Hinsdale, N.H., and enters a typical New England village community with a long main street shaded by great elms planted in 1815.

At 1 *m.* is Northfield Seminary (*see NORTHFIELD*).

NORTHFIELD, 2.5 *m.* (*see NORTHFIELD*).

Southwest of Northfield, State 10 crosses the Connecticut River. At 4.1 *m.* is a hill with the *Site of King Philip's Camp*. The stump of a large lookout tree together with defense trenches are on top.

At 4.9 *m.* is the entrance to *Mount Hermon School for Boys*, founded in 1881 by Dwight L. Moody (*see NORTHFIELD*) after the success of Northfield Seminary. It is a preparatory school of high standard that attempts to develop boys mentally and spiritually. Students spend two hours each day helping with farm work and care of buildings. It has a 1300-acre campus with 80 buildings and a large student body.

At 8.5 *m.* is BERNARDSTON (*see Tour 15*) at the junction with US 5.

TOUR 15B: *From* ADAMS *to* SPRINGFIELD, 70.5 *m.*, State 116.

Via Savoy, Hawley, Plainfield, Ashfield, Conway, Deerfield, Sunderland, Leverett, Amherst, South Hadley, Holyoke, and Chicopee.

B. & M. R.R. services this area.

Between Adams and Conway: hilly, part dirt roadbed, bad traveling in winter. Between Conway and Springfield: good conditions, open road.

SOUTH of Adams, State 116 passes through sparsely settled, hilly country. South of Deerfield are the flat lands of the Connecticut Valley with fields of tobacco and onions.

State 116 branches southeast from the junction with State 8 (*see Tour* 21) in Adams.

At 1.4 *m.* (R) is the *Old Brown House* (*open*), built 1778 by Eleazar Brown. The interior is low-ceiled, with plain paneled walls and wide floor boards. In the front yard is an old well-sweep. From the rear of the house is a view across the valley to beautiful Mt. Greylock.

At 2.6 *m.* is the junction with a dirt road.

> Right on this road at 1.3 *m.* is Stafford Hill, on the top of which is the site of the first settlement in Cheshire (*see Tour* 21), known as New Providence. Here there is a replica of an old mill at Newport, R.I., the *Norse Monument*, an open circular tower about 20 feet high, built of field-stone.

At 4.4 *m.* begins a gradual ascent with views of the Greylock Range (R).

SAVOY, 7.8 *m.* (town, alt. 1880, pop. 299, sett. 1777, incorp. 1797), is often called Savoy Hollow. One of the town's chief exports is Christmas trees. A typical section of young evergreens (spruce) being grown for this trade is at 9.1 *m.* (R).

State 116 continues through rather desolate country, the highest in Hampshire County.

Plainfield Pond, 12.2 *m.* (alt. 1720), is a lonely mountain lake surrounded by dense forests of spruce, white birch and hemlock.

At 13.1 *m.* State 116 turns sharply and descends steeply, affording a view of the winding valley. An *Old Sugar House* with a ventilated roof is left at 14 *m.*

PLAINFIELD, 15.5 *m.* (town, alt. 1660, pop. 332, sett. 1770, incorp. 1807), reached its industrial peak between 1850 and 1860; since then its manufacturing has dwindled away.

On the left in the village are the *Ruins of the Mill of Joseph Beals*, hero of Charles Dudley Warner's poem, 'The Mountain Miller.'

On the *Site of the School Attended by William Cullen Bryant* and maintained by the Rev. Moses Hallock is the present village schoolhouse.

Left from Plainfield, on a road running between the church and town hall, is the *Birthplace of Charles Dudley Warner* (1829–1900) (*private*), 1.1 *m.*, a farmhouse standing (R) at some distance from the road. Warner was an editor and popular author; he collaborated with Mark Twain in writing 'The Gilded Age.'

At 1.2 *m.* the road bears right, and then left at a crossroads, 2.4 *m.* At intervals along this road, the ranges to the north are visible.

HAWLEY, 3.8 *m.* (town, alt. 1760, pop. 380, sett. 1771, incorp. 1792), is a hilly, rural town, named in honor of Joseph Hawley, a leader of the opposition to the revivalist preaching of Jonathan Edwards and prominent in the Revolutionary struggle in western Massachusetts.

Between Plainfield and Spruce Corner, State 116 is a dirt road, bordered with apple orchards. The country is hilly and wooded, with occasional farms that have been converted into summer estates.

SPRUCE CORNER, 20.1 *m.* (alt. 1478, Town of Ashfield), is a crossroads settlement.

State 116 climbs to cross a series of hills, the highest of which is 1775 feet in altitude. At 24.1 *m.* (L) is the *Ashfield Country Club* with a course descriptively nicknamed 'The Mountain Goat Course.' This is a scenic area, popular with artists.

ASHFIELD, 24.4 *m.* (town, alt. 1360, pop. 918, sett. about 1743, incorp. 1765), unlike most New England towns, has no Green.

The *Town Hall* (R), originally the Ashfield Church (1814), has a fine Wren-type spire.

Sanderson Academy, occupying a two-story frame building constructed in 1888, with *porte-cochère*, dentiled cornices, and an octagonal belfry, was founded in 1816, and was early celebrated as having been attended by Mary Lyon, founder of Mount Holyoke College, who, after graduation, taught for a time on its staff.

Left from Ashfield on State 112 to a road junction at 0.2 *m.*; straight ahead on this road to (R) *Great Pond*, 0.6 *m.* (*picnic grounds; bathing*).

At 1.8 *m.* on this road is the junction (R) with Apple Valley Rd., which runs 1.2 *m.* to the beautiful orchards that give the valley its name.

On the road passing Great Pond is, at 1.9 *m.*, a magnificent mountain vista.

At 26 *m.* where State 116 bears left is the junction with a road.

Right (straight ahead) on the side road through heavily wooded hilly country is a cement bridge over Poland Brook at the head of *Chapel Falls*, 2.3 *m.* Just beyond the bridge, left on a footpath, following the bank of the brook, is the foot of the falls. The waters tumble in a series of cascades over a solid rock bed with moss-covered sides.

State 116 passes *Mt. Owen* (alt. 1400) (L), and enters the deep valley of the South River.

At 30.7 *m.* is the junction with a hard-surfaced road.

Right on this road across a *Covered Bridge*, one of the few remaining in Massachusetts, the road runs up through high farming country with rolling pastures extending to the base of heavily wooded mountains. The little village of Conway is visible below in the deep valley. At 1.7 *m.* the road runs between majestically towering cliffs. It traverses wild forest at 2.9 *m.* and crosses a small bridge; left, a sparkling brook dashes over rocks.

CONWAY, 31.5 *m.* (town, alt. 300, pop. 952, sett. 1762, incorp. 1786), formerly a part of Deerfield, was named for General Henry Conway, a member of the British ministry popular in the Colonies after he secured the repeal of the Stamp Act in 1766. Indian attacks retarded its early settlement. Always predominantly agricultural, Conway, in the early 19th century, reached its industrial peak, with woolen and cotton mills, tanneries, grist and oil mills, and factories making broadcloth, cutlery, combs and tinware. Marshall Field (1834–1906), the Chicago merchant, was born here.

The *Marshall Field Memorial Library* (L), given by Marshall Field in 1885, a limestone structure with a circular dome and roof of copper, contains a fine historical collection.

Right from Conway to the *Conway Town Forest* on *Cricket Hill* (alt. 1100), 0.1 *m.*

East of Conway, State 116 passes through a rocky cut, displaying (R) banded gneiss. For about a mile stately pines arch the highway.

SOUTH DEERFIELD, 37.9 *m.* (alt. 208, Town of Deerfield), is at the junction with US 5 (*see Tour* 15).

At 39.5 *m.* State 116 crosses the Connecticut River on a new bridge replacing one washed away in the flood of 1936.

SUNDERLAND, 39.7 *m.* (town, alt. 142, pop. 1182, sett. about 1713, incorp. 1718), granted to the inhabitants of Hadley in 1673, had to be abandoned during King Philip's War. Forty years later, the land, known as Swampfield, was granted anew, this time to 40 proprietors who divided it into lots.

The early industries included potash manufacturing, milling, hat and saddle manufacturing, and the home manufacture of covered buttons and braided palmleaf hats. Today the inhabitants specialize in growing tobacco, onions, and oats.

Left from Sunderland on State 63 at 0.1 *m.* (L) is a *Giant Sycamore Tree,* one of the largest of this species in New England. At 1.4 *m.* is the entrance (R) to *Taylor Park* (*open, privately owned*). At 0.2 *m.* along the roadway into the park, a trail leads left across a little brook; then right and a short distance along the bank to a high cliff over which the water flows.

At 1.5 *m.* is a fine view to the rear of *Mt. Sugarloaf* (alt. 709).

At 3.2 *m.* is the junction with a path leading 200 feet across a farm (*ask permission to enter grounds*) to a *Cave* penetrating a spur of *Mt. Toby* (alt. 1275) for 150 feet and emerging on the far side. The path to the cave passes an interesting formation, *Chimney Rocks.*

The highway south of Sunderland is lined with maples, many over 200 years old. The sugar maples of the area are a source of revenue to the farmers.

At 42.6 *m.* is the junction with a dirt road.

Left on this road at 1.4 *m.* is the junction with a second road; left on this second road at 3.3 *m.* is a road leading left into the woods to a picnic ground (*fireplaces*) in the *Mt. Toby State Demonstration Forest,* an area of 755 wooded acres. *Roaring Brook* is here, cascading down the side of Mt. Toby; a narrow wooded path winds around the mountain and up the *Summit of Mt. Toby* (alt. 1275), where a fire tower commands a panorama of the Connecticut River Valley.

At 3.2 *m.* on the main dirt road is LEVERETT (town, alt. 430, pop. 726, sett. about 1713, incorp. 1775), which has a box factory opened in 1875 and still in operation; the town also produces charcoal, maple sugar and maple syrup. Early industries were shingle and textile mills, tanneries and a shoe factory.

The *Field Tavern* or Bradford Field House (*open by permission*), west of the Center, has a sharply gabled, many-windowed ell, built about 1790. The old barroom upstairs and a large collection of old relics are of interest.

North of Leverett the road crosses an open country; right at 3.6 *m.*, then left to *Rattle Snake Gutter*, a ravine with steep stones, crags, and ledges.

At 4.5 *m.* (R) is a steep grass-grown slope; across a ravine is a perpendicular cliff honeycombed by small caves.

AMHERST, 47.3 *m.* (*see AMHERST*), is at the junction with State 9 (*see Tour* 8).

At 52.8 *m.* State 116 passes through the *Notch*, a natural pass pink and white with laurel in late spring, and winds its way down the wooded slope of the Mt. Holyoke Range.

At 57.2 *m.* is SOUTH HADLEY (*see SOUTH HADLEY*).

At 59.9 *m.* is the junction with US 202 (*see Tour* 13) in SOUTH HADLEY FALLS.

Between this point and HOLYOKE, 61.6 *m.* (*see HOLYOKE*), State 116 and US 202 (*see Tour* 13) are united.

In Holyoke, State 116 turns left and recrosses the Connecticut River.

CHICOPEE, 66.3 *m.* (*see CHICOPEE*).

The route turns right on Sargent St., Springfield, at Memorial Square, 69.3 *m.*, and left on Columbus Ave., 69.4 *m.*

SPRINGFIELD, 70.5 *m.* (*see SPRINGFIELD*).

Here is the junction with US 20 (*see Tour* 4) and US 5 (*see Tour* 15).

T O U R 1 5 C : *From* NORTHAMPTON *to* WESTFIELD, 14.6 *m.*, State 10.

Via Easthampton and Southampton.

Hard-surfaced road open all seasons.

STATE 10 branches southeast from US 5 (*see Tour* 15) at Northampton and passes through a rolling countryside, the heart of a prosperous farming country. This road is known as College Highway because it very conveniently connects Smith College and Yale University.

At 4.3 *m.* is the *Manhan Bridge*, from which are seen the remains of the old

Northampton–New Haven Canal, and the *Site of the Old Storehouse* where the canal boats used to stop.

EASTHAMPTON, 4.7 *m.* (town, alt. 169, pop. 10,846, sett. 1664, incorp. 1809), began industrial development in 1780, but the real foundation of its industries was laid in 1822 by Samuel Williston. Williston and his wife began by covering wooden button molds with cloth. At the end of ten years, during which time he engaged over a thousand families and spread his distribution to larger cities, Williston financed some mechanics in the construction of a button-making machine, and organized Williston, Knight & Co. About 1848 the first elastic-web mill in America was making shoe goring here. The looms were imported from England and skilled weavers were brought over to use them. By 1927 a dozen large factories had been established, most of them producing yarn, thread, buttons, and elastic.

Williston Academy, a boys' preparatory school, is between Main and Union Sts. and Payson Ave. The new campus begins at the dignified home of the principal; the sections of the fence around this property were given by the various classes, and are of wrought iron.

> Left from the village on Union St.; at 0.5 *m.* is the junction with a road leading (L) to a farm-road at 1.4 *m.* On this road is the *Old East Street Cemetery*, with a beautiful memorial fence and gates, a picturesque spot lying in the shadow of the Mt. Tom Range.
>
> Straight ahead at 1.7 *m.* is East St., which leads (L) to the *Pascommuck Boulder*, 2.7 *m.*, where an Indian massacre occurred in 1704.

At 6.3 *m.* (R) is a fine vista of the Berkshire Hills.

The bed of the Northampton–New Haven Canal is readily traced at 7.6 *m.* This waterway, completed at a cost of $1,000,000 in 1835, was in use until 1847.

Mt. Pomeroy (alt. 1233) is right at 8.1 *m.* In 1704, Mrs. Benjamin Janes, taken prisoner by Indians in retreat from a raid on Pascommuck, was scalped and left to die on its summit; she was found by friends, however, and recovered.

SOUTHAMPTON, 8.9 *m.* (town, alt. 229, pop. 954, sett. 1732, incorp. 1775), was named for Southampton, England. Tanneries, grist and cider mills, whip factories, and blacksmith shops were once important to the town. In the 19th century sawmills and woodworking enterprises used up the timber supply, and today agriculture is the main support of the community.

On a hill behind the *Old Southampton Church* is the *Old Edwards House* (*private*), where the townspeople took refuge during the French and Indian War raids. Charred spots on the floors, made when the refugees did their cooking, are still visible.

At 14.6 *m.* is the junction with US 202 (*see Tour* 13).

TOUR 15D : *From* WEST SPRINGFIELD *to* CON-
NECTICUT LINE (*Suffield*), 6.5 *m.*, State 5A.

Via Agawam.
Macadam paving, condition fair.

STATE 5A parallels the west bank of the Connecticut River and passes
through a suburban area.

State 5A proceeds southwest from its junction with US 5 (*see Tour* 15) at
Riverdale.

At 0.7 *m.* is WEST SPRINGFIELD (*see Tour* 4), at which is the junction
with US 20 (*see Tour* 4).

At 2 *m.* is junction with State 57.

Left on State 57 at 0.2 *m.* is STORROWTON (*open all year*), a permanent village on the Exposition Grounds, is a group of Colonial buildings
brought here from their original sites. The ancient dwellings, with their
old-fashioned walks and gardens, herb beds, carriage sheds and outhouses,
the village Green with its white church dominating the peaceful scene,
present a composite picture of early New England at its best. The
Gilbert Homestead, built in 1794 in West Brookfield, is an admirable example of the massive construction of the period. The *Lawyer's Office*, built
about 1806, was that of Zechariah Eddy, a contemporary and friend of
Daniel Webster. The *Potter House* from North Brookfield was built in
1760 by Captain Potter, and the nails, latches, hinges, and the elaborate woodcarvings were made by his own hands. The *Little Red Schoolhouse*, a red-brick building with a small tower and belfry, was brought
from Whately, and is furnished with red benches. The *Blacksmith's Shop*,
built 1750, is from Chesterfield, the *Meeting House*, built 1834, from Salisbury, the *Phillips House*, built 1767, from Taunton, and the *Town House*,
built 1822, from Southwick. The *Atkinson Tavern and Store* was built
about 1799 in Prescott; the living quarters and the store are separate,
and the taproom in the latter is still in use.

At 0.4 *m.* on State 57 is the *Eastern States Agricultural and Industrial Exposition Grounds*, 'The Show Window of the North Atlantic States,' a 175-
acre tract equipped with permanent buildings. The educational value of the
one-week annual exposition held in September is emphasized; more than
1000 boys and girls are brought to the display each year, all expenses paid,
for a week of education and instruction. About 1000 exhibitors from 30
states and many Canadian provinces are present. Musical concerts and a
horse show are major attractions.

At 3.9 *m.* is AGAWAM (town, alt. 85, pop. 7206, sett. 1635, incorp. 1855).

The Agawam (Indian, *Agaam*, 'Crooked River') River meanders along the northern boundary of the town and gave it its name. Until 15 years ago an agricultural community, Agawam Town is now partly a residential suburb of Springfield. Near-by farms at Feeding Hills are engaged in market gardening, dairying, and poultry and tobacco raising.

Right from Agawam on a paved road is the *Agawam Race Track* at 2.5 *m.* Originally an airport, it was taken over by the Agawam Breeders' Association and converted to its present use in 1935. Several runways have been left, however.

At 6.5 *m.* State 5A crosses the Connecticut State Line 20 *m.* north of Hartford, Conn.

T O U R 1 7 : *From* VERMONT LINE (*Pownal*) *to* CONNECTICUT LINE (*North Canaan*), 55 *m.*, US 7.

Via (*sec. a*) Williamstown, Hancock, New Ashford, Lanesborough, and Pittsfield; (*sec. b*) Lenox, Stockbridge, Great Barrington, and Sheffield.

B. & M., B. & A., and N.Y., N.H. & H. R.R.'s service this area.

Road is hard-surfaced throughout.

Sec. a. VERMONT STATE LINE to PITTSFIELD, 23.6 m.

US 7 is a scenic route between Vermont and Connecticut. South of the Vermont Line the road runs under Mt. Greylock and the Berkshire Hills and over the divide into the Housatonic Valley between the Hoosac and Taconic Ranges.

US 7 crosses the Vermont Line 13 *m.* south of Bennington, Vt.

WILLIAMSTOWN, 2.3 *m.* (*see WILLIAMSTOWN*), is at the junction (L.) with State 2 (*see Tour* 2) which unites with US 7 for several miles.

At 4.7 *m.* is the junction (R) with State 2 (*see Tour* 2).

At 5.6 *m.* is a view (L) of Mt. Greylock, identified by the marble shaft on its summit.

At 6.7 *m.* is SOUTH WILLIAMSTOWN (alt. 604, Town of Williamstown) and the junction with State 43.

Right from South Williamstown on State 43, which runs through a river valley, at 4 *m.* (R) is the *Edward Howe Forbush Wild Life Sanctuary*, a 500-acre reservation presented to the Commonwealth by the Federated Bird Clubs of New England and named for the ornithologist. Here are many varieties of birds, and fox and deer roam the woods.

At 9.8 *m.* on State 43 is the junction with the *Sky Line Trail*, which runs left through the *Pittsfield State Forest* 3 *m.* to *Berry Pond* (alt. 1013), set in a lovely dale and bounded on one side by the "'Ope of Promise,' a favorite hill of the Shakers. The Trail continues to the summit of *Tower Mountain* (alt. 2185), 3.5 *m.*, from which is a view of the Lebanon and Hudson Rivers, Equinox Mountain, and the Connecticut Hills.

HANCOCK, 10.1 *m.* on State 43 (town, alt. 1020, pop. 408, sett. 1767, incorp. 1776), first known as Jericho because of the high natural walls surrounding it, was given its present name to honor John Hancock. Though it at one time had gristmills and tanneries, it could not compete with rival industrial centers and is now a dairying community.

US 7 at 9 *m.*, starts an ascent, crossing and recrossing the Green River (*excellent trout fishing in season*).

At 10.6 *m.* (R) is the *Night Hill For Skiing* (*illuminated*) maintained by the Mt. Greylock Ski Club of Pittsfield.

NEW ASHFORD, 11.1 *m.* (town, alt. 1350, pop. 94, sett. 1762, incorp. 1835), was settled by emigrants from Rhode Island and Connecticut. The region once contained valuable quarries of blue and white marble, which were worked for some 20 years, but the cost of transportation became too great to allow a profit, and New Ashford relapsed into the peace of a farming community. Josh Billings, famous humorist, spent most of his summers here.

At 12.2 *m. Jones's Nose*, a giant proboscis, is visible (L).

Red Bat Cave (*open*), (L) 12.5 *m.* was so named because of tiny redheaded bats found on its walls. The cave, made up of four chambers, is 100 feet long and 150 feet deep.

US 7 passes the foot of a watershed that separates the Hoosac Valley from the Housatonic Valley. At 12.7 *m.* is the entrance (R) to the *Brody Mt. Ski Trails* (*adm.* 15¢).

At 15.1 *m.* (R) on Town Brook is *State Tourist Park* (*fireplaces, benches, tables, wading pools, trout fishing, camping*), located on what was once the roadbed.

At 16.3 *m.* is the junction with an improved road.

> Right on this road to *Disappearing Brook*, 1.2 *m.* (*entrance for cars; small fee*), which flows underground and through caves. *Quarry Cave* near-by once supplied a fine white marble. In a field is *Brown's Boulder* crowned by a natural rock garden. Rising west is *Potter's Mountain*, long ago a favorite of Herman Melville, author of 'Moby Dick.'

At 16.6 *m.* is the junction with Rockwell or Tourist's Rd. (*see Tour 17B*), which leads to the summit of Mt. Greylock.

At 16.7 *m.* (R) stands an old house known as the *British Headquarters*, a two-and-a-half-story, weather-beaten, brown-clapboarded structure with green tar-paper strips on its slanting roof and a small, central, red-brick chimney.

LANESBOROUGH, 17.8 *m.* (town, alt. 1210, pop. 1237, sett. about 1753, incorp. 1765), was originally known as New Framingham, but was incorporated as Lanesborough in honor of the beautiful Irish Countess of Lanesborough, a court favorite and a friend of the then Governor of Massachusetts. Except for variegated and pure white marble quarried in 1842–43, farming has always been the source of livelihood.

> Right from Lanesborough on Silver St. is *Constitution Hill* (R) 0.8 *m.*, named in memory of Jonathan Smith, who in a well-timed speech swung the State for the ratification of the Federal Constitution.

At the foot of the hill is an old farmhouse, the *Birthplace of Henry Wheeler Shaw* (1818–85), the humorist known as 'Josh Billings.' His 'Essa on the Muel' brought him national fame, and an almanac with his proverb, 'Tu sta is tu win: A man can outliv a not hoal,' sold 430,000 copies. The house is still occupied by the Shaw family.

At 19.2 *m.* is the junction with a country road.

Right on this road past the north shore of *Pontoosuc Lake* is *Balance Rock*, 1.9 *m.* This triangular mass of limestone, weathered gray, and weighing 165 tons, is thought to have been carried here from some point east of the Hudson River by glacial action, and is so poised, three feet above the ground on another rock, that it vibrates when touched, although it cannot be dislodged.

US 7 follows the east shore of *Pontoosuc Lake* at 19.8 *m.* Across the lake is visible the *Potter Mountain Group* of the Taconic Range. *Pontoosuc Lake Park* (*municipal bathhouses*) on the south shore, embraces 30 acres of pine grove. It is usually crowded in summer.

US 7 swings past the old *Pontoosuc Woolen Mill* (R) established in 1825, and into Wahconah St., once bordered by textile mills, now vanished.

At about 22.8 *m.* is the junction with First St., an alternate route through Pittsfield.

Straight ahead on First St. to East St.; left on East St. to the south end of the city park, left on South St. (US 20).

PITTSFIELD, 23.6 *m.* (*see PITTSFIELD*) is at the junction with US 20 (*see Tour* 4).

Sec. b. PITTSFIELD to CONNECTICUT STATE LINE, US 7, 20, 7, 31.4 m.

Following the Housatonic Valley, US 7, united with US 20 for 6 *m.*, winds between the Hoosac and Taconic Ranges and drops into level plains.

At 2 *m.* is the junction with a gravel road.

Right on this road 0.5 *m.* is the entrance to the *South Mountain Music Colony.* During the summer season a series of open-air concerts are given here by the Berkshire String Ensemble. Free instruction for promising young men and women is provided under the sponsorship of Mrs. Frederick Sprague Coolidge.

At 3.7 *m.* is the junction with New Lenox Rd.

Left on this road at 1.3 *m.* is NEW LENOX (alt. 1006, Town of Lenox). At 1.9 *m.* is the junction with a dirt road; right here to *October Mountain State Forest* (*see Tour* 8), a recreational area. Winding along the base of the mountain (L) the road crosses *Roaring Brook* at 2.3 *m.* In this area lies *Tory Cave*, which according to tradition was the hiding-place of Tories from Pittsfield during the Revolution.

At 6.1 *m.* (R) is the beautiful *Church on the Hill* (Congregational) built in 1805 and remodelled in 1840. It is a simple, but well-studied frame meeting-house, with square clock tower and octagonal belfry. This fine old church, which has been described as 'graceful without effort, solid and substantial without stolidness or dullness,' was probably designed by Isaac Damon from designs in one of Asher Benjamin's books.

LENOX, 6.6 *m.* (town, alt. 1210, pop. 2706, sett. about 1750, incorp. 1775), was named for Charles Lenox, Duke of Richmond, a defender of Colonial rights. Industries in the town included an iron foundry, marble works, a hearthstone mill, and a glass factory, but today only two tobacco mills operate. The town early became a summer resort with fine hotels and magnificent homes.

The *Lenox Library* (*open daily in summer*), at the town center, in the former County Courthouse, built 1816, has weekly exhibits of rare books and manuscripts. A side door opens into a shaded garden, with seats for readers.

The *Lenox Boys' School* (R), a group of fine, yellow-painted clapboarded buildings with extensive grounds, was formerly Mrs. Charles Sedgwick's School for Girls. Catherine Maria Sedgwick (1789–1867), first person to write of the natural beauties of the Berkshires, lived here.

Mrs. Edith Wharton's home, *The Mount*, is on the north shore of Laurel Lake. Here she was often visited by Henry James.

Right from Lenox on State 183 (Housatonic St.) at 1.5 *m.* (L) is the entrance of the Dixey estate, on the grounds of which is the *Site of the Hawthorne Cottage.* the little red house, in which Hawthorne wrote 'The House of the Seven Gables.' This estate, of 210 acres, is to be used by the Boston Symphony Orchestra, which will give concerts each summer in a natural outdoor bowl. At 1.7 *m.* is the junction (R) with a dirt road, the entrance to *Shadowbrook*, a Jesuit Novitiate, formerly the summer home of Andrew Carnegie. Left on the dirt road at 3.2 *m.* is the public entrance to *Lake Mahkeenac* or Stockbridge Bowl (*boating, fishing*).

At 6.7 *m.* US 7 bears right and US 20 (*see Tour* 4) runs left.

At this junction is the *Trinity Episcopal Church* (L), an edifice of cut stone with a beautiful stained-glass circular window.

At 12.3 *m.* is (L) the *Stockbridge School of Drama*, a remodeled rambling red barn.

STOCKBRIDGE, 12.8 *m.* (town, alt. 839, pop. 1921, sett. 1734, incorp. 1739), was named for an English municipality, and occupies a grant made by the General Court in 1734 for the purpose of establishing an Indian mission, with land set apart for four white families. At the time Stockbridge was the home of the Mukhekanews ('People of Ever-Flowing Waters'), a branch of the Algonquins. So successful was the mission that a number of the Mukhekanews were listed among the first officials of the church and town. Friendly relations between the whites and Indians were disturbed in 1755, and in 1785 the Indians left for New York State.

In 1745 a gristmill was established; and during the period between 1750 and 1850 the townsfolk were extensively engaged in the manufacture of hats and wrought nails.

Stockbridge support of the embargo on tea during the Revolutionary days was graphically shown by an experience of the Rev. Mr. Kirkland. On the eve of his departure for missionary work among the Oneida Indians, he invited to his home a colleague, who was shocked to see on the table a steaming pot of tea. Circumstances, however, seemed to warrant a compromise with patriotism, and behind locked doors the two men sat down to tipple, a pleasure suddenly ended by a loud knock on the door. In his haste to conceal the boiling pot of tea, the Rev. Mr. Kirkland upset it in his lap.

Grouped about the Common are the *First Congregational Church*, the old *Town Hall*, and the impressive *Field Chime Tower*, a memorial to the Rev. Dudley Field, father of three famous sons. First was Dudley Field, Jr., a noted lawyer permanently famous for his work to secure legal reforms; second was Stephen Field, United States Supreme Court Justice; third was Cyrus Field, promoter of the laying of the first transatlantic cable. A short distance west stands the *Jonathan Edwards Monument*, dedicated to the great preacher who taught the Indians for a time in the Mission House (*see below*).

At the junction with State 102 (L) is the *Red Lion Inn*, on the site of a tavern of that name established in 1774. The inn contains the *Plumb Collection* of Colonial china, pewter, and furniture.

East of the High School on State 102 is the entrance to the *Berkshire Playhouse* (*open in summer*), the principal Little Theater in the Berkshires, a rectangular frame structure, painted white, with an open cupola and a captain's walk.

The *Stockbridge Mission House* (*open summer* 10–12.30; 2–6; *Sun.* 2–6; *winter* 2–4, *and by appoint.; adm.* 25¢) is 0.3 *m.* west of the Center on State 102. This house was built in 1739 by the Rev. John Sergeant, first missionary to the Stockbridge Indians. Jonathan Edwards (1703–58), the great Calvinist clergyman whose writings and sermons at Northampton helped to touch off the Great Awakening that swept America, visited this house as a missionary in 1751 after he had been forced out of Northampton. In Stockbridge he wrote 'The Freedom of the Will.' With the adjacent buildings the Mission House constitutes a restoration of an early Colonial village. This beautiful memorial was conceived by Mabel Choate in honor of her parents. The magnificent landscaped gardens are the work of Fletcher Steele. The old house is a two-and-a-half-story unpainted clapboarded structure with two inner chimneys below the ridge-line on the rear slope of the roof, a very rare feature for a house of this period. The sole exterior embellishment is the front door with its fine panel work. The frame of the Connecticut Valley door has fluted sides and an intricate carved decoration over the center. Natural pine woodwork adorns the walls of the rooms. Enthusiasts about American antiques will delight in the displayed crewelwork of bird and flower designs. A partial list of other items includes a dole or livery cupboard, an extremely early and rare piece whose open front has tulip-like Gothic slats allowing a circulation of air for the food which was kept in it; candlestands whose height is adjustable by ratchet; an odd dresser with receding upper compartments; and an oak chest brought over from England by John Choate in 1643.

> Left from Stockbridge to *Ice Glen*, 0.6 *m.*, a wild and lovely gorge containing ice in its deeper crevices the year round. A trail to this point and to *Laurel Hill*, a knoll owned by the Laurel Hill Association, branches from the High School grounds.

South of Stockbridge US 7 climbs the slope of *Monument Mountain* (alt. 1640) and at 16.3 *m.* passes over *Squaw Peak* (*overnight cabins available*) to the *Monument Mountain Reservation*. The road here is flanked by a steep ravine (R) and a dense forest of deciduous trees (L). As the highway descends, an excellent view of the Berkshires unfolds. William Cullen Bryant's poem, 'Monument Mountain,' tells of an Indian girl who cast herself from the summit when forbidden to marry a member of a hostile tribe.

Right from this point, about 0.5 *m.*, on a steep, dangerous trail running along the face of a sheer cliff to the summit, is the *Devil's Pulpit*, an unusual white marble formation. The view of the valley and distant mountains from this point is very fine.

At 17.3 *m.* the majestic dome of *Mt. Everett* (alt. 2624), which appears in the works of Hawthorne and Bryant, is seen (R).

At 19.3 *m.*, *Belcher Square*, is the junction with State 17 (*see Tour 4A*).

Left from Belcher Square, on a trail is *Belcher's Cave*, a rift in the rocks, noted chiefly for a huge stone fragment that hangs like a spearhead in the entrance. Here a band minted false Colonial currency.

GREAT BARRINGTON, 20.4 *m.* (town, alt. 710, pop. 6369, sett. 1726, incorp. 1761). Both Dutch and English names are on the deeds here, given in 1724 by Chief Konkapot. The Great Road, running through the town, was the route of many expeditions during the French and Indian Wars.

The first telegraph line having a local station was run through the town in 1848 by Ezra Cornell, financier and founder of Cornell University. Anson Jones, last President of the Republic of Texas (1844–46), was born in Great Barrington in 1798. In recent years Great Barrington has become a winter and summer vacation center, and the summer home of many New York people.

On the grounds of the Searles High School, Bridge St., near the Housatonic River (L), is a stone monument marking the approximate site of an old *Indian Ford*. Here, in 1676, a band of fleeing Narragansetts was over taken by Major Talcott, and a sanguinary encounter took place, the last Indian engagement in the area.

The *William Cullen Bryant House* (R), now a summer tearoom, is in the garden behind the Berkshire Inn. The house (1739) is a two-and-a-half-story dwelling with a two-leaf door of the early Connecticut Valley type and with two interior chimneys. The interior is handsomely paneled, particularly the 'marriage room.' Here Bryant was married at the time he was practicing law and serving as town clerk (1815–25) of Great Barrington.

At 21.2 *m.* are the *Grounds of the Housatonic Agricultural Society (saddle horses; annual fair 4th Tues, in Sept.; grandstand, exhibition hall, race track)*.

US 7 passes over the *Green River* at 22.5 *m.*, near its junction with the *Housatonic River*, which runs parallel with the highway for a long stretch.

At 23.8 *m.* the *Appalachian Trail* (*see Tour 9*) crosses the road.

At 25.6 *m.* is SHEFFIELD PLAIN (Town of Sheffield).

1. Right from here on a dirt road is the *Bear's Den*, 0.8 *m.*, with a wooded knoll rising 200 feet. According to Indian tradition, savage bears used to come down from the cave to eat naughty papooses.

2. Left from Sheffield Plain, 0.5 *m.*, on a dirt road is an *Old Covered Bridge* over the Housatonic River; north of this bridge, 0.5 *m.*, is another *Old Covered Bridge*. Both bridges are more than 100 years old and are still in use.

SHEFFIELD, 26.6 *m.* (town, alt. 697, pop. 1810, sett. 1726, incorp. 1733), at one time depended on lime and marble for revenue, but today it depends on agriculture and summer visitors. Its wide main thoroughfare lined with elms is one of the most beautiful in the Commonwealth.

At 27.7 *m.* is a junction with a dirt road.

Right on this road 1.7 *m.* is *Bartholomew's Cobbles*, an outcropping of queerly shaped boulders in a pine-clad vale (*picnicking*).

At 30.8 *m.* (R) is an old *Red Mill* (*open* 8–5), which has been in operation continuously for over 200 years.

At 31.4 *m.* the road crosses the Connecticut State Line, 2 *m.* north of Canaan, Conn.

T O U R   1 7 A :   *From* PITTSFIELD *to* CONNECTICUT LINE (*Salisbury*), 31.7 *m.*, State 41.

Via West Stockbridge, Great Barrington, Alford, Egremont, Mount Washington, and Sheffield.

B. & A. and N.Y., N.H. & H. R.R.'s parallel the route at intervals.

Hard-surfaced road open all year except during severe snowstorms.

STATE 41 runs through hilly Richmond and the valley of the Williams and Housatonic Rivers. Passing infrequent tiny villages, lonely farms set in rugged country, and crisscrossed by innumerable streams, the route is paralleled throughout its length by an almost unbroken chain of forest-clad mountains.

South of its junction with US 20 (*see Tour* 4) 4.5 *m.* west of Pittsfield, State 41 runs through part of the *Shaker Settlement* (*see Tour* 4).

At 1 *m.* is *Richmond Pond*, with the summits of the Berkshire Hills rising behind it.

At 3 *m.* are the *Richmond Boulder Trains*, a geological curiosity. They are a band from two to three miles in width, extending southeast across Richmond. The rocks of a peculiar chlorite schist range from small pebbles to boulders of many tons, and were evidently transported across the Taconic Range during the glacial period.

RICHMOND, 5 *m.* (town, alt. 1107, pop. 628, sett. 1760, incorp. 1765), originally called Yokumtown, was incorporated as Richmont, but in 1785 became Richmond in honor of Charles Lennox, Duke of Richmond, and defender of Colonial rights. From 1827 to 1923 Richmond was active in the production of iron ore; Richmond iron was used for the cannon of the 'Monitor.' Competition ruined the mines and smelters here; today the town depends chiefly on agriculture, though two stone quarries and a small ironworks are still in operation.

> Left from Richmond on a gravel road, 0.7 *m.*, is a junction with a dirt road; right on this road to *Steven's Glen*, 1.7 *m.* (*picnicking*), a deep, cool ravine through which a brook winds its way.

RICHMOND FURNACE, 6.5 *m.* (alt. 1003), was named for the large iron smelters operating here until 1915. One of the old brick houses of this once thriving industrial center is adorned with floral paintings.

At 7.6 *m.*, near two ponds is *Troy's Baseball Field* where fast semi-professional games are played.

At 8 *m.* are *Crane Pond* (R), a breeding place for several species of fish; and *Shaker Mill Pond* (L), full of speckled trout.

At 8.4 *m.* is a junction with a hard-surfaced road, an alternate route to Great Barrington.

> Right on this road, 1 *m.*, is a junction with a dirt road. Left on this dirt road is WEST STOCKBRIDGE CENTER, 3 *m.* (alt. 915) in a former marble quarrying district.
>
> Left from the Center on West Rd., which winds through a valley of farms and summer homes, to ALFORD, 11 *m.* (town, alt. 960, pop. 210, sett. about 1740, incorp. 1775), named in honor of John Alford, founder of the Alford professorship of Moral Philosophy at Harvard University. Alford marble was used in New York's City Hall, and in the State House, the Market, and the Law Building at Albany. Quarrying has lately been discontinued.
>
> 1. Left from the village on East Rd. to *Tom Ball Mountain* (alt. 1930), 3 *m.* On its western slope is the *Devil's Den* (*reached by a 0.5 m. footpath*), a large cave unpleasant because of its constantly dripping cold water and its uneven floor. Two birch trees stand sentinel at the entrance.
>
> 2. Left from Alford on West Rd. to GREAT BARRINGTON, 14.5 *m.* (*see Tour 17*) and the junction with State 41.

WEST STOCKBRIDGE, 8.8 *m.* (town, alt. 744, pop. 1138, sett. 1766, incorp. 1775), is an attractive farming town nestled among valleys and wooded hills. William Bryant, the first settler, came from Canaan, Conn., to this region then called by the Indians *Qua-pau-kuk*. During the next few years some 40 families followed him. During the early 19th century, West Stockbridge enjoyed prominence and prosperity as the eastern terminus of the Hudson and Berkshire Railroad. In that period a paper mill, marble quarries, sawmills, and limekilns flourished, but of these industries there remain today only two limeworks. For many years the town has been well known as a summer resort.

At the junction with State 102 is an *Old Stone Mill* with a stone marked 'Anno 1830'; it is now the studio of an artist.

At 14.6 *m.* is the junction with an improved highway.

Left on this highway is HOUSATONIC, 0.3 *m.* (alt. 755; Town of Great Barrington), an industrial village, and the home of the *Monument Mills*, one of the largest textile plants in the State, named for *Monument Mountain* (alt. 1640), against which the town nestles.

VAN DEUSENVILLE, 16.5 *m.* (alt. 720; Town of Great Barrington), on the Williams River (*trout fishing in season*), one of the largest streams in Berkshire County, is another suburb of Great Barrington.

At 18.6 *m.* is the junction with US 7 (*see Tour* 17) with which State 41 unites through GREAT BARRINGTON (*see Tour* 17), 19.2 *m.*, to a junction (R) at 19.6 *m.*

West of its lower junction with US 7, State 41 crosses the *Green River*, 20.6 *m.*, a beautiful stream of clear water flowing over fragments of white marble; it inspired one of Bryant's poems. A marker (L) near the bridge is on the site of a camp of General Jeffrey Amherst on his way to Ticonderoga in 1758. General Knox also used the route here in 1776. The *Green River Mill* (R) is still in operation after a century of service to local farmers.

At 21.2 *m.* is the junction with State 69.

Right on State 69 is the *Great Barrington Airport*, 1 *m.*, on level ground of Egremont Plain.

NORTH EGREMONT, 2.1 *m.* (alt. 815), is a village with old houses shaded by tall maples and elms.

Right from North Egremont on a dirt road is *Prospect Lake*, 0.5 *m.* (*excellent pickerel and perch fishing; boating, bathing, camping*), a small deep pond.

SOUTH EGREMONT, 23.2 *m.* (town, alt. 740, pop. 569, sett. 1730, incorp. 1775), was named in honor of Charles Windham, Earl of Egremont, a liberal and a friend of the American cause in the Revolution. Prominent among the early plants utilizing the abundant water-power were a chair factory, cheese factories, sawmills, and axle works. A quarry producing a fine grade of marble is no longer worked owing to marketing difficulties.

At the Center is the *Olde Egremont Tavern*, built 1730, restored in 1931. Its Blue Grill overlooks an old swimming hole in the mountain brook at the foot of the shady lawns and its Cedar Grill has a large, ancient fireplace. Near-by is the restored *Egremont Inn*, built 1780, once a station on the stagecoach route. Adjacent to the inn is the *Old Blacksmith Shop* of 1730 (*open in summer*), now a store selling old furniture and other articles.

On Sheffield Back Rd. is the *Oldest Private House* (1761). This typical Dutch Colonial brick structure has the initials of John and Mary Tuller, original owners, and a huge heart inlaid at one end.

At 23.7 *m.* is the junction with Mt. Everett Reservation Rd.

Right on this road; left at 0.5 *m.* on a dirt road running through Guilder Hollow to *Jug End*, 1.1 *m.* (*privately owned*), containing *Bat's Den*, a group of four caves, two of which, *Growling Bear* and the *Pothole*, are difficult to reach (*beware of rattlesnakes*). The *Crystal Pool Cave*, though small, has beautiful stalactites and stalagmites.

The *Appalachian Trail* (*see Tour* 9) runs off Jug End from Mt. Everett. There is a fine ski trail (*private; fee charged*) here. Reservation Rd. follows *Goodale Brook* into a deep gorge. The mountains opposite rise higher and higher.

At 5.4 *m*. (R), and identified by large maples and a heap of stones, is the *Site of Sky Farm*, now almost obliterated by forest growth. Here lived the Goodale sisters, Elaine and Dora, the 'apple blossom poets' whose verse was popular throughout the country in the 1870's, and whose stories in *The Youth's Companion* were favorites.

At 5.6 *m*. is the junction with a dirt road.

Right (*straight ahead*) 0.5 *m*. is a foot trail (R) that winds through woods and meadows to *Profile Rock*, 1.5 *m*., a stone face on the brink of *Mt. Ethel* (alt. 1900).

At 1.3 *m*. (R) is a junction with a dirt road that runs into picturesque *Bash-Bish State Forest*, a 394-acre reservation.

At 3.7 *m*. is a parking area, whence a foot trail leads 0.3 *m*. to *Bash-Bish Falls* (*picnic tables, cut wood, fireplaces*). From points along the path are views of a deep cleft in the solid rock, 400 to 500 feet deep, at the base of which are the falls. The stream plunges the final 50 feet into a rock-bottomed pool, in which, in certain lights, it is reported, can be seen the image of an Indian girl who, disappointed in love, drowned herself in the waters.

At 3.9 *m*. (L) is a trail to the clearing near the Falls.

At the junction at 5.6 *m*. Reservation Rd. turns left; it passes through newly developed agricultural lands where potato-raising, once one of the principal industries of Mt. Washington, is being revived.

UNION CHURCH, 9.2 *m*. (alt. 1670, pop. 64, sett. 1692, incorp. 1779; Town of Mt. Washington), is the principal village of the town. The chief industry has always been farming, although considerable income is now derived from entertaining tourists. The community is without a post-office or store.

Left from Union Church an improved road leads into the *Mt. Everett Reservation*, a State park of 1200 acres.

At 1.3 *m*. on this reservation road is *Guilder Pond* (alt. 1975), surrounded by dense evergreens and almost covered in summer with pink and white water-lilies. A foot trail circles the pond.

At 1.7 *m*. are a picnic ground and parking area called *The First Level*. From this point a foot trail leads 0.5 *m*. to the *Dome* (alt. 2624). Here a steel tower with a sheltered observation platform provides a view extending to the dim outlines of the Green Mountains in Vermont and the Berkshires of Connecticut.

South of Union Church, on the main road 13.2 *m*., is ALANDER (alt. 1647), once the central village of Mt. Washington. From here the road passes through thick woods along the ridge to the Connecticut Line 16.2 *m*.

At 24.5 *m*. State 41, called here the Under Mountain Rd., winds its way close to the mountains, through an area of summer homes, meadowland, and pine groves.

At 26.4 *m*. is *Twin Fires*, the red-brick home of Walter Prichard Eaton, Associate Professor of Play-Writing at Yale University, author, and critic of the drama. The house, in a beautiful setting, has two large end chimneys from which it derives its name.

At 29.3 *m*. is a junction with a foot trail.

Right on this trail to *Race Brook Falls*, 0.5 *m*., are three lovely glens whose brooks cascade along the base of the Taconic Range. The Upper Falls are twin cataracts, one above the other.

At 31.4 *m.* is a junction with a foot trail (*private*).

Right on this trail, 0.7 *m.*, are high *Bear Rock Falls*. From their source in a beautiful lake in Race Mountain, the waters drop through a wild gorge.

At 31.7 *m.* State 41 crosses the Connecticut State Line, about 6 *m.* north of Salisbury, Conn. Here *Sage's Ravine Brook* passes under the highway and descends 50 feet in a series of cascades.

T O U R   1 7 B :   *From* LANESBOROUGH *to* SUMMIT OF MT. GREYLOCK, 10.3 *m.*, Rockwell Rd.

Improved dirt road. Impassable during winter except in lower stretch.

ROCKWELL ROAD, or Tourist Road as it is more commonly called, is the better of two roads to the summit of Mt. Greylock (alt. 3505) (*see Tour 17; for Notch Rd. from North Adams see Tour 2*). From its junction with US 7, 8 *m.* north of Pittsfield, Rockwell Rd. is marked Mt. Greylock Reservation Rd. It winds up through hill-farms and upland moor, providing wide, beautiful vistas of near-by vales and distant peaks swimming in blue haze. From the summit itself, five States are visible, a panorama like a brilliant-hued patchwork quilt whose blue-gray fringe is the vague horizon.

The picturesque area surrounding Mt. Greylock is ideal for winter hiking and sports. Miles of woodland trails stretching over mountains are easily accessible. The trails are suitable for leisurely progress, with here and there a downhill run for mild excitement. In winter the only sounds breaking the silence are the soughing of the wind through the bare branches of the trees, the snap of a twig, the soft plop of falling snow-fluffs, the startled cry of a grouse aroused by human approach.

At 1 *m.* there is a glimpse of Lanesborough (S) and the distant range of the Taconics (W). At 2.9 *m.* the whole valley comes into view, rimmed by the Taconic Range, with Mt. Petersburg (alt. 2510), towering aloft; the Green Mountains of Vermont loom up majestically.

At 3.2 *m.*, the junction with Bowen Rd., a magnificent view of the Hoosac Valley is obtained.

Continuing the ascent, the road enters wooded country clothed with spruce and small deciduous growth, and at 4.6 *m.* passes close to the base of *Rounds Rock*, a dark cliff rising abruptly from the wet lowlands, just within the boundaries of the *Greylock Reservation*. The road winds its way through thick woodland, making hairpin turns around rocky bluffs and promontories, until it emerges once more into open country at 5.5 *m.*

Jones's Nose (alt. 3000), a ledge-like cliff on *Saddle Ball Mountain* (alt. 3300), appears at 5.6 *m.* This cliff looks like the broad nose of a giant, the trees on its summit giving the appearance of a tangled mass of hair crowning a colossal head. The *Appalachian Trail* (*see Tour* 9) follows the entire length of Saddle Ball and runs directly up the Nose to join Rockwell Rd. near the summit.

At 6.9 *m.* Rockwell Rd. is joined (L) by the New Ashford Rd., used chiefly in January, when Rockwell Rd. becomes impassable. At the junction is (L) the *Site of Ash Fort* (1765), said to have been built of ash logs as the original block-house, center of the first settlement of the town of New Ashford.

Rockwell Rd. crosses Mitchell Brook, which plunges down a deep gorge, and at 7.7 *m.* reaches a junction with Stony Ledge Rd.

Left on this road at 1 *m.* is (1937) a Civilian Conservation Corps camp and at 2.3 *m. Stony Ledge.* This ledge offers one of the most spectacular and beautiful sights in all New England. Below is the *Hopper,* a deep, wooded gulf in the center of Greylock's several peaks, resembling a giant grain hopper plugged at its outlet by Mt. Prospect. The Ledge looks down on the tops of trees that in autumn are ablaze with color. Beyond the Hopper the peaks of Mt. Fitch and Mt. Williams rear their heads.

At 8.6 *m.* is the *Hopper Trail.*

At 8.8 *m.*, at the sharpest turn, the Appalachian Trail joins the route and follows it to the summit. At 9.3 *m.* the newly constructed *Notch Rd.*, a ski run, enters from North Adams (*see Tours* 2 *and* 21).

At 9 *m.* are the *Capes to the Berkshires Trail* and the *Cheshire Harbor Trail.*

At 9.9 *m.* the *Bellows' Pipe Trail* to North Adams is crossed, and just beyond, the *Thunderbolt Ski Run* leaps the road and catapults into the valley 1800 feet below. This run, on the east slope of Greylock, is one of the steepest courses east of the Rocky Mountains, but skiers who possess a moderate amount of skill need not fear it because its wide paths permit slowing movements. At the bottom of the drop the terrain opens up into about 200 acres of graded slopes giving opportunity for long slides.

Beyond the Thunderbolt, on the *Summit* (alt. 3505) is *Bascom Lodge* (*open winter and summer*), a rest-house of native stone and timber. From its piazza facing south, the view embraces the Berkshire Hills country for a distance of forty miles. Also on the summit is a *Memorial Tower,* 105 feet high, built of Quincy granite and dedicated to the soldiers and sailors of Massachusetts. From its top there is a magnificent view, extending as far as the White Mountains and New York Harbor.

T O U R   1 9 :   *From* BOSTON *to* BOURNE, 55 *m.*, State 28.

Via Milton, Braintree, Randolph, Holbrook, Avon, Brockton, West Bridge-water, Bridgewater, and Halifax.

N.Y., N.H. & H. R.R. services this area.

Hard-surfaced roadbed, heavy traffic during summer months.

SOUTH of the Blue Hills of Milton, State 28, one of the principal routes between Boston and Cape Cod, traverses a fairly level terrain.

South of its junction with US 1 (*see Tour* 1) in the Fenway in Boston, State 28 follows along the Arborway, lined with beautiful trees and estates. At 0.1 *m.* (R) is the *Arnold Arboretum* (*see BOSTON*).

State 28 bears right into Blue Hill Ave. at 2.6 *m.*, while State 3 (*see Tour* 27) continues straight ahead.

At 3.9 *m.* on State 28 is the junction with State 138 (*see Tour* 25).

MILTON, 5.1 *m.* (town, alt. 24, pop. 18,147, sett. 1636, incorp. 1662), originally Uncataquisset (Indian 'Head of Tidewater'), was formerly in the town of Dorchester. Factories utilizing the power created by the Neponset River were early established here, making powder, chocolate, bass viols, artificial legs, pianos, drugs, medicines, and dyestuffs.

The *Milton Library* (*open*) a red-brick structure on the corner of Canton Ave. and State 28, houses the James Whitman collection of etchings by Millet, Rembrandt, and Whistler, and exhibits the paintings of local artists. It is the headquarters of the Milton Historical Society.

The *Gulliver Elm,* junction of Elm St. and Canton Ave., is said to have been deeded in 1823 by the First Congregational Parish in Milton to Isaac Gulliver, who gave bond for its perpetual protection.

On Centre St., between Vose Lane and Randolph Ave., is *Milton Academy,* housed in several red-brick buildings. It was established in 1807, closed in 1866 when the first town high school was built, and reopened in 1885 as a private coeducational institution.

About 500 feet east of the academy on Centre St. is Milton Cemetery containing the *Grave of Wendell Phillips.*

1. Right from the Center 1.3 *m.* on Canton Ave., corner of Robbins St., 50 yards from the road, is the *Manassah Tucker House* (*private*). The original two-and-a-half-story, gray frame dwelling was built in 1707. The left half of the house was added later, bringing the end chimney to the center.

2. Left from the Center on Canton Ave. is MILTON LOWER MILLS, 1.2 *m.* (alt. 20; Town of Milton).

The *Vose House* (*private*), 38 Adams St., was built in 1773. Here delegates from Suffolk County on Sept. 9, 1774, adopted the Suffolk Resolutions drawn up at a preliminary meeting in Dedham (*see DEDHAM*).

Right from Milton Lower Mills, Adams St. climbs *Milton Hill,* the seat of Nanepashemet, sachem of the Neponset tribe, and the site of the first white settlement. In the provincial period, it was the most pretentious residential section of the town.

At 215 Adams St. on the estate of Mary Bowditch Forbes is a *Reproduction of the Cabin in which Abraham Lincoln was Born* (*open only Feb. 12, and May 30*).

Adams St. continues to EAST MILTON 2.2 *m*. (alt. 60, Town of Milton). At the junction with Granite Ave. is (L) a stone commemorating the *First Railroad Chartered in America*. In 1826 the Granite Railway Company laid tracks from Quincy to the Neponset River in Milton to carry granite blocks for the Bunker Hill Monument from the quarries to the harbor. The motive power of the railroad was furnished by horses and oxen.

State 28 bears (R) into Randolph Ave. at 5.7 *m*. and at 5.9 *m*. passes the G. H. Bent Company's celebrated *Water Cracker Factory* (L), where it is claimed water crackers were first made (1801).

At 6.8 *m*. is the junction with Hillside St.

Right on Hillside St.; 1.1 *m*. (R) is the *Barnard Capen House* (*private*), 427 Hillside St., erected in 1636, and said to be the second oldest farmhouse in New England. This white two-and-a-half-story salt-box house was in 1909 moved piece by piece to its present site from the corner of Melville Ave. and Washington St., Dorchester. The left half of the dwelling was added in the 18th century.

Five hundred feet west of the Barnard Capen House is a *Bridle Path* running along the southern slope of the hills of the Blue Hill Reservation.

At 9.7 *m*. is the junction with Pond St.

Left on Pond St. 1.3 *m*. to *Great Pond*, and a large boulder of pudding-stone known as *Weeping Willow Rock*, because of the pebbles that detach themselves and roll down its face. According to legend, Chicataubot, sachem of the Indians in this region, stood on this boulder and wept over his lost territories; since then the rock has shed sympathetic tears.

At 1.6 *m*. is the junction with State 128. Right (straight ahead) on this route by a side entrance to *Blue Hill Cemetery*, 1.9 *m*., where is a huge oak reputed to be more than 700 years old; its weakened branches, spreading 75 feet, are now artificially supported.

BRAINTREE, 3.6 *m*. (town, alt. 94, pop. 17,122, sett. 1634, incorp. 1640), early known as Monoticut (Indian, 'Abundance') formerly included Quincy and Randolph.

In 1665, to clear its title, the town bought the land from the Indian chief Wampatuck and his son, Chicataubot, paying £21, 10*s*.; fishing, and hunting rights were reserved by the sachem. Many followers of Roger Williams and Anne Hutchinson found temporary refuge here on their way from Boston.

Braintree was primarily agricultural until the middle of the last century when the railroad brought large industrial growth. Since 1910 the plants have become smaller and industries more diversified.

Increasing numbers of people employed in Boston, to which Braintree's excellent transportation service makes it easily accessible, have established homes here.

Thayer Academy (*open*), Washington St., was founded by General Sylvanus Thayer, superintendent of the United States Military Academy at West Point (1817–33), a native who gave the town its public library.

Left 1 *m*. from the Center on Union St. is the *Deacon Thayer House* (*now a tearoom*). This one-and-a-half-story yellow frame dwelling, built in 1803, with gable roof and central chimney, has been remodeled but still retains some of its old lines.

At 10.2 *m*. (R) is the *Boston School for the Deaf*, founded in 1899. Here nearly 200 children are cared for by the Sisters of St. Joseph, and taught lip reading and manual vocations. The surrounding 83-acre farm belongs to the school.

RANDOLPH, 11.7 *m.* (town, alt. 225, pop. 7580, sett. about 1710, incorp. 1793), originally called Cochato, was formerly the South Precinct of Braintree. It was named Randolph in honor of Peyton Randolph, first President of the Continental Congress.

Unable to compete with more fertile lands to the west, Randolph abandoned agriculture to become, in the 19th century, a pioneer in shoe manufacturing, its factories attracting Irish, Italian, and Canadian immigrants in great numbers. From 1860 to 1895 both shoe production and population decreased, and now the town is chiefly a residential suburb of Boston.

Mary Wilkins Freeman lived here, and in 'A New England Nun' and other works, told the stories of her neighbors.

The former *Home of Jonathan B. Hall* (*private*), built 1806, 0.5 *m.* north of the Town Hall, is now owned by the Ladies' Library Association; this organization, founded in 1855, is one of the oldest women's clubs in the State.

Left from Randolph on Union St. is HOLBROOK, 1.9 *m.* (town, alt. 200, pop. 3364, sett. 1710, incorp. 1872), originally in Randolph. Though one of the earliest towns to manufacture boots and shoes, it is now without a single shoe factory.

In *Union Cemetery* on Union St. are the graves of the early settlers; the stone on that of Levi Thayer (1765–1842) warns:

> 'Stop dear children and cast an eye.
> In these cold graves your parents lie.
> As you are now, so once was I;
> As I am now, so must you be.
> Prepare for death and follow me.'

The *Thayer House* (*private*), 56 Union St., the residence of Mrs. Maynard C. Thayer, contains many Colonial relics including a newspaper printed in Boston at the time of the Boston Massacre and containing a detailed account of this event and a newspaper printed the day after the assassination of Abraham Lincoln.

The *Nathaniel Belcher House* (*private*), 324 North Franklin St., built in 1754, is a broad gabled, two-story, white clapboarded dwelling with green blinds, and a small central chimney. The ell, added later, has a dormer window. The house sits back from the road on a knoll, with a solitary elm standing on the close-cropped lawn.

Left from the Square 0.5 *m.* on Plymouth St. to the junction with Pond St.; left here 1 *m.* on Pine St. to a *State Forest Fire Tower* on Turkey Hill (alt. 280), 1.2 *m.* (*tables for picnicking*), with an enclosed observatory offering a broad view of the countryside.

AVON, 13.9 *m.* (town, alt. 180, pop. 2362, sett. before 1700, incorp. 1888), was formerly part of the grant known as the 'land beyond the Blue Hills,' made to Dorchester in 1637. Its present name was suggested by the town schoolmaster to honor the Bard of Avon.

As East Stoughton, it was one of the earliest towns to begin the manufacture of boots and shoes, an important product by the middle of the 19th century. Today, however, it is a residential suburb of Brockton, to which most of its factories were transferred because of Brockton's superior transportation facilities.

At 122 East Main St. (State 28) is the *Blanchard House* (*private*), about 200 years old, a white frame dwelling with pillared porch and large central chimney.

At 17.5 *m.* is BROCKTON (*see BROCKTON*).

WEST BRIDGEWATER, 21.9 *m.* (town, alt. 92, pop. 3356, sett. 1651, incorp. 1822), was deeded to six people in trust for 56 proprietors of the Duxbury plantation. In 1645 Massasoit gave up his claims to the land for $30 worth of knives, hatchets, skins, hoes, coats, and cotton.

Although a number of mills and factories were established along its rivers during the course of the 19th century, the town is predominantly agricultural, growing potatoes and the smaller garden crops, and specializing in dairying and poultry-raising.

On the banks of the Town River near the Green is the new *Memorial Park* on the site of an old gristmill and shovel factory. The water of the river has been diverted through the park in a series of waterfalls.

The *Bridgewater Historical Society Museum* (*open*), 162 Harvard St., has the Massasoit deed given to the purchasers of the Bridgewater settlement.

At 58 South St. is the *Judge Baylies House* (*private*), a large yellow two-and-a-half-story frame dwelling with two inner chimneys. Here William Cullen Bryant studied law in 1814.

BRIDGEWATER, 24.5 *m.* (town, alt. 62, pop. 9210, sett. 1650, incorp. 1656), in the 18th century became one of the chief centers for iron manufacture. Many Revolutionary cannon were cast here, and, during the Civil War, some material for the 'Monitor.'

In the early part of the 19th century a young townsman, Eleazer Carver (b. 1785) set out for the Ohio River with a kit of millwright's tools; there he built a dugout and floated down the Ohio and Mississippi, stopping to do repair work at various plantations. On his return home in 1817 he established a factory to make cotton gins. Industry has attracted many Italians and Portuguese to the town, and the vineyards and bowling (*bocce*) alleys of the Italians are conspicuous. The Portuguese Holy Ghost festival, with colorful parades and feasting, held in July, is an annual event of local importance.

On a small plot near the Bridgewater Inn is a boulder of native sandstone containing a *Fossilized Paleozoic Tree Branch*.

The *Washburn House* (*private*), facing the Common, is a two-and-a-half-story gabled weather-beaten structure, built in 1700, and now surrounded by an iron fence. On either side of the wooden walk are bent trees, grown old with the house. A wooden sign identifies this building as the home of Colonel Edson, a Tory, from whom it was confiscated.

The *Unitarian Church of the Congregational Society* on School St., built in 1845, has a fine Christopher Wren type spire.

Directly across the street is the modern red-brick Georgian style administration building of the *Bridgewater Teachers' College*, established in 1840, and accommodating 500 students, mostly women. A group of paintings, prints, and objects of art are housed in the main building and in the Massachusetts School of Art building.

> 1. Right from Bridgewater on Broad St., at 0.9 *m.* is the junction with High St., right on High St. is (L) the *Deacon Joseph Alden House* (1700) (*private*), 1.5 *m.* The structure, built by the grandson of John Alden, is a two-and-a-half-story salt-box type, with unstained shingles, a large central chimney, and an open 'breeze-way' connecting the main house with a store shed. At the rear of the building are the original well and an iron-ribbed barrel, fed by a wooden trough. Except for the roofing and a few minor interior and exterior repairs, the house is unchanged from Colonial times.
>
> 2. Left from Bridgewater on an unnumbered road that unites with State 106, on which (R) is HALIFAX, 6 *m.* (town, alt. 84, pop. 817, sett. about 1670, incorp. 1734). Its former Indian name, Monponsett ('Near the Deep Pond') is the name of the twin lakes in the district. There were two Indian settlements in Halifax, one of which was captured by Colonel Benjamin Church during King Philip's War. A family of six banished Acadians was cared for here from 1760 to 1763. The church, dedicated in 1734, claims to have established the first Sunday School in New England. The town is a station for the uncommon chain fern *Woodwardia areolate*, and also grows unusually fine hothouse roses.

At 30.4 *m.* is the junction with US 44 (*see Tour* 10) which unites with State 28 to 31.4 *m.*, where State 28 turns right through open stretches of uninteresting country, with occasional thick pine groves to a junction with US 6 (*see Tour* 6) at 48.8 *m.*

State 28 and US 6 unite to BUZZARD'S BAY, 52.3 *m.* (alt. 17; Town of Bourne), the trading center of the town. The *Administration Building* at the State Pier, 0.5 *m.* southeast of the Center, was completed in 1932 to meet the needs of increased shipping through the canal.

At 53.8 *m.* is the *Bourne Bridge*, completed in 1935, spanning the *Cape Cod Canal* (*see Tour* 6, *SAGAMORE*). This simple and beautiful continuous-truss structure cost more than $1,500,000 and has a clearance of 135 feet at the central span. Cram and Ferguson were the consulting architects on this structure, which was planned and constructed by the engineering firm of Fay, Spofford, and Thorndike.

BOURNE, 55 *m.* (town, alt. 19, pop. 3336, sett. about 1640, incorp. 1884), originally the village of Monument in the Town of Sandwich, was named for its most prominent citizen, Jonathan Bourne. The making of freight-cars was an important industry here until 1928. In 1935 the Federal Government bought and dismantled the plant to make way for the enlargement of the Cape Cod Canal. Hundreds of the '40 and 8' box-cars made here were shipped to France during the World War. Catering to visitors, cranberry-growing, and dairying today form the inhabitants' principal occupations.

A reproduction of the *Aptuxcet Trading Post* (*open; 25¢ adm.*), is off Shore Rd. The cellar walls and hearthstones of the original structure, built in 1626, have been incorporated in the new building, a one-and-a-half-story unpainted structure with tiny diamond-paned windows and steep gable roof. The trading post was established by the colonists to facilitate barter with the Indians of the Narragansett country and with New Amsterdam, now New York City.

Right from Bourne, 1 *m.* on Shore Rd., is *Gray Gables Inn*, once the summer White House as the home of President Grover Cleveland. It has a newel post at the foot of the stairs on which the former President cut notches to mark the increasing height of his children.

T O U R 1 9 A : *From* ORLEANS *to* BOURNE, 61.8 *m.*, State 28.

Via Chatham, Harwich, Yarmouth, Barnstable, Mashpee and Falmouth.
N.Y., N.H. & H. R.R. services this area.
Hard-surfaced roadbed.

STATE 28 following the southern shore of Cape Cod passes through some of the most pleasant shore resort towns in the State. Delightful Cape Cod style cottages in gay dooryards rub shoulders with pretentious summer homes set in well-groomed lawns. Occasional groves of scrub pine hide from view the otherwise continuous panorama of Nantucket Sound and its numerous beaches, bays and rivers.

From its junction with US 6 (*see Tour* 6) in Orleans, State 28 runs south, skirting Pleasant Bay (L).

At 2.7 *m.* (R) is the *Kenrick House*, an admirable example of the Cape Cod cottage, built in 1792 by Jonathan Kenrick, a cousin of the adventurous Captain John Kenrick to whom the building of the cottage is often incorrectly attributed.

At 6.8 *m.* (R) is the *RCA Marine Station* (*private*), equipped with the most modern devices for transmitting and receiving commercial messages.

At 8.3 *m.* is the junction with a crossroad.

Left (straight ahead) on the *Chatham Shore Drive*, bordered by stately homes, the route provides a marvelous view of the harbor, the shoals, and the ocean beyond. The *Summer Home of Joseph C. Lincoln* (*private*), the popular Cape novelist, (L) at 0.9 *m.*, is a gambrel-roofed house behind a well-kept privet hedge.

At 1.5 *m.* are the *Chatham Light* (*open*) and *Mack Memorial Shaft.* The monument was erected in memory of a life-saving crew, commanded by Captain Mack, that set off in heavy seas to rescue the crew of a wrecked fishing vessel. All but one were drowned and old-timers say that he was so ashamed of being rescued that he would neither discuss the tragedy nor accept commendation. A sunrise service is held every Easter morning on the bluffs by the lighthouse.

CHATHAM, 9 *m.* (town, alt. 59, pop. 2050, sett. 1665, incorp. 1712), is a seaside town which numbers Justice Louis D. Brandeis among the summer residents. Although Chatham passed resolutions forbidding the use of tea during the pre-Revolutionary crisis, it voted against the adoption of the Declaration of Independence. The industries of Chatham have been fishing, whaling, and shipbuilding, saltworks and shoe factories; but today all but fishing have been discontinued.

At the Center, on the corner of Main St., is the *Congregational Church*, built in 1830 (*open daily*), a fine example of early architecture, containing two unusual modern murals of local religious concept by Alice Stallknecht Wight. One represents a Chatham fisherman preaching from a beached dory. The other depicts a church supper, at which all the participants are Chatham people, neighbors of the artist.

Left straight ahead from State 28 on an unnumbered road to *Oyster Pond*, 0.2 *m.*, beside which is a cluster of fishermen's shacks. At 0.7 *m.* (L) is the *Old Atwood House* (*open*), built 1752, now the headquarters of the Chatham Historical Society. It has a gambrel roof, central chimney, and gray shingled walls. The interior has fine paneling and H and L hinges.

The *Old Windmill* (1797) at 0.8 *m.* was in operation for 110 years and is one of ten remaining on the Cape. The settlement here lies on high land overlooking the harbor and Monomoy Point which extends ten miles out into the Atlantic Ocean. This point, a wild and lonely spit of sand dunes, covered with beach grass, heather, and wild plum, is one of the most beautiful spots on the Cape, and is much painted by artists. At the tip is *Monomoy Point Coast Guard Station*. Public cars with balloon tires make daily round trips from Chatham in summer, traveling by the hard sand beach. The trip by private car is dangerous.

At 13.3 *m.* is the junction with Depot Ave.

Right on Depot Ave. to the *Songless Aviary* (*open*), 2 *m.*, the home of manufacturers of wooden decoys.

SOUTH HARWICH, 13.6 *m.* (alt. 39; Town of Harwich), has a large summer colony and a good beach.

HARWICHPORT, 15.2 *m.* (alt. 18; Town of Harwich), is also a summer resort. *Wychmere Harbor* provides a scenic anchorage for pleasure craft. Along the shore are *Remnants of the Horse Race Track*, once the sporting center of the Cape, but inundated by a terrific storm in 1884.

Harwichport has an annual 'mutt show' which provides great amusement for lovers of dogs as dogs, without benefit of pedigree.

At 16.3 *m.* is JOHNSON JUNCTION at the junction with State 24.

Right on State 24 is HARWICH, 1.3 *m.* (town, alt. 80, pop. 2373, sett. after 1670, incorp. 1694). Queen Elizabeth called the English village for which it was named 'Happy-go-lucky Harwich,' a term that can be applied to this charming namesake. Embedded in the pavement at the entrance to Exchange Hall is an inscribed flagstone, the gift of the borough of Harwich, England. Harwich is generally considered the 'Harniss' of the novels of Joseph C. Lincoln.

In its early days, Harwich was a whaling and shipbuilding center, but in the 19th century cod-fishing largely supplanted whaling. Many of the former small industries have disappeared, superseded by the cultivation of cranberries and catering to summer visitors, who now own 70 per cent of the town area.

The *Old Powder House* (*private*), at the Center, a small square stone building built in 1770, served as a storehouse during the Revolutionary War. Adjoining is the *Brooks Library* (*open Sat. afternoons*), a two-story yellow frame building containing a permanent exhibit of American figurines by John Rogers, comprising 46 subjects.

WEST HARWICH, 17.6 *m.* (alt. 8; Town of Harwich), is a village whose beautiful homes are occupied the year round.

State 28 travels south and crosses Bass River at 21.1 *m.* with a view of the picturesque river and the handsome summer estates of the Bass River colony.

SOUTH YARMOUTH, 21.4 *m.* (alt. 37; Town of Yarmouth). An *Indian Burying Ground*, about 0.5 *m.* east of the Center off Station Ave., contains a pile of unhewn stones with a chiseled inscription: 'On this slope lie buried the last of the native Indians of Yarmouth.'

At 22.6 *m.* is the junction with an elm-shaded street with well-kept lawns and summer homes.

Sharp left on this street at 0.1 *m.* (R) on side road to the *Town Park* and *Beach,* 1.8 *m.,* facing Nantucket Sound. A large pine grove (*picnicking*) and a fine beach (*bathhouses, small fee*) make this a most attractive spot.

WEST YARMOUTH, 24.8 *m.* (alt. 13; Town of Yarmouth), is in a township that is one of the greatest cranberry-growing areas in the State.

Left from West Yarmouth 1 *m.* is *Englewood Beach* (*public*) on Lewis Bay.

At 26.2 *m.* is junction with East Main St.

Left (straight ahead) on East Main St. 1 *m.* is HYANNIS (Town of Barnstable), the summer business center of the Cape. Southwest of Hyannis is *Sunset Hill,* 2.6 *m.* from which there is a picturesque view of Centreville Harbor and the headlands of Wianno and Poponesset.

At 30.1 *m.* is junction with a hard-surfaced road.

Left on this road 1 *m.* is CENTREVILLE (Town of Barnstable), a popular summer resort. At 1.7 *m.* is *Craigville Beach* (*public bathhouses*), one of the finest in the country.

Passing between small patches of scrub pine and oak brush, State 28 comes to the junction with a road at 35.9 *m.*

Left on this road at 1.8 *m.* is COTUIT (Town of Barnstable), one of the summer recreation centers of the Cape.

At 36 *m.* is the junction with State 130.

Right on State 130 is MASHPEE ('Standing Water' or 'Great Pond'), 1.8 *m.* (town, alt. 51, pop. 380, sett. 1660, incorp. 1871), in an area with picturesque ponds, groves, streams, and stretches of woodland. It was originally inhabited by the Wampanoag tribe, which gave allegiance to Massasoit, and was later in the township of Sandwich.

The Mashpee Indians lived in rude shelters made of matting hung over bent saplings. Their religion centered about Kiehtan, the creator, and Habbamock, who governed health. Richard Bourne, a missionary, converted many of them and helped teach them self-government, managing in 1660 to have 10,500 acres set apart for them. In 1834 the area was incorporated under the supervision of a commissioner appointed by the State; in 1932, owing to the economic crisis, it was placed under a State Advisory Commission. Hunting and fishing, the chief occupations of the inhabitants until 1834, were superseded by employment in the cranberry bogs, practically all of which belong to outsiders. At the beginning of the 19th century, the full-blooded Indians had died out, and the present population is a mixture of native Indian, African Negro, Cape Verdean, and Portuguese.

One of the oldest local legends concerns Ahsoo, a Mashpee girl, so ugly that no man would have anything to do with her, but with such a lovely voice that birds, beasts, and fishes paused to listen to her. Most entranced by Ahsoo's voice was the largest of all trout, so large that he could not swim up the creek to hear her sing. In his efforts to reach her, he burrowed his nose farther and farther into the beach each night and thus made the Cotuit River. Grateful for this engineering feat and sympathizing with the big trout's passion, the chief of a pygmy tribe changed Ahsoo into a trout and placed her in Santuit Pond. In his efforts to tunnel his way to the new home of his love, the big trout died from exhaustion, and Ahsoo of a broken heart. The Indians buried them side by side in a large mound, called Trout Cave, near the brook dug by the chief of the trout.

On the road between South Mashpee and Waquoit is a brush pile known as the *Indian's Tavern* (to the Indians 'tavern' meant a place in the woods where two roads met). By placing a piece of wood on a pile that accumulated there, a passer-by would indicate to his friends the direction he had taken. Today it is called a 'wishing pile'; the inhabitants, in passing, place sticks on it 'just for luck.'

At 37.6 *m.* is the junction with a dirt road.

Right on this road 0.1 *m.* are an *Old Indian Church* (*services in summer*) with box pews and organ gallery and a *Burial Ground* in which is a marker with a plaque bearing the following inscriptions: 'Old Indian Church, built in 1684, remodeled in 1717, rededicated in 1923. In memory of friends who labored among the Indians. ...' The date of erection indicated is questionable.

A significant tale narrates how during an argument with the Rev. Richard Bourne the Indian pow-wow lost his temper and, chanting a bog-rhyme, mired Bourne's feet in quicksand. They then agreed to a contest of wits which lasted 15 days, during which Bourne was kept from thirst and starvation by a white dove which placed a succulent 'cherry' in his mouth from time to time. Unable to cast a spell upon the dove, and exhausted from his own lack of food, the medicine-man finally fell to the ground and Bourne was free. In the meantime one 'cherry' brought by the dove had fallen into the bog and had grown and multiplied. Thus the cranberry came to Cape Cod.

At 38.2 *m.* is the junction with an unnumbered road.

Left on the unnumbered road to a fork at 2.7 *m.*; left at the fork; right at the next intersection, to *Poponesset Beach* 4 *m.* (*bathing, camping; adm.* 15¢ *per person during summer; nominal sum for trailers*).

WAQUOIT VILLAGE, 41.4 *m.* (alt. 39; Town of Falmouth), is noted for its strawberries and asparagus.

At 46.5 *m.* is a junction with a good tar road.

Left on this road is FALMOUTH HEIGHTS, 1 *m.* (alt. 20, Falmouth), a well-known summer resort. From Great Hill the shores of Martha's Vineyard are clearly visible. Nantucket Island, 30 miles distant, is also seen on a clear day.

FALMOUTH, 47.4 *m.* (town, alt. 44, pop. 6537, sett. about 1660, incorp. 1686), called Succanessett by the Indians, was settled by a group of Quakers led by Isaac Robinson. In 1779 the townspeople were obliged to repel attacks by British ships. During the War of 1812 the British again attacked this section, and one of their ships was captured. Agriculture, shipbuilding, fishing, whaling, and the manufacture of salt and glass were important industries furnishing periods of prosperity.

Facing the Green is the *Congregational Church.* In the church belfry is a Revere bell with the popular inscription: 'The living to the church I call: Unto the grave I summon all.'

The *Falmouth Historical Society Headquarters* right of the Green on Palmer Ave., is a large square Colonial house topped by a 'widow's walk.'

A *Barn (open daily, except Wed. and Fri.*, 2–6), adjoining the house, is used for exhibition purposes.

At 16 Main St. is the *Birthplace (open) of Katharine Lee Bates* (1859–1929), Professor of English at Wellesley College until her death, and author of 'America the Beautiful.'

> Left from the Center on Locust St. (Woods Hole Rd.) is *Fay Rose Garden*, 3.5 *m.*, where the rambler and other species of the rose were first cultivated. Old trees spreading their shade over green lawns and vari-hued blossoms make this a spot of delicate beauty.

> At 3.6 *m.* is the junction with a road leading left 0.2 *m.* to the *Buoy Yard* and *Government Wharf*, where hundreds of bright-red buoys are piled ready to replace those brought in for reconditioning. From here is seen (L), the *Nobska Light*, which has been flashing its signal since 1828.

> At 3.9 *m.* is WOODS HOLE (alt. 8, Falmouth town). The *Woods Hole Oceanographic Institution*, Main St., founded in 1930 and endowed $2,000,000 by the Rockefeller Foundation. Staffed by eminent scientists, it utilizes deep ocean waters and the continental abyss, as well as inshore waters, to study not only marine biology, but winds, ocean currents, temperature changes, and their effects. From this base the Institution operates the 'Atlantic,' a completely equipped floating laboratory.

> The *Clapp Marine Biological Laboratory* (R), also on Main St., supplies facilities to qualified investigators for the study of marine life. Summer courses are conducted and the experimental work is stimulated by a library and a museum of local flora and fauna. An important study is now being made of the teredo, or shipworm, a bivalve that destroys wooden piers, piling, and boats. In front of the laboratory stands the *Old Candle House* (1836), one of the few relics of days when Falmouth was a center for the manufacture of candles from whale oil.

> A branch of the *U.S. Bureau of Fisheries* and an *Aquarium* are located at the corner of Main and West Sts. The Bureau of Fisheries here studies utilization of fish by-products, such processes as the extraction of oils and gelatines, and the habits and distribution of sea life for the purpose of regulation and conservation. It hatches some four million fish each year.

> (ELIZABETH ISLANDS *off Woods Hole, MARTHA'S VINEYARD and NANTUCKET, see Tour* 14.)

North of Falmouth are numerous roads running west from State 28 to fine stretches of beach.

At 54.7 *m.* is the junction with Depot St.

> Left on Depot St., straight ahead on County St. to Chester St., 0.5 *m.*; left here is *Silver Beach*, 3 *m.*, famous for its smooth silvery sand and crystal clear water.

BOURNE, 61.8 *m.* (*see Tour* 19).

T O U R   21 :   *From* VERMONT LINE (*Stamford*) *to* CONNECTICUT LINE (*Winsted*), 68.6 *m.*, State 8.

Via Clarksburg, North Adams, Adams, Cheshire, Dalton, Hinsdale, Washington, Becket, Otis, and Sandisfield.

B. & M., B. & A. R.R.'s parallel the road at intervals.

Macadam road, frequently hilly and therefore slippery in winter.

STATE 8 crosses the Vermont Line 2 *m.* south of Stamford, Vt., and winds through the delightful forested and rural country of the Berkshire Hills, sometimes at an altitude of nearly 2000 feet. For the most part it crosses sparsely settled towns; with little traffic it provides a leisurely alternate to US 7.

At 0.1 *m.* is the *Clarksburg Reservoir* (*boating*).

BRIGGSVILLE, 2.8 *m.* (alt. 1000, pop. 1333, sett. 1769, incorp. 1798, Town of Clarksburg), is in an industrial section with small woolen mills where the workers are chiefly of Scottish descent. The village is perched on the watershed that annually sends down floods threatening the city of North Adams.

At 3.1 *m.* is the junction with a dirt road.

Right on this road 0.5 *m.* to the *Natural Bridge* of marble, hanging above Hudson's brook and spanning a ravine. Hawthorne described the grandeur of this spot in his 'American Notebook.'

At 3.9 *m.* is the junction with State 2, the Mohawk Trail (*see Tour* 2).

NORTH ADAMS, 4.8 *m.* (*see Tour* 2).

The west entrance of the Hoosac Tunnel may be seen (L) at 6.5 *m.*

ZYLONITE, 9 *m.* (alt. 726, Town of Adams), once a thriving settlement, received its name from a mineral deposit found here and formerly used in manufacturing. That industry is now gone, but some limestone is still quarried in the hills behind the old village. South of the village *Mt. Greylock* (alt. 3505), the highest mountain in the State, is visible (R). Here, at 9.1 *m.*, is *Blue Lake*, an artificial pond deriving its deep blue tint from the waste deposits of the limeworks.

RENFREW, 10 *m.* (alt. 752, Town of Adams), is a mill village.

ADAMS, 10.8 *m.* (town, alt. 799, pop. 12,858, sett. 1762, incorp. 1778). One hundred years after its incorporation the town of Adams, named in honor of Samuel Adams, Revolutionary propagandist, was divided into North Adams and Adams.

Adams has always contended that she is the Mother Town. The following story (for which, however, we do not vouch) illustrates the point: When the Mohawk Trail was opened in 1920, Adams felt slighted at having no share in that great event. Her indignation exploded when the City of North Adams erected a sign on the Trail, reading: 'This is the City of North Adams, the Mother of the Mohawk Trail.' The Town of Adams erected a sign at their joint boundary, reading: 'You are now leaving Adams, the Mother of North Adams and the Grandmother of the Mohawk Trail.'

Industrial development here began in the first half of the 19th century when William Pollock, who is said to have secured capital by selling an old horse for a lottery ticket that won a prize, built and operated the old stone mill now known as Broadly Mill. Paper and textile print works have long been the leading industries. Both lime and marble are quarried in the vicinity.

The *Friends Meeting House* (*open*), at the corner of Friend and Maple Sts., erected in 1784 and continuously used for over 64 years, is a two-and-a-half-story gable-end structure that is still in an excellent state of repair. The two outer doors and the movable partitions, raised during regular services, provided privacy during separate meetings. No provision was made for lighting. Women were allowed to sit on the left to receive more heat from the fireplace.

The Quakers, who were the first settlers here, maintained justice with a minimum of legal proceeding as exemplified by the case of two neighbors who quarreled over straying cattle. The difference was taken to the meeting for settlement. After a period of silent prayer and waiting, a member quietly remarked, 'Six railes and a rider make good neighbors.' The two parties to the dispute shook hands and departed amicably to put up better fences.

1. Left from Adams on Hoosac St. at 1 *m.* is the junction with East Rd.; left on East Rd. to the *Birthplace of Susan B. Anthony* (1820–1906), (*open by permission*), 1.5 *m.*, a two-story buff frame dwelling with a pitched roof, built about 1810. Miss Anthony's favorite room is preserved intact with its furnishings. Beyond the house is the little schoolhouse (*now a private dwelling*) which the pioneer woman suffrage leader attended as a girl. It has a brick facing, unstained shingle roof, and small central chimney.

2. Right from Adams on Maple St. at 0.4 *m.* is the junction with West Rd., left on West Rd. (marked 'Thunderbolt,' 'Thiel Farm,' and 'Open Slopes') at 1.2 *m.*, is a junction with the Thunderbolt Rd.; right on Thunderbolt Rd. at 1.9 *m.* is the lower end of the State-owned *Thunderbolt Ski Run*, one of the most difficult runs in the East, used in several inter-collegiate meets annually. The run drops 2060 feet in 1.55 miles. At the bottom are slopes for amateur skiing and tobogganing; near-by is Thiel Farm with overnight accommodations.

At 13.3 *m.* the highway passes over an artificial hill, constructed in 1935 to eliminate a dangerous hairpin turn. This hill overlooks CHESHIRE HARBOR (Town of Cheshire), where slaves were 'harbored' during the days of the Underground Railroad.

Right from Cheshire Harbor is a road that is the end of the ancient *Cheshire Harbor Trail* up Mt. Greylock, popular with hikers and ski-runners, and a part of the Capes-to-the-Berkshires Bridle Trail.

CHESHIRE, 16 *m.* (town, alt. 945, pop. 1660, sett. 1766, incorp. 1793), has always depended to some extent on dairying. In 1801 a local cheese weighing 1235 pounds was laboriously carted down to President Jefferson by admirers. The town has had the usual minor industrial activities — small saw, grist, and iron mills — and for about 80 years local calcium carbonate has been mined and made into lime.

The *Cole House* (*open*), opposite the Baptist Church, is now a tearoom. Built about 1804, the large two-and-a-half-story structure with central chimney has a 'Christian' door with eight panels forming a double cross — supposed to protect the house against witchcraft. In 1809 the house served as a meeting-place for the Franklin Masonic Lodge and a few years ago, when five layers of wallpaper had been removed, a number of Masonic emblems were found — the royal arch, beehive, Bible-balance, square and compass — painted on the walls in brown with a blue-green background.

At 16.6 *m.* is *Hoosic Lake* (*Cheshire Reservoir; excellent pickerel fishing*).

At 17.1 *m.* is the *Site of the Glass Sand Plant,* where the first plate glass in America is said to have been made (1853) by James N. Richmond.

At 18.2 *m.* is the junction with a dirt road.

> Right on this road is a lime-making plant, 0.2 *m.,* which from the sifting dust of powdered lime has the appearance of a snow house. West on this road, trails lead to a tunnel drilled through half a mile of solid rock to facilitate the carrying of limestone from a quarry on one side of the hill to kilns in the village on the other side.

At 23.4 *m.* is the junction with State 9 (*see Tour* 8). Between this point and Dalton, State 8 and State 9 are united; right at Dalton, 25.8 *m.,* on State 8.

HINSDALE, 29.6 *m.* (town, alt. 1431, pop. 1144, sett. 1763, incorp. 1804), soon after its settlement became an industrial town, utilizing the plentiful water-power of the Housatonic River. Raising sheep to supply wool for local mills had some importance between 1800 and 1840. About 1895 there was brief excitement over an apparent discovery of gold. With the decline of textile industries, dairying and catering to the summer tourist trade have become the most profitable occupations.

At the Center is the junction with State 143 (*see Tour 8A*).

South of Hinsdale, State 8 passes through a plateau of grassy meadow and brush-grown swamps. The upper reaches of the Housatonic River winding in and out through the alders offer good trout fishing.

At 30.4 *m.* is the junction with Middlefield road (*see Side Tour 4B*).

At 34.9 *m.* is the junction with a crossroad.

> Left on this road is the *Washington Station* (alt. 1497) of the Boston and Albany Railroad, 1.2 *m.,* the highest station on the line. The old village Center was here until development of the motor road created a more modern village farther south. Near the station is a swamp that recently overflowed and covered the road paralleling the railroad, the streams having been dammed by beavers.

At 35.5 *m.* is a pond (L), a local recreational center, and a junction with a dirt road.

> Right on this road about 1 *m.* is a view of *Eden Glen,* a gorge through which the waters of Washington Brook froth along in a series of small cascades.

BECKET, 38.5 *m.* (town, alt. 1207, pop. 723, sett. 1740 and 1755, incorp. 1765), lacking good farming land originally depended for income upon its abundance of granite and hemlock bark. Scarcity of water-power and exhaustion of some of the natural resources arrested development in the latter part of the 19th century. Basket-making and quarrying are now the only year-around non-agricultural activities. This section of Becket was inundated by 25 feet of water pouring from the broken Ballou Dam in 1927, and the ruined factories were abandoned.

> Right from Becket on the old Pontoosuc Turnpike, a former stagecoach route running between Springfield and Pittsfield, is the junction with a trail at 0.2 *m.* that leads across a bridge and part-way up a steep bank to a point below a limestone ledge, over which *Becket Falls* plunges 25 feet into a grotesquely worn rock channel. At the foot of the cascade is a popular swimming hole.

At **3.7** *m.* is *St. Andrew's Chapel*, the only active church in Washington, a stone structure of Gothic design, given to the town by George F. Crane of New York.

WASHINGTON, 4.5 *m.* (town, alt. 1437, pop. 252, sett. about 1760, incorp. 1777), is the center of one of the first towns named for George Washington. At one time the inhabitants made considerable income by collecting hemlock bark for tanning purposes, but today farming and poultry-raising are the means of livelihood.

Left from Washington is a road running into the heart of the *October Mountain State Forest*, comprising 13,861 acres of high land covered with spruce, hemlock, and hardwood forests, of which 12,000 acres is a wild-life sanctuary. In the forest is *Schermerhorn Park* (*picnic grounds, trails, camp sites*). At 3 *m.* right into *Whitney Park*, a popular recreational spot named for the former owner of most of the Forest, Harry Payne Whitney, who held it as a private game preserve; when this area was acquired by the State, the elk and buffalo on it were shipped to the West, but the moose remained and still roam the area. In the park is a high *Observation Tower*.

At 6.2 *m.* on the Pontoosuc Turnpike is the junction with a dirt road leading (L) 0.3 *m.* to *Ashley Lake*, the principal reservoir of the Pittsfield water system. Near here is a large bed of sand that has been used by a glassworks in Lenox for the manufacture of an unusually clear glass.

At 39 *m.* on State 8 is the junction with a road.

Left on this road to *Center Pond Brook*, 1.3 *m.*; near its entrance into the West Branch of the Westfield River, reached by a footpath, it forms a 25-foot waterfall.

At 40 *m.* is the junction with a dirt road.

Right on this road at 1 *m.* to the junction with another road; left here past *Yokum Pond*, 2 *m.*, (alt. 1800) to the Becket section of *October Mountain State Forest* (*see above*).

At 40.4 *m.* (R) is the *Site of the Ballou Reservoir* (*see above*).

At 42.8 *m.* State 8 plunges erratically through thickly wooded hills and (R) passes the north end of *Center Pond* (*bathing, boating, fishing*), curtained by heavy foliage.

BECKET CENTER, 43.5 *m.* (alt. 1600, Town of Becket), has a fine old *Church*, dating from about 1780, with a Revere bell made from copper utensils contributed by the citizens of the town just after the Revolution.

Traversing rolling hills, State 8 reaches, at 45.1 *m.*, BONNY RIGG FOUR CORNERS (alt. 1400) and the junction with US 20 (*see Tour* 4). Between this point and West Becket, State 8 and US 20 are united, crossing Jacob's Ladder.

WEST BECKET (alt. 1039), 50.4 *m.* is a crossroads village where State 8 turns left and US 20 (*see Tour* 4) continues right.

At 51.3 *m.* on State 8 is *Shaw Pond* (*camping, bathing, fishing*).

At 52.3 *m.* is an *Old Rake Shop* (R.) (*open as a tearoom*), a two-and-a-half-story red clapboarded structure. Near-by is a wooden dam.

OTIS, 56.1 *m.* is at the junction with State 17 (*see Tour* 4A).

South of Otis, the highway parallels the West Branch of the Farmington River. The State-leased waters of this stream and its tributaries are public fishing grounds. Inviting areas for camping and picnicking border the roadway.

At 59.1 *m.* is COLD SPRING (alt. 1173), once a thriving section with a prosperous foundry that was destroyed by fire and never rebuilt.

At 61.3 *m.* is a junction with a dirt road.

Left on this road and across a bridge to an extensive picnic area in the *Tolland State Forest*, 0.2 *m.*

NEW BOSTON, 64.6 *m.* (Town of Sandisfield, alt. 880, pop. 471, sett. 1750, incorp. 1762), has had a variety of industrial interests, including tanneries, woolen and silk mills, shoe and hat factories and cooperages. Today, however, agriculture and dairying are the chief occupations, and maple sugar, and cheese the leading products.

Edmund H. Sears, Unitarian clergyman and editor of the *Religious Magazine and Monthly Review*, a native of this town, in 1849 wrote the Christmas hymn, 'It Came Upon the Midnight Clear.'

Right from New Boston on a road paralleling the Buck River are at 1.5 *m.* public fishing grounds on the Buck and Clam Rivers, near the village of WEST NEW BOSTON (alt. 920; Town of Sandisfield). At 2.6 *m.* is MONTVILLE (alt. 1150, Town of Sandisfield) with a *Jewish Colony* of a score or more families, started 25 or 30 years ago, as an experiment in a 'back-to-the-land' movement from New York City.

Crossing the West Branch of the Farmington River, State 8 passes the spectacular *New England Ski Hill* at 64.9 *m.*, one of the highest leaps in the State. At 66.1 *m.* (R) is a view of *Hanging Mountain*, a perpendicular cliff of rock about 300 feet high. Jutting out above the base are masses of rock that appear ready to plunge into the Farmington River; fragments loosened by the rain and frost do sometimes come crashing down with tremendous force.

At 68.6 *m.* is a junction with a dirt road.

Right on this road to *Simon Pond* (Lake Marguerite) 1 *m.*, a spot popular with anglers.

At this same point State 8 crosses the Connecticut Line about 8 *m.* north of Winsted, Conn.

TOUR 23 : *From* ATHOL *to* RHODE ISLAND STATE LINE (*Providence*), 63.5 *m.*, State 32 *and* 122.

Via (*sec. a*) Petersham, Dana, Barre, Oakham, Rutland, Paxton, and Worcester; (*sec. b*) Millbury, Grafton, Northbridge, Sutton, Uxbridge, Douglas, Millville, and Blackstone.

B. & A., B. & M., N.Y., N.H. & H. R.R.'s service part of this area.

Hard-surfaced road throughout.

Sec. a. *JUNCTION WITH STATE 2 to WORCESTER*, 37.3 *m.*

THE northern section of this route runs through heavily wooded country that gradually opens up into the Ware River Valley.

State 32 branches from State 2 (*see Tour 2*), 1.8 *m.* east of Athol. At 3.8 *m.* is the office and laboratory of the *Harvard Forest* (*see below*).

At the crest of a long hill, 4.7 *m.*, is the *Petersham Country Club* (*open to visitors;* 18-*hole golf course, greens fee* $1.50; *tennis courts*). In the low-ceiled rooms of the clubhouse is a collection of prints relating to sports.

PETERSHAM, 7.1 *m.* (town, alt. 1100, pop. 718, sett. 1733, incorp. 1754), was first called Nichewaug and Volunteers Town, and later named for Petersham in Surrey, England.

The *Town Hall*, an interesting building in Georgian Colonial style, is surmounted by a small gilt-domed cupola.

    1. Right from Petersham on New Salem Rd. into the *Massachusetts Federation of Women's Clubs State Forest* (*hiking; picnicking facilities*), 4.5 *m.*, an area of 1000 acres presented to the Commonwealth by the Federation in 1933; about one sixth of the park is a bird sanctuary.

    2. Right from Petersham on an improved road is DANA, 5.9 *m.* (town, alt. 515, pop. 387, sett. 1733, incorp. 1801). A plant was established here for the shaping of pianoforte legs and later included the making of picture and billiard-table frames. When the business was transferred in 1880, the building was used as a satinet factory. Numerous home industries were finally supplanted by agriculture.

Between 8.4 *m.* and 10.5 *m.* is *Harvard Forest*, a 2100-acre tract, including 1000 acres maintained as a bird refuge. It was acquired by Harvard in 1908, and used as an experiment station by the University's School of Forestry. In October the rich variety of foliage shows at its best in the varied hues of autumn.

The *Rocking Stone Park* is at 11.8 *m.*, and back from the road and to the right of the entrance is the famous *Rocking Stone*, a boulder so perfectly poised upon another that originally it could be rocked slightly by the mere pressure of the hand. According to Indian tradition, this was the work of Manitou, the Great White Spirit, who placed the boulder in that position. It is said to have been used as an altar of sacrifice or shrine by the Indians. A more credible explanation, however, is that given by Professor Agassiz to the effect that the formation occurred accidentally as a result of glacial action. The twin boulders remain today, but have been so affixed that the Rocking Stone no longer rocks. A literal-minded farmer, incensed at the trespassers who crossed his land to view the wonder, fastened the boulders together and undid the work of the glaciers — or of Manitou, as the case may be.

BARRE, 15 *m.* (town, alt. 650, pop. 3509, sett. about 1720, incorp. 1774), is a town incorporated as Hutchinson and renamed in 1776 for Colonel Isaac Barre, a friend of the colonists in the English Parliament. During the latter part of the 18th century flax-growing was profitable here and two linseed oil refineries established. Today dairying is the most important occupation, though woolen mills, founded in the early 19th century, and foundries help maintain local prosperity.

1. Left from Barre on South St. at 0.2 *m.* is a private road leading to *Cook's Canyon* (*open by permission of owner*), 0.6 *m.*, a particularly beautiful spot, comprising about 40 acres of rocky gorge.

2. Left from Barre on an improved road to *Barre Falls*, 4.5 *m.* a series of cataracts and pools where Dick Brook has cut its way through the rocks.

At 16.2 *m.* State 32 branches right (*see Tour 23A*); left on State 122.

WHITE VALLEY (alt. 652, Town of Barre), 18.7 *m.* on State 122, is a rapidly disappearing mill village. The *Headhouse Shaft* No. 8 of the tunnel connecting the Enfield and Wachusett Reservoirs of the Metropolitan Water System is at 19 *m.* on State 122. Here the waters of Ware River are caught from October to June, falling 270 feet through a series of gates in the shaft into the tunnel, where they can be diverted in either direction.

At 19.9 *m.*, on the *Site of the Village of Coldbrook Springs*, razed by the Water Commission, is the junction with an improved road.

Right on this road is OAKHAM, 3.2 *m.* (town, alt. 730, pop. 441, sett. 1749, incorp. 1762), named for the English village from which the majority of the settlers came. The town, originally relying on farming and lumbering, made attempts at industrial development, but dairying and the production of hay today provide the townspeople with income.

The *Forbes Memorial Library* (1908) on the Common houses Oakham Historical Society and its collection of old documents and relics. The Library, built of local field-stone, has granite and Indiana limestone trim, and a red slate roof with copper flashing.

In flat wooded country at 23.5 *m.* is the junction with State 122A.

Left on State 122A; at 1.5 *m.* is the junction with Charnock Rd. (L), on which, near-by, is the *Site of the Revolutionary War Barracks* built to hold the Hessians captured in 1778.

A short distance beyond the site of the barracks is a marker indicating the *Site of a Dugout* said to have been occupied by the family of the famous Madame Jumel when the latter was a child. This unfortunate family, who had the reputation of being ne'er-do-wells, had been hounded from pillar to post by the town officials of Providence, Rehoboth, Taunton, and North Brookfield, lest they become town charges. For three years Betsey Bowen lived in the workhouse at Providence, while her sister Polly, her mother, Phoebe, and her stepfather, Jonathan Clark, existed wretchedly in the dugout. Betsey, however, proved to be far from a ne'er-do-well. She did very well, indeed, for herself by marrying a wealthy trader named Stephen Jumel with whom she lived for many years in Paris. When she returned to the land of her humble birth and early humiliations, it was to create in New York City a furore (which doubtless reached Rutland) by her elegant establishment, her Paris wardrobe, and a famous collection of fine furniture and rare paintings. After the death of Jumel she married Aaron Burr.

The *General Rufus Putnam House* (*open daily*, 2–5; *adm.* 10¢) 2 *m.*, was the home of the Revolutionary officer from 1781 to 1788 (*see Tour 23, SUTTON*). Here he planned the expedition to settle the great Northwest, founding the town of Marietta, Ohio. Near-by is the *Rufus Putnam Memorial Park.*

At 2.6 *m.* is RUTLAND (town, alt. 1001, pop. 2406, sett. 1716, incorp. 1722). After the Revolution the bankrupt citizens of Rutland joined the insurgents headed by Daniel Shays and the town was used as headquarters of the forces that marched to Worceste

Because of the altitude, the first of several tuberculosis sanitariums was established here at the end of the 19th century; these institutions have contributed to the town's stability and prosperity, providing jobs and a market for dairy and garden products and poultry.

On Central Tree Ave., 0.5 *m.* left of the village, is a lopsided elm, identified by a marker as on the exact geographic center of the State.

At 27.9 *m.*, State 122 passes through an area of many ponds and slow-flowing brooks containing muskrats.

PAXTON, 29.3 *m.* (town, alt. 1133, pop. 731, sett. about 1749, incorp. 1765), was named for Charles Paxton, Commissioner of Customs at the Port of Boston and Marshal of the Admiralty Court. Some years later this gentleman so infuriated the colonists by his participation in the drafting of the notorious tea tax that he was driven out of Boston. The village, loyally supporting the Colonial cause, tried to rid itself of its name, but in vain.

Bottomley's Pond, 30.6 *m.* (R), at the corner of Leicester Rd., facetiously called 'the Paxton Navy Yard,' is said to have derived this nickname from the query of a drunken sailor, who, having arrived by coach within view of the pond, mistook the bare trunks and branches of a tree at the water's edge for the masts of ships.

Left from Paxton Center on Maple St. to *Three Mountain Corner*, 0.7 *m.*, which offers views of Mts. Wachusett, Monadnock, and Greylock.

At 36.4 *m.* is the junction with State 9 (*see Tour* 8) and State 12 (*see Tour* 11).

At 37.3 *m.* is WORCESTER (*see WORCESTER*) and the junction with State 70 (*see Tour* 7).

Sec. b. WORCESTER to RHODE ISLAND STATE LINE, 26.2 *m.* State 122.

South of Worcester, State 122, a heavily traveled, main artery, passes through a series of manufacturing districts.

At 0.9 *m.* is the junction with State 122A, a more direct and perhaps more interesting route between Worcester and Farnumsville.

Right on this road at 5.5 *m.* is MILLBURY (town, alt. 407, pop. 6879, sett. 1716, incorp. 1813). Before its settlement by the English this section must have been an important center of Indian life as more than 1000 relics of indigenous handicraft have been found in the vicinity of Ramshorn Pond.

The opening of the Blackstone Canal in 1828 gave impetus to its growth and within a few years its manufacturing capacity doubled. When the canal was closed in 1848, because of serious trouble between mill-owners and operators of the waterway, the Providence and Worcester Railroad was already an accomplished fact, so that the progress of the town was in no way hampered.

The peak of industrial growth was reached about 1910. Since that time, owing to changes in economic conditions and competition with new regions, the cotton textile enterprise in the town has declined. Today, however, Millbury is still primarily an industrial community, with textiles, spindles, thread, felt, and tools the leading products and a large percentage of the inhabitants employed in manufacturing these articles.

The second *Asa Waters Mansion* (*open*), Elm St. (L), is a two-and-a-half-story structure, said to have been the finest residence in the county at the time of its erection (1826–29). It is distinctive in its academic correctness and skillful treatment of detail and is one of the later examples of the Georgian Colonial style. The gathering of materials for the house took two years. Hard pine was brought from the South, mahogany from Central America, marble from Italy, and bricks from Baltimore. The finishing timber was 'pumpkin pine' from Maine. As woodworking machinery had not yet been invented, boards and moldings, joinery and carving had to be wrought by hand. The present occupant, Father James M. Burke, has a notable collection of colored glass.

Right from Millbury on a paved road is SUTTON, 3.7 *m.* (town, alt. 346, pop. 2408, sett. 1716, incorp. 1718). The town land was purchased from the Indians in 1704 by a group of Boston residents. Because of the rich soil, settlement progressed rapidly. Textile factories and a paper mill were established about 1800, but industrial activity declined when the railroads ignored the town in laying out routes. Today three small shuttle factories are the only industries, and fruit-growing, dairying, and market gardening are the profitable enterprises.

The *First Congregational Church* (organized in 1719), on the village Green, has a beautiful spire of the Wren type and a graceful green-shuttered fan window over the entrance. The building was erected in 1813.

Right from Sutton 0.5 *m.* on the Oxford Rd. is (L) the *Cole-Woodbury House* (*open*), built in 1724, a rambling white frame house with faded blue blinds, set back from the road, surrounded by a stone fence and gay-hued gardens. The spacious living-room has a large fireplace, exposed framing, and on three sides windows offering attractive vistas.

At 1.3 *m.* on the Oxford Rd. is a granite *Milestone*, five feet high and eight inches thick, marked '48 ML to Boston 1771 — B.W.' In 1771 the county commissioners undertook to place milestones along what was then called the Connecticut Rd.

Colonel Bartholomew Woodbury, a local innkeeper, was quick to sense the advertising advantage of a milestone at the front door of his tavern. Unfortunately, the proper location of the milestone was several hundred feet south of the tavern. The colonel overcame this obstacle by persuading the commissioners to waive the mere matter of accuracy and to authorize the setting of the stone where he desired. He promised that if they would do so, he would erect at his own expense a milestone that would be 'the queen of all milestones.' It is interesting to speculate whether the traveling public ever discovered the discrepancy in the local mileage.

On the *Site of the Birthplace* (1738) *of General Rufus Putnam*, is a monument dedicated to him by the town of Sutton. General Putnam planned the fortification of Dorchester Heights and was made chief engineer of the new army; in 1779 he assisted Israel Putnam in completing the defenses of West Point. His crowning achievement, however, was one of peace: he was a founder of the Ohio Company and superintended the settlement of Marietta, Ohio.

Between Millbury and Farnumsville, State 122A parallels the Blackstone River. At FARNUMSVILLE, 9.7 *m.* (alt. 292, Town of Grafton), is the junction with State 122.

State 122 winds down easy grades to Lake Ripple, 7.5 *m.*, at the junction with State 140 (*see Tour 23B*).

At 8.9 *m.* on State 122 is an old *Indian Cemetery* marked by a large boulder bearing the inscription, 'Eliot's band of Praying Indians.' There are 13 stones within the fenced plot. John Eliot commenced his benevolent labors among the Natick Indians (*see Tour 8*) with whom the Nipmucks of Worcester County had friendly and constant intercourse. It is probable that the favorable report of the Naticks induced the Nipmucks to listen to his sermons. Eliot's success in this area caused the General

Court in 1654, on his petition, to set it apart for the use of the tribes in order to prevent conflicting claims between them and the English.

At 10.4 *m.* is FARNUMSVILLE (alt. 292, Town of Grafton), the junction with State 122A (*see above*).

At 14.8 *m.* is the junction with a road.

> Right on this road is WHITINSVILLE, 1.3 *m.* (alt. 302, pop. 10,577, sett. 1704, incorp. 1772; Town of Northbridge). Through the influence of 12 families of Friends in the community, this town did not participate very actively in the Revolutionary War. Abundant water-power attracted industries. In 1826 Paul Whitin opened a cotton-textile factory and his descendants are still the leading manufacturers, though the production of mill machinery is now of primary importance, with textile and paper manufacturing ranking second.

> Right from Whitinsville on Sutton Rd. 3.2 *m.* is *Purgatory Chasm State Park* (*picnic facilities*), opened in 1919 and comprising 80 acres. The chasm is about a quarter of a mile long, 70 feet deep, and 20 to 50 feet wide. The bottom is strewn with huge blocks of stone resting at strange angles. On the sheer sides of the chasm are towering hemlocks, seemingly growing out of the very stone. Geologists generally agree that an earthquake caused the cleft.

At 17.4 *m.* is NORTH UXBRIDGE (alt. 243, Town of Uxbridge), a small village.

> Right from North Uxbridge on Hartford Ave. 0.3 *m.* to the junction with a road; right on this road at 0.7 *m.* is a small white house formerly known as the *Taft Tavern* (*private*). Here on Nov. 6, 1789, George Washington and his suite found accommodations on his return journey to New York after his tour of New England. He had planned to stay with his old friend Colonel Amidon in Mendon, but, owing to a misunderstanding, the Presidential party was refused lodging there by a slow-witted maid and was forced to travel to Uxbridge. The day was cold and rainy and the trip most uncomfortable. Colonel Amidon and his daughter rode post-haste from Mendon to Uxbridge to try to induce Washington to return, but the President had no desire to add to the miserable miles he had traveled that day; in fact, he had retired. Clad in dressing-gown, nightcap, and slippers, he did, however, chat a few minutes with his disappointed friend. So pleased was Washington with his entertainment at Taft's that he wrote a letter from Hartford, accompanied by a piece of chintz for each of the host's daughters and a gift of money for one of them.

> At 3.7 *m.* on Hartford Ave. is *East Douglas* (alt. 522, pop. 2403, sett. about 1721, incorp. 1746, Town of Douglas), the political and industrial center of Douglas Township. Douglas was first incorporated as New Sherburn and renamed a year later in honor of Dr. William Douglas, a Boston physician, who, in acknowledgment, gave the town $500 and 30 acres of land. Douglas, an industrial town, has had two principal industries, the making of axes that achieved a wide reputation in the 18th century, and the making of woolens on which the prosperity of the present town depends.

UXBRIDGE, 18.5 *m.* (town, alt. 259, pop. 6397, sett. 1662, incorp. 1727), called Wacantuck by the Indians, was another town of the Nip-muck Praying Indians. Agriculture was the main occupation of the first settlers until the abundant water-power led to the erection first of several small industrial plants and later of textile factories. The mills are locally owned and Uxbridge has had no serious industrial retrogression.

At the Center is the junction with State 126 (*see Tour 1C*).

MILLVILLE, 23.2 *m.* (town, alt. 225, pop. 1901, sett. 1662, incorp. 1916). Although in the beginning the town was part of Mendon, its history belongs chiefly with that of Blackstone, which separated from

Mendon in 1845, including Millville. In 1729, Daniel Darling erected a grist mill here. The first woolen mill on the river was established in 1814, after which industry developed rapidly. The Lawrence Felting Company had mills here in 1877, and during the World War subsidiary plants of large rubber and knitting companies were established in Millville. The recent depression, however, witnessed the departure of all industries.

Left from Millville a short distance on a marked road is the *Chestnut Hill Meeting House* (1769) now used by the Congregationalists. It is almost square in plan devoid of spire or ornament, and the severe aspect of the interior has been carefully preserved. A high pulpit, reached by a narrow winding stair and surmounted by a sounding board, dominates the interior. A drop-leaf, semi-circular shelf, hinged to the chancel rail, serves as a Communion table. The white box pews with battened doors are on a platform eight inches above the floor to protect the feet of the worshipers from chilly drafts. On three sides runs a gallery with plain wooden benches. In the window behind the pulpit are several panes of early rolled glass.

BLACKSTONE, 25.1 *m.* (town, alt. 190, pop. 4588, sett. 1662, incorp. 1845), was named for the Rev. William Blackstone, an Episcopalian clergyman who was the first white settler on the banks of the river, also named for him. In 1809 the first cotton mill was established, followed by a woolen mill erected in 1814. The industrial growth of the town was rapid and reached its height in the second decade of the 20th century when the Blackstone Cotton Manufacturing Company attained a capitalization of $1,000,000 and the Laramac Mills of the American Woolen Company approximated this amount. Since 1924, however, the industrial development of Blackstone has retrogressed and today there is no manufacturing carried on. The inhabitants are employed, for the most part, in the near-by Rhode Island towns.

Roosevelt Park, on St. Paul St., is well planned and equipped as a recreational center for the community.

St. Paul's Church (Catholic) (1852), near the park on St. Paul St., is on the Rhode Island Line, which cuts diagonally through it; half the congregation sits in Rhode Island and the other half in Massachusetts. Its organ is played in Massachusetts and produces its tones in Rhode Island.

At 26.2 *m.* State 122 crosses the Rhode Island State Line, about 15 *m.* north of Providence, R.I.

T O U R　2 3 A: *From* BARRE *to* CONNECTICUT STATE LINE (*Willimantic*) 36.7 *m.*, State 32.

Via New Braintree, Hardwick, Ware, Palmer, and Monson.
B. & M. R.R., B. & A. R.R., and Central Vt. R.R. parallel the route.
Hard-surfaced roadbed throughout.

STATE 32 in the northern part runs through hilly country with many attractive views; south of Palmer, it runs between hills.

South of the junction with State 122, at Barre (*see Tour* 23), State 32 passes a cemetery at the edge of which (R) stands a *Wineglass Elm*, so called from its shape.

BARRE PLAINS, 2.6 *m.* (alt. 630, Town of Barre).

> Left from Barre Plains on State 67, at 4.4 *m.* is the junction with an unnumbered hard road; right on this is NEW BRAINTREE, 5.8 *m.* (town, alt. 985, pop. 436, sett. 1709, incorp. 1775), an agricultural community. The town was originally a gore between Rutland and Hardwick owned by Braintree inhabitants. The Indians in this region were active during King Philip's War. Manufacturing was unsuccessfully attempted during the 19th century. Agriculture and dairying are the chief means of livelihood.

At 5.8 *m.* is the village of OLD FURNACE (alt. 660, Town of Hardwick).

State 32 climbs *Hardwick Hill*, an ascent of more than one mile, from the top of which is a wide view of the Ware River Valley.

HARDWICK, 9.2 *m.* (town, alt. 986, pop. 2379, sett. 1737, incorp. 1739), is an agricultural community whose inhabitants are of English, Polish, French, and Lettish stock. The land comprising the present township was purchased in 1686 from the Nipmuck Indians by eight Roxbury residents. No settlement was made at the time, however, because the owners were afraid that the Royal Governor, Sir Edmund Andros, would expropriate the land. At first called Lambstown, the district was incorporated as Hardwick, probably for Philip York, first Lord Hardwick. One of the largest herds of Guernsey cattle in the world was, until recently, pastured in this town.

On the *Old Barn* (R) at 11.8 *m.* are three clock dials, all operated by a single mechanism constructed from junked metals and springs.

At 15.5 *m.* is the junction with State 9 (*see Tour* 8) which is followed (R) to WARE, 17.2 *m.*

At 20.4 *m.* is the junction with a dirt road.

> Right on this road, which forks (L) at 5.9 *m.*, is the *Old Babcock Tavern* (*private*), 6.2 *m.*, a two-story, gable-end Colonial house that was a Colonial inn for a stage-coach route. The house, situated on a high bank, has been remodeled and has a new door and a colored glass window.

At 22.3 *m.*, is *Forest Lake* (*fishing, boating, bathing*).

The *Massachusetts State Fish Hatchery* (*open* 9–5), 23.6 *m.*, stocks the important local brooks, rivers, and ponds with trout, bass, perch, and pickerel.

At 24.7 *m.* is PALMER CENTER (alt. 335, Town of Palmer). Opposite the Green is *Frink Tavern* (*private*), built in 1733, which was open to the public for over a century. It is a frame structure with hip roof and central chimney. On each side of the front door are pilasters supporting a pediment. Above the door is a semi-circular fanlight. The windows of the second floor have the original small-paned sashes set with wavy glass.

At the *Home of Walter S. Allen* (*open by permission*), 21 Church St., Palmer, are a spinning wheel that came from Londonderry, Ireland, at the time of the settling of Palmer, a device for making musket bullets, a pot for melting lead, and a contrivance for pulling teeth.

Next to the Catholic Church, 76 Thorndike St., is the *Site of the Bear Tree*, cut down in 1920. One Sabbath morning Deacon Thomas King, armed against Indians, was walking through a lonely piece of forest when he was alarmed by the sight of a bear skulking behind this tree. Forgetting the Sabbath laws for the moment, the deacon raised his gun and fired. The shot had been heard and the corpse could not be concealed. Deacon King was tried for violating the Sabbath, and so hot was the debate that it was referred to the church council, which ultimately decided, after long and grave debate, that the deacon had committed a 'work of necessity and mercy.'

PALMER, 26.6 *m.* (town, alt. 332, pop. 9437, sett. 1727, incorp. 1775), has developed into an industrial town making a large variety of products.

Here is the junction with US 20 (*see Tour* 4).

At 28.1 *m.* State 32 crosses the Quaboag River, by a bridge at the southern approach of which is the *Site of Fellows Tavern* (L). Fellows was granted a tract of land on condition that he open a tavern for the convenience of travelers on the Bay Path, between Boston and Springfield, the latter a new settlement on the banks of the Connecticut. Since Brookfield was the only plantation between these points at the time, the enterprise promised success. The Indians, however, were hostile, and after a few years Fellows abandoned the attempt.

At the *Tufts House*, 30.5 *m.*, Eugene Field and his brother Roswell, in 1865–66, studied under James Tufts, the 'grand old man' of Monson. In the mill pond opposite, the two brothers were nearly drowned when carried over the dam in a boat of their own construction.

MONSON, 31.8 *m.* (town, alt. 380, pop. 5193, sett. 1715, incorp. 1775), was originally a district of Brimfield. Provincial Governor Thomas Pownall named the town for his friend, Sir John Monson, President of the British Board of Trade. Although the town is now essentially a farming community, a granite quarry and woolen mills furnish employment to many.

The *Flynt House* (*private*), on High St. facing Fountain St., built in 1824, contains a collection of about 400 unusual old articles from all parts of the world.

Monson Academy, an endowed preparatory boarding and day school for boys, incorporated in 1804, is on State 32. Three Chinese students brought to America by Robbins Brown, a missionary, were enrolled at the Academy in 1847, and were among the first Chinese to study in America.

State 32 now passes through farming country broken at intervals by stretches of wild land. At 36.7 *m.* the road crosses the Connecticut State Line, 5 *m.* north of Stafford Springs, Conn.

T O U R   2 3 B :   *From* GRAFTON *to* NEW BEDFORD, 67.5 *m.*, State 140.

Via (*sec. a*) Grafton, Upton, Bellingham, Franklin, Wrentham; (*sec. b*) Foxborough, Mansfield, Norton, Attleboro, Taunton, Freetown, Acushnet, New Bedford.

B. & A., N.Y., N.H. & H. R.R.'s service this area.

Hard-surfaced road.

Sec. a. Grafton to Wrentham, 27.9 m.

SOUTHEAST from its junction with State 122, 8 *m.* east of Worcester, State 140 passes through rolling hills, where poultry-raising and dairying provide much of the income.

GRAFTON, 0.7 *m.* (town, alt. 380, pop. 7681, sett. 1718, incorp. 1735), was originally the village of Hassanisco ('Place of the Falling Stones'), established in 1654, one of John Eliot's Praying Indian towns. Grafton underwent a period of industrial development, but today it is a residential suburb of Worcester, with many Colonial buildings.

Grafton Common, selected as typical of New England, was used in filming the motion-picture version of Eugene O'Neill's 'Ah, Wilderness.'

WEST UPTON, 5.3 *m.* (alt. 287; Town of Upton), is the home of the largest factory for ladies' felt and straw hats in the world; the work is seasonal.

UPTON, 6.4 *m.* (town, alt. 240, pop. 2163, sett. 1728, incorp. 1735), was named for a village in Worcestershire, England. Small industries were inaugurated here, stimulated by the water-power supplied by the Mill River. By 1835 shoes were the most important manufactured products, but these were in time superseded by straw hats and bonnets; dairying and truck-gardening, however, are now the chief occupations.

1. On the southern slope of Pratt Hill and on the right hand of Upper Mendon Rd., just beyond Brooks farm, are the *Devils Footprints* (R), impressions in solid rock, over two miles apart; both are about five feet long and two feet wide and both point southward.

2. Right from Upton on Mendon St. at 1 *m.* (R) is a fine specimen of *Glacial Boulder.* Opposite is a wide grassy lane leading uphill, the first road from Upton to Milford. The bordering stone walls and tall elms give the old road a quiet charm. A walk of several hundred yards on the lane leads to Upton's first *Burying Ground.* This one-acre enclosed plot with huge pine trees contains the grave of *Elisha Fish,* Upton's first long-term minister (1751–95). On the stone is a figure in ministerial garb and curled peruke. Here also is the *Site of Upton's First Meeting House* (L). It was never completed, but served for 12 years without a pulpit or pews, for five years without windows.

3. Left from Upton on a road marked 'Hopkinton' at 0.1 *m.* is a junction with a road; left on this road and then right to the *Deacon Johnson Tavern* 0.3 *m.*, a one-and-a-half-story red, painted frame structure with a massive gray stone central

chimney on which is the date '1750.' This well-preserved house was a stagecoach stop.

At 6.6 *m.* is the junction with Hopkinton Rd.

Left on Hopkinton Rd. at 0.1 *m.* in a private garden (L) is a *Stone Cave* or hut constructed of huge untooled stones set in a gravel bank. The entrance tunnel is 14 feet long and 3 feet wide. The hut has a diameter of 12 feet and a height of 11. Four huge slabs form the roof. Rough field-stone forms the walls, and the domed ceiling is of lapped slabs topped by a large flagstone. Many of the stones are cracked and the softer ones show signs of crumbling. There is no trace of smoke on the walls or any vent except the long tunnel. It is known to be over 300 years old, but its builders are still unidentified. Similar huts found in Ireland are presumably of sixth-century Pictic origin. Iceland also has huts of this description. Because the American Indians were not skilled in masonry construction, it is possible that Norsemen built this hut.

At 11.5 *m.* is the junction with State 126 (*see Tour 1C*).

BELLINGHAM, 16.2 *m.* (town, alt. 240, pop. 3056, sett. about 1713, incorp. 1719), when settled by Jacob Bartlett, was called No Man's Land. The town was settled around the Congregational Church and much of its earliest history is identified with that institution. The production of leather and textiles became important to the town after 1800.

Left from Bellingham on an improved road that swings right is NORTH BELL-INGHAM (alt. 200), 2.5 *m.* William T. Adams, author of juvenile fiction under the pen name of Oliver Optic, was born here in 1822. At 73 years of age, he had written over 1000 short stories and 126 books, of which 2,000,000 copies were sold.

FRANKLIN, 20.7 *m.* (town, alt. 294, pop. 7494, sett. 1660, incorp. 1778). In 1660 ten men left the colony at Dedham to break ground in Wollomonopoag, as the region was then called. Serious financial difficulties, however, were encountered in bargaining with the Wampanoag Indians for the purchase of the land. Finally, Captain Thomas Willett, a noted tactician in Indian affairs, lent his able efforts and secured a purchase price of about £35.

When the time came for incorporation, the town decided at first on the name of Exeter, but this choice was dropped in favor of Franklin, in honor of the great statesman, scholar, and humanist. Mr. Franklin was not insensible of the honor, and, after wavering for some time between presenting a church bell or a collection of books to his municipal namesake, he decided in favor of the latter, because it is said he 'considered sense more essential than sound.'

Industrial history began in 1713 when the falls of Mine Brook were utilized for a sawmill. Asa and Davis Thayer, 99 years later, started Franklin's first factory, and by 1865 seven local factories were turning out more than a million hats and bonnets a year.

Today the mill area is the industrial core of the town; about it are the homes of the workers, mostly owned by themselves, small single houses with neat dooryards and gardens, lacking the drab monotony of the usual mill homes. Greenhouses, vineyards, and well-cultivated farms beautify the southwest section.

On Main St. the *Ray Memorial Library*, built in the Greek revival style, contains Benjamin Franklin's gift. Frescoes of Greek scenes by Tommasco Juglaris decorate the interior.

Opposite is *Dean Academy*, a co-educational boarding-school sponsored by the Universalist Church and named in honor of Dr. Oliver Dean, a native son, whose gift to the Universalists of $60,000 and 9 acres of land made the Academy possible.

> 1. Left from the Center on Main St. to Lincoln St. at 0.7 *m.*; straight ahead on Lincoln St. is the *Baker Homestead* (*open*), 1.1 *m.*, now a shop specializing in the sale of early New England glass.

> 2. Right from Franklin on Summer St. is *Camp Unity*, 1.3 *m.*, a summer camp operated by and for working people, most of whom are trade-unionists. In addition to the 20 cabins on a hill overlooking a lake, there is a children's camp, a recreational hall, and a large recreational field.

The *Horace Mann Memorial*, 21.4 *m.* (L), marks the birthplace of the pioneer in public school administration. The son of a poor farmer, Horace Mann had, up to his fifteenth year, only eight or ten weeks of schooling a year. He worked his way through Brown University, studied law, was admitted to the bar in 1823 and during the next 14 years built up a brilliant law practice.

Serving in both the Massachusetts House of Representatives and State Senate, two years as president of the latter body, he was directly responsible for the enactment of several reform measures, and assisted in creating the State Board of Education. In 1837 he accepted the post of secretary to the newly established Board.

During the next 11 years, he supervised the foundation of two normal schools, the erection of hundreds of common schools, the first insane hospital, and a school for the deaf and blind.

Dr. Mann's last venture was the presidency of Antioch College (co-educational), Yellow Springs, Ohio. Hampered by pecuniary limitations and by lack of co-operation, worn with toil and ceaseless battle, he never gave up the struggle. A few weeks before his death in 1859 at a baccalaureate address, he uttered his famous admonition: 'Be ashamed to die until you have won some victory for humanity.'

At 23.5 *m.* is the junction with Creek St.

> Right on Creek St. to *Lake Pearl Park*, 0.4 *m.*, a privately owned amusement park (*swimming, boating, picnicking, dancing, and amusement facilities*).

Lake Archer, 24 *m.*, is surrounded by towering pines and maples.

WRENTHAM, 24.8 *m.* (*see Tour 1B*), is at the junction with State 1A (*see Tour 1B*).

Jordan Marsh Company Rest Home, 25.8 *m.*, standing on large grounds with maples, oaks, and elms, was once the home of Helen Keller and her teacher, Mrs. John Macy. In 1917 the Jordan Marsh Company purchased this two-and-a-half-story dwelling for its employees.

At 27.9 *m.* is the junction with US 1 (*see Tour 1*).

Sec. b. JUNCTION US 1 *to NEW BEDFORD*, 39.6 *m.*   State 140.

Southeast from its junction with US 1, State 140 enters a textile manufacturing region with pleasant, fairly level fields between the cities and
villages.

At 0.8 *m.* is the junction with Lakeview Rd.

> Right on this road over Laundry Brook, to *Foxborough State Forest*, 1.3 *m.*, 795
> acres containing *High Rock*, which affords an excellent view of the countryside.

At 1.2 *m.* is the junction with Chestnut St.

> Left on this street to *Foxborough State Hospital for Mental Diseases*, with 300 em-
> ployees and 1228 patients.

FOXBOROUGH, 2 *m.* (town, alt. 296, pop. 5834, sett. 1704, incorp.
1778), was named for Charles James Fox, British champion of the
American Colonies.   In 1781 the Foxborough Foundry was established
for casting cannon and cannon balls for the Continental Army.   As a
result of its rapid industrialization, the town in 1798 passed a pioneer
eight-hour-day law for heavy industry providing '66 cents for eight
hours' work and $1.33 for eight hours' work of a man and a team suffi-
cient to carry a ton weight.'

It was the straw bonnet industry, however, which built up the town.
Women and children braided and wove straw to help the finances.   A
certain Mrs. Cornelius Metcalf conceived the ingenious idea of adopting
orphan children and putting them to work in the preparation of straw —
a profitable combination of baby-farm, child labor and sweatshop.

After the decline of the straw bonnet industry, the production of indicating, recording, and controlling instruments gained importance.

On near-by Sunset Lake is the summer home of Bruce Barton, author
of 'The Man Nobody Knows.'

MANSFIELD, 5.5 *m.* (town, alt. 178, pop. 6543, sett. 1659, incorp. 1775),
was named for Lord Mansfield and occupies the site of an Indian winter
camping ground.   The town has been predominately industrial since 1800
when a large tack factory was opened.   In 1921 the town-manager form of
government was adopted.

The extensive gardens around the village devoted to the commercial
cultivation of gladioli are the result of experiments started here in 1917
by a native of Holland.

The *Mansfield Tavern*, on North Main St., a three-story stucco building
was given to the town by Mr. Lowney, candy manufacturer.

> Left from Mansfield, 1 *m.*, on North Main St., is (R) the large *Walter M. Lowney
> Chocolate Factory* (*open by permission*), erected in 1906, and (L) the model village
> built for the employees.

NORTON, 10.1 *m.* (*see NORTON*).

Between Norton and Taunton is a gently sloping sparsely settled country.

> Right on State 123 5.4 *m.* is ATTLEBORO (city, alt. 133, pop. 21,835, sett. 1634,
> incorp. town 1694, city 1914).   William Blackstone, the first settler, was a recluse
> who left England because he was 'no longer able to endure the power of the lord-

bishops,' and later informed Bradford that he also 'couldn't endure the power of the lord-brethren.' Named for an ancient town in England, Attleboro began its jewelry business in 1780. Today its 20 or 30 jewelry establishments have earned the city the sobriquet, 'the hub of the jewelry industry in America.' Other industries include bleaching and dyeing and the manufacture of optical goods, automobile accessories, pressed steel, cotton machinery, textile fabrics, and paper boxes. The *L. G. Balfour Company* (*open* 9–5), on County St., is one of the largest emblem manufacturers in the United States.

The *Watson Company* (*open* 9–5), on Mechanic St., is situated in a park with waterfall, pond, and stream mingling with woodland and meadow. Here, silver bullion of Government assay is transformed into sterling ware of great variety and beauty. The *Peck Homestead* (*open*), 3 Elizabeth St., is now the headquarters of the Attleboro Chapter of the D.A.R. Built in 1706, this red gambrel-roofed one-and-a-half-story dwelling is the oldest house in Attleboro, and has been the homestead of a single family for 230 years. The low-ceilinged interior is furnished in early American style with many relics and antiques. Each room contains a fireplace and the doors have their original latches.

TAUNTON, 17.9 *m.* (*see TAUNTON*).

At the Center are the junctions with State 138 (*see Tour* 25) and US 44 (*see Tour* 10).

South of Taunton, State 140 passes through a long stretch of thinly settled country.

At 23.7 *m.* is the junction with Myricks St.

Right on Myricks St. is the junction with Forge St. Left here to Evans's Farm 3.7 *m.* (R), from which (10¢ *fee*) is seen the *Old Man of the Mountain*, a geological phenomenon sometimes called the Indian of the Mountain.

EAST FREETOWN, 29.7 *m.* (town, alt. 98, pop. 1813, sett. 1675, incorp. 1683), first called 'ye freeman's land on Taunton River,' is today a rural area with much wooded land and abundant water-power. Its timber tracts have been somewhat depleted by serious fires. In *Rocky Woods* King Philip is supposed to have spent the last night of his life.

Squaw Hollow derives its name from the legend that an Indian woman used to sit by the side of the road 'busily spinning away despite the fact that her head lay in her lap.'

At 35.3 *m.* is a junction with Acushnet Ave.

Left on Acushnet Ave. to the junction with Tarklin Hill Rd., 1.3 *m.*; left here over the *Old Stone Bridge*, 1.4 *m.*, spanning the Acushnet River, is ACUSHNET (Indian, 'A Bathing Place'), 1.8 *m.* (town, alt. 138, pop. 3962, sett. about 1659, incorp. 1860). This village was completely devastated during King Philip's War. In September, 1776, there was a pitched battle between the Minutemen and the British troops at the present bridge on Main St.

The influence of the many groups of recent immigrants living in the town is evident in the local cuisine; in addition to the hasty pudding, fishcakes, and pumpkin pie of the Yankee, there are the hard-crusted breads and salads of the French-Canadians, the strongly spiced sausages called *linguica* and *chourico* of the Portuguese, and the thick cabbage soup of the Polish. The French-speaking residents are so numerous that a bilingual school has been established.

Clement Nye Swift, the painter of Breton subjects, and William Bradford, the marine painter, were both natives of Acushnet, the latter maintaining a studio here.

The *Methodist Episcopal Church*, on Main St., an ivy-covered field-stone structure, has a slender, shingled spire surmounted by a gilded dolphin.

Near-by is the *Summerton House* (1712), an unpainted, shingled two-story gambrel-roofed structure, with massive chimney and irregularly placed windows in the end. Also on Main St. is the *Precinct Cemetery* containing headstones dating back to 1700. Opposite is *Russell Memorial Library* (R), a field-stone building. The junction of Compton and Main Sts. is still known as 'Parting Ways.'

NEW BEDFORD, 39.6 *m.* (*see NEW BEDFORD*). Here is the junction with US 6 (*see Tour* 6).

T O U R 2 5: *From* BOSTON *to* RHODE ISLAND STATE LINE (*Tiverton*) 47.2 *m.*, State 138.

Via Boston, Canton, Stoughton, Sharon, Easton, Raynham, Taunton, Berkley, Dighton, Somerset, and Fall River.

N.Y., N.H. & H. R.R. services this area.

Hard-surfaced road throughout.

STATE 138, south of Boston, passes through the beautiful Blue Hills, where woods cover the undulating acres. At its southern end it traverses a dairying and poultry-farming country.

State 138 branches south from US 1 at Jamaicaway Circle in Boston, passing the *Arnold Arboretum* (*see BOSTON*).

At 2.7 *m.* State 138 turns right on Blue Hill Ave. and at 4 *m.* State 28 (*see Tour* 19) bears left.

At 8 *m.* (L) rises *Great Blue Hill* (alt. 635) (*foot and bridle trails*) which commands a view 150 miles in radius. *Blue Hill Observatory*, on the summit, is maintained by Harvard University.

At 8.3 *m.* a tablet marks the *Site of Doty's Tavern*, meeting-place for the preliminary drafting of the Suffolk Resolves.

At 10.2 *m.* is the junction with Randolph St.

1. Left on Randolph St. is the *John Fenno House* (*open by permission*), 0.8 *m.* (L) built in 1704, a two-and-a-half-story frame structure with a gable roof and central chimney. The clapboarded exterior is painted black.

2. Right on Randolph St. is CANTON, 2.8 *m.* (town, alt. 113, pop. 6505, sett. 1630, incorp. 1797), which received its present name by whim of a prominent citizen who estimated that the town was exactly antipodal to Canton, China. During the latter part of the 18th century and the early part of the 19th, the town was a busy manufacturing center, among other activities making muskets for the War of 1812. The Rising Sun Stove Polish Factory was opened here in 1858.

The *Plymouth Rubber Mill* (*open*), also on Revere St., is on the site of a foundry Paul Revere set up in 1808, the first copper-rolling mill in the country, which supplied the rolled copper for the State House dome and the copper boilers used in

Fulton's first steamboat. This versatile hero also operated a powder mill here during the Revolution and the War of 1812.

At 13.7 m. is the junction with Central St.

Left on Central St. to *Swan's Tavern*, 1.4 m., corner of Central and Turnpike Sts., now called the Century Farm (*private*). In 1807, the date of its erection by the Boston and Taunton Turnpike Company as a stagecoach station, it was christened the Washington Hotel.

STOUGHTON, 14.4 m. (town, alt. 239, pop. 8472, sett. about 1713, incorp. 1743), was named for William Stoughton, Lieutenant-Governor of Massachusetts (1694–1791), whose father, Colonel Israel Stoughton, commander of the Colonial forces during the Pequot War of 1636, was a large landholder in Dorchester, of which Stoughton was originally a part. During the American Revolution, Stoughton was the supply center for Colonial forces in the area, though there was little industrial development before 1800. By 1830, shoe manufacturing had begun; but the Civil War, depriving the town of its large Southern markets, threatened the prosperity of the factories for a time.

In 1921 the town adopted the city-manager form of government, the manager performing all executive functions and advising the board of selectmen, who have legislative powers.

The *Town Hall*, corner of Pearl and Porter Sts., contains the rooms of the Stoughton Musical Society, which in 1790 competed with singers of the First Parish of Dorchester, winning the contest by singing the 'Hallelujah Chorus' without books.

On the outskirts of Stoughton is a large field adorned with a rustic bandstand, rustic arches, and skeletal booths. In July all these bloom forth in foliage and blossoms, for here is held the Portuguese Festival in honor of Mary Magdalen. From several hundred miles around come the dark-skinned Portuguese in gala attire and mood. The Taunton City Band plays from the bandstand, the young people dance the latest American step, and folk-dances in native costumes are given. Steak barbecues, Portuguese style, supplement purely American edibles. Besides tables laden with all sorts of articles for sale, there is a grand auction block from which is sold everything from livestock to Madeira embroidery.

Right from Stoughton on State 27 at 2.7 m. is the junction with Bay St. At 36 Bay St. (L) is *Cobb's Tavern*, a long two-story frame structure, over 200 years old, with a red-brick end-wall and ells in the rear.

SHARON, 4.8 m. (town, alt. 234, pop. 3683, sett. about 1650, incorp. 1775), lies in the territory once known as Massapoag ('Great Waters'). Unable to farm to any advantage or to compete with industrial centers, Sharon has become a delightful residential center and health resort.

1. Left from the village 1 m. on Billings St. to East St. which leads left to the pre-Revolutionary *Gannet* (*Sampson*) *House*, 1.1 m., the home of Benjamin Gannet, whose wife, born Deborah Sampson, served in the Colonial army disguised as a young man (*see Tour 10*).

2. Left from Sharon on Ames St. along the shore of Lake Massapoag to the junction with Quincy St. 0.7 m.; left here to the *Site of the Ames Knife Factory*, 0.8 m., where in former days such interesting articles as banana and boot knives and machetes were produced.

At 18 *m.* is the junction with Elm St.

Right on Elm St. is NORTH EASTON, 0.5 *m.* (alt. 140). On the corner of Main St. is the *Unity Church*, in the transepts of which are stained-glass windows by John La Farge.

The *North Easton Library,* a memorial to Oakes Ames (1877), displays the vigorous individuality of H. H. Richardson — his fearless adaptation of plan to function, his vigorous use of simple mass, and for material rock-faced Milford granite, trimmed with Longmeadow granite. The long row of windows in the stack wing is considered the best feature of the building, and the most noticeable feature is the low Syrian arch. Norman, Southern French Romanesque, late Gothic, and other influences are mingled here, but are dominated by the architect's own creative genius.

At 18.3 *m.* is the former Lothrop Ames estate, now occupied by the Catholic *Seminary of Our Lady of the Holy Cross.*

At 20.4 *m.* is the junction with State 123.

Right on State 123 is EASTON CENTER, 1.1 *m.* (town, alt. 124, pop. 5294, sett. 1694, incorp. 1725), one of the seven villages whose population is largely of Swedish, Irish, and Portuguese birth. Many are employed in the factories of Easton, Brockton, and Taunton. Even in the early days there was a trend here toward industrialism, swamp land allowing the creation of artificial ponds supplying water-power. Peat and bog iron were extracted, the latter leading to the building of forges and foundries. The manufacture of iron products is still carried on, but the local bog is not utilized today.

Opposite the Town Hall is the Rankin Farm on which reached by a beaten'path from the house is a *Rock with Hoofprints.* Theories differ as to whether the impressions were carved by the Indians or by the elements.

At 2.7 *m.* where State 123 merges with State 106 is *Furnace Village* (Town of Easton). On Highland St. is the *Leonard Home* (*open*), containing numerous Indian relics, unearthed along Mulberry Brook, among them a trowel painstakingly fashioned along modern lines, the sides of it as finely polished as a machine-made implement, and banner-stones made in the shape of hearts, each with a hole bored lengthwise for the insertion of a stick. These stones were used for marking boundaries and traps. The Indians also used the sides of the stones as score boards in keeping track of their catches. A small nick denoted an ordinary catch and a deep nick denoted an extraordinary one.

The *Josiah Keith House* (1717) (*private*), on Bay Rd. is a red-shingled dwelling with white window casements and two interior chimneys. The lower floor has been cut away and the second story rests upon the original foundation.

At 27.9 *m.* is PRATTVILLE (alt. 99, Town of Raynham), the center of a poultry-raising and farming community.

Left from Prattville on King Philip St. at 1 *m.* is *Fowling Pond,* now a swamp, but formerly the site of King Philip's hunting lodge. Philip left Raynham unharmed because the local forge provided him with tools and repaired his weapons.

At 30.4 *m.* the road enters a heavily congested area.

TAUNTON, 30.6 *m.* (*see TAUNTON*). Here is the junction with State 140 (*see Tour 23B*) and US 44 (*see Tour 10*).

Left from Taunton on Weir St. through the stove manufacturing area to a junction with Plain St., 1.2 *m.*; left on Plain St. to Berkley St.; right on Berkley St. to BERKLEY, 4.5 *m.* (town, alt. 616, pop. 1156, sett. 1638, incorp. 1755), a rural town where shipbuilding flourished for about a century.

Berkley Common is described by Nathalia Crane, 'the child poet,' in 'The Janitor's Boy.'

The *Congregational Church* is a two-story building with a high peaked roof and windows with diamond-shaped panes of stained glass. The little church has two entrances, one beneath a tiny turret standing up about 6 feet and the other beneath the tower.

Left from Berkley on Bay View Rd. (the third road left, is Assonet Neck, from the tip of which is visible *Conspiracy Island*, where King Philip formed his confederacy and planned the war against the white interlopers.

DIGHTON, 37 *m.* (town, alt. 29, pop. 3116, sett. 1678, incorp. 1712), is a market-gardening community, inhabited by Yankees and Portuguese. Shipbuilding along the Taunton River and the netting of herring were profitable occupations. Some mulberry trees, planted in an abortive attempt at silkworm culture, still stand.

At the junction of State 138 and Elm St. stands the *Council Oak*, with wide-spreading branches. Here King Philip often met with the Pocassets, who had their settlement in the present Dighton.

Left on Hart St. to Pleasant St., 0.2 *m.*, and the *Segreganset River*, which boasts a legend. Many years ago a mill stood here. The miller put over a sharp deal one day on an old woman who, unfortunately for him, turned out to be a witch. The hag cursed the mill and from that hour never a peaceful moment did the miller know. Shafts and chains kept breaking; flour mildewed in the bins. Finally the curse reached its climax in a fire of supernatural origin which burned the mill to the ground; and the discouraged miller, a ruined man, did not attempt to rebuild.

At 0.5 *m.* is the *Perry Tavern (private)*. Built by David Perry (1750), it was used but a short time as a tavern. On the slope of a knoll, it appears from the road to be a two-and-a-half-story structure. The first floor is in reality a basement and the main entrance to the house is from the porch. An open porch on the second floor is reached on both sides by outdoor stairs. The house has two interior chimneys, and three dormer windows.

Almost directly opposite, on the shores of Berkley, may be seen the *Dighton Rock*, a granite boulder 11 feet long, the face of which is pockmarked with pecked incisions, many of them apparently alphabetic or pictorial. Some of the alphabetic writings are apparently meaningless scribbles done by the Indians in imitation of the white man's writings. Some were made by the Taunton haymakers of 1640, who cut hay for their stock at various points along the Taunton River and transported it on rafts. The remainder are believed to be a record of the story of Miguel Cortereal, a Portuguese explorer whose vessel was wrecked in 1502. He survived the catastrophe, made his way here to Assonet Neck, became a sachem of the local tribe of Indians, and left a record of his adventures with his name and the date carved on the rock. An Indian legend relates how a 'wooden house,' from which issued 'thunder and lightning,' came up the river and how the strange men which it carried fought with them and slew their sachem. This is thought to be an account of the arrival of Cortereal.

SOMERSET, 38 *m.* (town, alt. 17, pop. 5656, sett. 1677, incorp. 1790), is known for Rhode Island johnnycake, a delectable white corn-meal fritter of soft batter, served with either butter or syrup.

Jemima Wilkinson came to Somerset from New York in 1779, claiming she had died three years before and that her body had been reanimated by the soul of Christ. Garbed in a picturesque costume she held outdoor meetings in a walnut grove and chose twelve disciples from her followers. Sitting on a white horse, she is said to have asked her followers if they believed she could walk on the waters of the Taunton River. They said they did; she replied, 'Such faith cannot be strengthened by a miracle,' and rode off complacently.

At 38.7 *m.* is the junction with South St.

Left on South St. is the *Jarathmeal Bowers House*, 0.6 *m.*, built in 1770, a spacious structure with a hip roof and central chimney.

Henry Bowers, son of the founder of Somerset, purchased and brought home as a slave the son of an African chief. All efforts to tame his free wild spirit failed and he was shipped to sea. He made his escape at the island of Haiti and participated in the slave uprising then in progress there. The revolt was successful and he became emperor under the name of *Toussaint L'Ouverture*. In 1802, Napoleon's army overthrew his empire and he died in 1803 after a term of imprisonment in an Alpine dungeon.

At 41.3 *m.* is the junction with US 6 (*see Tour* 6).

At 43 *m.* is FALL RIVER (*see FALL RIVER*).

State 138 crosses the Rhode Island State Line at 47.2 *m.*, about 7 *m.* north of Tiverton, R.I.

T O, U R 2 7: *From* BOSTON *to* BOURNE 51.8 *m.*, State 3.

Via Quincy, Weymouth, Norwell, Hanover, Pembroke, Kingston, and Plymouth.

N.Y., N.H. & H. R.R. services this area.

Heavy traffic in summer on this hard-surfaced road, one of the main arteries to Cape Cod.

IN BOSTON State 3 branches southeast from US 1 (Jamaicaway), just south of Jamaica Pond. At 5.4 *m.* it crosses the Neponset River and traverses a thickly populated area.

At 7.4 *m.* State 3 enters the Southern Artery which by-passes the city of Quincy.

Right (straight ahead) at the junction to QUINCY, 0.8 *m.* (*see QUINCY*).

At 9.4 *m.* is the junction with State 3A (*see Tour* 27*A*).

At 11.5 *m.* the highway crosses the Weymouth Fore River, the lower end of which is one of the most traveled water areas of its size.

WEYMOUTH, 11.7 *m.* (*see WEYMOUTH*).

At 12.7 *m.* is the junction with State 18 (*see Tour* 27*B*).

State 3 skirts a heavily wooded section; at ASSINIPPI CORNER, 19.2 *m.*, is the junction with State 123.

Left on State 123 is NORWELL, 3.1 *m.* (town, alt. 137, pop. 1666, sett. 1634, incorp. 1888). For a number of years the Indians of this vicinity were friendly, but on May 20, 1676, following an attack on Hingham, they descended upon the hamlet, killing several persons and burning a number of buildings, including a mill.

In its early days shipbuilding yards occupied the banks of the North River; in the 19th century the manufacture of trunks and boxes was important and shoes and tacks were produced on a small scale; today the chief means of livelihood is truck gardening.

The *First Parish Church* (Unitarian), built in 1742, and reached by a broad flight of steps with iron railings, has three green doors with Colonial locks and hinges. Over the entrance rises a hexagonal steeple in the base of which is a four-faced clock.

Kent Memorial Building (*open*), River St., built before 1680, contains a museum of historical relics.

South of the Kent Memorial is *Thomas Garfield Park*, a wooded recreation center for children, presented to the town in 1895.

Right from the village on River St. to the junction with Cornet Stetson Rd., 5.4 *m.*; left on this road is the *Sargent S. Stetson House* (*private*), 6.2 *m.* a one-and-a-half-story frame dwelling with an addition of a single story. Although many alterations have been made, at one end of the house the original roof slopes to within seven feet of the ground. The inside timbers of the central part of the roof resemble the 'knees' of a ship, having been bent to the angle of the roof. The frame of the structure is held together by treenails. Across the road near an old barn is a lattice-enclosed well with an ancient iron wheel and ballast.

At 22.7 *m.* is the junction with Rockland Rd.

Right on this hard-surfaced, tree-lined road is HANOVER CENTER, 1.3 *m.* (town, alt. 54, pop. 2709, sett. 1649, incorp. 1727), named by the early settlers in honor of King George I, the former Elector of Hanover. Predominant among the early industries was the manufacture of anchors and fittings for ships, cannon balls, hollow ware, and other articles from bog-iron ore.

On the Green adjacent to a granite shaft memorial are *Two Ship's Howitzers* made about 10 years before the Civil War. East of the Town Hall on Hanover St. is (R) the *Samuel Stetson House* (*open; adm.* 15¢), built in 1694, a yellow, shingled, two-and-a-half-story frame dwelling, owned by the Society for the Preservation of New England Antiquities. The house has its original wide plank floors and contains an exceptional collection of old pictures and Colonial and Indian relics. Among these is a stone water bottle about the size and shape of a full-grown summer squash, with a brown stain on one side where it rubbed the horse's side as it hung from the saddle.

At 22.9 *m.* is the junction with Broadway.

1. Right on this hard-surfaced street to Elm St., 0.3 *m.*; left on Elm St. to the *Site of Luddam's Ford* and the *Old Forge*, 0.9 *m.*, where the anchor of the U.S. Frigate 'Constitution' was forged. In 1632, Governor Winslow and a guide crossed the stream here. Luddam, the guide, carried the Governor across on his back and Winslow named the ford for him.

2. Left on Broadway is a junction with Old Country Rd. formerly State 3, at 0.2 *m.*; right on Old Country Rd. is the *Old Bridge* spanning the North River at 0.7 *m.* On one side a bronze tablet tells of the many shipyards that once made this spot a center of activity.

At 23.2 *m.* State 3 crosses the North River, and passes through low level country.

At 23.6 *m.*, corner of Schoosett St., is the *Friends Meeting House* (1706) (*not open*), a one-and-a-half-story wooden building. Plain benches are lined up on a bare wooden floor. A heavy rope serves as a hand-rail on the steps leading to the balcony, which can be shut off by a movable wooden partition. The walls lack adornment of any kind. Only occasional meetings are held here. Adjacent to the meeting house is the *Friends Burying Ground* with headstones all about the same size and shape in keeping with Quaker traditions.

Left on Schoosett St. at 0.3 *m.* is a crossroad that leads (L) to the *Old Briggs House*, 0.7 *m.*, the home of a shipbuilder on the bank of the North River. In the yard adjoining, a bronze plaque on a granite post marks the *Site of Brick Kiln Shipyard* (1730–1848). More than 121 vessels, weighing from 15 to 375 tons, were built here. The 'Beaver,' one of the ships whose cargo inspired the Boston Tea Party in 1773, and the 'Bedford,' the first ship to display the United States flag in British waters, were among these.

At 24.1 *m.* is the *Birthplace and Home of Ichabod Thomas* (*open as a tearoom*) (1761–1859), the eminent shipbuilder. The structure has wings and ells, and recently added porches; the interior has many secret passages.

NORTH PEMBROKE, 24.8 *m.* (alt. 20, Town of Pembroke), is at the junction with State 14.

Right from North Pembroke on State 14, 0.3 *m.*, is the *Squire Keen House* (*private*), built in 1745, a two-and-a-half-story structure with a clapboarded front, shingled ends, and kitchen and open woodshed at right angles to an ell. Twin pines of noble proportions shade the lawn.

PEMBROKE, 1.6 *m.* (town, alt. 160, pop. 1621, sett. 1650, incorp. 1712), founded as an Indian outpost, honors, as its first settlers, Dolor Davis and Robert Barker. Barker acquired a liberal area from the Indians in Herring Brook district in exchange for a quart of sack. Until the early 19th century, shipbuilding on the North River was the major industry. This is the setting for 'Leave the Salt Earth,' by Richard Warren Hatch, and Whittier's 'Songs of Three Centuries.'

It is said that there was once a stump surrounded by water-lilies in near-by Hobomoc Pond that rose three feet above the surface regardless of the rise and fall of the water. To the Indians the stump was Hobomoc, an evil spirit, and the lilies were his pale-faced children, brought over the Great Water in a canoe; when the Indians assaulted the stump, it groaned, the waters were agitated, and the flowers danced. Unable to destroy the spirit, they offered him tribute, throwing choice morsels of food into the pond. The gifts, however, did little good — sicknesses came and eventually the Pale-Faced triumphed. 'Queen Patience,' the Indians' seeress, advised them to leave the region, though she had decided to remain by the grave of her father. When this Indian woman died in 1785, her burial was directed by the first minister of the First Parish of Pembroke.

On the front lawn of the Town Hall is the *Town Pound*, a stone-walled area 20 feet square, with a small wooden gate. On State 14 at 3 *m.* is *Furnace Pond* (*picnic grounds*), on the edge of which is the *Site of an Iron Mill* (1702). This mill was dependent upon bog iron obtained in the vicinity.

At 31.3 *m.* is the junction with State 3A (*see Tour 27A*).

KINGSTON, 32 *m.* (town, alt. 35, pop. 2743, sett. 1620, incorp. 1726). Passengers of the 'Mayflower,' the 'Fortune,' and the 'Ann' selected this spot on the navigable Jones River for settlement; it was in Plymouth Town until 1726. Shipbuilding, once a thriving industry, ceased in 1887, but a few wharves are a reminder of former commercial activity.

The *First Congregational Parish Church* (Unitarian), Main St., was erected in 1717. This gray frame building with wooden quoins, has an open belfry with a balustrade at its base, and round-headed windows and blinds. Its architecture is early Georgian Colonial. A *Granite Shaft* about four feet high served as the 'town post,' or bulletin board, until 1911.

The *Squire William Sever House* (*seen by appointment*), Linden St., is a frame structure, built in 1760. It is painted yellow, with white trim and dark green blinds. Three large chimneys, with caps painted black, top a roof surrounded by a white railing. The clapboards on the ell are graduated and the windows have multiple panes. Two aged linden trees flank the red-brick walk leading to the house.

> Left from the Center on Bay Rd. at about 0.6 *m.* is *Bradford House* (*open, adm.* 25¢), of frame construction, with weather-beaten unstained shingles. Built in 1674, it retains its original appearance and contains some of the early furnishings. Windows with diamond-shaped panes, a fireplace of huge dimensions with a Dutch oven, looms, an old rack for hooking rugs, and an old well with wooden lever and fulcrum are well preserved.

State 3 here traverses a rolling country of low hills and shallow valleys.

At 34.3 *m.* is the *William Crowe House,* the oldest house in Plymouth (*see PLYMOUTH*).

At 36.3 *m.* is PLYMOUTH (*see PLYMOUTH*).

Southeast of Plymouth, State 3 traverses flat, sandy country, sparsely covered with dwarf pine; at intervals are acres of cranberry bog.

The Sagamore Canal Bridge, 51.8 *m.* is at the junction with US 6 (*see Tour* 6).

T O U R   2 7 A: *From* QUINCY *to* KINGSTON, 28.2 *m.*, State 3A.

Via Weymouth, Hingham, Hull, Scituate, Cohasset, Marshfield, and Duxbury.
N.Y., N.H. & H. R.R. services this area.
Hard-surfaced road, mostly macadam.

STATE 3A closely parallels the South Shore of Massachusetts Bay and gives access to several old seaports now famous as summer resorts.

State 3A branches east from its junction with State 3 (*see Tour* 27) 0.8 *m.* north of QUINCY (*see QUINCY*), and crosses the Fore River, 0.6 *m.*, over the *Fore River Bridge,* an impressive structure.

NORTH WEYMOUTH, 1.5 *m.*, alt. 11 (*see WEYMOUTH*).

At 2.6 *m.* is the first *Drive-in Theater* (*cinema*) in New England, with terraced levels to allow an uninterrupted view of the screen without passengers' leaving their cars.

At 5.4 *m*. is the junction with North St.

Right on North St. 0.3 *m*. is HINGHAM (town, alt. 21, pop. 7330, sett. about 1633, incorp. 1635), named for the former English home of most of its settlers. Originally inhabited by Algonquin Indians, the territory was conveyed to the English by three Algonquin representatives in 1665.

In the early 19th century fishing and related occupations developed; by 1831, over 55,000 barrels of mackerel were landed on Hingham wharves. In the post-Civil War period both industry and agriculture declined, and are almost non-existent today.

The *Site of Captain Benjamin Church's Home*, now occupied by the Norton House, is at 102 North St. It was Captain Church whose company defeated King Philip.

The *Old Garrison House* (*open*), 123 North St., has been occupied by nine generations of the Perez Lincoln family, who settled in Hingham, 1633–35. Some of the walls are filled with a mixture of clay and straw, bound with a tough grass for protection from musket balls during Indian raids.

The *Cushing House* (*open as an inn*), 127 North St., a three-story frame structure antedating the Revolution, was formerly the Old Union Hotel and Little and Morey's Tavern. It was built by Dr. Bela Lincoln, a brother of the General.

On Liberty Pole Hill is *Glad Tidings Rock*. Legend says that friends of a famous hunter, John Jacob, on learning that he had been slain by the Indians, but not tortured, so named it in gratitude for his quick death.

The *Samuel Lincoln House* (*private*), at the fork of North and Lincoln Sts., is a two-and-a-half-story wooden structure, parts of which were built in 1667.

The *New North Church* (*open by arrangement with pastor*), nearly opposite the Samuel Lincoln House, erected in 1807, is architecturally interesting. The portico, with triangular pediment supported by four Doric columns, the corner pilasters, and the distinctive cupola supported by classic columns, are of characteristic Bulfinch design.

A part of the *Old Ordinary* (*open daily, June to Sept.*), 19 Lincoln St., was built in 1650. This two-and-a-half-story unpainted structure now houses the *Hingham Historical Society Collection* of old furniture. The front door and the two windows to the right mark the original length; the two windows to the left identify the addition made about 1740.

The *Old Ship Church* (Unitarian), on Main St., was built in 1681 by ship's carpenters and is believed to be the only 17th-century church now standing in Massachusetts. Its design, plain to the point of being severe, is devoid of any suggestion of the classical tradition. The roof is in the form of a truncated pyramid surmounted by a belfry and a lookout that gives the building its name.

In *Hingham Cemetery* at the rear of the church is the grave of General Benjamin Lincoln (1733–1810). Marked by an obelisk are (L) the *Remains of the Old Fort* that protected the early inhabitants from Indian attack. A local tradition says that when Major Samuel Thaxter, reported killed by the Indians, was returning to Fort William Henry, he met Caleb Bates who had just heard Dr. Gay preach the funeral sermon. 'Why, Major,' Bates exclaimed, 'we have just buried you!'

At 5.5 *m*. is the junction with Jerusalem Rd.

Left on Jerusalem Rd. at 2.5 *m*. is *Nantasket Beach*, three miles long, one of the most popular places for surf bathing on the Atlantic seaboard. Opposite it and extending half its length, *Paragon Park* (*small fee*) offers a variety of amusements. The State has just completed a modern bathhouse and solarium.

Straight ahead on Nantasket Ave. at 4.8 *m*. is *Strawberry Hill* (L), which affords a comprehensive view of the Atlantic side of the peninsula as well as the bay. There is an unsupported belief that Thorwald, son of Eric the Red, was slain and buried on Point Allerton (Hull) in 1004. Tradition says that many of the hundreds of vessels wrecked in early days on the rocks off Point Allerton were drawn off their courses by false lights hung by wreckers who wished to salvage the cargoes. At 6.8 *m.* is junction with Spring St.; right on Spring St. is HULL, 7.5 *m.* (town, alt. 23, pop. 2619, sett. 1624, incorp. 1647), which has a beach lined with summer cottages and hills covered with homes. The first building in this region was a trading post erected by traders from Plymouth. The first settlers were John Oldham, John Lyford, and Roger Conant. Oldham and Lyford had been expelled from Plymouth Colony for sedition and alleged profanation of the church. Oldham was killed by the Indians after his companions had moved on to Cape Ann and thence to Salem. Other settlers from Plymouth remained and developed the fishing industry to such an extent that the colony was taxed one eleventh of the Boston total in 1630.

The *Public Library*, originally the Hunt House, built in 1644, was the first rectory in Hull. It has been much remodeled. The last regular minister to occupy it was Samuel Veazie. It is told that the parishioners were once so far behind in his wages that Mr. Veazie was forced to sue them; in the meantime he was in such desperate straits that, hearing the carcass of a horse was on the beach, he hurried there to get the skin, only to find a parishioner had arrived ahead of him. In desperation, the clergyman removed the horse's shoes, which he sold to the village blacksmith for 25¢.

The *Cushing House* (*private*), 0.2 *m.* northeast of the center on Spring St., was built in 1725, a one-and-a-half-story gabled dwelling, with a large square central chimney; it was at one time the home of James Otis, the Revolutionary orator.

At 7 *m.* is the *Beal House*, now an evergreen-shaded tearoom, built in 1690.

At 8.3 *m.* is the *Bancroft Bird Sanctuary* (*open*), a nine-acre reservation in the custody of the South Shore Nature Club.

At 8.7 *m.* is the junction with Sohier St.

Left on Sohier St. is the junction with Main St., 1.2 *m.*; right on which is COHASSETT, 1.3 *m.* (town, alt. 24, pop. 3418, sett. about 1647, incorp. 1770), formerly a part of Hingham. It boasts a history beginning with the landing of Captain John Smith in 1614. From 1737 to 1885 fishing and farming were the leading occupations. From 1708 to 1880 small vessels were built. Lobster fishing is now engaged in mainly by Portuguese residents. Many permanent inhabitants commute to Boston. The natural beauty of the town, and its fine bathing beaches and yacht harbor, are natural assets bringing summer visitors, the main source of revenue.

The *Town Hall* with a fine auditorium is the headquarters of the South Shore Players, who present several plays every summer.

The *St. Stephen's Episcopal Church* (1900), 0.1 *m.*, south of the Center on Main St., designed by Cram, Goodhue, and Ferguson, is notable for its beautiful stained-glass windows and *Carillon* of 51 bells. It is built of seam-faced granite, varied with wood and plaster. Its design is modified perpendicular Gothic.

Right from the village 0.4 *m.* is the junction with Summer St.; left here and right on Border St. to the *John Smith Tablet*, 0.7 *m.*, commemorating the discoverer of Cohasset and bearing excerpts from Smith's 'Generall Historie' describing his fight with the Indians. From the roof of the colonnade behind the tablet is a view of the Atlantic and the rocky ledges offshore, scene of many shipwrecks, including that of the Danish ship 'Maria' in 1783. On *Grampus Rocks*, one and a half miles offshore the brigantine 'St. John' of Galway foundered Oct. 7, 1849, and many Irish immigrants lost their lives. These and other tragedies brought about the erection of *Minot's Light*, 2.5 *m.* offshore. The original light, an iron structure, completed in 1850, was destroyed in 1851 by a storm that killed its two keepers. The present granite tower, 114 feet high, was built in 1860. The 1-4-3 flash of its 75,000 candlepower beam is a familiar sight on Massachusetts Bay.

State 3A here traverses a wooded country. At 10.4 *m.* is *Bound Rock*, which was a marker on the boundary between Massachusetts Bay Colony and Plymouth Settlement.

At 12.6 *m.* is the junction with First Parish Rd.

Left on this road at 0.8 *m.* is the junction with Branch Rd.; left, Branch Rd. passes through EGYPT (Town of Scituate), which is largely occupied by *Dreamwold*, a magnificent estate owned by Thomas W. Lawson, the spectacular Boston financier, who made and lost a series of fortunes in stock-market speculations. The place is surrounded by a mile or so of white fence, covered in season with pink rambler roses. At strategic intervals Lawson made retreats to this place where he bred prize horses and pedigreed bulldogs, and listened to the notes of a carillon installed in a tower on the estate.

At 2.5 *m.* on First Parish Rd. is SCITUATE (Indian, *Satuit* or *Seteat*, 'Cold Brook'), 0.7 *m.* (town, alt. 46, pop. 3846, sett. about 1630, incorp. 1636). The village suffered during the Indian wars and, in a decisive battle near the Stockbridge Mansion, was barely saved from total destruction.

The War of 1812, bitterly opposed by the town, injured local business. According to a local legend, when an English man-of-war burned vessels in the harbor, two little girls, Rebecca and Abigail Bates, scared off a landing party at Lighthouse Point by beating on dishpans, firing guns, and otherwise simulating a lively force of defenders hidden behind a shed.

Scituate was early engaged in shipbuilding, fishing, and brickmaking, and later had saw, grist, fulling, and clothing mills. Today it is one of two communities in the United States preparing Irish moss, a marine alga growing on rocks and used in brewing and dyeing, and in making a delicate blanc mange peculiarly suitable for the diet of invalids.

The *Cudworth Cottage* (*open weekdays*, 9–5 *during July and Aug.*), near the Town Hall, built in 1723, is an unpainted two-and-a-half-story structure housing a collection of relics of the local historical society.

At 14.1 *m.* is the junction with State 123 and Old Oaken Bucket Rd.

1. Right on Old Oaken Bucket Rd. at 0.2 *m.* before a white frame house shaded by elm and horse-chestnut trees, is the *Well* made famous by a native, Samuel Woodworth (1785–1842), in his poem 'The Old Oaken Bucket.'

2. Left at the junction with State 123 is a dirt road leading left to *Stockbridge Pond*, 0.1 *m.* and the *Site of the Stockbridge Mansion*, built before 1660. The house was used as a garrison to protect near-by mills. A story is told of a Mrs. Ewell, who, hearing the war-whoops of approaching Indians, left her infant grandson sleeping and ran to the Stockbridge garrison, sixty rods away, to spread the alarm. Refusing to stay in the garrison, she ran back home, where she found the baby still asleep and unharmed. At the lower end of the pond stands a restored *Old Mill*, a small building with unpainted, shingled walls.

At 14.2 *m.* on State 3A is the large *Judge William Cushing* (1732–1810) *Boulder.* Cushing held important legal offices in Massachusetts, and was a member of the convention that framed the State Constitution of 1779, and of the first United States Supreme Court; in Chief Justice Jay's absence, he administered the oath of office to George Washington in 1793.

MARSHFIELD, 20.2 *m.* (town, alt. 24, pop. 2073, sett. 1632, incorp. 1642). The British garrison stationed here was withdrawn in 1775, before the attack of Colonial soldiers.

In the 19th century, after the construction of a marsh-drainage canal, strawberries and cranberries became the most important crops.

Marshfield was the scene of 'The Dike Shanty,' by Maria Louise Pool; 'The Children of Old Park's Tavern,' by Frances A. Humphrey; and 'Into the Wind' and 'Leave the Salt Earth,' by Richard Warren Hatch.

The *Fairgrounds of the Marshfield Agricultural and Horticultural Society*, founded in 1867, are on South St. (*Annual fair, Aug.* 26–29). The State maintains a *Pheasant Farm* in Marshfield.

Left from the village on South River St. at 2.2 *m.* is the junction with Peregrine White Rd.; on which at 2.7 *m.* is the *Site of Peregrine White's Homestead.* Peregrine, born on the 'Mayflower,' Nov. 20, 1620, lived here after his marriage.

At 20.8 *m.* is the junction with Ocean St.

Left on this road 0.7 *m.* is the junction with Webster St.; right here to a gravel road at 2.4 *m.*; which leads to the *Winslow Burying Ground*, 0.5 *m.*, containing the *Grave of Daniel Webster* (1852), which is on a knoll about 200 yards from the road. About 50 feet behind, and enclosed by an iron fence, is Webster's grave, and nearby are the graves of Peregrine White, Adelaide Phillips, and other notables.

At 2.5 *m.* on Webster St. is (L) the entrance to *The Site of the Daniel Webster House* on the former Winslow estate. The present two-and-a-half-story, yellow frame building was erected by the orator's daughter-in-law after his house was burned in 1890.

At 2.9 *m.* on Webster St. stands the *Adelaide Phillips House* (*open*), easily identified by the life-size statue of the singer in the front yard. The music-rooms of the three-story house are arranged as the owner left them.

At 3.2 *m.* is the *Winslow House* (*now a tearoom; adm.* 25¢), corner of Caswell St., built in 1699. It is a large hip-roofed house with central chimney, quoin trim, and vestibule entrance; and it has wide fireplaces and a secret chamber.

At 21 *m.* is *Tea Rock Hill*, where Marshfield patriots staged a tea party after seizing and burning tea from a local store. A small wooden marker identifies the hill.

At 24.7 *m.* is the junction with Alden St.

Left on Alden St., at 0.3 *m.*, is the *John Alden House* (1653) (*open*).

At 0.6 *m.* on Alden St. is the junction with St. George St., right on which at the corner of Washington St., is the *Transatlantic Cable Station* (*open by permission*), 1.1 *m.*

At 25.2 *m.* is DUXBURY (town, alt. 31, pop. 2244, sett. about 1624, incorp. 1637), a residential community. Shortly after 1624, Miles Standish, Elder Brewster, John Alden, and other Pilgrims entered this region, seeking additional land for the growing settlement and pasturage for recently acquired herds of cattle.

Between 1633 and 1636 a canal was cut across Gurnet Headland, facilitating travel between Plymouth and Boston. In 1637 an enactment by the General Court of Plymouth made 'Ducksburrow' a township. The origin of the name is uncertain, but it may have been taken from the Lancastershire seat of the Standish family.

An annual fair, the first in America, was sanctioned for Duxbury by the Colonial Government in 1638. This promoted travel to such an extent that in the same year Francis Sprague was licensed by the Colony 'to keep a victualling on Duxburrow side.' In 1639 a gristmill and a fulling-mill for the finishing of homespun cloth were built, and the next year a large tract of land was set aside as a Common to be used for pasturage.

During the first quarter of the 19th century the town carried on shipbuilding and shipped cod, mackerel, and clams.

'Standish of Standish,' a novel by Jane Austin (1831–94), uses Duxbury for much of its background. 'Hobomok,' by Lydia Maria Child (1802–80), tells a story of the Praying Indians of the area.

> Right from Duxbury on Depot St. to HALL'S CORNER and the junction with Chestnut St., 0.9 *m.*; right on Chestnut St. 0.2 *m.* is the *Old Burying Ground* in which are the graves of Miles, Lora, and Mary Standish. Miles Standish (1584–1656) directed in his will that he be buried beside his daughters, Lora and Mary, who had died before him. The grave of John Alden is known to be here, but has not been identified. The oldest original tombstone (1700) is that of the Rev. Ichabod Wiswall, third minister of the settlement. One of the ancient inscriptions reads:
>
> 'Aseneath Soule
The Chisel cant help her any.'
>
> Straight ahead from Hall's Corner on Standish St. to Crescent St.; right on Crescent St. to Monument Rd., on which, left at 1.3 *m.*, is the *Standish Monument* (*open*), 130 feet high, on the crest of *Captain's Hill.* Slabs set in the walls of the base give the Pilgrim history. From the top of the monument there is an extensive view, including the twin *Gurnet Lights*, which stand on an 80-foot bluff. This bluff was, in 1777, the site of a fort to which signals were sent from a lookout on Captain's Hill.
>
> Straight ahead on Crescent St., 0.5 *m.*, is the *Alexander Standish House* (*open*), a plain two-story, gambrel-roofed, frame building with a large central chimney, built by the son of Miles Standish in 1666.

At 28.2 *m.* is the junction with State 3 (*see Tour* 27).

T O U R   2 7 B :   *From* WEYMOUTH *to* EAST BRIDGE-WATER, 15.1 *m.*, State 18.

Via Abington, Rockland, Whitman, and Hanson.

N.Y., N.H. & H. R.R. services this area.

Three-lane concrete highway over most of route.

STATE 18 is a cross-country route connecting two heavily traveled routes running south from Boston. It passes through several rural towns in a hilly and forested countryside.

State 18 runs south from its junction with State 3 about 1 *m.* southeast of Weymouth (*see WEYMOUTH*).

At 7 *m.* is the junction with State 123.

> Left on State 123 is ABINGTON, 0.3 *m.* (town, alt. 104, pop. 5696, sett. 1668, incorp. 1713), occupies a section called by the Indians Manamooskeagin ('Many Beavers'). This name and the beavers appear on the corporate seal of the town. Agriculture and lumbering were at first the main occupations, but very early Colonel Aaron Hobart operated a foundry. The town is now a manufacturing community producing shoes, dresses, textile machinery, curtains, and ice cream. (*See WHITMAN, below.*) About 1815, Jesse Reed invented a machine with which

he could make 80,000 and later, 250,000 tacks a day. During the Civil War, Abington is said to have furnished one half of the shoes worn by the Union Army; the large output resulted from the invention of the McKay stitcher.

In the *Dyer Memorial Library* (1932), on Center Ave., are Indian relics, jewels, paintings, ivories, rare china, bric-à-brac, and glassware from the Dyer homestead, all imported by Samuel W. Dyer during his term as United States envoy to France.

The *Masonic Building*, Washington St., originally erected as a church, has beams that were cut for the U.S. Frigate 'Constitution,' but were rejected by government inspectors.

Island Grove Park, Wilson Place, off Washington St., remains very much in its natural state, its wild beauty enhanced by a pond. Anti-slavery and temperance meetings held beneath the shelter of its majestic old trees, were addressed by Webster, Garrison, Sumner, Phillips, Andrew, and many other stirring orators. A *Memorial Boulder*, erected in 1909, by Captain Moses N. Arnold of the 12th Massachusetts Volunteers, is inscribed:

> Meetings in the cause of abolition of slavery were held in this Grove yearly from 1846 to 1865. On this spot William Lloyd Garrison, Wendell Phillips and others addressed the people. Suffering all manner of abuse, the abolitionists stood steadfast until the slave was made free. Reader, take heed! Stand for the right, though power and wealth and all your fellows turn against you and persecute you. 'I am in earnest — I will not equivocate — I will not excuse — I will not retreat a single inch — and I will be heard.' Erected by an Abington Soldier, who served and was wounded in the war which ended slavery.

The *Memorial Bridge and Arch*, an impressive structure commemorating the soldiers and sailors of several wars, was dedicated on June 10, 1912, the 200th anniversary of the town, with President William Howard Taft as the guest of honor. This bridge, which, including the piers, is 300 feet long, is of concrete with iron railings. Fifty feet above the water, the arch is surmounted by a bronze eagle 11 feet in height. On the supporting columns facing the water are life-size figures in bas-relief, representing a soldier and a sailor of the Civil War.

The *Shedd House* (*private*), 770 Washington St., near Wilson Place, has a two-story brick front. It was built before 1700, and the first Dame School in the town was established here in 1732.

Kay's Goat Dairy (*open*), 365 High St., is one of the few modern goat farms in the State.

Left from Abington on State 123 is ROCKLAND, 3.7 *m*. (town, alt. 124, pop. 7890, sett. 1673, incorp. 1874), a manufacturing town; pleasant with shaded sidewalks and neat homes, it produces shoes and allied products including welts and dyes.

King Philip's Headquarters occupied a field back of the cemetery on Webster St. An ancient map of the town shows a round-house in this field which legend says was used by King Philip in a raid.

About 4.2 *m*. south of the Center on State 123, in the bend of the road opposite the pond, is the *First Frame House of Rockland* (*private*), built by the Thatcher family shortly after they established a sawmill on Cushing Rd. in 1703. The old dwelling housed slaves who worked at cutting logs for the mill.

At 8.7 *m*. is the junction with State 27.

Left on State 27 is WHITMAN, 0.6 *m*. (town, alt. 76, pop. 7591, sett. about 1670, incorp. 1875). Known as 'Little Comfort,' or South Abington, Whitman was named for Augustus Whitman when it became a separate town. Among the early products were ship timbers and box wood. The white oak timbers of the Frigate 'Constitution' were cut in near-by forests and were squared in local mills. Agriculture is limited, but Whitman is noted for fine specimens of poultry. The dominant industry is shoes; Whitman excels in the production of shanks and shoe finding.

Straight ahead from Whitman on State 27, the *G. G. Roberts Corporation* (*open by permission*), 1.2 *m.*, manufacturers of tacks, occupies the factory built by Benjamin Hobart, pioneer in this industry. This is the site of the foundry of Colonel Aaron Hobart, where Paul Revere learned to make copper and bronze bells. Colonel Aaron Hobart, among the first in the country to cast church bells, is also believed to be the first person to cast cannon in America.

At 1.3 *m.* is the *Regal Shoe Company* (*open*), one of the largest shoe manufactories in the East, shipping to foreign countries as well as to all parts of the United States. Near-by are the *Commonwealth Shoe and Leather Company*, a large shoe manufacturing plant, and the *United Shank and Finding Company*, a subsidiary of the United Shoe Machinery Corporation, and one of the largest factories of its kind in the world.

At 1.4 *m.* is the junction with South Ave.; straight ahead on South Ave. is the junction with State 58; (R) on State 58 is NORTH HANSON, 4.1 *m.* (alt. 68, Town of Hanson). On the corner of Washington and Liberty Sts. is the *Elijah Cushing House*, built about 1724, a large, commodious two-story house. Part of it is used as an antique shop. From this house Lucy Cushing presented a silk flag to the Pembroke Light Infantry at the outbreak of the War of 1812.

At 5.1 *m.* on State 58 is HANSON (town, alt. 66, pop. 2417, sett. 1632, incorp. 1820), a residential town, named for Alexander Conte Hanson, a patriot, assaulted by a Baltimore mob in 1812 for criticizing the Federal administration. The surrounding country is generally level, with many lakes, slowly meandering streams, and a large cedar swamp in the southern part.

Extensive cranberry bogs annually produce about 8,500,000 cans of cranberry sauce and employ many Portuguese who form a foreign-speaking community near *Monponsett Pond* in the south of the town. This is the only industry surviving from the brief industrial period of 75 years ago when practically every citizen maintained a shoe shop in his home and did piece-work for neighboring towns.

At 9.4 *m.* is the *Toll House* (*open as a dining-room*), built in 1709, in the section of Whitman known as Westcrook. The road between Westcrook and Joppa was owned by a private corporation during the height of the whaling industry in New Bedford, and this house was the toll house, where the passengers dined, horses were changed, and toll was paid. A rambling yellow clapboarded Cape Cod cottage with varicolored shingled roof, it has dormer windows, an ell, and an extension to the rear. It was restored in 1930. A garden and a terrace were added, neatly enclosed within a picket fence and shaded by two great elms. From the swinging sign at the front to the old lamp-post at the rear topped by its ancient oil-lamp, from the big central chimney of the main block, painted white with a black band at the top to the lively rooster on the weathervane of the remodeled, attached barn, the Toll House is a charming restoration.

EAST BRIDGEWATER, 12.1 *m.* (town, alt. 68, pop. 3670, sett. 1649, incorp. 1823), is a small industrial town, rich in bog iron. From the beginning this natural resource influenced the development of the town. The establishment here of the first triphammer shop in America initiated a period of manufacturing progress that lasted for almost 200 years.

Among the ingenious residents of the community were Samuel Rogers, inventor of a machine for cutting and heading a nail in one operation; Melville Otis, who devised the 'spring nipper,' an economical machine for salvaging outmoded nail-making machines; and Eleazer Carver, whose improvements on the cotton gin led to his decoration by the Government of India. Today only three small factories offer local employment; most of the workers commute between East Bridgewater and Brockton.

The *Unitarian Church*, Central St., was erected in 1794, and altered in 1850. In the belfry of this church hangs a Revere bell, bearing the name of Paul Revere's father and the date 1724.

Left from the Center on Central St. is the junction with Plymouth St., 0.3 *m.*; right on this street at 0.6 *m.* is *Sachem's Rock*, called by the Indians *Wonnocoote*. Here Miles Standish, Samuel Nash, and Constant Southworth met with Ousamequin in 1649, and purchased from him 'all land running seven miles in each direction from weir.' The Indians were to be paid in the following goods: 7 coats, a yard and one half of cloth in each coat; 9 hatchets; 8 hoes; 20 knives; 4 moose skins; and 10½ yards of cotton.

At 15.1 *m.* is the junction with State 28 (*see Tour* 19).

CHRONOLOGY

1000–08 Norsemen from Greenland visit New England.

1524 Giovanni da Verrazano cruises along New England coast

1602 Bartholomew Gosnold reaches Massachusetts Bay.

1603 Martin Pring explores coast of Maine and Massachusetts.

1604–05 De Monts and Champlain explore Maine and Massachusetts coast.

1605 George Weymouth explores Massachusetts coast.

1607–08 George Popham attempts to colonize 'Northern Virginia' (New England).

1609 Henry Hudson cruises along New England coast.

1614 Adriaen Block, from Manhattan, passes through Hell Gate and sails along as far as Nahant Bay. John Smith maps New England coast line, and region thereafter is known as New England.

1620 *Mayflower* lands at Plymouth with cargo of Pilgrims, John Carver elected first Governor. Plymouth Hill fortified.

1621 Pilgrims celebrate Thanksgiving and build their first church.

1623 Miles Standish conducts first organized war against the Indians while the men of Dorchester establish a fishing post on Cape Ann.

1630 John Winthrop arrives with a fleet of eleven ships and nine hundred settlers; Boston begins.

1631 Maritime history of Massachusetts commences when Governor Winthrop launches the *Blessing of the Bay* on the Mystic River.

1634 Mistress Anne Hutchinson outrages Boston's clergy.

1635 Boston opens a Public Latin School for Boys.

1636 General Court establishes a college in Newtowne, later Cambridge.

1638 First printing press in America north of Mexico set up in Cambridge by Stephen Daye. Lynn has a shoe factory.

1639 A fulling mill is in operation in Rowley.

1641 Enterprising men in Salem produce salt by the evaporation of sea water.

1642 Harvard holds first commencement.

1643 Colonists organize the New England Confederation to combat Indians and the Dutch of New Amsterdam.

1645 A Latin school opens in Roxbury.

1646 John Eliot translates the Bible into the Indian tongue.

1647 Popular education begins with law requiring elementary schools in towns of fifty persons and secondary schools in towns double that size.

1648 Margaret Jones of Charlestown is hanged for being a witch.

1649 General Court passes legislation controlling the practice of medicine.

1652 Property ownership and church affiliation is required for the franchise. The first book store opens in Boston.

1657 Halfway Covenant allows baptized as well as converted church members to vote.

1660 Council for Trade and Plantations commences its activity in London.

1675 King Philip makes war on colonists.

1677 Massachusetts produces a medical treatise on small pox and measles.

1684 Era of Bible Commonwealth passes with revocation of Massachusetts Charter.

1687 Britain sends Andros to govern the Dominion of New England.

1689 Irate colonists overthrow Andros.

1691 New Massachusetts Charter abolishes church membership as prerequisite for voting.

1692 Witches abound in Salem and the hysteria spreads.

1699 Early law to avoid spread of infectious diseases.

1704 *Boston News Letter*, first American newspaper, appears.

1734 Jonathan Edwards preaches hell-fire sermons at Northampton and begins Great Awakening.

1742 Faneuil Hall becomes Boston's Town Hall and market place.

1745 Governor William Shirley leads Massachusetts troops in the capture of Louisburg.

1761 Lawyers organize Bar Association in Suffolk County.

1763 Pontiac's braves devastate Massachusetts frontier in second serious Indian uprising.

1764 Great Britain commences policy of imperial control and passes Sugar Act.

1765 POPULATION: 240,433. Stamp Act, designed to increase imperial revenue, follows Sugar Act.

1766 Colonials inaugurate boycott and Great Britain repeals Stamp Act and modifies Sugar Act.

1767 Britain passes Townshend Act placing duties on paint, glass and tea. Massachusetts is in a fever of excitement; Boston merchants are especially alarmed by appearance of imperial customs officials.

1768 Massachusetts develops the Circular Letter to provide a bond of unity for colonies. Cargo of Hancock's sloop *Liberty* lands in defiance of authorities. British troops arrive in Boston.

1770 British sentry fires on crowd collected near Old State House and Boston resentment runs high. Colonial pressure results in repeal of Townshend Act.

1773 Britain passes Tea Act which leads to Boston Tea Party; Britain answers with coercive measures, closes port of Boston.

1774 Angry colonists vote to resist British taxation at mass meeting in Faneuil Hall.

1775 Paul Revere rides, Bunker Hill is fought, Gage evacuates Boston and George Washington takes command of the Continental Army.

1776 POPULATION: 299,841. Massachusetts unanimously approves the Declaration of Independence, publicly proclaimed from the Old State House.

1778 A popularly elected constitutional convention meets in Cambridge.

1780 Massachusetts ratifies State Constitution containing Bill of Rights; John Hancock elected Governor. Judicial interpretation of Constitution abolishes slavery. Academy of Arts and Sciences is organized in Boston.

1781 Massachusetts Medical Society is founded.

1784 *Empress of China* makes her maiden voyage to the Orient.

1785 Massachusetts surrenders her western lands to the National Government.

1786 Bridgewater develops machinery for the manufacture of cotton. Shays leads rebellion of debt-ridden farmers. General Rufus Putnam and other Massachusetts men organize the Ohio Land Company starting the New England movement of population to the Ohio frontier.

1788 Massachusetts ratifies the Federal Constitution and becomes the sixth state to enter Union. Massachusetts suggests amendments to the Constitution from which the Bill of Rights develops.

1789 President George Washington visits Boston; Governor John Hancock refuses to call on him, insisting that the Governor of Massachusetts is a more important personage than the President of the United States. The *Franklin* of Boston is the first American ship to reach Japan; the *Atlantic*, another Boston vessel, sails into the harbors of Bombay and Calcutta. A steam-propelled paddle boat invented by Nathan Reed is used on Wenham Pond and begins operation between Danvers and Beverly.

1790 POPULATION: 378,787.

1792 Paul Revere opens a bell foundry in Boston.

1794 The Middlesex Canal, 27 miles long, connecting the Merrimack and Mystic Rivers, is an 18th century wonder.

1796 John Adams of Massachusetts elected President of the United States. Boston creates Boston Dispensary to provide medical aid for the poor in their homes and in clinics.

1800 POPULATION: 422,845. Thomas Jefferson elected President of the United States. Massachusetts Federalists are in a panic of apprehension.

1802 Dr. Benjamin Waterhouse employs Jenner method of vaccination at Harvard.

1803 Massachusetts with other New England States and New York threaten to secede from the Union in protest over the Louisana Purchase. War with Tripoli (1801–05); Massachusetts makes history with Captain Preble and the *Constitution*.

1810 POPULATION: 472,040. Philharmonic Society becomes first orchestra in New England.

1812 Massachusetts House of Representatives condemns Federal Government for leading country into second war with England.

1814 Hartford Convention convenes; conservative Federalist delegates from Massachusetts condemn War of 1812, threaten nullification and secession. Steam power looms of Francis C. Lowell hum in Waltham and lead to industrialization of Lawrence, Lowell, Fall River and New Bedford.

1815 *North American Review* and the Handel and Haydn Society are founded. A Peace Society, the first of its kind in the world, is organized in Boston.

1818 People discuss building canal across Cape Cod at Sandwich, which materializes almost a hundred years later (1909).

1820 POPULATION: 523,287. Conservative Massachusetts reacts to westward expansion; calls a constitutional convention which incorporates cities, removes religious tests for office holders and discards all qualifications for the franchise excepting a small property tax which Daniel Webster, John Adams and Judge Joseph Story resist because it allows 'the poor and the profligate to control the affluent.' Maine acquires statehood making the Missouri Compromise possible.

1821 Boston has a real public high school.

1822 City Charter is granted Boston.

1823 Jonas Chickering manufactures a piano.

1824 John Quincy Adams elected President of the United States.

1825 The American Unitarian Association organizes in Boston and first High School for Girls in the United States opens.

1826 Massachusetts boasts its first railroad (horse-drawn), constructed for hauling granite blocks from Quincy to the Bunker Hill Monument in Charlestown. Prohibitionists commence activity in Massachusetts and Total Abstinence Societies make their appearance.

1829 Perkins Institution for the Blind is founded.

1830 POPULATION: 610,408.

1831 Garrison commences anti-slavery crusade and founds *The Liberator* in Boston.

1832 New England Anti-Slavery Society forms in Boston.

1833 A constitutional amendment completely separating church and state passes Legislature. Abolition sentiment grows; New England Anti-Slavery Society becomes American Anti-Slavery Society. The Boston Academy of Music comes into existence.

1834 Angry mob burns Ursuline Convent at Charlestown in outburst of anti-Catholic feeling.

1835 Horace Mann at work and normal schools are first created in Massachusetts.

1837 Mary Lyon establishes Mount Holyoke College in South Hadley, claimed to be the first American college for women. Emerson delivers 'America's Intellectual Declaration of Independence' in his Phi Beta Kappa Address at Harvard.

1838 Lowell Mason introduces Music in the public schools of Boston. Evening medical courses are offered at Tremont Temple.

1840 POPULATION: 737,699.

1846 Anaesthesia successfully used at Massachusetts General Hospital.

1847 Louis Agassiz lectures on embryology at Lowell Institute.

1849 Garrison submits a petition for the suffrage of women.

1850 POPULATION: 994,514. A national Women's Rights Convention convenes in Worcester.

1852 Boston Public Library, made possible by public subscription, opens its doors.

1855 Know-Nothing Legislature appoints 'Nunnery Committee' to pry into secrets of Catholic convents and schools.

1856 Massachusetts gives its electoral vote to John C. Fremont, the Republican candidate for the presidency.

1860 POPULATION: 1,231,066.

1861 Baltimore mob attacks Sixth Massachusetts Regiment on its way to Washington.

1863 Marie Jakrysewka founds the New England Hospital for Women and Children.

1864 State Board of Charities is established.

1865 Law forbids discrimination against any race in public places. Massachusetts Institute of Technology opens its doors. Labor of children under ten in factories is prohibited.

1867 New England Conservatory of Music begins its career in Boston. Mary Baker Eddy founds Christian Science in Lynn.

1869 First State Board of Health is established. Evening schools established. The last whaler sails from New Bedford.

1870 POPULATION: 1,457,351. Massachusetts Woman's Suffrage Association elects Julia Ward Howe president.

1872 Dr. Susan Dimock has a training school for nurses at the New England Hospital for Women and Children. A fire sweeps Boston, causing a loss of $70,000,000.

1876 Alexander Graham Bell successfully experiments with telephone.

1880 POPULATION: 1,783,085. An Art Museum for the public opens at Copley Square in Boston.

1881 Henry Lee Higginson endows the Boston Symphony Orchestra.

1882 Henry Wadsworth Longfellow dies at Cambridge; Ralph Waldo Emerson dies at Concord.

1887 Labor Day is declared a legal holiday. The Legislature passes the Employers' Liability Act. Clark University is established as second purely graduate school in America.

1889 Cotton spinners organize a National Cotton Mule Spinners Union.

1890 POPULATION: 2,238,943.

1891 Death of James Russell Lowell.

1892 First Church of Christ, Scientist, Boston. John Greenleaf Whittier dies.

1894 Boston and Maine Railroad opens North Station.

1897 Boston has first subway in the United States.

1899 South Station opens.

1900 POPULATION: 2,805,346.

1907 Savings banks permitted to conduct life insurance business.

1908 Ford Hall Forum is established in Boston.

1910 POPULATION: 3,366,416.

1911 Workmen's Compensation Act is passed.

1912 A minimum wage law is passed. Textile workers in Lawrence and street car operators in Boston strike. A department of Labor and Industry is established.

1918 German submarine appears in Cape Cod waters near Orleans, bombards tug and three empty coal barges, causing great consternation; air forces ordered to Cape region.

1919 Boston Police Strike.

1920 POPULATION: 3,852,356.

1923 Calvin Coolidge of Massachusetts succeeds Warren G. Harding as President of the United States.

1924 Massachusetts women vote.

1926 Beverly shoe machine plant is the largest in world. Drs. Minot and Murphy discover cure for pernicious anemia for which they receive Nobel Prize.

1928 Roger Babson predicts unusually good business year in 1929. The submarine S-4 sinks off Provincetown with 40 men.

1929 Earthquake rocks state. Ex-President Calvin Coolidge returns to his law practice in Northampton. Boston University celebrates 60th anniversary.

1930 POPULATION: 4,249,614. Massachusetts Bay Colony Tercentenary Celebration.

1933 Convicts fire Charlestown State Prison.

1934 Massachusetts textile workers answer call of general textile strike.

1935 POPULATION: 4,350,910. Boston Public Latin School celebrates 300th anniversary. Teachers' Oath Bill, requiring all teachers in public schools and colleges to take an oath of allegiance to the Constitution, becomes law.

1936 Harvard University celebrates 300th anniversary.

1937 Child labor amendment with significant national implications again defeated. Repeal of Teachers' Oath Law, passed in Legislature, vetoed by Governor.

FIFTY BOOKS ABOUT
MASSACHUSETTS

Adams, Brooks. *The Emancipation of Massachusetts*. Boston, 1887.
Adams, Charles Francis, Jr. *Massachusetts: its Historians and its History*. Boston, 1893.
Adams, Charles Francis, Jr. *Three Episodes of Massachusetts History*. 2 vols. Boston, 1892.
Adams, Henry. *The Education of Henry Adams*. Boston, 1930.
Adams, James Truslow. *New England in the Republic*. Boston, 1926.
Adams, James Truslow. *Revolutionary New England*. Boston, 1923.
Adams, James Truslow. *The Adams Family*. Boston, 1930.
Adams, James Truslow. *The Founding of New England*. Boston, 1927.
Bacon, Edwin M. *Historic Pilgrimages in New England*. New York, 1898.
Bayley, Frank William. *Five Colonial Artists of New England: Badger, Blackburn, Copley, Feke, Smibert*. Boston, 1929.
Bolton, Charles K. *The Real Founders of New England*. Boston, 1929.
Brooks, Van Wyck. *The Flowering of New England*. New York, 1936.
Clark, Arthur Hamilton. *The Clipper Ship Era*. New York, 1911.
Cousins, Frank, and Riley, Phil M. *Colonial Architecture of Salem*. Boston, 1919.
Cousins, Frank, and Riley, Phil M. *The Wood Carver of Salem (Samuel McIntire)*. Boston, 1916.
Crawford, Mary Caroline. *Old Boston Days and Ways*. Boston, 1909.
Crawford, Mary Caroline. *Social Life in Old New England*. Boston, 1914.
Daniel, Hawthorne. *The Clipper Ship*. New York, 1928.
Digges, Jeremiah. *Cape Cod Pilot*. Federal Writers' Project. Provincetown, Mass., 1937.
Dow, George Francis. *Domestic Life in New England in the 17th Century*. Topsfield, Mass., 1925.
Drake, Samuel Adams. *Old Landmarks and Historic Personages of Boston*. Boston, 1906.
Duniway, Clyde Augustus. *The Development of Freedom of the Press in Massachusetts*. New York, 1906.
Earle, Alice Morse. *Customs and Fashions in Old New England*. New York, 1894.
Early, Eleanor. *And This is Boston!* Boston, 1930.
Eliot, Samuel Atkins (editor). *Biographical History of Massachusetts*. 3 volumes. Boston, 1911.
Ellis, George E. *Puritan Age and Rule in the Colony of the Massachusetts Bay, 1629–1685*. Boston, 1888.
Forbes, Harriette Merrifield. *Gravestones of Early New England and the Men Who Made Them*. Boston, 1927.
French, Allen. *The Day of Concord and Lexington*. Boston, 1925.
Hart, Albert Bushnell (editor). *Commonwealth History of Massachusetts*. 5 vols. New York, 1930.

Hitchcock, Henry Russell, Jr. *The Architecture of H. H. Richardson and His Times.* New York, 1936.

Howe, M. A. DeWolfe. *Boston, The Place and the People.* New York, 1924.

Kimball, Fiske. *Domestic Architecture of the American Colonies and of the Early Republic.* New York, 1922.

Kittredge, George Lyman. *Witchcraft in Old and New England.* Cambridge, 1929.

Kittredge, George Lyman. *The Old Farmer and His Almanack.* Boston, 1904.

Lockwood, John Hoyt (editor). *Western Massachusetts, 1636–1925: A History.* 4 vols. New York, 1926.

Major, Howard. *The Domestic Architecture of the Early American Republic: The Greek Revival.* Philadelphia, 1926.

McKay, Richard C. *Some Famous Sailing Ships and their Builder, Donald McKay.* New York, 1928.

Martin, George H. *The Evolution of the Massachusetts Public School System: A Historical Sketch.* New York, 1915.

Mathews, Lois Kimball. *The Expansion of New England.* Boston, 1909.

Moore, Ernest Carroll. *Fifty Years of American Education (1867–1917).* Boston, 1917.

Morison, Samuel Eliot. *Builders of the Bay Colony.* Boston, 1930.

Morison, Samuel Eliot. *Maritime History of Massachusetts.* Boston, 1921.

Morison, Samuel Eliot. *Three Centuries of Harvard.* Cambridge, 1936.

Nutting, Wallace. *Massachusetts Beautiful.* Framingham, Mass., 1923.

Parrington, Vernon L. *Main Currents in American Thought.* 3 vols. New York, 1927–30.

Phillips, James Duncan. *Salem in the Seventeenth Century.* Boston, 1933.

Phillips, James Duncan. *Salem in the Eighteenth Century.* Boston, 1937.

Place, Charles A. *Charles Bulfinch, Architect and Citizen.* Boston, 1925.

Usher, Roland G. *The Pilgrims and Their History.* New York, 1918.

Weeden, William B. *Economic and Social History of New England, 1620–1789.* 2 vols. Boston, 1894.

Winsor, Justin (editor). *Memorial History of Boston, 1630–1880.* 4 vols. Boston, 1881.

Wright, T. G. *Literary Culture in Early New England, 1620–1730.* New Haven, 1920.

INDEX

INDEX